Third Edition

THE IRWIN HANDBOOK OF TELECOMMUNICATIONS

JAMES HARRY GREEN

IRWIN
Professional Publishing®
Chicago • London • Singapore

Times Mirror
Higher Education Group

Library of Congress Cataloging-in-Publication Data

Green, James H. (James Harry)
    The Irwin handbook of telecommunications / James Harry Green.
        p.   cm.
    Includes index.
    ISBN 0-7863-0479-0
    1. Rev. ed. of: The Irwin handbook of telecommunications
management. 1995. 2. Telecommunication systems—United States.
3. Business enterprises—United States—Communication systems.
I. Green, James H. (James Harry) Irwin handbook of
telecommunications management. II. Title.
TK5102.3.U6G74   1997   96–23791
621.382—dc20

Printed in the United States of America
1 2 3 4 5 6 7 8 9 0 BB 3 2 1 0 9 8 7 6

The flood of new products and unbridled competition is hardly the essence of the telecommunications industry. All of this must fit into a structure that has evolved over the past century or so, and all of the parts must interact. The purpose of this book is to explain in overview how the North American telecommunications system functions. Each chapter is devoted to a particular aspect of the technology. The coverage is aimed at breadth instead of depth. Each chapter covers subject matter that would easily require a volume of its own.

The structure of this third edition follows that of the second. The book is divided into five parts.

Part I covers concepts that are common to the industry, and which are necessary for an understanding of the elements. Chapter 1 is a high-level overview of the telecommunications network and how it fits together. Chapter 2 discusses transmission concepts and the means by which quality of transmission service is assured. This is followed by two chapters on data communications, and one on digital multiplexing. Part I concludes with chapters covering the telecommunications infrastructure: outside plant and premise wiring.

Part II discusses circuit switching, the means by which circuits are interconnected, and the historical method of dial-up communications. Included are chapters on switching concepts, local switching, and toll switching, including a discussion of how operator services are handled. One chapter discusses common equipment, which includes the relay racks, distributing frames, and power equipment that all telecommunications systems employ. Part II concludes with a discussion of signaling and the methods by which signaling supports delivery of advanced customer services.

Part III deals with transmission equipment. We start with an explanation of fiber optics, which has captured a significant part of the market that was once filled by products that have a longer history, such as microwave and satellite. These technologies are covered in this part along with chapters discussing cellular telephone and a service that is just emerging as this book is written: personal communications service (PCS) and other wireless services. The final chapter in this part discusses video transmission and conferencing.

Part IV covers the only equipment many users see: customer premise equipment. The discussion begins with chapters on station and key telephone equipment and turns to a detailed discussion of private branch exchanges (PBXs) and automatic call distributors (ACDs). One chapter covers the emerging technology of computer-telephone integration, which merges computers with telephone systems to bring a host of new products and labor-saving applications. Other chapters cover voice processing, electronic messaging, Centrex, and facsimile.

PREFACE

These are exciting times for people in the telecommunications business. The breakup of the Bell System in 1984 trigged an onslaught of change greater than the sum of all change from the invention of the telephone more than 100 years earlier, and still the change continues. AT&T has broken itself into three more companies, voluntarily this time. Cisco purchased Stratacom, and IBM acquired Lotus. The telecommunications and media giants dance with one another looking for combinations to help them achieve critical mass. Time-Warner, for example, found a successful fusion with Turner Broadcasting, but not with US West. Congress has passed new telecommunications legislation that will cost local exchange companies their monopolies, while opening the way for them to enter new markets, and that has spawned more changes such as the pairs of ex-Bell companies that are combining. Southwestern Bell Corp. has merged with Pacific Bell, and Hynex and Bell Atlantic have announced plans to combine.

This has been a wrenching time for those accustomed to the old ways of doing business: guaranteed returns on investment, rigid and protective tariffs, and government regulation in lieu of competition. Hundreds of thousands of people have found their once steady and predictable jobs realigned or lost in the tumult of change. Service quality that once was taken for granted has often been all but forgotten in the jockeying for competitive position.

But a revolution without discomfort is no revolution at all, and what we are witnessing is revolutionary change in an industry that once was accustomed to stability. Hundreds of new companies and countless products have emerged since the Bell System breakup, and we have barely seen the beginnings of what human ingenuity can devise when the shackles are removed.

Since the second edition of this book was published, many changes have occurred that affect telecommunications. Then, the very term asynchronous transfer mode (ATM) was unknown to most within the industry. Today it has become a mantra. Although ATM has still not been widely deployed, nor are standards complete, it has generated more interest than any technology in recent memory. Structured wiring standards had not been developed, computer-telephony integration was unknown to most users, and LAN internets were in their infancy. Today these technologies are either mainstream or rapidly gaining acceptance.

Part V discusses networks. It opens with a chapter on integrated services digital network (ISDN), a switched service offering that, after more than two decades of development, is finally beginning to realize its promise. Two chapters cover local area networks, a technology that has advanced from theory at the time of the first edition of this book to a mainstream application by the second edition, and is now at the heart of virtually every corporate network. Three chapters discuss data networks. Chapter 31 deals with traditional and some newly emerging wide area networks. Chapter 32 discusses broadband networks, which are at the threshold of new technology. The following chapter covers internetworks, which have become the glue that binds the corporate enterprise network together. Chapter 34 discusses private voice networks, and the next three chapters deal with network design, testing, and management.

The book concludes with a chapter on the near-term future of telecommunications. We attempt to look only as far as technology currently under development will lead. Following that chapter is a series of appendices that form a handy reference that anyone associated with telecommunications needs. Appendix A is a brief explanation of the principles of electricity. Readers who are unfamiliar with terms such as resistance, capacitance, voltage, and current may want to read this appendix as a prerequisite to understanding terms the book uses throughout.

Appendix B lists some of the principal ITU standards pertaining to telecommunications. The end of each chapter lists selected manufacturers and suppliers of equipment covered in the text, and Appendix C lists their locations and telephone numbers. Appendix D lists sources of telecommunications information, including standards agencies and publications. Appendix E consists of network design tables that are used for determining trunking quantities, dial-up ports, and other resources that involve queuing. Appendix F lists country and North American area codes in both numeric and alphabetic order. Appendix G is a dictionary of acronyms, with which the telecommunications industry is replete. These and other terms are defined in the glossary that follows.

A few words are in order about the intended audience of this book. It is written for anyone who needs an overview of how the various elements of the North American telecommunications network operate and interact. The book is primarily intended for newly appointed telecommunications managers who need a reference for the technology they manage. Earlier editions of the book have been used as a text, although it does not include standard textbook features such as an instructor guide and sample questions. The book is also useful to vendors who need a clear understanding of the environment in which their equipment exists.

New and improved telecommunications products continue to reach the market. We take the approach in this book of avoiding a detailed description of the present state of development of emerging products. Instead, we focus on how the service or product fits into the scheme of things, how it works, and role it is intended to fill. This book's objective is to give you a foundation from which you can evaluate products and services and accomplish your role in tele-communications, whatever it may be.

CONTENTS

Chapter 4

Data Communications Protocols   99

Chapter 5

Pulse Code Modulation   121

Chapter 6

Outside Plant   157

Chapter 33

Internetworking   785

Chapter 34

Enterprise Networks   799

Chapter 35

Network Design Principles   815

Chapter 36

Network Testing Principles   839

Chapter 37

Network Management   865

Chapter 38

Future Developments in Telecommunications   887

Appendix A

Principles of Electricity Applied to Telecommunications   900

Appendix B

Principal Voice and Data Standards of the International Telecommunications Union   921

Appendix C

Telecommunications Manufacturers and Vendors   937

Appendix D

Sources of Additional Technical Information: Standards Institutions, Trade Associations, and Trade Publications   948

LIST OF FIGURES

LIST OF TABLES

I

PRINCIPLES OF TELECOMMUNICATIONS SYSTEMS

1

INTRODUCTION TO TELECOMMUNICATIONS

To the user on the end of a telephone, the public switched telephone network (PSTN) looks like a single monolithic entity; a black box with telephone lines that somehow mysteriously get connected to one another. It is a tribute to the inventive genius of the thousands of scientists, engineers, and technicians who design, install, and maintain the many parts of the network that its complexity is hidden so well that users don't have to know any more about the network than how to dial and answer telephone calls. In reality, however, the network is composed of countless assemblies of circuits, switching systems, radio and fiber-optic systems, signaling devices, and telephone instruments that act as part of a coordinated whole even though they are owned by many companies with no organizational connection to one another. Every day, the industry adds brand-new devices to the network, and they must function with other devices that were designed and installed more than 30 years ago.

The word "network" has become an ambiguous term. It can describe the relationship of a group of broadcasting stations or a social fabric that binds people of similar interests. In telecommunications the usage is somewhat more specific, but the precise meaning of the term must be derived from context, and this can be confusing to those outside the industry. In its broadest sense a telecommunications network is the combination of all the circuits and equipment that enable users to communicate. All the switching apparatus, trunks, subscriber lines, and auxiliary equipment that support communication can be classified as elements of the network. In another sense, the word narrows to mean the circuits that interconnect the inputs and outputs of a switching system. At the circuit level a third meaning describes the interconnection of components to form a filter or level-reducing attenuator. The only way the ambiguity can be dealt with is to become familiar enough with the technology to take the meaning of the term from its context.

The direct interconnection of two stations meets the definition of a network in the strictest sense of the word, but this is a restrictive kind of private network because it lacks accessibility. In a broader sense public voice networks provide the capability for a station to reach another station anywhere in the world without the need for complex addressing. The same, unfortunately, cannot yet be said for data networks.

To understand the systems discussed in this book, it is necessary to understand how they fit as part of a coordinated whole. This chapter discusses the major building blocks of the telecommunications network without explaining how or why they work. Many terms are introduced and explained in detail only later in the book. You are cautioned that despite its origins in scientific disciplines, the vocabulary of telecommunications is frequently highly ambiguous, and the meaning of many of its terms must be taken from context. Therefore, when we use terminology, we will define it in context to illustrate its meaning.

Just as the human body can be viewed either as a unit or as an assembly of systems such as the digestive, respiratory, and circulatory systems, the telecommunications network can be understood from its systems. We will first discuss the major systems in broad terms, and in subsequent chapters examine them in greater detail.

THE MAJOR TELECOMMUNICATIONS SYSTEMS

Figure 1–1 shows the major classes of telecommunications equipment and how they fit together to form a communications network. In the telecommunications industry, as with the computer industry, the manufacturers often set the standards, and compliance with equipment standards set by others is voluntary. In the past few years, international standards-setting organizations have been more active, so we are now threatened by too many rather than too few standards. The topic of setting standards is examined in more detail in a later section. Unlike the systems of the human body, the systems in telecommunications are not tightly bound. Each element in Figure 1–1 is largely autonomous. The telecommunications network is created by the systems' exchanging signals across the interfaces.

FIGURE 1-1

The Major Classes of Telecommunications Equipment

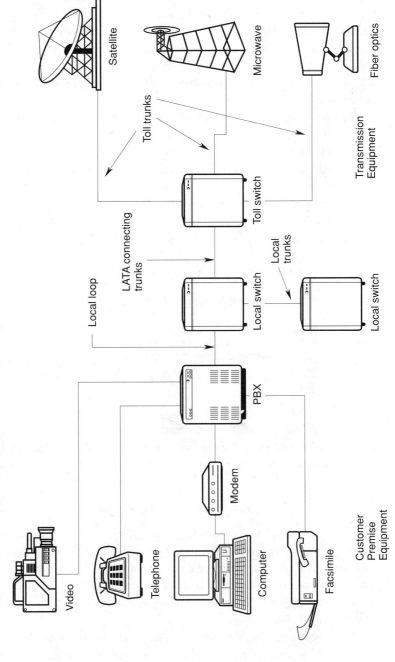

Customer Premise Equipment

Located on the user's premises, *station* or *terminal* equipment is the only part of the telecommunications system the users normally contact directly. It includes the telephone instrument itself and the wiring in the user's building that connects to local exchange carrier (LEC) equipment. For our purposes, station equipment also includes other apparatus such as *private branch exchanges* (PBXs) (sometimes also called computer branch exchanges or private automatic branch exchanges), and local area networks (LANs) that normally belong to a single organization. It also includes multiple line key telephone equipment used to select, hold, and conference calls. Data equipment such as modems and multiplexers, and auxiliary equipment such as speakerphones, automatic dialers, answering sets, and the like also fall into the station equipment classification.

Customer premise equipment has two primary functions. It is used for intraorganizational communication within a narrow range, usually a building or campus, and it connects to private or common carrier facilities for communication over a wider range.

Subscriber Loop Plant

The *subscriber loop,* also known as the *local loop,* consists of the wire, poles, terminals, conduit, and other outside plant items that connect customer premise equipment to the LEC's central office. Before deregulation, LECs had a monopoly on the local loop. Now alternatives are becoming available. For some services it is possible to transport information over cable television, and in other cases to use facilities such as microwave radio or fiber optics to bypass LEC equipment. A class of common carrier known as an alternate access carrier (AAC) provides such service in most major metropolitan areas. AACs and LECs as well as some CATV companies offer service over fiber-optics-based facilities.

Local Switching Systems

The objective of the telecommunications system is to interconnect users, whether they are people communicating over a telephone line or systems communicating over specially designed data circuits. These connections are either dialed by the user or the connections are wired in the LEC's central office and remain connected until the service is discontinued. This latter kind of circuit is called *private line* or *dedicated.*

The local switching office (often called an end office) is the point where local loops terminate. Loops used for switched services are wired to computer-driven systems that can switch to other loops or to *trunks,* which are channels to other local or long-distance switching offices. Loops used for private line services are directly wired to other loops or to trunks to distant central offices. Until recently, local switching was a monopoly service of the LECs, but the Telecommunications Act of 1996 opens local switching to competitive carriers.

Interoffice Trunks

Because of the huge concentrations of wire that converge in local switching offices, there is a practical limit to how many users can be served from a single office or *wire center*. Therefore, in major metropolitan areas, the LECs strategically place multiple central offices according to population density, and connect them with *interoffice trunks*. Central offices exchange signals and establish talking connections over these trunks to set up paths corresponding to telephone numbers dialed by the users.

Tandem Switching Offices

As the number of central offices in a region increases, it becomes impractical to connect every office to every other office with trunks. For one thing, the number of groups of trunks would be unmanageable. Also, some central offices have too little traffic demand between them to justify the cost of directly connected trunks. To solve these problems, the telephone network is equipped with *tandem switches* to interconnect trunks. *Local tandem* switches connect local trunks together, and *toll tandem,* also called *interexchange tandem* switches, connect central offices to interexchange trunks leading outside the free calling area. A special type of tandem switch known as a *gateway* interconnects the telephone networks of different countries when their networks are incompatible.

Privately owned tandem switches also may interconnect circuits under the control of a single organization. Before the breakup of the Bell System, the telephone companies owned the toll tandem switches. Now, with multiple interexchange carriers (IECs) offering service, each carrier connects tandem switches to the end office or to a LEC-owned *exchange access tandem.*

Interexchange Trunks

LECs divide their serving areas into classifications known as *exchanges.* Most exchanges correspond roughly to the boundaries of cities and their surrounding areas. Interexchange trunks that connect offices within the local calling area are known as *extended area service* (EAS) trunks, while those that connect outside the local calling area are called *toll* trunks. Trunks that connect the LEC to an IEC are called *interLATA connecting trunks.*

Transmission Equipment

The process of transporting information in any form including voice, video, and data between users is called *transmission* in the telecommunications industry. The earliest transmission took place over open wire suspended on poles equipped with crossarms and insulators, but that technique has now all but disappeared. For short ranges, some trunks are carried on pairs of copper wire, but most trunks now are carried on fiber optics. For longer ranges, interoffice and interexchange trunks are transported over primarily fiber optics, with microwave radio and satellites used to a limited degree. *Multiplexing* equipment divides these backbone transmission facilities into voice channels.

FUNDAMENTALS OF MULTIPLEXING

The basic building block of the telephone network is the *voice-grade* communications channel occupying 300 to 3,300 Hz of bandwidth. Bandwidth is defined as the information-carrying capacity of a telecommunications facility. The bandwidth of a voice-grade channel is far less than the bandwidth of high-fidelity music systems that typically reproduce 30 to 20,000 Hz, but for ordinary voice transmission this bandwidth is entirely satisfactory. For the first six or seven decades of telephony, open wire or multiple-pair cables were the primary transmission medium. At first, each pair of wires carried one voice channel. However, these media, (known as *facilities* in telecommunications vernacular) have enough bandwidth to carry multiple channels. Today's fiber-optic equipment, for example, can carry more than 30,000 voice channels on a single pair of fibers.

The telecommunications industry has always invested heavily in research and development. Much of it has been directed toward how to superimpose an increasing amount of information on a single transmission medium. The process for placing multiple voice or data channels over one facility is known as *multiplexing*.

Frequency Division Multiplexing

With the arrival of the vacuum tube in the 1920s, a form of multiplexing known as *carrier* became possible. The earliest carrier systems increased the capacity of a pair of wires by frequency division multiplexing (FDM). Broadcast radio is an example of FDM in action (except that it does not allow two-way communications). In an FDM carrier system, as Figure 1–2 shows, each channel is assigned a transmitter-receiver pair, or *modem* (a term derived from the words

FIGURE 1-2

Frequency Division Multiplexing System

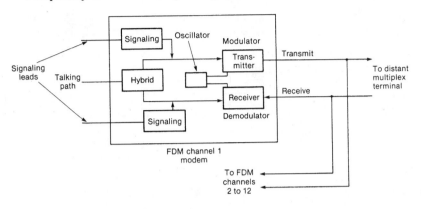

modulator and demodulator). These units operate at low power levels, are connected to cable rather than an antenna, and therefore do not radiate as a radio does. Otherwise, the concepts of radio and carrier are similar. FDM carrier systems were once the backbone of the telecommunications network, but they have been all but completely replaced by digital multiplexing systems today.

Time Division Multiplexing

Although FDM is an efficient way of increasing the capacity of a transmission medium, the techniques used for its manufacture do not lend themselves to large-scale integration. Therefore, FDM is gradually being replaced by *time division multiplexing* (TDM). In TDM, shown conceptually in Figure 1–3, the voice is digitized and inserted on the transmission medium in eight-bit segments. Instead of the bandwidth of the transmission medium being divided into frequency segments, each user has access to the full bandwidth of the system for a stream of time segments that repeat 8,000 times per second. The capacity of the transmission medium is so great that users are not aware they are sharing it. Chapter 5 describes the concept of time division multiplexing in more detail.

Higher Order Multiplexing

The basic building block of both analog and digital multiplexing systems is the *group*. A group has 12 voice-grade circuits combined into a band of analog frequencies, or into a stream of digital data. Groups are formed in equipment

FIGURE 1-3

Time Division Multiplexing System

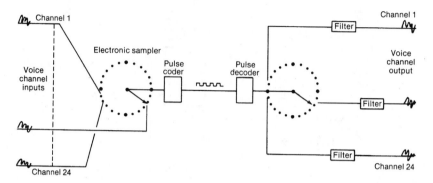

called a *channel bank*. Analog channel banks consist of 12 circuits; digital channel banks derive 24 circuits known as a *digroup*. Higher order multiplexing combines the output of channel banks into hundreds and thousands of circuits that can be transmitted over broadband facilities such as coaxial cable, microwave radio, and fiber optics.

Data Multiplexing

When data communications people speak of multiplexing, they are usually using it in a different sense than voice people. Data multiplex equipment subdivides a voice channel into several lower bandwidth data channels. In later chapters we will discuss this multiplexing in more detail. For now it is important to know that the term "multiplex" must be understood in context because it is a term that has many different meanings.

ANALOG AND DIGITAL TRANSMISSION CONCEPTS

When people speak into a telephone instrument, the voice actuates a transmitter to cause current flowing in the line to vary proportionately, or *analog*ously to the changes in sound pressure. Because people speak and hear in analog, there was, until a few decades ago, little reason to convert an analog signal to digital. Now, there are three primary reasons digital transmission has replaced analog in all parts of the network but the local loop. First, digital equipment is less expensive to manufacture than analog; second, an increasing amount of communication takes place between digital terminal equipment such as computers; and third, digital transmission provides higher quality in most respects than analog.

The higher quality of digital signals results from the difference in the methods of amplifying the signal. In analog transmission, an audio amplifier known as a *repeater* boosts the signal, together with any noise on the line. With digital transmission, regenerators detect the incoming bit stream and create an entirely new signal that is identical with the original. If a digital signal is regenerated before noise causes errors to occur, the result is a channel that is practically noise-free.

The system for generating and transmitting telephone signals digitally is known as *pulse code modulation* (PCM). A PCM channel bank samples the voice 8,000 times per second, converts each sample to an eight-bit digital word, and transmits it over a line interspersed with digital signals from 23 other channels. Repeaters spaced at appropriate intervals regenerate the 24-channel signal. This technique results in a 1.544 megabit-per-second (mb/s) digital signal known as T-1. T-1 is the basic building block of the North American digital hierarchy. Most other parts of the world use a 2.048 mb/s signal known as E-1.

The theory of PCM is not new—an IT&T scientist in England developed it in 1938. Though the system was technically feasible then it was not economical because of the high cost of the electronics needed to make the analog-to-digital conversion. With the invention of the transistor, the development of solid-state electronics, and particularly large-scale integration, the economics shifted in favor of digital transmission. PCM has replaced analog techniques in all parts of the telecommunications system except at the source, the telephone, and some parts of the local loop. Telephone sets in which the voice is digitized in the instrument, however, are common in PBXs. Presently, digital telephone sets are not widely used in public telephone networks for technical and economic reasons, but the drawbacks will disappear in time with the advent of the *Integrated Services Digital Network* (ISDN). ISDN is the architecture that is being used to upgrade the local network, which has changed little in its basic architecture since the invention of the telephone.

SWITCHING SYSTEMS

For many applications, fixed circuits between points, known as *point-to-point* or *dedicated* circuits, are desirable. Usually, however, the real value of a telecommunications system is in its ability to access a wide range of users wherever they are located. This is the role of telephone switching systems.

Early Switching Systems

The earliest switching systems were manually operated. Telephone lines and trunks were terminated on jacks, and operators interconnected lines by inserting plug-equipped cords into the jacks. Figure 1–4 shows a manual toll switchboard

FIGURE 1–4

A 1926 Toll Switchboard.

Courtesy, AT&T Archives.

from 1926. Note the headsets worn by the operators and the large clock mechanism used for timing calls.

In 1891 a Kansas City undertaker named Almon B. Strowger patented an electromechanical switch that could be controlled by pulses from a rotary dial. The Strowger system, also known as *step-by-step,* has largely been replaced by modern electronic switching systems. Step-by-step's distinguishing feature was that electrical pulses created by a dial directly controlled the motion of the switches. The switching system had no intelligence and limited ability to vary the destination of the call. This limitation, coupled with high maintenance cost, led to common control switching.

Common Control Switching Offices

All switching offices have a common characteristic: they contain a limited amount of equipment that many users share. With manual and step-by-step systems, all the equipment used to establish a talking path remained connected for the duration of the call. As technology advanced, it became evident that keeping the equipment occupied for the duration of the call was not the most economical way to switch. More important, it was also inflexible. As a call progressed through the switching system, if it encountered blockage, the system was incapable of rerouting the call to a different path. It could only signal the user to hang up and try again. These drawbacks were overcome by use of *common control.*

Common control switching equipment sets up the talking path through a switching fabric and releases when the connection is established. The common control equipment is not called on again until the connection is to be taken down. In this respect, common control equipment serves a function similar to the manual switchboard operator. Although common control equipment is more complex than directly controlled switching, it is also more efficient and much faster.

Contrasted to step-by-step where the user builds a connection gradually with pulls of the dial, under common control the user transmits dial or tone pulses into a circuit that registers the digits. An advantage of this method is that when dialing is complete, logic circuits can inspect the digits, determine the destination of the call, and choose an alternative route if all trunks in the preferred route are busy. This capability, known as *alternate routing,* is a characteristic shared by all modern switching systems.

The earliest common control equipment, introduced in the 1920s, was a system known as *panel,* followed about two decades later by the *crossbar* system. The systems take their names from the method of interconnecting lines and trunks.

Computer Controlled Switching Systems

Common control offices use electromechanical relays in their logic circuits. Relays have an electronic counterpart, the logic gate. Both gates and relays are binary logic devices. That is, they are either on or off, and if a decision can be reduced to a series of "yes/no" responses to outside conditions, both logic gates and relays can do the same functions.

The electronic equivalent of a common control central office was a natural outgrowth of computer and switching technology. Early electronic switching systems used wired logic, that is, they were not programmable. In the middle 1960s the age of the stored program control (SPC) central office was born. The No. 1 ESS, which is still in use today, has a reed relay switching fabric driven by a software program.

Digital Central Offices

When large-scale integrated circuits were perfected in the 1970s, it became technically feasible to develop a digital switching fabric to replace the analog electronic network in SPC central offices. The current state-of-the-art of central office technology has a digital switching fabric controlled by a programmable central processor. Most modern switching equipment, ranging from small PBXs to large toll tandem switches that can handle thousands of trunks, uses this technology. Now, further research is under way to develop even less costly switching systems capable of switching light streams directly rather than electrical pulses.

NUMBERING SYSTEMS

Switching systems route calls between themselves and selected terminating stations by *addressing*. Station addresses in North America consist of an area code and telephone number. From overseas locations a country code is added. Without controlled assignment of telephone numbers, the telephone system could not function. In this section we will look briefly at how telephone numbering operates both in this country and worldwide.

The Switching Hierarchy

The public telephone network operated by AT&T and connecting LECs was divided into five classes of switching systems as illustrated in Figure 1–5. Since divestiture, AT&T and other IECs have reduced the number of levels in the switching hierarchy, but the class designation remains for Class 5 central offices, the lowest class in the hierarchy. Class 5 offices, also known as *end offices,* are the systems that directly serve subscriber lines. Higher class offices are tandem offices used for connecting toll trunks.

Trunks between switching systems are classified as either *high-usage* or *final* trunks. Within certain limits, high-usage trunks can be established between any two offices if the traffic volume justifies it. Common control switching systems contain the intelligence to enable them to decide what group of trunks to choose to route calls to the destination, always attempting first to connect to a distant central office over a high-usage trunk. Calls progress from system to system until the terminating office is reached. Systems route calls by exchanging signals over either the trunk that provides the talking path, or over a separate data network.

Figure 1–5 shows that if all high-usage trunks are busy, a call from a Class 5 office could theoretically be routed over as many as nine final trunks in tandem before it reached the terminating Class 5 office. In practice, this rarely, if ever, happened. Traffic engineers monitor the amount of traffic flowing between terminating points, and order the proper quantity of trunks to cause calls to complete over the most economical route.

The North American Numbering Plan

Every telephone line in the United States and Canada plus some Caribbean countries has a unique 10-digit address. The first division is a three-digit *area code.* This code is also sometimes called the *numbering plan area* (NPA) code. Until 1995 the NPA was identified by a 0 or 1 as the second digit. Several forces have converged to exhaust the pool of available numbers, so on January 1, 1995, the new North American numbering plan was introduced. This plan permits any digit from 0 to 9 in the second position.

Within the NPA, each central office is assigned at least one three-digit *central office code.* Within the central office, each customer has a *line number* between 0000 and 9999. Each central office code, therefore, can support 10,000 lines. In larger cities it is for a single switching system to serve multiple central office codes. Appendix F lists the North American dialing codes.

The Worldwide Numbering Plan

Not all nations in the world use the same numbering plan as the United States. This is of little consequence if the gateway offices that interconnect the countries can translate the dialed digits to their destination. Each nation in the

The Predivestiture Switching Hierarchy

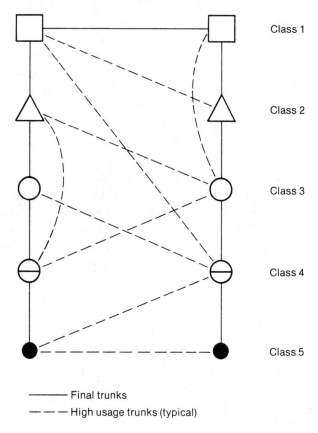

Class 1

Class 2

Class 3

Class 4

Class 5

——— Final trunks

— — — High usage trunks (typical)

worldwide plan is assigned a two- or three-digit country number. Worldwide dialing is accomplished without operators by dialing an international direct distance dialing (IDDD) access code, a country code, and the terminating telephone number. Appendix F includes the country codes for the worldwide dialing plan.

INTEREXCHANGE CARRIER ACCESS TO LOCAL NETWORKS

The ten-digit telephone addresses we have been discussing allow completing a call to any telephone in the country after you have obtained access to the IEC you select to handle your long-distance calls. Until the 1984 breakup of the Bell System, AT&T, through its Long Lines division, the Bell Operating Companies, and independent telephone companies owned the only public switched network that spanned the country. The Bell Operating Companies generally handled intercity communications within state boundaries, and in a few instances between states. The bulk of the interstate calling, however, was handled by Long Lines.

The toll network was accessed by dialing "1." In the early years of user-dialed long-distance calls, operators identified the calling telephone number by bridging on the call momentarily and asking the calling party for the billing number. This process was called *operator number identification* (ONI). Gradually, the LECs added *automatic number identification* (ANI) equipment to identify the billing number.

In 1976 the Federal Communications Commission (FCC), which regulates interstate telephone service, opened long-distance telephone service to competition from other IECs. These IECs gained access to the local telephone network through an ordinary seven-digit telephone number. This form of access had technical drawbacks that resulted in poorer quality transmission for reasons that Chapter 2 explains. An equally important drawback was the necessity of dialing a seven-digit telephone number for access to the long-distance network instead of the digit "1" that all callers used for access to AT&T's network. Also, ANI was not feasible over this method of access, so users had to dial a personal identification number (PIN). With a five- or six-digit PIN, this form of access required dialing as many as 22 or 23 digits to reach the terminating telephone number.

Equal Access

In 1982, AT&T and the Department of Justice signed a consent decree that resulted in AT&T's divesting its operating telephone companies. An element of the decree required the LECs to give equal access to all IECs. Under equal access, all carriers have connections that are identical to AT&T's connection to end offices. When a user originates a call, the switching equipment must decide which IEC the user wants to handle the call. The selected IEC is known in the industry as the *primary interexchange carrier* (PIC). In central offices equipped with stored program controllers that are programmed for equal access, each user presubscribes to a preferred IEC. The central office routes the call to that IEC when the user dials "1." Callers can reach other IECs by dialing a carrier access code, 10XXX or 101XXXX, where XXXX is a number assigned to the IEC. Automatic number identification is a standard equal-access feature, so PIN dialing is not required. The Bell companies programmed equal access into most SPC offices by 1986, which the consent decree between

AT&T and the Department of Justice required. In many locations, equal-access tandem offices allow access to multiple IECs. It should be understood that except for GTE, independent telephone companies are not required to provide equal access, though most of them have voluntarily done so. GTE agreed in 1983 to provide equal access from its central offices as a condition imposed by the Department of Justice in permitting GTE to purchase Sprint. Subsequently, GTE divested itself of its ownership in Sprint.

Another significant feature of the agreement between AT&T and the Department of Justice is the subdivision of the country into serving areas called local access transport areas (LATAs). Under the terms of the agreement, the local Bell Operating Companies can offer toll telephone service only within the LATA. Between LATAs, AT&T and any other authorized IEC can furnish long-distance services. Conditions established by the 1996 Telecommunications Act permit the LECs to offer long-distance service. Some other conditions of the consent decree are modified or eliminated under this legislation.

THE 1996 TELECOMMUNICATIONS ACT

In 1996 Congress passed the first major modification of the 1936 telecommunications legislation that established the Federal Communications Commission and regulated the radio, telephone, and telegraph industries. The 1996 bill affects all elements of telecommunications in the United States. This section briefly discusses the major provisions of the bill.

Local Telephone Service

Local service can be offered by a variety of companies, including IECs, CATV companies, electric power companies, and other utilities in competition with the LECs. Users will be permitted to keep their telephone numbers if they change service providers. Other companies are not permitted to offer local and long-distance service as a package until the ex-Bell company serving the area is permitted to offer long-distance service. Low-income rural users are to receive a range of services at reduced rates. Schools, libraries, and rural health care facilities are entitled to preferential rates for selected services.

Long-Distance Telephone Service

Ex-Bell LECs are permitted to enter long-distance markets, but the FCC can bar their entry if it is not deemed to be in the public interest. The FCC will weigh Justice Department recommendations in deciding whether to permit entry.

Local Bell companies cannot enter the long-distance market until their local customers have the option of selecting competitive services. All long-distance carriers are prohibited from changing a customer's long-distance provider without permission.

Broadcast Services

The transmission of sexually explicit and indecent materials to minors over computer networks is prohibited. Television set manufacturers are required to provide computer chips to enable blocking of shows that are labeled as potentially offensive. A single company would be permitted to own stations that reach up to 35 percent of the viewers in the United States. The existing limit was 25 percent. Companies would now be permitted to own a TV station and a CATV system in the same market. Additional spectrum is allotted to permit the transition to high definition television.

Cable Television

LECs and others are permitted to deliver video to homes and businesses. Rates of CATV systems with fewer than 50,000 subscribers are deregulated. All other CATV systems will be deregulated by 1999 if the cable company competes against the local telephone company for cable customers.

PRIVATE TELEPHONE SYSTEMS

Many organizations operate private telecommunications systems. These systems range in size from small PBXs to the Federal Telephone System (FTS), which is larger than the telecommunications systems in many countries.

Private networks normally must be connected to the public network so users can place calls to points that the private network does not cover, and so people outside the private network can reach them. This is done by connecting to an end office in a manner similar to the pre-equal-access connection described for IECs. These connections are usually switched through a PBX or through private tandem switching systems.

Private network operators design their networks to transmission and numbering plan criteria similar to networks operated by the LECs. There is no reason that private systems must conform to the nationwide numbering plan. If they do not, however, the result is often a dual numbering system, one for calls placed on the private network, and another for calls placed on the public network.

BROADBAND SYSTEMS

Overlaying the voice network of switches, CPE, and transmission equipment is a vast array of services. The PSTN is only one of the many services that ride these facilities, and it is not a single network; instead, it is a system of many networks under multiple ownership, which all come together in the local exchange network. Even the local exchange, which has been the remaining bastion of monopoly ownership, is gradually becoming competitive.

The power of the PSTN lies in the fact that to place a telephone call it isn't necessary to know anything about the network's structure. The addressing method is simple, and the system decides which carrier's network will handle which type of call. You can, for example, pick up a telephone in New York City, place an 800 call to San Francisco, and the network automatically switches the call to the IEC that serves the 800 number you dialed. New York Telephone on the originating end and Pacific Bell on the terminating end handle the local exchange portion of the call, the IEC handles the intermediate portion, and the revenues are divided accordingly.

The only exception to the rule that you don't need to know anything about the network in order to use it is public telephones such as pay phones and phones in hotel rooms, where calls may be handled by a service that charges unexpectedly high prices. Here, users may need to know how to bypass the service in favor of their preferred carrier.

Although the PSTN is orderly and easy to use, the same cannot be said for data networks. Data networks use the same backbone facilities as voice: the copper cable local loop and the fiber-optics transmission facilities, but there is no guarantee that one data network can communicate with another, and no easy way to reach another user who subscribes to a different network. The data equivalents of the PSTN are value-added networks using packet switching or frame relay and a broadband service some LECs offer called switched multimegabit data service (SMDS). These technologies, which will be explained in later chapters, enable users to send traffic across a public network over permanent virtual circuits. A virtual circuit is one that is defined in the network software. The path doesn't occupy a fixed hardware circuit as does a dedicated circuit. Furthermore, switched virtual circuits, which enable data users to address stations that are not addressed as part of a private network, do not exist at the time of this writing. As a result, users cannot dial an end-to-end data connection over a public data network. That role is supposed to be assigned to ISDN, but at the present state of ISDN development only a small percentage of the stations in North America can be reached with end-to-end digital connections.

Some demand for switched digital connectivity exists today, but apparently not enough to inspire the LECs to make it universally available. A new form of network is gradually beginning the long process of replacing what we now have. With a few exceptions such as frame relay, today's network services are largely composed of fixed-bandwidth circuits. Information can be encoded and compressed, and more squeezed into circuits, but once they are full they are full, and when no information is being transmitted, their bandwidth goes to waste. Some services, such as voice, survive nicely in a fixed-bandwidth environment, but many of today's applications require a lot of bandwidth for a very short time, and then none.

Take, for example, the case of a physician on the West Coast reading a digitized X-ray of a patient on the East Coast. The X-ray may contain one million or more bytes (eight megabits) even after it is compressed. To download this file over today's analog networks using the fastest modem available would take nearly five minutes. Over the full bandwidth of a T-1 circuit it would take a little over five seconds, which isn't bad, but you can't dial up a T-1 connection, hold it for a few seconds, and release it. Our physician needs the ability to dial a broadband circuit, hold it long enough to transfer the file, and pay only for the bandwidth used.

Switching is at the heart of many applications. The beauty of the PSTN is that you can connect to anyone anywhere with a PSTN connection, but that type of connection isn't sufficient for the kind of application we have been discussing. A new switching and multiplexing system is needed to enable users to connect to anyone they choose, and get the bandwidth they need while they need it, and pay for usage instead of a full-time connection. Such a service is asynchronous transfer mode (ATM), which is being developed to fulfill broadband switching needs. We will discuss ATM frequently in this book, even though it has not yet reached the point of common application.

STANDARDS

The close interrelatedness of the telecommunications network requires standards for devices to communicate successfully with one another. Unfortunately, the need for standards and the need for technical progress sometimes conflict because standards often are not set until the technology has been proven in practice, and the only way to prove the technology is through extensive use. Therefore, when it comes time to set a standard, a large base of installed equipment is already in place designed to proprietary standards. The policies of many standards-setting organizations preclude their adopting proprietary standards, even if the manufacturer is willing to make them public.

Also, competing manufacturers are represented on the standards-setting bodies of the United States, which is an incentive for bodies to not accept proprietary standards. As a result, even after standards are adopted, a considerable amount of equipment exists that does not conform to the standard.

Some standards are set before they are tested in commercial applications. A good example is the Open Systems Interconnect (OSI) model of the International Standards Organization (ISO), which is discussed in Chapter 4. The model was developed first, well before any practical demonstration of its technical feasibility. Vendors have adopted standards from one or more of its seven layers, but at the time of this writing, few commercial products use the entire model.

How Standards Are Developed

The field of players in the standards process is vast, and sometimes not closely coordinated. There are four key stages that occur in moving a standard from conception to adoption:

◆ Conceptualization
◆ Development
◆ Influence
◆ Promulgation

In the United States, just about anyone can conceptualize the need for a standard. Before development begins, however, some recognized body must accept responsibility for the task. For example, local area network standards could have been developed by several different organizations; the Institute of Electrical and Electronic Engineers (IEEE) accepted the task. The Electronics Industries Association (EIA) is another organization that has developed many standards that the American National Standards Institute (ANSI) has accepted.

The development of a standard is usually assigned to a committee within the organization. If the committee is not broadly represented across interest groups, the standards work may never begin. Participation is largely voluntary, and is usually funded by the standards' influencers, who are the companies or associations with the most to gain or lose. Governmental organizations also wield influence in the standards process. Companies with vast market power also fill the role of standards influencers. Often, their influence is enhanced because they have already demonstrated technical feasibility of the standard in practice.

The standards promulgators are the agencies that can accredit standards and produce the rules and regulations for enforcing them. In the United States ANSI is the chief organization that accredits standards developed by other organizations such as IEEE and EIA.

Standards Organizations

In the United States and internationally many organizations and associations
are involved in the standards process. The following is a brief description of the
role of the most influential of these.

International Telecommunications Union (ITU)

The International Telecommunications Union (ITU) was formed in 1865 to
promote mutual compatibility of the communications systems that were then
emerging. The ITU, now a United Nations–sponsored organization to which
160 countries belong, distributes international standards. The two principal
groups of interest to telecommunications are the ITU-T (telecommunications)
and ITU-R (radio). These groups were formerly known as the Consultative
Committee on International Telephone and Telegraph (CCITT) and Consultative Committee on International (CIR).

ITU does its work through study groups that work in four-year time increments. After a four-year session, the study groups present their work to a
plenary assembly for approval. Plenary assemblies coincide with leap years.
The principal standards adopted by ITU-T are listed in Appendix B.

In some countries where a state-owned agency operates the telecommunications system, ITU recommendations bear the force of law. In the United
States, compliance is largely voluntary, although the standards of the ITU are
accepted by international treaty.

International Standards Organization (ISO)

The International Standards Organization (ISO) is an association of standard-
setting organizations from the various nations that participate in the process. In
the United States, ANSI is the ISO representative and adviser to the State Department on ITU standards. The most familiar ISO standards in the telecommunications industry are the standards that support the OSI model.

International Electrotechnical Commission (IEC)

The IEC accredits standards on much the same basis as ISO. IEC promulgates
electrical standards, in contrast to ISO standards, which are primarily logical.

American National Standards Institute (ANSI)

ANSI is the standards body in the United States that promulgates standards of
all types, not just information processing and telecommunications. ANSI is a
nongovernmental, nonprofit organization comprising some 300 standards
committees. The ANSI X.3 committees handle information-related standards;

T1 committees handle telecommunications standards. Both consumers and manufacturers are represented on ANSI committees, and cooperating trade groups that follow ANSI procedures do much of the work. The Institute of Electrical and Electronic Engineers (IEEE) and the Electronic Industries Association (EIA) are two prominent organizations that promulgate standards through ANSI.

Industry and Professional Associations

Two of the most important industry and professional associations are IEEE and EIA. EIA has produced many standards that are important to the telecommunications industry. For example, most data terminal devices use the EIA-232 interface standard in their interconnection with circuit equipment. More recently, EIA collaborated with the Telecommunications Industry Association (TIA) to produce commercial building telecommunications wiring standards, which are discussed in Chapter 7.

The IEEE is a professional association that has had an important effect on standards activities such as the local area network standards that its "802" committee developed. These standards, discussed in more detail in Chapter 29, use the framework of ISO's Open Systems Interconnect model and CCITT protocols to develop three local network alternatives. IEEE is also responsible for metropolitan area network standards that most LECs are now deploying.

Other associations include the United States Telephone Association (USTA), Corporation on Open Systems (COS), an industry group that is promoting open architectures; Computer and Business Equipment Manufacturing Association, Exchange Carrier's Association, Open Software Forum, and in Europe, the Standards Promotion and Applications Group (SPAG).

Defacto Standards

Large companies such as IBM and AT&T have enough market power to set proprietary standards, which others must follow to be compatible. IBM's Systems Network Architecture (SNA) is the most widely used data communications architecture in the world. Yet, however, SNA is not an international standard, although it is closely aligned in concept to OSI.

The voice networks in the United States are largely designed to AT&T's proprietary standards. Before divestiture, AT&T released these standards to other manufacturers through the United States Independent Telephone Association (now United States Telephone Association). Sometimes others manufactured equipment through cross-licensing agreements with AT&T, but usually compatibility information was unavailable until several years after AT&T successfully introduced the technology.

Sometimes, ITU has adopted AT&T standards. For example, the standards for the United States version of digital multiplex is an ITU recommendation, but it is not compatible with the European version, which is also an ITU standard. In other cases, ITU standards and AT&T proprietary standards conflict. For example, signaling between AT&T's long-distance switching offices for several years used a protocol known as Common Channel Interoffice Signaling (CCIS). The international standard is ITU Signaling System No. 7, which is incompatible with CCIS.

The Importance of Standards

In the years before the FCC and the courts opened AT&T's network to interconnection and competition, users could avoid compatibility problems by turning the responsibilities over to the LEC (except in data communications where incompatible protocols were a frequent problem). Now that station equipment is no longer owned by the LEC and long-distance networks are a complex combination of common carrier and private facilities, compatibility is a concern of almost every user. The need for compatibility thrusts the issue of standards to the forefront because users' options are limited if the manufacturer's interfaces are proprietary and not made publicly available.

One cannot help being awed by the intricacy of the nation's telecommunications system. The complexity is evident from this brief overview, but it becomes even more impressive as the details emerge. The marvel is that the system can cover such a vast geographical area, can be administered by hundreds of thousands of workers, contain countless pieces of electrical apparatus, and still function as reliably as it does. As we discuss these elements in greater detail, the techniques that create this high quality service will become more understandable.

CHAPTER

2

VOICE TRANSMISSION PRINCIPLES

Before the dissolution of the Bell System, telecommunications managers and users had little reason to concern themselves with transmission quality. Over the years, quality gradually improved, and as it did, users' expectations grew. The improvements did not, however, simply happen. They occurred because engineers and scientists, principally from the Bell Laboratories, developed procedures for measuring transmission quality and equipment that delivered an increasing degree of freedom from the principal enemies of good transmission: loss, noise, and echo.

Today the idea of a unified network transmission design no longer exists. The former Bell Operating Companies through their research and development arm, Bell Communications Research (Bellcore), develop and publish the standards to which the local exchange networks are designed. Interexchange carriers are free to design their networks to any standard they choose, but most follow the standards previously published by AT&T.

Private networks are under no transmission restrictions, other than the acceptance of their users, and with the mixture of circuits and equipment that is available today, there is a risk that users will find certain connections unacceptable. This chapter discusses the fundamentals of transmission design and explains how common carriers achieve quality in their networks. Most of the principles are equally applicable to private networks.

FIGURE 2-1

Typical Telecommunications Circuit

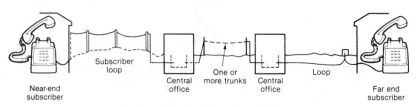

In common carrier and private telecommunications systems, systematic maintenance, careful circuit design, and high-quality equipment help assure quality. Transmission quality is entirely different from switching-system quality. Switching systems are go/no-go devices. The connection is either established or it isn't. With transmission systems, quality is a statistical measure. The telecommunications system always introduces some impairments into the talking path between users. Transmission design is a compromise between quality and cost. Although it is possible to build a telecommunications system that will reproduce voices with near-perfect fidelity and clarity, such quality is neither necessary nor economical.

TRANSMISSION IMPAIRMENTS

For voice communication, four variables are particularly important in ensuring the adequacy of communications: level or volume, noise, bandwidth, and echo. For data communications over analog circuits, envelope delay and amplitude distortion are also important. Over digital circuits, the main concern in a data network is bit error rate (BER), which is the number of errored bits expressed as a portion of transmitted bits. For example, a BER of 10^{-9} means one bit is received in error for each 1 billion bits transmitted.

Volume or Level

Consider the simple telecommunications circuit illustrated in Figure 2–1. The telephone instrument converts the changes in sound pressure from a talker's voice to a varying electrical current that is an analog of the acoustic signal. (Refer to Chapter 19 for an explanation of how the telephone instrument functions.) The electrical characteristics of the circuit between the sending and receiving telephones modify the signal to reduce its volume (or increase its loss), change the bandwidth of the signal, and introduce extraneous signals such as noise, crosstalk, and distortion.

The unit of loss is the *decibel* (dB). A decibel is a logarithmic unit that expresses the relationship between the power or voltage levels of signals. Appendix A discusses the decibel in more detail for those who are unfamiliar with it.

An increase in signal volume that doubles the power of the signal is a 3 dB increase. Similarly, a drop in signal power that halves the signal is a 3 dB reduction. The smallest change that the human ear can detect is about 1 dB; a 3 dB change is apparent to a listener concentrating on hearing the change. It is essential to understand that the dB is not an absolute unit of measurement, as are the volt, the ampere, and the watt. The dB measures only the ratio of two quantities of the same unit. A signal power of one milliwatt (mw) is an almost universally used standard power against which other power levels are compared. The dB is often used to express power levels compared to one milliwatt; for example, 0 dBm = 1 mw.

The amount of loss that users can tolerate in a circuit depends on noise impairments, the tolerance of the listener for weak signals, and other distortions that alter the character of the received signal. This, of course, depends on individual preference and varies among users, ranging from those with hearing impairment to those with acute hearing sensitivity. Because of the wide differences in preference, transmission objectives are statistically based with signal and noise standards designed to satisfy most users.

Amplification easily overcomes loss in telecommunications circuits. Amplifiers, or *repeaters,* however, may introduce undesired side effects along with the desired effect of reducing loss. Not only do they add cost to the circuit, but they add distortion as limited bandwidth, additional noise, and other undesirable changes to the signal they amplify. Designers attempt to minimize the use of repeaters to the greatest extent possible, particularly in local subscriber loops. With more than 150 million subscriber loops in the United States, the cost of amplifying more than a small fraction of them would be substantial. Instead, designers provide amplification for trunks, which all users share, and for some long loops. The characteristics and economics of the ordinary telephone and the subscriber loop drive the design of the elements of the telecommunications network, which Chapters 6 and 35 discuss.

Increasingly, the use of digital trunk facilities minimizes loss and noise impairments. The vast majority of the subscriber loops are still analog, however, and are the source of a large share of the transmission impairments in today's connections. In the Integrated Services Digital Network, which Chapter 28 discusses, digital subscriber loops permit end-to-end digital connections. With digital connections, transmission impairments are controlled by designers and will be of little concern to users. ISDN is not widely displayed in North America today, however, so analog impairments remain.

Noise

Noise is any unwanted signal in a circuit. Noise is an analog phenomenon. Digital circuits are susceptible to errors, but even a high error rate still results in a noise-free voice connection. Hum, crackling or frying, and crosstalk from adjacent circuits are all examples of unwanted signals that careful design and maintenance of a circuit can control. There are definite trade-offs between the various noise impairments and the quality of the signal as the listener perceives it. A uniform level of hiss, for example, may be tolerable if no other impairments exist and the signal level is high. The most important measurement of noise is the signal-to-noise ratio (expressed in dB).

Data signals exhibit an entirely different tolerance to noise than do humans. A data signal may be satisfactory in the presence of uniform steady hissing noise (white noise) that would be bothersome to humans. On the other hand, impulse noise (clicks, pops, or sometimes frying noise) will destroy a data signal on a circuit that might be acceptable for speech communication.

Circuit noise originates from three primary sources. The first is interference from external sources. Electric power lines, lightning, industrial apparatus such as electric motor commutators, crosstalk from adjacent circuits, and other sources can cause circuit noise.

The second source is thermal noise developed within the telecommunications apparatus itself. Any conductor carrying current at a temperature higher than absolute zero (–273°C), generates noise from internal electron movement. Some types of circuit elements, such as vacuum tubes, generate more thermal noise than others, but it is present in all circuit elements, including such passive elements as wire.

The third source of noise is distortion generated by nonlinearities in circuit elements, primarily amplifiers. Amplifiers do not precisely reproduce their input signals. The small imperfections in an amplifier's transfer characteristic (the output of the amplifier compared to the input) distort the amplified signal so that extra components appear in the output signal. The effect is aggravated by operating the amplifier beyond its design capability. This effect is called *intermodulation distortion*.

Bandwidth

Bandwidth is the circuit attribute that, with frequency response, controls the naturalness of transmitted speech. As with level, this is a subjective evaluation. The human ear can detect tones between about 20 Hz and 16,000 Hz, but because the voice has few frequency components below about 300 Hz or above 3,500 or 4,000 Hz, a telephone circuit that transmits a band of frequencies in this range is adequate for voice communication. Channels for voice transmission are usually designed to pass a nominal bandwidth of 300 Hz to 4,000 Hz. Telephone receivers are designed to be most sensitive to the frequency spectrum between 500 Hz and 2,500 Hz, because research has shown that most of the frequency components of ordinary speech fall into this range.

Echo

When telephone signals traverse a transmission facility, they move with a finite, although very high, speed. Electrical signals propagated in free space, a radio broadcast signal for example, travel at the speed of light (300,000,000 meters per second). Signals on a physical transmission circuit, on the other hand, propagate at about 50 to 80 percent of the speed of light, depending on the type of transmission medium and the amount of amplification or filtering applied to the circuit. A signal is delayed, therefore, as it transits any type of network.

If, in traversing the circuit, the electrical signal encounters an impedance irregularity, a reflection will occur just as a reflection occurs to a sound propagated in a large, empty room. The reflected signal returns to the sending end of the circuit and sounds to the talker like the echo from a long, hollow pipe. The greater the distance from the talker to the irregularity, the greater the time delay in the reflected signal.

Echo is detrimental to transmission in proportion to the amount of delay suffered by the signal and the amplitude of the echoed signal. A communication circuit that displays even a small amount of echo is unfit for service if the delay is too long. On the other hand, a small amount of echo occurs in the ordinary telephone where the user hears it as *sidetone,* which is the sound of the speaker's voice in his or her receiver. Because sidetone is not delayed, it does not interfere with communication. In fact, designers deliberately introduce a certain amount of sidetone in a telephone to help users regulate their voice level. A lack of sidetone gives talkers the perception that the instrument is dead, while a sufficient amount causes talkers to lower their voices somewhat.

The most serious form of echo in communications circuits arises from *four-wire terminating sets,* or *hybrids.* These are devices that convert the transmission circuit from four-wire to two-wire, as Figure 2–2 shows. Economics impels the designer to make as much of a communications network two-wire as possible to minimize costs. Carrier and radio systems inherently transmit in only one direction so that a separate path or channel is required in each direction to obtain two-way transmission. The two directions of transmission must be combined into a single two-way two-wire circuit at each end by a four-wire terminating set, or hybrid, for extension through two-wire switching systems and to two-wire local loops.

F I G U R E   2–2

Typical Long-Haul Connection

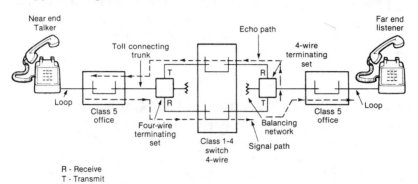

In digital networks the hybrid is still required at the two-to-four-wire junction point, such as the line circuit where the two-wire loop connects to the switching network in a digital switching system. The hybrids in a digital switch serve the same purpose as they do in an analog switch, but the hybrid circuitry is digital instead of analog. In today's networks, virtually all of the interexchange circuits and switches are digital, and many of the local switching systems are analog. An interexchange call will usually be four-wire and digital from the interLATA access trunks of the local switch to the interLATA access trunks of the local switch at the distant end. The only opportunity for echo to occur, therefore, is in the hybrids at each end of the connection.

In a hybrid the two-wire portion of a circuit is balanced against a network that approximates the electrical characteristics of the two-wire transmission line. When the balancing network is identical with the transmission line, the hybrid is in balance, and energy received over the four-wire transmission path is coupled to the two-wire path. Because the balancing network fails to match the two-wire line perfectly, a signal feeds back to the talker at the distant end as an echo. The farther away from the talker the echo occurs, the greater the time delay introduced into the return signal and the greater the impediment to good transmission. Figure 2–2 shows the configuration of a typical analog long distance circuit showing four-wire terminating sets, four-wire transmission facilities, and the echo path.

The loss of a signal traversing a circuit through the hybrid and back to the sending end is called *return loss.* If the return loss of the circuit does not equal or exceed the amplification in both paths of the four-wire circuit, oscillation, or *singing,* occurs. This is the same effect observed when the volume is advanced on a public address system until the system squeals or sings. The hybrid's balancing network must be adjusted to at least 10 dB more loss than needed to prevent the circuit from singing. Adjustments to the hybrid balance network become more important as the circuit becomes longer. At about 2,000 miles, the round-trip delay on a circuit becomes excessive and any appreciable echo becomes disturbing to the talkers. *Echo suppressors* in analog circuits and *echo cancelers* in digital circuits control echo.

Echo suppressors are devices that automatically insert loss in the return path of a four-wire circuit. The echo suppressor switches back and forth between the two transmission paths following first one talker then the other. Properly adjusted, an echo suppressor inserts only enough loss in the circuit to allow the listener to interrupt the talker, but otherwise attenuates the reflected signal by approximately 15 dB. Long circuits such as satellite circuits with round-trip delays of about 0.5 second require a more effective method of eliminating echo. On such circuits, echo cancelers are used. Echo cancelers perform the same function as echo suppressors but operate by creating a replica of the near-end signal and subtracting it from the echo to cancel the effect.

Circuit loss is adjusted in shorter circuits to control echo. The whole subject of loss and echo control is embodied in the *via net loss plan,* which is a set of design rules that optimize transmission performance and economics in an analog telecommunications network. The advent of modern digital transmission and switching facilities has caused the loss plan to evolve toward a fixed-loss plan that integrates zero loss digital transmission facilities and digital echo cancelers into the network.

Amplitude Distortion

Telecommunications channels rarely have a perfectly flat response across the voice frequency band. Figure 2–3a shows an equalized channel; Figure 2–3b shows the frequency response characteristic of a channel before equalization. Although equipment used in voice frequency channels is manufactured to close tolerances, the accumulated small deviations inherent in the manufacturing process produce the irregular response illustrated. The channels can be brought into close tolerance by adding equalizers where the demands of the service justify the extra cost.

Envelope Delay Distortion

The design of electronic amplifiers and multiplexers requires components that introduce varying amounts of delay to frequencies within the voice frequency pass band. This varying delay is known as *envelope delay*. Envelope delay has

FIGURE 2–3

Voice Channel Attenuation

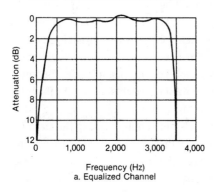
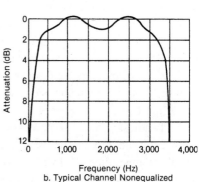

Frequency (Hz)
a. Equalized Channel

Frequency (Hz)
b. Typical Channel Nonequalized

no discernible effect on voice frequency signals, but for data signals, which are composed of complex voice frequency tones, envelope delay results in tones arriving at the receiver slightly out of phase with one another. So high-speed modems, which use phase characteristics to encode the data signal, may not operate properly. Envelope delay distortion can be compensated by the addition of delay equalizers either in the telecommunications circuit or in the data terminal equipment.

ELEMENTS OF TRANSMISSION DESIGN

Transmission design is the process of balancing loss, noise, and echo against circuit costs. The fourth variable, bandwidth, is not adjustable; it is inherent in the design of amplifiers and multiplex equipment. The remainder of this chapter discusses transmission from the point of view of the quality requirements of voice frequency circuits. Data circuits traveling over the switched telephone network must accept the characteristics of the circuits as they are, but as the network evolves toward all-digital, it is increasingly congenial toward data. On analog private line data circuits, transmission can be controlled more closely by *conditioning,* which Chapter 31 discusses.

Telecommunications circuits are either switched or dedicated; that is, the user dials the connection and releases it on call termination, or the circuit is permanently connected between two or more points. The characteristics of dedicated or private-line circuits can be specifically designed for the application, but because of the random originations and terminations and the variation of the characteristics of switched circuits, design control is less exact. Switched-

FIGURE 2-4

Transmission Levels and Transmission-Level Points

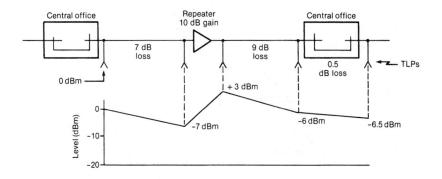

circuit design is a compromise based on the probability of the user's receiving a connection that is of satisfactory quality a high percentage of the time.

Each switched connection is composed of three types of circuits: a subscriber loop on each end, an interLATA connecting trunk on each end, and one or more interoffice trunks between. These types of circuits are designed using different rules. Each circuit type is allocated a share of the end-to-end impairment, with the objective of providing a total connection of satisfactory quality to the user.

Variables in Transmission Quality

It is important to remember the difference between loss and level in a circuit. Level is a measurement of signal power at a specified point in the circuit known as a *transmission-level point* (TLP). Loss is the difference in level between TLPs. A voice frequency signal is a complex amalgam of tones that vary widely in frequency and amplitude.

A voice signal is impractical for measuring level and making adjustments to circuits, in which level is adjusted in 0.1 dB increments. Level is measured by applying a 1,004 Hz single frequency tone to the circuit at a standard TLP and then measuring the test tone at another TLP. The measured tone is then compared to a standard one-milliwatt (0.001 watt) test source to establish a test tone level. Most transmission testing equipment is calibrated against a one-milliwatt source so that measurements can be made directly with the test set. Figure 2–4 illustrates the concept of TLPs, loss, and gain.

Transmission-Level Points

Several measurement points in circuits are traditionally set at a specified level. For example, the output of a switch is considered a 0 TLP. This does not, however, mean that signals leave the switch at 0 dBm; usually they are less. For example, if a 0 dBm signal is inserted at the end of a subscriber loop that has 5 dB of loss and if the switch inserts an additional 0.5 dB of loss, the output measurement at the 0 TLP will be –5.5 dBm.

Carrier channels are normally designed with TLPs of –16 dBm into the transmitting port and +7 dBm out of the receiver. Thus, a carrier system introduces into the circuit 23 dB of gain that can be used to overcome other circuit losses. If this is more gain than needed, it is adjusted with fixed-loss attenuators, which are known as *pads*.

Insertion Loss

Circuit design is simplified by treating certain elements as black boxes with identifiable loss characteristics. For example, when a connection traverses a switching machine, it is generally assumed to have a 0.5 dB loss. Some PBXs have a loss of as much as 6 dB between lines. Circuit designers call this *insertion loss,* or *inserted connection loss* (ICL). Insertion losses are additive. If two trunks, each with 5 dB of loss, are connected into a circuit, they will introduce 10 dB of loss into the connection.

Reference Noise

Noise is measured with respect to an arbitrary reference noise (rn) level of–90 dBm. This level, defined as 0 dBrn, is at the threshold of audibility. As mentioned earlier, not only the level but also the frequency of noise determines its interfering effects. If noise is evenly distributed across a voice frequency band (called white noise), the noise in the 500 Hz to 2,500 Hz range will be more annoying to the listener than low- and high-frequency noise because both the ear and the telephone are more sensitive to these middle frequencies. Therefore, noise is measured through a *C message weighting* filter. This weighting, shown in Figure 2–5, passes noise in roughly the same proportion as the sensitivity of the human ear. The interfering effect of noise on voice communication is usually expressed as dBrnc, with the c indicating the use of a C message weighting filter. When noise is measured at a zero TLP or mathematically adjusted to a 0 TLP, it is expressed as dBrnc0. Special service circuits, such as data and broadcast audio, do not have the same tolerance for high- and low-frequency noise. Therefore, they are measured without the C message weighting filter.

FIGURE 2-5

C Message Weighting Response Curve

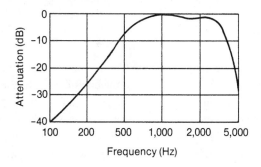

A noise measurement is a measure of the noise power in a connection and is not directly additive in the same way as loss. Doubling the noise power in a circuit increases the noise by 3 dB. If two circuits, each with 20 dBrn of noise, are connected in tandem, the result will be a noise level of 23 dBrn.

Echo Return Loss

As mentioned previously, listeners are most sensitive to interference in the frequency spectrum between about 250 Hz and 2,500 Hz. Measuring a circuit's return loss in that band produces a value called *echo return loss*. The measurement is made by transmitting a band of white noise that filters limit to 250 Hz to 2,500 Hz and measuring the returned noise energy. A useful companion measurement is the *singing point* in which an amplifier is inserted into the circuit to increase the gain to the point at which the circuit just begins to oscillate, or sing. The circuit sings at the frequency at which it has the poorest return loss. Measurements of echo return loss, singing loss, and singing frequency are important indicators of circuit performance.

Subscriber Loop Transmission

Of the circuit elements, subscriber loop transmission is the most difficult to control because of the varying distance of users from the telephone central office and the varying composition of the circuits that serve them. Subscriber loop losses vary from 0 dB (some are inside the telephone central office) to as much as 8 or 10 dB. It is technically possible to design all subscriber loops to some target figure, say 5 dB. This could be done by inserting resistance networks (pads) into shorter loops and amplifiers into loops with more than 5 dB of loss. With so many subscriber loops, however, the cost of designing them all to a fixed loss is prohibitive while the network remains analog. With an all-digital network, fixed-loss loops will become a reality.

Loop Loss

Designers select cable gauge and loop length with the objective of allowing at least 23 milliamps of current to flow in the combination of the telephone set, cable circuit, and central office battery feed circuitry. Of these elements, the loss of the cable is the most variable because its resistance varies with the wire gauge and the length of the loop. Cables are built to design objectives that typically result in circuits of 8 dB of loss or less. Except for those few that are derived on multiplex equipment or fed on fiber optics, subscriber loops are connected to the central office with twisted-pair cable. Loop design balances cost against transmission quality. To the greatest extent possible, fine-gauge cable is used because its cost is lower and its smaller diameter fits into conduit more readily. Most loops leave the central office in cables composed of 26-gauge wire. This provides adequate transmission to about 15,000 feet from the central office. The effects of loss in longer loops are overcome by using coarser gauge cable—24 gauge, 22 gauge, and, rarely, 19 gauge.

The frequency response of cable is reasonably linear. Cable loss is a composite of resistance and capacitance loss. Cable pairs, acting like large capacitors, attenuate the high more than the low frequencies. The effects of high-frequency loss are overcome in loops more than 18,000 feet long by using inductance coils in series with the conductors. This technique, known as *loading*, improves the loss of the loop at the expense of frequencies above 4 kHz, which the load coils attenuate. Figure 2–6 shows the frequency response of loaded and nonloaded cable pairs. While loading improves the voice frequency characteristics of cable, it precludes the use of digital signals and limited distance modems on the circuit. These modems, which are discussed in Chapter 3, are inexpensive devices that permit data transmission at 19.2 kb/s or higher.

Shielding

Properly constructed loops are enclosed in shielded cables and are not greatly affected by external noise. Many loops in the United States are built jointly with electric power transmission lines, which are a potential source of noise. Continuity of the metallic shield that surrounds cable pairs must be strictly maintained if noise influence is to be minimized. Failure to attend to shielding and balance, described in the next section, accounts for most noise problems in telephone circuits.

FIGURE 2–6

Loss-Frequency Response of 10,000 Feet of 26-Gauge Cable

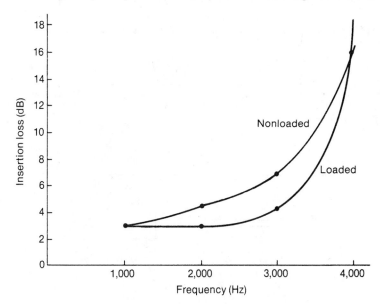

Balance

Induction, by itself, is not necessarily detrimental to telephone circuits. In rural areas, unshielded open wires often shared pole lines with electric power circuits without excessive interference. The degree of interference depends on the *balance* of the telephone circuit. In a balanced environment, each wire in the cable has the same amount of exposure to interference; interference induced in one wire of the pair is canceled by the interference induced in the second wire. As Figure 2–7a shows, when the two wires of a cable pair are identically balanced in resistance and isolation from ground, induced voltages are equal when measured from each side of the pair to ground. Telephone sets and amplifiers, which detect voltages across the two wires of a pair, are insensitive to these balanced voltages, but any imbalance results in noise in the output circuit, as Figure 2–7b shows. Chapter 6 describes how cable balance is controlled. For now it is necessary only to understand its effects. Noise on most subscriber loops should be in the order of 5 or 10 dBrnc0. When the noise exceeds 20 dBrnc0, corrective action is usually required.

Loops exist in a hostile environment. They are exposed to weather, flooded manholes, icing, winds, disruptions by excavation; the hazards are many and difficult to avoid. Therefore, this portion of a connection exhibits

FIGURE 2-7

Noise Current Flow in a Cable

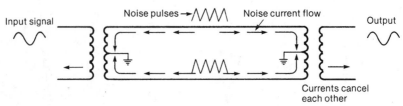

a. Balanced Cable Pair

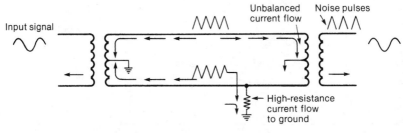

b. Unbalanced Cable Pair

the greatest variability in transmission performance. Bandwidth, envelope delay, and amplitude distortion are less affected by the hazards that confront subscriber loops, but the variability of subscriber loops greatly affects loss and noise.

InterLATA Connecting Trunks

Trunks connecting an IEC's switching office to an LEC's end office are called *interLATA connecting trunks.* These trunks connect directly from the IEC's point of presence to the LEC's end office, or they connect through an access tandem. InterLATA connecting trunks are the circuits that connect the user to an IEC's operator and to recording and billing equipment for directly dialed calls, and that terminate calls from a distant IEC's switching office to the local central office. Some of these trunks are connected over voice frequency cable circuits, but the majority are digital carrier. In any event, these trunks almost invariably have adjustable gain. Loss, therefore, can be controlled within close limits. The design objectives for interLATA connecting trunks as prescribed by *BOC Notes on the LEC Networks* range from 3.0 dB for digital trunks to 4.0 dB for analog trunks without gain.

Intertoll Trunks

Intertoll analog trunks are circuits that interconnect IEC switching offices. These trunks are, with rare exception, deployed over carrier facilities where the loss and gain are controllable, and the causes of noise found in cables are of small concern.

Intertoll circuits are designed with loss complying with via net loss design rules to aid in controlling the interfering effects of echo. Analog intertoll trunks, which are rapidly disappearing, operate with a variable amount of loss determined by via net loss rules and are tested with 2 dB pads in each end to optimize the signal level with respect to the TLPs. Similarly, digital trunks operate at zero loss and are tested with 3 dB pads in the receiving path at each end to provide consistency with the analog environment. When analog circuits are connected in tandem to build up a long circuit, the overall connection of intertoll trunks operates at via net loss. Similarly, digital circuits operate at zero loss when connected in tandem.

Via Net Loss

The variable component in trunk design is determined by a factor known as the via net loss factor (VNLF) of the circuit. A VNLF of 0.0015 dB per mile is used for analog terrestrial carrier circuits; for example, a circuit 1,000 miles long would require 1.5 dB of loss. In practice, designers add somewhat more loss than this for administrative reasons. The amount is unimportant for this discussion.

The IECs administer intertoll circuit loss. Private network users who obtain circuits from a carrier are provided with circuits with a net loss that the carrier designs and controls.

The net loss of circuits is subject to variation because of maintenance actions, component aging, and equipment troubles. Statistically, the variations between circuits should compensate for one another. However, because of the random nature of connections through the switching network, it is possible for some connections to be established with either so much loss that it is difficult to hear or so little that the circuit sounds hollow or, in the worst case, oscillates or sings.

Noise Sources

Intertoll circuits are susceptible to the same noise sources as interLATA connecting trunks. A primary advantage of lightwave circuits is that, because the signals are digital and are regenerated at every repeater point, noise is not a problem. The noise levels of long-haul digital circuits are not appreciably higher than those of local digital circuits, and as a result, cross-country circuit quality has improved dramatically as the IECs have shifted their circuits from the older microwave radio to lightwave.

Some analog circuits remain, however, and the analog microwave and the multiplex equipment used on microwave and coaxial cable is subject to intermodulation noise. As mentioned earlier, both thermal noise and intermodulation noise are present in electronic communications systems. The overall noise effect on a circuit is the sum of both types of noise. The effect of noise is optimized by adjusting the operating level of the signal applied to the circuit. When the signal level is very low, the thermal noise becomes controlling, and when the signal level is high, a high level of intermodulation noise is apparent.

Analog microwave radio systems are also susceptible to other noise sources, particularly noise in the first receiver amplifier stages. This noise becomes perceptible when the received radio signal fades. As the received signal falls, it approaches the noise level generated in the front end of the receiver. This noise is then amplified with the desired signal and appears as a deteriorated signal-to-noise ratio. Microwave systems are usually equipped with standby transmitters and receivers that can take over when the regular channel fades or fails. Chapter 14 discusses protection, or diversity, more fully.

Echo Control

Echo is an important variable in intertoll network design. As previously mentioned, echo of short time delay is controlled by introducing a small amount of loss proportional to the delay of the circuit. Beyond a delay in the order of 10 to 20 milliseconds, however, the loss begins to be too great for satisfactory transmission, and echo suppressors or cancelers must be inserted in the circuit.

Local Interoffice Trunks

In a metropolitan network composed of more than one central office, the end or local central offices are linked by local interoffice trunks. These trunks are normally designed to a nominal loss of 3 dB, but the loss may be as high as 5 dB. They are used for calls within a local calling area and are not used for access to interexchange facilities. Therefore, loss and noise are less critical than in inter-LATA connecting trunks, and echo is of no consequence. Balance is still important because a poor return loss results in hollowness or singing. The facilities and equipment used in interoffice trunks are identical with equipment used in inter-LATA connecting trunks, and the same loss and noise considerations apply.

Special-Purpose Trunks

LECs and IECs use a variety of trunks for special applications. Examples are directory assistance, intercept (used for recorded announcements and operator transfer of disconnected numbers), repair service, and verification (used by operators to verify busy/idle status of lines). The design of these trunks is wholly within the purview of the LEC and is of little concern to the user. *BOC Notes on the LEC Networks* covers these design variables in detail.

Private networks may employ special-purpose trunks for a variety of applications. Examples are PBX tie lines, WATS lines, 800 (INWATS) lines, point-to-point voice and data, broadcast audio, wired music, and telemetering. These circuits are deployed over private facilities within the user's premises, over private or common carrier facilities in a metropolitan area, or over leased or common carrier facilities worldwide. Satisfactory transmission quality is obtained only by careful design of these circuits. Common carriers usually offer design assistance. However, the common carrier often lacks knowledge of the total makeup of a circuit and cannot control transmission variables. It is, therefore, essential that all users of special services understand the effects of transmission design on the systems they are purchasing.

Loss and Noise Grade of Service

Transmission measurements can be made with precision, and with modern equipment a high degree of level stability and noise performance is achievable. This does not answer the question of how good a circuit must be to satisfy its users because telephone connections are subjectively evaluated. A person who is hard-of-hearing finds perfectly satisfactory a connection that others complain is too loud and is dissatisfied with circuits that others find acceptable. Clearly, transmission quality must be evaluated against a varying base of opinion.

Transmission objectives are based on the results of many opinion samples measured by Bell Laboratories. In these tests, varying amounts of loss and noise were introduced into connections and users rated the quality. The result of these samples is a family of loss-noise grade-of-service curves. These opinion curves are translated into design and maintenance objectives for both loss and noise. Figure 2–8 is a set of curves that show the rating assigned by users to connections with varying combinations of loss and noise. Note the relationship between loss and noise. Generally, more noise is tolerable if accompanied by less loss, and more loss is acceptable if the noise level is low.

FIGURE 2-8

Loss-Noise Grade-of-Service Curves

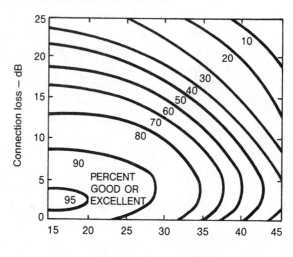

Noise to listener — dBrnC

Designers assure transmission quality by controlling three elements:

♦ Circuit design
♦ Circuit maintenance
♦ Overall connection evaluation

In circuit design, loss is the only adjustable characteristic. The other variables, principally noise and echo, are functions of how well telecommunications circuits and equipment are designed and maintained. It is unrealistic to expect equipment design and maintenance to overcome the effects of poor circuit design. Circuits with excessive loss will be unsatisfactory to users. Circuits with too little loss will result in singing, increases in intermodulation noise, and complaints from users of excessive level or hollowness.

Conversely, properly designed circuits cannot be expected to provide satisfactory transmission service when equipment is not maintained to high standards. The nation's telecommunications networks are composed of equipment ranging from new to several decades old. Although most new equipment provides excellent transmission performance with minimum maintenance, regular testing is required to ensure satisfactory performance.

Equipment and circuit maintenance are not enough to ensure that most connections will be satisfactory to the user. In both public and private networks, a regular sampling program of end-to-end connection quality is an important quality assurance technique. By making repeated loss and noise measurements to terminating locations resembling the calling patterns of the users, irregularities can be detected before they result in user complaints.

TRANSMISSION MEASUREMENTS

Transmission quality assurance requires systematic measurement with accurately calibrated test equipment. This section describes transmission measurement techniques and equipment.

Loss Measurements

Loss is measured with a transmission-measuring set (TMS) that has a tone generator, or oscillator, and a level detector with a meter or digital readout. Many TMSs also include noise-measuring apparatus. A TMS measures level at specified TLPs and at impedances that match the impedance of the TLP. Loss is nominally specified at 1,000 Hz. In practice, measurements are made at 1,004 Hz to prevent interference with digital carrier equipment.

Measurements are made by sending a single tone into the circuit at a transmitting TLP and measuring the level at a receiving TLP. Levels are adjusted by either changing physical pads or setting software pads so the design loss is achieved within specified limits. A TMS can also measure the equalization of a circuit by sending and receiving a band of frequencies instead of a single tone.

Most common carrier and many private networks are equipped to make automatic transmission measurements on circuits. Both the transmitting and receiving ends have testing systems that automatically send and measure test tones in both directions. Equipment at the far end, known as a *responder,* records measurements from the near end and reports the results over a data circuit. Most automatic test equipment also measures noise and tests signaling.

Noise Measurements

Noise is measured with a noise-measuring set that can be either a separate instrument or part of a TMS. Noise measurements are made at a TLP with the far end terminated in its characteristic impedance. If the circuit is used for voice communication, measurements are made through a C message filter. If the TLP is not a 0-level point, noise measurements are adjusted to 0 and expressed as dBrnc0. For example, if noise measures 27 dBrnc at a +7 TLP, the 7 dB gain would be subtracted and the circuit noise expressed as 20 dBrnc0.

Return Loss Measurements

Return loss measurements are made by sending a signal into the input port of a four-wire terminating set and measuring the signal returned to the output port. If a 1 kHz tone is used for the test signal, the resulting measurement may not reveal the worst-case return loss, because the hybrid balance is never uniform across the voice frequency spectrum. To find the degree of hybrid balance in a working circuit it is necessary to measure return loss at enough frequencies across the voice band to permit plotting a return loss curve that shows the worst-case frequency.

To simplify testing, a white noise source in the band of 250 Hz to 2,500 Hz is used as a test signal. Typical return-loss-measuring instruments are equipped with a white noise source, band-limiting filters, and high- and low-pass filters so return loss measurements can be made over the entire voice frequency band.

Envelope Delay Measurements

Envelope delay measurements are made with test sets that send a pair of closely spaced frequencies from the sending end of the circuit to a synchronized test set at the receiving end. The combination measures directly the relative delay of signal frequencies at various points within the circuit pass band. The ideal circuit would display linear delay across the pass band so that all components would be transmitted in a perfect phase relationship.

APPLICATIONS

A satisfactory transmission grade of service must be designed into every common carrier and private network. This chapter has discussed transmission in only the broadest terms to give the reader an understanding of the importance and principles of transmission quality control. In public networks, transmission design is under the control of the company supplying the service. When only one network existed in the United States, AT&T and its subsidiaries controlled transmission design. The independent companies that connected to the network designed their circuits to the same objectives, so the network could be considered a single entity. Private networks were composed primarily of circuits obtained from telephone companies and were also designed to AT&T-specified standards and objectives.

Today, the nation's telecommunications system is composed of a multitude of networks designed and controlled by the seven RBHCs, the independent telephone companies within their territories, and many IECs, of which AT&T is only one. Each IEC sets its own transmission objectives, and the quality is therefore not necessarily uniform.

Users need to be aware that the facilities offered by the carrier of their choice may offer different grades of service. This is not to imply that the service will be unsatisfactory. The nature of today's network is to provide choices at different cost levels, and for some applications, lower transmission quality may be acceptable. It is important to evaluate quality and to understand the implications of the different alternatives.

The most important implication of the multiple networks of the kind we have in the United States today is that the vendor may not assume responsibility for end-to-end circuit performance. If the user has telephone sets made by one vendor, cable by another, a PBX by a third vendor, connected by circuits provided by a LEC and one or more IECs, it may be difficult to find which vendor is at fault when transmission quality is impaired. This makes it imperative to develop a network transmission design before procuring equipment and circuits.

The design of a telecommunications network must include performance specifications for each element. For example, in designing a PBX tie trunk to a particular net loss, it is important to know how much of each impairment to assign to the loops, the PBXs, the interexchange access lines, and the long-haul trunks provided by the IEC. If calculations are made in advance and each vendor agrees to provide equipment and services that meet these specifications, offending circuit elements can be readily identified.

Designers should not assume that shortcomings in one part of a circuit can be compensated for in another part. For example, if the interexchange trunk has excessive loss, it cannot be made up by amplifiers at the station. To do so would likely result in noise in the receiving direction and excessive output level in the transmitting direction. Excessive output causes crosstalk and distortion.

Standards

Transmission standards are derived from a variety of experiments and studies performed by AT&T and ITU. In the United States, suppliers of telecommunications circuits and services are free to design their networks to whatever criteria they choose. Users should be alert to differences in transmission quality and may wish use ITU recommendations as references in comparing alternative sources.

Transmission Traps for the Unwary

This section presents examples of some common causes of unsatisfactory transmission in private networks. We do not attempt to describe all the traps that can occur; the purpose is to show that users must be alert to avoid telecommunications services that provide unsatisfactory results.

Add-on Conferencing

Local loops are designed to a maximum loss of 8 dB to 10 dB. With these losses, most connections will be satisfactory, depending on the talker's volume, circuit noise, and room noise. Many PBXs and key telephone systems allow multiparty conferencing by directly connecting lines together. When two lines are tied together, the received signal power divides equally between them. This introduces 3 dB of loss, turning a loop with 8 dB of loss into one with 11 dB of loss. Depending on the loop loss, the number of stations tied together, and the loss of the circuits connecting them, this form of conferencing may be satisfactory; however, the results are not dependable because of the variability in the end-to-end circuit loss.

The most reliable, although more expensive, way to handle multiport conferencing is through special apparatus known as *conference bridges.* These devices are mounted in the LEC's central office where they can be dialed up, or on the user's premises where they can be connected by dialing or by a PBX operator. Bridges insert gain into the legs of the conference circuit and ensure that circuits are properly terminated so that gain can be regulated without hollowness or singing.

High-Loss PBX Switching Networks

Modern digital PBXs use four-wire switching networks. In contrast to older two-wire electromechanical PBXs, these machines have hybrids in all line interface circuits. To reduce costs, some hybrids insert 2 dB of loss in each line circuit, so on line-to-line connections, the loss across the switching network is 4 dB. Trunk hybrids are usually zero loss, so the line-to-trunk loss is 2 dB. For connections within most offices, the amount of cross-PBX loss is inconsequential. Several special situations can, however, result in transmission problems.

The first case involves a PBX with many off-premises lines. If lines to these distant stations have, say, 5 dB of loss, users in that location will experience 14 dB of line-to-line loss (two 5 dB loops plus 4 dB switching loss). This loss is tolerable to most talkers, provided the room and circuit noise are not too high. With high noise, these connections are apt to be the source of complaints. Calls from long subscriber loops (up to 10 dB) connected to the PBX through a trunk that may have 5 dB of loss and out to an off-premises station (5 dB of loss plus 2 dB loss through the PBX) will encounter losses of up to 22 dB.

As Figure 2–8 shows, only half the users will rate such a connection as good at low noise levels. As noise increases, the degree of user satisfaction drops rapidly. It is important, in choosing a PBX that must serve many off-premises stations, to ensure that the PBX inserts a negligible amount of loss into an off-premises line port.

A contrast in volume is also a frequent source of complaint. Users at the off-premises location may find it difficult to understand why connections to phones in the main PBX location are better than to phones in the next room.

When the PBX includes tie trunks to a distant machine, the extra loss from the PBX may result in complaints. Such trunks are designed to a net loss of about 5 dB. The quality of the connection depends on noise and other losses in the circuit. When long loops are present in both ends of the connection, loss is likely to be excessive. When add-on conferencing is used with these trunk calls, transmission is almost certain to be poor.

The solution to PBX transmission problems is careful evaluation of the system before purchase. The PBX should be evaluated in an environment similar to that in which it will be used. Transmission calculations should be made on all worst-case combinations of line and trunk connections. When services are procured from interexchange carriers and the LEC, the companies' transmission specifications should be obtained. Sometimes it may be necessary to purchase a higher grade of service to obtain satisfactory transmission. In other cases it may be necessary to make regular end-to-end loss and noise measurements to ensure that circuit elements are meeting their specifications. Sometimes it is necessary to insert variable gain amplifiers into the connection. These devices vary the amount of gain based on the signal level.

Enhanced Transmission Performance Charges

Before divestiture, LECs were responsible for total transmission performance and designed their circuits accordingly. Residence and business classes of service were nominally designed to have a maximum loop loss of 8.0 to 8.5 dB. PBX trunks, Centrex lines, off-premises extensions, and other special services were designed to a loss of 3.0 to 5.0 dB. In most LECs, if the loss exceeded the maximum allowable threshold, amplification was added to reduce the loss to the lowest practical limit—generally approximately 3.0 dB.

After divestiture, several LECs changed their tariffs to levy an additional charge for enhanced transmission performance. The old objective of 8.0 to 8.5 dB loss for residence and business lines was left intact and applied to all classes of service. Customers, including PBX customers whose circuits formerly were designed to no more than 5.0 dB of loss, were guaranteed loops that did not exceed 8.5 dB; if lower loss was required, the customer paid an extra charge.

With the responsibility for transmission performance put on the shoulders of the user, it is important that telecommunications managers understand the alternatives. First, it is not always necessary to pay the improved transmission performance charge to the LEC; gain devices can be installed at the customer's premises—usually with equally good results. Determine from the LEC what the expected transmission loss will be without gain devices and consider adding enough gain to reduce the circuit loss to 3.0 dB to 5.0 dB.

A second option is to consider digital trunks. These may either be ISDN trunks or regular central office trunks furnished over a T-1 line. The trunk loss of digital trunks is inherently low; from 0 dB to 3 dB of loss. In some cases digital trunks cost more, but the improved performance may be worth the extra cost. In other cases the cost may even be less considering the reduced cost of equipment in the PBX.

A third option is to live with the loss as designed. If a PBX has no off-premises extensions and uses T-1 carrier for the connection to the IEC, the chances are excellent that a loss of up to 8.5 dB will not be objectionable. Determine what the line-to-trunk loss of the switch is. If it is or can be adjusted to zero loss, the overall loss probably will not be objectionable. If a few off-premises extensions are connected to the PBX, they may experience poor transmission without gain devices on the trunks. If there are fewer off-premises extensions than trunks, voice-regulating repeaters can be added to the extensions.

The fourth option applies to PBXs that are far enough from the central office that they are beyond the 8.5 dB limit. In some LECs, circuits that existed before divestiture are charged for improved transmission performance even though the circuit loss would exceed the limit without it. It should be possible to have the charge for improved transmission performance removed while retaining the equipment because it is necessary to meet the LEC's standards.

It is important to understand that loss is only one of several criteria affecting subscriber loop performance. Loop current is an even more important consideration, because with insufficient current, PBXs and DTMF dials will not work. Refer to Chapter 35 for a discussion of loop current calculations.

Satellite Services

Geostationary satellites orbit the earth at an altitude of 22,300 miles. Although the cost of private satellite circuits may be less than the cost of terrestrial circuits, the 0.25 second path delay of a satellite circuit makes it unsatisfactory for certain types of communication. Voice communication users usually become accustomed to the delay and are not adversely affected by it, but many data protocols will not function over a satellite. Sometimes, two satellite connections may be required. Most users find that amount of delay intolerable for normal conversations.

Voice Compression Circuits

With the arrival of inexpensive voice compression equipment, more private circuits are being implemented over circuits that may cause transmission impairments. First, there is a limit to the number of times a circuit can be converted

FIGURE 2–9

Transmission Problems with Off-Premise Equipment

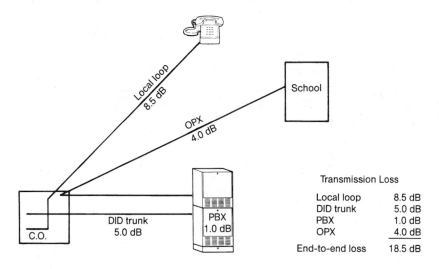

Transmission Loss

Local loop	8.5 dB
DID trunk	5.0 dB
PBX	1.0 dB
OPX	4.0 dB
End-to-end loss	18.5 dB

between analog and digital. With pulse code modulation (Chapter 5) as many as seven analog-to-digital conversions may be made without affecting voice transmission. Manufacturers use several proprietary methods to compress voice into much narrower bandwidths than the 64 kb/s bandwidth of PCM, however. The narrower the bandwidth, the less natural the connection will sound, and connecting several highly compressed circuits in tandem may make them unsatisfactory for voice transmission. Telecommunications managers should be aware that compressed voice algorithms will limit data and facsimile to speeds lower than they can achieve on PCM.

Off-Premises Extension Network

The experience of a rural school district illustrates the transmission problems that can occur with off-premises extensions. The district originally had Centrex service, in which the local loops were designed to have a maximum loss of 5.0 dB, even for the longest loops, which were some eight miles long. Residence lines in the same area were designed to have a maximum loss of 8.5 dB. A call from a residence to the neighboring school would have a maximum loss, therefore, of 13.5 dB, which is generally acceptable.

The school installed a new PBX and served the elementary schools over off-premises extensions, which the LEC designed to have a maximum loss of 4.0 dB. As shown in Figure 2–9, however, a call placed from a residence to the school encountered the loop loss of 8.5 dB, a DID trunk of 5.0 dB, an off-pre-mises extension of 4.0 dB, and the loss of the PBX and wiring, which averaged 1.0 dB. Altogether, the loss of the call was now at least 18.5 dB and the result was complaints from parents, who had difficulty in calling the school although it was only a short distance away. Calls from within the PBX or from other schools were satisfactory.

The school district solved the problem by installing gain-regulating re-peaters on the off-premises lines at the PBX. These repeaters, which sense the volume of the talker's voice, automatically insert gain or loss to regulate vol-ume on the service.

3

DATA COMMUNICATIONS SYSTEMS

Data communications can be considered to have begun more than a century and a half ago with Samuel F. B. Morse's invention of the telegraph in 1844. The telegraph, and its successor the teletypewriter, played an important part in communications for the first century, but these early communications systems were used almost exclusively for messaging. Although messaging is still an important part of communications, in terms of volume it takes a backseat to today's data communications, which is remote access to computers, file transfers between computers, interconnection of LANs, image transfer, and a host of other applications that require high bandwidth, real-time connections, and absolute data integrity.

Several factors caused the current explosion in data communication, the most important being the dramatic drop in computer prices. Applications that formerly required expensive mainframe computers can now be processed on microcomputers, bringing computing power to the end user. As the white-collar workforce increasingly turns to computers for help, the demand for computing resources has burgeoned, and this demand has in turn spawned a need for information to be shared over telecommunications facilities.

Meanwhile, we are left with a network that is part analog and part digital, and the issue of how best to carry out data communication remains very much alive. Data is far more complex than voice and is likely to remain so for several reasons. First, data demands a precision that is totally unnecessary in voice communication. A voice session has so much redundancy that a few audible noise bursts on an analog circuit or thousands of missing bits in a digital circuit have little effect on the intelligibility of the message. If the message is garbled, the receiving party simply asks the sender to repeat, and both parties are satisfied, unless the noise is excessive, in which case they hang up and try another circuit. With data, on the other hand, a single missing bit can cause a serious problem, and every effort is made to get error-free transmission.

The second difference is the multiplicity of standards in data communications. The major computer manufacturers have developed proprietary networking systems, and although progress is being made toward developing international standards, proprietary standards are still in common use. Many international standards are in use today, but the dozens of options and alternatives make data communications complex.

The third difference lies in the nature of the network itself. Voice communication lends itself to circuit switching, in which the parties to a session are connected with a physical circuit that is exclusively theirs until the session ends, at which time the circuit returns to a pool. Some forms of data communications (facsimile, for example) are suited to circuit switching. Other forms, such as remote terminals connected to a host, are unsuited for circuit switching and must operate on dedicated circuits or one of the emerging forms of switching such as asynchronous transfer mode (ATM) . Other forms of data communication, such as multiple remote terminals feeding a single host, operate effectively under packet switching or frame relay, which provide time-shared access to a network of dedicated circuits.

Telecommunications and the computer are partners in a marriage that is changing the way people store, access, and use information. The merger of the computer and telecommunications makes possible many new applications, including automatic teller machines, airline reservation systems, and credit card verification networks. The telephone network was designed and constructed for voice, however, which means that the computer, a digital device, must either use a separate digital network or adapt to the analog portions of the voice network.

This chapter is the first of several in this book that deal with data communications. This chapter sets the foundation. We will discuss how data travels across a circuit, how errors are corrected, and how the major components of a data network function and interact.

DATA COMMUNICATIONS FUNDAMENTALS

The objective of a data communications network is to provide devices with a connection that is equivalent to directly-connected devices. Some applications can tolerate an occasional error, which is defined as any pattern of received bits that is not identical to the transmitted pattern. Most applications, however, require absolute data integrity. As shown in Figure 3–1, a host computer may have directly attached and remote terminals. With the short, secure connections of a directly attached device, errors are rare, but not unheard of. When the circuit extends across town or across a continent, data errors will occasionally occur. A major objective of a data network, therefore, is to present to the host computer an error-free data stream.

The devices in a data network that originate and receive data are collectively called *data terminal equipment* (DTE). These can range from computers to simple receive-only terminals. DTE is coupled to the telecommunications network by *data circuit-terminating equipment* (DCE), which includes any device that converts the DTE output to a signal suitable for the transmission medium. DCE ranges from line drivers to complex modulator/demodulators (*modems*) and multiplexers.

The basic information element processed by a computer is the binary digit, or *bit*. A bit is the smallest information element in the binary numbering system and is represented by the two digits, 0 and 1, corresponding to two different voltage states within the DTE. Processors manipulate data in groups of eight bits known as *bytes* or *octets*. Within the computer's circuits, bytes travel over parallel paths that may be extended to output ports for connection to peripherals such as printers.

The range of parallel ports is limited to a few feet. Although the range can be extended with electronic regenerators, extending eight circuits in parallel over long distances is uneconomical because one circuit would be required for each parallel path. Therefore, most DTE is equipped with an interface to convert the eight parallel bits into a serial bit stream, as Figure 3–2 shows. This serial bit stream can be coupled to telecommunications circuits through a modem or line driver, or directly to circuits up to about one kilometer.

Coding

The number of characters that can be encoded with binary numbers depends on the number of bits in the code. Early teletypewriters used a five-level code called *baudot* that had a capacity of 2^5, or 32 characters. A five-level code lim-

FIGURE 3-1

Data Network Showing Locally and Remotely Attached Terminals

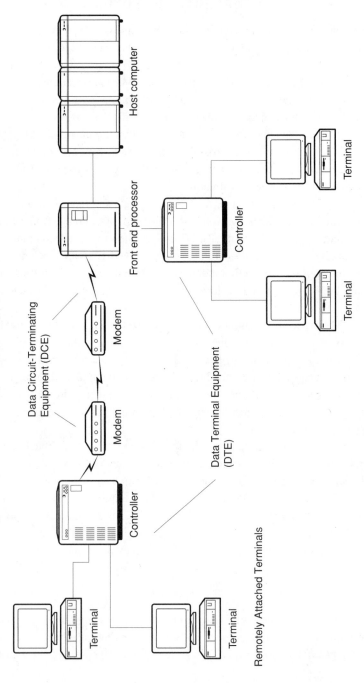

FIGURE 3-2

Parallel and Serial Data Conversion

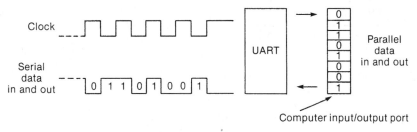

UART = Universal Asynchronous Receiver/Transmitter

its communications, because there are insufficient combinations to send a full range of upper and lower case plus special characters. In the baudot code, upper and lower case are indicated by shift characters. The receiving device continues in upper- or lower-case mode until it receives a case-shifting character. If it misses a shift character for some reason, the transmission will be garbled, because special characters are shifted numeric characters in the baudot code.

To overcome this limitation, a seven-level code known as the American Standard Code for Information Interchange (*ASCII*) was introduced. This code, which Table 3–1 shows, provides 2^7 or 128 combinations. In ASCII transmissions, although seven bits are used for characters, eight bits are transmitted. The eighth bit is used for error detection, as described later.

Several other codes are used for data communications. The most prominent is the Extended Binary Coded Decimal Interchange Code (*EBCDIC*), which Table 3–2 shows. EBCDIC is an eight-bit code, allowing a full 256 characters to be encoded. It is used extensively in IBM applications.

Code compatibility between machines is essential. Because EBCDIC and ASCII are both widely used, in some applications code conversion will be required. Most intelligent terminals can be programmed for code conversion, but with nonprogrammable terminals, external provisions are necessary. This can be a separate code converter or a value-added function of the network.

Data Communications Speeds

Table 3–3 shows the range of speeds for typical data communication applications. The speed that a circuit can support depends on its bandwidth, which as Chapter 2 explains, is 300 to 3,300 Hz over voice frequency telephone chan-

TABLE 3–1

American Standard Code for Information Exchange

$b_7\,b_6\,b_5$ $b_4\,b_3\,b_2\,b_1$	000	001	010	011	100	101	110	111
0000	NUL	DLE	SP	0	@	P	´	p
0001	SOH	DC1	!	1	A	Q	a	q
0010	STX	DC2		2	B	R	b	r
0011	ETX	DC3	#	3	C	S	c	s
0100	EOT	DC4	$	4	D	T	d	t
0101	ENQ	NAK	%	5	E	U	e	u
0110	ACK	SYN	&	6	F	V	f	v
0111	BEL	ETB	´·	7	G	W	g	w
1000	BS	CAN	(	8	H	X	h	x
1001	HT	EM	)	9	I	Y	i	y
1010	LF	SUB	*	:	J	Z	j	z
1011	VT	ESC	+	;	K	[	k	{
1100	FF	FS	,	<	L	\	l	|
1101	CR	GS		=	M	]	m	}
1110	SO	RS	.	>	N	^	n	~
1111	SI	US	/	?	O	_	o	DEL

nels. Where wider bandwidths are required, special service or digital circuits must be obtained over private facilities or through common carrier tariffs.

Two terms used to express the data-carrying capacity of a circuit are bit rate and *baud* rate. Bit rate and baud rate are often used interchangeably, but to do so is not technically accurate. The bit rate of a channel is the number of bits per second the channel can carry. For example, with complex modulation schemes, a voice-grade channel can carry 28,800 bits per second or more. The baud rate of a channel describes the number of cycles or symbols per second the channel can handle. The 3,000 Hz bandwidth of a voice channel can pass a 2,400 baud signal with the extra bandwidth used for guard bands between signals. If the data is encoded at one bit per Hz, the channel is limited to 2,400 b/s. Higher bit rates are transmitted by encoding more than one bit per Hz. A 19,200 b/s signal can be carried on a voice-grade channel, for example, by encoding eight bits per Hz. The latest version of high-speed modems using the V.34 modulation method use higher baud rates, which will work on some, but not all voice channels, depending on the total bandwidth available and the absence of impairments.

TABLE 3-2

Extended Binary Coded Decimal Interchange Code (EBCDIC)

BITS 4 3 2 1 ↓ \ 8 7 6 5 →	0000	0001	0010	0011	0100	0101	0110	0111	1000	1001	1010	1011	1100	1101	1110	1111
0000	NUL	DLE	DS		SP	&	-									0
0001	SOH	DC$_1$	SOS				/		a	j			A	J		1
0010	STX	DC$_2$	FS	SYN					b	k	s		B	K	S	2
0011	ETX	DC$_3$							c	l	t		C	L	T	3
0100	PF	RES	BYP	PN					d	m	u		D	M	U	4
0101	HT	NL	LF	RS					e	n	v		E	N	V	5
0110	LC	BS	EOB	UC					f	o	w		F	O	W	6
0111	DEL	IL	PRE	EOT					g	p	x		G	P	X	7
1000		CAN							h	q	y		H	Q	Y	8
1001		EM							i	r	z		I	R	Z	9
1010	SMM	CC	SM		¢	!			:							
1011	VT				.	$	,	#								
1100	FF	IFS	DC$_4$		<	*	%	@								
1101	CR	IGS	ENQ	NAK	(	)	_	'								
1110	SO	IRS	ACK		+	;	>	=								
1111	SI	IUS	BEL	SUB		¬	?	"								□

PF Punch Off
HT Horizontal Tab
LC Lower Case
DEL Delete
SP Space

UC Upper Case
RES Restore
NL New Line
BS Backspace
IL Idle

PN Punch On
EOT End of Transmission
BYP Bypass
LF Line Feed
EOB End of Block

PRE Prefix (ESC)
RS Reader Stop
SM Start Message
Others Same as ASCII

TABLE 3-3

Data Transmission Speeds and Applications

	50 b/s	75 b/s	100 b/s	150 b/s	300 b/s	1200 b/s	2.4 kb/s	4.8 kb/s	7.2 kb/s	9.6 kb/s	19.2 kb/s	56 kb/s	64 kb/s	1.5 mb/s	10 mb/s	100+ mb/s
Telemetry	↕	↕														
Telex	↕	↕														
Teleprinters			↕	────	────	↕										
Interactive Terminals					↕	────	────	────	────	────	↕					
Medium-Speed Data							↕	────	────	────	↕					
High-Speed Data											↕	────	────	↕		
Digital Video												↕	────	────	↕	
Local Area Networks														↕	────	↕
Image Transmission														↕	────	↕

60

FIGURE 3-3

Data Modulation Methods

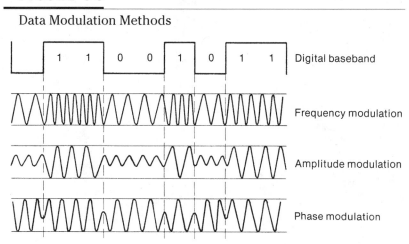

1	1	0	0	1	0	1	1	Digital baseband

Frequency modulation

Amplitude modulation

Phase modulation

Modulation Methods

A data signal leaves the serial interface of the DTE as a series of *baseband* voltage pulses, as Figure 3–3 shows. Baseband means that the varying voltage level from the DTE is impressed without modulation directly on the transmission medium. Baseband pulses can be transmitted over limited distances from the serial interface or over longer distances by using a *limited distance modem* or a *line driver* that matches the serial interface to the cable. For transmission over voice-grade channels, a modem modulates the pulses into a combination of analog tones and amplitude and phase changes that fit within the pass band of the channel.

The digital signal modulates the *frequency,* the *amplitude,* or the *phase* of an audio signal, as Figure 3–3 shows. Amplitude modulation by itself is the least used method because it is susceptible to noise-generated errors. It is frequently used, however, in conjunction with frequency and phase changes. Frequency modulation is an inexpensive method used with low-speed modems. To reach speeds of more than 300 b/s, phase shift modems are employed.

Quadrature Amplitude Modulation

Modems use increasingly complex modulation methods for encoding multiple bits per Hz to reach speeds approaching the capacity of a voice-grade circuit. Since an analog channel is nominally limited to 2,400 baud, or symbols per second, to send 9,600 b/s, for example, four bits per Hz must be encoded. The

FIGURE 3-4

Signal Constellation in a 16-Bit (2^4) Quadrature Amplitude
Modulated Signal

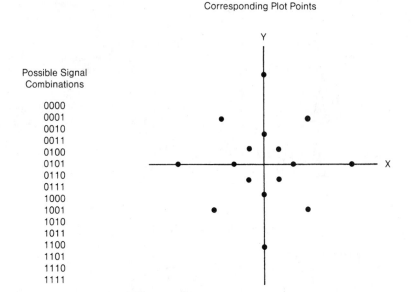

resulting 2^4 encoding yields a total of 16 combinations that each symbol can represent. High-speed modems use *quadrature amplitude modulation* (QAM) to send multiple bits per Hz. In QAM two carrier tones combine in quadrature to produce the modem's output signal. The receiving end demodulates the quadrature signal to recover the transmitted signal. Each symbol carries one of 16 signal combinations. As Figure 3–4 shows, any combination of four bits can be encoded into a particular pair of *X-Y* plot points, which represent a phase and amplitude combination. This combination modulates the carrier signals. This two-dimensional diagram is called a *signal constellation.*

The receiving modem demodulates the signal to determine what pair of *X-Y* coordinates was transmitted, and the four-bit signal combination passes from the modem to the DTE. If line noise or phase jitter affects the signal, the received point will be displaced from its ideal location, so the modem must make a best guess which plot point was transmitted. If the signal is displaced far enough, the receiver makes the wrong guess, and the resulting signal is in error.

Even higher rates can be modulated, with each additional bit doubling the number of signal points. A 64 QAM signal encodes 2^6 bits per symbol, and a 128 QAM signal results in 2^7 combinations, bringing the signal points closer together and increasing the susceptibility of the modem to impairments. As discussed later, the performance of the modem can be improved by using forward error correction to process the incoming bit stream.

Trellis-Coded Modulation

Trellis-coded modulation (TCM) is a more reliable method of encoding data signals. In a 14,400 b/s modem, for example, data is presented to a TCM modulator in six-bit groups. Two of the six bits are separated from the signal, and a code bit is added. The resulting signal is two groups, one three-bit and one four-bit. These are combined, and the resulting 2^7 bits are mapped into a signal point and selected from a 128-point signal constellation. Since only six of the seven bits are required to transmit the original signal, not all the 128 points are needed, and only certain patterns of signal points are defined as valid. If a line impairment results in an invalid pattern at the receiver, the decoder selects the most likely valid sequence and presents it to the DTE. TCM reduces the signal's susceptibility to line impairments, but as discussed later, some means of correcting errors must be added to the session.

Full- and Half-Duplex Mode

Full duplex data systems transmit data in both directions simultaneously. *Half duplex* systems transmit in only one direction at a time; the channel reverses for transmission in the other direction.

Full duplex circuits use separate transmit and receive paths on a *four-wire* circuit, or a *split channel modem* on a *two-wire* circuit. Two- and four-wire circuits refer to the type of facility that the local and interexchange carriers furnish. In the interexchange portion circuits are inherently four-wire, and the two directions of transmission travel over separate paths. It is possible, however, to purchase two-wire local loops, in which case the two directions of transmission must be combined in a single path for transmission and reception.

Split-channel modems provide the equivalent of four-wire operation by dividing the voice channel into two segments, one for transmit and one for receive. The 2,400-baud bandwidth of a channel limits a full duplex modem to 1,200 b/s in each direction when straight frequency modulation is used. Modems with more sophisticated modulation are available at higher cost to provide 2,400 b/s full duplex communication over two-wire circuits using the ITU V.22 *bis* modulation method, 9,600 b/s using V.32, 14,400 b/s with V.32 bis, and 28,800 b/s with V.34 modulation.

FIGURE 3-5

Asynchronous Data Transmission

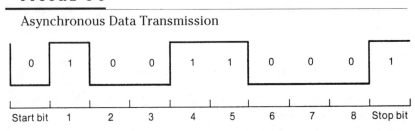

Synchronizing Methods

All data communications channels require synchronization to keep the sending and receiving ends in step. The signal on a baseband data communications channel is a series of rapid voltage changes, and synchronization enables the receiving terminal to determine which pulse is the first bit in a character.

The simplest synchronizing method is *asynchronous,* sometimes called stop-start synchronization. Asynchronous signals, illustrated in Figure 3–5, are in the one or *mark* state when no characters are being transmitted. A character begins with a start bit at the zero or *space* level followed by eight data bits and a stop bit at the one level. The terms mark and space are carried over from telegraphy, where current flowed in the line to a teletypewriter to hold it closed when it was not receiving characters. Current loop lines have largely disappeared from public networks because they generate noise. Some asynchronous terminals, however, still operate in a current loop state because their range is greater than the range of EIA serial interfaces.

Asynchronous signals are transmitted in a character mode; that is, each character is individually synchronized. The chief drawback of asynchronous communication is the extra two bits per byte that carry no information. These noninformation bits are called *overhead* bits.

To reduce the amount of overhead, data can be transferred in a *synchronous* mode, as illustrated in Figure 3–6. Synchronous data is sent in a block mode with information characters sandwiched between header and trailer records. The header and trailer contain the overhead bits; the information bits are transferred without start and stop bits. A clock signal that the modem extracts from the incoming bit stream keeps the two devices in synchronization. The drawbacks of synchronous signals are their complexity and their lack of standardization. Variables in the data block, such as block length, error-checking routine, and structure of the header and trailer records, are functions of the *protocol.* Protocols, which are discussed in the next chapter, are handshaking signals that devices go through to establish their readiness and ability to communicate.

FIGURE 3-6

Synchronous Data Transmission (IBM SDLC Frame)

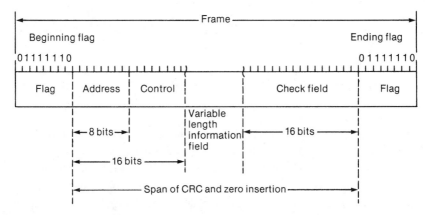

Although there are many standard protocols, such as High-Level Data Link Control (HDLC) recommended by ITU, many data manufacturers have their own protocols, which are incompatible with one another.

Whereas asynchronous data terminals can communicate with each other if the speed, code, and error-checking conventions are identical, synchronous terminals require protocol compatibility and intelligence in the DTE or terminal controller. Synchronous data communication systems have offsetting advantages of greater throughput and the ability to use sophisticated error correction techniques.

Error Detection and Correction

Errors occur in all data communications circuits. Where the transmission is text that people will interpret, a few errors can be tolerated because the meaning can be derived from context. In many applications, such as those involving transmission of bank balances, computer programs, and other numerical data, errors can have catastrophic effects. In these applications nothing short of complete accuracy is acceptable. This section discusses causes, detection, and correction of data communication errors.

Causes of Data Errors

The type of transmission medium and the modulation method have the greatest effect on the error rate. Any transmission medium using analog modulation techniques is subject to external noise, which affects the amplitude of the signal.

FIGURE 3-7

Character Parity

	BIT 8	BIT 7	BIT 6	BIT 5	BIT 4	BIT 3	BIT 2	BIT 1
ASCII a		1	1	0	0	0	0	1
Even Parity	1	1	1	0	0	0	0	1
Odd Parity	0	1	1	0	0	0	0	1

Atmospheric conditions, such as lightning, that cause static bursts can induce noise into data-carrying analog radio and carrier systems. Relay and switch operations in electromechanical central offices, switching to standby channels in microwave, fiber-optics, and carrier systems all cause momentary interruptions that result in data errors. Changes in the phase of the received signal, which can be caused by instability in carrier supplies or radio systems, also can cause errors because the modem is incapable of determining accurately which of many possible signal patterns was transmitted.

Any communication circuit is subject to errors during maintenance actions and external damage or interruption by vandalism. Even local networks within a single building are subject to occasional interruptions due to equipment failure or damage to the transmission medium. Whatever the causes, errors are a fact of life in data circuits. The best error mitigation program is a design that reduces the susceptibility of the service to errors. Following that, the next most important consideration is to design the application to detect, and, if possible, correct the errors.

Parity Checking

The simplest way of detecting errors is *parity checking,* or *vertical redundancy checking* (VRC), a technique used on asynchronous circuits. In the ASCII code set, the eighth bit is reserved for parity. Parity is set as odd or even, referring to the number of 1s bits in the character. As Figure 3–7 shows, DTE adds an extra bit, if necessary, to cause each character to match the parity established for the network.

Most asynchronous terminals can be set to send and receive odd, even, or no parity. When a parity error occurs, the terminal registers some form of alarm. Parity has two drawbacks: There is no way to tell what the original character should have been, and worse, if an even number of errors occurs, parity checking will not detect the error at all. Therefore, parity is useful only for showing that an error occurred; it is ineffective when transmission accuracy is required.

In terminals operating at 300 or 1,200 b/s or more, characters arrive so fast that it is difficult to determine which character was in error when the parity

TABLE 3–4

Commonly Used Asynchronous File Transfer Protocols

Protocol	Definition
Xmodem	A half duplex file transfer protocol that has been widely accepted since the late 1970s.
Ymodem	A protocol similar to Xmodem, but with larger data blocks, which results in higher throughput on low error rate circuits.
Zmodem	A refinement of Xmodem and Ymodem, offering greater efficiency in file transfers.
Kermit	A file transfer protocol that is widely supported by personal computers, mainframes, and minicomputers.
Sealink	A full duplex version of Xmodem.
CompuServe B	An efficient file transfer protocol used on CompuServe's network.

alarm was registered. DTE can be programmed to flag an error character by substituting a special character, such as an ampersand, in its place. The error can be corrected by communication with the sending end. In today's data networks, parity is of little value, and is set at zero by many networks.

Echo Checking

Over full duplex circuits, errors can be detected by programming the receiving device to echo the received characters to the sending end. This technique, called *echo checking*, is suitable for detecting errors in some forms of text. It is, however, subject to all the drawbacks of proofreading; it is far from infallible. Besides, an error in an echoed character is as likely to have occurred on the return trip as in the original transmission. At 300 b/s, a reader can keep up with echoed characters, but with machine transmission at 1,200 b/s or more it is impossible to read with any degree of reliability. The DTE can be programmed to make the echo check automatically, but correcting errors is just as difficult as with parity. Echo checking is widely used in asynchronous computer and terminal combinations.

Most dial-up modems in use today have built-in error correction using the V.42 error correction standard. File transfers over dial-up lines also use error-correcting protocols to ensure data integrity. Several protocols, as listed in Table 3–4, are widely supported by telecommunications programs and value added carriers for end-to-end error correction. These protocols operate on an *automatic repeat request* (ARQ) much the same as synchronous error-correcting protocols, which are described in the next section. Most popular telecommunications software packages support one or more of these protocols. They are required for most transfers of binary files and are easy to use; the user specifies the file to be up- or downloaded. The protocol automatically takes care of the transfer, signaling the user when the transfer is completed.

Cyclical Redundancy Checking

Most synchronous data networks use cyclical redundancy checking (CRC). All the characters in a block are processed against a complex polynomial that always results in a remainder. The 16-bit remainder is entered in an error check block that is transmitted following the data block. The synchronous data block illustrated in Figure 3–6 contains a CRC field in the trailer record.

At the receiving end the data block is processed against the same polynomial to create another CRC field. If the locally created CRC field fails to match the field received in the data block, the protocol causes the block to be retransmitted. The probability of an uncorrected error with CRC is so slight that it can be considered error-free. Synchronous data link protocols use ARQ to initiate retransmission of errored blocks.

When a block is received in error, it makes no difference how many bit errors were received; the entire block must be retransmitted. Therefore, the block error rate (BLER) is the best measure of the quality of a data link. BLER is calculated by dividing the number of errored blocks received over a period of time by the total number of blocks transmitted. A device such as a front end processor or a protocol analyzer can compute BLER.

Forward Error Correction

When the BLER of a circuit is excessive, *throughput,* which is the number of information bits correctly transferred per unit of time, may be reduced to an unacceptable level. The error rate can be reduced by a technique known as *forward error correction* (FEC). In FEC systems, an encoder on the transmitting end processes the incoming signal and generates redundant code bits. The transmitted signal contains both the original information bits and the additional bits. At the receiving end, the redundant bits are regenerated from the information bits and compared with the redundant bits that were received. When a discrepancy occurs, the FEC circuitry on the receiving end uses the redundant bits to generate the most likely bit combination and passes it to the DTE. Although FEC is not infallible, it reduces the block error rate and the number of retransmissions.

Throughput

The critical measure of a data communication circuit is its throughput, or the number of information bits correctly transferred per unit of time. Although it would be theoretically possible for the throughput of a data channel to approach its maximum bit rate, in practice this can never be realized because of overhead bits and the retransmission of error blocks. The following are the primary factors that limit the throughput of a data channel:

◆ Modem speed. Within a single voice channel, modems at speeds up to 28.8 kb/s can be accommodated.

◆ Half or full duplex mode of operation. With other factors equal, full duplex circuits have greater throughput because the modems do not have to reverse between transmitting and receiving.

◆ Circuit error rate. The higher the error rate, the lower the throughput.

◆ Protocol, including quantity of overhead bits and method of error handling such as selective retransmission or "go back N."

◆ Overhead bits, including start and stop bits, error checking, and forward error correction bits.

◆ Size of data block. The shorter the data block, the more significant the overhead as a percentage of information bits. When the data block is too long, each error requires retransmitting considerable data. Proper block length is a balance between time consumed in overhead and in error retransmission.

◆ Propagation speed of the transmission medium.

The throughput of a data channel is optimized by reaching a balance between the above variables using complex formulas. Because of the volume of calculations required to optimize the network, a computer program is generally required to generate throughput curves similar to those in Figure 3–8.

DATA NETWORK FACILITIES

Facilities is the generic term used to describe the combination of local loops and long-haul circuits that support communications. For data applications that require nearly full-time use of a channel between fixed points, *dedicated,* or *private line,* facilities are the most economical. Many applications, however, require switching because they transmit data between multiple points or send only a few short messages each day.

The variety of data communications applications means that no single facility type is universally suitable. For example, the following types of applications illustrate the need for a variety of facilities:

◆ *Interconnected Local Area Networks.* Nearly every office worker today has a desktop computer, and most of these are connected to a LAN. Multilocation companies interconnect their LANs so users can easily share files, use E-mail, and access public networks such as Internet.

FIGURE 3–8

Effects of Line Error Rate on Throughput

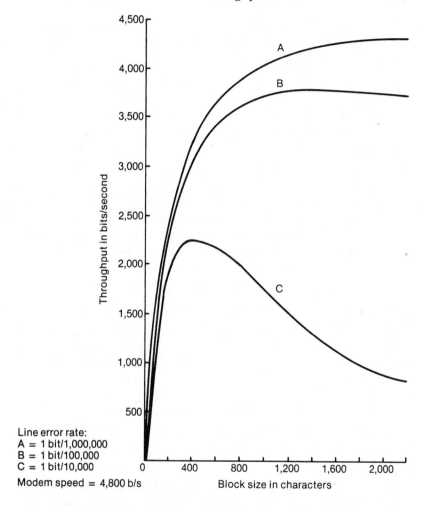

Line error rate:
A = 1 bit/1,000,000
B = 1 bit/100,000
C = 1 bit/10,000
Modem speed = 4,800 b/s

◆ *Automatic Teller Machines.* These devices are available in nearly all banks and in many public locations such as shopping centers and airports. They demand perfect transmission, high security, and rapid response. The transactions are short, and even a heavily used machine makes use of only a fraction of the data-carrying capacity of a circuit.

◆ *Credit Card Verification.* Nearly every retail establishment has a credit card machine, and many of these verify each transaction. The

applications vary from large department stores with dozens of
terminals to small, remote stores with a single, seldom-used terminal.
For the former a high-speed dedicated line is needed; for the latter a
dial-up line is more cost-effective.

◆ *Single Host Supporting Multilocation Terminals.* This application is
typical of many large businesses, such as airlines, banks, and order
bureaus, that use a mainframe computer linked to terminals over wide
area networks. Since input is from a keyboard, the data rate is limited
to typing speed, yet near-instantaneous communication is required.
This application requires a network of shared lines to reduce circuit
costs.

◆ *Point-of-Sale Terminals.* Large department stores with multiple
locations are typical of this application. Data is transmitted at high
speed, but each terminal is used only a fraction of the time. High
security and perfect accuracy are essential.

◆ *Electronic Mail.* Several nationwide carriers such as AT&T and MCI
offer electronic mail services to the public. The messages can
originate from and be retrieved from any residence or business in the
nation. The dial-up telephone network is the most practical facility to
support this kind of application except for large users who need a real-
time connection.

Private line networks can be constructed over all-digital facilities, but for
the next several years most switched data communications will be handled over
analog voice facilities. Many applications do not use the full capacity of a circuit, so the only economical way they can be implemented is by sharing the capacity of the circuit. Generally, the facilities they share can be classed as one
of seven types: point-to-point, multidrop, circuit switched, message switched,
packet switched, frame switched, or cell switched.

Point-to-Point Circuits

A *point-to-point* circuit, shown in Figure 3–9, is directly wired between the stations on the network. Point-to-point circuits are cost-effective for high-speed
communications between two processors but are expensive for most keyboard
applications. For slower or keyboard-driven applications, the circuit capacity
can be shared by subdividing it with a *multiplexer,* which is discussed later.

Low-speed point-to-point *voice-grade* circuits are known in the industry
as 3002 circuits, following the nomenclature used in AT&T and LEC tariffs.
Voice-grade circuits can carry data from the slowest speed up to 28.8 kb/s.

FIGURE 3-9

Point-to-Point Circuits

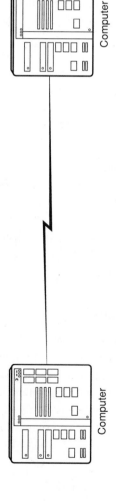

A. Computers directly connected with a point-to-point circuit

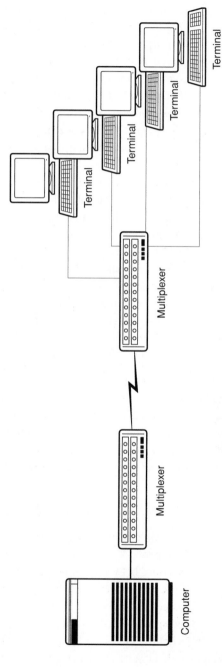

B. Point-to-point circuit shared with a multiplexer

With data compression, even greater speeds can be carried if the data is not already compressed by the application. Digital circuits can carry data at 2.4, 4.8, 9.6, 19.2, 56, and 64 kb/s. Digital circuits are not technically voice grade, but they can be used to carry either voice or data, as discussed in Chapter 5.

Multidrop Circuits

The simplest point-to-point circuits connect directly between two stations that share exclusive access to the circuit. More complex configurations are *multidrop* circuits such as that shown in Figure 3–10, in which a station can transmit only when polled. The host computer or an attached unit called a *front-end processor* does the polling. The processor sends a polling message to each station in turn. If the station has traffic, it sends it. Otherwise, it responds negatively. The central unit also sends output messages to the remote stations.

The intelligence to respond to polling messages is sometimes built directly into the terminal. In other configurations the terminals connect through a controller. A polling system keeps circuits fully occupied. Much circuit time is consumed with polling messages and negative responses, however, and these messages, which are collectively known as *overhead,* do not contribute to information flow. In a widely distributed network, where no single station takes up more than a fraction of the circuit time, a multidrop circuit is an effective way of sharing capacity.

Circuit Switching

In a circuit-switched network, a central switch is connected to stations in a star configuration as shown in Figure 3–11. Communication is between the stations and the switch, or the switch establishes circuits between two or more stations. The stations signal the switch to set up the connection, and when the stations have sent their traffic, they signal the switch to disconnect the circuit. The switch can be a data PBX, a voice/data PBX, or a telephone central office, all of which are discussed later in this book.

In circuit-switched networks, the circuits to the stations (called *loops*) are not fully occupied. When the circuits are short, the cost of idle time is acceptable, but with long circuits costs may be excessive if usage is light. Utilization can be improved by using a hierarchical network. In a hierarchical network, the switch is placed close to the stations so the circuits can be short and less costly. The more costly long circuits between the switches (called *intermachine trunks*) are engineered for a higher occupancy rate.

FIGURE 3-10

A Polled Multidrop Circuit

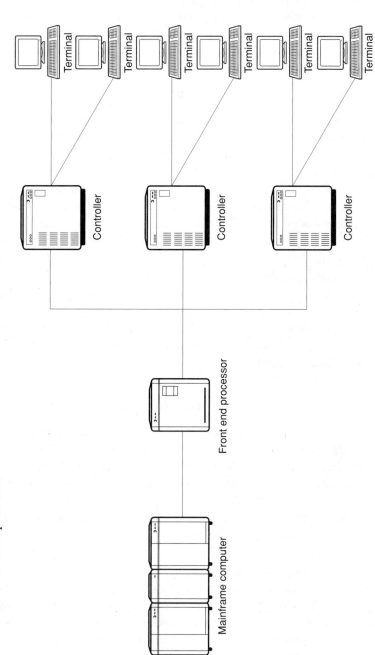

Mainframe computer

Front end processor

Controller

Controller

Controller

Terminal

Terminal

Terminal

Terminal

Terminal

Terminal

FIGURE 3–11

Circuit-Switched Networks

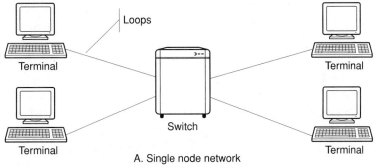

A. Single node network

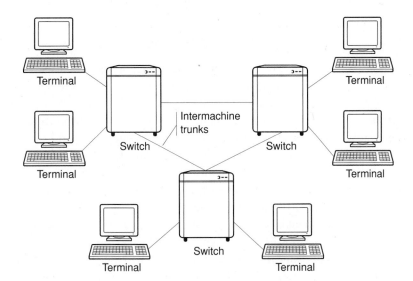

B. Hierarchial network

Message Switching

Message-switching networks are sometimes called *store-and-forward*. Stations home on a computer that accepts messages, stores them, and delivers them to their destination. The storage turnaround time can be either immediate for interactive applications, or the message may be delayed for forwarding when circuits are idle, rates are lower, or a busy device becomes available.

In its earliest form, message switching existed as a torn tape system. Teletypewriter messages were punched into paper tape by a perforator. The tape was torn at the end of the message and transmitted over another circuit, sometimes after being clipped to the wall and stored for a time. Magnetic storage media made paper tape systems obsolete, but the principle remains of receiving messages, formatting them, storing them (if only for an instant), and forwarding them to another location. Message switches route and queue messages, clearing them to their destinations at the scheduled delivery times according to the priority the sender establishes.

Store-and-forward networks include private networks and both domestic and international Telex. Access may be through public value-added networks such as MCI Mail, AT&T Mail, or electronic mail offered by one of the on-line services such as CompuServe or America Online. Most networks offer speed and code conversion and may also offer protocol conversion.

Packet Switching

A *packet-switched* network has control nodes that host the stations, as Figure 3–12 shows. In a packet network, nodes are interconnected by sufficient trunks to support the traffic load. Data travels from the station to the node in *packets,* which are blocks of data characters delimited by header and trailer records. The node moves the packet toward its destination by handing it off to the next node in the chain. Nodes are controlled by software, with algorithms that determine the route to the next station. In contrast to a circuit-switched network, where circuits are physically switched between stations, a packet-switched network establishes *virtual circuits* between stations.

A virtual circuit is one that appears to the user as if it exists, but does not exist except as a defined path through a shared facility. Virtual circuits are of two types. In a *permanent virtual circuit* mode, the routing between stations is fixed and packets always take the same route. In a *switched virtual circuit* mode the routing is determined with each packet.

Frame Relay

The architecture of a frame relay network is similar to a packet-switching network, but with some significant differences. Packet networks were designed in the 1970s when the network was largely analog and error rates were high. Frame relay networks were designed in the late 1980s when digital networks operating over fiber-optic facilities were common. Where a packet network checks for errors between each pair of nodes, frame relay networks do not

FIGURE 3-12

A Packet-Switched Network

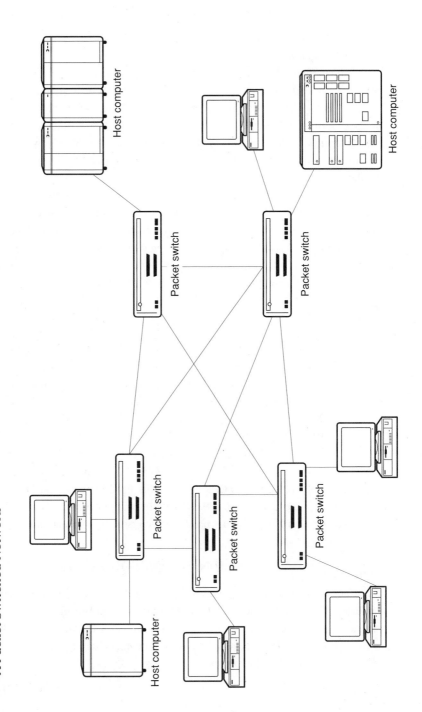

check for errors. Instead, it is up to the end devices to check for and correct errors. As we will discuss in the next chapter, a frame is a lower protocol level than a packet, and carries less overhead across the network.

The method of charging on frame relay networks is also different. Packet networks typically base their charges on kilopackets transmitted. Frame relay network costs are not usage sensitive. Instead, the cost of the network is based on the cost of the access circuit, the speed of the access port, and the committed information rate (CIR) of carrying data between stations. The network allows the information rate to burst up to the speed of the access port if capacity is available.

A user could, for example, purchase a 64 kb/s access circuit and port, but choose a lower CIR, such as 16 kb/s. The network would guarantee to carry 16 kb/s. If capacity was available, the network would carry data up to 64 kb/s. If capacity was not available, the network would notify sending stations of congestion so they slow their output. In the worst case the network can mark frames as discard-eligible, and discard them to prevent overload.

Cell Relay

Cell relay, the most significant example of which is ATM, is a combination multiplexing and switching protocol. The architecture of the network is similar to a packet network except the nodes are high-speed switching devices instead of packet store-and-forward devices. Data is sliced into short cells, 48 bytes in ATM, and forwarded across the network with a short header, which is five bytes in ATM.

ATM is used in both private and public networks. Unlike frame relay, packet switching, message switching, and multidrop, cell relay is designed to be used in both voice and data networks. It is used in *broadband* networks, which are high-speed networks used for multiple applications including imaging, voice, data, video, and other bandwidth-consuming applications.

DATA COMMUNICATION EQUIPMENT

An effective data communication network is a compromise involving many variables. The nature of data transmission varies so greatly with the application that designs are empirically determined. The network designer arrives at the most economical balance of performance and cost, evaluating equipment alternatives as discussed in this section.

Terminals

Terminals can be grouped into three classes—dumb, smart, and intelligent. They are also categorized as synchronous and asynchronous or ASCII terminals. This section discusses the characteristics of terminals and how they differ.

Dumb Terminals

Dumb terminals are so called because they contain no processing power. They are not addressable and, therefore, cannot respond to polling messages. They have no error-correcting capability and so are most often located near the host computer, or they operate behind a controller or multiplexer that has addressing and error correction capability. Most asynchronous dumb terminals do support parity checking and can flag when errors are occurring. Since they are not addressable, dumb terminals are incapable of line sharing.

Smart Terminals

Smart terminals are nonprogrammable devices, but they are capable of addressing and can be used on a multidrop line. Unlike asynchronous terminals that transmit one character at a time, smart terminals can often store data in a buffer and transmit in block mode. In block mode the terminal can detect errors and, through an ARQ process, retransmit errored blocks. A smart terminal contains only limited processing capability. For example, it may have limited editing capability, but it relies on the host for processing.

Intelligent Terminals

An intelligent terminal contains its own processor and can run application programs. The most common type of intelligent terminal is the personal computer (PC), although PCs do not always operate in intelligent terminal mode.

An intelligent terminal, being capable of running application programs on its own, provides better line utilization than dumb and smart terminals. Certain tasks can be delegated from the host to the terminal, which reduces the amount of data that flows between the two. It is important to note that some kind of communication software must run in an intelligent terminal. By changing applications software, the operator can function with different applications on the host.

Terminal Emulation

As the prices of desktop computers have fallen over the past few years, many companies have replaced terminals with desktop computers. Depending on the applications program running on the computer, it can emulate any of the three classes of terminal.

Since a serial (EIA-232) port is a standard feature of most desktop computers, it is simple for a computer to emulate an asynchronous terminal. Telecommunications software ranges in features from simple dumb terminal emulation to full-featured intelligent terminal applications. In the latter category, a desktop computer can upload and download files from and to its own disk, select and search for files on the host, and even interact with the host without a human attendant.

Interaction with a synchronous host is considerably more complex. Not only is the protocol specialized and more difficult to implement, the physical interface is likely to be something other than EIA-232; coaxial cable and twinax are common. In such a case, terminal emulation involves placing an interface board in a desktop computer expansion slot and running emulation software in the computer. Emulation boards and software are available for most of the popular synchronous protocols such as IBM's Synchronous Data Link Control (SDLC).

Modems

Since the early 1980s, modems have undergone a striking evolution. To discuss modems, it is useful to classify them as dial-up and private line. In the latter category, there is risk of incompatibility between modems of different manufacture, although more and more modems are being built to ITU standards. In the dial-up category, modems have almost become a commodity, and prices have dropped to a fraction of their former level.

The primary issue in selecting modems is compatibility. The interface between DTE and the modem is standardized in the United States, with the predominant interfaces the EIA-232, EIA-449, and ITU V.35. Figure 3–13 illustrates these interfaces. EIA and ITU standards specify the functions of the interface circuits but do not specify the physical characteristics of the interface connector. Connectors have been adopted by convention; for example, the DB-25 connector has become a de facto standard for the EIA-232 interface. Not all the 25 pins of the DB-25 are necessary in most applications. Therefore, many manufacturers use fewer pins as a way of conserving chassis space. The DB-9 nine-pin connector has become common in personal computers. The physical

FIGURE 3-13

CCITT V.35, EIA 449 Interfaces, and EIA-232

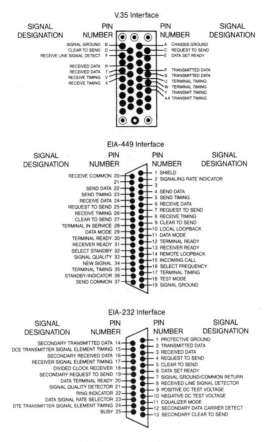

connector is only a minor problem to users because units can be easily inter-connected with adapters if they are electrically compatible.

Compatibility of older modems is often related to the Bell System modem numbering plan. Modems may be designated as *compatible* with a Bell modem, which means they are end-to-end compatible, or they may be designated as *equivalent,* which means that they perform the same functions but are not necessarily end-to-end compatible with the Bell modem of that number. Table 3–5 lists the most common Bell and ITU modem standards.

Dial-Up Modems

Like other telecommunications products, modems have steadily become faster, cheaper, and smarter. The ready availability of inexpensive personal computers

TABLE 3-5

Bell and CCITT Model Compatibility Chart

Type	Speed (b/s)	Synchronization	Mode
103 A/J	300	Asynch	FDX Dial-up
113 A/D	300	Asynch	FDX Dial-up
103 F	300	Asynch	FDX P/L
212 A	1200	Synch/Asynch	FDX Dial-up
202 S	1200	Asynch	HDX Dial-up
202 T	1800	Asynch	FDX/HDX/P/L
201 B	2400	Synch	FDX P/L
201 C	2400	Synch	HDX P/L
208 A	4800	Synch	FDX P/L
208 B	4800	Synch	HDX Dial-up
V.21	300	Asynch	FDX Dial-up
V.22	1200	Synch/Asynch	FDX Dial-up P/L
V.22 bis	2400	Synch/Asynch	FDX Dial-up P/L
V.23	1200	Asynch	FDX P/L
V.24	2400	Synch/Asynch	FDX/HDX Dial-up P/L
V.26	2400	Synch	FDX P/L
V.26 bis	2400	Synch	HDX Dial-up
V.27	4800	Synch	FDX P/L
V.27 bis	4800	Synch	HDX Dial-up
V.29	9600	Synch	FDX P/L
V.32	9600	Synch/Asynch	FDX Dial-up
V.33	14,400	Synch	FDX P/L
V.34	28,800	Synch/Asynch	FDX Dial-up

FDX = Full Duplex
HDX = Half Duplex
P/L = Private Line

has expanded the demand for modems, and where a few years ago 2,400 b/s modems were the norm, now 9,600 b/s is common, and the newer V.34 28,800 b/s modems are rapidly becoming accepted. Chips containing the circuitry to support the V.22 or V.32 format are the essence of modems, with most vendors also supporting the Hayes command set.

The Hayes command set is a proprietary group of instructions that receives commands preceded by the letters AT from the DTE. The modem translates these into instructions to handle functions such as dialing a number and hanging up when the session ends.

Matched with telecommunications software, dial-up modems enable users to upload and download files, converse with databases, access packet-switching networks, exchange files, and perform other functions that once required a highly trained operator.

Dial-up modems either plug into a desktop computer expansion slot or are self-contained devices that plug into the computer's serial port. Most modems support the V.42 error correction protocol and are therefore useful between devices that lack error correction capability. Most modems also implement V.42 *bis* data compression, which, on V.34 modems, may result in a data transfer rate approaching 100 kb/s.

The switched telephone network carries a considerable share of asynchronous data communication. Therefore, many modem features are designed to emulate a telephone set. The most sophisticated modems, in combination with a software package in an intelligent terminal, are capable of fully unattended operation. Modems designed for unattended, and many designed for attended, operation include these features:

◆ Dial tone recognition.
◆ Automatic tone and dial pulse dialing.
◆ Monitoring call progress tones such as busy and reorder.
◆ Automatic answer.
◆ Call termination.

Dial-up modems operate in a full duplex mode. When two modems connect, they go through an elaborate exchange of signals to determine the features the other modem is equipped with. Such features as error correction and compression are examined. High-speed modems test the line to determine the highest speed with which they can communicate.

Private Line Modems

Like dial-up modems, private line modems have dropped in price and improved in functionality, but there is such a diversity of features that they have not reached commodity status, and probably never will. Analog private lines are rapidly becoming a thing of the past, and private line modems are replaced by their digital equivalents. Different manufacturers use proprietary formats to encode the signal, to compress data, and more important, to communicate network management information.

Private line modems can be classed as synchronous or asynchronous, as half or full duplex, and as two-wire or four-wire, with the latter being the most common. When synchronous modems are used at speeds above 4,800 b/s, they may require *line conditioning* from the common carrier. Line conditioning is not available on the switched-voice telephone network, but most manufacturers offer modems equipped with *adaptive equalization,* which is circuitry that automatically adjusts the modem to compensate for irregularities in the telephone channel. Adaptive equalization substitutes for line conditioning and enables the use of 9,600 b/s or higher on a voice-grade private line.

Circuit throughput can be improved by using data compression, a system that replaces the original bit stream with a stream that has fewer bits. With data compression techniques and adaptive equalization, it is possible to operate at 19.2 kb/s or higher over nonconditioned voice-grade lines.

The following is a list of the most important features of private line modems. Not all manufacturers use these terms to describe their equivalent features.

Adaptable Inbound Rate   On multidrop circuits where the modems contain adaptive rate capability, one drop suffering from impairments can bring the speed of the entire line down to the speed of the worst-case drop. With adaptable inbound rate, each modem establishes its own rate with the host and transmits at the maximum supportable speed.

Adaptive Line Rate Capability   This feature enables a modem to sense line conditions and adjust its transmission speed to the maximum speed the line will support.

Fast Reversal   In half duplex circuits, the modem flip-flops between send and receive. The time required to reverse itself is an important factor in determining throughput. A fast-reversal modem minimizes turnaround time.

Internal Diagnostics   With this feature the modem automatically runs real-time diagnostics and displays information about its status. Some models also display the condition of the communications facility.

Loop-around   Line troubles can be isolated by forcing the modem into a loop-back configuration, as discussed in Chapter 36. Most modems permit looping the analog and digital sides of the signal to isolate whether a problem is on the line, in the modem, or in the DTE.

MNP Error Control   The Microcom Network Protocol has become a widely accepted method of obtaining data integrity and data compression on asynchronous lines. Modems equipped with MNP monitor incoming data for errors and request retransmission of errored frames. This protocol is standardized as ITU-T V.42.

Modem Sharing Capability   A modem sharing unit separates the transmission line into two or more channels, providing multiple slow-speed channels without the use of a multiplexer. For example, a modem with a bandwidth of 9,600 b/s could support four 2,400 b/s channels.

Network Management   Many proprietary network management systems collect information from modems and other devices in real time. The modem provides a narrow channel for transmitting network management information such as analog line parameters back to the host for continuous line quality evaluation. With this capability, the network administrator or network management software can test, monitor, and reconfigure the modem from a central site.

Reverse Channel Capability   In half-duplex applications, it is sometimes desirable to send a small amount of information in the reverse direction. For example, it may be necessary to interrupt a transmission. Reverse channel capability provides a narrow band of frequencies for slow-speed operation in the reverse direction, while the forward direction transmits wider band data.

Signal Constellation Generator   The bit patterns of the modem's signal constellation are brought out to test points for monitoring with external test equipment.

Special-Purpose Modems

The market offers many modems that fulfill specialized requirements. This section discusses some of the equipment that is available.

Digital Simultaneous Voice and Data (DSVD)   This new technology enables PC users to share collaborative applications and voice conversation simultaneously over a single standard telephone line using a V.34/V.FC modem. The use of digital voice compression allows additional bandwidth for simultaneous data transmission.

Dial-Backup Modems   A dial backup modem contains circuitry to restore a failed leased line over a dial-up line. The restoration may be automatically initiated on failure of the dedicated line. The modem may simulate four-wire private line over a single dial-up line, or two dial-up lines may be required.

Fiber-Optic Modems   Where noise and interference are a problem, fiber-optic modems can provide high bandwidth at a moderate cost. Operating over one fiber-optic pair, these modems couple directly to the fiber-optic cable.

Limited Distance Modems   Many LECs offer limited-distance circuits, which are essentially a bare nonloaded cable pair between two points within the same wire center. LDMs are inexpensive modems operating at speeds of up to

19.2 kb/s. Where LDM capability is available, the modems are significantly less expensive than long-haul 19.2 kb/s modems.

Data Service Units/Channel Service Unit

A DSU/CSU connects DTE to a digital circuit. It provides signal conditioning and testing points for digital circuits. For example, the bit stream out of a data device is generally a unipolar signal, which must be converted to a bipolar signal for transmission on a digital circuit. The CSU/DSU does the conversion, and also provides a loop-back point for the carrier to make out-of-service tests on the circuit. Operating at 56 and 64 kb/s, DSUs are full duplex devices. They are available for both point-to-point and multidrop lines.

Multiplexers and Concentrators

Many data applications, by their nature, are incapable of fully using the bandwidth of a data circuit. Rather than flowing in a steady stream, data usually flows in short bursts with idle periods intervening. To make use of this idle capacity, data *multiplexers* are employed to collect data from multiple stations and combine it into a single high-speed bit stream.

Data multiplexers are of two types, *time division multiplexers* (TDM) and *statistical multiplexers* (statmux). In a TDM, each station is assigned a time slot, and the multiplexer collects data from each station in turn. If the station has no data to send, its time slot goes unused. TDM operation is illustrated in Figure 3–14.

A statmux, illustrated in Figure 3–15, makes use of the idle time periods in a data circuit by assigning time slots to pairs of stations according to the amount of traffic they have to send. The multiplexer collects data from the DTE and sends it to the distant end with the address of the receiving terminal.

Statistical multiplexers improve circuit utilization by minimizing idle time between transmissions. They are more costly than TDMs, however, and must be monitored to prevent overloads, with stations added or removed to adjust the load to the maximum the circuit will handle while meeting response time objectives.

Analog, or frequency division, multiplexers are also available to divide a voice channel into multiple segments for data transmission. These devices assign each data channel to a frequency and use frequency shift techniques similar to those used in a modem. Their primary use is to connect multiple slow-speed data terminals over voice channels.

FIGURE 3-14

Time Division Multiplexing

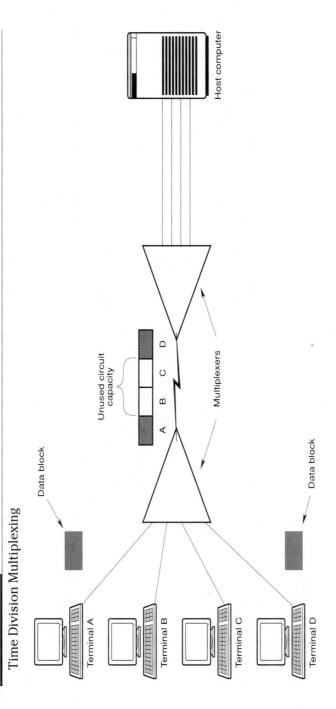

FIGURE 3-15

Statistical Multiplexing

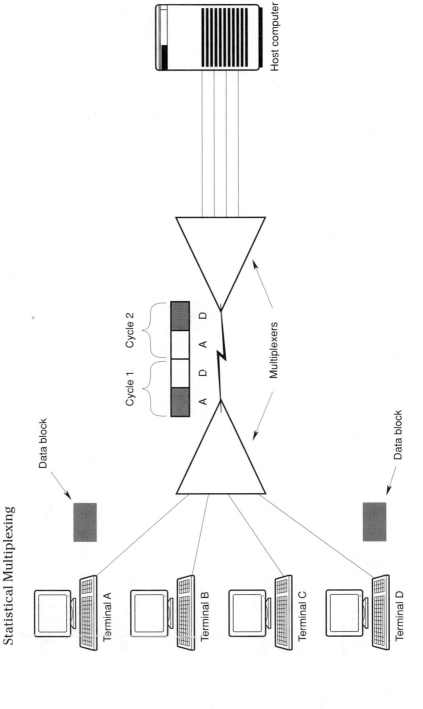

A *concentrator* is similar to a multiplexer, except that it is usually a single-ended device. At the terminal end, devices connect to the concentrator exactly as they would connect to a multiplexer, and the concentrator connects to the facility. At the host end, the facility is routed directly into the host or front-end processor. A concentrator matches the characteristics of the host processor.

The primary application for multiplexers is in data networks that use asynchronous terminals. Since many of these terminals cannot be addressed and have no error correction capability, they are of limited use by themselves in remote locations. The multiplexer provides end-to-end error checking and correction and circuit sharing to support multiple terminals.

Multiplexer Features

Multiple Multiplexer Support   Some statistical multiplexers have the capability of talking to more than one distant multiplexer in the network. Lacking this capability, multiplexers must be implemented in pairs.

Alternate Routing   Multiplexers with alternate routing capability can transmit data around network congestion and circuit failures.

Terminal-to-Host Mapping   With this feature, users can log onto a network and address any host. The multiplexers determine the route.

Network Management Capability   With this feature a remote network management system can monitor the network through an interface into the multiplexers. It is possible to perform such functions as determining system status, changing port assignments, and diagnosing trouble.

Integrated CSU/DSU   Many multiplexers have a built-in CSU/DSU, which eliminates the need for a separate outboard device.

Packet-Switching Equipment

Packet switching can be implemented on either public or private networks. A device known as a packet assembler/disassembler (PAD) creates the packets. The PAD accepts a data stream from the DTE and slices it into packets of a length that the network designer determines. The packets are handed off to a packet node, which terminates the circuits and routes packets to the destination. The nodes may be specialized computers or devices that closely resemble multiplexers. The interface between the PAD and the packet node is ITU X.25. The standard does not establish the protocol between nodes, so networks are assembled from nodes of identical manufacture.

Packet networks are usually interconnected in a mesh configuration with at least two alternate routes for handing off traffic. The network uses one of several routing algorithms, which Chapter 31 discusses, to deliver packets to the next node. The transmission is checked for errors in each link and packets are sequenced and handed off to the PAD. The PAD disassembles received packets and presents the original bit stream to the receiving device.

A packet-switching network is robust compared to other data communications facilities. Because of its alternate routing capability, the network can usually survive a link failure, although throughput may be diminished. The end-to-end transmission delay through a packet network is usually greater than through a multiplexer network because of the processing time required in each node. Packet networks were developed for a time when circuit error rates were high and speeds were low. With today's digital circuits, packet-switching technology is giving way to techniques such as frame relay, which Chapter 31 discusses. Some observers believe that packet switching in its present form will probably not survive beyond the turn of the century.

Frame Relay Access Device

Many users employ routers to access frame relay networks. Routers are covered in more detail in Chapter 33, which discusses internetworks. Routers are expensive compared to simple frame relay access devices (FRADs). The FRAD connects to a network such as Ethernet and conditions the frames for connection across the network.

Ancillary Equipment

This section discusses the ancillary equipment that is available on the market to aid the user in assembling unique applications.

Protocol Converters

When incompatible devices must be used on the same data network, it is often necessary to use a protocol converter. The most common conversion is between synchronous and asynchronous devices. For example, an ASCII-to-SDLC converter can be used to enable asynchronous terminals to function on an IBM network. Protocol converters to enable asynchronous and synchronous devices to communicate with X.25 networks are also available. Special types of protocol converters known as gateways are often used to interconnect incompatible networks. A gateway physically connects to each network and implements all the protocol functions of each, making the incompatibility transparent to the users. Gateways also enable local area networks to interface with host computers.

Modem-Sharing Devices

The total bandwidth of a circuit is often greater than a single attached device requires. A modem-sharing device performs much the same function as a multiplexer, but it is less expensive to purchase and less complex to administer. It receives information from the line and directs it to the appropriate device, which could be a terminal or a printer. It accepts data from the attached computer and buffers it, if necessary, until line capacity is available to receive it.

Dial Backup Units

Dial backup capability, to provide continuity of service if a dedicated line fails, is either contained in a modem or provided as a stand-alone device. A dial backup unit normally requires two dial lines to provide the equivalent of full duplex private line capacity. The service may be established manually, or the dial backup unit may monitor the dedicated line and automatically switch with a short interruption in service when a failure occurs.

Multidrop Bridges

Multidrop circuits are established by *bridging* multiple point-to-point lines. A bridge terminates each line in its characteristic impedance and may provide amplification to make up for bridging losses. The LEC or IEC often provides bridging, but it also may be installed on the customer's premises. Customer premises bridging is effective when a network of T-1 private lines is available and in a campus environment where twisted pair cable supports multiple controllers. It is important to understand that this type of bridge is different from bridges used in local area networks. A LAN bridge is used to extend the range of or segment a network.

APPLICATIONS

Unlike voice applications, which usually can be handled by equipment vendors and common carriers with little participation by the customer, data applications require direct involvement of the manager. Few applications have a single design alternative. It is usually possible to design an array of solutions to any problem, with the principal trade-offs being ease of use, first cost, ongoing cost, maintainability, and survivability in case of failure. The manager needs a fully defined set of requirements and objectives to select the most effective alternative. This section discusses some important considerations in evaluating data communications services and equipment.

Standards

ANSI, EIA, and ITU are the principal data communications standards agencies affecting equipment used in the United States. Although much of the data communications equipment being manufactured today conforms to ITU standards, some older nonconforming equipment is in use. Many data communications systems operate under proprietary protocols such as IBM's Binary Synchronous Communication (BSC) and Synchronous Data Link Control (SDLC).

Evaluation Considerations

This section discusses considerations in evaluating the major items of data communications equipment. Some factors, including the following, are common to all classes of equipment:

♦ Compatibility with standards.
♦ Compatibility with existing equipment.
♦ Support of the manufacturer and its representatives.
♦ Compatibility with network management systems.

Evaluating Network Alternatives

The first question to ask in evaluating network facilities is whether the application requires a switched or dedicated circuit network. Circuit switching is advantageous where the simple addressing scheme and universal connectivity of the PSTN is required. Consider circuit switching whenever multiple short sessions to widely distributed terminal points are required. When switched virtual circuits become available for ATM and frame relay, they will become a suitable substitute for circuit switching in some applications.

The type of network service is often determined by the application. If you are expanding an existing network the choice is usually clear: Continue to grow the network with an extension of existing services.

In a new network or when the existing network must be redesigned, the protocol used by the application may determine the shape of the network. Multidrop networks are feasible when the host computer uses a polling protocol and usage on the network is light. When usage is high, point-to-point circuits may be required. Host computers that use asynchronous terminals usually require point-to-point circuits and statistical multiplexers or connection to an X.25 network. Increasingly, Ethernet is used in lieu of serial ports on the host. If the computer is a member of a LAN, a router provides the interface to the LAN. Routers can be interconnected by point-to-point circuits. When the circuit complexity grows, frame relay networks become cost-effective. If the bandwidth required is T-1 or less, frame relay is an obvious choice. ATM, at the time of this writing, is not feasible at bandwidths below T-3, but lower bandwidth implementations will likely reach the market.

Message switching is used in some private networks. Most new applications will likely use one of the other alternatives as this technology becomes obsolete.

Evaluating Modems

The following are the most important considerations in choosing a modem.

Dial-up vs. Private Line.   Although some modems are designed for both dial-up and private line use, most models are designed for one or the other. Units that are designed for both are more expensive than single-purpose units.

Standards Compatibility   Many of today's modems conform to one or more ITU standards, older Bell standards, or both. If modems that do not conform to one of these standards are chosen, they will probably be compatible only with modems of the same manufacture.

Another important consideration in standards compatibility is what form of data compression and error correction capability the modem supports. ITU V.42 and V.42 *bis* standards provide error correction and compression.

Modem Reversal Time   Half-duplex modems require a finite time to reverse the line from send to receive. This variable is specified as turnaround time or RTS/CTS delay. Fast-reversal modems have delay times of less than 10 ms. Other modems may have reversal times as high as 100 ms.

Modulation Method   The modulation method normally will be a function of the ITU or Bell compatibility specification if the modem conforms to one of those standards. Since nearly all dial-up modems conform to a standard, the modulation method depends on speed. Private-line modems may follow a proprietary modulation scheme, but most will be phase shift keying (PSK), quadrature amplitude modulation (QAM), or trellis-coded modulation (TCM).

Speed   Next to standards compatibility, speed is the primary factor in selecting a modem. Generally, the higher the speed, the higher the price. To save money, choose the lowest speed that meets respose time and throughput requirements.

Operating Mode   Modems operate in either full- or half-duplex mode, synchronous or asynchronous. The application often drives the mode. For example, IBM's BISYNC protocol is inherently half-duplex synchronous. Dual-mode modems are available and are generally more expensive than single-mode modems.

Equalization Method   Most modems are equalized to match the characteristics of the transmission facility. Equalization is either fixed or adaptive. The latter is more expensive, but it may enable the modem to function over an unconditioned line, which will save recurring costs on leased circuits.

Diagnostic Capability   Most external modems display the status of the line and major signal leads on the front panel. More elaborate models display status information on alphanumeric readouts. The most elaborate private-line modems include network management information that can be linked to a diagnostic center.

Evaluating Multiplexers and Concentrators   Multiplexers can be classified in several ways. First is the time division versus statistical multiplexer classification. Statistical multiplexers are divided into two classes, high-end multiplexers that support multiple lines and 30 or more ports and can wrap around line failures, and low-end units that simply permit multiple devices to share a single line. This section discusses evaluation considerations of multiplexers and concentrators.

Line Speed   Most multiplexers on the market can support at least 9,600 b/s analog and digital lines. Higher speeds including 19.2 kb/s, 56 kb/s, and 64 kb/s are available. An important factor is whether the multiplexer can be upgraded to higher speeds by replacing a card.

Number and Speed of Ports Supported   The multiplexer must be evaluated based on the number of EIA input devices it can support. Also, the speed of the input ports is important. In some multiplexers, port contention permits multiple input devices to contend for access to a group of ports, which effectively increases the port capacity of the system.

Redundancy   High-end multiplexers have redundant power supplies and processors, which makes them less vulnerable to equipment failures.

Protocol Support   Multiplexers usually support asynchronous devices. Some applications require support of other protocols such as SDLC and BSC. Some multiplexers support X.25 connections from packet assembler/disassemblers (PADs) and X.25 connections to a packet node.

Security   Multiplexers may require users to log in and enter a password, adding a second level of security to the host environment.

Network Management Capability   The multiplexer may be required to support a network management protocol such as SNMP (Simplified Network Management Protocol) to simplify the task of managing the network and its resources.

Evaluating Packet-Switching Equipment

Evaluation considerations for packet switching equipment and multiplexers are equivalent. The same factors discussed in the preceding section should be considered.

Absolute Delay   Absolute delay, or latency, affects throughput. The more nodes a signal traverses, the greater the delay and the lower the throughput. A packet switch vendor should be able to quote the absolute delay through its packet-switching equipment.

Access Method   Packet networks are accessed by one of three methods: dial-up to a PAD located on the vendor's premises, a dedicated circuit to a vendor-supplied PAD, or an X.25 connection from the user's PAD to the node. The link between the user's premises and the node may not be protected from errors in the first two access methods. Unless an X.25 circuit from the premises to the node is employed, an error-correcting protocol between terminal devices may be required.

SELECTED DATA COMMUNICATIONS EQUIPMENT MANUFACTURERS

Modems

Note: This is only a partial list of the most prominent manufacturers of private-line modems and high-speed dial-up modems. The list omits many manufacturers of dial-up modems.

Concord Communications

Data Race

Digital Equipment Corporation

Gandalf Technologies, Inc.

General Datacomm, Inc.

Hayes Microcomputer Products, Inc.

IBM Corporation

Micom Communications Corp.

Microcom, Inc.

NEC America Inc.

Network Equipment Technologies, Inc.

Paradyne Corp.

Racal-Datacom, Inc.

Telebit Corp.

US Robotics

X.25 Packet-Switching Equipment

Alcatel

Andrew

Ascom Timeplex

Memotec Communications

Tellabs, Inc.

Telematics International

Frame Relay Switches

ACT Networks

Alcatel

Ascom Timeplex
Bay Networks/Wellfleet
Dynatech Communications
Frame Relay Technologies
Gandalf Technologies
Hughes Network Systems
Memotec Communications
Network Equipment Technologies
Newbridge Networks
Nortel
RAD Data Communications
Stratacom
Telematics International

Frame Relay Access Devices (FRADs)

ACT Networks
BBN Systems and Technologies
Cray Communications
Dynatech Communications
FastCOMM Communications
Frame Relay Technologies
Memotec Communications
Newbridge Networks
RAD Data Communications
Stratacom
Telematics International

Time Division and Statistical Multiplexers

Ascom Timeplex
Cray Communications
General Datacomm, Inc.
HT Communications
Micom Communications Corp.
Motorola Information Systems Group

Multi-Tech Systems, Inc.

Paradyne Corp.

RAD Data Communications

Video Display Terminals

Digital Equipment Corp.

Harris Corp.

IBM Corp.

Wyse Technology

Unisys Corp.

4

DATA COMMUNICATIONS PROTOCOLS

When diplomats speak of protocols they refer to the etiquette, customs, and procedures by which political relations are conducted. In the telecommunications world protocols fill a similar purpose. Devices exchange signals, sometimes called a "handshake," that establish the terms and conditions under which they will communicate. Unlike human beings who have the ability to adjust to an unfamiliar protocol, however, data devices are unable to communicate at all unless their protocols match within narrowly defined limits.

Protocol compatibility and standardization are the most important issues in data communications. Most major computer manufacturers have developed proprietary protocols that are incompatible with those of other manufacturers. Even standard protocols developed by international agencies, such as ITU's HDLC and X.25, provide multiple options and are not always interchangeable between applications.

Incompatible protocols can communicate with each other through *protocol converters*. A protocol converter known as a *gateway* communicates with both connecting protocols using their languages. Certain value-added networks also offer protocol conversion. They communicate with the DTE using that DTE's own protocol, convert it to the network protocol, and transport it to the distant DTE in its own language. The incompatibility of protocols has long been a stumbling block in the path of full interconnectability of data networks. Although international standards have progressed significantly, the problems of incompatibility are likely to remain for many years.

The simplest protocols have been established by common usage. For example, asynchronous protocol is used by every device that has a standard serial interface. It is universally accepted, and when the device is initialized with the proper speed, parity, stop bits, and data bits, it can communicate with any other device that is identically set up. Such simplicity is achieved at a price, however. As we have seen, the asynchronous protocol does not provide for such an important function as error correction. The lack of error correction was a serious drawback of the asynchronous protocol until development of file transfer protocols such as X-Modem, Kermit, and the like. Now, many modems have built-in error correction using another protocol, Microcom's MNP, which is the international standard V.42.

The hundreds of different protocols in the data communications industry are at the root of traits that make data communications more complex than voice. Not only is the sheer number of protocols enormous, but most of them have options and variations that must be satisfied before devices can communicate. Many protocols are proprietary. The major computer manufacturers have proprietary networks derived from protocols of their design. Most have been released into the public domain or licensed to allow other manufacturers to interoperate, but the standard remains under the manufacturer's control.

This chapter discusses the kinds of functions data protocols perform and the terminology that is common to most protocols. We will discuss the International Standards Organization's Open Systems Interconnect model (OSI), which is at the heart of most current protocol designs. We will review two examples of protocols that are in common use today: transmission control protocol/internet protocol (TCP/IP) and point-to-point protocol (PPP). These protocols are complex, and will be reviewed in concept only as a way of illustrating how protocol functions are carried out. For a more detailed bit-level discussion of these and other protocols, readers are referred to publications listed in the bibliography. Subsequent chapters will discuss many other protocols in the context in which they are used.

PROTOCOL TERMINOLOGY AND FUNCTIONS

Data protocols may be implemented in firmware (a chip), hardware, or a combination of both. Just as computer programs are usually written in modules to simplify administration, layered protocols allow developers to write software to a clearly defined interface. Each layer has a defined function. If a function or specification changes, it isn't necessary to change the entire protocol stack; only the affected layer and its interfaces with other layers are changed.

A good example of layered protocols in action is found in LAN standards. These standards, which are discussed in more detail in Chapter 29, are designed to work at the first two layers of the OSI model. Hardware vendors can build network interface cards (NICs) to connect to any of the transmission media that LAN standards support (twisted-pair cable, fiber optics, coaxial cable, and so on). Network operating system developers such as Novell, Banyan, Microsoft, and others can develop higher layer protocols that talk to any NIC. The card manufacturers provide software drivers to enable the functions in their cards to communicate with the network operating system.

LAN standards further illustrate how the protocol is deployed. The portion of the protocol that describes how the NIC communicates with the transmission medium is implemented in firmware. The card manufacturers use chips that implement the access protocol. The drivers and all of the network operating system are implemented in software. The result is a complete network that can be composed of NICs from one manufacturer, bridges or routers from another, a network operating system from a third manufacturer, and computers from a mixture of companies. Although interoperability is not completely assured, manufacturers are able to design to known interfaces, and when problems occur the standard makes it easier to determine what corrective action is appropriate.

Protocol Functions

To continue with the analogy of a diplomatic protocol, the way people behave in a situation is dictated by a complex set of rules. Diplomatic protocols suggest who is seated next to whom, how officials of different ranks are to be addressed, what kind of response is appropriate to another's statement, who is introduced to whom, and other such niceties that govern diplomatic affairs. Data protocols dictate some of the same types of relationships. In this section we will discuss some of the major functions of protocols. In a layered protocol these functions are usually assigned to one layer, but the rules regarding this are not rigid. For example, every Ethernet NIC has an address embedded in firmware. That address permanently belongs to the station, and is not duplicated anywhere else in the world. That address is used to identify the station in intraLAN transactions. If the LAN is connected to a distant LAN, the internetworking protocol is likely to be TCP/IP. IP, a higher level protocol, uses an addressing scheme entirely different from that used on the LAN. We will discuss TCP/IP later in this chapter. In this section we will discuss the major functions of protocols without concern for where or how they are implemented.

Session Control

The major objective of interactions between protocols is to establish a session across a network. A session begins when devices establish communication, and ends when the communication terminates. In dial-up communications a session begins when parties establish a connection across the network, and ends when one party hangs up. In data communications a session may begin when a user logs on a distant computer, and ends with log-off. The protocol authenticates the parties before permitting communication to begin.

Data networks handle sessions in two distinct ways: *connectionless* and *connection-oriented*. In a connection-oriented protocol the devices have a physical or logical connection across the network; the connection is set up at the start of the session and remains for its duration. The connection can be circuit-switched as in the telephone network, or it can be a *virtual* connection, which is defined in a software path that shares circuits with other sessions.

A connectionless session is one in which data is launched into the network and delivered to the distant end based on its address. The postal service is an example of a connectionless operation. The user doesn't care how a letter gets to its destination. Each letter is individually addressed and handed to the post office for delivery to the addressee. Most LANs are also connectionless. A stream of information is launched onto the network. All stations copy the message but retain it only if they are the addressee. In a data network, connectionless operation means that each packet or frame must contain the address of the sending and receiving stations. In a connection-oriented session the packets or frames typically contain a path identifier, but do not need the address of either the sender or the receiver after the session is set up.

Communications Control

Protocols can be classified as peer-to-peer or master-slave. In the latter protocol the master controls the functioning of the data link and controls data transfer between the host and its terminals. All communication between slaves goes through the master. A peer-to-peer protocol does not use a controller, so devices can communicate with one another at will.

Link Management

After the session is set up, the protocol controls the flow of data across the data link.

Synchronizing

At the start of a session data devices exchange signals to determine such variables as the bit rate of the modems, whether compression or error correction will be used, and so on. Modems exchange signals to determine the highest speed at which they can exchange data, falling back to a lower speed if the circuit will not support the maximum.

Addressing

Every session requires an address to set up a connection if the protocol is connection-oriented, or to route packets if it is connectionless. Not all protocols contain addresses. Many of them rely on higher or lower layers for addressing.

Routing

In data networks having multiple routes to the destination, the protocol determines the appropriate route based on variables such as cost, congestion, distance, and type of facility.

Data Segmenting and Reassembly

A continuous data stream from the source is segmented into frames, cells, or packets as appropriate and equipped with header and trailer records for transmission over the network. At the distant end the protocol strips the overhead bytes and reassembles the data stream for delivery to the receiver.

Data Formatting

The bit stream may require conditioning before transmission and restoration after reception. For example, conditioning could include encryption or compression.

Flow Control

Protocols protect networks from congestion by sending signals to the source to halt or limit traffic flow.

Supervision

The protocol establishes a connection, determines how the session will be started and ended, which end will control termination of the session, how charging will be handled, and so on.

Error Detection and Correction

Protocols check for errors, acknowledge correctly received data blocks, and send repeat requests when blocks contain an error. In the most primitive type of error correction, each packet is separately acknowledged, so the sending device must wait for an acknowledgment before sending another packet. More sophisticated protocols can acknowledge multiple packets using one of two types of acknowledgment. A *selective repeat* acknowledgment enables the receiving device to request specific packets to be repeated. In the *go-back-n* method the receiver instructs the sender to resend an errored packet and all subsequent packets.

Failure Recovery
If the session terminates unexpectedly, the protocol determines how to keep the application from being corrupted.

Sequencing
If data blocks are received out of their original sequence, the protocol delivers them to the receiving device in the correct order.

Setting Session Variables
The protocol determines such variables as whether the session will be half or full duplex, network login and authentication, file transfer protocols that will be used, and so on.

THE OPEN SYSTEMS INTERCONNECT MODEL

The standardization efforts in protocols have resulted in layered protocols. A layer is a discrete set of functions the protocol is designed to accomplish. The International Standards Organization (ISO) has published a seven-layer protocol model, the Open Systems Interconnect (OSI) model, which is illustrated in Figure 4–1.

Controlling communications in layers adds some extra overhead because each layer communicates with its counterpart through header records, but layered protocols are easier to administer than single-layer protocols and provide greater opportunity for standardization. Although protocols are complex, functions in each layer can be modularized so the complexity can be dealt with separately by system designers. Layered control offers an opportunity for standardization and interconnection between the proprietary architectures of different manufacturers. Generally, the degree of standardization is greatest at the first layer, and becomes increasingly disparate in the higher layers. The seven OSI layers are defined below. Table 4–1 lists the OSI layers and some of the standards that apply to each layer. The higher layers in the protocol stack are more abstract and in some cases less well-defined than the first three or four layers, which have been in common use for many years.

FIGURE 4-1

International Standards Organization Open Systems Interconnection Model

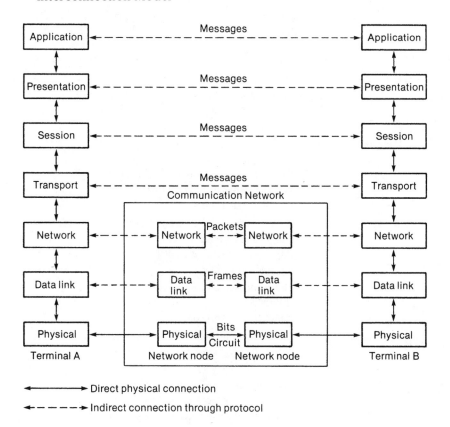

Direct physical connection

Indirect connection through protocol

Layer 1—Physical

The first layer describes the method of physical interconnection over a circuit. The physical layer contains the rules for the transmission of *bits* between machines and standardizes pin connections between DCE and DTE. The standards discuss modulation methods and multiplexing over the physical medium, which is wire, fiber optics, coaxin cable, or wireless. For example, EIA-232 is a common standard for serial port connections. Its speed and distance limitations are overcome by using balanced interfaces such as EIA-422 or V.35. Two devices can communicate using nothing but the physical layer. For example, if the serial ports of two computers are connected through an adapter

TABLE 4-1

Representative Protocols of the OSI Layers

Layer	Common Standards
1. Physical	EIA-232 EIA-422 V.35
2. Data Link	High-level data link control (HDLC) Balanced link access procedure (LAPB) Designated link access procedure (LAPD) IEEE 802.2 logical link control
3. Network	X.25 packet level protocol Internet protocol (IP) Connectionless network protocol (CLNP) Address resolution protocol (ARP) IBM/SNA Path control
4. Transport	Transmission control protocol (TCP) User datagram protocol (UDP) Netware control protocol (NCP) ISO transport protocol
5. Session	ISO connection-oriented session protocol NETBIOS IBM/SNA data flow control
6. Presentation	ISO connection-oriented presentation protocol Microsoft server message block protocol Netware file service protocol
7. Application	X.400 Message handling service (MHS) ISO file transfer, access, and management (FTAM) ISO office document architecture (ODA) ISO virtual terminal service Simple mail transfer protocol (SMTP) Virtual terminal (TELNET)

known as a *null modem,* they can send data to each other. The null modem connects the transmitting data and signaling leads of each computer to the corresponding receiving leads of the other.

Layer 2—Data Link

Data link protocols are concerned with the transmission of *frames* of data between devices. The protocol in the data link layer detects and corrects errors so the user gets an error-free circuit. The data link layer takes raw data characters, creates frames of data from them, and processes acknowledgment messages from the receiver. When frames are lost or mutilated, the logic in this layer arranges retransmission.

Protocols contain flags and headers so DTE can recognize the start and end of a frame. A frame of information, as Figure 3–6 shows, has flags to signal the beginning and ending of the frame, a header containing address and control information, an information field, and a trailer containing CRC bits for error correction. The principal international standard, high-level data link control, has numerous subsets, of which balanced-link access procedure and designated-link access procedure are common. The former is used in packet-switched data networks, and the latter as the access protocol for ISDN.

Layer 3—Network

The network layer accepts messages from the higher layers, breaks them into *packets,* routes them to the distant end through the link and physical layers, and reassembles them in the same form in which the sending end delivered them to the network. The network layer controls the flow of packets, controls congestion in the network, and routes between nodes to the destination. The X.25 protocol is a connection-oriented protocol for access to a packet-switched data network. Internet protocol (IP) is one of the most widely used protocols in the world which, together with transmission control protocol, forms a common language used in most internets.

Layer 4—Transport

The transport layer controls end-to-end integrity between DTE devices, establishing and terminating the connection. It segments data into manageable protocol data units (PDUs), and reassembles them at the receiving end. It is responsible for flow control and end-to-end error correction. If the lower layers have any shortcomings in their ability to deliver data with complete integrity, it falls to the transport layer to overcome them. Transmission control protocol, (TCP), which is discussed later in this chapter, is the most widely used transport layer protocol. User datagram protocol (UDP) is a connectionless protocol that is used by simple network management protocol (SNMP).

Layer 5—Session

The user communicates directly with the session layer, furnishing an address that the session layer converts to the address the transport layer requires. The conventions for the session are established in this layer. For example, the validity of the parties can be verified by passwords. The session can be established as a full-duplex or a half-duplex session. The session layer determines whether machines can interrupt one another. It establishes how to begin and terminate a session, and how to restore or terminate the connection in case a failure interrupts the session. If a user attempts a file transfer, for example, the file must be opened, the data moved across the network, and the file closed at the end of the session. If anything happens to disrupt the transfer, the file could be left in limbo. It is the job of the session layer to ensure that the transfer is as orderly as if the distant device was directly connected to the host.

Layer 6—Presentation

This layer interprets the character stream that flows between terminals during the session. For example, if encryption or bit compression is used, the presentation layer may provide it. This layer is the least well developed of the OSI model, and is skipped in many implementations.

Layer 7—Application

The application layer is the interface between the network and the application running on the computer. Examples of application layer functions now in use are ITU's X.400 electronic mail protocol and its companion X.500 directory services protocol. Message-handling service (MHS) is an important protocol for enabling X.400 E-mail systems to communicate. ISO's file transfer, access, and management (FTAM) is a protocol for managing and manipulating files across a network. Other protocols include virtual terminal (VT), which provides a standard terminal interface, and electronic document interchange (EDI), which uses the MHS platform for transferring electronic documents across networks.

The objective of the OSI reference model is to establish a framework that will allow any conforming system or network to connect and exchange signals, messages, packets, and addresses. The model makes it possible for communications to become independent of the manufacturer that devised the technology, and to shield the user from the need to understand the complexity of the network. It should be understood that although the OSI model can be used to develop standards, it is not a standard itself. Manufacturers are increasingly announcing support for OSI, and proprietary networks may eventually evolve into compatible standard networks.

TRANSMISSION CONTROL PROTOCOL/INTERNET PROTOCOL (TCP/IP)

TCP/IP is a collection of protocols that were developed in the late 1970s by the Department of Defense as a way of providing interoperability among equipment manufacturers. The protocols emerged from research that spanned three decades under the auspices of Advanced Research Projects Agency (ARPA). The agency is now called Defense Advanced Research Projects Agency (DARPA). ARPANET, as it was called in its early days, was a loosely confederated collection of networks operated by colleges, universities, and defense-related companies and agencies. Unlike OSI, TCP/IP is not a true international standard, although it is an open standard that is widely used internationally. The standard is administered through the Internet Engineering Task Force, which is a voluntary body. The IETF distributes its recommendations through Internet Requests for Comments, which are open to anyone.

In late 1989 the original ARPANET gave way to a network that now is known as the *Internet*. Internet is a collection of independent packet-switched networks that are interconnected to act as a coordinated unit. Governmental agencies, military branches, educational institutions, and commercial companies operate the networks, but no single body has overall control. The protocols compensate for the unreliability of the underlying networks and insulate users from the need to understand the network's architecture and addressing scheme. Internet has four primary purposes:

◆ To provide electronic mail service to the users.
◆ To support file transfer between hosts.
◆ To permit users to log on to remote computers.
◆ To provide users with access to information databases.

A TCP/IP internet fits in a three-layer framework atop the physical and data link layers, as shown in Figure 4–2. The application services layer defines the interface to the basic network, which consists of the transmission control and internet protocols. The transport layer has two separate protocols, TCP, which is a connection-oriented protocol, and UDP, which is connectionless. Figure 4–2 compares TCP/IP to the OSI model.

The best known protocols in the TCP/IP suite are transmission control protocol (TCP), internet protocol (IP), file transfer protocol (FTP), simple mail transfer protocol (SMTP), and TELNET. The latter three are application layer protocols that correspond to FTAM, X.400, and VT in the OSI structure. TELNET is a protocol that allows users to log on a remote computer over the network and operate as if they were directly attached.

The user datagram protocol (UDP) is a connectionless version of TCP. It is used by simple network management protocol (SNMP), trivial file transfer protocol (TFTP), and versatile message transfer protocol (VMTP). See Chapter 38 for a discussion of SNMP. In addition, the protocol family includes address resolution protocol (ARP) and reverse address resolution protocol (RARP), which are discussed later. Routing information protocol (RIP) is used by UNIX-based computers for exchanging routing information, although it is

F I G U R E 4–2

Comparison of TCP/IP to the OSI Model

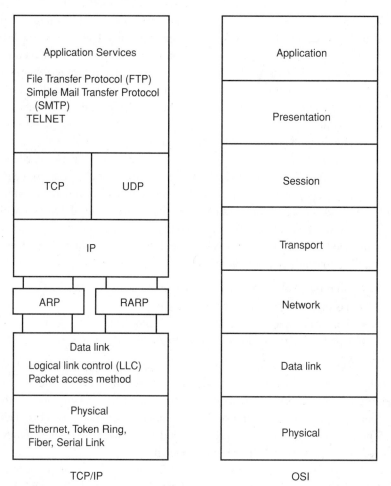

TCP/IP   OSI

inefficient and is being replaced by another routing protocol, open shortest path first (OSPF). The internet control message protocol (ICMP) handles control and error functions for IP.

The TCP/IP protocol has evolved over the years to become increasingly sophisticated. Although no international standard-setting agencies sponsor TCP/IP, it is so widely used that most computer manufacturers support the protocol. It has achieved the status of a common language between otherwise incompatible computers and will remain a de facto standard for the foreseeable future, particularly because it is evolving to meet new demands. TCP/IP is designed for operation on the Internet, but it is equally adaptable to communication within a closed network.

How TCP/IP Functions

TCP/IP became an important protocol because it was available at a time when the world needed a standard, and nothing else was available. The network structure has a simple three-level hierarchy. The lowest level is the subnetwork, or segment as it is often called in LANs. Numerous subnetworks linked together, usually through routers, comprise *domains*. Domains, in turn, are linked by an enterprisewide internetwork as shown in Figure 4–3. An IP network has two types of nodes: hosts and gateways. The functions of gateways are usually built into routers. A host is a source or destination of information. Gateways select routes to a host based on the address, which is unique for every device. See Chapter 31 for a more complete description of the functions of routers.

Gateways are of two types—core gateways and noncore gateways. Core gateways have, through routing tables, information about the structure of the network. Noncore gateways have incomplete routing information; they know the route to a core gateway but have no knowledge of routing beyond the core. From their routing tables, core gateways boost each packet toward its ultimate destination, handing it from gateway to gateway until the packet reaches a gateway that has direct connection to the addressee. A stream of packets can travel over different routes to the destination and can arrive out of sequence, mutilated, duplicated, or not at all.

The physical networks, which can be LANs, public networks such as frame relay, or private networks made up of individual circuits, are connected by the gateways. All devices on the network are given addresses that correspond to their physical position in the hierarchy. The hierarchical addressing scheme of TCP/IP is the key to efficient traffic flow. Networks can be broken into subnetworks with each device on the network having a unique address.

The operation of TCP/IP is simple. For example, assume the application is file transfer using FTP. The application transfers the file to the TCP layer, which adds a header and passes it to the IP layer. The IP layer recognizes the destination from the address, segments the file into datagrams, and passes it over the physical network to the destination. The IP layer determines the route from its internal tables based on the addressing structure. If the network is configured as a star, static routing works fine because only one path exists from a network to the world, but few networks are configured that way, so some form

Hierarchy of TCP/IP Networks

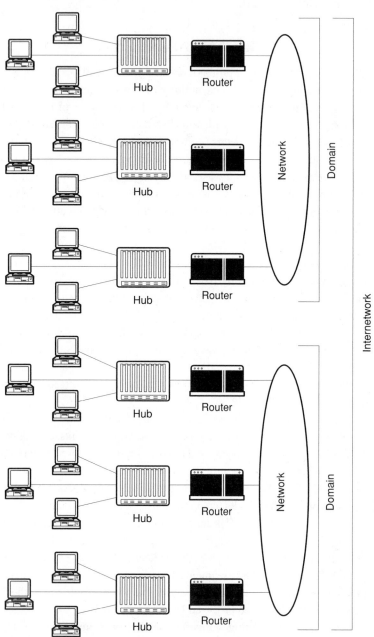

of routing algorithm is needed. Early systems used a protocol known as routing information protocol (RIP), but it proved to be inefficient in adapting to network configuration changes. The routing algorithm used currently in most networks is open shortest path first (OSPF), in which nodes need only know the shortest route to the destination.

IP is roughly analogous to the OSI network layer, but it has some important differences. First, it is a connectionless protocol, compared to X.25, which is connection-oriented. IP's protocol data unit is the datagram, which, as discussed earlier, is a unit of information carried through the network without assurance of delivery. Unlike OSI's data link protocol, which ensures message integrity from link to link, IP lacks end-to-end error checking and acknowledgment. TCP takes care of those functions.

TCP is analogous to OSI's transport layer. Its function is to discipline an otherwise chaotic path through the Internet. TCP performs end-to-end error checking, correction, and acknowledgment. It resequences packets that arrive out of sequence and communicates directly with the application program in the host. Some host operating systems even include a TCP module.

TCP/IP Addressing

The IP addressing system is both the strength and the weakness of the TCP/IP protocol. The address consists of four segments separated by a decimal, with each segment providing 255 addresses. A sample address would be 188.12.2.1. The addresses are carefully chosen to identify the network to which the device attaches as well as the address of the device itself.

IP addresses are composed of three parts: class, network portion, and host. The addresses are classed as A, B, C, and D. Class A addresses have 24 bits for hosts and eight bits for networks, one bit of which identifies the network class, leaving seven bits for network number. Therefore a maximum of 2^7, or 128, class A networks are available, each of which can have 2^{16}, or 65,536, hosts. Class B addresses allocate 14 bits for host addresses and 16 bits for networks. Class C addresses have 8 bits for hosts and 21 bits for the network address. Class D addresses are multicast addresses. The 32-bit address makes it difficult to connect Ethernets, which have 48-bit addresses embedded in hardware. A special address resolution protocol (ARP) enables a host to find its target given its Internet address. Address classes can be recognized from the digits in the first octet. Addresses from 1 to 126 are class A, 127 to 191 are class B, and 192 to 223 are class C.

Although the theoretical addresses are enormous (2^{32}), the hierarchical nature of the system precludes using all of them. An expanded addressing

TABLE 4–2

Internet Suffixes

Commercial	COM
Government	GOV
Organization	ORG
Military	MIL
Network	NET

method known as IPNG (IP Next Generation—also known as IP Version 6) is under development and will be used before the reservoir is exhausted. IPNG provides 128-bit addresses, which should be plenty to handle all conceivable devices that might connect to Internet. Networks that will never connect to the Internet are free to use any addresses they like, but any organization doing so should be aware that a future Internet connection will require changing existing addresses, which may be no small task. Internet addresses are assigned by the National Information Center (NIC). Of the four segments of IP addresses, the NIC assigns only the first segment in class A addresses, the first two segments in class B addresses, and the first three in class C addresses. The network administrator assigns the lower address levels. Anyone using TCP/IP is advised to obtain an address from the NIC. Class A addresses are given only to the largest organizations, which can make efficient use of the lower level addressing structure.

Numerical IP addresses are not particularly easy to remember, so Internet has adopted a naming convention that is easy to use. Each user is assigned to a domain, which is the name of the company or service provider having direct connection to Internet. The domain name is separated from a three-letter suffix by a period. A typical address might be jsmith@acme.com. Table 4–2 shows the common suffixes. The suffix is either functional (COM, EDU, and so on) or it is geographical (US, UK, JP, and so on). Users send messages across Internet using the domain name, which must be translated into a numerical address. The translation function is assigned to domain name servers (DNS), each of which knows about every connected domain. When a host needs to know an IP address, it sends a message to the DNS, which reports back the whole IP address. Each Internet host has in its root directory the address of its DNS for its domain.

The dots between domain names are not directly related to the dots between the numeric address. The addresses are used for routing, which depends on the physical structure of the network, but address names are more related to the organization structure.

Address Resolution

When computers share a physical network, they are assigned a network address, which, in the case of LANs, is encoded permanently in the NIC. Even though the NIC contains the address, it isn't permanently associated with the address of the machine. For example, if a card fails and is changed, its physical address changes, but if the computer is a member of an internetwork, its IP address remains the same. Hosts and gateways must have a method of mapping IP addresses to physical addresses in order to send data across the Internet. The objective of address resolution is to hide physical addresses and allow communication using only IP addresses. The problem is further complicated with Ethernet, which has a 48-bit address that cannot be encoded directly into the 32-bit IP address.

The solution to the problem is called address resolution protocol (ARP). When a host needs to know the physical address of a station, it sends a broadcast message requesting the physical address of a station with a given IP address. The station with that IP address responds with its physical address. The host that sent the ARP message retains the IP-physical address mapping in cache memory to avoid the need of sending repeated ARP messages. This is on the theory that when devices are in session, it is likely that multiple exchanges will take place.

A special case occurs with devices such as diskless workstations that are unable to store their IP addresses permanently. Before they can operate they must determine their IP address when all they know is their physical address. This is done through reverse address resolution protocol (RARP). At start-up, such stations broadcast their physical address, asking hosts to respond with their IP address, which is contained in a table. Once this initial transaction is completed, the workstation is able to respond to ARP messages.

Gateways

Gateways are the key to a host's finding its way through the Internet. The host does not have to know the route to the destination; it needs only the route to the nearest gateway. Gateways contain routing tables that the programmer enters or that the gateway builds by querying neighboring gateways. A gateway has detailed routing information for all directly attached networks and knowledge of where to send traffic for remote networks. If a gateway is unable to identify an address, it broadcasts an ARP (address resolution protocol) message, which causes other gateways to aid in resolving the dilemma. Ultimately, if traffic cannot be delivered because there is no valid route to the destination, the network returns a delivery failure message to the originator.

Internet Protocol

The IP protocol routes information between devices. It is an unreliable, connectionless, best-effort, datagram protocol that delivers data across an internet.
An unreliable protocol is one that does not guarantee delivery. Packets may be
lost, discarded, delayed, delivered out of order, or duplicated, but the protocol
does not detect the irregularity or inform the higher layer protocols. The protocol is called best-effort because it tries to deliver packets, and does not discard
them without a good reason.

IP routes packets and defines the rules under which hosts and gateways
handle packets. It also defines the basic PDU of traffic passing across an Internet, which is an internet datagram. An IP datagram is a simple PDU that contains a 24-octet header plus a data area that can be up to 65,535 octets long. The
24-octet header will be replaced by one 40 octets long when IPNG addressing
arrives. The data area length is too long to allow the IP datagram to fit inside
the maximum length frames of many networks. The maximum length permitted by a network is called its maximum transfer unit (MTU). For example,
Ethernet has a maximum data field length of 1,500 octets. When it is necessary
to send an IP datagram across a network with a shorter MTU than the datagram's data field, the protocol divides the datagram into fragments and reassembles it at the destination.

IP is a *laissez-faire* protocol. The Internet lacks flow control and has no
way of detecting duplicate, out-of-sequence, or lost packets. The gateways attempt to send messages over the shortest distance to the destination, but there is
no assurance that a packet is always heading toward its destination. Every packet,
therefore, contains a time-to-live field that has a maximum value of 255 seconds.
If the time-to-live timer expires before delivery, the network discards the packet.
This process prevents undelivered packets from traveling the Internet forever.

Internet control message protocol (ICMP) enables gateways and hosts to
send messages over the Internet to other gateways and hosts to do functions that
lower levels handle in the OSI model. For example, flow control is achieved by
sending a source quench message to throttle back a host that is outstripping the
recipient's ability to handle traffic. A destination-unreachable message is returned when a route to the destination does not exist, and a time-exceeded message is returned when a packet is killed because its time to live has expired.

Transmission Control Protocol

TCP is a connection-oriented guaranteed delivery protocol. It provides reliable
end-to-end data delivery, and is also responsible for sequencing, flow control,
deleting duplicate packets, and arranging delivery of missing packets. TCP can

be used with a variety of networks, not just IP. Its function is to receive messages from the application program and break them into packets, which may be further fragmented for transmission on the Internet. Datagrams are received at the destination and reassembled into the original message. TCP hosts, therefore, must contain adequate buffering to resequence packets. TCP provides positive acknowledgment of the receipt of packets from the distant end. The sender waits for the acknowledgment, and if it fails to arrive before a transmission timer has expired, it retransmits the packet. This may result in duplicate packets, so the receiving TCP host must be prepared to discard them.

TCP uses a sliding-window protocol to control the session between two hosts. The receiving machine acknowledges the number of correctly sequenced bits it has received and the number it is prepared to accept. If its buffers have plenty of space, it opens the window further, and when they begin to overflow, it reduces the size of the window in its next acknowledgment.

TCP/IP vs. OSI

The above discussion shows that there are significant differences between TCP/IP and OSI. TCP/IP's primary advantage is that it is an existing protocol that is widely supported, whereas OSI is not a protocol but an architectural model against which protocols can be designed. The designers of TCP/IP intended that it would be used only until the arrival of suitable international standards, and then it would evolve to be compatible with the standard. The almost universal acceptance of TCP/IP, however, has given it a life that is not likely to end soon.

A major difference between the two is that TCP/IP lacks link-by-link error correction and flow control. These exist only in the transport layer. By contrast, in OSI, which also has end-to-end error correction in the transport layer, the data link and network layers presents a more disciplined architecture. OSI has additional overhead, however, that may prove unacceptable for applications that need greater throughput. Also, error checking is unnecessary with the lower error rate of today's fiber-optic circuits, which leads to development of networks such as frame relay and ATM that omit error checking inside the network and leave it to external protocols.

Communicating between incompatible networks has been, and remains, a problem that the OSI model is expected to solve sometime in the future. Meanwhile, enough computers and other devices support TCP/IP that it has achieved the status of a de facto internetworking standard. Some observers believe that TCP/IP will disappear when OSI becomes more widely accepted. Meanwhile, applications developers have no choice but to support TCP/IP because it is so universally accepted.

TCP/IP has several benefits:

◆ It is a well-defined and widely accepted protocol.
◆ It carries less overhead than OSI and may provide better performance.
◆ There are plenty of experienced programmers who can implement TCP/IP.

OSI offers several advantages that may cause it to replace TCP/IP in the future:

◆ It is an international standard.
◆ It probably has greater longevity than TCP/IP applications.
◆ It provides for accounting chargeback.

POINT-TO-POINT PROTOCOL (PPP)

PPP was designed by the Internet Engineering Task Force to route multiple protocols over dial-up and dedicated point-to-point links. Most dial-up Internet programs support PPP in addition to the less effective synchronous line interface protocol (SLIP). PPP permits interoperability of hosts, routers, and bridges over serial links. Various types of networks such as Ethernet, token ring, Apple Computer's LocalTalk, and FDDI can communicate simultaneously over serial links. Figure 4–4 shows how PPP compares to the OSI model.

The datalink control protocol is HDLC. Operating above HDLC are two higher level protocols, link control protocol (LCP) and network control protocol (NCP). LCP is responsible for negotiating link options and authenticating the link between devices. Link negotiation can include frame compression, adjustment of frame size, and setting up link monitoring. The protocol also provides for compression of the address and control fields in the HDLC header to save transmission time.

Authentication is particularly important in dial-up applications compared to dedicated lines where the link remains intact until dismantled. PPP has two methods of authentication. The simplest is by password through the password authentication protocol (PAP). In this option the originator sends a password. The receiver either accepts the password or closes down the link. In the second, called challenge handshake authentication protocol (CHAP), the host transmits to the distant station a challenge that contains a random character string. The distant station responds with a calculated value using a private algorithm and the receiving station's identifier. The host looks up the station in a table, checks the response against the station's key, and either accepts or rejects the connection. The authentication can be repeated during the session if desired.

Comparison of PPP to the OSI Model

	Application
	Presentation
	Session
	Transport
	Network

LCP	NCP		Data link
HDLC			
Full-duplex serial link			Physical

PPP   OSI

Once the link is established, the NCP provides a framework to enable the network layer protocols, such as IP or AppleTalk, to establish a connection. When the connection is established, data transfer can take place. A link quality monitoring protocol provides for checking link quality during the session. For example, link quality reports include the number of PDUs and octets that have been transmitted and received, plus a count of errored and discarded packets and correctly received octets. If quality is unacceptable, the protocol can decide when it is appropriate to terminate and reestablish the connection over another facility.

Although PPP operates as a leased-line protocol, the most common use will be over networks that include dial-up connections. With the increasing use of dial-up access to Internet, especially by users with little or no data protocol experience, PPP will become increasingly important because of its ease of setup and use.

CHAPTER
5
PULSE CODE MODULATION

From its beginnings as the basic modulation method for T-1 carrier, pulse code modulation (PCM) has developed into the fundamental building block of today's switching and transmission systems. Almost every telephone session outside the bounds of the user's serving central office is carried over a system that converts voice into a digital stream of eight-bit words.

Alec Reeves, an ITT scientist in England, first patented the PCM method of multiplexing voice circuits on digital facilities. Although the system was technically conceivable then, it wasn't economically feasible. Pulse-generating and -amplifying circuits required vacuum tubes, and their size and power consumption consigned PCM to the shelf for another 20 years. Following the development of the transistor, PCM became commercially feasible in the 1960s, and with the development of large-scale integration in the following decade, cost, size, and power consumption continued to drop, even in the face of high inflation.

Today, digital technology has all but replaced analog technology in transmission systems and is rapidly replacing it in switching systems. Besides the lower cost of integrated circuitry, digital systems have the added advantage of directly interfacing digital switching systems and data circuits without an intervening voice frequency conversion. Digital circuits are also less susceptible to noise. In analog circuits, noise is additive, increasing with system length, but in digital carrier the signal is regenerated at each repeater. Over a properly engineered system, the signal arrives at the receiving terminal with quality unimpaired and a bit error rate several orders of magnitude less than analog.

DIGITAL CARRIER TECHNOLOGY

A T-1 digital carrier system samples a voice signal, converts it to an eight-bit coded digital signal, interleaves it with 23 other voice channels, and transmits it over a line that regenerates the signal approximately once per mile on twisted-pair copper wire. Although this discussion refers to voice channels, the T-1 signal is channelized only if the terminating equipment does so. The entire bandwidth of the T-1 signal can be used between devices such as routers, which are used to interconnect LANs. Other devices such as T-1 multiplexers can divide part of the bit stream into voice channels and part into a wider channel for LAN interconnection.

T-1 also can be transmitted over digital radio and over fiber optics with regenerators spaced at wider intervals. The digital signal is encoded and decoded in a digital central office or one of several types of terminal devices. A *channel bank* combines 24 voice and data circuits into a T-1 bit stream. Figure 5–1 is a photograph of a Newbridge® *3624 MainStreet*® intelligent T-1 channel bank. A *T-1 multiplexer,* which is described later, breaks the T-1 bit stream into smaller increments than a channel bank and supports both voice and data signals. T-1 lines can be directly connected to digital PBXs and a variety of other devices such as automatic call distributors, all of which are discussed in later chapters.

A digital signal is developed by a five-step process, consisting of the following:

- ◆ Sampling
- ◆ Quantizing
- ◆ Encoding
- ◆ Companding
- ◆ Framing

Sampling

According to Nyquist's theorem, if an analog signal is sampled at a rate twice the highest frequency contained within its bandwidth, enough intelligence is retained in the samples to reconstruct the original signal. The range of human hearing is approximately 20 Hz to 20,000 Hz, but the frequency range in a voice signal is much narrower. Communications channels filter the voice to a

FIGURE 5-1

A Newbridge® *3624 Mainstreet*® Intelligent T-1 Channel Bank

Courtesy Newbridge Networks Corp

nominal bandwidth of 4,000 Hz (actually 300 to 3,300 Hz). Therefore, a sampling rate of 8,000 times per second is sufficient to encode a voice signal for communications purposes. A PCM system does exactly this. The output of the sampling process is a *pulse amplitude modulated* (PAM) signal, shown in Figure 5–2.

FIGURE 5-2

Voice Sampling

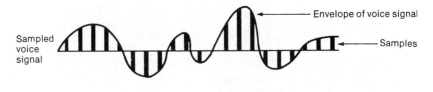

FIGURE 5-3

Companding in a PCM Channel Bank

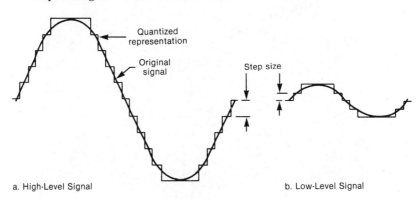

a. High-Level Signal   b. Low-Level Signal

Quantizing, Encoding, and Companding

The amplitude of the pulses from the sampling circuit is encoded into an eight-bit word by a process called *quantizing*. The eight-bit word provides 2^8, or 256, discrete steps, each step corresponding to the instantaneous amplitude of the speech sample. The output of the encoder is a stream of octets, each representing the magnitude of a single sample.

The quantizing process does not exactly represent the amplitude of the PAM signal. Instead, the output is a series of steps, which, as shown in Figure 5–3a, does not precisely represent the original waveform. The error is audible in the voice channel as *quantizing noise,* which is present only when a signal is

FIGURE 5-4

PCM Frame

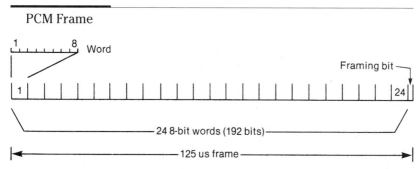

being transmitted. The effects of quantizing noise are greater with low-amplitude signals than with high. To overcome this effect, the encoded signal is compressed to divide low-level signals into more steps and high-level signals into fewer steps, as shown in Figure 5–3b. When the signal is decoded at the receiving terminal, it is expanded by reversing the compression process. The combination of expansion and compression is called *companding*. In the United States companding follows a formula known as *mu law* coding. In Europe, the companding formula is a slightly different form known as *A law* coding. Although the two laws are incompatible, they differ only slightly.

Framing

The PAM voice signal is encoded in the terminating device and merged with 23 other voice channels. Each channel generates a bit rate of 64 kb/s (8,000 samples per sec. ×8 bits per sample). The 24 channels produce the frame format shown in Figure 5–4. A single framing bit, required in earlier systems for synchronization of the terminal equipment, is added to the 192 bits that result from the 24 eight-bit words. A 193-bit frame, 125 microseconds in duration, results. The frame repeats 8,000 times per second for a total line rate of 1.544 mb/s. The framing bits follow a fixed pattern of zeros and ones throughout 12 frames. This repetitive sequence of 12 frames is called a *superframe*. The 1.544 mb/s rate results from the following:

$$
\begin{array}{rl}
8{,}000 & \text{samples per second} \\
\underline{\times 8} & \text{bits per sample} \\
64{,}000 & \text{bits per channel} \\
\underline{\times 24} & \text{channels} \\
1{,}536{,}000 & \text{bits per second} \\
\underline{+\,8{,}000} & \text{framing bits per second} \\
1{,}544{,}000 & \text{bits per second total}
\end{array}
$$

European digital carrier systems, which are known as E-1 systems, use the same 64 kb/s channel bit rate but multiplex to 32 rather than 24 channels for a 2.048 mb/s bit rate. Of the 32 channels, 30 are used for voice or data. One channel is used for frame alignment, and one for signaling. Companding and bit rate differences make North American and European digital carrier systems incompatible.

Bit-Robbed Signaling

T-1 carrier's original purpose was interoffice trunking in metropolitan areas. Analog carrier systems required, with a few exceptions, outboard devices to signal over the channel. Since signaling is a binary function, it was feasible to use a portion of the T-carrier signal itself to convey the on-hook or off-hook status of the channel. See Chapter 11 for further discussion of how signaling systems work.

The original digital channel banks used the least significant bit in every sixth frame for signaling. This technique is known as *bit robbing*. Within a super frame, the bit robbed from the sixth frame is called the *a bit*. The bit robbed from the 12th frame is called the *b bit*. The distortion resulting from bit robbing has no effect on voice signals or data signals modulated with a modem. The circuit would be unusable, however, for a 64 kb/s digital data signal. Therefore, a conventional channel bank uses only seven of the eight bits for data. At a sampling rate of 8,000 samples per second, this leaves a usable signal of 56 kb/s. Special data channel units provide direct digital access to the usable bandwidth.

Extended Superframe

Within a superframe, the framing bits synchronize the channels and signaling, but otherwise carry no intelligence. Also, the signaling bits reduce the data-carrying capacity of a T-1 channel by 8,000 bits per second. As the LECs and IECs convert to common channel signaling, the inband signaling capability of T-1 is no longer required. *Clear-channel* capability, which is one of ISDN's features, eliminates the bit-robbed signaling and introduces a revised T-1 format known as *extended superframe* (ESF). Under ESF, the 8,000 b/s framing signal, also called the Fe channel, is multiplexed to provide 2,000 b/s for six-bit cyclical redundancy checking (CRC) on the data. A 4,000 b/s facility data link (FDL) is used for end-to-end diagnostics, network control, and maintenance functions such as forcing loopback of a failed channel. The remaining 2,000 b/s are used for framing and signaling. ESF is supported by ANSI as the T1.403 standard.

The CRC code operates in the same manner as data link error detection, which is discussed in Chapter 3. It does not, however, correct errors; it only detects them. The CRC code is calculated at the source and then again at a terminal or intermediate point. If an error is detected, the equipment can flag the fault before a hard failure occurs. The receiving equipment calculates the performance of the facility from the CRC results and stores it or sends the information back to the originating equipment over the FDL.

ESF requires a change in terminating equipment and repeaters. Some ancillary equipment, such as the channel service unit (CSU), which is described later, can be designed to operate under either SF or ESF rules. ESF requires a change in the line coding, using a coding method known as bipolar with 8-zero substitution (B8ZS), which is discussed later.

DIGITAL TRANSMISSION FACILITIES

The basic digital transmission facility is a T-1 line, which has an office repeater at each end feeding twisted-pair wire, with digital regenerators spaced every 6,000 feet. The function of the office repeater is to match the output of the channel bank to the impedance of the line and to feed power over the line to the repeaters. The line repeaters regenerate the incoming pulses to eliminate distortion caused by the cable. The 6,000-foot spacing was selected because manholes are placed at 6,000-foot intervals to match the spacing of load coils in voice frequency cables.

Digital signals are applied to twisted-pair wire in groups of 24, 48, and 96 channels called T-1, T-1C, and T-2. The signals for all three originate in channel banks, digital central office switches, T-1 multiplexers, PBXs, and other T-1 compatible devices. The higher bit rates of T-1C and T-2 are developed by higher order multiplexing as described later. Digital signals also can be applied to fiber optics, microwave radio, satellite, or coaxial cable for transmission over longer distances. Digital transmission over these facilities is described in Chapters 13, 14, 15, and 18.

Digital Signal Timing

T-1 signals are synchronized by loop timing, in which synchronizing pulses are extracted from the incoming bit stream. The PCM output of the terminating device is encoded in the bipolar format that is described later. The transition of each 1s bit is detected by the repeaters and the receiving terminals and is used to keep the system in synchronization. If more than 15 consecutive zeros are transmitted on a digital facility, the receiving end may lose synchronization. To prevent this, the channel bank inserts a unique bit pattern that is detected by the receiving end and restored to the original pattern. This technique, called *bit stuffing,* is used by digital carrier systems to prevent loss of synchronization.

FIGURE 5-5

Block Diagram of a T-1 Carrier System

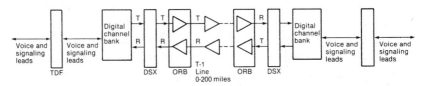

TDF - Trunk Distributing Frame
DSX - Digital Signal Cross-connect Frame
ORB - Office Repeater Bay
  T - Transmit
  R - Receive

FIGURE 5-6

Block Diagram of a PCM Channel Bank

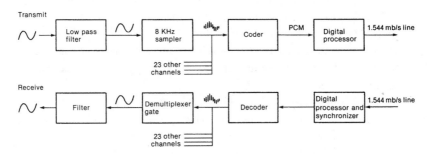

The T-1 Carrier System

Figure 5–5 is a block diagram of a T-1 carrier system. The primary elements of the system are the channel banks and the repeaters. The other elements, distributing frame and digital crossconnect frame, are provided for ease of assignment and maintenance.

Channel Banks

A basic digital channel bank consists of 24 channels called a digroup. Some manufacturers package two digroups in a 48-channel framework. The 48 channels share a common power supply and other common equipment, failure of which can interrupt all 48 channels simultaneously. Figure 5–6 is a block diagram of a digital channel bank. The channel bank has a metal framework with backplane wiring designed to accept plug-in common equipment and channel units.

T A B L E 5–1

Digital Carrier Typical Channel Unit Types

Code	Function
2W E&M	Two-wire E&M signaling trunk
4W E&M	Four-wire E&M signaling trunk
SDPO	Sleeve control dial pulse originating
DPO	Dial pulse originating
DPT	Dial pulse terminating
2W FXO	Two-wire foreign exchange office
4W FXO	Four-wire foreign exchange office
2W FXS	Two-wire foreign exchange subscriber
4W FXS	Four-wire foreign exchange subscriber
2W DX	Two-wire duplex signaling
4W DX	Four-wire duplex signaling
2W ETO	Two-wire equalized transmission only
4W ETO	Four-wire equalized transmission only
2W FXO/GT	Two-wire foreign exchange office with gain transfer
2W FXS/GT	Four-wire foreign exchange office with gain transfer
4W SF	Four-wire single-frequency signaling
PLR	Pulse link repeater
PG	Program
RD	Ringdown
PLAR	Private line automatic ringdown
OCU DP	OCU dataport

A major advantage of digital channel banks over their analog counterparts is the availability of many channel unit plug-ins. Integrated in these plugs are electrical functions that require external equipment in analog carrier systems. These functions include integrated signaling, voice frequency gain, wide-band program transmission, and data transmission capability. Table 5–1 lists the channel units available from most major manufacturers. Most of these special service units have unique signaling options, which are explained in Chapter 11; the transmission functions are covered in this chapter.

Special Transmission Functions

The plug-in units listed in Table 5–1 provide several special transmission functions in addition to the signaling functions that will be described in Chapter 11. Foreign exchange (FX) service is a combination of special signaling and transmission service. It is used by LECs to connect a telephone line in one exchange to a station located in another. FX channel units are also used in PBXs to connect the PBX to off-premises station lines or to foreign exchange trunks extended between PBXs. FX channel units are equipped for direct connection to metallic loops and have provisions for ringing telephones and for adding gain to long loops (gain transfer option).

Program (PG) channel units replace two or more voice channel units and use the added bit stream to accommodate a wider channel for use by radio and television stations, wired music companies, and other applications that require a wide audio band. Program channels with 5 kHz bandwidth replace two voice channels, and 15 kHz units replace six voice channels.

Transmission Only (TO) channel units are used for circuits that do not require signaling and for data services in which signaling is part of the application. TO channel units are also used to connect channels in channel banks wired back-to-back. Back-to-back wiring is used at intermediate points on a T-carrier line when it is necessary to drop off individual voice channels.

Digital Crossconnect Panel

In most multiple channel bank installations a digital signal crossconnect (DSX) panel, shown in Figure 5–7, is provided. The transmit and receive circuits of the channel bank are wired through jacks in this panel to provide test access and to enable the channel bank to be connected to another T-1 carrier line. The transfer of the T-1 bit stream to another line is called *patching* and is used for rearranging circuits and for manually transferring to a spare line when repeaters fail.

The ability to patch to spare lines is a vital part of service restoration in common carrier applications and is provided in most installations. In private networks the DSX panel is useful for temporary rearrangement of facilities. For example, a T-1 facility might be used for multiple low-speed point-to-point terminal communications during working hours and patched to a high-speed multiplexer for transfer of data after hours.

Automatic protection switching is often used for manual patching where rapid restoral is essential and where one or both terminals are unattended. The automatic protection system monitors the bit stream of the protected channel banks and switches automatically to a spare line when the working line fails.

Distributing Frame

The voice frequency side of a channel is wired to crossconnect blocks on a distributing frame. A crossconnect block provides a convenient location for concentrating lines between the channel banks and their interfacing equipment. Where temporary rearrangements are needed, the voice frequency and signaling leads of a

FIGURE 5-7

DSX-BEST-56 DSX Panel

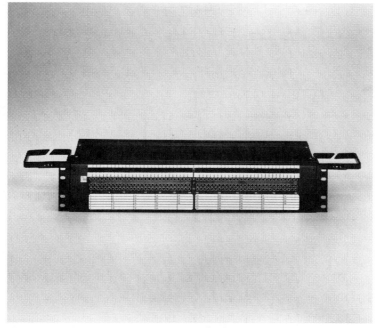

Courtesy of ADC Telecommunications

channel are wired through jacks. These jack panels are a convenient place for rapidly restoring circuits and for temporarily rerouting equipment to another channel.

T-Carrier Lines

T-1 carrier lines can be extended on twisted-pair wire for about 200 miles, although most private and common carrier applications are considerably shorter
because longer circuits are usually deployed over radio or fiber-optic facilities.
A T-carrier line accepts a *bipolar* signal from the channel bank, as shown in Figure 5–8. A bipolar signal, also called *alternate mark inversion,* assigns 0s to a
zero voltage level. Ones signals are alternately ± 3 volts. The bipolar signal offers two advantages. First, the line signaling rate is only half the data rate of 1.544
mb/s because in the worst case of a signal composed of all 1s, the signal would
alternate at only 772 kb/s. The second advantage is the ability of a bipolar signal
to detect line errors. If interference or a failing repeater adds or subtracts 1s bits,
a bipolar violation results, which indicates a fault in a T carrier system. A bipolar
violation occurs when two 1s bits of the same polarity arrive in sequence.

FIGURE 5-8

T-1 Carrier Line Signals and Faults

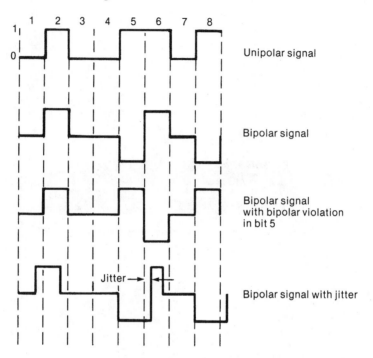

Clear channel capability requires the T-carrier system to support any pattern of bits, including long strings of 0s. ESF systems replace the straight bipolar signal with a coding scheme known as *bipolar with 8-zero substitution* (B8ZS). In this system, any string of eight 0s is replaced with an intentional bipolar violation at the fourth and seventh bits. The receiving equipment, normally the channel service unit, detects the bipolar violation and replaces it with a string of eight 0s. The B8ZS coding scheme is not compatible with earlier T-carrier lines, which may correct bipolar violations, but most modern regenerators, office repeaters, and channel service units are ESF-compatible.

Office Repeaters and Channel Service Units

An office repeater terminates the T-1 line at each central office. In the receiving direction, the office repeater performs normal repeater functions, but it is passive in the transmit direction. Its transmit function is to couple the bipolar signal to the line and to feed power to the line repeaters. A special type of office repeater called a channel service unit (CSU) terminates the customer end of a T-1

FIGURE 5–9

Block Diagram of a T-1 Repeater

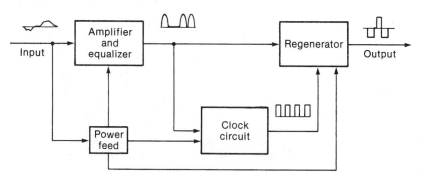

line feeding customer premises. Not to be confused with a CSU that operates on a single 56/64 kb/s channel, a T-1 CSU terminates the entire T-1 line.

The CSU was considered part of the network before divestiture, but the FCC has ruled that the CSU is network channel terminating equipment (NCTE) and is therefore to be furnished by the customer. Unlike a DDS signal, where a DSU is required to convert the line signal from bipolar to the unipolar signal required by the terminal equipment, the bipolar signal is produced by the T-1 multiplexer or channel bank. Increasingly, the CSU function is built into the channel bank or the multiplexer. The CSU fulfills the following functions:

◆ Terminates the circuit, including lightning and surge protection.
◆ Regenerates the signal.
◆ Loops the digital signal back to the originating end upon command.
◆ Monitors the incoming line for bipolar violations.
◆ Generates a signal—usually all 1s—to maintain synchronization on the line if the terminal equipment fails.
◆ Maintains the 1s density requirement of the line.
◆ Provides signal lamps and line jacks for testing and monitoring.
◆ Provides line build-out (LBO) if necessary.

Line Repeaters

Line repeaters are mounted in an apparatus case holding 25 units. Apparatus cases are watertight for mounting on poles and in manholes. Repeaters, shown in a block diagram in Figure 5–9, perform these functions:

◆ Amplify and equalize the received signal.
◆ Generate an internal timing signal.
◆ Decide whether incoming pulses are 0s or 1s.
◆ Regenerate pulses and insert them the in correct output time slot.

FIGURE 5-10

Slip in Digital Transmission

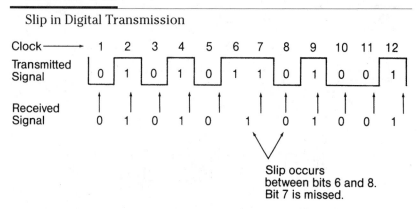

Slip occurs
between bits 6 and 8.
Bit 7 is missed.

Incoming pulses are received in one of three states—plus, minus, or 0. If the incoming pulse, which has been distorted by the electrical characteristics of the line, exceeds the plus or minus threshold, the repeater generates a 1 output pulse. Otherwise it registers a 0.

Phase deviations in the pulse, which are additive along a T-carrier line, are known as *jitter*. Excessive jitter, as illustrated in Figure 5-8, can cause errors in data signals. Errors occur when the receiver in a repeater or a terminal incorrectly interprets the incoming signal.

The transmit and receive paths of T-1 signals must be isolated to prevent crosstalk coupling. If excessive crosstalk occurs between the high-level pulses of a repeater's output and the low-level received pulses of adjacent repeaters, errors will result. These are prevented by assigning the transmit and receive directions to separate cables, to partitions within a specially screened cable, or to separate binder groups within a single cable. Cable binder groups are explained in Chapter 6.

T-1C and T-2 lines operate on the same general principles as T-1 lines except that their bit rates are higher and greater isolation between the pairs prevents crosstalk. Design rules for these systems require either a screened cable, which contains a shield to separate transmit and receive pairs, or separate transmit and receive cables.

T-1 Carrier Synchronization

When T-1 carrier is used in a private network that carries end-to-end digital signals, it is important that the network be kept in synchronization. To understand why, consider the timing diagram shown in Figure 5–10. If the clock of one terminal device runs slightly faster or slower than the clock at the other end, a point will be reached where an extra bit will be inserted or a bit will be lost, and the entire frame will lose synchronization momentarily. This condition is known as a *slip*.

When T-1 carrier was introduced, the circuits riding on the network were mostly analog, and synchronization between the two ends of a circuit was not important. The two directions of transmission were independent of each other, and the receiving end extracted timing from the line. If a slip occurred, it was heard as a slight pop and had little effect on voice transmission. With the advent of end-to-end digital circuits, however, slips became a matter of concern because the loss of one frame of 193 bits causes one or more data blocks to be rejected. To prevent slips and consequent data errors, the entire digital network must be kept locked in synchronization.

In a private network of only two devices linked by T-1, one device is a master and the other is a slave. A precise clocking rate is not important. If the slave extracts clocking from the 1s bits in the received signal, synchronization is maintained. The more nodes that are added to the network, the more critical the provision of a master clock becomes. When the network is connected to a common carrier network, as with a T-1 long-distance service, it is vital that the entire network slave from the common carrier because the carrier is tied to a higher level in the national clocking structure.

Nationally, digital network synchronization is maintained through a four-level hierarchy of clocks. ANSI standard T1.101 defines the four levels, which are known as Stratum 1 through Stratum 4 timing levels. Stratum 1 clocks use highly accurate oscillators using cesium and rubidium clocks with a maximum drift of 1×10^{-11}. Stratum 2 clocks, which are used in common carriers' toll centers, are slightly less accurate—1×10^{-10} in the short term (one day)—but if synchronization is lost with the Stratum 1 clock, it will still maintain an acceptable amount of stability. Stratum 3 and 4 are less stable and generally depend on synchronization from higher levels to maintain an acceptable degree of performance. Private network equipment generally contains Stratum 3 or 4 clocking.

THE DIGITAL SIGNAL HIERARCHY

Digital signals from a T-1 source are multiplexed to higher rates. Figure 5–11 shows the bit rates of the North American digital hierarchy. T-1 signals are applied to a standard repeatered line as described in the next section. Higher rate signals are applied to wire, coaxial cable, fiber optics, and digital microwave radio.

FIGURE 5–11

North American Digital Signal Hierarchy

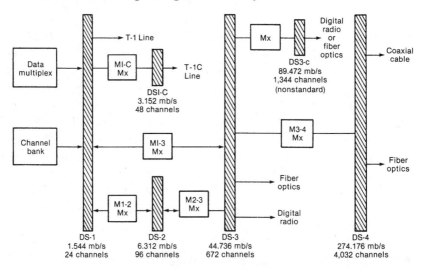

A family of multiplexers raises the basic digital group to higher bit rates. Multiplexers are designated according to the digital signal levels they interface. For example, an M1-3 multiplexer connects DS-1 to DS-3. An M1-3 multiplexer accepts 28 DS-1 inputs and combines them into a single 45 mb/s bit stream. (The bit stream is 45.736 mb/s, but it is commonly called 45 mb/s in the industry.) Multiplexer output can be directly connected to a digital radio or to a fiber-optic system.

The primary use of the DS-4 signal level is to feed T-4 coaxial cable. The DS-4 signal speed is too high to apply to the limited bandwidth of a digital microwave. Lightwave systems can easily support 274 mb/s, but their bandwidth can transport much higher bit rates, so most manufacturers are producing equipment that operates at bit rates of 1 gb/s or more and are undefined in the digital hierarchy. This ambiguity is being corrected as the world adopts synchronous optical network (SONET) standards, which are discussed in the next section.

SYNCHRONOUS OPTICAL NETWORK (SONET)

SONET is a hierarchy of optical standards that is replacing the present digital signal hierarchy over single-mode fiber-optic cable. Internationally, SONET is known as the Synchronous Digital Hierarchy (SDH). SONET standards are defined in 192 increments up to 10 gb/s. The basic building block of SONET is

T A B L E 5–2

SONET and SDH Line Rates

SONET	SDH	Speed MB/S
STS-1		51.840
STS-3	STM-1	155.520
STS-9	STM-3	466.560
STS-12	STM-4	622.080
STS-18	STM-6	933.120
STS-24	STM-8	1,244.160
STS-48	STM-16	2,488.370
STS-192	STM-64	9,953.280

an octet repeated every 125 microseconds, which corresponds to the 64 kb/s rate of T-1. SONET offers the following advantages:

♦ It offers bandwidths more commensurate with today's fiber-optic systems than the older digital signal hierarchy.

♦ It merges North American and European hierarchies at higher rates.

♦ It offers multivendor interoperability over fiber-optic systems. By contrast, non-SONET networks use a proprietary frame overhead that mandates equipment from the same manufacturer at both ends of a fiber-optic cable.

♦ It offers centralized end-to-end network management and performance monitoring.

♦ Network costs are lower because SONET permits direct access to any signal level from DS-0 to the top of the hierarchy. It permits drop-and-add capability without the use of back-to-back multiplexers.

♦ It provides support for new switching standards such as ATM and B-ISDN.

The SONET hierarchy is specified in terms of OC (Optical Carrier), which is an optical interface, and STS (Synchronous Transport Signal) layers. STS is the designation for the electrical interface. OC-1 is the lowest level on the SONET hierarchy. OC-1 can carry, and becomes the envelope for, a DS-3 (45 mb/s) signal. At OC-3, which is 155–520 mb/s, the North American and European standards converge, which eliminates the past incompatibility of the two standards. At present, the top level of the SONET hierarchy, OC-192, is 9,953.28 mb/s. Table 5–2 lists the line rates of the principal SONET levels. The standard supports up to 10 gb/s now, but it can be extended to higher rates in the future.

SONET begins with an 8-bit byte repeated every 125 microseconds, the same as the European and North American voice channel of 64 kb/s. Sets of 810 bytes form a 51.840 mb/s OC-1 signal. Multiple OC-1 signals interleave to form the higher levels. The OC-1 signals contain payload (customer data) and overhead signals. The payload of an OC-1 signal is 49.536 mb/s. The remaining 2.304 mb/s is a multilevel line, path, and section overhead signal. Section overhead carries framing and error-monitoring signals that all devices on the line can monitor and process. Line overhead extends between central offices. It carries performance information plus automatic protection switching and control information. Path overhead provides performance and error information plus control signaling between the end points of a SONET network.

SONET is being used by LECs to deliver clear-channel DS-1 and DS-3 digital services between offices and directly to end users. Private network users also employ SONET over private fiber-optic systems. As bandwidth demand increases, SONET will likely be the physical layer technology that the LECs use to carry services from the customer premises to the central office, where they can access a variety of services including broadband ISDN. B-ISDN standards are not part of SONET, but the two standards are compatible. OC-3 will be used as the primary transport for the B-ISDN signal.

DIGITAL CROSSCONNECT SYSTEMS

Short-haul carrier systems converge in central offices in both private and common carrier networks for connection to long-haul facilities. If 24-channel digroups are connected through the office to a single terminating point, no channel bank is required. Instead the incoming T-1 line is connected to the outgoing line with an express office repeater with channel banks needed only at the terminating ends. If fewer than 24 channels are needed, or if channels from a single originating point must be split to separate terminating points, back-to-back channel banks or a drop-and-insert multiplexer must be used to access the bit stream for channel crossconnection.

Back-to-back channel banks are undesirable for several reasons:

◆ Cost of the channel banks.
◆ Channel banks are an added source of potential circuit failure.
◆ Labor cost of making channel crossconnections.
◆ Extra analog-to-digital conversions, which are a source of distortion.

For smaller networks, a drop-and-insert multiplexer, which splits a certain number of channels out of the T-1 bit stream, can be used. For larger networks, the *digital crossconnect system* (DCS) is a specialized electronic switch that terminates T-carrier lines without channel banks and routes the individual channel bit streams to the desired output line. Unlike the electronic digital switches covered in Chapters 8, 9, and 10, a DCS establishes a semipermanent path for the bit stream through the switch. This path remains connected until it is disconnected or changed by programmer order or administrative action.

The DCS system eliminates most of the labor associated with rearrangement, eliminates extra analog-to-digital conversions, and offers a high degree of flexibility in rerouting circuits. Also, routing changes can be controlled from a central location over a data link. If the organization uses a mechanized database to maintain records of facility assignments, the same source that updates the data-base can drive the DCS assignments. DCS is a space-saving system because it eliminates the distributing frame blocks and wire required to interconnect the large numbers of voice frequency and signaling leads that back-to-back channel banks would require.

DCS is the key to implementing the intelligent digital network described in Chapter 31. Linked to the user's network control system, DCS allows the user to reconfigure the network to meet changes in demand or to accommodate changes that occur with time, such as assigning network capacity to a voice switch during normal working hours and to a computer center for high-speed data transfer during off hours.

Private network managers are increasingly becoming attuned to the problem of network restoral, a function in which DCS plays a key role. When a major switch node fails, a DCS system can quickly reroute traffic around the point of failure. It also increases the traffic carried by T-1 systems. Many of today's T-1 networks are only partially filled. With DCS it is feasible to combine channels to fill a T-1, though it may mean routing a circuit over greater distance than it would otherwise span.

Privately owned DCS systems are not the only alternative available to network operators who need DCS capability. Most large LECs offer DCS as a contracted or tariffed service. Since the T-1 lines may extend through the LEC's central office anyway, using a centralized DCS may make sense technically and economically. The principal issue, however, is the degree of control the LEC provides over the DCS facility. If the network operator has full control over circuit configuration, the use of private versus common carrier DCS is primarily an economic issue.

T-1 MULTIPLEXERS

Channel banks are somewhat inflexible devices for subdividing the T-1 bit stream. Voice channels and data occupy a full 64 kb/s each, though the data channels may operate at lower speeds. Also, even intelligent channel banks lack the ability to switch and reroute signals. A more versatile (and expensive) device is the T-1 multiplexer, which uses TDM techniques to combine multiple low-speed bit streams into a 1.544 mb/s signal. By using external multiplexers, it is possible to divide the bandwidth of a single T-1 into more than 2,000 fragments. Figure 5–12 shows a Newbridge® *3630 MainStreet®* primary rate multiplexer.

T-1 multiplexers contain control logic to provide clocking, generate frames, and enable testing. The control logic and the power supply are common to the entire multiplexer and may be redundant to improve reliability. The diagnostic capabilities include alarm and loop-back facilities and may include a built-in test pattern generator to help in trouble diagnosis. Multiplexers can generally handle synchronous data from 50 b/s to 1.544 mb/s, and asynchronous data from 50 b/s to 19.2 kb/s. Voice input is accommodated by using PCM or voice compression methods such as adaptive differential pulse code modulation (ADPCM), which compresses the voice into 32 kb/s.

T-1 multiplexers divide the bit stream into a series of subslots. Some provide slow-speed subslots; others provide larger subslots, which require external multiplexers to use the capacity of the subslot for low-speed data. Figure 5–13 shows how a network might be constructed by multiplexing data over T-1 lines. It also shows drop-and-insert capability, another feature of multiplexers. This allows the multiplexer to extract selected channels while extending others on to another destination.

T-1 multiplexers are more expensive than channel banks. Some products cost two to four times the price of a channel bank, but multiplexers offer significantly increased functionality. Multiplexers can be networked, as Figure 5–14 shows, to form an integrated voice and data network with alternate routing capability and sophisticated network management. A channel bank can theoretically derive as many channels from a T-1 line as a multiplexer can, but to do so would require external data multiplexers and voice compression equipment. The external equipment would be more costly than providing the same facilities in a multiplexer, and the channel bank would still lack the management capabilities and flexibility of a multiplexer.

A valuable feature of T-1 multiplexers is their network management capability. Some multiplexers have the capability of monitoring multiple points in the network, reporting malfunctions and keeping the network manager supplied with usage and performance information from all the nodes. Another vital feature of many multiplexers is their ability to reroute circuits during failure or congestion. Two different systems are used to keep data flowing. A *table-based* system is composed of fixed routing tables that instruct the multiplexer how to act in the face of a failure. A *parameterized,* or rule-based, system develops a global view of the network and responds flexibly.

FIGURE 5–12

A Newbridge® *3630 MainStreet*® Primary Rate Multiplexer

Courtesy Newbridge Networks Corp.

FIGURE 5-13

T-1 Multiplexer Layout Showing Drop-and-Insert Capability and Submultiplexing Low-Speed Channels

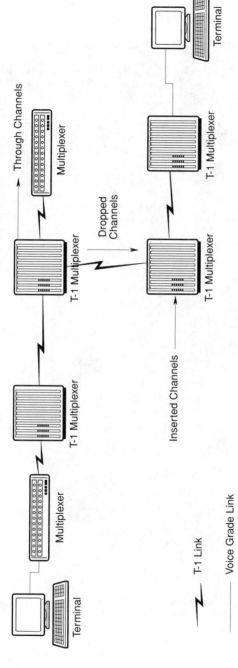

FIGURE 5-14

Networked T-1 Multiplexers

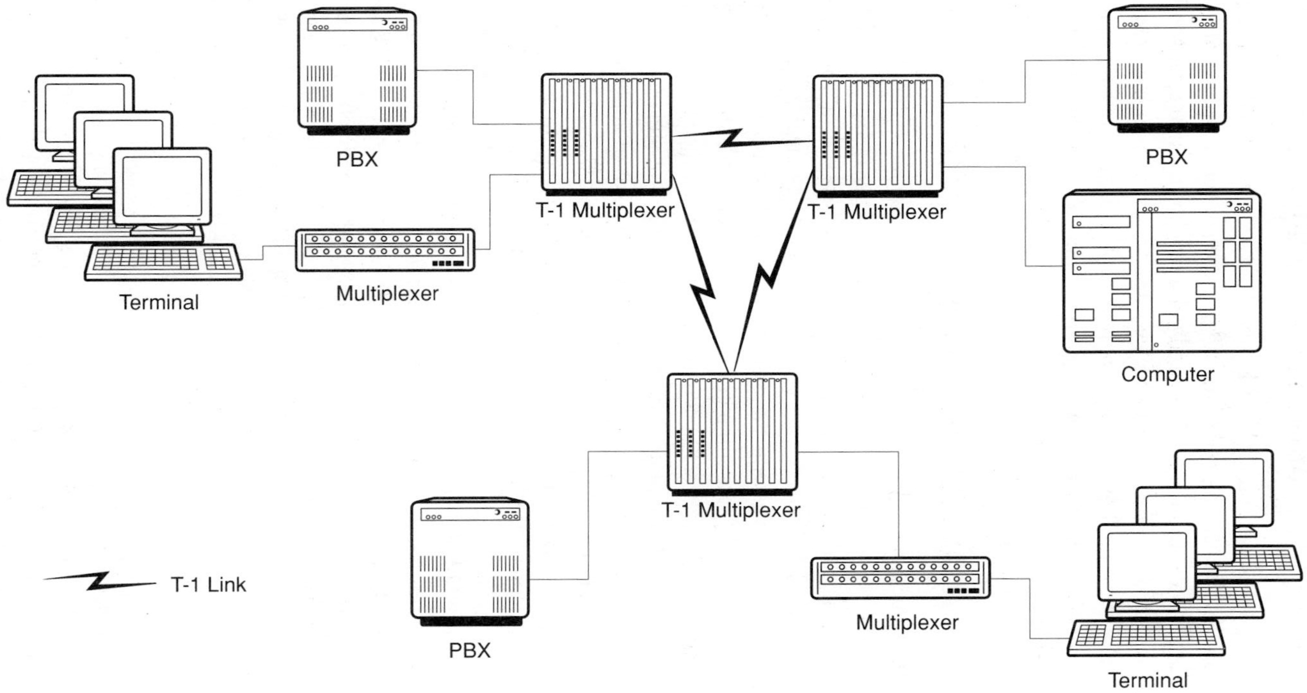

Drop-and-Insert Multiplexers

A drop-and-insert multiplexer is similar to a channel bank with respect to the channels that are dropped or inserted. These are connected as individual channels or as a portion of the T-1 bandwidth to a host computer or similar device. A portion of the T-1 line is connected straight through the multiplexer, usually continuing on to the next terminal point or terminating in a PBX, as shown in Figure 5–15. Drop-and-insert capabilities may also be contained in a T-1 multiplexer.

ADAPTIVE DIFFERENTIAL PULSE CODE MODULATION

Pulse code modulation uses an efficient encoding algorithm that provides excellent fidelity and clarity for a voice signal. Its use of bandwidth, however, is inefficient, and other coding methods can compress several voice channels into the same 64 kb/s bandwidth that a single PCM channel requires. Bandwidth costs are dropping with the arrival of nationwide fiber-optic networks, but transmission costs are still high enough that decreased circuit costs often repay the cost of the hardware to compress voice and combine it with data.

ADPCM equipment compresses two PCM bit streams into a single bit stream that can be transmitted over T-1 carrier lines or applied to M1-3 multiplexers and transmitted over fiber-optic or radio facilities. An ADPCM transcoder encodes a digital signal at 32 kb/s rather than 64 kb/s, enabling transmission of 48 channels over a 1.544 mb/s line.

ADPCM uses the same 8,000 times-per-second sampling rate as PCM, but instead of quantizing the entire voice signal, it quantizes only the changes between samples. A circuit known as an *adaptive predictor* examines the incoming bit stream and predicts the value of the next sample. ADPCM quantizes the difference between the actual sample and the predicted sample into 16 levels, which can be coded with 4 bits. The encoder adapts to the speed of change in the difference signal; fast for speech-like signals and slow for data signals. Figure 5–16 compares PCM and ADPCM, both of which result in a 1.544 mb/s line signal.

ADPCM can use the bit-robbed signaling methods of PCM, but to do so presents two problems. First, the voice compression techniques of ADPCM make it necessary to rob a bit from every fourth rather than every sixth frame. This makes ADPCM incompatible with the DS-1 signal format. Second, the robbed bit can degrade 4,800 b/s data on a voice channel. To address this problem, the standard offers an optional 44-channel format, in which one channel of every 12 is devoted to signaling. Some manufacturers provide either 44- or 48-channel operation as options.

FIGURE 5-15

Sharing an IEC Entrance Facility between Voice and Data

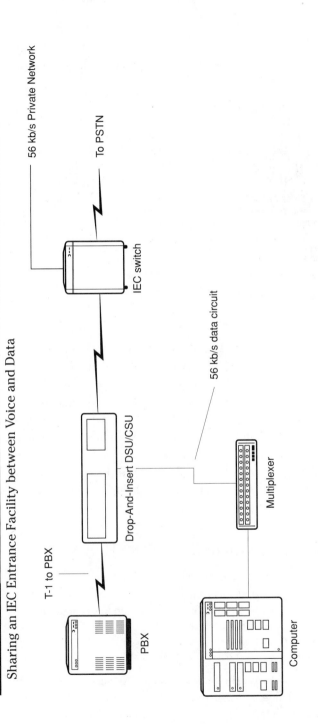

FIGURE 5–16

Comparison of Pulse Code Modulation and Adaptive Differential
Pulse code Modulation

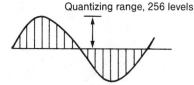

Quantizing range, 256 levels

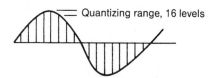

Quantizing range, 16 levels

Sampling: 8,000 times per second
Quantize: 256 levels/sample
Code: 8 bits/sample

8,000 samples/sec
x   8 bits/sample
x   24 circuits
1,536 kb/s
+   8 kb/s framing
1,544 kb/s

Sampling: 8,000 times per second
Quantize: 16 levels/change
Code: 4 bits/change

8,000 samples/sec
x   4 bits/sample
x   48 circuits
1,536 kb/s
+   8 kb/s framing
1,544 kb/s

The primary disadvantages of ADPCM are the extra expense of the transcoder, which is required besides PCM channel banks, the inability of ADPCM to handle data reliably above 4,800 b/s, and the loss of two voice channels per digroup for signaling. The data speed restriction is apt to be most critical with companies that need to send Group 3 facsimile or V.32 data over ADPCM circuits. The facsimile machines will automatically downshift to compensate for the lack of bandwidth, and transmission will take approximately twice as long. Several ADPCM products on the market provide 64 kb/s clear-channel capability by using two voice channels for high-speed data transmission.

OTHER COMPRESSION METHODS

Some compression methods are commonly enough used that they are virtually a standard. Others are proprietary, and may carry names such as vector quantization coding, high capacity voice, and code-excited linear prediction (CELP).

Delta Modulation

Delta modulation is a less sophisticated method of signal compression than AD-PCM. Delta modulation, also called continuously variable slope delta (CVSD), uses a one-bit code to represent the voice frequency waveshape. If a sample is greater in amplitude than the previous sample, it transmits a one . If the sample

FIGURE 5–17

Delta Modulation

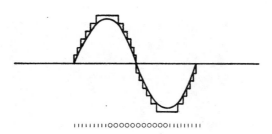

is less, it sends a zero. These signals result in a code that represents the instantaneous slope of the voice frequency waveshape, as Figure 5–17 shows.

The primary advantage of delta modulation is its ability to compress more voice channels into a bit stream at a lower cost than PCM, ADPCM, or other adaptive low-bit-rate systems. A reasonably good-quality signal can be obtained at 16 kb/s per channel. It is a simple and inexpensive method that several manufacturers support, although their products are not necessarily compatible.

The main weakness of delta modulation is its inability to follow rapid changes in the voice signal. Fortunately, however, voice signals are predictable in their behavior, so the effect is not noticeable in most conversations. A second weakness of delta modulation is the inability of the system to handle direct data transmission through data port channel units or to transport high-speed data using modems.

Time Domain Harmonic Scaling

Several companies that make voice/data integration equipment use the time domain harmonic scaling (TDHS) algorithm. Voice is digitized, and compressed by algorithms that remove redundancy and compress silent periods in a voice session. Most products that use this technology provide a combination of voice and data services over one or more 56 kb/s lines. Some products packetize the voice signal, which causes delay. A limited amount of delay can be tolerated by most users, so the quality approaches that of a "toll grade" circuit.

VOICE/DATA MULTIPLEXERS

Voice/data multiplexers, also called *line expanders* and *bandwidth managers,* are devices that enable a private line circuit to carry a combination of digitized voice and data signals. Figure 5–18 shows a Newbridge® *3600 Mainstreet*®

FIGURE 5–18

Newbridge® *3600 Mainstreet*® Bandwidth Manager

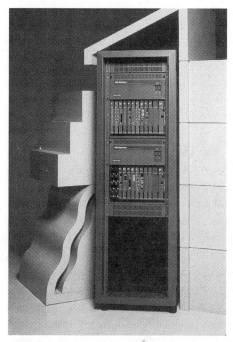

Courtesy Newbridge Networks, Inc.

multiplex Bandwidth Manager, which combines the functions of an integrated voice and data multiplexer, intelligent channel bank, digital cross-connect switch, LAN bridge, and frame relay switch. A sampling and compression algorithm such as CVSD digitizes the voice signals. The algorithms used in the products on the market are proprietary, so the devices on each end of the circuit must be furnished by the same manufacturer.

   With fractional T-1 prices dropping, these devices are becoming increasingly popular. For a modest capital investment, from two to five voice channels can ride with data for no additional cost. A voice/data multiplexer is connected, as Figure 5–19 shows. The data channel connects to a data multiplexer to subdivide the bandwidth, and voice channels connect to a PBX as tie lines.

   Currently available products compress voice signals into bandwidths as narrow as 9,600 b/s, with some manufacturers suggesting that 4,800 b/s systems are technically feasible. Some products vary the amount of data band-

FIGURE 5-19

Connection of a Voice-Data Multiplexer

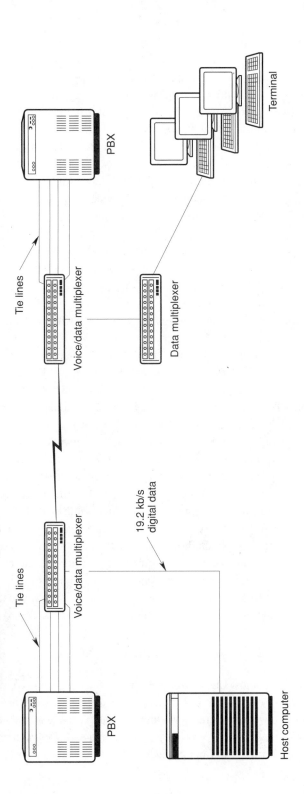

width available, expanding it when voice does not need it, and contracting it when the channel fills with voice signals. This strategy can slow data down when there is heavy voice traffic, but it keeps the bandwidth fully occupied when the demand exists. At night, when there is little voice traffic, the multiplexer can expand the data channel to occupy the entire bandwidth for high-speed data transfer.

The compression algorithm used by voice/data multiplexers will not handle high-speed modem data. Some systems provide automatic recognition of modem signals, a feature that also permits the multiplexer to pass facsimile traffic. Other products have integrated facsimile capability, which permits them to recognize a fax signal and allocate the necessary bandwidth.

FRACTIONAL T-1

Digital service users have, until recently, been faced with two alternatives: leasing service one channel at a time or leasing a full 24-channel T-1 line. With the advent of fractional T-1, a much wider choice is available. For example, AT&T's fractional T-1 offering, Accunet Spectrum of Digital Services (ASDS), provides service at 56, 64, 128, 256, 512, and 768 kb/s. Other vendors offer fractional T-1 in multiples of 64 kb/s. The basic building block is the DS-0 channel. Higher bandwidths are available for services such as slow-speed digital conferencing, high-speed data, and local area network bridging.

Technically, fractional T-1 is little different from a full T-1 channel. The IEC subdivides an existing T-1 channel with a digital crossconnect system (DCS) or a drop-and-insert multiplexer. Until the LECs file fractional tariffs, the local loop portion of the service requires the bandwidth of a full T-1 service, though less than a full T-1 is used. The most cost-effective way for many companies to use fractional T-1 is to bring the data channels in over the same T-1 that carries incoming and outgoing long-distance service. At the customer's premises the T-1 is connected to a drop-and-insert multiplexer to separate the voice and data channels. The voice channels are connected directly to the PBX, and the data channels to a computer or multiplexer.

T-3 SERVICE

The major IECs and most LECs offer T-3 service at a cost that is considerably lower than the cost of 28 separate T-1 channels. Any company that needs 10 or more T-1 lines between two cities or within a local exchange area will find T-3 an attractive option. T-3 is delivered as a single intact 45.736 mb/s bitstream, often over a self-healing fiber-optic ring.

APPLICATIONS

Digital carrier systems have wide application in both common carrier and private networks. Most metropolitan common carrier networks use digital carrier today, with analog carrier confined to expansion of existing systems. Satellite common carriers also offer digital circuits, which are multiplexed with T-1 equipment.

Standards

T-carrier standards are primarily set by manufacturers in North America with voluntary adherence to the standards originally developed by Bell laboratories. Many North American standards have been adopted by ITU. Extended super-frame standards are supported by ANSI as the T1.403 standard, and T-carrier synchronization standards are published as ANSI standard T1.101.

Evaluating Digital Transmission Equipment

Originally, digital transmission equipment was used almost exclusively by common carriers, but most large companies now have T-1 service in their network. T-1 is widely used for tie lines between PBXs and for access to the IEC. Terminal equipment is owned by the network user, and digital lines are implemented over common carrier or privately owned facilities. The criteria for evaluating digital transmission equipment are the same for both private and public ownership.

Availability of Special Service Features

T-carrier channel banks can be equipped with a range of special services channel units to match the user's requirements. Most private networks will require data and foreign exchange channel units plus a variety of voice channel units to match the PBX or station equipment they interface. Compatibility with the extended superframe should be considered for all equipment purchased. Even if ESF is not used now, it will likely be required for future applications.

Maintenance Features

The design and layout of a T-carrier system has a substantial effect on the cost of administering and maintaining it. Channel banks and line equipment should be equipped with an alarm system that registers local alarms, which can be interfaced to telemetry or SNMP for unattended operation. Test equipment needed to keep the system operative also should be considered. Typically this includes a bit error rate monitor, repeater test sets, a T-1 signal source, and extender boards to obtain access to test and level monitor points on the plug-in units.

The physical layout of the system should be designed to aid maintenance. Voice frequency and signaling leads should be terminated on a distributing frame. If more than one T-carrier line is terminated, DSX jacks should be provided. If temporary rearrangements will be made, voice frequency and signaling leads should be jack-equipped.

Spare channel and common equipment plug-in units should be provided for rapid restoral, with quantities related to the number of units in service and the failure rate of the system. Carrier group alarm (CGA) may be required to lock out switching systems from access in case of channel bank failure. CGA should restore circuits automatically when the failure is corrected.

Power Consumption

Differences in power consumption are found between products of the various manufacturers. Digital carrier is normally left operating continually, so any saving in power will involve a substantial cost saving over the life of the system. Power consumption varies with the mix of channel units installed in the channel bank, so if alternative products are being evaluated, economic comparisons should be made assuming a similar mix of channel units.

Backup Power

Most digital channel banks require -48 volts DC to match the storage batteries in telephone central offices. Converters to power the equipment from commercial AC sources are available. If continuous service during power outages is required, a battery plant should be provided. T-1 multiplexers that use random access memory to store the multiplexer configuration should be equipped with battery power to prevent loss of the configuration when the power fails. See Chapter 12 for power plant and common equipment considerations.

Operating Temperature Range

The operating temperature range of a digital channel bank is rarely a consideration in either private or common carrier networks. Most digital channel banks can operate between about 0° and 50° C, which is well within the limits of most operating environments. T-1 multiplexers, which are not usually designed for a telephone central office environment, may have narrower limits that should be evaluated against the environment in which they will be installed. Forced-air circulation may be required for reliable operation at higher temperatures.

Compatibility

T-1 channel banks built for use in the United States are generally compatible with each other and with the standard T-1 line format. T-carrier repeaters are not only compatible with the signal but are also plug-compatible so that any manufacturer's repeater fits in the same slot in an apparatus case. Other than these two elements, compatibility is a matter of concern. Any T-1 multiplexer will be end-to-end compatible only with one of like manufacture unless it was specifically designed to be compatible with that of another manufacturer. Voice compression systems that follow ITU standards are compatible; other systems are proprietary and will be found incompatible with one another. Any system purchased today should be compatible with the ESF frame format or it will be obsolete before the end of its service life. Compatibility with fractional T-1 is also a concern in devices such as multiplexers and CSUs.

Evaluating T-1 Multiplex

Several features are unique to T-1 multiplexers and should be considered along with the above factors:

- *Vendor support.* Multiplexers are normally deployed over a wide area and in locations where the company may not have staff. Vendor support is critical to minimize outage time.
- *Granularity.* This is the bandwidth of a single time slot and affects the ability of the multiplexer to use the total bandwidth of the T-1 signal.
- *Minimum bandwidth required.* Wide bandwidths may require submultiplexers to use lower speed DTE. Some multiplexers provide narrow bandwidth channels that require no submultiplexing.
- *Data channel interface.* The multiplexer will normally support cards of different types to interface EIA-232, V.35, asynchronous, and other standard interfaces.
- *Bypass or nodal delay.* This variable refers to the propagation delay that occurs between nodes on a T-1 multiplexer network.
- *Rerouting capability.* This is the ability to reroute traffic automatically when the primary link fails. The routing method, table routing or parameterized routing, and the time required to effect a reroute are important.
- *Channel bypass and drop-and-insert.* These capabilities may be required to enable flexible use of time slots.
- *Redundancy.* The amount of redundancy in the power supply and central logic improves reliability. Also, the type of redundancy in the power supply is important. Load-sharing supplies are more reliable than hot standby supplies, which must switch when the working supply fails.

♦ *Configuration backup*. Determine whether configuration is maintained in software or hardware. PROM memory tends to be inflexible; RAM memory is flexible but can be lost during power failures. If RAM memory is used, a backup method of restoring the configuration, such as booting from floppy disk or tape, should be provided. Also, nondisruptive reconfiguration, which is the ability to reconfigure channels without affecting other channels in service, is important.

♦ *Circuit trace*. This is the capability to trace the lines and nodes through which a circuit passes.

♦ *Network management*. This capability provides at least performance reporting, configuration management, and problem diagnosis. Consider whether the device is SNMP compatible.

♦ *Voice compression capability*. The type of modulation used for voice channels is important. Compression limits the speed of data and facsimile that can be transmitted over a voice channel.

♦ *Self-diagnostic capability*. The more capability the multiplexer has to diagnose its own trouble, the more rapid restoral will be.

Evaluating Channel Service Units

The following features should be considered in evaluating CSUs for T-1 or fractional T-1 service:

♦ *Diagnostic capability*. Loop-back capability should be a feature of any CSU. Some CSUs permit more advanced testing, particularly when devices of the same manufacture are on both ends of the circuit. ESF-compatible circuits can take advantage of accumulated statistical information, which evaluates the overall health of the circuit. ANSI T1.403 standards establish the reporting capabilities of the CSU. A CSU that is not ESF-compatible may not be compatible with T1.403 standards, and may or may not be capable of reporting line variables such as clock synchronization and framing errors.

♦ *Powering*. When CSUs were part of the network, they were usually powered from the T-1 line. The main reason for line powering was to use the CSU to maintain synchronization if the terminal equipment lost its power. Many LECs no longer furnish power, in which case the end user must provide power for the CSU.

♦ *Monitoring capability*. The CSU should contain 1s density and bipolar violation monitoring capability. Discrepancies should be reported to an outboard management system, displayed on panel lamps, or both.

SELECTED DIGITAL CARRIER EQUIPMENT MANUFACTURERS

Channel Banks

Hubbell Pulsecom Division

Lucent Technologies

Newbridge Networks

Nortel Inc.

Reliance Comm/Tec

Telco Systems Network Access Corp.

Tellabs

T-1 and T-3 Multiplexers

Ascom Timeplex

Coastcom

Codex Corp.

Cray Communications

Fibermux Corp.

Gandalf Data, Inc.

General Datacomm, Inc.

Micom Communications

Motorola Information Systems Group

Network Equipment Technologies

Newbridge Networks, Inc.

Nortel Inc.

Pacific Communication Sciences

Paradyne Corp.

Racal-Datacom

RAD Data Communications Ltd.

Retix

StrataCom, Inc.

Telco Systems Fiber Optics Div.

Tellabs Inc.

CSU/DSUs

ADC Kentrox
Adtran
Cray Communications
Digital Link
General Datacomm
Larscom
Motorola Information Systems Group
Paradyne Corp.
Racal Datacom
RAD Data Communications
Tylink

Data Compression Devices

Compression Technologies
Magnalink Communications
Newbridge Networks
Western Datacom

Digital Crossconnect Systems

Ascom Timeplex
Dynatech Communications
Frederick Engineering
Larus
Lucent Technologies
Tellabs, Inc.

CHAPTER

6

OUTSIDE PLANT

Outside plant is the network of cables, poles, conduit, and fiber optics that interconnects central offices and connects the local central office to the customer's premises. The link between the customer's premises and the local central office—the local loop—is the most expensive and the least technically effective portion of the entire telecommunications system today. Wide bandwidth signals travel across the country in ribbons of fiber-optic cable, are digitally routed and switched, but finally must be converted to analog and piped to the customer over a pair of wires that may cut off any frequency higher than 4 kHz. The local loop is referred to as the "last mile," and it consists largely of twisted-pair copper wire enclosed in large cables that are routed through conduit, buried in the ground, or hung on poles to reach the end user. Except for metropolitan areas where many buildings are served by fiber optics, the local loop hasn't changed much over the years. Insulation has improved, cable sheaths have evolved from lead to nonmetallic, and improved splicing techniques have increased the productivity of the LECs. Much of the outside plant that once was aerial has migrated underground, which makes it less vulnerable to damage. Otherwise, a cable placed today is technically about the same as one placed in 1920.

The portion of outside plant that connects central offices has changed substantially over the past two decades. Local trunks are a critical part of maintaining customer service, so most trunk routes were constructed in underground conduit with manholes placed every 6,000 feet. High-quality cables provided voice-grade trunks between offices. As the conduits filled, cable capacity was expanded with multiplex; at first analog, then with T-carrier as digital multiplexer became feasible. Today, the conduit remains, but the copper wires are being replaced with fiber optics, which can expand the capacity of a conduit system almost indefinitely.

Although interoffice plant has changed significantly, the local loop has not kept pace in most LECs. The local loop is the choke point of telecommunications, and technology has many solutions to offer, most of which are not yet economically practical. The obvious approach is to replace copper with fiber optics. The raw material is unlimited, the bandwidth it delivers is far greater than most applications need, and fiber is immune to the noise and corrosion that sometimes attack copper cables. Eventually, today's copper cables will undoubtedly be replaced, but now it is impractical to do so for several reasons. First is the matter of simple economics. Fiber-optic cable has enormous bandwidth, but it must be multiplexed, and multiplexing equipment is expensive and must be housed somewhere. Then there is the matter of powering station equipment. Today's copper cable carries power to the customer premises, and with the power equipment in the central office, telephone service is effectively immune to commercial power failures. Since fiber-optic cable is nonconducting, station equipment must be locally powered.

A third drawback is the sheer magnitude of the task of replacing today's copper facilities. Where the type of service requires it, LECs are replacing copper plant with fiber, but extending fiber to millions of residences and small businesses is an enormous undertaking that must be justified by benefits, and the benefits are not yet great enough. Many observers believe that video-on-demand will be the technology that drives the conversion to fiber in the local loop. The industry has even given the technology the name FITL, an acronym for "fiber in the loop," but it has yet to make a significant impact in the local loop except for fiber feeds to large businesses.

This chapter discusses how outside plant is constructed and deployed in the United States. The chapter includes a discussion on electrical protection, which is an issue that all private network managers must consider when metallic cable is used between buildings. Although this chapter primarily discusses the application of outside plant by LECs, the same fixtures are used for wire facilities in private networks. Also, because nearly every private network requires a local loop obtained from the telephone company, it is important for private network managers to understand the characteristics of the loop and how it affects the performance of the network.

OUTSIDE PLANT TECHNOLOGY

Outside plant (OSP), diagrammed in Figure 6–1, consists of the following components:

- Pole lines
- Conduit
- Feeder cable
- Distribution cable
- Terminals
- Subscriber loop multiplex equipment
- Aerial and drop wire

Protection equipment and range extension devices located in the central office and on the user's premises are also included in this discussion, though the LECs do not normally consider them as part of outside plant.

Supporting Structures

Most subscriber loops are routed from the user's premises to the telephone central office over twisted-pair cable, which is classified according to its supporting structure:

- *Aerial cable*, supported by pole lines.
- *Underground cable*, supported by conduit.
- *Buried cable*, placed directly in the ground without conduit.

Aerial cable is being discontinued as rapidly as economics permit because of environmental concerns and because of its vulnerability to damage. Aerial cable requires an external strength member to relieve tension on the conductors. Self-supporting aerial cable contains an internal strength member; all other cable requires an external *messenger* that is attached to poles. The messenger is a multistrand metallic supporting member to which cable is lashed with galvanized wire applied with a lashing machine. Down guys and anchors are placed at the ends and offsets in pole lines to relieve strain on the poles.

Direct burial is the preferred method for placing cable underground in rural areas because it is less expensive than conduit. Buried cable is either placed in an open trench or plowed with a special tractor-drawn plow that feeds the cable underground through a guide in the plow blade. Where the LECs place several cables simultaneously, or where future additions and rearrangements will be required, they also place empty conduit to avoid the expense of opening streets more than once. Manholes are located in conduit runs at intervals corresponding to the maximum length of cable that can be handled physically and at 6,000-foot intervals to house T-carrier repeaters and load coils.

FIGURE 6–1

Major Components of Outside Plant

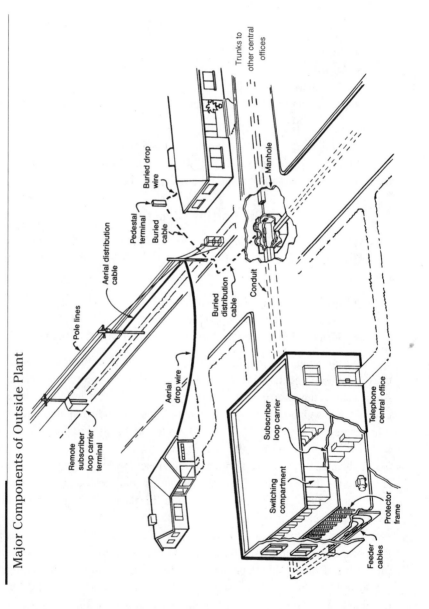

Cable Characteristics

Twisted-pair cables are classified by the wire gauge, their sheath material, their protective outer jacketing, and the number of pairs contained within the sheath. Sizes available range from one- or two-pair drop wire to 3,600-pair cable used for central office building entrance. The upper limit of cable size, which depends on wire gauge and the number of pairs, is dictated by the outside diameter of the sheath. Sheath diameter, in turn, is limited by the size that can be pulled through 4-inch conduit. Cables of larger sizes, such as 2,400 and 3,600 pairs, are used primarily for entrance into telephone central offices, which are fed by conduit in urban locations. Wire gauges of 26, 24, 22, and 19 AWG are used in loop plant. Cost considerations dictate the use of the smallest wire gauge possible, consistent with technical requirements. Therefore, the finer gauges are used close to the central office to feed the largest concentrations of users. Coarser gauges are used at greater distances from the central office as needed to reduce loop resistance.

Cable sheath materials are predominantly high-durability plastics such as polyethylene and polyvinyl chloride. Cable sheaths guard against damage from lightning, moisture, induction, corrosion, rocks, and rodents. In addition to the sheath material, coverings of jute and steel armor protect submarine cables. Besides the outer sheath, a layer of metallic tape, which is grounded on each end, shields the cables from induced voltages.

The twist of cable pairs is controlled to preserve the electrical balance of the pair. As Chapter 2 discusses, unbalanced pairs are vulnerable to noise induced from external sources, so the twist is designed to ensure that the amount of coupling between cable pairs is minimized. This is done by constructing cable in units of 12 to 100 pairs, depending on the size of the cable. Each unit is composed of several layers of pairs twisted around a common axis, with each pair in a unit given a different twist length.

Cable pairs are color coded within 50-pair complements. Each complement is identified by a color-coded string binder that is wrapped around the pairs. At splicing points, the corresponding pairs and binder groups are spliced together to ensure end-to-end pair identity and continuity. Cables can be manually spliced with compression sleeves or ordered from the factory cut to the required length and equipped with connectors.

Splicing quality is an important factor in preserving cable pair balance. Many older cables are insulated with paper and have been spliced by twisting the wires together. These older splices are often a source of imbalance and noise because of insulation breakdown and splice deterioration. To prevent crosstalk, it is also important to avoid splitting cable pairs. A split occurs when a wire from one pair is spliced to a corresponding wire in another pair. Al-

FIGURE 6–2

Pedestal-Mounted Splice Case

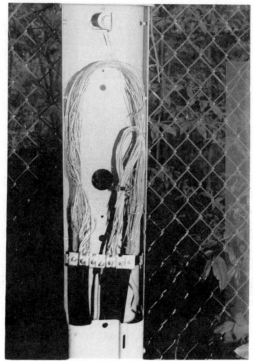

Courtesy, Preformed Line Products Company

though electrical continuity exists between the two cable ends, an imbalance between pairs exists, and crosstalk may result.

Cable splices are stored in above-ground closures in splice cases such as the one shown in Figure 6–2. Cables must be manufactured and spliced to prevent water from entering the sheath because moisture inside the cable is the most frequent cause of noise and crosstalk. In a later section we will discuss methods of keeping cables impervious to moisture.

Loop Resistance Design

Outside plant engineers select the wire gauge to achieve an objective loop resistance. All telephone switching systems, PBXs, and key telephone systems are limited in the loop resistance range they can tolerate. The loop resistance a system can support is specified in ohms and includes the following elements:

- ◆ Battery feed resistance of the switching system (usually 400 ohms).
- ◆ Central office wiring (nominally 10 ohms).
- ◆ Cable pair resistance (variable to achieve the design objective of the central office or PBX).
- ◆ Drop wire resistance (nominally 25 ohms).
- ◆ Station set resistance (nominally 400 ohms).

The cable gauge is selected to provide the desired resistance at the maximum temperature under which the system will operate. This method of design is called resistance design. Telephone central offices have total loop resistance ranges from 1,300 to 1,500 ohms or more; most PBXs have less, with many supporting ranges of 400 to 800 ohms. The range can be extended with subscriber carrier or range extension devices, which are described later. The range limitation of subscriber loops depends on the current required to operate PBX trunk circuits, DTMF dials, and the telephone transmitter. Range is also limited by the supervisory range of the central office, the range over which ringing can be supplied and tripped on answer (ring trip range), and the transmission loss of the talking path. Depending on the type of switching system, one of these factors becomes limiting and determines the loop design range.

A further consideration in selecting cable is the capacitance of the pair, expressed in microfarads (mf) per mile. Ordinary subscriber loop cable has a high capacitance of 0.083 mf per mile. Low-capacitance cable, used for trunks because of its improved frequency response, has a capacitance of 0.062 mf per mile. Special 25-gauge cable used for T-carrier has a capacitance of 0.039 mf per mile.

Special types of cable are used for cable television, closed-circuit video, local area networks, and other applications. Some types of cable are constructed with internal screens to isolate the transmitting and receiving pairs of a T-carrier system. These types of cable are beyond the scope of this book; however, the reader should be aware that they exist and may be required for certain telecommunications applications such as high-capacity T-carrier systems.

Feeder and Distribution Cable

Cable plant is divided into two categories—*feeder* and *distribution*. Feeder cables route cable pairs directly to a serving area without intervening branches to end users. Feeder cable is of two types, main and branch feeders. Main feeders are large backbone cables that exit the central office and are routed, usually through conduit, to intermediate branching points. Branch feeders are smaller cables that route pairs from the main feeders to a serving area. Distribution cable extends from a serving area interface to the user's premises. Figure 6–3 shows the plan of a typical serving area.

FIGURE 6–3

Feeder and Distribution Service Areas

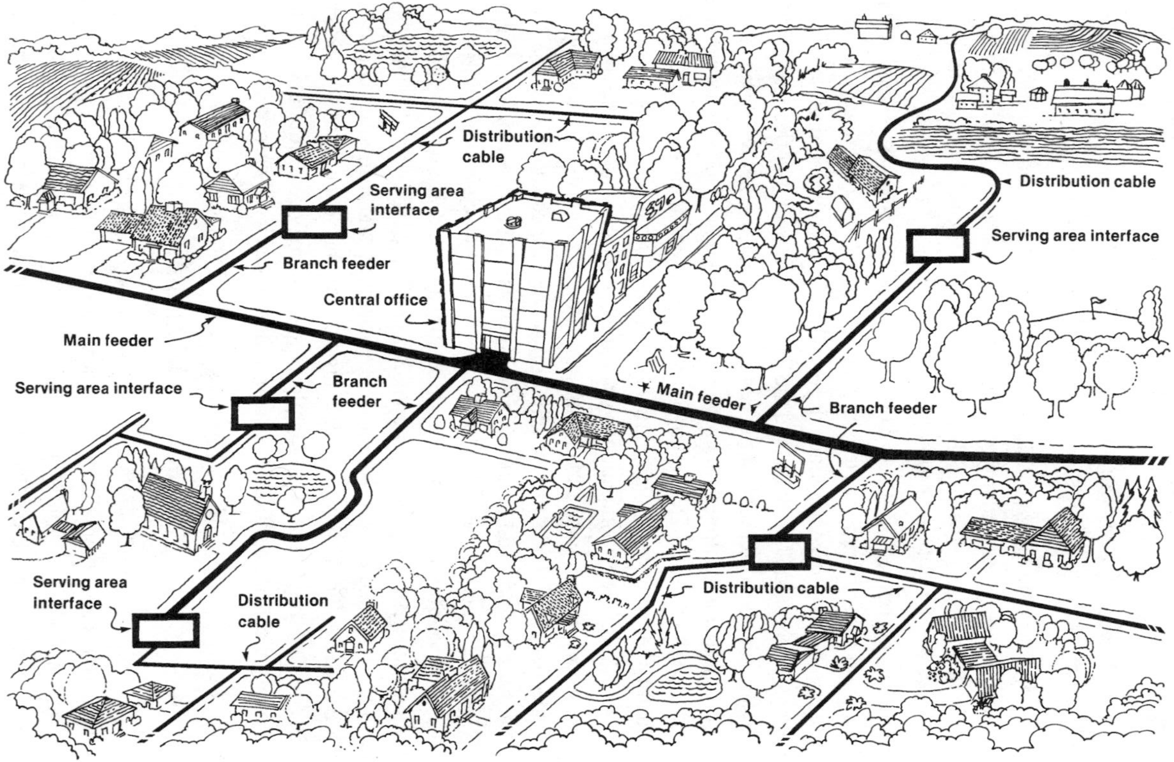

FIGURE 6–4

Aerial Cable Showing Splice Cases, Distribution Terminals, and
Load Coil Cases Mounted on Pole

Courtesy, Preformed Line Products Company

Where enough pairs are needed in a single building to justify wiring an
entire complement into the building, the interface between feeder and distribution plant is a direct splice. Otherwise, the interface may be a crossconnect cabinet where provision is made to connect cable pairs flexibly between feeder and
distribution plant.

Distribution cable is terminated in *terminals* similar to the ones shown in
Figure 6–4 to provide access to cable pairs. Terminals may be mounted on the
ground in pedestals, in buildings, on aerial cable messenger, or underground.
Aerial or buried *drop wire* connects from the terminal to the protector at the
user's premises.

To the greatest degree possible feeder cables and distribution cables are
designed to avoid *bridged tap,* an impairment shown in Figure 6–5. Bridged tap
is any portion of the cable pair that is not in the direct path between the user
and the central office. It has the electrical effect of a capacitor across the pair
and impairs the high-frequency response of the circuit. Bridged tap can render
DTMF dials and data modems inoperative because of amplitude distortion, primarily at high frequencies. It can be detected by measuring the frequency response of a metallic circuit.

FIGURE 6–5

Bridged Tap in Cable Pairs

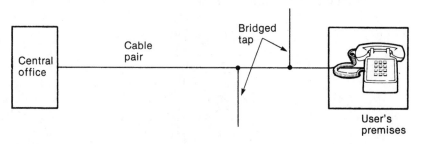

FIGURE 6–6

Toroidal Load Coil

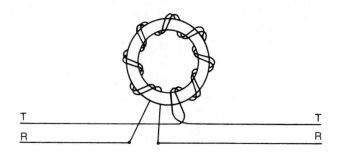

The frequency response of long subscriber loops is improved by loading, as discussed in Chapter 2. Load coils are small inductors wound on a powdered iron core, as shown in Figure 6–6. They are normally placed at 6,000-foot intervals on loops longer than 18,000 feet. Load coils are contained in weatherproof cases that are mounted on poles or in manholes.

ELECTRICAL PROTECTION

Whenever communications conductors enter a building from an environment that can be exposed to a foreign source of electricity, it is essential that electrical protection be used. Protection is required for two purposes—to prevent injury or death to personnel and to prevent damage to equipment.

Common carriers are responsible for protecting cables between their central offices and the user's premises. The type of protection provided is sufficient to prevent injury or death, but may not be sufficient to prevent damage to delicate telecommunications and computer equipment. Also, interbuilding cables may require protection, and the carrier will be responsible only if it provides and owns the cable.

Protection requirements are based on the National Electrical Safety Code. Much of the information in this section is based on AT&T practices, which often are more stringent than the code.

Determining Exposure

The first question that must be answered in determining electrical protection requirements is whether the cable is considered *exposed*. An exposed cable is one that is subject to any of the following hazards:

- ◆ Contact with any power circuit operating at 300 volts rms (root mean square) or more from ground.
- ◆ Contact by lightning.
- ◆ Induction from a 60 Hz source that results in a potential of 300 volts rms or more.
- ◆ Power faults that cause the ground potential to rise above 300 volts rms.

Bearing in mind that safety considerations must not be compromised in designing a protection plan, it is natural to wonder why 300 volts rms is chosen as the apparent threshold of danger. Actually, any shock that results in more than about 10 milliamps of current flowing through the body is painful. More than 20 ma is dangerous, and more than 50 ma of current flow through the heart is likely to result in ventricular fibrillation, a condition that usually results in death.

The amount of current that flows through the human body in contact with electricity is unpredictable. It depends on the skin resistance (damp skin has a much lower resistance than dry skin), on the body parts in contact (current flow between two fingers of the same hand is less dangerous than current flow between the two hands), and several other factors that circuit designers cannot control. Despite the danger that contact with less than 300 volts can be fatal, this value is chosen because it is the value from which terminal equipment is designed to insulate the user.

All cables with aerial sections should be considered exposed. Even though a short section of aerial cable may not be in proximity to power at the time it is constructed, aerial power may be added later and expose the cable. Therefore, it is advisable to protect all aerial cables, which include any cable that contains any pairs that may be exposed. For example, a 600-pair cable, only 25 pairs of which are connected to aerial cable, is considered exposed in its entirety. Buried and underground cables should be considered exposed unless one or more of the following conditions exist:

- ◆ There are five or fewer thunderstorm days per year and the earth resistivity is less than 100 meter-ohms. (See Figure 6–7 for thunderstorm activity and earth resistivity in the United States.)
- ◆ A buried interbuilding cable is shorter than 140 feet and has a shield that is grounded on both ends.
- ◆ A cable is totally within a cone of protection because of its proximity to buildings or other structures that are grounded (see Figure 6–8).

In metropolitan areas, some cables may be considered to exist under a *zone of protection* that diverts lightning strikes and shields the cable from damage. As Figure 6–8 shows, if a shielding mast is 25 or fewer feet high, a high degree of protection is afforded to objects within a radius equal to the height of the mast. A satisfactory degree of protection is also afforded to objects within a radius equal to twice the height of the mast if the mast is 50 or fewer feet high. To illustrate, assume that a cable runs between two buildings, each of which is 50 feet high. Each building extends a zone of protection of 100 feet, which means that a cable 200 feet long would not be considered exposed to lightning. For structures higher than 50 feet, the zone-of-protection concept does not apply on the same basis as for lower structures. To visualize the protection zone that surrounds higher objects, visualize a ball 300 feet in diameter rolled up against the side of the structure, as in Figure 6–9. The zone of protection is shown as the shaded area in Figure 6–9. Note that the zone of protection applies only to lightning, not to power exposures.

A cable also should be considered exposed to lightning, even though it is in an area that would otherwise be excluded by the earth resistivity and lightning requirements, if it rises above the elevation of surrounding terrain—on hilltop, on a tower, and so on.

Normally, ground is considered to be at zero potential, or the potential of the earth. In practice, ground has some resistance, and when current flows through it, the ground potential can rise. The hazard of a ground potential rise from commercial power is most severe near a power substation, but ground potential rise can occur anywhere from a lightning strike.

Induction occurs when power lines and telephone cables operate over parallel routes. Under normal conditions the magnitude of the induction is not so great as to constitute a hazard, but when telecommunications lines are unbalanced or when a fault occurs in the power line, the amount of induced voltage can rise to hazardous levels. This is not a concern in most private networks,

FIGURE 6-7

Average Annual Number of Days with Thunderstorms

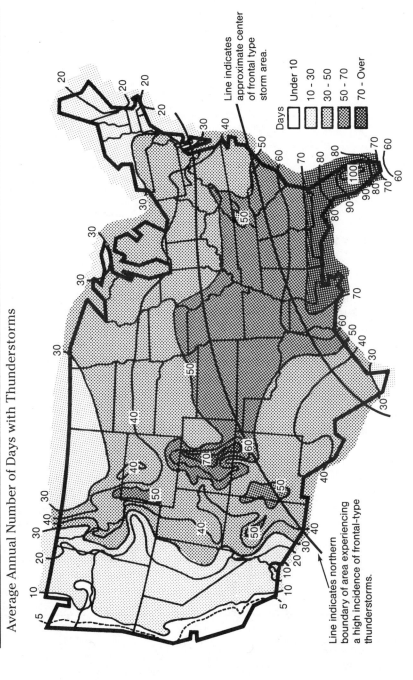

Line indicates approximate center of frontal type storm area.

Days

Under 10
10 - 30
30 - 50
50 - 70
70 - Over

Line indicates northern boundary of area experiencing a high incidence of frontal-type thunderstorms.

Courtesy of AT&T Archives

FIGURE 6–8

Cone of Protection Provided by Vertical Grounded Conductors

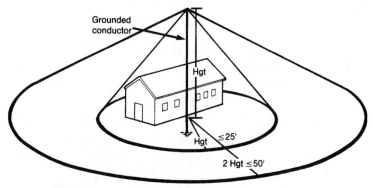

Courtesy of AT&T Archives

FIGURE 6–9

Lightning Strike Radius of 150 Feet Using "Roling Ball" Model for Structures Greater Than 50 Feet Tall

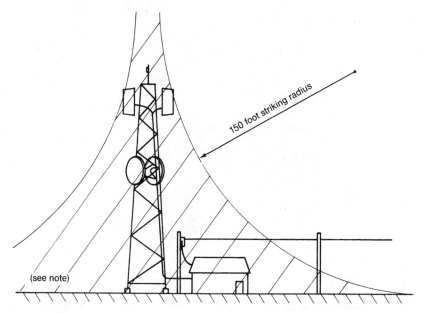

Note: shaded areas are strike-free,
protected zones.

Courtesy of AT&T Archives

but designers should be alert to the possibility of induction whenever power and telecommunications circuits share the same route, though they may not share a pole line.

Even though a circuit is protected to eliminate hazards to users, the equipment attached to it may be sensitive to foreign voltages. Since the equipment provider is in the best position to know of this sensitivity, all requests for proposals and purchase orders should require the vendor to specify the level of protection required.

Protection Methods

Personnel and equipment can be protected from the hazards of unexpected contact with a foreign source of electrical potential by the following methods:

◆ Insulating telecommunications apparatus.
◆ Shielding communications cables.
◆ Grounding equipment.
◆ Opening affected circuits.
◆ Separating electrical and telecommunications circuits.

This section discusses how each preventive measure is applied to telecommunications circuits.

Insulating Telecommunications Apparatus

Nearly all telecommunications circuits installed today are insulated with some kind of protective coating that serves as the first line of defense against accidental cross with foreign voltage. Polyethylene, which is the insulation used with most copper cables, has a conductor-to-conductor breakdown value of from 1,000 to 4,000 volts. Although this is enough to guard against a high value of foreign voltage, it is possible that the insulation will be damaged by the fault. A lightning strike or power cross may cause a burning effect that will destroy the insulation even if the voltage itself does not pierce the insulation.

Not only are the conductors insulated, but most apparatus is constructed to insulate the user from foreign voltage. If the magnitude of the voltage is great enough to arc from the supply conductors to the chassis, however, the inherent insulation of the equipment may not be enough to protect the user from dangerous shock, and the equipment will be destroyed or heavily damaged.

Although insulation is the first line of defense against the invasion of foreign potential, it alone is not enough to solve electrical protection problems.

Shielding Communications Cables

Cables can be shielded from lightning strikes by placing a grounded conductor above the cable so it intercepts the lightning strike. A grounded shield wire can be placed above aerial cable to serve the same function as a lightning rod serves on a building—it attracts the lightning strike to itself. Shield wires also can be buried above a communications cable. If there is enough separation to prevent arcing between the shield and the cable, this method is effective.

Grounding Equipment

An important principle of electrical protection is to provide a low impedance path to ground for foreign voltage. Both carbon and gas tube protectors, which are illustrated in Figure 6–10, operate on the principle of draining the foreign voltage to ground.

The simplest form of protector is the *carbon block*. One side of the carbon block is connected to a common path to ground. It is essential that the ground path be a known earth ground. In most buildings the grounding point for the power entrance is a suitable grounding point. A metallic cold-water pipe may be a satisfactory ground, but if the water system has any nonmetallic elements in it, the effectiveness of the ground may be lost. To ensure an effective water pipe ground, the pipe should be bonded to the power ground with a copper wire of at least #6 AWG.

The other side of the carbon block protector is open, with a mating block separated from ground by a narrow gap. The communications conductors are connected to the mating block. When voltage rises to a high enough level to arc across the gap, current flows, the block fuses, and the communications conductors are permanently connected to ground. When a carbon block protector is activated, it is destroyed and must be replaced.

A *gas tube protector* is connected between the communications conductors and ground. Like the carbon block protector, its purpose is to provide a low impedance path to ground for foreign voltage. The electrodes of the gas tube are farther apart than the carbon block electrodes, however, and they are contained in a glass envelope that is filled with an inert gas. When the breakdown voltage is reached, the gas ionizes and current flows until the voltage is removed. When the voltage is removed, the tube restores itself. Although gas tubes are more expensive than carbon blocks, the self-restoring effect may repay the additional cost. They may be particularly effective in sensitive apparatus that is easily damaged by relatively low voltages.

FIGURE 6-10

Station and Central Office Protection Equipment

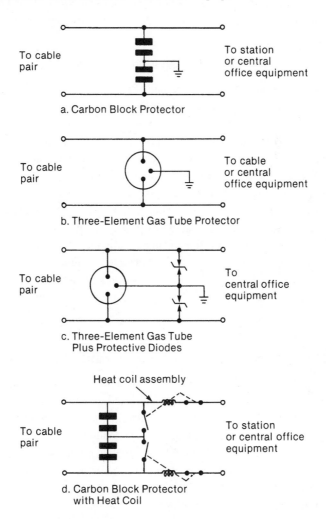

a. Carbon Block Protector

b. Three-Element Gas Tube Protector

c. Three-Element Gas Tube
Plus Protective Diodes

d. Carbon Block Protector
with Heat Coil

Another type of grounding protector is the *heat coil*. A heat coil is a spring-loaded device that, when released, connects the communications conductors to ground. Heat coils protect against *sneak currents*, which are currents that flow from voltages that are too low to activate a carbon block or gas tube protector. The heating effect of the sneak current is sufficient to melt a low-melting-point metal that keeps the electrodes separated. When the metal is melted, the spring forces the electrodes together and the circuit is grounded until the heat coil is replaced.

Protectors cannot operate effectively unless they are connected to a good ground. It is essential that all protector frames and apparatus such as PBXs and key telephone systems be connected to a good ground, and that the ground be bonded to the power system ground or other known low-impedance ground.

Opening Affected Circuits

Everyone is familiar with the next method of protecting circuits and equipment, the *fuse* or *circuit breaker*. If the communications conductors are opened before they enter the building or before they reach the protected equipment, current cannot flow and damage the equipment or reach the operator. The LEC often installs a *fuse cable* between its distribution cable and the building entrance. A fuse cable is a short length of fine-gauge cable, usually 26-gauge. If the distribution cable is of coarser gauge, the fuse cable will open before the protected cable opens. To restore the circuits, a new fuse cable is spliced in. Although this is an inexpensive method of protection, it can be detrimental to good service because of the length of time required to replace the fuse cable.

A fuse, by its nature, takes time to operate. Current flows during lightning strikes tend to be very short, lasting less time than the duration of most lighting strikes. Therefore, fuse cables are effective against power crosses, but not against lightning.

Separating Electrical And Telecommunications Circuits

Another method of protecting from accidental cross with electrical power is adequate spacing. Many buildings are served by buried power and telecommunications cables that share a joint trench. (Although joint trenches offer adequate spacing, joint power and telecommunications conduits are never acceptable.) The minimum acceptable separation between power and telecommunications circuits in a joint trench is one foot; more separation gives an additional measure of protection. The sharing of a joint trench with at least the minimum separation does not, of itself, create an exposure condition.

Each cable pair in a central office is protected in a frame, as described in Chapter 12. At the user's end of the circuit, protectors range from a simple single-pair device to multiple-pair protected terminals. Although station protectors are adequate to prevent injury to users, they are often inadequate to prevent damage to delicate electronic equipment. The owners of all devices connecting to the network, including modems, PBXs, key telephone systems, and answering recorders, must be aware of the degree of protection offered by the telephone line and the ability of their equipment to withstand external voltage and current.

SUBSCRIBER LOOP CARRIER

Subscriber loop carriers are increasingly used to deliver multichannel service to large concentrations of users. Analog subscriber carriers provide from one to eight subscriber circuits on a single cable pair. Single-channel carrier derives one carrier channel in the frequency range above the voice channel. Because of the high-frequency cutoff of load coils, single-channel subscriber carrier cannot be used on loaded cable. Therefore, single-channel carrier must be used within the range 18,000 feet of nonloaded cable to obtain satisfactory transmission from the voice channel.

Digital subscriber carriers operate over T-1 lines using either PCM or delta modulation techniques. These modulation methods, as described in Chapter 4, derive from 24 to 40 voice channels over two cable pairs. T-1 repeaters are placed at 6,000-foot intervals to provide a line equivalent to that used for trunk carrier. Digital carrier is replacing analog carrier in the subscriber loop as it is in trunks, and for the same reasons. Digital carrier operates effectively over either fiber optics or copper cable and provides excellent transmission quality.

Some subscriber carriers use concentration to increase the number of voice channels that can be transmitted over a T-1 line. Concentration operates on the probability that not all users will require service simultaneously. Users are not permanently assigned to digital time slots in concentrated systems. Instead, when the user requests service, the system selects an idle time slot and identifies the line to the distant terminal with a data message. Concentrated carriers allow the termination of as many as 48 subscribers on a 24-channel T-1 line.

A line concentrator, diagrammed in Figure 6–11, is similar to subscriber carrier except that it is specifically designed for concentrated service and terminates multiple T-carrier trunks to a larger number of subscriber lines to reduce the probability of a trunk being unavailable when a user requests service. Contrasted to concentrated subscriber carrier with a 2:1 concentration ratio, a remote line concentrator may assign, say, 250 users to five T-1 lines, a concentration ratio of 5:1. Concentrators are equipped with circuits to collect usage information that an administrator can use to avoid overloads. They must be engineered and monitored in the same manner as central office switching equipment, administration of which is described in Chapter 35.

Concentrators also may include circuitry known as *intracalling,* which enables users within the concentrator to connect to one another without using channels to the central office and back. Intracalling features require only one channel for the central office to supervise the connection. With intracalling, a concentrator may provide service between the users it serves even though the carrier line is inoperative. Without this feature a carrier line failure disrupts all service to its users.

FIGURE 6-11

Block Diagram of a Remote Line Concentrator

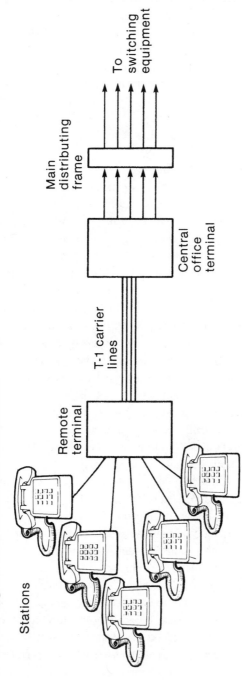

The term *pair gain* describes the degree to which subscriber carriers and concentrators increase the channel-carrying capacity of a cable pair. The pair-gain figure of a carrier or concentrator is the number of voice circuits that are added above the single voice circuit that a cable pair supports. For example, a 24-channel digital subscriber carrier requiring separate transmit and receive pairs has a pair gain of 22. The families of single and multiple channel subscriber carriers and concentrators are called *pair-gain devices*. A pair-gain device has a central office terminal and a matching remote terminal with intermediate repeaters if required. The remote terminal is contained in a pole-mounted cabinet or a ground-mounted enclosure.

Pair-gain devices provide better transmission quality than cable facilities. The transmission loss is fixed, normally at 5 dB, despite the length of the system. Pair-gain devices also provide quieter channels than the cable pairs they replace. An advantage of digital subscriber carrier is its ability to use special service channel units to provide the range of special services listed in Table 5–1. Pair-gain devices must be powered from an external source, so backup battery power is required to maintain telephone service during power outages.

RANGE EXTENDERS

Another family of loop electronic devices is classified as *range extension*. Although these devices are normally mounted only in the central office, they are discussed here because they improve subscriber loop performance. Range extenders are single-pair devices that boost the line voltage and may include voice frequency gain. Battery boost range extenders overcome the DC loop limitations of the switching system and station equipment. Range extenders increase the sensitivity of the switching system line circuits in detecting dial pulses and the on-hook/off-hook state of the line.

A second type of range extender increases the central office sensitivity and feeds higher voltage to the station. This latter type boosts the normal -48 volt central office battery to -72 volts, which increases the line current when the station is off hook, supporting greater DTMF dial range and providing greater line current to the telephone transmitter. If the voice frequency transmission range of the cable pair is limiting, range extenders with built-in amplification to boost the voice level can be used. These devices either contain a fixed amount of gain or adjust gain automatically in proportion to the line current.

CABLE PRESSURIZATION

Cable pressurization is used by LECs to keep moisture out of the cable and should be considered in private networks when cable is exposed to moisture for long distances. In a cable pressurization system, a compressor pumps dehy-drated air into the cable. At terminals where pairs are exposed, the cable sheath is plugged with a watertight dam, and air bypasses the dam through plastic tub-ing. A flow meter at the source shows the amount of leakage. When leakage exceeds a specified amount, it indicates sheath damage, which must be located and repaired to ensure watertight integrity. When a cable run is long with mul-tiple branches, low air pressure alarms help locate trouble.

APPLICATIONS

Loop plant is part of every network application. Even in private networks that bypass the local telephone company by routing circuits directly to an interex-change carrier, a connection may made from the network terminal to the station over metallic cable facilities that must be designed as part of the total network. Increasingly, however, fiber optic connections are available to large compa-nies. Where available, fiber optics eliminates the transmission problems that are inherent with copper facilities. This section includes only electrical consid-erations. The evaluation of supporting structures involves mechanical consid-erations that are beyond the scope of this book.

Standards

With the exception of wire, which meets American Wire Gauge standards, out-side plant is not manufactured to the standards of an independent agency. Man-ufacturers' specifications determine cable size, construction, and sheath char-acteristics. Outside plant is selected according to its specifications to meet the requirements of the application.

Evaluating Subscriber Loop Equipment

This section includes the principal considerations for both LECs and private network users for selecting metallic outside plant facilities.

Cable Structural Quality

Cable is selected to match the pair size and gauge required by the network design. The sheath must be impervious to the elements if it is mounted out-side. Crosstalk and balance characteristics are of paramount concern. When cables support special applications such as local area networks and high-speed data transmission, the cable must meet the specifications of the equip-ment manufacturer.

Insulation resistance and DC continuity measurements should be made on all new cables. On loaded cables, structural return loss, gain frequency response, and noise measurements, as described in Chapter 36, should be made to ensure the electrical integrity of the cable. When cable facilities are obtained from a common carrier, these measurements also should be made when trouble is experienced.

Air Pressurization

Air pressurization should be considered on long cables and on any cable that carries essential services and is exposed to weather. The system should be equipped with a dehydrator, a compressor, a flow meter, and a monitoring and alarm system to detect leakage.

Protection

All metallic circuits, both common carrier and privately owned, are subject to lighting strikes and crosses with external voltage. It is not safe to assume that the protection provided by the telephone company is enough to prevent damage to interconnected equipment. Private network users should determine the characteristics of the input circuits of their equipment and obtain external protection if needed.

MANUFACTURERS OF OUTSIDE PLANT PRODUCTS

Cable and Wire Products

Alpha Wire Crop
Anaconda Ericsson Inc. Wire and Cable Div.
Belden Corp.
Brand-Rex Co.
General Cable Co.
Siecor Corporation
Standard Wire and Cable Co.

Cable Air Pressurization Equipment

Chatlos Systems, Inc.
General Cable Co.

Concentrators and Digital Loop Carrier Equipment

Alcatel

Lucent Technologies

Ericsson, Inc. Communications Div.

Hubbel, Pulsecom Div.

NEC America

Northern Telecom, Inc.

Protectors

See Chapter 12.

Terminals and Crossconnect Boxes

General Cable Co.

3M Co. Telcomm Products Div.

Northern Telecom, Inc.

Preformed Line Products Co.

Reliance Comm/Tec

Siecor Corporation

7

STRUCTURED WIRING SYSTEMS

Wiring has long taken a backseat to electronics in the quest for improved tele-communications technology. In the past, premise wiring systems have been dictated by the interface needed by the equipment. The result has been a mix of quality and wire sizes—2-pair, 3-pair, 4-pair, 6-pair, 12-pair, and 25-pair have been common. Some low-quality wire is susceptible to crosstalk because little attention was paid to the amount of twist during manufacture. Different manufacturers have required different wiring types, including shielded twisted-pair and coaxial cable for their apparatus. The lack of uniformity in station wiring was tolerable for voice, but when data devices became common the situation demanded standards. Conduits and raceways became clogged with special-purpose cabling, designation and labeling was haphazard, and new wire was often installed with older, undesignated wire left in place.

In the early 1990s the Electronic Industries Association (EIA) and the Telecommunications Industries Association (TIA) collaborated to produce standards for a structured wiring system. They determined that if wire is carefully manufactured and installed to high-quality standards, it can support data rates in excess of 100 mb/s over distances of up to 100 meters. To obtain this kind of performance required new standards that had not existed in the past. These standards, which are listed in Table 7–1, were developed and published to bring order from chaos. These standards do not have the same force

TABLE 7–1

List of EIA/TIA Wiring Standards

EIA/TIA-568	Commercial Building Telecommunications Cabling Standard
EIA/TIA-569	Commercial Building Standard for Telecommunications Pathways and Spaces
EIA/TIA-606	Administration Standard for the Telecommunications Infrastructure of Commercial Buildings
EIA/TIA-607	Commercial Building Grounding and Bonding Requirements for Telecommunications
EIA/TIA-570	Residential and Light Commercial Telecommunications Wiring Standard

Global Engineering Documents is the primary distributor of all TIA and EIA technical documents. To purchase a document, call 1-800-854-7179 or send a fax to 303-397-2740.

as the National Electric Code. Compliance is not, in most jurisdictions, required by local building codes, but any company planning a wiring system is well advised to follow the standard because it ensures compatibility with future equipment.

Structured wiring includes other media besides twisted-pair wire. Fiber optics and coaxial cable are both covered in addition to both shielded and unshielded twisted-pair wire. The standards are voice and data oriented. Where video is planned, coaxial cable outside the standards may be needed.

This chapter presents an overview of structured wiring. Readers are referred to the standard itself, sources of which are listed in Appendix D, for more detailed design information.

OVERVIEW OF STRUCTURED WIRING

Structured wiring brings numerous benefits to the using organization:

◆ Since manufacturers design their equipment to work on standard structured wiring, the using organization is assured of compatibility with future applications.

◆ Problem detection and isolation are enhanced by a standardized layout and documentation method.

◆ It ensures that wiring is installed within recommended distance limits.

◆ The system promotes an efficient and economical wiring layout that technicians can easily follow.

◆ It eases the job of network segmentation by providing network interfaces for LAN hubs.

◆ Moves, adds, and changes are facilitated.

Most of the above advantages are absent with nonstandard wiring systems. The advantages of structured wiring may be lost, however, with a substandard installation job. Unless wire is terminated in accordance with the manufacturer's instructions, the wiring system may fail to meet the specifications even though the hardware is manufactured to standards.

Elements of a Structured Wiring System

A structured wiring system as shown in Figure 7–1, which is extracted from EIA/TIA 568A, is composed of the following elements:

- ◆ Equipment rooms (ER), which are building areas intended to house telecommunications equipment. Equipment rooms also may fill the functions of a telecommunications closet.
- ◆ Telecommunications closets (TC) are rooms in which wiring is terminated. A building may have multiple TCs.
- ◆ Backbone wiring (riser cable) is the wire that connects ERs to TCs.
- ◆ Work area (WA) is the user's work space. Telecommunications outlets (TO) are located in the work area.
- ◆ Horizontal wiring is the wiring from the ER or TC to the work area.
- ◆ Entrance facility (EF) is the physical structure and cable connecting the main ER to the common carrier's facilities.

A major objective of a structured wiring system is to ensure that it is capable of supporting future broadband applications. Any transmission facility offers a trade-off between bandwidth and distance: The greater the bandwidth requirement, the shorter the distance it can support with other factors equal. Applications such as FDDI (100 mb/s) and ATM (155 mb/s) are designed to operate over either fiber optics or unshielded twisted-pair (UTP) wire. Structured wiring standards specify that horizontal wiring is limited to a maximum distance of 90 meters, which yields a maximum UTP end-to-end length of 100 meters including patch cords. Within this distance the specifications of a properly manufactured and installed wiring system will support high-bandwidth applications that are designed for UTP.

The three main variables that are of concern with a structured wiring system are attenuation, impedance, and crosstalk. Attenuation is affected by the wire gauge, which is specified in the standard as 22 or 24 AWG, and by its capacitance, which is a function of the manufacture and type and structure of insulation. The characteristic impedance of the wire is affected by the same factors. Neither of these is likely to be affected greatly by the installation job, but the third characteristic, crosstalk, is highly dependent on good installation practice.

FIGURE 7–1

Typical Telecommunications Cabling System

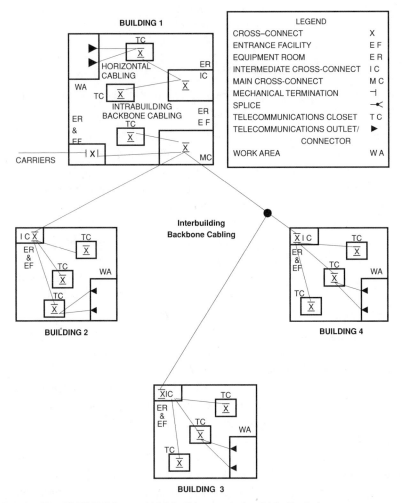

Reproduced from EIA/TIA-568A Commercial Building Telecommunications Cabling Standard

Crosstalk refers to the amount of coupling between adjacent wire pairs. The EIA/TIA standard specifies four-pair UTP to each workstation, so the wire has strict crosstalk specifications between pairs. It is measured by injecting a signal into one pair and measuring it on each of the other pairs. Crosstalk is referred to as near-end and far-end crosstalk (NEXT and FEXT). In wire installations,

NEXT is the most important because at the near end the signal source is at its highest level, while the received signal is lowest, having been attenuated by the loss of the wire. In any telecommunications circuit it is important that the ratio between the wanted and unwanted signal is at a maximum. Since the received signal level can be predicted from the output specifications of the transmitting end, by knowing the amount of crosstalk coupling it is possible to calculate the wanted-to-unwanted signal ratio.

The amount of crosstalk coupling is a function of both the wire itself and the telecommunications outlets in which it is terminated. Crosstalk is kept to a minimum in the wire by carefully controlling the length and tightness of twist. If the installer untwists too much wire to terminate it on the outlet or jack panel, the amount of isolation between pairs will be reduced.

EIA/TIA STANDARDS

Four parts of the EIA/TIA standards are of particular interest to telecommunications managers: wiring, pathways, grounding and bonding, and administration. The residential and light commercial standards may be of interest in branch offices.

Wiring Standards

Wire is installed in a star configuration with horizontal wiring extending from the work area to the TC or ER with no splices or bridged tap. The standard recognizes four types of wire:

◆ Four-pair 100 ohm UTP.
◆ Two-pair 150 ohm shielded twisted-pair wire (STP).
◆ 62.5/125 micron graded index multimode fiber-optic cable.
◆ 50 ohm coaxial cable.

The standard calls for at least two four-pair UTPs to each WA; additional media are optional. UTP wire is listed in five categories, as shown in Table 7–2. Categories 1 and 2, which are older wire types that predate the standard, are recognized, but not specified by the standards. The minimum wire to be installed to the WA is Category 3. Categories 1 and 2 wire are acceptable for voice, but are not recommended for data. Category 4 wire is rarely installed. It is intended for 16 MHz token ring LANs. Since token ring installations may be upgraded to 100 mb/s in the future, most companies install Category 5 wire as the data standard. Most companies install at least one Category 3 for voice plus one or more Category 5 for data. In most commercial installations one Category 3 and one Category 5 should be the minimum to be installed.

TABLE 7–2

EIA/TIA 568 Unshielded Twisted-Pair Categories

Unshielded Twisted Pair Categories				
Category	Maximum Data Rate	Attenuation dB/1,000 feet	Capacitance	NEXT
1				
2	4 mb/s	8 dB @ 1 MHz		
3	10 mb/s	30 dB @ 10 MHz	20 pF/ft	26 dB @ 10 MHz
		40 dB @ 16 MHz		23 dB @ 16 MHz
4	20 mb/s	22 dB @ 10 MHz	17 pF/ft	41 dB @ 10 MHz
		31 dB @ 20 MHz		36 dB @ 20 MHz
5	100 mb/s	32 dB @ 10 MHz	17 pF/ft	47 dB @ 10 MHz
		67 dB @ 100 MHz		32 dB @ 100 MHz

Users often ask why four-pair wire is recommended when the typical telephone system uses only one or two pairs, and both Ethernet and token ring use two pairs. The answer lies in future applications. Some high-speed LAN applications such as 100VG-AnyLAN (see Chapter 29) require four pairs, and all LANs are designed to use specific pairs out of the four-pair cable. By using four-pair wire in a standard manner you can apply future applications to the wire without rewiring the jacks.

The telecommunications outlets in the work area must also meet the standards. Multiple outlets can be installed in those installations where multiple wire runs are terminated. The standard does not specify the physical jack arrangement, and a variety of configurations are available from different manufacturers. The wire is terminated on RJ-45 jacks. Most voice systems require one or two pairs. To use spare pairs for additional ports for modems or other such applications, T adapters can be used to access the vacant pairs.

The data pairs should not be used for more than one simultaneous application. LAN protocols such as Ethernet and token ring use two pairs, but putting a different application on the unused pairs can lead to data errors. Devices equipped with RS-232 or V.35 connectors can be connected to the TO with adapters.

The standard recommends two wiring patterns for jacks and patch panels: T-568A and T-568B. The two standards are shown in Table 7–3.

Shielded versus Unshielded Wire

For some applications, the bandwidth of UTP may not be sufficient. For these, the standard recognizes fiber-optic cable, shielded twisted-pair, and coax. Users often intuitively assume that STP is superior to UTP, but for most prop-

TABLE 7–3

EIA/TIA 568 Jack-Wiring Standards

T568A		
Pair	**Pin**	**Color**
1	4–5	W-BL/BL
2	3–6	W-O/O
3	1–2	W-G/G
4	7–8	W-BR/BR
T 568B		
Pair	**Pin**	**Color**
1	4–5	W-BL/BL
2	1–2	W-O/O
3	3–6	W-G/G
4	7–8	W-BR/BR

Color Codes:
W = white
BL = blue
O = orange
BR = brown

erly designed applications, it is not. Shielding is a metallic braid or layer of foil surrounding all or some of the conductors in the cable. The purpose of the shield is to reduce electromagnetic interference (EMI). The shield reduces EMI by attenuating the electrical energy radiated from the cable and minimizing energy coupled from outside sources. Shielding operates through one of two effects, the *field effect* or the *circuit effect*. The field effect theory holds that the shield reflects and absorbs the interfering waves. The circuit effect assumes that interfering signals generate a secondary field in the shield, canceling the original field. It is difficult to connect the shield to ground in some types of connectors, so most shielded cables include a drain wire, which is in direct contact with the shield throughout the cable length.

The key to using UTP lies in balance, which is discussed in Chapter 2. Network equipment that is designed to use UTP is designed for a balanced transmission medium. That means that it takes its signal across the two wires of a pair, or in some applications across the wires of two or four pairs. If an interfering signal is induced into the cable, the two wires of a pair will receive an equal voltage if they are twisted so they have equal exposure to the interfering signal. If the voltage on both wires is equal, the receiving device does not detect a voltage difference across the pair, so the interference has no effect. In practice, balance is not perfect, but the circuit has enough margin that it does not have to be.

TABLE 7–4

Comparison of Characteristics of Shielded and Unshielded 4-Pair
Solid Conductor Twisted-Pair Wire

	Attenuation dB/1,000 Ft.		Characteristic Impedance	
	1 Khz	1 Mhz	1 Khz	1 MHz
Shielded	.43	9.4	500 ohms	65 ohms
Unshielded	.41	6.1	600 ohms	105 ohms

Many organizations choose shielded wire for one of two convincing reasons: The equipment manufacturer specifies it, or it seems the most conservative approach. Both are rational reasons for using shielded wiring, but the reasons for avoiding it if possible are equally convincing. Shielded wiring is significantly more expensive than unshielded. It is more difficult to install and terminate, and it has higher loss. As Table 7–4 shows, shielding affects the electrical characteristics of the wire. The effects are not significant at voice frequencies, but at the higher frequencies typical of LANs, shielding can increase loss by 50 percent or more.

Some services are inherently unbalanced, which makes them susceptible to interference. The most frequently used DTE-to-DCE connection is EIA-232, which uses a common signal ground path for transmit and receive. This limits the transmission distance, which the specification lists as 50 feet. Many organizations violate this limit, however, without encountering trouble.

To sum up the shielded versus unshielded question, most administrators should consult an expert on their particular installations before making the decision. A properly installed UTP system should support any forthcoming technology up to 100 mb/s, and probably up to 155 mb/s. Bear in mind, however, that the terminating equipment must be designed and manufactured with a high degree of balance. If the equipment specifies shielded wire, then the manufacturer's recommendations should be installed.

Connectors and Patch Panels

In the TC and ER, two methods are available for terminating wire: punch-down connectors and patch panels. The latter are preferred for data wiring, and the former for voice. Data wiring usually connects to a hub that is equipped with RJ-45 jacks, and hub ports can easily be connected to wire runs with patch cords. Crossconnects of Category 5 wire should be avoided because it is difficult to make crossconnections and still retain Category 5 compliance. Most manufacturers do not produce Category 5 jumper wire because it is impossible to control its manufacture and installation, to the degree that can be achieved with patch cords. Jumper wire is preferred for voice wiring, on the other hand, because it is less expensive and the typical voice connection is from horizontal wiring to riser cable. With the proper kind of administration system, the cross-connection in the TC remains in place after the service is disconnected.

Telecommunications Pathways and Spaces

Every building supports one or more methods of running telecommunications wiring. The method is inherent in the design of the building itself, whether through the design or lack thereof by the architect. In a new building it is a grave error to leave the communications wiring method to chance. In older buildings designers could not foresee the impact of telecommunications, so wiring methods are often a compromise between utility and aesthetics.

EIA/TIA 569 standards cover commercial building telecommunications pathways and spaces. Figure 7–2 shows the elements of building pathways as described in the standard. The pathways include the conduit, floor cells, and cable troughs that support the backbone and horizontal cables. They also support entrance cables and pathways for the grounding systems. Standards are an excellent starting place for installing wiring in new buildings. In older buildings the wiring technicians often have to use what is available.

Fire codes also regulate pathway choices. In any building that uses air plenum space for wiring, the insulation must be plenum rated. Plenum cable uses a smokeless sheath such as Teflon® to minimize toxic fumes in case of fire. Schools and hospitals may be required in some jurisdictions to use plenum-rated wiring everywhere including nonplenum space. Nonplenum wire can be installed in plenum spaces in conduit.

Building codes also require that the length of outdoor cable sheath brought into the building not exceed 50 feet unless the cable is in conduit. For that reason, as well as for ease of rearrangement, the pathway provided for the building entrance cable should always be conduit if at all possible. Otherwise it may be necessary to splice the cable near the entrance.

Conduit also facilitates placing the backbone cable. Campus backbone cable can be buried directly, but the major cost of installation is opening a trench. Placing conduit adds a small increment to the total cost. If space permits, good practice is to place an inner duct for future fiber-optic cable. It is also good practice to place empty conduit while a trench is open.

Horizontal cable is usually installed in four-pair increments. Twenty-five-pair cable is available in both Category 3 and 5, and can be used effectively

FIGURE 7–2

Elements of Building Pathways

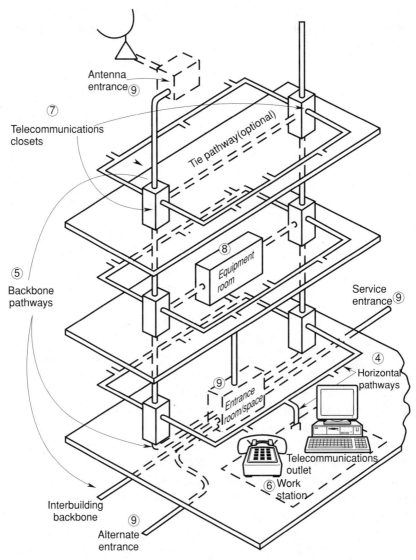

Reproduced from EIA/TIA-569 Commercial Building Standard for Telecommunications Pathways and Spaces

where multiple TOs are clustered. Horizontal cable is brought to the work area from the TC by one of the following pathways:

Ceiling Area Pathway   The area above a suspended ceiling is an excellent space for concealing horizontal wire. Wire must be fastened to the building structure, and not resting on the ceiling grid. Wire is brought into the work area through conduit stubbed into the ceiling, run in surface-mounted raceway, fished through walls, or placed in telepower poles.

Floor Cells   Many buildings are constructed with cells under the floor for power and telecommunications. Access into the cell is by core drilling. TOs are mounted in monuments that fasten to the floor.

Raised Flooring   Some buildings are equipped with raised flooring built on a metal framework. Cable is placed under the floor and brought into the work area through holes in the floor tiles.

Cable Trays and Raceways   Cable trays are an effective way of routing large quantities of wiring along both horizontal and vertical surfaces. Cable trays are particularly effective in warehouses, factories, and other areas where appearance is not important. Enclosed raceways can be surface-mounted to conceal wire. Surface-mounted raceway comes in a variety of colors to blend with the decor.

Telecommunications Closets

Telecommunications closets must be placed with close attention to the maximum horizontal and backbone wire length. Good practice limits the number of TCs while limiting the wire length to 90 meters. Note that the locations must take into consideration the route the wire will follow to the work area so the maximum is not exceeded. TCs must be built large enough to provide adequate wall space for terminating horizontal and backbone cables. Many TCs also contain hubs, routers, and other active equipment that is often relay-rack mounted. Swing-out relay racks are available for this purpose. Figure 7–3 is a photograph of a TC enclosed in a wall cabinet with rack-mounted equipment. As with equipment rooms, telecommunications closets need to be well lighted and secure.

Telephone wiring is normally terminated on punch-down connectors. Closets that contain 10-Base-T or token ring hubs should have the wire terminated in patch panels such as the one shown in Figure 7–3. Connections between the hub and the horizontal wiring are made with modular patch cords.

FIGURE 7-3

A Telecommunications Closet Enclosed in a Wall Cabinet

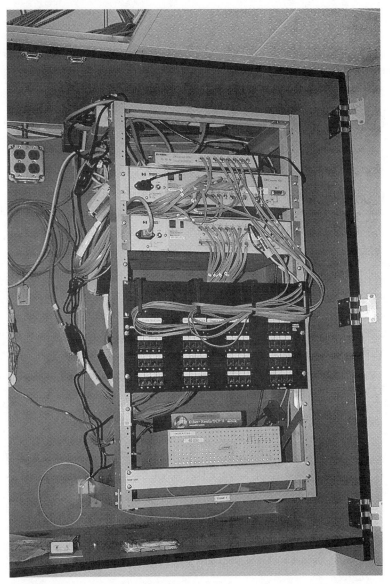

Photo by author

Work Area

The work area is the area in which telephone instruments and data workstations are installed. Horizontal wiring terminates in modular jacks. Connections are made into most devices with modular cords, but some devices that are EIA-232 equipped require a modular-to-EIA adapter.

Wire Administration

TIA/EIA 606 covers administration of telecommunications wire. To make it easy to administer, wire and terminations must be numbered, labeled, color-coded, and designated in a manner that is easy to follow. Before the standard was developed most wire installation companies had a preferred method of documentation, although many wiring systems have been installed with no documentation whatsoever. Figure 7–4 shows schematically the labeling method used in TIA/EIA standards. Separate designations are used for backbone, horizontal, and grounding paths. The standards are not the only way of designating wire plans, and the designations themselves have no effect on technical performance. In time, however, as companies adopt this standard, it will become the most cost-effective system to use because technicians will be familiar with it. Poorly documented wiring systems cause technicians to spend unnecessary time in toning and tracing. A properly documented system solves this problem.

The TIA/EIA 606 standard specifies the types of records that are to be kept. Records include required information and linkages and optional information and linkages. Linkages are the logical connections between identifiers and their corresponding records. Identifiers are the designations that are assigned to items of plant such as cables, manholes, conduits, and bonding and grounding locations.

Bonding and Grounding

Modern electronic equipment is sensitive to grounding. Many cases of erratic operation, unexplained noise, and periodic equipment failure have been cured by clearing grounding deficiencies. EIA/TIA 607 describes bonding and grounding requirements in commercial buildings. The standard, which is illustrated in Figure 7–5, specifies a single grounding point called the telecommunications main grounding busbar (TMGB), with all equipment room and telecommunications closet grounds brought back to this point. The TMGB is bonded securely to the building's electrical power ground and to the building's metal framework.

FIGURE 7–4

Scope of Telecommunications Administration in EIA/TIA Standards

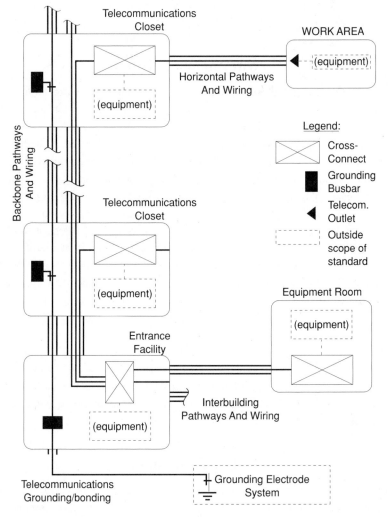

Reproduced from EIA/TIA-606 Administration Standard for the Telecommunications Infrastructure of Commercial Buildings

FIGURE 7-5

Bonding and Grounding Standard

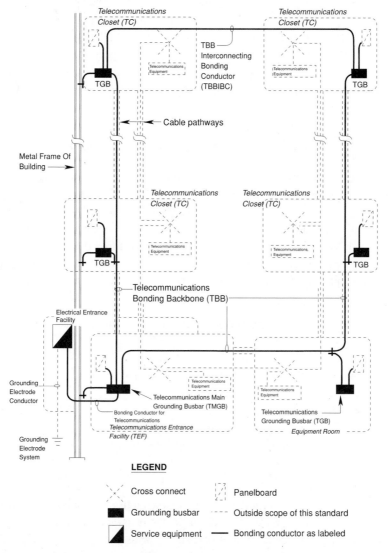

LEGEND

✕ Cross connect	⬚ Panelboard
⬛ Grounding busbar	--- Outside scope of this standard
◣ Service equipment	— Bonding conductor as labeled

Reproduced from EIA/TIA-607 Commercial Building Grounding and Bonding Requirements for Telecommunications

Each TC and ER must contain a telecommunications grounding busbar (TGB) that is connected to the TMGB over the telecommunications bonding backbone (TBB). The purpose of the TBB is to equalize, as far as possible, the ground potential of the various building telecommunications locations. It is sized according to the size and structure of the building. The minimum size is #6 AWG, but it may be as large as #3/0 AWG. Each TGB also is bonded to the metal building frame with a #6 AWG wire. It is important that architectural drawings specify the installation of these grounding and bonding elements when a building is constructed, and that an electrical engineer specify the ground wire size.

NATIONAL ELECTRICAL CODE (NEC)

The National Electrical Code (NEC) specifies fire resistance standards for communications cables to protect people and property from fire hazards. The code, covered by the National Bureau of Standards Handbook H43, addresses the methods of limiting the hazards of cable-initiated fires and cable-carried fires. The code requires that communications and signaling wires and cables in a building be listed as suitable for the purpose. The following summarizes the code requirements. Further information can be obtained by consulting the code itself.

Article 800 Communications

This article lists six categories of communications cables:

- ◆ CM cables for general purpose use except plenums and risers.
- ◆ CMP cables for use in plenums.
- ◆ CMR cables for use in risers.
- ◆ CMX cables for residential and for use in raceways.
- ◆ CMUC cables for undercarpet use.
- ◆ MP cables for multipurpose use (must satisfy requirements for CM, CMP, and CMR).

Any cable used for telephone communications must be tested and listed as meeting the fire resistance, mechanical, and electrical standards of the testing laboratory. The code requires that jumper wire be fire resistant. It also requires that equipment intended to be electrically connected to a telecommunications network be listed for the purpose. The NEC specifies requirements for separation between communications and power conductors, and states what types of cables can share raceways and closures.

APPLICATIONS

The type of telecommunications wiring should always be dictated by the application. In the past many buildings were constructed with inadequate attention to communications wiring and pathways. It may be difficult to bring these up to standard, but whenever rewiring is considered, the EIA/TIA standards should be followed. In any new building the wiring plan should be constructed as part of the building and not left as an afterthought. A properly designed and installed structured wiring system can and should have a life at least as long as the electrical wiring, and it should be installed with the same degree of forethought. The EIA/TIA standards remove the uncertainty with which equipment designers have had to contend in the past. Building owners now can proceed with structured wiring, knowing that the wiring will be compatible with the applications.

In new buildings the telecommunications wiring design must be part of the building's architecture, just as the electrical wiring is. TCs and ERs must be located to keep backbone and horizontal wiring lengths within specified limits. The design of a multitenant building is necessarily different than a single-tenant building. In a single-tenant building the backbone extends from the carrier's point-of-presence throughout the building. In a multitenant building each tenant may have its own backbone and a separate equipment room, depending on the amount of floor space it occupies and the number of floors. Where it is impossible to foresee future wiring requirements as, for example, in unoccupied space that hasn't been built out, the designer must provide pathways to avoid building roadblocks that are expensive to overcome.

Category 5 wiring systems are often installed with the expectation of future applications, but immediately used on 10-BaseT or token ring. These systems do not begin to test the ultimate capabilities of Category 5 wiring, and even many handheld testers cannot test wire to the limits of Category 5 specifications. To cope with this problem, owners are advised to consider extended performance warranties, which are offered by most of the major wiring manufacturers. These warranties, most of which run for 15 years, warrant that if the system fails to support a 100 mb/s application, the manufacturer (not the vendor) stands behind the installation. This warranty, which may carry an additional cost, ensures that the installation meets the manufacturer's specifications. Since the manufacturer offers the warranty, it survives the potential demise of the vendor. Without a performance warranty you are left with the manufacturer's materials warranty, which is of limited value considering that labor is usually more than half the cost of an installation.

Case History: A Suburban School District

A large suburban school district with 1,200 classrooms in 41 schools initiated a project to bring network connections to every classroom. The computers, video devices, printers, and other devices are used for instructional purposes. Each school has a connection to a backbone network over channels provided by the cable television company connecting the school to the administration building.

The schools in the district were built over a period stretching from the 1920s to the 1990s, which raises interesting problems in installing wiring. The typical elementary school is structured in three pods. In some schools the pods are in separate buildings, and in others they are areas of a single building. Middle and high schools are similarly constructed except with more pods. The backbone cabling architecture is also shown in Figure 7–6. Each school has a main distributing frame linked to one or more intermediate distributing frames by a backbone of UTP and fiber-optic cabling plus coaxial cable for video. The UTP is for voice services and the fiber optics for linking 10-Base-T hubs in each frame location. The photograph in Figure 7–3 is one of these distributing frame locations.

Two four-pair Category 5 cables were run to two different locations in each classroom, providing four wire drops per classroom. To multiply the number of ports available, eight-port minihubs were installed in each classroom. In addition, one RG-6 coaxial cable was run to one of the two locations for video.

Since the schools were built over a considerable time span, different wiring methods had to be employed. In schools with fixed ceilings, cable was run through surface-mounted raceways. Breakouts from these raceways, usually installed near the ceiling, were used to bring cabling into the classrooms through smaller raceways that terminated in matching boxes to hold the TOs.

In schools that were built with suspended ceilings, drops were either fished down the walls, installed in surface-mounted raceways, or installed in telepower poles. Many classrooms were built with open construction that did not permit running and terminating wires on walls, so telepower poles, such as the one shown in Figure 7–7, provided a good alternative.

MANUFACTURERS OF STRUCTURED WIRING PRODUCTS

For fiber optics products see Chapter 13.

FIGURE 7-6

Elementary School Wiring Layout

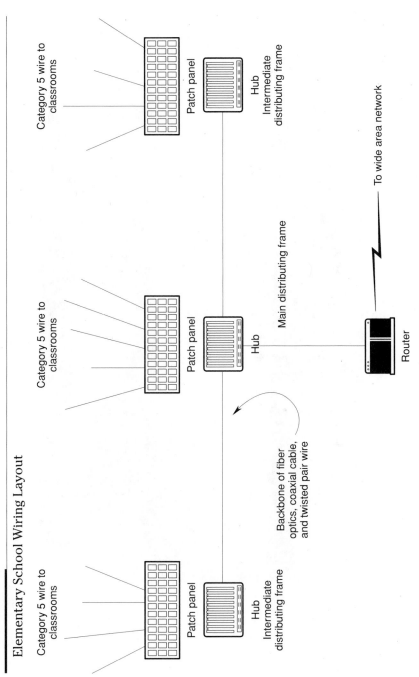

FIGURE 7-7

Telepower Poles are a Convenient Way of Terminating
Telecommunications Wire and Power in Open Floor Areas

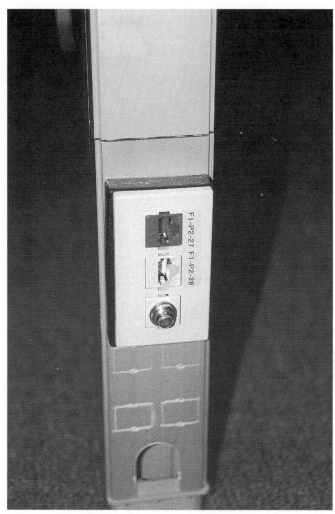

Photo by author

Manufacturers of Structured Wiring System Products

AMP, Inc.

Amphenol Corporation

Alpha Wire

Belden Electronic Wire and Cable

Berk-Tek

CommScope, Inc.

Hubbell Premise Wiring, Inc.

Leviton Telecom

Lucent Technologies

Nortel, Inc.

MOD-TAP

Siecor Corp.

Siemon Company

Simplex Wire and Cable Corp.

Standard Wire and Cable Co.

PART

II

SWITCHING SYSTEMS

8

CIRCUIT SWITCHED NETWORK SYSTEMS

In telephone parlance, a *circuit* is any path that connects two or more users. In the first few years of the telephone's existence, circuits ran from point to point, and they were always connected over a physical facility, such as a pair of wires. To solve the obvious impracticality of running a circuit between each pair of users that wishes to communicate, a circuit switch connects the output of one circuit, such as a telephone line or a trunk, to the input of another so information can be passed. Circuits can be switched in tandem so users can reach the desired destination over a series of built-up connections.

In the early days of telephony, subscriber loops terminated in jacks, and operators used long patch cords to connect circuits. As the number of telephones grew, the size of the jack panels increased until it became impractical to switch circuits with plug-equipped patch cords.

The next stage in the evolution of circuit switching brought manual cord boards like the one pictured in Figure 8–1. Circuits still terminated on jacks, but they were wired within reach of an operator, who sat at a fixed position that was equipped with several pairs of cords; key switches to control talking, monitoring, and ringing; and lamps to show the on-hook/off-hook status of the circuits. Circuits were connected in *multiple,* which is to say that each circuit appeared in front of several operator positions. As antiquated as manual circuit

FIGURE 8–1

A Manual Switchboard of the Pennsylvania Bell Telephone
Company at Easton, PA, circa 1890.

Courtesy, AT&T Archives

FIGURE 8-2

A Bank of Step-by-Step, or Strowger, Switches

Courtesy, AT&T Archives

switching seems, it survived in the public telephone network well beyond the middle of the 20th century and exists today in some countries.

Manual switching was fine when labor was cheap and the telephone was a rarity, but it was an obvious candidate for mechanization. In 1891, a Kansas City undertaker named Almon Strowger became convinced that telephone operators were reporting false busy signals on his line and connecting callers to wrong numbers, depriving him of business. He designed an electromechanical replacement for the operator and invented the switch that today bears his name. Figure 8–2 is a photograph of a bank of Strowger switches, which still have not completely disappeared from the scene despite the many advantages that computer control brings to circuit switching. With Strowger's invention, the automatic circuit-switching system, which is the subject of this chapter, was born.

The nature of telephone systems requires that subscriber stations be accessible to one another. Accessibility is achieved by using switching to control routing choices and to provide a point of entry to the network. An effective tele-communications network has these attributes:

◆ *Connectivity.* Any station can be connected to any other station if they are compatible with the network's protocols.

◆ *Ease of addressing.* Stations are accessed by sending a simple address code. Using that address, the network does the translation and code conversions to route the call to the destination.

◆ *Interconnectability.* Network ownership rarely crosses national borders, and in the United States multiple ownership is the rule. For greatest utility, interconnection across sovereign or proprietary boundaries is required.

◆ *Robustness.* Networks must contain sufficient capacity and redundancy to be relatively invulnerable to overloads and failures and to recover automatically from failures that do occur. They must offer some form of flow control to prevent users from accessing the network when overloads occur.

◆ *Capacity.* Networks must support enough users to meet service demands.

Some type of switching is required to fill all the above demands. Networks employ three forms of switching: packet switching, in which traffic is divided into small segments and routed to the destination by nodes that are interconnected by circuits; message switching, in which traffic is stored and forwarded when a path to the destination is available; and circuit switching, in which users are interconnected directly by a path that lasts for the duration of the session. Message switching is practical only for data communications. Packet-switched voice is technically feasible and some systems use forms of packet switching for voice traffic, but voice signals are time-sensitive. Any delay in forwarding packets is noticeable, and may impair effective communications. Therefore, special switching types such as ATM are needed to prevent disruptive delay. Until ATM becomes more ubiquitous, circuit switching is the most feasible form for public voice networks. Circuit switching is also feasible for some data traffic, and a significant portion of the traffic carried by the public switched telephone network (PSTN) is data and facsimile.

NETWORK TERMINOLOGY

Network terminology is often confusing because of the ambiguity of the vocabulary. In this discussion of networks the following terms are used:

♦ A *node* is a network element that provides a point at which stations can access the network; it is the terminating point for internodal trunks. In circuit-switched networks, nodes are always switching systems. In packet- and message-switched networks, they may be computers. This chapter discusses the differences between switching systems and computers.

♦ *Trunks* are the circuits or links that interconnect nodes. In switching systems the equipment that interfaces the internodal trunks to the switching system is also called trunk equipment, or sometimes trunk relay equipment.

♦ *Stations* are the terminal points in a network. Telephone instruments, key telephone equipment, data terminals, and computers all fall under the station definition for this discussion.

♦ *Lines* are the circuits or paths that connect stations to the nodes.

NETWORK ARCHITECTURE

Chapter 3 discusses five basic network topologies—ring, bus, branching tree, mesh, and star. Circuit-switched networks use the star and mesh topologies almost exclusively. Lines radiate from the central office to stations in a star topology, and the nodes are usually interconnected as a mesh. For survivability, switching systems are often connected by fiber-optic rings.

The fundamental network design problem is determining how to assemble the most economical configuration of circuits and equipment based on peak and average traffic load, grade of service required, and switching, circuit, and administrative costs. It is practical to connect a few nodes with direct trunks between nodes, as Figure 8–3 shows. Direct connection is feasible up to a point, but as the number of nodes increases, the number of circuit groups increases as the square of the number of nodes, and the number of trunks soon becomes unwieldy. To control costs, a hierarchical network can be formed using tandem switches to interconnect the nodes.

The number of levels in a network hierarchy is determined by the network's owner and is based on a cost/service balance, as explained in Chapter 35. In the past, the AT&T and Bell Operating Company network was connected in a five-level hierarchical structure. With divestiture and the increasing power and intelligence of switching systems, the hierarchical arrangement is giving way to a more flat network structure.

FIGURE 8-3

Direct and Tandem Trunks in Single-Level and Hierarchical
Networks

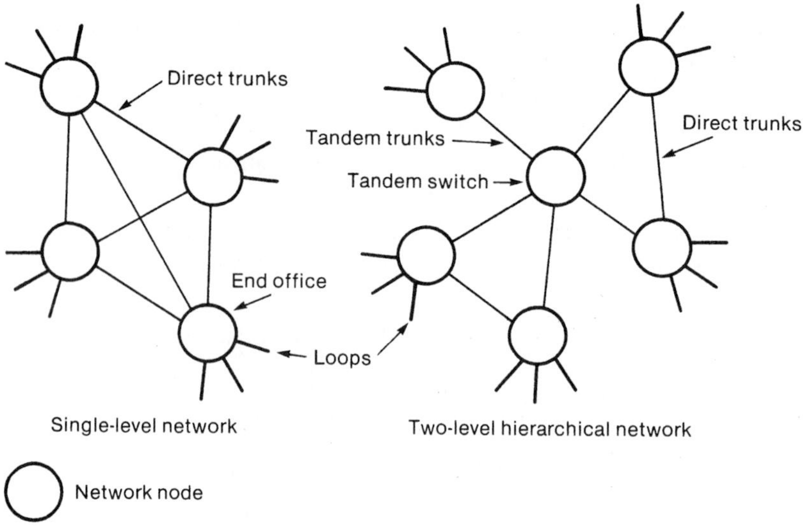

Single-level network   Two-level hierarchical network

Network node

The Changing Network Environment

Telecommunications networks exist in an environment that is continually
changing. Service demands are not constant—they vary by time of the day, day
of the week, and season of the year. Demand is continually evolving in response to changing calling habits and business conditions. Competition and
new technology have a substantial effect on cost and demand. Also, network
design is always a compromise that seeks to balance the use of existing equipment with the provision of satisfactory service. Because of these diverse forces,
any network is a complex of modern and obsolescent equipment that is continually being shrunk or expanded to match demand. Even a new private network
assembled with the latest technology is soon made partially obsolete by technical advances.

The remainder of this chapter explains the characteristics of the switching equipment that serves North American telecommunications users. This
technology is common to the three major classes of switching systems—local
central offices, tandem switches, and PBXs, which Chapters 9, 10, and 21 discuss. The distinctions between these three types of switching systems are not
absolute. A single system can serve any or all functions.

FIGURE 8–4

Block Diagram of a Switching System

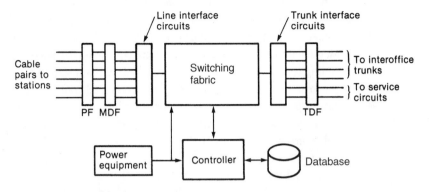

PF—Protector Frame
MDF—Main Distributing Frame
TDF—Trunk Distributing Frame

Switching System Architecture

All switching systems include the following elements, as shown in Figure 8–4:

- ◆ A *switching network,* or fabric, that connects paths between input and output ports.
- ◆ A *controller* that directs the connection of paths through the switching network. Direct control switching systems, which we will discuss later, do not employ a separate controller. The user controls the switch by dialing digits.
- ◆ A *database* that stores the system configuration and addresses, and features of lines and trunks. In direct control systems the database is not a separate element.
- ◆ *Line ports* that interface outside plant for connection to users. All local and PBX switching systems include line ports; tandem switches may have only a few specialized line ports.
- ◆ *Trunk ports* that interface interoffice trunks, service circuits, and testing equipment.
- ◆ *Service circuits* that provide call progress signals such as dial tone, ringing, and busy tones.
- ◆ *Common equipment* such as battery plants, power supplies, testing equipment, and distributing frames.

Switching System Control

When a user signals a switching system with a service request, the switch determines the terminating station's address from the telephone number dialed and translates the number to determine call routing. Translation tables specify the trunk group that serves the destination, an alternate route if the first choice route is blocked, the number of digits to dial, any digit conversions needed, and the type of signaling to use on the trunk. Some switches lack translation capability. These systems, called *direct control* systems, route calls only in direct response to dialed digits. *Common control* systems include circuitry that enables them to make alternate routing choices; that is, when one group of trunks is blocked, another group can be selected. Electromechanical common-controlled switching systems use wired-relay logic. Modern electronic switching systems use stored-program control (SPC) to direct call-processing functions. In central offices the controller is a special-purpose computer. In most PBXs, a commercial processor is the heart of the controller.

Switching Networks

Switching systems can be classified by type of switching network. Direct-controlled switching systems have inflexible networks that follow dial pulses to a single destination. Most common control and stored-program control systems use one of four types of switching fabric:

- ◆ Crossbar analog.
- ◆ Reed relay analog.
- ◆ Pulse amplitude modulated (PAM) analog.
- ◆ Pulse code modulated (PCM) digital.

Of the above types, nearly all currently manufactured systems use PCM switching fabric. The basic function of the switching fabric is to provide paths between the inputs and outputs. Like all other design tasks, the network design objective is to provide enough paths to avoid blocking users while keeping costs to a level users are willing to pay. The first two network types use electromechanical relays for the switching medium and are more expensive than the last two types, which employ digital logic circuits to provide and control the network paths. Electromechanical networks have some restrictions on the number of users that can be served at once. A network that contains fewer paths than terminations is called a *blocking network* because not all users can be served simultaneously.

A *nonblocking network* enables a connection to be made between any two ports independently of the amount of traffic. Nonblocking networks are not economically feasible with electromechanical switching systems because the cost of the network increases directly with the number of switch points. With digital networks where the switching medium is entirely solid state, nonblocking networks are not only economically feasible, they are common in PBXs; vendors frequently stress nonblockage as a selling point.

It is easy to exaggerate the importance of a nonblocking network, which can deliver a full 36 CCS of capacity to every station. (CCS, a measure of traffic intensity, is discussed in Chapter 35.) Not only is the need for this kind of capacity rare, it must be remembered that the switching network is but one element of the switching system; another element invariably arises to limit capacity. The phrase *virtually nonblocking* has evolved in the industry to describe a network that is not designed to be totally nonblocking but provides enough paths that users rarely find themselves blocked by the network. In switching terminology, the situation in which an incoming call cannot be connected to a port because of blockage in the switching network is called *incoming matching loss* (IML). The percentage of IML is a useful factor in evaluating the health of the system. In a nonblocking switch, the IML should always be zero. In a virtually nonblocking network the IML should rarely be anything but zero. In a switch with concentration and a satisfactory degree of load balance, IML should be a fraction of 1 percent.

A nonblocking switch network does not ensure that users will not encounter blockage. Trunking is always designed to some level of blockage, as discussed in Chapter 35. If the switching system is configured without enough common equipment, users will encounter delays that they will interpret as blockage. For example, too few digit receivers results in slow dial tone. Switches are also subject to processor overloads, which can result in a variety of call-processing delays. Switches are rated by the number of busy hour call attempts (BHCA), which is the factor that describes the number of calls the system can handle during the peak hour of the day. The term *call attempt* may bear little relationship to the actual number of calls handled by the system. Not only are call originations counted as call attempts, but accesses to features such as call pickup, call transfer, and call waiting, which require attention by the central processor, count as call attempts in most switches.

Modern switching networks are wired in grids, as Figure 8–5 shows. Each stage of the grid consists of a switching matrix that connects input links to output links. Links, which are often called *junctors,* are wired between switching stages to provide a possible path from any input port to any output port. The network shown in Figure 8–5 is nonblocking because it has an equal number of input and output ports, and the number of possible paths equals the number of ports.

FIGURE 8–5

Nonblocking Switching Network

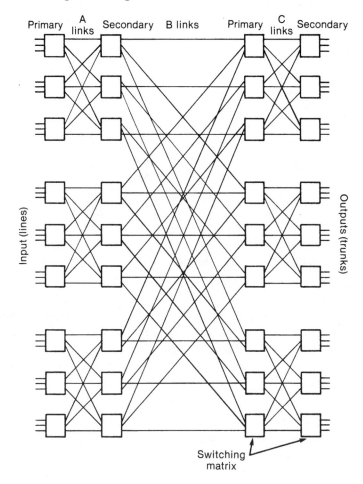

Many switching networks use concentration to reduce network cost. If the primary switch on the input side of the network has six input ports, as in Figure 8–6, the network would have a two-to-one concentration ratio because only three of the six inputs could be serviced simultaneously. Local central offices and PBXs that use electromechanical networks typically use a line switch concentration ratio of 4:1 or 6:1. It should be understood that even though a switch may have a nonblocking network, it can still be blocked in the line switch networks if these use concentration. Trunk switches usually use no concentration.

FIGURE 8-6

A Switching Network with Two-to-One Concentration

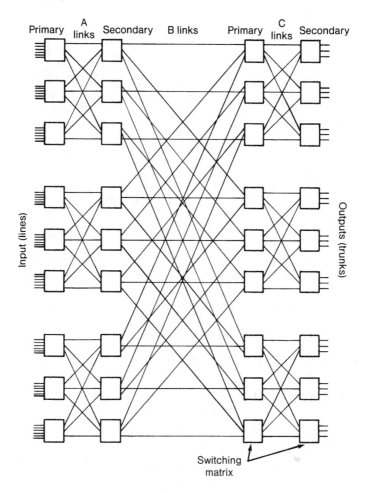

The capacity of a switching network relates directly to the number of switching stages it has. The switching matrix is physically limited by the number of terminations it can support. To avoid blocking, the controller must have multiple choices of paths through the network. These paths are obtained by providing multiple switching stages so that each stage has enough choices that the probability of blocking is reduced to a level consistent with grade of service objectives.

Derivation of Terms Tip, Ring, and Sleeve from the Operator's
Switchboard Plug

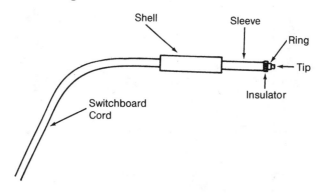

DIRECT CONTROL SWITCHING SYSTEMS

The earliest type of switching system was a manual switchboard similar to the
one shown in Figure 8–1. Manual switchboards employed operators to make
connections. An incoming signal, actuated by taking the receiver off hook or
turning a crank, operated a signal on the switchboard to notify the operator of
an incoming call. The operator answered the call by inserting a cord in a jack,
obtaining the terminating number, and inserting the matching cord in the jack
of the called line or of a trunk to a distant office. Disregarding the cost of the
manual switchboard, it was efficient because the operators could make alternate routing decisions.

Many terms in common use today originated with the manual switchboard. Incoming calls to some switchboards were signaled by a hinged cap
that covered the jack and dropped down when a ring arrived. The term *drop*
has survived to signify the equipment toward the central office from the line.
The operator's cord had three connections, as Figure 8–7 shows—the tip, the
ring, and the sleeve. The *tip* and the *ring* connected to the two sides of the subscriber's line, and this terminology survives today. The operator detected the
busy or idle status of the line by touching the tip of the plug to the sleeve of
the jack. If the line was busy at another position in the lineup, a click could be
heard in the headset from the battery on the *sleeve,* which supervised the connection. The operator's reach imposed a practical limit on the number of lines
that a single switchboard could serve. Switchboard positions were connected
in multiple, another term that remains today to describe the parallel connection of several devices.

FIGURE 8–8

Direct Control Step-by-Step Switching System

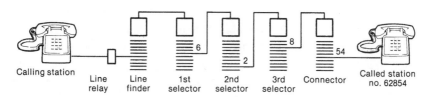

| Calling station | Line relay | Line finder | 1st selector | 2nd selector | 3rd selector | Connector | Called station no. 62854 |

The operator monitored a connection by observing lamps on the switchboard console. A lighted lamp meant the line was on hook; when the telephone was off hook the lamp was extinguished. The operator *supervised* the connection by watching the lamps. The term supervision survives today to describe the process, now entirely electronic, of determining when a party answers or terminates a call. Supervision today not only directs the equipment to establish and take down a connection but also determines when to start and terminate billing for the call.

As the telephone system expanded, it exceeded the practical limitations of manual operation. Mechanical switching systems were necessary to keep the costs under control and to contain the equipment in a reasonably-sized area. The Strowger, or step-by-step, switch is an electromechanical device that operates through two axes; it steps vertically to one of 10 levels and rotates horizontally to one of 10 terminals. It is actuated by pulls on the telephone dial or by an internal operation, depending on the function of the switch. Figure 8–8 is a block diagram of a simple step-by-step central office. Although these systems have nearly disappeared from use in North America today, their structure provides insights into how switching systems work, and some of the problems modern systems are designed to overcome.

Subscriber lines connect to line relays that operate when the user lifts the receiver. Line relays connect to line finders that are wired in line groups to serve as many as 200 lines with up to 20 switches per group, depending on the traffic volume. When all switches in a line group are busy, new users cannot get dial tone until someone hangs up. Line finders automatically step vertically and rotate horizontally to locate a calling telephone line. A first selector switch, permanently wired to the line finder, furnishes dial tone to the user. As digits are pulsed, selector switches step upward to a level corresponding to the digits dialed and automatically rotate horizontally to find the first path to the next selector.

The final two digits in the train actuate a connector switch, which connects to the user's line. The next-to-last digit drives the connector to the appropriate level; the last rotates the connector to the correct terminal. If the terminal is busy, the connector returns a busy signal. If it is idle, the connector attaches a ringing signal, which remains attached until the called party answers or the calling party hangs up.

The step-by-step office has a theoretical concentration ratio of 10:1, which is established by 200 subscribers assigned to a line group of 20 switches. In practice, it is important that line groups contain a mix of heavy and light users to maintain a reasonable grade of service. Network administrators vary the concentration ratio by changing the number of switches in the line group or the number of subscribers assigned.

Two other problems, *permanent signals* and *calling party hold*, also plague step-by-step offices. A permanent signal results when a user takes the receiver off-hook and leaves it off without dialing. A line finder-first selector combination is seized and cannot be released except by manual intervention. A calling party hold condition occurs when the calling party fails to hang up at the end of a session. The switch train remains connected through to the called party, who cannot use the telephone until the caller releases the path.

A step-by-step central office can be visualized as a concentrator in which many originating stations route over fewer paths through the selector train. The selector switches find vacant paths to the expansion side of the office, which contains all the telephone numbers terminating in the central office. A step-by-step office lacks translation capability. It routes to lines and trunks directly based on the dialed digits. Different selector levels are wired to internal switches or to trunks to distant offices. The initial digit 1 is reserved for dialing to service circuits such as long distance, directory assistance, and repair service.

Here are some reasons step-by-step systems are no longer suitable for service:

◆ Step-by-step switches are incapable of making routing decisions. When a caller encounters blockage, the switch can return only a reorder or a busy signal. The user must hang up and try again.

◆ The switch can be driven only by dial pulses. To provide DTMF service, a separate converter is wired to the first selector to convert DTMF signals to dial pulses.

◆ The switching speed is regulated by the speed of the telephone dial and depends on the number of digits in the dialed number and the dialing speed of the user.

◆ The feature set is limited. Step-by-step switches can provide few of the modern enhancements such as conferencing and call waiting that make telephone service more valuable.

◆ All equipment used for a call remains connected for the duration of the call; the system cannot release equipment to another user.

- ◆ Each call causes wear on the mechanical equipment. Unless periodic adjustments and replacements are made, service deteriorates.
- ◆ The switches and relays in a step-by-step office cause noise that couples into other circuits. Therefore, data transmission is likely to be impaired by errors in a step-by-step office, particularly when the equipment is improperly maintained.
- ◆ A step-by-step office lacks a database of subscriber connections. Each valid user is wired to a line group, which establishes the originating equipment number, and to a connector, which establishes the telephone number.
- ◆ Step-by-step central offices have few defenses against misuse of the telephone by subscribers who take their instruments off-hook without dialing or who fail to hang up after a session. These actions cause service difficulties for other users, and the central office cannot correct them without manual intervention by a technician.

Common Control Central Offices

Common control switching systems employ electromechanical logic circuits to drive the switching network. These logic circuits are brought into a connection long enough to establish a path through the switching network, then release to attend to other calls. Figure 8–9 is a block diagram of a crossbar common control switching system.

Several types of switching networks are used with common control systems, but the most common is the crossbar switch shown in Figure 8–10. The crossbar switch is a matrix consisting of horizontal and vertical connections. Switches are manufactured in several different sizes, but for illustration, a 10-by-20 switch will be considered. With this type of switch, 20 input paths assigned to the vertical portion of the matrix can be connected to 10 output paths assigned to the horizontal side of the matrix, providing a 2:1 concentration ratio.

A set of cross points is wired to the horizontal and vertical paths at each matrix intersection, as Figure 8–11 shows. The common control equipment operates and releases the crosspoints. For example, to make the connection between vertical 3 and horizontal 5 as the figure shows, an impulse from the common control operates a horizontal select magnet. This magnet moves a finger against an actuating card on the switch contacts, where the vertical hold magnet clamps it. The select magnet is then released. The hold magnet keeps the contacts in operation until the common control equipment releases it when the call ends. The function of the common control equipment is to select an idle path through the switching network and to operate crosspoints in all switches simultaneously to establish path continuity.

FIGURE 8-9

Block Diagram of a Crossbar Switching System

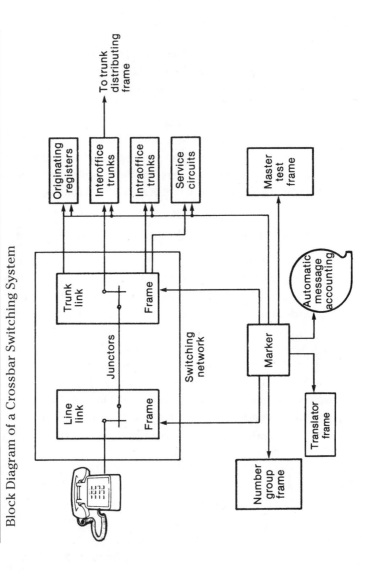

FIGURE 8–10

Crossbar Switch

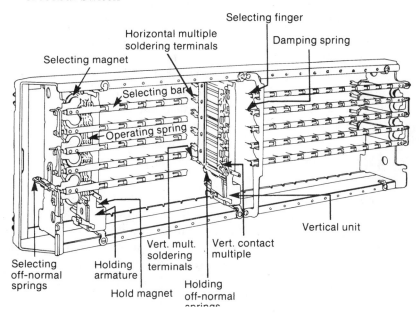

FIGURE 8–11

Crossbar Switch Schematic Diagram

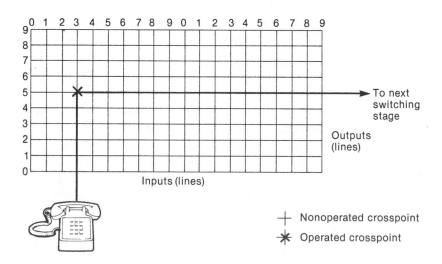

The brain of a crossbar switch is the *marker,* an electromechanical device that performs functions analogous to those of the central processor in a computer. Instructions from the marker drive the switching network and auxiliary equipment in a crossbar office. Markers are provided in a quantity sufficient to serve the traffic load in the office. A minimum of two is provided for redundancy.

When a line goes off-hook the marker detects the change of state and connects the line to an originating register trunk. The register provides dial tone and receives the dialed digits. Registers are of two classes, dial pulse and DTMF. Dial pulse registers can detect only dial pulses; DTMF registers can detect either type of signal. The register stores dialed digits in a relay circuit and signals the marker when dialing is complete. If dialing has not been completed in a specified interval, the register times out and the marker connects the line to a reorder trunk.

After dialing is complete the marker calls a *translator,* a device that stores routing and signaling information. If the translator informs the marker that the call is to a chargeable destination, the marker calls in automatic message accounting (AMA) equipment and records the initial entry. If the number is within the same office, the marker tests the status of the terminating number, and if busy, attaches the calling line to a busy signal trunk. If the called line is idle the marker reserves a path through the network, connects the called number to a 20 Hz ringing trunk, and connects the calling number to an audible ringing trunk. When the called party answers, the marker removes audible and 20 Hz ringing and connects a path through the network. When the first party hangs up, the marker takes down all the connections.

When a call comes in from a distant office, the marker recognizes the trunk seizure from the change in status of the signaling leads and attaches an incoming register to receive the digits. Based on the trunk classification, the marker tells the register how many digits to expect. When dialing is complete, the register signals the marker, which connects a path from the trunk to the terminating number.

The most significant advantage of common control offices compared to direct control offices is the flexibility of common control. If, for example, an office has direct trunks to another office but they are all busy, it can attach an outgoing call to an alternate route to a tandem office. This capability is designed into most networks. Direct circuit groups, called *high usage* (HU) groups, are established to terminating offices if the traffic volume is sufficient to justify the cost. The capacity of HU groups is engineered to keep the circuits fully occupied during heavy calling periods. Overflow traffic is routed over tandem trunks that are more liberally engineered to support the overflow. Chapter 35 discusses alternate routing concepts in more detail.

Crossbar offices take considerably less manual attention than step-by-step offices. The switches do not have the wiping action that wears down contacts. When troubles occur, the marker calls a trouble recorder into action and punches a card to show the state of the various leads when the trouble occurred. Crossbar offices solve the problems of permanent signals and calling party hold. If a customer remains off-hook without dialing, the register times out, and the marker connects the line to a permanent signal holding trunk, which applies tones to alert the customer to hang up the telephone. If a calling party fails to disconnect at the completion of a call, the marker recognizes the termination from the called party and takes down the connection.

Crossbar offices are not bound by a fixed numbering plan that relies on the digits dialed to route the call. They can insert and translate digits, choose alternate routes to the destination, and offer *Centrex* service, which is a PBX-like service provided from the central office. Chapter 25 discusses Centrex.

The following characteristics are significant in common control switching systems:

- ◆ Alternate routing capability offers flexibility in handling overloads.
- ◆ Crossbar offices require less maintenance than step-by-step because their internal circuitry has no wiping action to generate wear. Also, trouble indications are detected by the marker and recorded in a trouble recorder for analysis.
- ◆ Although crossbar offices are not as electrically noisy as step-by-step offices, relay and switch operations cause noise that can cause errors in switched data circuits.
- ◆ Common control switches are vulnerable to total central office failure. When markers are all occupied or out of service, no further users can be served, even though idle paths are available.
- ◆ Common control offices are much faster than step-by-step offices. Dial pulses are registered in shared circuits to avoid tying up equipment with slow users or long dial pulse strings.

Stored Program Control

Stored program control (SPC) central offices have been in operation in the United States since 1965 and in either analog or digital form have essentially replaced their electromechanical counterparts. The primary economies of SPC offices lie in their lower maintenance cost and their ability to provide enhanced features that are impractical with electromechanical central offices. Analog SPC systems, diagrammed in Figure 8–12, use concepts similar to common control electromechanical offices except that electronic logic replaces wired relay logic.

FIGURE 8–12

Block Diagram of a Stored Program Switching System

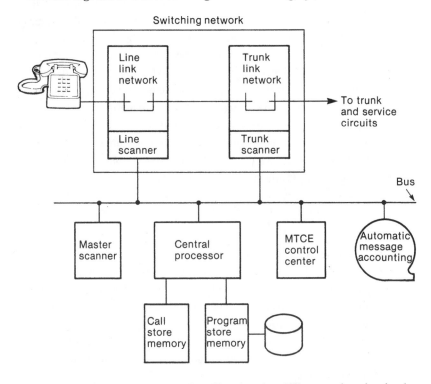

The central processor controls call processing. When service circuits detect an off-hook signal, the processor attaches a dial pulse or DTMF receiver to
the originating line. The receiver supplies dial tone and registers the incoming
digits. The processor stores the details of the call in a temporary *call store*
memory. Translation tables are stored in semipermanent memory. The processor establishes a path through the switching network, attaches 20 Hz ringing to
the called party, and an audible ringing trunk to the calling party. When the
called party answers, the processor marks completion of the connection.

The central processor in SPC central offices is similar to that used in
mainframe computers, but with some important differences. First, the SPC processor is not only fault tolerant; it is almost fail-safe. Although SPC central offices do fail, their design objective is no more than one hour's outage in 20
years, which is an outage tolerance several orders of magnitude better than that
of most mainframe computers. A second difference is in the nature of the processing task. Call processing is highly input/output intensive, with little requirement for arithmetic operations compared to other data-processing tasks.

Where a mainframe computer is overseeing several dozen peripherals, a central office processor is managing tens of thousands of individual terminals, any of which can spring to life at any time and demand service within a second or less.

Although call processing is similar to that in a common control electromechanical office, the SPC processor offers much greater flexibility. The processor operates under the direction of a *generic program,* which contains the call-processing details. Features can be added by replacing the generic program with a new issue. Because of this factor, SPC systems are far more flexible than their electromechanical counterparts. The generic program contains special features that Chapters 9, 10, and 21 discuss. These can be activated, deactivated, or assigned to a limited group of users by making translation changes. SPC systems also can collect statistical information and diagnose circuit and system irregularities to a much greater degree than electromechanical systems.

Electronic Switching Networks

Over the past two decades many changes, which can be broadly classed as analog or digital, have been made in SPC switching networks. Most analog systems use reed relay networks. A reed relay has contacts enclosed in a sealed glass tube and surrounded by a coil of wire. The contacts are closed by a short pulse of current and remain closed until opened by a second pulse. The switches are wired in a matrix of horizontal and vertical paths to establish a DC circuit through the network.

Many electronic switching systems in use in the United States today are analog switches using reed relay networks; however, this technology is obsolescent and is rapidly being replaced by digital switching. Reed switches are more expensive to manufacture and require more maintenance than the digital networks that are replacing them. Analog systems are also incapable of supporting ISDN, which is gradually being provided by many LECs.

Pulse Amplitude Switching

The earliest all-electronic switching networks used pulse amplitude modulation (PAM), a concept that Chapter 4 discusses. At the heart of the network is a high-speed time-multiplexed bus that provides talking paths for all connected conversations. The bus is divided into time slots. Stations are interconnected by assigning them to the same time slot, during which they are allocated the full bandwidth of the bus long enough to send a single pulse. Line circuits sample the voice signal 8,000 times per second and generate a PAM signal. Line and trunk ports connect to the bus through gating circuits, as Figure 8–13 shows. At the proper time slot instant the gate opens to connect the parties to the bus

FIGURE 8–13

Time Multiplexed Bus System

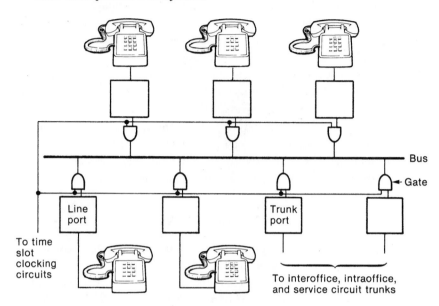

for the duration of one pulse. By allowing a port to send during one time slot and receive during another, full duplex operation results.

PAM networks remain in some obsolescent switching systems today, but most modern systems use PCM switching fabric.

Pulse Code Modulated Networks

The latest generation of switching systems uses PCM switching networks. PCM networks are similar in concept to the analog matrix shown in Figure 8–5 with some important exceptions.

First, PCM networks connect the encoded signal over parallel paths. The incoming serial bit stream from the line or trunk circuits is converted to a parallel signal and assigned to a *time slot*. At the proper time slot instant, all eight bits of the input PCM signal are gated to the output port in parallel. The output circuits convert them to serial for application to trunk and line circuits.

The second exception is in the mode of switching employed in PCM networks. Analog networks use *space division* switching exclusively. That is, input paths are physically connected to output links. Digital networks use a combination of space division and time division switching. Although the term

FIGURE 8–14

And Gate Truth Table

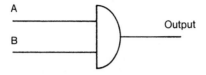

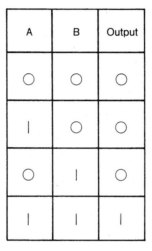

A	B	Output
○	○	○
|	○	○
○	|	○
|	|	|

space division implies a relay operation, the switches used in digital networks contain no moving parts. Integrated logic gates form the switching element to direct the PCM pulses from one path to another.

Consider the diagram in Figure 8–14. The switching element is an *and gate*, which is a device with two inputs and a single output. If a pulse appears on both inputs simultaneously, the pulse is gated to the output. If either input is 0, which means no pulse, the pulse is blocked. The logic of a gate is shown in its truth table in the lower part of the figure. The central processor controls the opening and closing of the many gates that comprise a space division switch.

The other form of electronic switching is time division switching, which is implemented in a *time slot interchange* element (see Figure 8–15). A TSI receives digital pulses during one increment of time, stores them for one processor cycle, and releases them during the proper time slot in the next cycle. Two stations can talk to one another if they are connected to the same time slot.

FIGURE 8–15

Time Slot Interchange

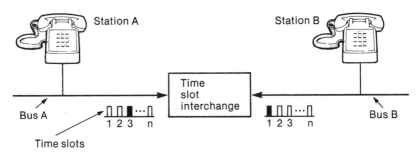

FIGURE 8–16

Time-Space-Space-Time Digital Switching Network

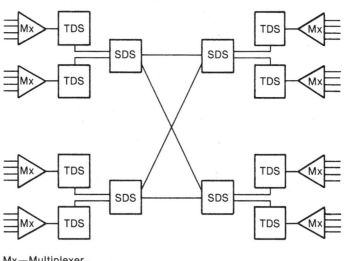

Mx—Multiplexer
TDS—Time Division Switch
SDS—Space Division Switch

Time slot assignments are made by the processor and released when the call terminates. The time slot interchange process introduces an absolute delay of one processor cycle for each time division switching stage.

Practical digital switching networks contain a combination of space and time division switches. For example, Figure 8–16 shows a time-space-space-time (TSST) network. This is a four-stage network that is the functional equivalent of the space division networks of older analog switching systems.

Control Systems

Electronic switching systems are designed as *central control, multiprocessing,* or *distributed control.* In a central control system, all the call processing is concentrated in a single location. A multiprocessing system has two or more central processors that share call-processing functions. The sharing takes the form of dividing the call-processing load or assigning one set of functions to one processor and another to its mate. For example, one processor could handle call processing and the other maintenance. If either failed, the other could assume the entire load. The third method of control, distributed, uses multiple processors, each of which handles a designated part of the switch. There might, for example, be a separate processor for each shelf or each frame.

Electronic switching systems have four kinds of software. Although not all manufacturers use the same terminology, and there may be architectural differences between systems, the functions are contained in every SPC switch.

The *operating system* is the system that keeps the switch alive even though it is not processing calls. The operating system ties the elements of the switch together, takes care of input and output functions, and supervises the general health of the system. Closely tied to the operating system is the call-processing software, which in many systems is called the *generic program.* This software contains all the features of the switch and maps the connections through the switching fabric.

The third type of software is the *parameters.* These are a database that contains the types, quantities, and addresses of the major hardware components. By maintaining records of the busy/idle status of components, the processor sets up a path through the network, assigns it while a call is in process, and releases it when the call ends.

The fourth type of software is the *translations,* which are a database of how ports are assigned and what feature is assigned to each port. Each trunk and each station in a switching system is assigned through the translation tables, and the features associated with that port are defined within the table. For example, the trunks are translated as to location, signaling, and type. Stations are translated as to location, restrictions, and features.

Synchronization

Networks of digital switches must be closely synchronized to prevent transmission errors. If two interconnected systems do not have a common synchronizing source, their clocks will run at slightly different rates. This means that occasionally the receiving end will miss a bit or will sample the same bit twice, either of which results in a bit error in data transmission. These momentary losses of framing are known as *slips*. Slips have little effect on voice transmission, but their effect can be serious on data.

Circuit-switched networks are kept in synchronization by slaving switches on a master clock known as the Basic Standard Reference Frequency (BSRF). Each office has its own clock that can run freely with a certain degree of stability. The highest level clock below the BSRF is a Stratum 1 clock, which has an accuracy of at least 1×10^{-11}. There are three lower levels of clocking, which offer progressively less accuracy and lower cost. Timing passes down from each higher class office to the offices that home on it. This type of synchronization is called plesiochronous. When clocking is lost from a higher level office, lower level devices run freely. The greater the differences in clocking between two such devices, the higher the number of slips that will occur. Clocking principles are the same as those discussed in Chapter 5.

Comparison of Digital and Analog Switching Networks

Digital switches have several advantages over their analog counterparts:

- ◆ The switching networks are less expensive to manufacture because of the ability to use low-cost integrated components.
- ◆ T-1 circuits can interface the switching system directly without using a channel bank to bring the circuits down to voice frequency.
- ◆ High-speed data can be switched without the use of modems if digital line interface circuits are provided.
- ◆ Digital switches can be made to support ISDN.

Line, Trunk, and Service Circuits

All switching systems are equipped with circuits to interface the switching network to stations, trunks, and service circuits such as tone and ringing supplies. In some systems, these circuits are external devices. In other cases, they are integral to the switching equipment. For example, some digital central offices develop tones internally by generating the digital equivalent of the tone, so when it is applied to the decoder in a line or trunk circuit it is converted to an analog tone.

Line Circuit Functions

In a digital central office, line circuits have seven basic functions that can be remembered with the acronym BORSCHT. Analog central office line circuits require five of the seven functions; because they have two-wire switching networks, the hybrid and coding functions are omitted. The BORSCHT functions are:

> *Battery* feeds from the office to the line to operate station transmitters and DTMF dials.
>
> *Overvoltage protection* is provided to protect the line circuit from damaging external voltages that can occur during the time it takes the protector to operate.
>
> *Ringing* connects from a central ringing supply to operate the telephone bell.
>
> *Supervision* refers to monitoring the on-hook/off-hook status of the line.
>
> *Coding* converts the analog signal to a PCM bit stream in digital line circuits.
>
> *Hybrids* are required in digital line circuits to convert between the four-wire switching fabric and the two-wire cable pair.
>
> *Testing* access is provided so an external test system can obtain access to the cable pair for trouble isolation.

In PBXs and digital central offices, line circuits reside on plug-in cards. Because much of the cost of the system is embedded in the line circuits, shelves are installed, but to defer the investment, line cards are added only as needed. In analog central offices, line circuits are less expensive because they omit the analog-to-PCM conversion and the two- to four-wire conversion. Analog line circuits are permanently wired in frames that are connected to a distributing frame for crossconnection to the cable pairs.

Trunk Circuits

Trunk circuits interface the signaling protocols of interoffice trunks to the internal protocols of the switching system. For example, in an SPC office a trunk is seized by an order from the central control to a trunk distributing circuit in the trunk frame. This seizure causes the trunk circuit to connect battery to the M lead toward the carrier system. When a trunk is seized incoming, the ground on the E lead passes from the trunk circuit to a scanner that informs the controller of the seizure.

Digital central offices interface analog trunks using external trunk circuits just as analog offices do. Digital trunks interface without the use of trunk circuits. Digital offices have interface circuitry that allows the 1.544 mb/s bit stream direct access to the switching network.

Service Circuits

All types of switching systems require circuits that are used momentarily in routing and establishing connections. These applications are briefly discussed so readers will understand how the services are obtained and applied in all types of switching systems.

Ringing and Call Progress Tone Supplies

All switching systems that interface end users require 20 Hz ringing supplies generating approximately 90 volts to ring telephone bells. In addition, switching systems require audible ringing supplies, busy tones operating at 60 interruptions per minute (IPM), and reorder tones operating at 120 IPM. In digital switching systems, these tones are generally created in firmware.

Recorded Announcements

Recorded announcements provide explicit information to the user when calls cannot be completed and tone signals are insufficient to explain the cause. For example, calls to disconnected numbers are connected to recorded announcements. When a transfer of calls is required, the system routes the incoming call to an intercept operator; otherwise, calls to nonworking numbers route to a recorder. Announcements are also used on long-distance circuits to indicate temporary circuit or equipment overloads. Often these are preceded by a three-tone code called *special identification tones* (SIT) so automatic service observing equipment can collect statistics on ineffective dialing attempts.

Permanent Signal Tones

A *permanent signal* occurs when a line circuit is off-hook because of trouble or because the user has left the receiver off-hook. Permanent signals in trunk circuits occur because of equipment malfunctions or maintenance actions. Combinations of loud tones and recorded announcements are used on most line switching systems to alert the user to hang up the phone. Permanent trunk signals are indicated by interrupting the supervisory signal at 120 IPM, which flashes the supervision lights attached to E & M leads in some signaling apparatus.

Testing Circuits

All end offices and some PBXs contain circuits that provide testing access to subscriber lines. These circuits connect the tip and ring of the line to a test trunk to allow a test position access to both the cable facility and, to a limited degree, the central office equipment.

All tandem switching systems, most end offices and some PBXs also include trunk-testing circuitry to make transmission and supervision measurements on central office trunks. These circuits vary from 1004 Hz tone supplies that can be dialed from telephones served by the switching system to trunk-testing circuits that enable two-way transmission and supervision measurements on trunks. Chapter 10 discusses trunk testing methods, and Chapter 36 discusses testing equipment.

ACCESS TO THE LOCAL NETWORK

Until AT&T's divestiture of its Bell Operating Companies (BOCs) on January 1, 1984, the telephone network was designed for single ownership. Divestiture, which intended among other objectives to open long-distance telephone service to competition, has far-reaching effects that should be understood by telecommunications managers. This section discusses the architectures of local and long-distance telephone networks, how the interexchange carriers (IECs) obtain local access, and the way IECs sometimes bypass the local networks to provide service directly to end users.

Predivestiture Network Architecture

Until the mid-1970s, AT&T had a monopoly on switched long-distance telephone service. The 22 BOCs and some 1,500 independent telephone companies (ICs) owned the local network up to that time. The local exchange companies (LECs) furnished all local telephone service, most intrastate long-distance service, and a limited amount of interstate long-distance service. AT&T's Long Lines Division furnished most interstate service.

The network was divided into five classes of switching systems and their interconnecting trunks. Class 5 central offices, the lowest class in the hierarchy, were owned and operated by the LECs, a situation that remains unchanged. Ownership of Class 4 and higher offices was established by agreement between the parties; many of these systems were owned jointly before divestiture, reflecting their use for both intrastate and long-haul traffic.

The Class 5 offices connected to higher class offices by toll connecting trunks, now called *interLATA connecting trunks.* The higher class offices are interconnected by intertoll trunks. The LECs and the independent telephone companies, as negotiated by the parties, own interLATA connecting trunks; AT&T other IECs own the intertoll trunks. The FCC and the courts regulate the regional Bell holding companies, a situation that exists as of this writing, but which will diminish as the effects of the 1996 Telecommunications act take hold.

FIGURE 8-17

Feature Groups A and D Access to the Local Exchange Network

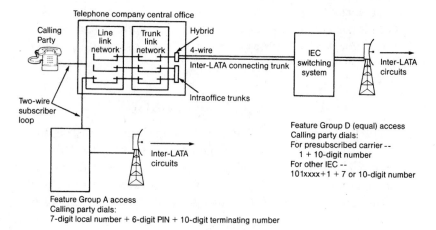

Beginnings of Competition in the Toll Network

In 1978, the FCC decided to permit other common carriers to offer switched long-distance telephone service in competition with AT&T. A key issue in the decision was how the carriers would obtain access to local telephone subscribers through Class 5 offices. Because the network was designed for single ownership, it was impossible to give other carriers access similar to AT&T's without extensive redesign of the local central offices. The AT&T Long Lines circuits terminated on trunk ports in the central offices as did circuits to independent telephone companies. This trunk-side access was not suitable for multiple common carriers, however, because local central offices were not designed for customer-directed access to a carrier. Switching systems routed calls based only on destination, not by customer-selected access code.

The BOCs filed tariffs to provide IECs other than AT&T access to the local network through line-side terminations in the central office. These tariffs were called the Exchange Network Facilities Interconnecting Arrangement (ENFIA) and were subsequently replaced by Feature Group tariffs that are discussed in a later section.

The line-side access to the local switching systems offered under ENFIA A tariffs allowed customers of the IECs to access the network by the arrangement shown in Figure 8–17. Compared to the trunk-side access offered to AT&T, line-side access has the following disadvantages:

◆ Callers obtained access to the IEC's network by dialing a seven-digit local telephone number. The IEC provided second dial tone to indicate attachment of its switching and recording equipment. Access to AT&T's network was by dialing 1.

◆ Automatic number identification, a feature that Chapter 9 discusses, is possible only over trunk-side connections. IEC users dial a personal identification number (PIN) for calling-party billing identification. Rotary dials cannot be used for dialing PIN numbers; only DTMF dial pulses can pass through the Class 5 office to the IEC's switching equipment.

◆ Line-side connections are inherently two-wire and provide inferior echo performance compared to the four-wire terminations of trunk side access.

◆ Answer and disconnect supervision are not provided over line-side connections. Call timing can be determined only by monitoring the originating party's holding time, a technique the IECs call *software answer supervision.*

◆ Multifrequency signaling, which is standard on trunks, is not available on line-side connections.

The BOCs filed another ENFIA tariff to improve access before divestiture. This tariff, ENFIA B (now Feature Group B), offers trunk-side access to the local switching system and most of the features of AT&T's access. The most notable exception to equal access under Feature Group B is that single-digit access is provided only to AT&T's network. Feature Group B uses the code 950-10XX, where XX is a two-digit code identifying the IEC, for access to the IEC's network. Although IECs have now converted to equal access, Feature Group B continues to be used for terminating calls within a LATA and for access to the IEC for some services.

Equal Access

AT&T's agreement with the Department of Justice required the BOCs to provide access substantially equal to that given to AT&T by September 1986, except where it was not technically and economically feasible to do so. Equal access, called *Feature Group D,* gives all IECs access to the trunk side of local switching systems. Users presubscribe to service from a preferred IEC and obtain access to that IEC by dialing 1. Callers reach other IECs by dialing 10XXX or 101XXXX where XXXX is a nationwide access code to the particular carrier. IECs choosing equal access receive automatic number identification, eliminating the need to dial a personal identification number.

FIGURE 8–18

Exchange Access Through LEC LATA Tandem

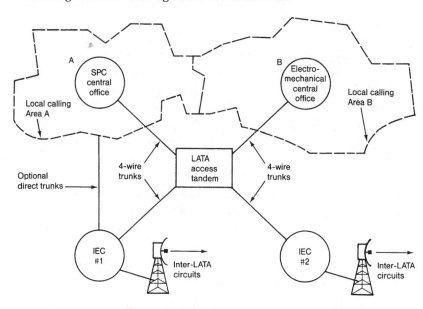

Equal access requires intelligence in the Class 5 office to route the call to the required IEC trunk group. This required changes in the generic programs in SPC offices. Electromechanical offices required extensive redesign to provide equal access; usually they were replaced instead of being converted.

Many LECs provide equal access through a tandem switching system, as Figure 8–18 shows. An equal access tandem registers the dialed digits from the end office and, based on originating telephone number, routes the call to the selected IEC. Where the LEC provides equal access tandems, IEC trunks' interfacing electromechanical central offices terminate on the tandem rather than the end office. The access tandem introduces some delay in call setup time, so it is advantageous for IECs to use direct trunks to the end office where practical. The equal access dialing plan is listed in Table 8–1.

Local Access Transport Areas

The terms of the agreement between AT&T and the Department of Justice prohibit the LECs from transporting long distance traffic outside geographical boundaries called *Local Access Transport Areas* (LATAs). LATA boundaries correspond roughly to Standard Metropolitan Statistical Areas defined by the Office of Management and Budget. Traffic crossing LATA boundaries cannot

T A B L E 8–1

Dialing Plan under Equal Access

	Access	Dialing Plan	Total Digits
Local		NNX-XXXX	
FGD	Toll Intra NPA (presubscribed)	1 -NNX-XXXX	
FGD	Toll Intra NPA (other carrier)	1O1XXXX 1-NNX-XXXX	15
FGD	Toll Inter NPA (presubscribed)	1 -NNX NNX-XXXX	11
FGD	Toll Inter NPA (other carrier)	1O1XXX X 1-NNX NNX-XXXX	16
FGA	Toll Intra NPA	NNX-XXXX (DT) XXXXXX NNX-XXXX	20
FGA	Toll Inter NPA	NNX-XXXX (DT) XXXXXX NNX NNX-XXXX	23

Legend:
FGA = Feature group A
FGD = Feature group D
N = Any digit from 2 to 9 or 0
1O1XXXX Carrier **access** number
XXXXXX Personal identification number (PIN)
(DT) = Dial tone

be transported by the LECs. State utilities commissions regulate traffic within LATA boundaries. Some states assign intraLATA traffic exclusively to the LECs; others permit IECs to carry intraLATA traffic, but where this is permitted, users must dial 101XXXX to access the IEC.

The North American Numbering Plan

The North American Numbering Plan underwent a significant transition on January 1, 1995, when the area code structure of the number changed. The area code had always been identifiable from the digits 0 or 1 in the second position. Several factors, however, cause the supply of available area codes to exhaust in 1994. These factors included rapid growth of cellular telephone, paging, direct inward dialing, facsimile, distinctive ringing, and other applications that consumed numbers. As prefixes filled up, area codes were split, until the available supply of numbers was consumed. The new numbering plan allows any digit from 0 to 9 in the second position. Equipment that once could distinguish an area code from a prefix had to be reprogrammed to comply with the new plan.

The carrier access codes, which had previously been 10XXX, also reached exhaust about the same time. The access code of 101XXXX was added to increase the quantity of available codes.

The 800 number supply was also exhausted in 1995, raising the need for another code for reverse charging. The industry selected the area code 888 as the new toll-free number. IECs began assigning these numbers as their supply of 800 numbers exhausted.

International Dialing

Each country is free to adopt its own numbering structure for internal calls, but international dialing requires countries to conform to a dialing plan standardized by ITU. The ITU standard in the past specified a country code of up to three digits and a national significant number (NSN) of up to 11 digits. The total number of digits could not exceed 12. Effective January 1, 1997, the international dialing plan is expanded to 15 digits. The three-digit country code does not change, but the NSN can be as many as 14 digits.

APPLICATIONS

Switching system applications and standards are covered separately by type of system in Chapters 9, 10, and 21. Also, refer to the Standards section of Chapter 2 for standards on the transmission performance of networks.

9

LOCAL SWITCHING SYSTEMS

Local switching systems, like all telecommunications products, have evolved with the availability of high-powered and inexpensive processors and memory. The earliest electronic switches used specialized processors and memory, but now many systems use commercial processors and RAM, which reduces both cost and complexity. The LECs, cellular operators, and local exchange competitors are the primary users of the switching systems discussed in this chapter, although some large organizations use modified or specially adapted local central office systems as PBXs and tandem switching applications. The key to the application of a local switch lies in the features provided in its generic program. Hardware differences between local switches, PBXs, and tandem switches are not significant. Some manufacturers produce systems that can handle all three applications, with software changes and hardware variations determining whether the switch is a central office, a tandem, a PBX, or a cellular mobile telephone switching office (MTSO).

Central office switching systems are occasionally used as PBXs or tandem switches. With the right software, a local central office can function in any of the three applications. The primary differences between these applications are:

♦ *Line Circuits.* Tandem switches have few or no line circuits. PBX line circuits often omit some BORSCHT functions, have less loop range, and use less expensive technology than central office line circuits.

◆ *Trunk Circuits*. Central office and tandem switch trunk interfaces must meet identical requirements. PBX trunk interfaces are built for private network applications, have a narrower range of features than central office trunks, and are frequently two-wire compared to central office trunks, which are invariably four-wire.

◆ *Maintenance Features*. Local central offices include features for subscriber line testing and maintenance. These features are usually omitted from PBXs and tandem switching systems. Trunk maintenance features are usually more sophisticated in tandem switches than in either local central offices or PBXs. Both tandem and local switching systems have administrative, self-diagnostic, and internal maintenance features that exceed the capability of all but the most sophisticated PBXs.

◆ *Capacity*. With some exceptions, local central offices have greater capacity than all but the largest PBXs. The switching network capacity of local and tandem switches is generally equivalent.

DIGITAL CENTRAL OFFICE TECHNOLOGY

DCOs fall into two categories: community dial offices (CDOs) that support un-attended operation serving up to about 10,000 lines, and central offices de-signed for urban applications of up to about 60,000 lines. The distinction be-tween these categories is not absolute. Both use similar technology, but CDOs use an architecture that limits their line size. When the system exceeds this ca-pacity, it must be replaced. The size of urban central offices, on the other hand, is limited primarily by the calling rate of the users. If the calling rate is low, some DCOs can support 100,000 lines or more, but with a high calling rate, the central processor or the switching network limits the capacity to fewer lines. As processing power continues to grow, central office switching capacity will grow with it. DCOs in operation today can handle more than 1,000,000 busy hour call attempts. Note that busy hour call attempts does not refer simply to the number of completed calls per line. Anytime a line requires the processor's attention, such as initiating a call transfer or activating other enhanced services, it represents one or more busy hour call attempts.

Switching systems are enclosed in cabinets or mounted in relay racks. CDOs tend to be housed in cabinets, and larger central offices are often rack mounted. Since DCOs operate at high frequencies, electromagnetic radiation must be controlled, so all components that radiate are enclosed in shielded cabinets. A small system can be installed with little labor, although skilled personnel and special equipment are required to install and test the system. The interconnecting circuits in cabinet systems are prewired, and installation involves cabling the system to protector and distributing frames and to power and alarm equipment. Figure 9–1 shows the major components of a DCO.

Distributed Processing

The earliest SPC switches used a central processor for all call-processing functions. With the advent of high-powered microprocessors, many SPC systems now use distributed processing, in which a central processor links to distributed microprocessors over a data bus. The central processor controls the primary call-processing functions, such as marking a path through the switching network. Processors or service circuits located in the line switch units control such functions as line scanning, digit reception, ringing, and supervision, which require no access to the system's database.

DCOs must process packet-oriented data required by ISDN and signaling system 7 (SS7). Also, some DCOs are capable of supporting frame relay and X.25 packet switching. These functions are typically assigned to a peripheral processor that is bus-connected to the main processor.

SPC Central Office Memory Units

DCOs require three types of memory. The *generic program* provided by the manufacturer is common to all switching systems of the same type. It resides in *program store memory* and directs call processing. *Parameters* also reside in a program store database and are unique to the particular central office. The generic program uses parameters to find the quantities and addresses of peripheral equipment. Parameters are developed when the office is engineered and remain constant until the office is reengineered.

The second type of memory is the *data store,* which contains *translations.* Translations are unique to the office and are input by the system administrator to enable the generic program to identify working lines and trunks, to determine the features associated with lines and trunks, and to provide trunk-routing information for interoffice calls. Each line is assigned a record in the line translation memory. The line translation includes information about each user such as the following:

◆ Class of service—one-party, two-party, or four-party PBX Centrex, and so on.
◆ Telephone number associated with the line.
◆ Optional features such as call waiting, call forwarding, three-way calling, and DTMF.
◆ Status of the line—working, temporarily disconnected, out of service, and so on.

FIGURE 9-1

Major Components of a Digital Central Office

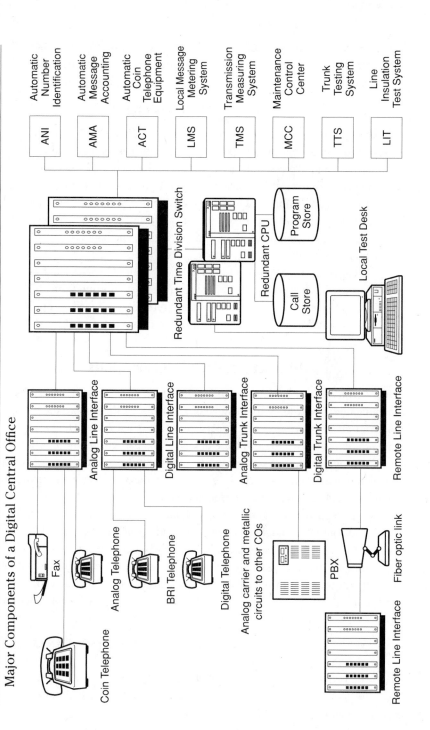

Trunk translations identify signaling and terminating characteristics of the trunk such as:

◆ Method of pulsing—dial pulse or multifrequency.
◆ Terminating office identity.
◆ Type of signaling on trunk—loop, E & M, and so on.
◆ Use of trunk—local, toll, service circuit, and so on.

The third type of memory is the *call store,* which is temporary memory the program uses to store details of calls in progress. Temporary memory is also used to store *recent change* information, which is line and trunk translations that have been added to the system but have not yet been merged with the semipermanent database.

Redundancy

Redundancy of critical circuit elements in the switching system provides local DCOs with reliability in the order of one hour's outage in 20 years of operation. This is not to imply that individual users experience that degree of reliability, because component and local loop failures can interrupt individual lines.

All local DCOs have duplicate central processors. In addition, other circuit elements that can cause significant outage, such as scanners and signal distributors, are duplicated. Redundant switching networks are usually provided in digital systems. In analog systems, the high cost and low probability of total network failure make redundant switching networks unnecessary. Other than network redundancy, the degree of duplication is similar in digital and analog systems.

Redundancy is provided on one of three bases:

◆ *Shared load* redundancy provides identical elements that divide the total load. When one element fails, the others can support service to all users, but during heavy loads a lower grade of service may be provided.
◆ With *synchronous* redundancy, both regular and duplicate elements perform the same functions in synchronism with each other, but only one element is on line. If the on-line element fails, the standby unit accepts the load with no loss of service. Either unit can carry the entire office load alone.
◆ With *hot standby* redundancy, one unit is on-line with the other waiting with power applied, but in an idle condition. When the regular unit fails, the standby unit switches on line with a momentary interruption.

The critical service considerations in evaluating redundancy are the degree to which the system diagnoses its own problems and initiates a transfer to standby, and the degree to which a transfer results in loss of service. With the first two forms of redundancy, little or no detriment to in-progress calls should be experienced. With the third form of redundancy, calls in progress are usually unaffected by a failure, but calls being established are often lost and must be redialed. When calls in progress are lost, many immediate reattempts can be expected, with the possibility of temporary processor overload.

Maintenance and Administrative Features

DCOs include many features to monitor the system's health from a local maintenance control center (MCC) or from a remote location. These features enable the system to respond automatically to abnormal conditions. These features can be classified as fault detection and correction, essential service and overload control, trunk and line maintenance features, configuration management, and database integrity checks.

Fault Detection and Correction

The central processor continually monitors all peripheral equipment to detect irregularities. When a peripheral fails to respond correctly, the processor signals an alarm condition to the MCC and switches to a duplicated element if one is provided. The MCC interfaces maintenance personnel to the fault-detecting routines of the generic program. At the MCC, the central processor communicates its actions with messages on a CRT, a printer, or both. Depending on the degree of sophistication in the program, the system may register the fault indication or may narrow the source of the fault down to a list of suspected circuit cards. For unattended operation the MCC transmits fault information to a control center over a data link.

The processor also monitors its own operation through built-in diagnostic routines. If it detects irregularities, the on-line processor calls in the standby and goes off-line. All such actions to obtain a working configuration of equipment can be initiated manually from the MCC or from a remote center. The ultimate maintenance action, which can be caused by an inadvertently damaged database or a program loop, is a restart or initialization. Initialization of the system is usually done only manually because it involves total loss of calls in progress and loss of recent change information.

Essential Service and Overload Control

Switching systems are designed for traffic loads that occur on the busiest normal business days of the year. Occasionally, peaks higher than normal yearly peaks occur. Heavy calling loads can occur during unusual storms, political disorders, and other catastrophes. During these peaks, the switching system may be overloaded to the point that service is delayed or denied to large numbers of users. Central offices include *line load control* circuitry that makes it possible to deny service to nonessential users so that essential users such as public safety and government employees can continue to place calls. Nonessential users are assigned to two groups. When line load control operates, one group is denied service while the other group is permitted to dial. The two groups are periodically reversed to give equal access to both groups.

Central offices also may be equipped with features that control overloads in the trunk network. These features are discussed in Chapter 10.

Trunk Maintenance Features

Local central offices have varying degrees of trunk maintenance capability. The system monitors trunk connections in progress to detect momentary interruptions or failures to connect. For example, if a trunk fails during outpulsing, the unexpected off-hook from the far end causes dialing to abort. The system registers the failure and enters it on a trunk irregularity report, which technicians use to pattern trunk trouble. The system marks defective trunks out of service and lists them on a trunk out-of-service list. When all trunks in a carrier system fail, the system detects a carrier group alarm, marks the trunks out of service in memory, and through its alarm system reports the failure to the MCC.

DCOs also include apparatus for off-line trunk diagnosis. Trunk test systems, which Chapter 10 discusses, interface with distant central offices to measure transmission performance and to check trunk supervision.

Line Maintenance Features

Switching systems contain circuits to detect irregularities in station equipment and outside plant. Like trunk tests, these are made on a routine or per-call basis. On each call, many systems monitor the line for excessive external voltage (foreign EMF), which suggests cable trouble.

Line insulation tests (LIT) are made routinely during low usage periods to detect incipient trouble. The LIT progresses through lines in the office on a preprogrammed basis and measures them for foreign voltage or low insulation resistance, which is low resistance between tip and ring or from each side of the pair to ground. These tests detect outside plant troubles such as wet cable, and terminal, drop wire, and protector problems.

Most local switching systems can deal with permanent signals, which are caused by a telephone off hook, cable trouble, or a defective station protector. Any of these irregularities places a short circuit on the line, and the line circuit attaches the line to a register, which furnishes dial tone and prepares to accept digits. If the central office could not protect itself, all its common equipment could become tied up with a single case of cable trouble, and other users would be blocked. Common control and SPS offices, therefore, have the capability of dealing with permanent signals. First, the line is disconnected from the register and connected to a permanent signal holding trunk. Then the line is connected to a series of tones and recordings such as a recording that asks the caller to hang up the line. Then after a suitable interval it may be connected to a progressively louder series of tones to attract the caller's attention. These are of no value during cable trouble, but identifying the lines connected to permanent signal holding trunks helps maintenance forces find which cable count is defective. Then the heat coils (see Chapter 6) can be removed to disconnect the cable from the central office until the fault is corrected.

Configuration Management

Portions of the central office configuration remain static until it is upgraded with additional circuit pack slots. When the office is upgraded the configuration management system modifies the parameters to inform the switch of the presence of new equipment. Daily service order activity modifies the software to add new subscribers, delete disconnected ones, or change features. The configuration management system enables technicians to enter order activity through a terminal or through a file transfer.

As discussed later, the system samples call activity and reports traffic information such as call counts, call completions, and line, trunk, and feature usage. The system monitors CPU activity and reports grade-of-service measurements such as dial tone delay and common equipment usage.

Database Integrity

Changes to a switching system's database of line, trunk, and parameter translations are made only after checks to ensure the accuracy of the input record and to assure that existing records will not be damaged. Update of the database may be allowed only from authorized input devices, and then limited with password control to ensure that only qualified personnel may access the files. A copy of the database also may be kept off-line in disk storage so it can be reinserted if the primary file is damaged or destroyed. The manner of assuring database integrity varies with the manufacturer and is an important consideration in evaluating local switching systems.

Line Equipment Features

Line switch frames in DCOs are constructed modularly with several line cards concentrated into a smaller number of links to the switching network. The ratio of lines to links is the *concentration ratio* of the office. Two different architectures are employed in the line interface, as Figure 9–2 shows. In the coder/decoder (*codec*) per-line architecture, each line card contains a separate analog-to-digital converter. The 64 kb/s bit streams from multiple cards combine in a multiplexer into a high-speed bit stream and route to the switching matrix. In the shared-codec architecture, the output of the analog line circuits is switched to a group of shared codecs. The former method, while more expensive, reduces the service impact of a single codec failure. The line card also provides testing access to the local test desk through a relay that transfers the cable pair to a testing circuit.

Line cards are produced in different varieties to provide features required by special types of subscriber equipment. The simplest card provides POTS (plain old telephone service) features to 2500-type telephone sets. Business-class line cards provide features for ground-start (see Chapter 11) and coin signaling. DCOs equipped for digital Centrex (Chapter 25) require digital line cards that communicate with proprietary telephone sets. Message-waiting line cards are available to light lamps on telephones associated with LEC-provided voice mail. DCOs offering ISDN service (Chapter 28) require line cards supporting T and U basic rate interfaces.

Transmission Performance

Because every line circuit in a digital switching system contains a hybrid circuit, line circuit balance is of particular importance in a DCO. The variability of outside cable plant makes it difficult to design an economical line circuit to balance a wide range of cable pairs. Some manufacturers compensate by designing loss into the line circuit hybrid. The addition of loss to the line circuit is undesirable because it degrades transmission performance.

Distributed Switching

Planning for service expansion is a difficult proposition in fast-growing areas. New business or residential developments can spring up rapidly, putting a strain on switching and outside plant facilities. Instead of bringing the lines to the central office with more copper or fiber outside plant facilities, it is often more economical to move the front end of the switch to the users. Most DCOs are capable of remote switching. As most line switches have a concentration ratio of four or more to one, distributed switching reduces the number of circuits needed between the central office and the users. Use of a remote line switch reduces the need for range extension and gain devices because the line circuit is moved close to the user and linked to the central office with low or zero loss trunks.

FIGURE 9-2

Digital Central Office Line Circuit Architecture

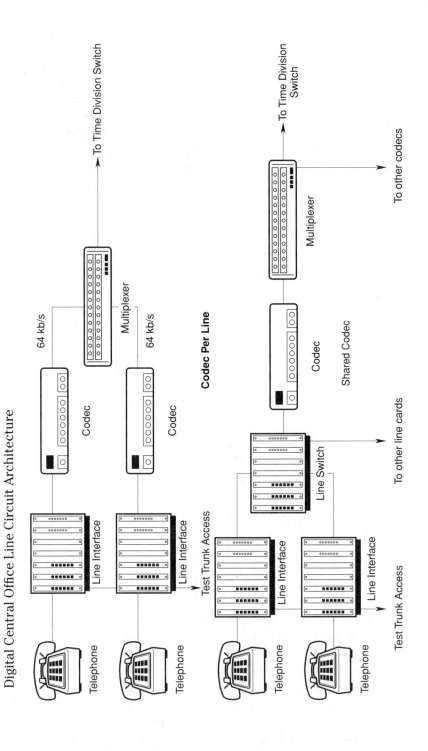

Remote switches can be located miles from the main switch, delivering up-to-date services to rural subscribers. LECs can replace obsolete electromechanical systems and offer services such as CLASS, ISDN, digital Centrex, and advanced intelligent networking without the cost of a total central office replacement.

Remote line equipment comes in two general forms, as illustrated in Figure 9–3. The first, a remote line switch, contains a switching matrix. Calls within the module are switched through an *intracalling* link. A single circuit to the central office sets up and supervises the connection. The second form, a *remote line module,* contains no intracalling features. A call between two stations within the module requires two central office links. If the *umbilical,* or data link, to the central office fails, calling within a remote line switch is still possible, but a remote line module can neither place nor receive calls without the umbilical.

Intracalling is essential for replacement of remote CDOs. In case of failure of the umbilical, local subscribers require service to each other, and must have access to local emergency services. Survivability of the remote is enhanced by using a SONET-based fiber-optic ring architecture between the host and the remote, as shown in Figure 9–3.

Subscriber carrier, as described in Chapter 6, also can interface digital central offices. Subscriber carrier differs from a remote line module in that carrier usually does not include concentration. The number of lines served at the remote location is equal to the number of trunks from the remote to the central office. Digital central offices can interface directly to digital subscriber carrier without using a central office terminal.

Trunk Equipment Features

DCOs provide both analog and digital trunk interfaces, although analog trunks are becoming rare. T-1 interfaces to other central offices and to customer premises are provided on DS-1 trunk interfaces. Both AMI and B8ZS interfaces are required (Chapter 5). DCOs supporting primary rate ISDN require trunk circuits and software to support PRI toward the station. Most DCOs support nonfacility associated signaling (NFAS), which permits one D channel to support multiple B channels. See Chapter 28 for more details on this feature, which is also known as nB+D, where n is the number of bearer channels supported by one D channel. Special trunks interface service circuits such as directory assistance, repair service, local test desk, and disconnected number intercept.

FIGURE 9–3

Digital Remote Line Equipment

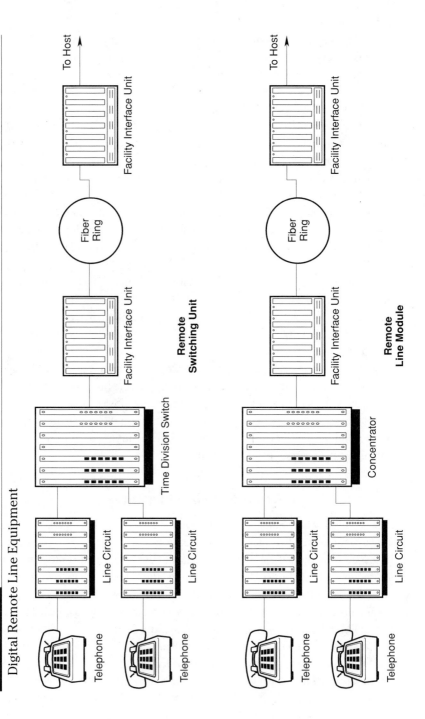

Trunk interface circuits must be capable of supporting multiple interoffice protocols including:

- *Feature Group A:* FGA is a line-side interface to IECs and subscribers. FGA is identical to any subscriber line except that usage is measured both originating and terminating.
- *Feature Group B:* FGB, discussed in Chapter 8, is a trunk-side interface to IECs and subscribers.
- *Feature Group D:* FGD is the equal access protocol discussed in Chapter 8. It permits subscribers to presubscribe to a particular IEC for all long-distance calls by dialing 1.
- *Signaling System 7:* SS7 is the out-of-band signaling protocol recommended by ITU and adopted by most LECs and IECs. SS7 provides interoffice signaling over a separate data network, as discussed in Chapter 11.
- *In-Band Signaling:* As discussed in Chapter 5, signaling between central offices and between the central office and subscribers using a T-1 interface may use bit-robbed signaling to exchange on-hook and off-hook signals.
- *D-Channel Signaling:* PRIs between the central office and subscribers exchange signals over the D channel, and provide full 64 kb/s bandwidth on the subscriber circuits.

Dialable Bandwidth

Services such as videoconferencing and medical imaging require more bandwidth than is available on the 64 kb/s circuits that central offices provide. This leads to a need for inverse multiplexing to combine multiple channels. Some ISDN-equipped DCOs provide the capability of $N \times 64$ service, which enables the user to dial the amount of bandwidth needed. This feature is the circuit-switched alternative to the variable bandwidth-on-demand provided by ATM switching. At the time of this writing most switching systems lack this capability, and most LECs have not begun to offer the service, but, depending on the cost and availability of alternatives such as ATM and SMDS, the service may become more widely available.

LOCAL CENTRAL OFFICE EQUIPMENT FEATURES

Local central offices contain peripheral equipment units that facilitate maintenance and special software features. The most significant of these features are listed below.

Alarm and Trouble Indicating Systems

As central offices have progressed, alarm systems have evolved from simple visual and audible alarms to systems that include internal diagnostics. In early switching systems, technicians located trouble by alarm lights on the ends of equipment frames and on the individual equipment shelf. Crossbar offices punch alarm indications into trouble cards that provide information on the status of the circuits in use when an alarm occurs.

SPC offices have internal diagnostic capability; the degree of sophistication varies with the manufacturer. In addition to audible alarms and aisle pilots, trouble indications register on the maintenance console and can be printed. Alarms also can be sent to remote surveillance centers. The console operator sends orders to the system to transfer to backup equipment, make circuits busy, and perform other actions designed to diagnose trouble or obtain a working configuration of equipment. Some systems carry the diagnostic capability to the level of directing which circuit card should be replaced to clear the trouble.

Automatic Number Identification (ANI)

ANI automatically identifies the calling party for billing purposes. Single-party lines are identified from their line circuit. In electronic offices this is a table lookup function. In electromechanical offices, separate equipment translates the billed telephone number from the line equipment. On two-party lines the ANI equipment decides which party to bill by determining whether the station ringer is wired from the tip or the ring of the line to ground. ANI should not be confused with calling line identification (CLID). The difference is explained later.

Automatic Message Accounting (AMA)

Automatic message accounting (AMA) equipment interrogates ANI equipment to determine the identity of the calling party. Where automatic identification is not provided, as with most four-party lines, the switching system bridges an operator on the line to receive the calling party's number and key it into the AMA equipment.

AMA equipment is classified as local AMA (LAMA), in which call collection is done in the local central office, or centralized AMA (CAMA). A CAMA office connects calling subscribers to a center where call details are recorded for all subtending central offices. AMA equipment records call details at each stage of a connection. The calling and called party numbers are registered initially. An answer entry registers the time of connection, and the terminating entry registers the time of disconnect. These entries are linked by a common identifying number to distinguish them from other calls on the storage medium.

The storage medium is tape, disk, or solid-state memory. Call records are sent to distant data-processing centers over a data link or dial-up connection, or AMA circuits may be polled from the remote processing center. AMA equipment also registers local measured service billing details, sometimes called local call detail recording (LCDR).

Coin Telephone Interface

As described in Chapter 19, private organizations own coin telephones in most states, in which case the telephone itself may provide all coin functions. In LEC-owned coin telephones, central office equipment is required to control the flow of coins. Three classes of coin operation are in use in the United States today:

- ◆ *Dial Tone First.* This class offers dial tone to the user without a coin so calls can be placed to operators and emergency numbers. When a call is placed to a chargeable number without coin deposit the central office signals the user that coins are required to complete the call.
- ◆ *Prepay or Coin First.* This class requires a coin deposit before dial tone is supplied. Calls to the operator and emergency numbers require a coin, which returns after the call is completed. Prepay is largely obsolete because of its inability to handle emergency calls.
- ◆ *Postpay.* The central office supplies dial tone to the phone, and a call can be placed to any number without a coin. However, a coin must be deposited before the parties can talk. This system, which is disappearing in the United States, is used in other countries.

Coin telephones are assigned to a separate class of service that provides access to special coin trunks. The coin trunk supports one of three classes of coin operation. Its function is to send coin collect and return signals to operate relays in the telephone to route the coin to the collection box or to the return chute. In an SPC office, the processor controls the coin trunk; in an electromechanical office, the coin trunk contains the logic to supply dial tone and to collect and return coins.

For long-distance calls the coin interacts with the operator or automatic coin equipment to transmit tones corresponding to the value of the coins deposited. The operator controls the collecting and refunding of coins with switchboard keys that control the coin trunk. This gives the operator the ability to collect coins before the call is placed and to refund them if the call is not completed. This is done by holding the coins in the coin phone and collecting them only when the called party answers.

COMMON EQUIPMENT

Chapter 12 discusses equipment common to all types of central office equipment. This section describes how common equipment items provide external interfaces for the central office.

Power Equipment

Power equipment consists of a commercial AC entrance facility, a backup emergency generator, a -48 volt DC storage battery string, and battery-charging equipment. Emergency generators are provided in all metropolitan central offices. CDOs may be wired with an external plug to couple to a portable generator. In either case, the battery string has sufficient capacity to operate the office until emergency power can assume the load during a power failure.

The switching system connects to the battery plant with heavy copper or aluminum bus bars. Where higher voltages are required, separate battery strings are provided in some offices, but in most applications DC converters raise the battery voltage to the higher voltage required by the equipment.

Trunks, subscriber lines, loop electronic equipment, and other central office equipment are wired to terminal strips mounted on protection and distributing frames. Distributing frames provide access points to the transmission and signaling leads and are used for flexible assignment of equipment to user services and to trunks. Equipment is interconnected by running crossconnects between terminals.

Local Measured Service (LMS)

Many telephone companies base their local service rates on usage. Flat-rate calling is often available, with LMS as an optional service class. With the LMS class of service, calls inside the local calling area are billed by number of calls, time of day, duration of call, and distance between parties. The method is similar to long-distance billing except that calls may be bulk-billed with no individual call detail.

Traffic Measuring Equipment

All central offices are engineered based on usage. Usage information is based on the number of times a trunk or line circuit is seized and the average holding time of each attempt. This information is collected by attaching two software registers to the equipment—one that measures the number of times the circuit is seized and one that measures elapsed time that the circuit is busy. Chapter 35 discusses the method of evaluating this information. The registers are periodically unloaded to a processing center for summary and analysis.

Most electromechanical central offices also provide dial tone speed registers, which are devices that attach to line circuits, periodically go off-hook, and measure the number of times dial tone is delayed more than three seconds. Dial tone speed is an important measure of the quality of local switching service.

Traffic measuring equipment can provide a variety of other data for administering the central office. For example, database statistical information is provided to update the availability of vacant lines and trunks. Point-to-point data collection enables the system administrator to detect the calling pattern of various subscriber lines to improve the utilization of the network by reassigning lines to different network terminations.

Subscriber line usage (SLU) measurements enable the administrator to distribute heavy usage lines among different terminations on the line switch frame to avoid overloading the line switch with several heavy users. The system makes service measurements to determine key indicators such as incoming matching loss (IML), which is the failure of an incoming call to obtain an idle path through the network to the terminating location.

Network Management

Many local offices have network management provisions to prevent overloads. For example, *dynamic overload control* automatically changes routing tables to reroute traffic when the primary route is overloaded. *Code conversion* allows the system to block traffic temporarily to a congested central office code. This feature enables the blocked system to take recovery action without being overwhelmed by ineffective attempts from a distant central office.

THE ADVANCED INTELLIGENT NETWORK (AIN)

LECs have long been hampered by the inability to react quickly to customer demands for specialized services. Until AIN the switching services the LECs offered were restricted to those provided by the particular central office manufacturer. If a LEC uses central offices from more than one manufacturer, the service offerings are not uniform across the serving area, but instead are confined to those offered in the wire center. New service offerings require the switching system manufacturer to upgrade the generic program, which may be unacceptable in this day of fast-moving competition.

AIN is a strategy conceived to assist LECs in being more competitive by controlling how and when they deploy new service offerings. With AIN the LEC can design and develop its own service offerings across multiple manufacturer switching platforms. AIN can be conceived as similar to computer-telephony integration (CTI) offered by most PBX manufacturers. The switching system offers an interface that provides information and accepts instructions from an outboard computer. The features can be provided via data link from a central point to all compliant switches in the LEC's network.

LOCAL CENTRAL OFFICE SERVICE FEATURES

Local central offices provide a variety of service features that enhance call processing. In SPC offices, these are provided primarily by software. The following is a brief description of the principal features provided by most electronic end offices.

Call-Processing Features

Call-processing features allow the customer to recall the central office equipment by a momentary on-hook flash. The system responds with stutter dial tone to show that it is ready to receive the information. Each of these features is optional to the user, generally at extra cost. Many call-processing features that once were reserved for business use are now becoming popular with residential subscribers. As residential users increasingly subscribe to second lines and custom-calling features, such services as call pickup and do-not-disturb are becoming popular. In addition, the following features are supported by most switching systems, although not necessarily offered by all LECs.

Three-way calling is a feature that allows the user to add a third party to the conversation by momentarily holding the first party while a third number is dialed. *Call transfer* is a similar feature that is exactly like three-way calling except one party can hang up, leaving the other two parties in conversation.

If a line equipped with *call waiting* is busy, the switching system sends a tone to signal that another call is waiting. The user can place the original call on hold and talk to the waiting call by pressing the switch hook. Most LECs offer a *cancel call waiting* feature that enables users to disable the service temporarily. This feature is important to anyone who uses a dial-up modem and wants to avoid having a modem call interrupted by call waiting.

Speed calling is different from the other features in that a switch hook flash is not used. This feature gives the user the ability to dial other numbers with a one- or two-digit number.

Call blocking enables subscribers to prevent long-distance or other billed calls from being completed from their line.

Call forwarding enables the user to forward incoming calls to another telephone number. While this feature is activated, calls to the user's number route automatically to an alternative telephone number. When the user of a forwarded line picks up the telephone, the system sends stutter dial tone to show the forwarded status of the line. *Call forward remote access* enables the user to activate or deactivate call forwarding from a remote location.

Distinctive ringing allows the LEC to assign as many as four separate directory numbers to a single line. Using an adapter that responds to the unique ringing pattern, as discussed in Chapter 19, the user can route calls to a separate telephone, fax machine, modem, or other analog device.

Gab line is a feature that enables callers to dial a number to which multiple callers can be simultaneously connected. Some LECs use the gab line, which is popular with teenagers, as a revenue-generating feature.

Custom Local Area Signaling Services (CLASS)

Most LECs offer a suite of services known as Custom Local Area Signaling Services (CLASS). CLASS services bring to residence and small business users features that are available in most PBXs. These additional features improve the service for the users and, in turn, generate more revenue for the LECs. Most CLASS features depend on SS7 for communication between central offices, and others will become available only through ISDN. The LECs have not fully deployed SS7, so CLASS features are not available from all central offices. Some of the services require special telephone sets or external adapters to use them. The following discusses the principal CLASS features that are defined to date. Additional services will undoubtedly be defined in the future.

Anonymous Caller Rejection   This feature allows the subscriber to reject calls from callers who have blocked identification of their telephone number.

Automatic Callback   When activated by a caller who has reached a busy line, the central office lets the subscriber know when the called line is available, and automatically redials the called number unless canceled by the caller.

Automatic Recall   This feature enables a called party to initiate a call to the number from which the last call arrived, which lets the caller return a missed call. The central office announces the call before completion of call setup so the called party can decide whether to continue with the call or drop it.

Calling Line Identification (CLID)   This feature delivers the calling number to the called party. The number can be displayed on a special telephone set, or it can be linked to a database in a computer to give the call certain treatment before it is delivered to the called telephone. For example, the calling number could be used to retrieve a customer record from the database before sending the call to an agent position behind an automatic call distributor. This feature has been subjected to court challenge based on the contention that it is an invasion of privacy. The issue has been resolved in most jurisdictions by allowing per-call blocking, which suppresses CLID if a Suppression code is dialed.

Calling Number Identification Blocking   This feature enables a calling party to block transmission of calling party identification. Blocking can be implemented on a per-call or per-line basis.

Customer-Originated Trace   With this feature the called party can initiate a trace on the last call placed. The service is useful for tracing harassing or obscene calls. The calling number is not delivered to the customer, but is entered on a log at the LEC or a law enforcement agency.

Distinctive Ringing/Call Waiting   This feature enables a user to enter a list of numbers, calls from which are to be announced with a special ringing tone. If the user subscribes to call waiting, the call waiting tone is also distinctive.

Ring Again   This service allows station users who encounter a busy signal to request the network to alert them when the busy station becomes idle and to place the call automatically. When callers encounter a busy, if they flash the switch hook, the central office returns a special dial tone. The caller dials the ring again code and can then use the telephone normally. When the called party hangs up, the central office signals the caller with a ring again signal. If the caller picks up the handset, the central office places the call. This feature is not only a convenience to the user, it also reduces the load on the central office from users who repeatedly dial against a busy number.

Selective Call Acceptance   This feature enables users to enter a list of numbers from which calls will be accepted. Calls from numbers not on the list route to an announcement and are rejected.

Selective Call Forwarding   This feature enables users to enter a call screening list in the central office. Only calls from stations on the list are forwarded to another number. Calls from stations not on the list ring at the dialed number.

Selective Call Rejection   Users of this feature can enter directory numbers into a screening list. Calls from these stations will be routed to an announcement that states that the called party is not accepting calls. Calls from other stations will be routed through normally.

Signaling Systems and Calling Line Identification

Calling line identification (CLID) is often confused with automatic number identification (ANI). The difference between the two is rooted in how signaling is handled in local central offices. This section discusses the differences between the two and explains when the delivered number may be identical in either case. The distinction is important to anyone who plans to capture calling numbers, whether for personal purposes or for business purposes such as routing calls in a call center.

Automatic number identification identifies the originating party's billing number. The ANI process sends the calling party's billing telephone number from the originating central office to the IEC, or retains it if the LEC is billing the call. The purpose of ANI is to bill long-distance calls. The IEC may deliver it to the called party for identification, but that is not its primary purpose. The ANI number may be the directory number of the line that originates a call, but often the ANI is another number assigned for billing purposes. This is often the case with large businesses that have all charges billed to a single telephone number. The same business may have numerous trunks, each of which the LEC sends to the IEC as calling line identification. If the call comes from a PBX equipped with ISDN trunks, the station number may show as the CLID if the PBX is programmed to send station numbers to the central office, and if the central office is programmed to send it forward.

IECs forward ANI to some accounts if the customer asks for, and sometimes pays extra for the service. This feature enables the customer to use ANI for such purposes as synchronizing a computer screen from the database with an incoming call. Originating callers can block CLID in most jurisdictions, but they cannot prevent the IEC from forwarding the ANI over an 800/888 trunk to the called subscriber.

Signaling methods are different for ANI and CLID. The LEC can pass ANI to the IEC via in-band signaling over trunks that use multifrequency signaling. (See Chapter 11 for a discussion of signaling). They can also pass ANI over an SS7 data link. CLID is passed between LEC offices only by SS7 technology. It identifies the calling line's directory number, which may be the same as the billing number. The two numbers are usually the same for single-line residences but different for multiline businesses. An SS7-equipped central office retains the CLID of both the originator and terminating party for later use if either party initiates subsequent calls between them using the special CLASS features. CLID is not used for billing.

CLID is usually not transmitted beyond LATA boundaries. It is transmitted on most calls carried on the LEC's network. Where SS7 signaling has not been installed, CLID is not transmitted because it is not sent over multifrequency trunks. In some cases LECs' central offices are connected via SS7, and they have agreed to carry CLID between companies. For CLID to work reliably, the LECs must have made specific arrangements. LECs that are equipped for SS7 usually forward CLID to the IECs, but the IECs often do not forward CLID even through the call terminates in the same LATA.

Voice Messaging Services

Most LECs offer centralized voice-messaging service to their subscribers. Central-office-provided voice mail provides similar features to stand-alone voice mail offered by service bureaus. Message waiting is indicated by either message-waiting lamps or stutter dial tone. With stutter dial tone indication, if a message is waiting the subscriber hears a burst of interrupted dial tone upon lifting the hand set. Calls can cover to voice mail on busy, no answer, or call forward.

Voice messaging services can include services such as automated attendant and interactive voice response (IVR). Fax messaging, fax-on-demand, and fax overflow (calls to a busy fax number) services are also available in central-office-based messaging services.

Centrex Features

Centrex is a PBX-like service furnished by telephone companies through equipment located in the central office (see Chapter 25). Usually the switching equipment is a partition in the end office called a *Centrex common block*. Centrex features allow direct inward dialing (DID) to a telephone number and direct outward dialing (DOD) from a number. For calls into the Centrex, the service is equivalent to individual line service. Outgoing calls differ from individual line service only in the requirement that an outgoing access code— usually 9—be dialed. Calls between stations in the Centrex group require four or five digits instead of the seven digits required for ordinary calls.

An attendant position located on the customer's premises is linked to the central office over a separate circuit. Centrex service provides PBX features without locating a switching system on the user's premises.

Emergency Reporting

In North America the code 911 is dedicated to fire, police, ambulance, and other emergency numbers. The local central office switches a 911 call over a dedicated group of trunks to a Public Safety Answering Point (PASP). Calls can be routed over the switched network to the PASP, but there is always a risk that calls will be blocked by normal telephone traffic, so dedicated lines are normally used. The PASP is staffed with personnel who have been trained in emergency call-handling procedures. Emergency centers can be classified as Basic 911 (B-911) or Enhanced 911 (E-911).

The telecommunications equipment in a B-911 center can be as simple as key telephone service, or calls can be delivered to an automatic call distributor (ACD). Emergency operators can be given features that enable them to trace calls and hold up a circuit to rering the calling party to obtain more information, but they cannot identify the caller. Almost all exchanges equipped for 911 provide coin-free dialing, which enables a caller to dial from a pay phone without a coin. The B-911 center also can force a disconnect on a 911 trunk that a caller is holding.

To provide calling party identification if E-911 service is used, the LEC or other bureau maintains a database of calling party information that is furnished to the PASP. Besides the originating telephone number, the database furnishes name and address, the address of the nearest emergency facility, and identification of which facility has emergency jurisdiction. Besides automatic number and location identification, E-911 provides selective routing, which, for overlapping jurisdictions, routes the call to the appropriate PASP.

Routing to Service Facilities

All central offices provide access to certain service facilities such as operator services and repair service bureau. All local switching systems also provide access to call progress tones—busy, reorder, vacant number tone, etc.—and recorded announcements for intercepted numbers and permanent signals. Some systems also provide access to local testing facilities.

Multiline Hunt

This feature, often called *rotary line group,* connects incoming calls to an idle line from a group of lines allocated to a user. In older central offices the numbers had to be in sequence; in electronic offices any group of numbers can be linked by software into a multiline hunt group.

Call Processing

Most DCOs use similar techniques for processing calls. The following is a short description of how calls typically are processed. The discussion assumes that the call originates and terminates in the same central office. The principal processing elements are:

◆ *Scanners,* which are circuits that detect changes in states of lines and trunks.

◆ *Signal distributors,* which transmit signals from scanners to call processing programs.

◆ *Registers,* which are circuits that furnish dial tone and accept and register dialed digits. Registers are normally dial pulse (rotary dial) or DTMF.

◆ *Generic program,* which is the call-processing instructions contained in the program store.

◆ *Call store,* which is the temporary scratch pad memory used to store the details of calls in progress.

◆ *Data store,* which stores the line translations.

◆ *Time slots,* which, in a digital switch, are units of time reserved for the parties to share during a session.

◆ *Network or switching fabric,* which contains the time slots to make connections between lines and trunks.

A call is initiated by the calling party's removing the receiver from the switch hook. A line scanner detects the change in the state of the line and sends a signal through a signal distributor to the generic program, which marks the line busy in call store memory and consults the data store about features and options available to the line. The processor marks a path through the network and reserves a time slot to a register.

The processor connects the line to a register and sends dial tone toward the line. The register receives tones or dial pulses and stores them in a call store register. The processor consults the data store about the address of the called number. It marks the called line and reserves two time slots through the network—one for the originating party and one for the terminating party.

The called number connects to a ringing source. The calling number is connected to an audible ringing source. The terminating line is monitored for ring trip, which is a short circuit on the line, indicating that the called party has answered.

When the called party answers, the ringing and audible ring signals are removed, and the two time slots that were previously reserved are linked through the network. The connection is supervised for an indication that either party has gone on-hook.

When either party hangs up, the processor restores the circuits, marks the time slots idle, and restores the call store registers. The line status is changed in memory from busy to idle, and the call is terminated.

Calls outside the same central office are handled similarly, except that two switching systems are involved. Chapter 11 explains how signals are exchanged between two central offices. During call processing, many events other than those described above may occur. One party may flash the switch hook, which recalls the processor to send a second dial tone and to be prepared for another process such as conferencing to occur.

APPLICATIONS

Digital central offices are used almost exclusively by local exchange and cellular companies, although a few have found their way into service as large PBXs. The selection of a digital switch is a complex process that depends on the maintenance strategies, service offerings, and cost objectives of the LECs. This section briefly describes the primary criteria used in selecting a DCO.

Standards

Few local switching system standards have been set by standards agencies. Subscriber line and trunk interface standards are published by EIA; the bulk of DCO performance criteria is a matter of matching the manufacturer's specifications to the user's requirements. Bell Communications Research (Bellcore) publishes a comprehensive list of requirements on behalf of the seven Bell regional operating companies. This publication, *Local Switching System General Requirements* (LSSGR), defines the features and technical specifications required of local central offices used by the Bell regions. LSSGR is not a standard; compliance by manufacturers is voluntary, but it is the most comprehensive publication available for local central office operation. The FCC specifies emission requirements in Part 15, Subpart J of its rules.

Grounding requirements are specified in Bellcore Technical Reference on Ground Arrangements, TR-EOP-00295. Most DCOs use a system ground that is isolated from the frame ground. Ground integrity is essential to system operation and for signaling.

EVALUATING DIGITAL SWITCHING SYSTEMS

The primary criteria in evaluating a DCO are cost, features, compatibility, maintenance features, and the ability of the office to provide the desired grade of service. The complexity of a DCO makes the provision of maintenance features particularly important. The following is a list of the primary DCO evaluation criteria:

Maintenance Features and Reliability

DCOs should be designed to provide a high degree of reliability with duplicated critical circuit elements and high-grade components. All processors should be duplicated, preferably on a synchronous basis. The processor should be capable of full self-diagnosis. In case of overload, automatic recovery, including discontinuing nonessential call-processing operations if necessary, is essential.

The system should be operable from a remote location except for changing defective circuit cards and running crossconnects. Manufacturers should provide an on-line technical assistance center to aid in solving unusual maintenance conditions.

The system should be fully documented with maintenance practices, trouble-locating manuals, software operation manuals, office-wiring diagrams, and a complete listing of database information.

The system should provide an interface to a local test desk for diagnosing subscriber line troubles. It also should have a complete suite of trunk tests to aid maintenance forces in diagnosing and correcting trunk faults.

Training and Documentation

The manufacturer must provide a full line of courses designed to train the using organization in designing, engineering, maintaining, and administering the system. A full range of installation, maintenance, and operating practices are required for system operation.

Transmission Performance

The central office should insert no more than 1 dB of loss into a line-to-line and 0.5 dB into a line-to-trunk or trunk-to-trunk connection.

Line Concentration

The system should be capable of providing line concentration ratios to match the expected usage. Line concentration ratios as low as two-to-one may be required in heavy usage systems, with ratios as high as eight-to-one acceptable in low usage systems. Local switching systems are usually not designed to be nonblocking.

Environment

The system should operate under the temperature extremes that could occur with power, heating, or air-conditioning failure. The normal operating temperature range of most central office equipment is at least 10° to 30° C (50° to 80° F). The amount of heat dissipation determines the size of air-conditioning equipment required. Switching systems are also sensitive to relative humidity. They normally operate in a humidity range of 20 to 60 percent. Both temperature and humidity ranges are expressed as normal and short-term. Short-term means the equipment can operate under those conditions for specified periods of time. Short-term temperatures of 0° to 50° C (32° to 120° F) and humidity up to 80 percent are typical.

Earthquake Resistance

Survivability of any local switching system during earthquake conditions is essential; not only because of the expense of restoring damaged equipment, but also because the safety and well-being of the community depends on continued telecommunications service. Switching systems should be constructed and installed to meet the requirements of the seismic zone in which they are installed.

Multiclass Operation

A DCO should contain the software needed for all end office functions. In addition, some applications require tandem software. If the DCO is used as a PBX, it must include the PBX features described in Chapter 21. Of major significance in PBX use is the ability to interface a local end office through the line side rather than the trunk side of the system.

Remote Line Capability

A DCO should include remote line capability to minimize range extension and subscriber loop costs. The remote should contain intracalling capability when used in remote communities or a locale with a strong community of interest. The user will notice no difference in operation if a system lacks intracalling capability unless the link to the central office is severed. The DCO should also be capable of interfacing subscriber carrier at the T-1 level.

Capacity

The system should have the capacity to handle the traffic load for the expected life of the system. The system should also be capable of terminating the required number of lines and trunks. All central offices must have the capability of measuring and recording usage, whether with built-in or external equipment.

Conversion and Technical Support

Conversion to a new switching system is a major task that requires assistance from the manufacturer. Data from the old switch must be converted and loaded into the new. Technical assistance is required to engineer, install, and test the new system. Postinstallation support is needed from the manufacturer to assist with trouble diagnosis and emergency repair.

MANUFACTURERS OF LOCAL SWITCHING SYSTEMS

CIT-Alcatel Inc.

Ericsson, Inc. Communications Div.

Lucent Technologies

NEC America, Inc.

Northern Telecom, Inc.

Siemens/Stromberg Carlson Corporation

10

TANDEM SWITCHING
SYSTEMS

Common carriers and many private companies use tandem switching systems to build up long-distance connections by switching trunks together. Both local central offices and PBXs can be equipped to serve as tandem switches. If trunking requirements are light, the most economical way to switch trunks is through a PBX or an existing end office switch, but the market offers switching systems designed specifically for trunk-switching applications. These are the subject of this chapter.

The primary users of tandem trunk-switching systems are:

◆ LECs that use tandem switches for switching local interoffice trunks.
◆ LECs that use tandem switches to provide IEC access to the LATA. These are known as *LATA tandems.*
◆ Interexchange and resale carriers that use tandem switches inside their networks.
◆ Large government and business organizations that use tandem switches for private message and data networks.

The technologies used in these systems are similar; however, the size varies considerably from a few dozen trunks to systems equipped with more than 100,000 trunk terminations.

Long-haul trunk facilities are owned primarily by private carriers and furnished to end users as individual circuits, as bulk groups of circuits, or as bandwidth that can be channelized at the user's discretion. Some large organizations own private facilities, but the majority of users obtain long-haul facilities through common carrier tariffs.

TANDEM SWITCH TECHNOLOGY

Tandem switch architecture is similar to local digital switch architecture except that a tandem switch has few, if any, line terminations. Otherwise, the typical tandem has a nonblocking switching fabric controlled by central or distributed processors. Digital trunks terminate in digital interface frames that couple incoming T-1 or T-3 bit streams directly to the switching network. Peripheral equipment detects signaling, and the central processor sets up a path through the switching network from the incoming time slot to an outgoing time slot that it assigns to an outgoing digital channel. Calls that cannot be completed because of trunk congestion or invalid dialed digits route to a tone or recorded announcement trunk. The digital switch acts as a large time slot interchange device that, except for some delay, is transparent to the bit stream in the terminated circuits.

Power, alarm, and control circuits are similar to those discussed in Chapter 9. Maintenance and diagnostic circuits are important in tandem switches, which cannot tolerate extended failures because they account for significant amounts of revenue. All critical elements are fully duplicated to provide a high degree of reliability.

Most digital switches designed for the public telephone network are equipped for signaling system 7 (SS7), which is an ITU signaling standard. See Chapter 11 for a discussion of common channel signaling. The SS7 interface is a circuit that interprets incoming data messages and communicates them to the call processor. This out-of-band signaling method replaces the bit-robbed signaling built into T-carrier.

Figure 10–1 shows how a tandem switch fits into the circuit switching scheme. Circuit groups of different types connect to end offices. As discussed in Chapter 1, Feature Group A trunks offer line-side access to end offices. Interstate Feature Group A connections provide usage-sensitive access to all locations in the LATA through the LEC's network. FGA connections are similar to foreign exchange (FEX) except that usage is measured in both directions. Feature Group B connections offer trunk-side connections to the end office switch. Feature Group D (equal access) connections are technically similar to FGB except they are accessed through the LEC's office when the user dials 1. IECs use

FIGURE 10-1

IEC Tandem Switch Network

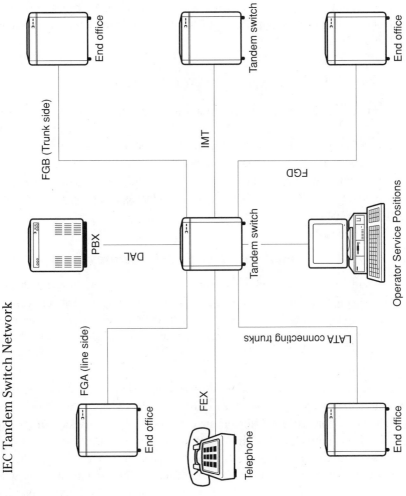

IMT= Intermachine trunk
DAL= Dedicated access line
FGA= Feature group A
FGB=Feature group B
FGD= Feature group D
        (Equal access)
FEX=Foreign exchange

LATA connecting trunks for direct access to the end office in lieu of connecting through a LATA tandem, which introduces call setup delay. Intermachine trunks (IMT) interconnect tandems. Finally, some tandem switches support operator service positions, which are used for providing call setup assistance.

Tandem switches offer two kinds of dedicated access lines (DALs) to their customers. Analog DALs are analog private lines from the customer's premises either directly to the tandem switch, or routed to an LEC end office where they are switched to the IEC. Analog lines are disappearing in favor of T-1 or T-3 facilities. Digital facilities are connected from the customer's premises to the tandem switch via LEC, alternate access carrier (AAC), or privately owned facilities such as microwave. The motivation for installing DALs is to bypass the LEC's local exchange facilities, reducing access charges.

TANDEM SWITCH FEATURES

Most tandem switching system features are implemented in software. Therefore, systems can be used in either public or private networks by changing the generic program. Although the architecture for private and public tandem switches is similar, feature differences between the two applications may be significant. In the discussion that follows, the features are segregated by public and private switch features, but depending on the generic program, the distinction between the two is not absolute.

Public Tandem Switch Features

Tandem switches for public telephone networks terminate large numbers of both analog and digital trunks. The primary features employed are discussed in the following sections. Private networks use some of these same features in private tandem switches as noted under the feature descriptions.

Routing
Public networks are designed to provide a high degree of facility utilization while still providing good service to customers. The competition for customers is intense among IECs. Customers are unlikely to tolerate blockage just to save a few cents on each call. Therefore, tandem switches must have the ability to sense overloads and reroute calls around congestion. Tandems should provide dynamic routing control to change their routing patterns automatically when congestion occurs. They also must provide circuit utilization information to enable administrators to change routing tables quickly to respond to changes in customer usage patterns.

TABLE 10–1

Trunk Maintenance Test Lines

Type	Function	Purpose
100	Balance	Provides off-hook supervision and terminates trunk in its characteristic impedance for balance and noise testing.
101	Communications	Provides talking path to a test position for communications and transmission tests.
102	Milliwatt	Provides a 1,004 Hz signal at 0 dBm for one-way loss measurements.
103	Supervision	Provides connection to signaling test circuit for testing trunk supervision.
104	Transmission	Provides termination and circuitry for two-way loss and one-way noise tests.
105	Automatic Transmission	Provides access to a responder to allow two-way loss and noise tests from an office equipped with a ROTL and responder.
107	Data Transmission	Provides access to a test circuit for one-way voice and data testing. Enables measurement of P/AR, gain/slope, C-notched noise, jitter, impulse noise, and various other circuit quality tests. See Chapter 37 for description of tests.

Testing Access

Because of their heavy reliance on trunk quality, all tandem switches require trunk test positions. Trunks are switched through the switching network to the test position for making continuity, transmission, and supervision tests. In a network of multiple tandem switches, technicians communicate between test positions by dialing a special access code, usually 101. This connects the two test positions so technicians can talk and test over the trunk. Several different codes are employed in the long-distance trunks of the IECs, LECs, and some private networks for testing, as Table 10–1 shows. These test lines can be used for both manual and automatic tests.

To test direct trunks between two offices automatically, computer-controlled test equipment dials a *remote office test line* (ROTL) over an IMT, as Figure 10–2 shows. The ROTL seizes an outgoing trunk and dials the test line number over the trunk. A *responder* at the distant office interacts with the ROTL and the responder at the near-end office to make two-way transmission, noise, and supervision measurements. The test system registers the test results, automatically takes defective trunks out of service at the switching system, and marks them for maintenance action.

FIGURE 10-2

Automatic Remote Testing System

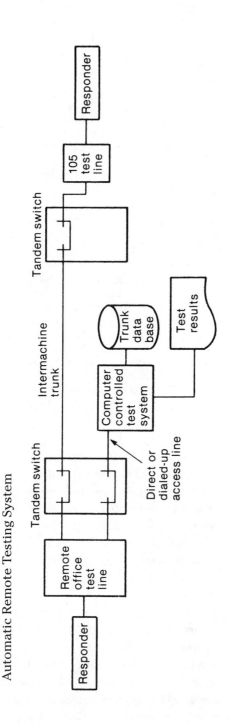

Signaling

Common channel switching is the rule for public toll tandem switching systems and is increasingly being employed on private systems. A common channel interface circuit connects between the processor and the data circuits that comprise the SS7 network. The switching systems select an idle path by exchanging data messages, test the path for continuity, and assign a path through all switches that are part of the connection. Chapter 11 discusses SS7 in more detail.

Operator Service Positions

Local exchange and interexchange carriers require operator service positions (OSPs) with some of their tandem switches. Most carriers that provide operator services centralize the function with one operator center serving multiple tandems. Therefore, an essential feature is the ability to support remote terminals. Operator service functions include intercept, directory assistance, and toll and assistance, which helps callers complete collect, third-number, and credit-card calls. Intercept is the function of assisting customers with calls to disconnected numbers. Directory assistance provides telephone number lookup for callers.

The objective of intercept systems is to complete as many calls as possible with an interactive voice response unit (IVR), which Chapter 24 discusses in more detail. IVR systems are used for essentially all intercept functions, where callers are informed of the new number if one exists. Some calls, such as those to numbers not yet in the database or where the caller remains on the line, must be completed manually. In these cases the system connects the call to an OSP. Directory assistance calls are handled by an operator who looks up the number, but transfers the caller to a voice announcement unit to read out the number.

Figure 10–3 shows the components of an OSP and a tandem switch system. Incoming and outgoing trunks terminate directly on the switching network or on analog trunk interfaces through channel banks. A central processor controls call processing. The system directly switches calls that do not require operator assistance. If the caller dials an assistance code, the processor routes the call through the switching network to the front end of the OSP, which is an automatic call distributor (ACD).

The ACD delivers calls to the appropriate position. The position controller receives calls from the ACD and supplies the circuitry to enable the operator to communicate with the various subsystems. Within limits, the larger the work group, the more efficiently positions can be staffed. The ACD delivers calls to operators in segregated groups that are called *splits*. During normal load conditions, the three types of calls—toll and assistance, intercept, and directory assistance—might constitute three splits. The ACD can be programmed to over-

F I G U R E   10–3

Components of a Tandem Switch and Operator Service System

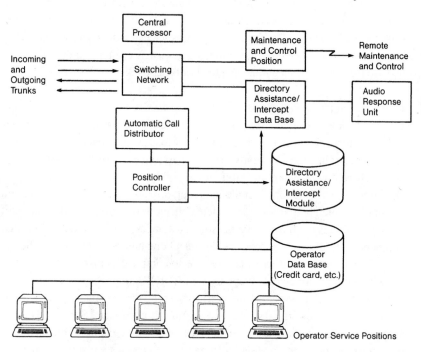

flow calls between splits when overloads occurred. During light load periods, the splits might be combined, with the ACD routing calls to a single set of OSPs. See Chapter 22 for further information on the functions and method of operation of an ACD.

User-Dialed Billing Arrangements

Special networks that register and verify charging information handle most coin and credit card calls. Credit-card calls are verified over a data link to a centralized database. The customer dials the desired number, then when signaled by the system, dials a credit-card number. The system sends a message to the database to verify the validity of the card number, after which it switches the call.

Coin calls are connected to a circuit that computes the rate, informs the user of the charge with a voice announcement unit, registers the values of the coins deposited, and connects the call. The equipment monitors the connect time and reconnects the voice announcement unit when the caller is required to make an additional coin deposit.

Operator service features include:

◆ *Center shutdown:* The operator service center should be able to close operations during certain periods of the day and transfer calls to another center.

◆ *Centralization:* The center should be able to provide operator service features for numerous tandem switches regardless of their location.

◆ *Interactive voice response:* The center should provide IVR to handle intercept calls, and should route calls to a live operator for user assistance.

◆ *Directory assistance:* The center should act as a directory assistance center, searching on such variables as phonetics, name and address, and key word.

Authorization Codes

Tandem switches provide authorization codes to identify subscribers, determine their class of service and features, and to collect call details by specific user within the subscriber's organization. Most carriers offer both verified and nonverified authorization codes. A verified authorization code is accepted by the switch only if it is listed in its database. This feature prevents unauthorized individuals from placing long-distance calls unless they happen upon a valid code. Most switches offer as many as seven digits for each authorization code, which makes it difficult to select a valid code by chance. An accounting code may also be required in addition to the authorization code. The system may also accept and verify bank cards and credit cards offered by the LECs and IECs. The authorization is handled by a data link to an external center.

A nonverified authorization code relies on the subscriber to assign code numbers; any valid digits will be accepted by the switch. Subscribers often use nonverified codes for such purposes as distributing costs among departments and to clients, but unlike verified codes, unverified codes do not offer security against unauthorized use. With either type of code the switch sends a tone to prompt the caller to enter the code. After an interval of unsuccessful or no attempts to enter the code, the switch terminates the call.

Virtual Networks

Some IECs offer virtual private networks to their customers, a service that requires support from the tandem switch. A virtual private network is one that operates as if it is composed of switched private lines, but that, in reality, is derived by shared use of the carrier's switched facilities. The database for a virtual private network is contained in a service control point (SCP), which is a computer connected to tandem switches by 64 kb/s data links. The switches in a virtual network are known as service switching points (SSPs). The concept is explained in more detail in Chapter 11 under SS7.

A virtual private network handles calls in three manners:

◆ Dedicated access line to dedicated access line.
◆ Dedicated access line to switched access line.
◆ Switched access line to switched access line.

A DAL-to-DAL call bypasses the LEC's access charges in both the originating and the terminating direction, reducing the cost significantly. The DAL-to-switched call is handled on a virtual private network the same way it is handled for a customer with conventional DAL service. The access charge is eliminated in the originating, but not the terminating direction. For switched-to-switched access line calls, the virtual private network handles calls like regular long-distance calls except for features and restrictions.

Virtual private networks also emulate many features of electronic tandem networks. For example, a reduced number of digits can be used to dial on-net stations. Virtual private networks offer a full restriction range such as blocking calls to overseas locations, selected area codes, central office codes, or even selected station numbers. If the virtual network is used in conjunction with account codes, calls can be restricted for certain station numbers. For example, a company could allow its accounting personnel to call the accounting department in another branch, but calls to all other numbers could be blocked.

Call Reorigination

This feature enables subscribers to place multiple calls through the network without redialing the carrier and reentering the authorization code. Manual call reorigination requires the caller to dial a digit such a * or # to place another call, after which dial tone is returned to the user, who can continue to dial calls. Automatic call reorigination returns dial tone automatically if the caller remains off hook after the called party hangs up.

Accounting Information

Tandem switches provide message accounting information to allocate communications costs to the users. This information is either provided in machine readable format for separate processing or processed by the carrier's accounting office to assemble completed message detail. IECs distinguish themselves by the type of billing information they provide, but billing is handled by an external accounting center. The switch's role is to provide the raw call details.

Network Management Control Center

Most tandem switching systems provide either a centralized or localized network management control center (NMCC) to administer service and performance on private and public networks. The center collects all network management information in a single location. Typical NMCC functions include:

◆ Manual and automatic testing of trunks using apparatus and techniques discussed above.

◆ Compilation and analysis of statistical information to determine loads and service levels and to determine when circuit types and quantities should be changed.

◆ System performance monitoring, including diagnostics and maintenance control of all system features and circuits.

◆ Alarm surveillance to detect and diagnose troubles and determine status of switching and trunking equipment.

◆ Performance and status logging to monitor and log system history, including records of trouble and out-of-service conditions.

Call Progress Toned and Recorded Announcements

Every tandem switch must be capable of inserting recorded announcements or tones to prompt callers on system usage or to inform them when the call has reached an unexpected termination. Callers are familiar with the most common progress tones such as busy, fast busy (reorder), dial tone, ringing, and ringback. Special tones such as queue tone and accounting code prompt tone are used in private systems, and users must be trained to use the feature.

Private Tandem Switching System Features

With the exception of the need for coin and operator services, private tandem switches require much the same feature set as public switches. Also, tandem switches provide other features unique to a private network. Many of these are the same as the PBX features described in Chapter 21. Circuit costs tend to drive the total network costs in a private system; therefore tandem switches make efficient use of circuit capacity. This section covers features that are generally included in switches that use all or a significant part of their capacity for tandem switching.

Queuing

Public networks are designed so that blockage occurs on 0.1 percent or fewer of the calls placed. When blockage occurs the call routes to a reorder trunk, and if the user wants to complete the call, he or she must redial. In a private network environment, circuit usage can be increased and costs controlled by queuing users for access to outgoing trunks. If calls always are backed up in the queue, trunk utilization can be increased during peak hours, but the feature must be used with care.

User dissatisfaction and lost productive time always result from queuing, so public networks, where the user can easily dial a competitor, do not use this technique. In private networks, however, the organization has control over the network and its users and may choose to pay the price of lost productive time by using queuing. An audible indication signals when the caller places a call in queue. Some systems use a tone, others a recorded announcement, and others use music in queue. Any network that employs queuing should collect statistical information to show the average length of queue, the number of calls abandoned from queue, and the average holding time in queue. This information indicates the number of productive hours that may be lost because of queuing.

Routing

Private tandem switches include least-cost routing features identical in concept to the LCR feature in PBXs, which Chapter 21 discusses. Other routing features are also available with most tandem switches and some PBXs. Code blocking prevents dialing certain digit combinations. With this feature an organization can block access to a given geographical area by blocking the area codes. This can be carried down to blocking individual terminating telephone numbers. For example, some organizations use this feature to block calls to 900 numbers, the cost of which is billed to the caller. The accounting information described in a later section can be sorted by called telephone number to identify heavily used numbers that might suggest abuse of communication services. Where abuse is found, the unauthorized number is blocked.

Another feature, code conversion, limits the number of digits a user must dial to make a connection. For example, a frequently-used number overseas or in another area code could be dialed with seven digits, and the call completed over either a tie line or IEC facilities. If the number completes over an IEC network, the switch appends the area code before forwarding the call. Calls off-net to an IEC over a Feature Group A connection may require dialing a PIN that differs from the user's on-net PIN. The users can dial their own PINs, but the switch dials the PIN required by the IEC.

Time-of-day routing allows the carrier or private system administrator to select facilities based on time of day or day of week. Each day of the year is classified as a weekday, Sunday, Saturday, or special day. The routing tables indicate which route to choose based on the schedules in the database.

Restrictions

Most systems optionally provide other methods of controlling costs. For example, some users may be denied the right to place overseas calls. Some users may be permitted to access a tie line network, but when a call is about to advance to a high-cost facility because lower-cost routes are full, a call warning tone sounds. The call will not route to the higher-cost facility until the user dials a positive action digit to instruct the system to proceed. When the call duration exceeds a threshold set in the user's file, a time warning signal can sound. These and other similar features are normally not available in public networks because the network owner has no interest in limiting usage.

Other features that are available for certain line classes include security blanking, which blanks the called telephone number on the billing record if the user wants to avoid leaving a record of calls to certain numbers. Some line classifications are given queuing priority to enable them to jump to the head of the queue when all circuits are busy. Most of these features are implemented in software and can therefore be provided for little or no cost, enabling an organization to customize a network to meet its individual needs.

Traveling Class Mark

Callers are assigned a class of service corresponding to the features and restrictions contained in the system's database. As a call advances through multiple switches, the class of service travels with the call so each switch in the chain recognizes the features to be accorded the call. This feature is called *traveling class mark.*

Remote Access

The remote access feature allows a user to dial a local telephone call to the tandem switch to complete long-distance calls over the private network. PIN identification is required to control unauthorized usage. Even with PIN control, security can be a problem with remote access. Many systems raise an alarm when they detect repeated attempts to dial with invalid PINs. It is advisable to deactivate this feature unless it is critical to company operations and is carefully policed.

Call Accounting

Tandem switches provide call details similar to the CDR in a PBX, as discussed in Chapter 21. Call details are forwarded to an outboard call accounting system where charges can be summarized by individual user, department, and accounting code, depending on the service class. For most effective communications cost control, calling habits can be analyzed and destinations evaluated to determine whether additional private trunks should be added to reduce overflow to more expensive common carrier circuits.

Network Statistical Information

Network administrators need information about calling patterns and habits to manage a network. They use information on the disposition of originating calls to size circuit groups and switching equipment. Most systems provide the following types of information:

◆ *Trunk information* for each trunk group on the network, including peak and average number of calls, holding time of calls, and number of ineffective attempts because of blockage, cutoff, or equipment trouble.

◆ *Queuing statistics,* including average and peak number of calls in queue, duration of calls in queue, and abandoned calls.

◆ *Service circuit statistics,* including number of attempts, holding time, and overflow to service circuits such as reorder, busy, and multifrequency receivers and senders.

The amount of statistical information collected from a system is apt to be overwhelming unless the system provides some form of analysis. Some tandem switches are linked to external processors that also can analyze usage information and recommend corrective action.

APPLICATIONS

Tandem switches find their primary applications in public networks. Large companies, which formerly used private tandem switches at the hubs of their private line networks, are finding the virtual network offerings of the IECs more attractive than their networks. The tandem function can be embedded in PBXs at major switching points of all but the largest users, which limits tandem switch applications in most private companies.

Standards

As with other types of switching systems, few standards are published with respect to tandem switching. Trunk interfaces in private network switches require FCC registration and must meet the standard technical interface information for compatibility. Most trunk connections are T-1 or T-3, standards that ITU and Bellcore publish. Operator service positions follow proprietary standards if they are provided at all.

Tandem Switch Evaluation Considerations

Most factors that are important for other switching systems are also important for tandem switches including reliability, capacity, compatibility of external interfaces, operational features, and internal diagnostic capability. This section covers the features that tandem switches include, primarily to control private network costs.

Queuing

Tandem switch manufacturers emphasize queue efficiency as an important way of improving circuit occupancy and controlling circuit costs. The method of handling calls during blocked circuit conditions is an important factor to evaluate in comparing tandem switches. Queuing can definitely increase circuit occupancy during busy periods, but the increase in efficiency must be evaluated. The time spent in queue is generally nonproductive and can easily outweigh the cost of the alternatives. Users may lose productivity while waiting in queue for calls to be completed. Also, the time required to administer the system is an expense that must be considered.

Three approaches can be used instead of queuing. The first is to return the call to reorder and force redialing. With a telephone that includes a last number redial feature, this approach is tolerable. The second approach is to increase the number of circuits. With adequate data from the queuing and circuit usage statistics, the cost of this option can easily be calculated. The third approach is to overflow to a higher-cost facility. IECs design their networks to a low blocking probability. Overflow to a common carrier is usually an effective way for network managers to limit delays.

Despite its hazards, queuing is an effective tool to use in managing a network. To be effective, a system should provide for variable queuing by class of service and time of day. The length of queue should be administratively variable. When a reasonable queue length is reached, additional callers should be turned back to avoid long queue holding times. The system should provide near real-time information about queue length so system administrators can take corrective action.

Network Management Control

An effective tandem switch should provide the tools needed to manage and control the network. The system should be equipped for unattended operation from a remote location. It should have complete flexibility in changing line classifications, restriction levels, trunk classifications, queuing parameters, and other factors that affect line and trunk administration. The system should provide real-time information about trunk status. Defective trunks should be removed from service and referred to the control center for corrective action.

The system should diagnose trunk performance automatically during light load periods. It should be equipped for transmission and supervision tests to distant tandem switches and, if permitted, to IEC and LEC responders. Direct access to individual circuits should be permitted for making transmission measurements and supervision.

A full range of statistical information should be available for evaluating service and for determining when trunk quantities should be adjusted. A method of automatically analyzing the raw statistical information should be included. The information should be formatted so the corrective action to be taken is apparent.

The system should diagnose its own troubles and direct technicians on what action to take, ideally to the point of specifying the circuit card to change. The manufacturer should provide remote diagnostic and technical assistance along with a method of keeping both hardware and software current with updates.

ISDN Compatibility

The system should be capable of supporting PRI. Basic rate is not supported on most tandem switches. The system should support ISDN features including calling line identification (CLID), call-by-call service selection, nonfacility associated signaling (NFAS), and network ring again.

Network Modeling

Networks are sized, as discussed in Chapter 35, by simulation or modeling techniques. If the vendor provides a simulation or modeling service to determine equipment and trunk quantities and to predict the effects of changes in load, tandem switch administration will be simplified. An effective tool should accept usage information from system-produced statistics and summaries of originating and terminating traffic to determine the most efficient use of equipment and facilities. The system also should accept cost information to find the best balance between options such as DALs, tie lines, and public switched networks.

Routing, Blocking, and Translations

A tandem switch should provide fully flexible routing to trunk groups based on class of service. It should have the capability of blocking area codes, central office codes, and line numbers. It also should filter calls so some users can complete calls only to selected codes. The system should block access to circuit groups to prevent unsuccessful attempts to access distant systems that are temporarily experiencing service difficulties. This capability allows the distant system to recover without being inundated with excessive call attempts. The system also should translate codes so users dial the same code to reach a destination despite the routing.

Common Channel Signaling

In a multitandem network, common channel signaling should be used to achieve more effective circuit utilization. The cost of SS7 equipment and the separate data network should be weighed against the improved circuit utilization from eliminating in-band signaling.

Remote Access

The value of remote access from a separate location should be considered. Security and transmission performance must be weighed against the benefits of remote access. A switch should provide an effective screen against unauthorized access and should alert the network administrator to unauthorized attempts. The transmission characteristics of the access circuits should be evaluated to predict whether service will be satisfactory.

High-Speed Switching Capability

If videoconferencing, closed-circuit TV, or high-speed data transfer is anticipated, the system should be evaluated for its capability to allocate the bandwidth on an $N \times 64$ basis. The system should be capable of reserving any segment of capacity required and should preempt occupied circuits when necessary to vacate the required bandwidth.

Billing Capability

The system must generate a call detail record for each call attempted. The record must distinguish between customer-dialed and operator-handled calls. Call details should be output to a variety of media including magnetic tape, hard disk, and solid-state storage. The system must permit the administrator to search for billing records. The system must produce billing records by ANI, personal identification number, or account code.

Operator Service Position Evaluation Considerations

A fundamental objective of operator service units is to reduce the average work time (AWT) per call to a minimum. A reduction in AWT is achieved by having automated equipment handle as much of the call as possible. For example, directory assistance positions almost universally use a voice announcement unit to read out the telephone number. The operator's function is to locate the name in the database and transfer the call to the announcement system. The more effective the search algorithm, the fewer the keystrokes the operator must make before the system finds a match. Work time is also reduced by enabling the operator to access the most frequently used functions with a single key. Less frequently encountered conditions may require menu access. For new operators, a help key is important.

Signaling System Compatibility

Another important feature is compatibility with the signaling format of the central offices served. Signaling System No. 7 compatibility is usually required. Compatibility with the exchange access operator service signaling (EAOSS) protocol also may be required. The system must interface to or provide a database for intercepted calls.

Force Management Capability

An important feature of operator service systems is force management software. The force management system provides productivity statistics such as the number of calls and the average work time per operator. It provides managers with service statistics such as the number of calls exceeding the waiting time objective and the number of calls abandoned without being served. The system provides service observing capability and enables operators to call a supervisor into the connection if necessary.

SELECTED TANDEM SWITCHING SYSTEM MANUFACTURERS

Harris Corporation, Digital Telephone Systems Div.

Lucent Technologies

Northern Telecom, Inc.

Rockwell Switching Systems Div.

Siemens Stromberg Carlson

11

SIGNALING SYSTEMS

The objective of any voice network is to establish a communication path between end users, to monitor the path while it is in use, to disconnect it when the users finish, and to compile information for billing the call. Users need to know nothing of how the network establishes the path; they supply the destination address and let the system select the route. Processor-driven controllers, which are the brains of the network, determine the route over signal paths that are the nerve system. Signals travel between controllers either over the talking path or over separate data networks. Telecommunications networks have a variety of methods for setting up and taking down circuit connections, which we will discuss under the blanket of signaling systems.

As with so many other telecommunications terms, *signaling* is somewhat ambiguous. The term is sometimes used to mean the method by which information is transported across data networks. In this vein, signaling refers to the information encoding method such as alternate mark inversion, Manchester, or non-return to zero. In this book we will refer to this as *encoding* (which in itself can ambiguously mean an encryption method). Signaling will refer to the process of setting up circuits, which, as we have seen, can be real or virtual. Virtual circuit setup is discussed in Chapters 4 and 32, which deal with data protocols and broadband. This chapter discusses signaling in circuit-switched networks. Bear in mind that circuit switching doesn't refer exclusively to voice, nor does packet switching refer exclusively to data transport. The methods of signaling and encoding are only loosely related to the type of information being carried.

Signaling can be separated into the two categories of in-band and out-of-band. In-band signaling means that signals are carried over the same circuit that carries information during the session. Out-of-band signaling uses a separate network to carry the signals. The two most prominent out-of-band signaling systems are the D channel of ISDN (Chapter 28) and signaling system 7 (SS7), which is a separate *common channel* signaling network that we discuss in this chapter.

In-band signaling has several drawbacks that common channel signaling overcomes. The most significant drawback of in-band signaling for long-distance circuits is its susceptibility to fraud. As we will discuss later in the chapter, in-band tone signaling on toll trunks uses a 2,600 Hz tone for transmitting supervisory signals. Toll thieves are able to defeat automatic message accounting systems by using devices that emulate signaling tones. Common channel signaling eliminates this form of toll fraud.

The second drawback is setup time. When circuits are built up with a series of signals, the time required to set up the call is much longer than it takes to manage call setup end-to-end from a central computer network. Furthermore, conventional signaling lacks look-ahead capability. A circuit can be connected only to find that the call cannot be completed because the called number is busy. This is undesirable from the network owner's standpoint because uncompleted calls waste circuit time.

Another major benefit of common channel signaling is in the service options it supports. In Chapter 10 we discussed virtual private networks, which are not feasible with conventional signaling. Common channel signaling supports credit-card authorization, cellular phone roaming, intelligent network services, and Custom Local Area Signaling Services (CLASS), which Chapter 9 discusses. Besides reducing call setup time, common channel signaling reduces the access charges that IECs must pay LECs for circuit connect time. In addition, the IECs' circuit utilization is improved by reducing holding time.

Signaling systems can also be classified by the method of exchanging signals: direct current (DC), tone, bit-robbed, and common channel. DC signaling is used in local loops. It was formerly used in metallic trunks, but few of these remain in service. Tone signaling was once used on all long-distance circuits, but it has largely been replaced by SS7 now. Local loops and tie lines still use both DC and tone signaling; the familiar dual-tone multifrequency (DTMF) signals are used in nearly all loops, including those served by T-carrier. The bit-robbed T-carrier signaling is a hybrid in-band system that is neither tone nor DC signaling.

Signals can be grouped into four functions:

◆ *Supervising* is monitoring the status of a line or circuit to determine if it is busy, idle, or is requesting service. Supervision is a term derived from the function telephone operators performed in monitoring manual circuits on a switchboard. Manual switchboards displayed supervisory signals by an illuminated lamp on the keyshelf to show a request for service on an incoming line or an on-hook condition of a switchboard cord circuit. In the network, the supervisory signals are conveyed as voltage levels on signaling leads, or the on hook/off hook status of signaling tones or bits.

◆ *Alerting* indicates to the addressee the arrival of an incoming call. Alerting signals are audible bells and tones or visual lights.

◆ *Call progress* signals such as busy and reorder tones inform the user of the status of the call setup process.

◆ *Addressing* is the process of transmitting routing and destination signals over the network. Addressing signals include dial pulses, tone pulses, or data pulses over loops, trunks, and signaling networks.

To illustrate these four functions, consider what happens when you lift a telephone handset to place a call. Lifting the handset sends a DC signal that notifies the central office of your intention to place a call. The central office responds by returning dial tone and preparing its circuits to receive the address of the call's destination. As you press the DTMF buttons on the telephone, the central office registers the address, sets up the path, and sends an alerting signal in the form of a ringing signal to the called station. If the called station is busy the central office sends a busy signal. If all circuits are busy it sends a reorder or fast busy tone.

In this chapter we will discuss the various types of signals the telephone network uses to accomplish these functions of supervising, alerting, call progress, and addressing.

SIGNALING TECHNOLOGY

With few exceptions, switched connections over the telecommunications network today involve at least some analog signaling; even though most of the facility is digital, the subscriber loop remains analog and requires analog signals. Even when T-carrier is used for the local loop, the addressing signals are, in most cases, DTMF. Supervisory signals using digital equipment is simple and inexpensive. As indicated in Chapter 5, it involves little more than robbing the lowest-order bit from every sixth frame, and using the binary status of this bit to signal the switching system or drive signaling leads in the channel units. Analog signaling is considerably more complex. Most analog carrier systems require separate signaling units, which add to the cost and complexity of the circuit.

When local networks are converted to ISDN, analog signaling is eliminated. Signals pass among IEC, LEC, and user as data messages. With today's signaling systems, when a station is busy, the signal stops at the end office (unless the user has chosen the call-waiting feature, which interrupts the call in progress). ISDN provides a separate out-of-band signaling channel that allows the network to send alerting messages to the user, where they can appear on a readout on the telephone. The user can choose how to handle the call without terminating or interrupting the original session.

Consider the general call state model shown in Figure 11–1. Call setup connects circuits together regardless whether the signaling is in-band or out-of-band. Let us consider the differences between these two signaling methods.

In-Band Signaling

In the idle state, subscriber loops have battery on the ring side of the line and an open circuit on the tip. No loop current flows in this state. Signaling equipment attached to the trunks between the local offices and the toll office furnishes a 2,600 Hz signaling tone, indicating idle circuit status. If the interoffice trunks are digital, signaling bits indicate the circuit status. With trunks the tone operates auxiliary single frequency (SF) signaling sets that show the line status by changing the status of DC voltages on their signaling leads.

The local central office continually scans the subscriber line and trunk circuits to detect any change in their busy/idle status. When station A lifts its receiver off hook, current flows in the subscriber loop, signaling the local central office of A's intention to place a call. The central office responds by marking the calling line busy (a status indication), and returns dial tone to the calling party. Dial tone is one of several call progress signals that telephone equipment uses to communicate with the calling party. It conveys the readiness of the central office to receive addressing signals.

Station A transmits digits to the central office using either DTMF or dial pulses. The system registers the digits and translates them to the address of the terminating station D. The switching system looks in its database to determine which is A's primary IEC. Included in the switching system's address translation is a routing table that tells it the path to take to the destination. From the address, the system determines that the call must be passed to tandem B. The local switch at A checks the busy/idle status of trunks to office B, and seizes an

FIGURE 11-1

General Call State Model

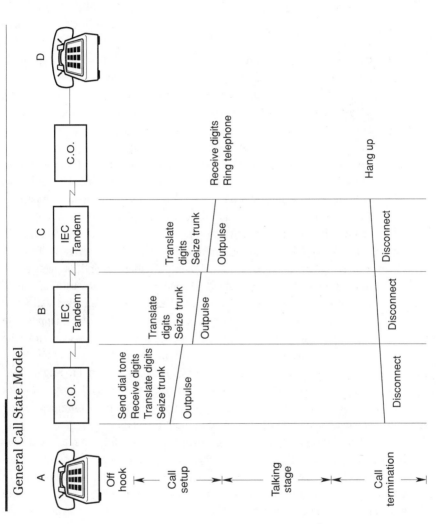

idle trunk. If no trunks are idle, central office A returns a reorder or fast busy call progress tone to station A. When the switch seizes an idle trunk, the caller at A hears nothing except, perhaps, the clicking of operating relays. If central office A has local automatic message accounting (LAMA) equipment, it registers an initial entry to identify the calling and called number, and to prepare the LAMA equipment to record the details of the call when D answers. If the office does not have LAMA it sends the initial entry to a centralized AMA office over a CAMA trunk.

The trunk seizure removes the 2,600 Hz SF tone from the channel to show the change in status. Tandem office B, detecting the change in status, returns a signal, usually a momentary interruption in the signaling tone toward A. This signal, called a *wink,* signifies that B is ready to receive digits. Detecting the wink, central office A sends its addressing pulses toward B. These pulses are either dial pulses, conveyed by interrupting the SF tone, or, usually, *multifrequency* pulses, conveyed by coding digits with combinations of two out of five frequencies. Tandem office B continues to send an on-hook tone toward office A, and will do so until station D answers. At this point, office A has completed the originating functions, and awaits the completion of the call.

Tandem B translates the digits and picks a route to local central office D through Tandem C, selects an idle trunk to Tandem C, and seizes it. Tandem C, detecting the seizure, sends a start signal to Tandem B, and prepares to receive digits. B detects the start signal and sends the digits forward. Tandem C repeats the process to local central office D. Office D tests the called station for its busy/idle status, and if busy, returns a busy tone over the voice channel. The calling party, recognizing the call progress tone, hangs up; the switches take the connection down. The originating switch adds no completion entry to the AMA record. If station D is idle, office D sends a 20 Hz alerting signal to ring the bell in D's telephone. It also returns an *audible ring* (another call progress tone) over the transmission path to the originating party. The line continues to ring until D answers, A hangs up, or the equipment times out.

When station D answers, central office D detects the change in status as line current begins to flow. This trips the ringing signal and stops audible ringing. Office D changes the status of its signaling set toward C from on-hook to off-hook by interrupting the SF tone. C sends the on-hook signal to B, which transmits the on-hook signal to A. The AMA equipment registers call completion, indicating the time that charging begins.

When either party hangs up, the change in line current indicates a status change to its central office, which forwards the change to the other end by restoring the SF tone. Office A registers a terminating entry in the AMA equipment to stop charging. The SF tones are restored to all circuits to show idle circuit status. All equipment then is prepared to accept another call.

This system, with minor variations that we will discuss later, can be used for signaling over both dedicated and switched circuits. Not all circuits use SF signaling, however. T-carrier and common channel signaling are making SF signaling obsolete. SF signaling can be transmitted over a digital circuit, and often is when a digital link connects to an analog link. SF and MF signaling have several drawbacks that are leading to their replacement in toll circuits. The primary reasons are toll fraud and wasted circuit time during call setup.

Common Channel Signaling

Referring again to Figure 11–1, consider what happens to a call with common channel signaling. To replace the in-band signaling equipment, common channel signaling uses a separate data communications network to exchange signals and route the calls. We will discuss the architecture of SS7, which is the international common channel signaling system, later. For now, assume that all central offices are *signaling points* (SPs) on the network, and are linked via data circuits to *signal transfer points* (STPs), which are network nodes that act as hubs for signaling messages. STPs are linked to a *service control point* (SCP), which is a database of network information that can be accessed by the network nodes.

In the end-to-end common channel mode, an ISDN station at A sends a setup message over its D (data) channel to local central office A. The message includes the address of the terminating station D plus information about the call, such as the type of call it is. Call types can be data, voice, video, and so on. Central office A selects the appropriate combination of B (bearer) channels based on the call type, and sends a data message to its STP. The STP sends a data message to the SCP's database to retrieve information about the originating and termination stations. For example, the user's class of service indicates whether the called and/or calling stations are members of a virtual network, and whether the connection is switched or dedicated. The STP selects a route to the destination, allocates circuits, and sends connect messages to the switches.

Each stage of the call—ringing, connect, and disconnect—is signaled with a data message. Although the capability isn't generally activated yet, the signaling network is fast enough that circuit connection can wait until the called party answers, further increasing circuit utilization.

E & M Signaling

By long-standing convention, signaling on interoffice circuits uses two leads designated as the E or recEive and the M or transMit leads for conveying signals. External signaling sets and the built-in signaling of T-carrier channels use E&M signaling to communicate status to attached central office equipment.

FIGURE 11-2

E&M Signaling Types

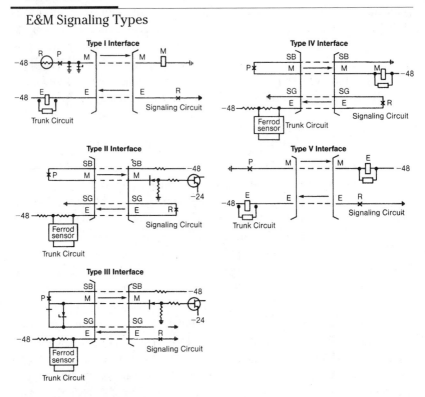

Signaling equipment converts the binary state of line signals, (tone on or off for analog and zero or one for digital equipment), to actuate the E&M leads.

There are five different types of E&M signaling interfaces, but in the most common type the M lead is grounded when on-hook. An off-hook seizure is indicated by applying -48 volt battery to the M lead. The E lead is open when on-hook; the signaling set applies ground to the E lead when it receives an off-hook signal from the distant end. Figure 11-2 illustrates the most common types of E&M signaling.

Direct Current Signaling Systems

DC signaling can be employed on metallic facilities, which include most sub-scriber loops and voice frequency interoffice trunks. The use of DC signaling over metallic facilities is not mandatory. In many applications it is desirable to use SF signaling from end to end. The simplest status signal on the local loop occurs when the caller takes the telephone receiver off-hook, closing a DC path between tip and ring and allowing loop current to flow. This system is called *loop start*. All subscriber loops that terminate in station sets use loop start signaling.

All of us have experienced situations where we pick up the telephone to place a call and find the line is already connected to an incoming call, but the bell hasn't rung. This condition, known as *glare,* occurs when both ends of a circuit are simultaneously seized. Glare is easy to resolve in ordinary telephone circuits (the parties both say hello), but it creates a problem in trunks. One way of preventing glare is by using one-way signaling on trunks. On small trunk groups the use of one-way trunks is uneconomical for reasons explained in Chapter 35. Therefore, to accommodate two-way trunks, signaling and switching systems must prevent glare or resolve it when it occurs. In the worst case, when glare occurs the equipment is unable to complete the connection, the circuit times out, and the user receives reorder.

Most PBXs connect to the central office over trunks equipped with two-way signaling, and are thus subject to glare. PBXs cannot use loop-start two-way trunks because the only indication the PBX has of a call incoming from the central office is the ringing signal, which occurs at six-second intervals. For up to six seconds the PBX would be blinded to the possibility of an incoming trunk seizure, and could seize a circuit for outgoing traffic when the trunk was carrying an incoming call that the PBX had not yet detected. To provide an immediate trunk seizure signal toward the PBX, central office line circuits are optionally wired for *ground start* operation. With this option the central office grounds the tip side of the line immediately upon seizure by an incoming call. By detecting the tip ground, the PBX is alerted to the line seizure before ringing begins. PBX users must specify to the LEC when ground start operation is required.

Metallic trunks and many special services use *duplex* (DX) signaling. DX signaling uses relays or electronic circuits that are sensitive to line status beyond the range of loop signaling. DX signaling equipment has either separate signaling sets, circuitry built into carrier channel units as discussed in Chapter 5, or network channel terminating equipment (NCTE). An older system, composite (CX) signaling, is similar to DX signaling, except that it includes filters to separate the voice frequency path from the signaling path. Figure 11–3 is a diagram of a DX signaling set.

TRUNK SIGNALING SYSTEMS

Trunk signaling requires the built-in signaling of digital carrier, a separate SF set, or, in some types of analog carrier, out-of-band tone signaling. Out-of-band tone signaling, rarely used in North America, passes a 3,700 Hz signaling tone over the channel. Narrow band filters separate the signaling tone from the voice frequency pass band.

FIGURE 11–3

Schematic of a DX Signaling Set

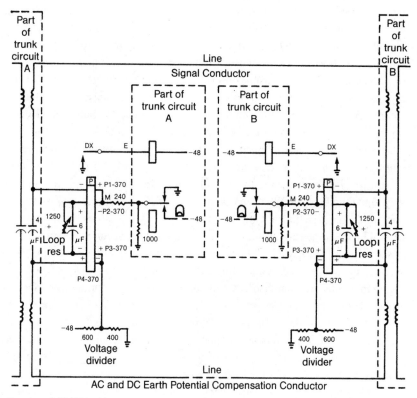

Courtesy of AT&T Archives

Single Frequency Signaling

The most common analog trunk signaling system is 2,600 Hz single frequency (SF) illustrated in Figure 11–4. The voice frequency leads from a carrier channel connect directly to the SF set. The SF set contains circuitry to change the state of the E&M leads in response to the presence or absence of the SF tone, and to turn the signaling tone on and off when the switching system or other central office equipment changes the status of its leads. The SF set blocks the voice frequency path toward the switching system while the signaling tone is on the channel. The user does not hear the tone, although short tone bursts are occasionally audible when one party hangs up.

FIGURE 11–4

Single-Frequency Signaling Simplified Block Diagram

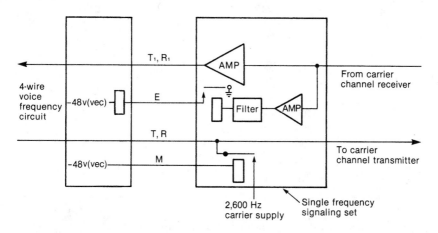

One hazard of SF signaling is the possibility of *talk-off,* which can occur when the user's voice contains enough 2,600 Hz energy to actuate the tone-detecting circuits in the SF set. Voice filters minimize the potential of talk-off, but the problem may occur, particularly to people with high-pitched voices.

Addressing Signals

Addressing signals between station and central office equipment use either dial pulse or DTMF signals, as described in Chapter 19. DTMF pulses require a DTMF receiver in the central office to convert the tones to the addressing signals. Because DTMF pulses travel over the voice path, they can be passed through the switching system after the connection is established. This capability is required to send addressing and identification information to interexchange carriers that use exchange access Feature Group A. It is also useful for converting the telephone to a simple data entry device. All electronic central offices can receive DTMF dialing. Some older electromechanical central offices require externally mounted DTMF receivers to convert the tones to dial pulses.

Addressing signals are transmitted over trunks as DTMF, dial pulse, or multifrequency (MF) signals, or over a common channel as a data signal. MF signals are more reliable and considerably faster than dial pulse signals, but require a *sender* to transmit the pulses. Modern central offices all support MF signaling, but older electromechanical central offices can receive only dial pulses. Dial pulse or DTMF signals are also used between PBXs and their serving central office.

TABLE 11-1

Single-Frequency Signaling Tone Frequencies

Tone Combination	Digit
700 + 900	1
700 + 1100	2
900 + 1100	3
700 + 1300	4
900 + 1300	5
1100 + 1300	6
700 + 1500	7
900 + 1500	8
1100 + 1500	9
1300 + 1500	0

MF senders use a two-out-of-five tone method to encode digits, as Table 11–1 shows. Digits are sent at the rate of about 7 digits per second, compared to the 10 pulses per second of dial pulsing. Since a dial-pulsed digit requires from 1 to 10 pulses plus an interdigital interval, MF pulsing requires substantially less time to set up a call than dial pulsing.

COMMON CHANNEL SIGNALING

As discussed earlier, in-band signaling systems have four major drawbacks in interexchange networks. First, they are vulnerable to fraud. In the 1970s, the loss of revenue to persons with devices that simulated in-band signaling tones was considerable, and was a prime motivating factor in developing common channel signaling. Second, in-band call setup takes several seconds, and third, call setup consumes circuit time. A separate signaling network reduces call setup overhead. Not only is reduced call setup time important to the IECs' competitive positions, it also represents a direct expense in the access charges paid to the LECs. The fourth drawback is important to the market strategies of the IECs: in-band systems are limited to transferring call setup and supervision information, and are therefore incapable of supporting virtual networks, which Chapter 34 discusses.

Common channel signaling uses a separate packet-switched network to pass call setup, charging, and supervision information. It also can access the carrier's database to obtain account information such as features and points served on a virtual network. The ITU has adopted signaling system No. 7 as the world standard common channel signaling system. The purposes of SS7 can be summarized as follows:

- *Improves call management:* The system handles call setup and disconnect. SS7 handles end-to-end call supervision, and call timing and billing.
- *Enhances network management:* SS7 is responsible for call routing and congestion control, functions that previously were handled by each switch in communication with a network management center. It provides status information to network elements, and collects performance information.
- *Separates network control from hardware:* With other signaling systems, network control is embedded in the underlying hardware. SS7 is a control system independent of the circuits and transmission equipment that make up the network.
- *Supports ISDN:* Common channel out-of-band signaling is inherent in ISDN.
- *Supports user database:* SS7 provides database information to form virtual networks, provide enhanced services, and identify and verify callers.
- *Handles addressing and supervision:* Common channel signaling protocols carry line status, calling and called numbers, credit-card numbers and other such information through the network.
- *Supports 800 number portability:* When an 800 number is dialed, an SS7 message to a central database returns with the identity of the IEC.

With in-band signaling, the process of setting up the talking path determines whether the path is operative since audible signals are passed over the channel that will be used for talking. With common channel signaling this test is not possible; therefore the equipment makes a separate path assurance test before establishing the call.

Signaling System No. 7 Architecture

Figure 11–5 shows the architecture of SS7. The system has three major components: the *service switching point* (SSP), the *signaling transfer point* (STP), and the *service control point* (SCP). The SSP is a tandem switch in the interexchange network, or an end office in the LEC network. The STPs are packet-switching nodes, and the SCPs are databases of circuit, routing, and customer information. Each carrier has its own signaling network; the networks are interconnected to enable carriers to interoperate.

FIGURE 11–5

Architecture of Signaling System No. 7

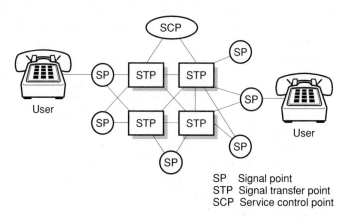

SP   Signal point
STP Signal transfer point
SCP Service control point

When the SSP receives a service request from a local end office or a user attached on a direct access line, it sends a service request to the SCP, and suspends call processing until it receives a reply. The SSP forwards the request to the STP over the packet network. The STPs are geographically dispersed, redundant nodes that are interconnected over a high-speed packet network that is protected from failure by alternative paths. STPs are deployed in pairs so that the failure of one system will not affect call processing. STPs pass the call setup request to an SCP over direct circuits or by relaying it to another STP.

The SCP is a high-speed database that is also deployed in pairs, each having duplicates of the database. The database has circuit and routing information, and for customers that are connected through a virtual network, the database contains customer information such as class of service, restrictions, and whether the access line is switched or dedicated. The SCP accepts the query from the STP, retrieves the information from the database, and returns the response on the network. The response generally takes the same route as the original inquiry.

Signaling System No. 7 Protocol

SS7 uses a layered protocol that resembles the OSI model, but has four layers instead of seven. Figure 11–6 shows the protocol architecture compared to the OSI model. The first three layers are called the message transfer part (MTP). The MTP is a datagram service, which means that it relays unacknowledged packets. The MTP has three layers, which form a network similar to X.25. The functions of these layers are:

FIGURE 11–6

SS7 Protocol Architecture Compared to the OSI Model

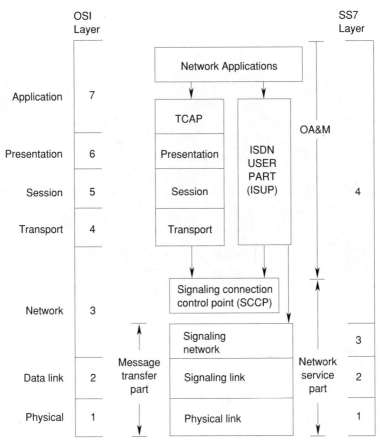

TCAP = Transaction Capabilities Application Part

♦ The *signaling data link* is the physical layer. It is a full duplex connection that provides physical links between network nodes.

♦ The *signaling link layer* is a data link that has three functions: flow control, error correction, and delivering packets in the proper sequence.

♦ The *signaling network layer* routes messages from source to destination, and from the lower levels to the user part of the protocol. Its routing tables enable it to handle link failures and to route messages based on their logical address.

FIGURE 11–7

Tellabs 334 SST Selective Signaling System

Courtesy Tellabs, Inc.

The fourth layer is called the Signaling Connection Control Part (SCCP). It is responsible for addressing requests to the appropriate application, and for determining the status of the application. An application, for example, might be an 800 service request. The ISDN Service User Part (ISUP) relays messages to ISDN users. The user in this context refers to the interface with the end user's equipment, and not to the user itself. The ISUP handles call setup, accounting and charging, and circuit supervision for ISDN connections.

PRIVATE LINE SIGNALING

Private or dedicated lines use all types of in-band signaling discussed so far plus *selective signaling,* an in-band system for operation of certain private line switching systems. Figure 11–7 shows the Tellabs 334 SST selective signaling system, which permits dial-selectable connections over a multipoint network.

Some dedicated circuits use signaling identical with that used by the telephone network. PBX tie trunks and large private switched networks require all the signaling capabilities of the telephone network. Many private networks use tie trunks with out-of-band signaling links. Some use SS7 between tandem switches, some use ISDN, and others use proprietary networking protocols, which most PBX manufacturers offer. Special dedicated circuits require signaling arrangements that use the same techniques and equipment as the telephone network, but have no direct counterparts in switched systems. Examples are:

♦ *No Signaling.* Some private lines require no signaling. Examples are data circuits that include signaling in the DTE and circuits that use microphones and speakers for alerting. Other examples of circuits requiring no signaling are program and wired music circuits.

♦ *Ringdown Circuits.* In ringdown circuits a 20 Hz generator signal rings the bell of a distant station. The 300 Hz cutoff frequency of carrier channels prevents 20 Hz ringing signals from passing over the channel. Ringdown circuits require equipment to convert the 20 Hz ringing supply to SF or E&M signals and vice versa. A similar circuit actuates ringing when the receiver goes off-hook. This type of circuit requires a loop-to-SF converter. The signal at the far end may activate a light instead of a bell by using additional converter circuits.

♦ *Selective Signaling.* Some private line networks use a four-wire selective signaling system to route calls without the use of switching systems. Dial pulses generate in-band tones to drive a simple switch to build up a connection to the desired terminating point.

Coin Telephone Signaling

Coin telephones owned by the LECs use the dialing and ringing signals of ordinary telephones plus DC signals that operate apparatus within the telephone to collect and return coins. Coin tones are also generated in the telephone to enable the operator to distinguish between coin denominations. Privately owned coin telephones are not connected to coin control circuits in the central office, and since supervisory signals are not repeated over the local loop, they must rely on internal circuitry for coin control, as discussed in Chapter 19.

APPLICATIONS

All public and private networks, except some data communications networks that supply their own signals, use signaling systems and equipment. Equipment used in these networks is identical and does the same functions of alerting, addressing, supervising, and indicating status in both private and common carrier networks.

All major PBXs provide methods of network signaling to support features such as voice mail, automatic callback, and message lamp illumination across the network. The methods are proprietary, and although some vendors use signals that resemble international standards, signaling is not carried through to the LECs or IECs. As the LECs deploy ISDN, PBXs will be integrated into the international signaling system.

Standards

Few published standards exist on the conventional single-frequency signaling system used in North America. Most standards have evolved by practice, and are followed by signaling equipment manufacturers. Internationally, most carriers use the ITU No. 6 and 7 standards for common channel signaling and ITU No. 4 and 5 line signaling systems. These standards are of little concern to users because the IECs administer them. In North America, carriers have adopted similar systems for SF and MF signals.

Evaluating Signaling Equipment

A circuit design is essential before selecting signaling equipment. So many alternatives exist for interconnecting signaling equipment that it is necessary to determine the most economical design to minimize signaling costs. The most economical configuration in digital systems is the use of the built-in equipment in the T-carrier channel. With the wide range of special channel units listed in Table 5–1, it is feasible to provide nearly any conceivable combination of signaling services to operate station signaling equipment.

Where built-in signaling is not included as part of the channel unit, external signaling converters are required. Table 11–2 lists the most common converters. These units are often available with amplifiers contained in the same package, and are built into plug-in units that mount in a special shelf. The voice frequency and signaling leads are cabled to distributing frames as discussed in Chapter 12 for connection to carrier and subscriber loop equipment.

Signaling compatibility is also an important consideration in acquiring signaling equipment. Compatibility is rarely a problem with respect to signaling equipment of different manufacturers. Signal frequencies, ringing frequencies, and E&M lead connections are universal with all manufacturers. However, the timing of signals, which is controlled by switching and transmission equipment connected to signaling sets, is a frequent cause of incompatibility, but this has little to do with the signaling equipment itself.

Plug compatibility is an issue that must be addressed by the manufacturer. Several types of plug-in shelves exist on the market; all are designed to

TABLE 11–2

Voice Frequency Terminating and Signaling Units

Two-wire repeater
Four-wire repeater
Four-wire terminating set
Automatic ringdown unit
Conference bridge
DX signaling module
Data channel interface
Dial long-line unit
Dial pulse-correcting unit
Echo suppressor
Line transfer relay
Loop extender
Loop signaling repeater
Program amplifier
Pulse link repeater
Repeat coil
Signaling converter, 20 Hz to E & M
Signaling range extender
Single-frequency signaling unit
Toll diversion unit
Voice frequency equalizer

manufacturer's specifications, and no standards exist. Some manufacturers make equipment that is designed to be plug-compatible with shelves of others.

Another important consideration in evaluating signaling equipment is testing capability. Circuits have either end-to-end signaling or link-by-link signaling, illustrated in Figure 11–8. End-to-end signaling is the easiest to test. If SF tones are used between both ends of a circuit, signaling status can be determined by listening to the tone over the voice channel or monitoring the signaling leads of a T-carrier channel. The operation of the SF set is determined by measuring the electrical state of the E&M leads. With link-by-link signaling the signals are extracted at intermediate points and connected by a pulse link repeater, which interconnects the E&M leads. In most private networks with station, PBX, and NCTE equipment furnished by the user, the local loop by the LEC, and the intercity circuits by an interexchange carrier, link-by-link signaling is the rule. For the user to diagnose signaling problems, testing capability is required to evaluate signaling in the station and NCTE.

FIGURE 11–8

End-to-End versus Link-by-Link Signaling

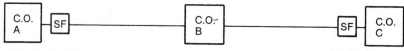

A. End-to-End Signaling

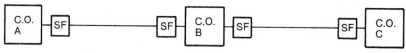

B. Link-by-Link Signaling

SELECTED SIGNALING EQUIPMENT MANUFACTURERS

ADC Telecommunications

Lucent Technologies

Northern Telecom, Inc.

Pulsecom Div., Harvey Hubbel, Inc.

Telco Systems, Inc.

Tellabs, Inc.

12

COMMON EQUIPMENT

Common equipment supports all classes of telecommunications. Common equipment, as covered in this chapter, includes:

◆ Relay racks and cabinets
◆ Distributing frames
◆ Ringing and tone supplies
◆ Alarm and control equipment
◆ Power equipment

RELAY RACKS AND CABINETS

Central office equipment mounts either in cabinets or open relay racks, with the latter the most common. PBXs, ACDs, and small tandem switches are usually enclosed in cabinets. In cabinetized equipment the interbay cabling is sometimes contained within the cabinet. In relay rack-mounted equipment the cabling is external and is supported by overhead cable troughs or run through raceways in the floor. Because of the quantities of cables involved and the need for physical separation in some cables, overhead racking is the most common method in both central offices and large PBXs. Cables can be run through closed cable trays, or in open ladder racks. The latter are generally less expensive than cable trays, and permit airflow around the cables.

To control noise and crosstalk in telecommunications equipment the manufacturer's specifications must be followed for the type and layout of cabling. As with outside plant cable, the twist in interbay cable controls crosstalk and prevents unwanted coupling between circuits. Also, cables often must be run in separate troughs that are segregated by signal level and kept physically separated by enough distance that signals from high-level cables cannot crosstalk into low-level cables. For some types of cable, shielding is required to further reduce the possibility of crosstalk.

In central offices and PBXs alike, many critical leads have maximum lengths that cannot be exceeded. If lead lengths are exceeded signal loss between components may be excessive, signals may be distorted, or in high-speed buses timing may be affected by propagation delay. Manufacturer's specifications must be followed rigorously with respect to lead length.

DISTRIBUTING FRAMES

Temporary connections or those requiring rearrangement terminate on crossconnect blocks mounted in distributing frames. Distributing frames also provide an access point for testing cable and equipment. The size and structure of a distributing frame are dictated by the quantity of circuits to be connected. Cabling to the central office equipment routes through openings at the top of the frame, fastens to vertical members, and turns under a metal shelf or mounting bracket that supports the crossconnect blocks. The crossconnect blocks are multiple metallic terminals mounted in an insulating material and fastened to the distributing frame. Equipment and lead identity are stenciled on the blocks.

Technicians make crossconnects by running "jumper" wire in a supporting wire trough. Between blocks connections are made at the block by one of three methods. In the oldest method, rarely used in modern equipment, the wire is stripped and soldered to the block. The second type uses wire-wrapped connections in which the wire is stripped and tightly wrapped around a post with a wire-wrap tool. The third type of connection uses a split quick-clip terminal that clamps the wire and pierces the insulation as a special tool inserts it in the terminal. The quick-clip method has several variations that operate on the same principle of piercing the insulation and gripping the wire against a metallic connection.

Some installations use modular distributing frames, which keep the length of crossconnects to a minimum, and are often administered by a computer. In small installations distributing frame administration is not enough of a problem to require computer administration. In large centers with thousands of subscriber lines and trunks terminated in the office, however, distributing frame congestion becomes a significant problem as quantities of crossconnect wires are piled in troughs. In large installations it is important that the distributing frame be carefully designed and administered to keep the wire length to a minimum.

Large PBXs may use the same hardware as central offices, or they may use a wall-mounted backboard that holds 66-type blocks or the newer 110 connectors offered by most manufacturers. Wall-mounted frames are satisfactory in small installations, but in PBXs with more than about 1,000 stations the frame becomes too large to be administered efficiently. Jumpers are long and wiring trough congestion becomes a problem. To relieve jumper congestion, hardware is available to mount wiring blocks on double-sided freestanding frames.

Protector Frames

Incoming circuits that are exposed to power or lightning are terminated on protector frames. The protector module forms the connection between the cable pair and the attached equipment. As described in Chapter 6, if excessive current flows in the line, the protector opens the circuit to the central office equipment and grounds the conductors. If excessive voltage strikes the line, carbon blocks inside the protector module arc across to ground the circuit. Modules are manufactured with gas tubes where these are needed to protect vulnerable central office equipment such as digital switches.

Combined and Miscellaneous Distributing Frames

Small installations use combined protector and distributing frames. The incoming cable pairs terminate on the protector frame, where they are crossconnected to equipment that terminates on the distributing frame. In large central offices the size of the frame may dictate separate protector and distributing frames. One or more distributing frames terminate trunks, switching machine line terminations, and miscellaneous equipment such as repeaters, range extenders, and signaling equipment. In offices large enough to need multiple frames, tie cables permit crossconnecting between cable and equipment terminated on different frames. Buildings with multiple floors almost invariably require several distributing frames linked with tie cable.

RINGING AND TONE SUPPLIES

Common equipment includes ringing, dial tone, call progress tone, and recorded announcement apparatus. In digital central offices many of these tones are generated in software, so no external equipment is needed. Electromechanical and analog electronic central offices require external supplies.

Ringing machines are usually solid-state supplies that generate 20 Hz ringing current at about 90 volts. Dial tone supplies with precisely generated tones are required. Busy tone and reorder supply tones are generated in the same manner as dial tones.

Recorded announcements are stored in digital form in solid-state memory or in analog form on magnetic tapes or drums. Most recorders contain multiple tracks for the several types of messages used in central offices.

ALARM AND CONTROL EQUIPMENT

Most telecommunications equipment has integral alarms in any circuit that can affect service. The extent and type of alarming varies with the manufacturer, but generally alarms draw attention to equipment that has failed or is about to fail, and direct the technician to the defective equipment.

Equipment alarms light an alarm lamp on the equipment chassis and operate external contacts that are used for remoting the alarm and for operating external audible and visual alarms. Most central offices contain an office alarm system to aid in locating failed equipment. Alarms are segregated into major and minor categories to show the seriousness of the trouble; different tones sound to alert maintenance personnel to the alarm class and location. Besides audible alarms, aisle pilots and bay alarm lamps guide maintenance personnel to the room, equipment row, bay, and the specific equipment in trouble.

In offices designed for unattended operation, telemetering equipment transmits the alarms to a distant center over telephone circuits. The alarm remote is generally a slave that reports only the identity of the alarm point. The center typically is equipped with a processor and database that pinpoint the trouble and also may diagnose the cause. Some equipment, including most electronic switching systems, communicates with a remote that provides the equivalent of the local switching machine console. Other remote alarms report building status such as open door, temperature, smoke, and fire alarms.

Central offices designed for unattended operation frequently include control apparatus for sending orders from a distant location over a data circuit. For example, microwave and fiber-optic equipment usually have control systems that enable technicians to transfer working equipment to a backup channel. Offices equipped with emergency generators frequently are arranged for engine start and shutdown, and transfer to and from commercial power.

The more extensive private telecommunications networks use central office techniques for reporting alarms and diagnosing trouble. Most PBX manufacturers support their systems with a remote maintenance and testing system that enables technicians to diagnose trouble remotely, and, sometimes, switch around failed apparatus. Alarm systems range from simply reporting a contact opening or closure over a circuit to more elaborate systems that report values to a remote center, support remote diagnostics and maintain a trouble clearance database.

POWER EQUIPMENT

Most central office equipment operates from direct current, usually -48 volts, which is the typical voltage supplied by central office charging and battery plants. PBXs operate either on -48 volts or on commercial AC. Figure 12–1 shows a battery plant and charging equipment in an AT&T toll office. PBX DC power systems use a similar type of power plant, only smaller. Microwave equipment usually works on -24 volts DC in radio stations and -48 volts DC in central offices. Some central office equipment operates from alternating current (AC) and requires a DC-to-AC converter known as an *inverter* to provide an uninterrupted power source during power failures. AC-operated equipment includes tape and disk drives, computers, and other equipment that is not normally designed for DC operation. Commercial uninterruptable power supply (UPS) equipment, which we will discuss later, is an alternative family of equipment that contains a built-in battery supply.

Most central offices and PBXs in hospitals and other organizations that cannot tolerate system failures have an emergency generator to carry the load and keep the batteries charged during prolonged power outages. The emergency generator connects to the charging equipment through a power transfer circuit that cuts off commercial power while the generator is on-line. Offices lacking emergency power equipment often have circuitry for connecting an external generator.

Storage batteries use technology similar to automobile batteries. Lead acid and nickel cadmium cells are common, and some equipment uses batteries with solid electrolyte called gel cells. Power is distributed from the battery plant to the central office equipment over *bus bars,* which must be designed large enough to carry current for the total equipment load. Bus bars connecting the batteries are visible in the foreground of Figure 12–1. To minimize the amount of voltage drop, batteries are installed as close to the equipment as possible.

Some types of central office equipment require voltage higher or lower than the nominal -48 or -24 volts used by most equipment. These voltages are supplied by either a separate charging and battery plant or by using solid-state power converters. Except for very high current loads, power converters are the preferred method of supplying other voltages.

FIGURE 12–1

A Central Office Power Plant

Courtesy of AT&T Archives

Uninterruptable Power Supplies (UPS)

Any telecommunications apparatus that operates from commercial alternating current (AC) power, is vulnerable to failure from irregularities that cannot be predicted or controlled. The following are the principal types of commercial power irregularities:

◆ *Blackouts,* which are total failures of commercial power.

◆ *Brownouts,* which are reductions in voltage.

◆ *Surges,* which are momentary voltage changes.

◆ *Transients,* which are momentary open circuit conditions.

◆ *Spikes,* which are sharp pulses of high voltage that rapidly rise and decay.

◆ *Frequency variations,* which are momentary or prolonged deviations from the nominal 60 Hz power line frequency.

Many power line irregularities have no effect, but others can damage equipment, interrupt service, or both. The severity of the problem varies with locale and season. In some parts of the United States outages happen so infrequently that protective measures are unnecessary. In other parts of the country outages are a regular occurrence, particularly in bad weather.

Equipment that can be categorized as *power line conditioning* equipment removes spikes, transients, and surges. Blackouts and brownouts require some form of backup power. Equipment such as computers, tape and disk drives, many PBXs, and most key telephone systems operate from commercial AC. These are protected from failure by an *uninterruptable power supply* (UPS).

UPS devices come in many sizes and capacities. Capacities range from enough to enable a small shared device such as a file server to shut down gracefully, to ones with enough capacity to operate a mainframe computer, a PBX, and auxiliary equipment such as modems, multiplexers, and voice mail through a prolonged power outage. If the UPS does not have the capacity to operate through an outage, the protected device should have circuitry connected to an alarm port on the UPS and shut itself down. Some UPS supplies can dial a pager to notify the administrator of the power outage. Some supplies are SNMP-compatible so they can be monitored and controlled from a network management system.

UPS supplies are available in three general types: *off-line* or *standby power source, on-line,* and *line interactive.*

Off-Line UPS

An off-line supply, sometimes known as standby power source or standby UPS, monitors the power line and switches the load to its internal inverter when the power falls outside limits. Figure 12–2 shows schematically how this type of supply works. The inverter converts DC to AC. It connects permanently to a storage battery that charges from the AC source. The AC source carries the load, and on failure the load switches to the output of the inverter. A short break in power occurs when the load transfers. The break runs from 5 to 20 milliseconds,

FIGURE 12–2

An Off-Line UPS

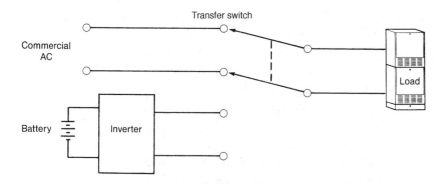

which is short enough to keep most apparatus working. During brownout conditions, however, the switching time may be longer. Some off-line UPSs have ferrite core transformers that provide a flywheel effect to keep power supplied to the load long enough to prevent any interruption. Many inexpensive off-line UPS supplies lack line conditioning, have no frequency regulation, and provide limited or no surge and spike protection.

On-Line UPS

An on-line UPS, which Figure 12–3 shows, supplies power continuously to the protected apparatus. The commercial power source keeps the UPS battery charged. When the power fails, the inverter continues to function without a break in power because the power is supplied directly from the inverter. The charging apparatus keeps the equipment completely isolated from power line irregularities. Some types of on-line supplies have a dangerous flaw in that if the UPS itself fails, the load is isolated from the commercial source. When selecting equipment of this type, be certain that the unit has bypass circuitry to connect the protected equipment directly to the commercial source in case of UPS failure.

Line-Interactive UPS

A line-interactive UPS has some of the characteristics of both an on-line and an off-line UPS. The protected equipment is powered from commercial power during normal conditions, but the UPS has circuits that can boost or reduce (buck) the voltage from the source. This technique provides voltage regulation,

FIGURE 12–3

An On-Line UPS

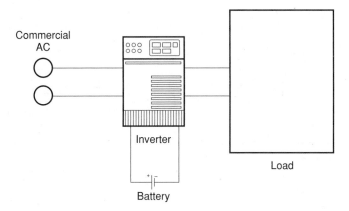

which the off-line supply lacks. If the commercial supply fails, the UPS increases the amount of voltage boost in a time interval approaching that of an on-line supply.

Battery Supplies

Both central office and PBX equipment that operates from direct current connects to a 48-volt bus, as Figure 12–4 shows. A string of batteries connects between the bus and ground. Charging equipment keeps the batteries charged and furnishes DC power to the equipment. When commercial power is on-line the charging equipment carries the central office load; the batteries draw only enough power to compensate for internal leakage and to filter noise on the power bus.

When commercial power fails, the equipment is unaffected because it draws its operating current from the battery supply. As the batteries discharge, the bus voltage drops. Equipment is designed with a tolerance for a variance in supply voltage. Under normal operation the -48-volt bus is actually "floated" from the charger at approximately -52 volts. Most central office equipment can tolerate a drop to 44 volts or less without affecting equipment operation.

The length of time equipment can operate under power failure conditions depends on the current drain and the capacity of the batteries. For example, if equipment draws 10 amperes and the battery string can supply 100 ampere-hours, the equipment could operate for 10 hours under power failure conditions. As a practical matter, it may operate for fewer than 10 hours because of

FIGURE 12–4

Central Office Power Plant

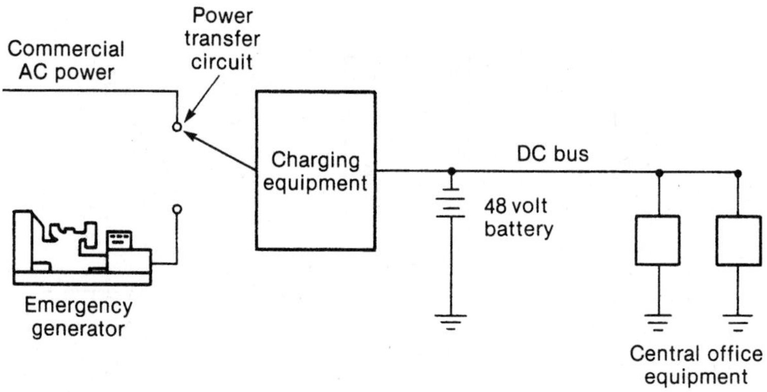

reduced battery capacity, which is discussed later. The operating time under power failure conditions can be extended by three methods: paralleling battery strings, end cells, and emergency generators.

Paralleling Battery Strings

Battery capacity can be extended by connecting a paralleling battery string. Each string contributes its capacity to the load. For example, if three 100 ampere-hour strings are connected in parallel, the total string will furnish approximately 300 ampere-hours.

End Cells

As battery voltage begins to deteriorate, it can be boosted by switching in auxiliary cells known as *end cells*. Switching apparatus, which is either manual or automatic, connects the end cells in series with the existing battery string so they contribute their voltage to the overall bus voltage. When end cells are not in use they are switched out of the circuitry and an auxiliary charger keeps them charged.

Emergency Engine Generator

Common carriers and organizations such as hospitals and public safety organizations that require continuity of telecommunications service must use an auxiliary engine generator to furnish power. The generator connects through a transfer switch to the charging equipment. If a generator is available, less battery capacity is needed because the battery must furnish power only until the generator starts.

Battery Capacity

A storage battery has three principal elements: positive and negative plates, electrolyte, and case. The plates, which are made of a metallic substance such as lead or nickel-cadmium, are suspended in electrolyte from the case, which is made of an insulating material. In contrast to automobiles, which normally have the negative pole grounded, in telecommunications equipment the positive pole is grounded to aid in preventing electrolysis. Some central office batteries have open cells, which require periodic maintenance to measure the specific gravity and add water. More recent telecommunications applications use sealed batteries. These batteries normally have a jellylike electrolyte that requires no maintenance.

Temperature has a significant effect on battery life and capacity. Battery capacity is highest during warm temperatures, but as temperature increases, battery life is shortened. Conversely, cooler temperatures extend battery life, but below freezing, battery capacity is greatly reduced.

To maintain the best balance between capacity and life, batteries should operate at approximately room temperature. Obviously, this is impractical in remote locations, such as repeater sites, that may be unheated and have no air-conditioning. In such locations, batteries should be placed to minimize their exposure to temperature extremes. For example, they should be placed in the shady side of a building to reduce heat.

APPLICATIONS

Common equipment is separately engineered in central offices. In private networks the switching equipment supplier will usually engineer and furnish common equipment. This section discusses the primary considerations in evaluating common equipment in a local private network environment.

Standards

Common equipment is generally built to manufacturer's standards. The principal voltages used in central offices, -48 and -24 volts, are accepted by convention, but are not regulated by telecommunications standards. The National Electrical Safety Code and local codes apply to wiring commercial power to charging equipment, but the voltages used on central office equipment are too low to be considered hazardous.

Most manufacturers in the United States follow the Bellcore Network Equipment Building System (NEBS) guidelines in their bay dimensions. Relay racks are standardized at 7, 9, and 11.5 feet in height and support equipment with 19- or 23- inch-wide mounting panels. The mounting screw holes are also spaced at standard intervals. In other countries metric dimensions must be supported.

Evaluating Common Equipment

Evaluation considerations discussed in previous chapters are equally applicable to common equipment. As with all telecommunications equipment, high reliability is imperative. Compatibility is important with alarm and control systems, but with power, distributing frame, and cabling, compatibility is generally not a problem if the equipment meets the specifications of the manufacturer of the interfacing equipment.

Environmental Considerations

An early consideration in planning a telecommunications system is to provide the floor space and environment required for its operation. The manufacturer's recommendations should be followed with respect to heating, air-conditioning, air circulation, cabling, and mounting. The primary considerations are provision of:

- ◆ Administrative work space.
- ◆ Sufficient floor space for expansion.
- ◆ Sufficient air-conditioning and heating capacity.
- ◆ Ducts and raceways where required.
- ◆ Separate power equipment room where recommended by the manufacturer.
- ◆ Adequate security.

Work Space

Equipment areas should provide a physical working environment with adequate space and lighting for equipment maintenance. The manufacturer should install equipment to its standards and should specify aisle space between equipment lineups, lighting standards, and commercial AC outlets for powering test equipment.

Protection and Distributing Frames

Frame terminations should be provided for all equipment that requires rearrangement or reassignment. The primary considerations are the density of frame blocks and the amount of trough space provided for jumper wire. Block density is a trade-off between the amount of floor space consumed by the distributing frames and the difficulty of running multiple wires to small or congested blocks. Distributing frames should always conform to a plan that is designed to eliminate congestion and support productivity in placing and removing crossconnects.

All cable pairs exposed to lightning strikes or power cross should be protected (see Chapter 6). This includes all pairs furnished by the LEC. The manufacturer's recommendations should be followed with respect to gas tube protection.

UPS Equipment

The primary criterion in evaluating UPS equipment is whether the supply is on-line, off-line or line-interactive. This can usually be determined by evaluating the manufacturer specifications. If the supply has any transition time before it assumes the load, it is not an on-line supply. If it lacks any kind of power line conditioning equipment, it is most likely an off-line supply.

A second important evaluation criterion is the *crest factor ratio*. This factor evaluates the supply's capability of handling load peaks. Technically, it is the ratio between the nonrepetitive peak load the supply can provide and the linear RMS (root mean square) load it supplies. The ratio should be at least 2.5; the higher the better.

The output wave shape is another evaluation factor. Commercial AC is a pure sine wave, and the more effective UPS supplies also furnish sine wave output. Less expensive supplies provide square wave output, which could affect the operation of the power supply in the supported equipment. If the vendor is unable to provide photos of the output wave, this factor is easy to evaluate by looking at the wave under load with an oscilloscope.

The amount of voltage regulation and the backup time are two more important factors in evaluating a UPS. The supply should maintain voltage within ±3 percent. The amount of backup time is determined by comparing the power drain of the protected equipment to the power furnished by the UPS, and how long the equipment is to be protected. A key telephone system or PBX normally is protected through the longest expected power outage. It may be necessary to power a file server or computer only long enough to allow a graceful shutdown since desktop devices are down anyway.

Batteries and Charging Equipment

Storage batteries are evaluated by their capacity, usually stated in ampere-hours, type of plate material, and electrolyte. Central office batteries are usually strings of individual cells, each having a nominal voltage of 2.17 volts. The cells must be in leakproof and crackproof cases, preferably with a sealed electrolyte. Private telecommunication equipment batteries are usually purchased in 12-volt increments. A 48-volt string consists of four such batteries.

Manufacturers also specify batteries by their expected service life. Long-life central office batteries have sufficient plate material to last for up to 20 years with proper maintenance.

If a plant powers a switching system, it is important to ensure that it has enough spare capacity to power external transmission and signaling equipment. In a private network the provision of batteries depends on whether the network must remain in operation during power failures or whether it will be allowed to fail until the power is restored. The decision whether to provide an emergency generator depends on whether the battery reserve is enough to survive a long power outage.

Cabling

The number of leads to cable to distributing frames is an important consideration in installing equipment. Apparatus such as T-1 carrier and NCTE usually has many wiring options designed to fit special services. If not all leads are cabled to the distributing frame, the use of certain options may be precluded in the future unless the equipment is recabled. If unneeded leads are cabled to the distributing frame, however, extra costs will be incurred in cabling, frame blocks, and installation labor, and more frame space will be consumed by the extra terminations.

Also of importance is proper segregation of cables. For example, cables carrying low-level carrier signals usually are separated from high-level cables, or the cables are shielded to prevent crosstalk. Data bus cables in many SPC switching systems must be isolated from other cables to prevent errors. The manufacturer's specifications must be rigidly adhered to in designing cable racks and troughs.

The manufacturer usually specifies maximum cable length. Most telecommunications equipment has critical lead lengths that must not be exceeded.

SELECTED COMMON EQUIPMENT MANUFACTURERS

Cable and Central Office Structural Components

3M Co. Telcomm Products Div.

Amphenol

Anaconda-Ericsson Inc.

Belden Electronic Wire and Cable

General Cable Co.

Lucent Technologies

Newton Instrument Co. Inc.

Saunders Telecom

Siecor Corporation

Standard Wire and Cable Co.

Distributing and Protector Frames and Equipment

3M Co. Telcomm Products Div.

Lucent Technologies

Northern Telecom Inc.

Porta Systems Corp.

Reliance Comm/Tec

Alarm and Control Equipment

Communication Manufacturing Co.

Lucent Technologies

NEC America

Rockwell International

SNC Manufacturing Co.

Power Systems and Storage Batteries

American Power Conversion

Analytic Systems

Citel

Clary

Exide Corporation

Geist

Kohler Central Office

Liebert

Lorain Products

Minuteman

Northern Telecom, Inc.

Panamax

Power Conversion Products, Inc.

Quality Power Systems

Reliance Comm/Tec

Sola Electric

Superior Electric

Tripp Lite

III

TRANSMISSION SYSTEMS

CHAPTER

13

LIGHTWAVE COMMUNICATIONS

Since its introduction in the late 1970s, fiber optics has been the telecommunications growth industry. It fueled a hectic decade of construction in the 1980s as IECs installed enormous quantities of fiber to replace their older microwave systems and to meet the burgeoning demand brought about by competition and long-distance rate reductions. As a result, the world has a huge supply of high-quality telecommunications circuits. Continents are laced with fiber, and undersea cables have multiplied the number of available circuits, increased the quality, and reduced the cost.

Fiber optics is one of the most remarkable developments in telecommunications, a field that has given the world such developments as satellite, digital switching, microwave radio, and the telephone itself. Fiber optics arrived at an opportune time in telecommunications history. It provides unlimited bandwidth in a world that was rapidly exhausting microwave frequencies. It provides interference-free communications of a quality that matters not whether the parties to a session are next door or half a world apart. The cable is fabricated from silicone, the most abundant substance on earth, and in terms of energy consumption the electronics are far more efficient than the technologies they replace.

The next step in the transformation of telecommunications networks is to introduce fiber into the local loop. All of the major LECs have experimented with

FITL. Its growth will depend to some degree on regulatory decisions that permit the LECs to offer entertainment services and CATV companies to offer telephone service.

Fiber's growth has not been limited to common carrier applications. It is now the medium of choice for building and campus backbones. Fiber-optics interfaces are the most economical and effective way of interconnecting LAN hubs. Many switching products offer remote modules that are connected to the host over fiber optics. The Fiber Distributed Data Interface (FDDI) is a 100 mb/s standard for campus data backbones. An emerging standard, Fiber Channel, provides speeds approximating 1 gb/s for interconnecting data hosts and peripherals.

A major controversy today is whether fiber optics on customer premises should be extended all the way to the desktop. Its proponents point out that the cost of fiber is about the same as Category 5 UTP (see Chapter 7), and provides bandwidths several orders of magnitude higher. Opponents point to the lower cost of UTP devices and contend that UTP can handle ATM at 155 mb/s, a speed that is likely to satisfy most foreseeable needs.

Controversy notwithstanding, the importance of fiber optics in telecommunications' future is unquestioned. As we have discussed in previous chapters, the analog network is disappearing. Digital devices work well over copper, but only if installation and manufacture are carefully controlled. Advances in fiber splicing and connectorizing techniques are bringing fiber to the point that handling skills for are no longer confined to a highly trained few.

One reason fiber optics is so effective is that once the cable is in place, it can be expanded by further developments in electronics without the need of adding cable. Every year development laboratories announce new speed and distance records, and soon the manufacturers translate experimental devices into commercial products. Fiber's enormous success does not mean that further developments will not occur. Considerable work remains to be done in the area of optical switches, optical amplifiers, and linear lasers.

Fiber-optic cable is an important replacement for twisted-pair cable in local trunking applications because of its greater capacity and smaller physical diameter. Diameter is important when conduits are congested and must be augmented to contain more voice frequency or T-carrier cables. Replacing a single copper cable with fiber optics can usually gain enough conduit capacity to forestall additions for many years to come. Because the medium does not radiate into free space, the FCC does not require licensing as they do with microwave.

As we approach the 21st century, most of the cross-country fiber-optics networks are in place, and manufacturers are looking to other applications to increase demand. The potential demand in the local loop outweighs the scope of the long-haul projects that were completed in the 1980s, but there are significant barriers preventing this demand from materializing immediately. The technology is understood, but some new revenue source is needed to justify the cost. The revenue source could be entertainment, but, most neighborhoods are already served by coaxial cable, and the CATV carriers have limited motivation to replace coax with fiber.

Lightwave communication is not without its drawbacks. Where the application needs enormous amounts of bandwidth, it is without equal, but where only a few circuits are needed it cannot compete economically with copper cable. Also, its enormous bandwidth makes it vulnerable. The natural enemy of fiber optics is the backhoe; a single cable cut can disrupt traffic to a large section of the country. It is not enough, therefore, for a common carrier to have a lightwave system. The network must be protected by diversity and automatic protection of cable routes to prevent a service disaster when a fiber route is lost.

As with other telecommunications technologies, there is a constant debate on standards. The digital input side of lightwave has standards that are derived from the digital signal hierarchy discussed in Chapter 5. On the line side, however, standards of many systems are proprietary. A light signal from one manufacturer will not work with a signal from another manufacturer unless they are designed for compatibility. This is one of the principal driving forces behind the synchronous optical network (SONET) standards (see Chapter 5).

LIGHTWAVE TECHNOLOGY

The use of light for communication is an idea that has been around for more than a century, but has become feasible only within the past two decades. Alexander Graham Bell, in the first known lightwave application, received a patent for his "Photophone" in 1880. The Photophone was a device that modulated a light beam that was focused from the sun and radiated in free space to a nearby receiver. The system reportedly worked well, but free space radiation of light has several disadvantages that the devices available at the time could not overcome. Like many other ideas this one was ahead of its time. Free space light communication is now technically feasible if the application can tolerate occasional outages caused by fog, dust, atmospheric turbulence, and other path disruptions.

Two developments raised lightwave communication from the theoretical to the practical. The first development was the laser in 1960. A laser produces an intense beam of highly collimated light; that is, its rays travel in parallel paths. The pulses from a digital signal trigger the laser on and off at the speed of the modulating signal. The second event that advanced lightwave was the development of glass fiber of such purity that only a minute portion of a light signal emitted into the fiber is attenuated. With a laser source that is triggered on and off at high speed, the zeros and ones of a digital communication channel can be transmitted to a detector, usually an avalanche photo diode (APD) or PIN diode. The detector converts the received signal pulses from light back to electrical pulses and couples them to the multiplex equipment. Figure 13–1 shows the elements of a lightwave communication system. Repeaters or regenerators are spaced at regular intervals with the spacing dependent on the transmission loss of the fiber and the *system gain* at the transmission wavelength. System gain is discussed in a later section.

A standby channel, which assumes the load when the regular channel fails, protects most lightwave systems. The two directions of transmission are normally protected separately between the digital signal input and output points. If a failure occurs, the protection equipment switches the signal to a new combination of cable, terminal equipment, and repeaters.

The advantages of lightwave accrue from the protected transmission medium of the glass fiber. These tiny waveguides isolate the digital signal from the fading and interference characteristics of free space. The optical fiber attenuates the light signal, however, and as Figure 13–2 shows, the loss is not uniform across the spectrum. As the figure shows, there are three regions or *windows* that lightwave communication can use.

The earliest fiber-optic systems used the 850 nm window because suitable lasers were first commercially available at that wavelength. Slower-speed LANs also use this window because LEDs to operate at that wavelength are economical. As lasers became available at 1,300 nm applications have shifted to this wavelength because of its lower loss. Single-mode fiber, discussed later, exhibits slightly lower losses in its third window at about 1,550 nm.

The first commercial fiber-optics system, installed in 1977, operated at 45 mb/s with repeaters required at four mile (6.4 km.) intervals. Current systems operate at OC-48, which has a bit rate of 2.49 gb/s. At OC-48 a pair of fibers, one for transmit and one for receive, can carry about 32,256 voice frequency channels. At OC 192, the highest SONET range that has been specified, a pair of fibers could support 129,024 voice channels.

LIGHTGUIDE CABLES

A digital signal is applied to a lightguide by pulsing the light source on and off at the bit rate of the modulating signal, and the signal propagates to the receiver at slightly less than the speed of light. The lightguide has three parts, the inner core, the outer *cladding,* and a protective coating around the cladding. Both the core and the cladding are of glass composition; the cladding has a greater *refractive index* so that most of the incoming light waves are contained within the

FIGURE 13-1

Block Diagram of a Typical Fiber-Optic System

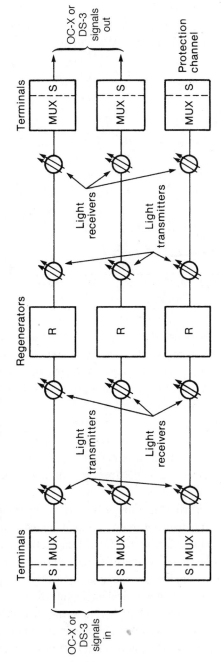

FIGURE 13-2

Spectral Loss for a Typical Optical Fiber; Loss Disturbances Labeled OH⁻ Result from Hydroxyl Ion Absorption

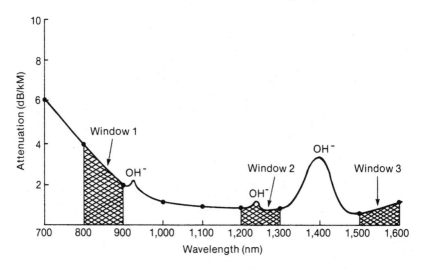

core. Light entering an optical fiber propagates through the core in *modes,* which are the different possible paths a lightwave can follow. Optical fiber is grouped into two categories, *single mode* and *multimode.* In single-mode fiber light can take only a single path through a core that measures about 10 microns in diameter, which is about the size of a bacterium. (A micron is one one-millionth of a meter). Multimode fibers have cores of 50 to 200 microns in diameter, with 62.5 microns the standard recommended for most applications. Multimode fiber is used almost exclusively in customer premise applications. Most LANs and high-speed networks such as FDDI specify multimode fiber with a 62.5 micron core.

Single-mode fiber is more efficient at long distances for reasons that we discuss below, but the small core diameter requires a high degree of precision in manufacturing, splicing, and terminating the fiber. Despite the greater precision needed, single-mode fiber is less expensive than multimode, primarily because of the vast quantities of single mode manufactured.

Lightwaves must enter the fiber at a critical angle known as the *angle of acceptance.* Any waves entering at a greater angle can escape through the cladding, as Figure 13–3 shows. The reflected waves take a longer path to the detector than those that propagate directly. The multipath reflections arriving out of phase with the main signal attenuate the signal, round, and broaden the shoulders of the light pulses. This pulse rounding is known as *modal dispersion.* It

FIGURE 13–3

Light Ray Paths through a Step-Index Optical Fiber

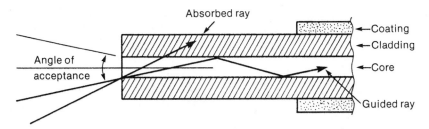

can be corrected only by regenerating the signal. The greater the core diameter, the greater the amount of modal dispersion. Single-mode fiber propagates only one mode of light, and therefore does not suffer from modal dispersion.

Both single- and multimode fiber are subject to another form of dispersion called *chromatic dispersion*. The term chromatic comes from the multiple wavelengths or colors of light that propagate through the core. Single-mode fiber is immune to modal dispersion because its core propagates only one path, but it is affected by chromatic dispersion. The amount of dispersion, in turn, is affected by the quality of the laser. High-quality lasers emit a narrower band of wavelengths.

Fiber also is classified by its refractive index into two general types, *step index* and *graded index*. With step-index fiber the refractive index is uniform throughout the core diameter. In graded-index multimode fiber the refractive index is lower near the cladding than at the core so that lightwaves propagate at slightly lower speeds near the core than near the cladding. The result is pulse rounding. When pulse rounding becomes too severe, the receiver cannot distinguish ones from zeros, and errors result. In graded-index, fiber dispersion is lower and the distance between regenerators can be lengthened. Figure 13–4 shows wave propagation through the three types of fiber.

Besides the effects of dispersion, fiber optic regenerator spacing is controlled by loss. Loss is caused by two factors, *absorption* and *scattering*. Absorption results from impurities in the glass core, imperfections in the core diameter, and the presence of hydroxyl ions or water in the core. The water losses occur most significantly at wavelengths of 1,400, 1,250, and 950 nm, as Figure 13–2 shows. Scattering results from variations in the density and composition of the glass material. These variations are an inherent by-product of the manufacturing process. Single-mode fiber has its lowest chromatic dispersion at the 1,300 nm wavelength, but minimum loss is at 1,550 nm, which has led to the development of *dispersion-shifted fiber*. Dispersion-shifted fiber shifts the

FIGURE 13-4

Wave Propagation through Different Types of Optical Fibers

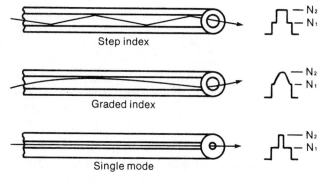

Step index

Graded index

Single mode

N - Refractive index

TABLE 13-1

Typical Fiber-Optic Characteristics

Type	Core/ Cladding Diameter μm	Attenuation dB/km 850 nm	Attenuation dB/km 1,300 nm	Bandwidth MHz/km
Plastic	985/1000	230		20
Multimode	62.5/125	4	2.5	200
Single mode	9/125		0.8	20,000

minimum chromatic dispersion wavelength to the 1,550 nm window to provide the lowest combination of loss and bandwidth at the same wavelength.

Most LANs operating at under 50 megabaud use 850 nm LEDs. Those operating between 50 and 250 megabaud generally use 1,300 nm LEDs. Applications running more than 250 megabaud use 1,300 nm lasers on single-mode fiber.

Not all fiber is made of glass. Plastic fiber, which has attenuation in the order of 160 to 200 dB per km, is also available. By comparison, glass fiber has attenuation of 2.5 dB/km or less. Plastic absorbs moisture, which increases attenuation, and it has a narrower bandwidth. Its primary application is in low-cost systems. Table 13–1 shows the loss range of different qualities of fiber.

FIGURE 13–5

The Modified Chemical Vapor Deposition Process

Courtesy of AT&T Archives

Manufacturing Processes

Glass fibers are made with a process known as *modified chemical vapor deposition* (MCVD) or an alternative process called *outside vapor deposition*. The MCVD process starts with a pure glass tube about six feet long and one and one-half inches in diameter. The tube is rotated over a flame of controlled temperature while a chemical vapor is introduced in one end, as Figure 13–5 shows. The vapor is a carrier for chemicals that heat from the flame deposits on the interior of the glass. The deposited chemicals form a tube composed of many layers of glass inside the original tube. The OVD process deposits high-purity glass on the outside of a ceramic rod, which is removed after the process is complete. When the deposition process is complete the tube is collapsed under heat into a solid glass rod known as a *preform.* The preform is placed at the top of a drawing tower where the fiber is heated to the melting point and drawn through into a hair-thin glass strand, as Figure 13–6 shows

Multiple fiber strands are wound together around a strength member and enclosed in a sheath. Like copper cable, fiber cable sheaths are made of polyethylene and can be enclosed in armor to protect against damage. Fiber-optic cable is suitable for direct burial, pulling through conduit, suspension from an aerial strand, or submersion in water.

Fiber Is Pulled through a Die into a Single Strand

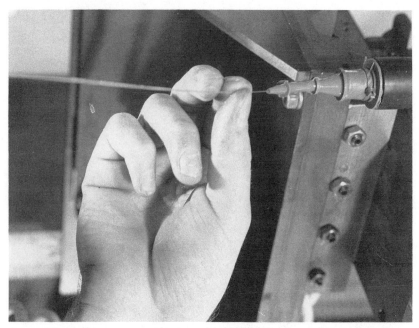

Courtesy of AT&T Archives

Fiber cables are spliced by adhesion or fusion. In the adhesion process, a technician places fibers in an alignment fixture and joins them with epoxy. The fusion method employs a splicing fixture that precisely aligns the two ends of the fiber under a microscope and fuses them with a short electric pulse. After splicing, the loss is measured to ensure that splice loss was acceptable. Splices are made with enough slack in the cable that they can be respliced, if necessary, until the objective loss is achieved.

Cable Connectors

In midspan, fiber cables are joined by splicing, but at terminal locations they are connectorized for coupling to terminal devices and for ease in rearrangement. The physical structure of connectors is of utmost importance because of the exceedingly close tolerances that are required to match cable to the transmission device. Connectors must be made from thermally stable materials, and have tightly locking keyed parts and highly polished mating surfaces. They also must be field-installable while maintaining factory-level performance.

Connector performance is rated by two criteria, the amount of insertion loss and the amount of reflection attenuation or return loss. A reflection is light that travels down the lightguide, strikes a discontinuity, and reflects toward the source, causing instability or errors. The amount of loss that is considered acceptable depends on the application. LAN applications, which use multimode cable almost exclusively, are more tolerant of performance. The loss of a LAN connector can usually be as much as 1.0 dB and still remain well within the loss budget. LANs can tolerate return loss as low as 20 dB, but as higher-speed applications such as FDDI are applied to the medium, a higher return loss is needed. A suitable connector for common carrier applications should have an insertion loss of 0.5 dB or less, and a return loss of at least 40 dB.

Couplers are made either free-hanging or for bulkhead mounting. Connectors use an epoxy and polishing arrangement for termination. The fiber is stripped and inserted into the connector. The ends are then polished to an optical finish. The durability of the connector is important. The connector is constructed to hold the ends of the fiber in contact, and it should remain so even under the strain of pulling or sideways motion. The types of connectors in use differ primarily in their method of latching the mating ends together. SC connectors use a push-pull type of latch with a plastic housing. They are rugged connectors that are used for high performance. FC connectors use a screw coupling. They are popular for single-mode and other high-performance applications.

ST® connectors are made by Lucent Technologies, and use a bayonet-style of housing. These are popular for multimode fiber. They come in both pullproof and nonpullproof versions. Biconic connectors have a dual cone-shaped barrel, which is the source of the name. They were one of the first types of connectors produced, and are primarily used today for additions to existing systems. FDDI connectors are a dual connector used for the separate transmit and receive fibers of FDDI.

FIBER-OPTIC TERMINAL EQUIPMENT

Fiber-optic systems have separate transmit and receive fibers, the opposite ends of which terminate in a light transmitter and receiver. The light transmitter employs either a light-emitting diode (LED) or a laser as its output element. Lasers have a greater system gain than LEDs because their output is higher and because a greater portion of the light signal can be coupled into the fiber without loss. The primary advantage of a LED transmitter is its lower cost. In applications that do not need high system gain such as local area networks, the cost saving can easily justify the use of LED transmitters.

FIGURE 13–7

Wave Division Multiplex

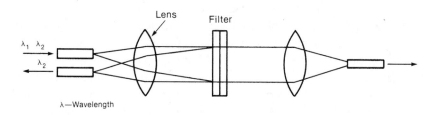

λ—Wavelength

The multiplex equipment connects to the input of the transmitter, and the fiber-optic cable couples to the output through a precision connector. Most fiber-optic systems use digital modulation, but analog transmitters vary the intensity of the light signal, or they modulate the pulse rate or pulse width. Although analog modulation is normally not linear enough for transmitting analog multiplex, it is suitable for transmitting a video signal, and is used in cable television systems.

The light receiver is an APD or PIN diode that couples to the optical fiber on the input end and to the multiplex equipment on the output end. The diode converts the light pulses to electrical pulses, which the receiver reshapes into square wave pulses. A lightwave regenerator has back-to-back receiver and transmitter pairs that connect through a pulse reshaping circuit.

Fiber-optic systems accept standard digital signals at the input, but each manufacturer develops its own output signal rate. Error checking and zero suppression bits are inserted to maintain synchronization and to monitor the bit error rate to determine when to switch to the protection channel. Because of differences in the line signals, lightwave systems are usually not end-to-end compatible between manufacturers unless they meet SONET standards.

Wavelength Division Multiplexing

The capacity of a fiber pair can be multiplied by using *wavelength division multiplexing* (WDM). WDM assigns services to different light wavelengths in much the same manner as frequency division multiplexing applies multiple carriers to a coaxial cable. Different wavelengths, or "colors" of light, are selected by using light-sensitive filters to combine light wavelengths at the sending end and separate them at the receiving end, as Figure 13–7 shows. Because the filter introduces loss, WDM reduces the distance between regenerators, and limits the path length by the wavelength with the highest loss. When engineers design lightwave systems, they normally provide enough system gain to compensate for future wavelength division multiplexing even if it is not used initially.

LIGHTWAVE SYSTEM DESIGN CRITERIA

Fiber-optic systems are designed by balancing capacity requirements with costs for cable, cable placing, terminal equipment, and regenerators. In most systems a prime objective is to eliminate midspan regenerator points so regenerators are placed only in buildings housing other telecommunications equipment. This objective may require reducing bit rates, providing higher-quality cable, and stretching the system design to preclude future WDM. The three primary criteria for evaluating a system are:

- ◆ Information transfer rate
- ◆ System attenuation and losses
- ◆ Cutoff wavelength

Information Transfer Rate

The information transfer rate of a fiber-optic system depends on the bandwidth, which in turn depends on dispersion rate and on the distance between terminal or repeater points. Manufacturers quote bandwidth in graded-index fiber as a product of length and frequency. For example, a fiber specification of 1,500 MHz-km could be deployed as a 150 MHz system at 10 km or a 30 MHz system at 50 km. Fiber-optic transmission systems are quoted according to the number of DS-3 systems they can support, with current commercial products ranging from fewer than one to more than 48 DS-3 systems per pair. Typical values are the same as the SONET optical carrier levels discussed in Chapter 5. Special-purpose fiber-optic systems intended for short-range private data transmission have much lower bit rates, and typically use cables with considerably more bandwidth than the application requires.

System Attenuation and Losses

In any fiber system a key objective is to avoid placing repeaters between terminals, if possible, because of the expense of right-of-way and maintenance. Therefore the system loss and attenuation, together with available bandwidth, is a key factor in determining usable range. System gain in fiber optics is the algebraic difference between transmitter output power and receiver sensitivity. For example, a system with a transmitter output of -5 dBm and a receiver sensitivity of -40 dBm has a system gain of 35 dB.

From the system gain, designers compute a *loss budget,* which is the amount of cable loss that can be tolerated within the available system gain. Besides cable loss, allowances must be made for:

◆ Loss of initial splices plus an allowance for future maintenance splices.
◆ Loss of connectors used to couple fibers and terminal equipment.
◆ Temperature variations.
◆ Measurement inaccuracies.
◆ Future WDM.
◆ Aging of electronic components.
◆ Safety margin.

These additional losses typically subtract about 10 to 12 dB from the span between terminal points, which leaves a loss budget of about 25 dB for cable. Cable cost depends on loss, so system designers choose a cable grade to match the loss budget.

FIBER OPTICS IN THE LOCAL LOOP

Now that a substantial portion of the interexchange network is converted to fiber optics, the LECs and CATV companies are turning to the next potential application, the local loop. The rationale behind fiber in the loop (FITL) is the assumption that video-on-demand will eventually require fiber. When this service develops, the user will select from a menu of educational and entertainment programs and have the program delivered to the premises over the loop. FITL could be particularly advantageous when high-definition television (HDTV) standards are established.

Local loop fiber will likely assume one of several architectures. The easiest application is to replace feeder cable with fiber. Fiber extends from the central office to a serving area interface point where it connects to digital loop carrier (DLC). The loop from the serving area interface to the customer's premises is copper cable, which simplifies the interface problem and overcomes the problem of feeding power to the customer's station. The second form of local loop fiber-optic option provides fiber direct to the customer's premises. In some applications, two fibers are installed, one for voice and data communication and the other for video; in other plans a single fiber is installed, using WDM to separate the directions of transmission.

A promising method of bringing fiber to the home is the Passive Optical Network (PON). This method places all the active equipment in the central office. A passive signal is brought to the residence, either directly to the home or to the curbside. The same fiber could be multipled into several residences, with the signals to and from the different premises multiplexed by time division multiple access (TDMA), which is similar to the method cellular radio uses to multiplex digital channels on the airwaves.

The real demand for fiber in the local loop now is for business. The two driving factors are an increase in DS-3 services, which cannot be transmitted for long distances over twisted-pair wire, and an increase in the demand for broadband services. Many LECs and AACs already provide fiber-optic capacity in metropolitan areas to serve business, so this form of growth does not greatly affect local loop technology. Fiber optics will eventually become a dominant local loop medium, but before that happens it must become cost-competitive with copper, and bandwidth requirements must grow to a level that cannot be economically served with alternative media.

UNDERSEA FIBER-OPTIC CABLES

Intercontinental communications services, which once were the province of satellite and conventional voice cables, are rapidly shifting to fiber-optics. The first transoceanic fiber optic cable, AT&T's TAT-8, became operational in 1988. TAT-8 can carry 40,000 simultaneous conversations. By comparison, the first undersea cable between Europe and the United States, TAT-1, could carry 36 simultaneous calls. During its 22-year life span, TAT-1 carried 10 million calls, which TAT-8 can handle in two days. TAT-8 has six fibers; two pairs in use and a third pair for backup, with regenerators placed at 79 km. intervals. The cable is buried one meter below the ocean floor where the water is less than one km. deep. Figure 13–8 shows TAT-8 beside its much larger predecessor, TAT-7, which is a coaxial cable. The rapid growth of undersea cable will inevitably bring down the price of circuits and switched services, just as it has domestically. The availability of satellite and fiber-optic circuits between continents makes route diversity feasible for those services that must have a high degree of availability.

APPLICATIONS

Lightwave communications systems have applications in both private and public communications systems. The primary applications are:

- ◆ Long-haul transmission systems.
- ◆ Trunking between local central offices.
- ◆ Metropolitan area backbone systems.

TAT-8 Transatlantic Fiber-Optic Cable Shown with the Larger TAT-7 Coaxial Cable

Courtesy of AT&T Archives

- ◆ Digital loop carrier feeder systems.
- ◆ Local area networks.
- ◆ Cable television backbone transmission systems.
- ◆ Private network backbone systems.
- ◆ Short-haul data transmission systems through noisy environments.

Standards

Several standard-setting bodies propose fiber-optic standards. The standards for customer-premises applications are prepared by the Electronic Industries Association and Telecommunications Industry Association in their Commercial Building Wiring Standards (see Chapter 7). Optical transmission standards, the lack of which once held back the industry, are now published in ITU's SONET standards. These standards, which are discussed in Chapter 5, set data rates, signal formats, and performance-monitoring standards.

Application Criteria

The high cost of right-of-way often stands in the way of companies' installing fiber-optic systems, but the advantages of this medium make it attractive for private applications. A major impediment to many applications is the common carriers' refusal to offer dark fiber. Most common carriers provide bandwidth, but where the application requires dark fiber, its use must be confined to the customer's premises. The following discusses the variety of ways companies can apply fiber optics.

Campus and Building Backbone Networks
Fiber optics is an excellent medium for a campus or building backbone. Most LANs now employ a fiber backbone. Fiber optics not only provides bandwidth, but also offers security and noise immunity that no other medium can match. Any campus or riser cable system should at least consider the potential future need for fiber optics. Either fiber pairs should be installed for future expansion, or empty conduit should be installed to support future fiber. Current applications use multimode fiber almost exclusively, but future applications such as Fiber Channel are apt to use single mode. Companies installing fiber today should consider installing both varieties in separate cables.

Fiber to the Desktop
The experts are in agreement about using fiber as a backbone in a building or campus network, but the question of carrying it all the way to the desktop is still open. Unshielded twisted pair (UTP) is about the same price as fiber, and has enough bandwidth for most applications. Since fiber is not an option for voice, UTP must be installed to every desktop; the question is whether to install fiber as well. Fiber optics is an ideal transmission medium for LANs, but the terminating equipment is twice as costly for fiber than for UTP. The fiber premium will undoubtedly decrease as the volume increases. In today's environment, fiber to the desktop can be justified only if the application has a genuine need for high bandwidth, or if there is an overriding consideration, such as security or need for noise immunity, that mandates the use of fiber.

If fiber is not feasible today, should it be installed today and left dark to support a future application? The answer to this question depends on economics. Many buildings are difficult to wire, and placing a composite fiber and UTP cable to desktops may make economic sense because so much of the cost is in installation labor. The chief question to evaluate here is whether the location of future applications can be foreseen reliably enough to justify the expense of fiber optics.

Video Systems

Until the last few years, the lack of reasonably priced linear modulators has limited the use of fiber optics for video. Fiber is an ideal medium for digitized video, but the high cost of compression equipment has made video prohibitive for many noncommercial applications. Now, the transmission of analog television signals over fiber is technically feasible, although fiber is more expensive than coaxial cable.

Environmental Concerns

Fiber optics has a far greater ability to survive in hostile environments than copper cable. The fiber itself is essentially immune to damage from water, caustic chemicals, and a corrosive atmosphere. In such applications, however, care should be taken that the outer sheath is equally immune to the environment.

Fiber is also immune to electromagnetic interference, which may impair UTP or even coaxial cables. This makes fiber ideal in industrial environments where heavy equipment may radiate interference. The elevator shaft is an acceptable housing for riser cables in some buildings, but the motors and controls may cause noise in twisted pair, but not in fiber.

Security Concerns

Fiber-optic systems offer a high degree of security. They are almost impossible to tap undetected, and if properly constructed they can meet TEMPEST standards. (TEMPEST is a Department of Defense specification that stands for Transient Electromagnetic Pulse Emanation Standard.) Equipment that meets TEMPEST standards must restrict the radiation of energy that could be picked up by nearby devices. Organizations that have sensitive information that could be compromised will find that fiber optics offers security that is unequaled by other media.

Evaluation Criteria

Fiber-optic equipment is purchased either as an integrated package of terminal equipment and cable for specialized private applications, or it is purchased as separate components assembled into a system for trunking between switching nodes. For the former applications, which include local area, point-to-point voice, data, and video networks, the evaluation criteria discussed below are not critical. In such systems the main question is whether the total system fits the application. In all fiber-optic systems the questions of reliability, technical support, cost, and compatibility are important. Fiber-optic systems do not vary widely in their power consumption or space requirements, so these criteria may usually be safely disregarded. In longer-range trunking applications the following criteria should be considered in evaluating a system.

System Gain

In selecting lightwave terminating equipment, the higher the system gain, the more gain that is available to overcome cable and other losses. The cost of a lightwave system relates directly to the amount of system gain. High-output lasers and high-sensitivity diodes are more expensive than devices producing less system gain. The least expensive transmitters use light-emitting diodes for output and have less system gain than lasers. When the limits of lightwave range are being approached, obtaining equipment with maximum system gain is important. For applications with ample design margin, low system gain is acceptable.

Cable Characteristics

Cable is graded according to its loss and bandwidth. The cable grade should be selected to provide the loss and bandwidth needed to support the ultimate circuit requirement. For systems operating at 100 mb/s or more, bandwidth becomes the limiting factor as opposed to loss. If the cable can support ultimate requirements there is little reason to spend extra money to purchase a higher grade. In public networks, unless some compelling reason exists for purchasing multimode cable, single-mode cable should be purchased for all applications. The price of single-mode fiber is less than multimode, and its greater bandwidth and lower loss makes it considerably more valuable for future expansion. The cable composition should be selected with inner strength members sufficient to prevent damage when cable is pulled through conduits or plowed in the ground. Armoring should be considered where sheath damage hazards exist.

In private applications the core size of multimode cable is an important consideration. EIA/TIA standards specify 62.5/125 micron cable, but some applications require 50/125 cable. (The 62/125 designation means the cable has a core of 62.5 microns and an external diameter of 125 microns.) If the application has not been selected, and cable is being placed for future applications, the safest choice is 62.5/125 micron cable.

Wavelength

With present technology the most feasible wavelength to choose is 1,300 nm. FDDI specifications call for 1,300 nm cable with a bandwidth of at least 500 MHz-km. Cable should be purchased with a 1,550 nm window if circuit requirements will ultimately justify the use of WDM. For most applications 850 nm should be avoided because of its greater loss. Exceptions are in local networks and private networks implemented by using leased fibers. With leased fibers the 850 nm window can be used with WDM as a way of increasing capacity without leasing more fiber, providing the distance between terminals supports the use of 850 nm and WDM. In other applications such as local networks the wavelength may be predetermined by the manufacturer. If the total system has enough gain and bandwidth to support the application, the wavelength is of little or no concern to the user.

Light Source

The two choices for light source are laser and LED. Both are semiconductor devices that emit light when an external voltage is applied. A laser has much higher power output than a LED, and can operate at higher bit rates. A LED is lower cost, and has a longer life, but it produces a wider beam of light and has a wider spectral width, which means that its light wavelength is broader than that of a laser.

LEDs are typically used where the distance between terminals is short; normally 10 km or less, and the bandwidth of the signal is lower than about 150 mb/s. A LED is generally satisfactory for local networks. In long-haul networks where long repeater spacing and high bandwidth are important, a laser is the device of choice.

Wavelength Division Multiplexing

The question of whether to plan a fiber-optics system with future WDM designed into the transmission plan is a balance between future capacity requirements and costs. WDM can double or triple the capacity of a fiber pair for little additional cost, or it can convert a single optical fiber into a full-duplex mode of operation by transmitting in both directions on the same fiber. It accomplishes this by reduced regenerator spacing, however, which is important in long systems but unimportant on systems that do not require an intermediate regenerator. On very short systems the cost of the WDM equipment may be greater than the cost of extra fibers.

SELECTED LIGHTWAVE PRODUCT MANUFACTURERS

Lightguide Cable

AMP, Inc.

Belden Wire and Cable

Berk-Tek

Brand-Rex Co.

CommScope, Inc.

Fibertron

Lucent Technologies

Mohawk/CDT
Northern Telecom, Inc. Cable Group
Optical Cable Corporation
Siecor Corporation

Lightwave Transmission Products

Alcatel Network Systems Corp.
Canoga Perkins
Fujitsu Network Transmission Systems
Hewlett-Packard Co.
Jerrold Communications
LDC Inc. Fiber Optics Communications
Lucent Technologies
NEC America Inc., Radio & Transmission Div.
Northern Telecom Inc., Optical Systems Division
Optelecom, Inc.
Preformed Line Products Fiberlight Div.
Rockwell International Network Transmission Systems
Rycom Instruments, Inc.
Telco Systems Fiber Optics Corp.

Splicing Equipment and Connectors

3M Telecom Systems Div.
Alcoa Fujikura LTD
AMP, Inc.
Amphenol Fiber Optics Products
Canstar
Fibertron
Gould, Inc. Fiber Optics Div.
Lucent Technologies
MOD-TAP
Porta Systems Corp.
RIFOCS Corp.
Siecor Corp.

Fiber-Optic Test Equipment

Alcoa Fujikura Ltd.

Anritsu Wiltron

Antel Optronics, Inc.

Broadband Communications Products

Hewlett-Packard Corp.

Laser Precision Corp.

LightScan Advanced Technologies

Lucent Technologies

Nextest Communications Products, Inc.

Opto-Electronics, Inc.

Photon Kinetics, Inc.

Siecor Corporation

Rycom Instruments, Inc.

Tektronix, Inc.

Wandel & Goltermann

Optical Switches

DiCon Fiberoptics

E-TEK Dynamics, Inc.

Fiberoptic Switch, Inc.

Fibersense & Signals, Inc.

CHAPTER

14

MICROWAVE RADIO SYSTEMS

As a communication medium, microwave had its birth during World War II. In the expansion that followed the war, microwave advanced from an experimental technology to become the workhorse of long-haul telecommunications. The North American continent was crisscrossed with networks of microwave routes, which became the information superhighways of the 1950s and 1960s. Now, most of those systems lie dormant, replaced by the fiber-optics-building boom of the 1980s. Microwave technology itself, however, is far from dead. Satellites, which we will discuss in the next chapter, are microwave repeater sites in the sky. Personal communications service, discussed in Chapter 17, is preempting some of the lower microwave frequencies and pushing the services that resided there into still-higher frequencies. Private organizations that have difficulty acquiring right-of-way for fiber routes can use microwave to bridge obstructions such as highways, lakes, and rivers. Short-haul microwave in the 18 GHz and 23 GHz bands has assumed increasing importance in metropolitan areas. (GHz is the abbreviation for gigahertz, which is one billion hertz.)

MICROWAVE TECHNOLOGY

The microwave bands constitute an enormous amount of bandwidth. Figure 14–1, which is a logarithmic scale, shows how the microwave frequency

345

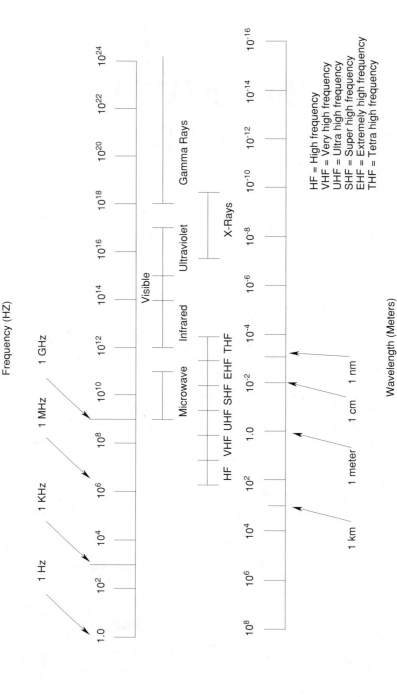

FIGURE 14-1

The Electromagnetic Spectrum

TABLE 14-1

Common Carrier and Operational Fixed (Industrial) Microwave
Frequency Allocations in the United States

Common Carrier	Operational Fixed
2.110–2.130 GHz	1.850–1.990 GHz
2.160–2.180 GHz	2.130–2.150 GHz
3.700–4.200 GHz	2.180–2.200 GHz
5.925–6.425 GHz	2.500–2.690 GHz (television)
10.7–11.700 GHz	6.575–6.875 GHz
	12.2–12.700 GHz*

* Based on noninterference with direct broadcast satellite service.

spectrum fits into the total radio and light spectrum. The usable portion stretches from approximately 1 to 40 GHz, with frequencies above that largely experimental. Considering that the frequency spectrum below microwave occupies a total of 1 GHz of bandwidth, you can see that microwave provides at least 40 times the bandwidth that is available below the microwave bands. This submicrowave bandwidth supports all the broadcast services, virtually all two-way radio, and countless other radio services.

Although the available microwave bandwidth is enormous, it is still a limited resource, and users must coordinate microwave paths to prevent interference. Because of congestion in metropolitan areas, it is often impossible to obtain frequency assignments in the lower end of the band. Table 14–1 lists the microwave common carrier and operational fixed-frequency band assignments in the United States. Microwave services are classified as operational fixed, which are commercial and private microwave systems, government, and common carrier. Other services such as radar occupy the unlisted parts of the spectrum.

As discussed in Appendix A, different parts of the radio frequency spectrum propagate through the atmosphere by different means. Frequencies higher than about 30 MHz travel in straight lines, which makes them ideal for short-distance line-of-sight communications. The higher the frequency, the more a radio signal takes on the characteristics of light. Microwaves are focused by the antenna so a maximum amount of energy is radiated in the desired direction, where they are picked up by the receiving antenna. Provided a microwave system is properly engineered, it is a cost-effective and reliable method of communication.

Microwave signals are affected by the following conditions that the engineer takes into account in designing the system:

♦ *Free-space loss,* which is the attenuation the signal undergoes as it travels through the atmosphere.

♦ *Atmospheric attenuation* is closely related to free-space attenuation. Changes in air density and absorption by atmospheric particles and water density attenuate the signal.

♦ *Reflections* can occur when the signal traverses a body of water or a fog bank. The signal takes multiple paths, which arrive at the receiving antenna out of phase, and cause the signal to fade.

♦ *Diffraction* occurs as a result of the terrain the signal crosses.

♦ *Rain attenuation* occurs when raindrops absorb or scatter the microwave signal. The effect is greater at higher frequencies and varies with the size of the raindrops. Larger drops are more detrimental.

Both analog and digital microwave systems are available, but as with other telecommunications technologies, digital predominates in current products. A digital microwave system consists of three major components: the digital modem, the radio frequency (rf) unit, and the antenna. The modem modulates an intermediate frequency (if), which is transmitted to the rf unit over coaxial cable. The rf unit is typically connected directly to the antenna, and mounted on a rooftop, tower, building mast, or tripod. At the rf unit a signal from a microwave generator is mixed with the if signal to generate the microwave output.

Units with the rf unit separated from the antenna are also available. In such systems the antenna connects to the rf unit with *waveguide,* which is a rectangular or round section of low-loss pipe.

The antenna focuses and radiates the signal to the receive location. To comply with zoning restrictions that regulate appearance, the antenna is sometimes mounted indoors behind glass. The glass must be chosen to avoid loss. Loss varies with the thickness of the glass, and lead compounds in the glass result in high attenuation. The angle of incidence, or the angle at which the signal penetrates the glass, affects the amount of loss. Reflections also attenuate the signal.

Microwave antennas are susceptible to snow and icing. A radome can be installed on the antenna to keep ice and snow from affecting the parabolic shape of the antenna. Heaters prevent interfering elements from building up on the radome.

Microwave signals can cover only a limited range. Repeaters are used to extend the range. Repeater stations are transmitter and receiver units connected back-to-back with the frequency shifted to prevent the transmitted signal from

FIGURE 14-2

A Billboard Microwave Reflector

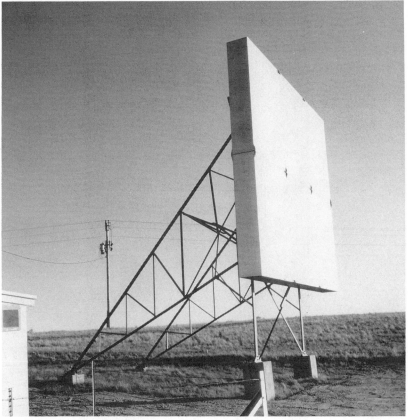

Courtesy, Gabriel Electronics, Inc.

leaking back into the receiving antenna and causing feedback. Passive repeaters are used in some installations where line of sight cannot be obtained between stations. A passive repeater can be two antennas connected back-to-back. Billboard reflectors, such as the one in Figure 14-2, are used to redirect the signal from one path to another.

MICROWAVE CHARACTERISTICS

The general principles of microwave radio are the same as those of lower frequency radio. A radio frequency (rf) signal is generated, modulated, amplified, and coupled to a transmitting antenna. It travels through free space to a receiving

FIGURE 14–3

Gabriel TH-10 Horn Reflector Antennas

Courtesy of Gabriel Electronics, Inc.

antenna, where a receiver captures a portion of the radiated energy and amplifies and demodulates it. The primary differences between microwave and lower frequency radio are the wavelength and behavior of the radio waves. For example, VHF television channel 2 has a wavelength of about 20 feet. To gain the maximum efficiency, a half-wave antenna receiving element is about 10 feet long. A 4 GHz microwave signal has a wavelength of about 3 inches, so an effective antenna at microwave frequencies is small compared to those at lower frequencies.

Since microwave frequencies behave similarly to light waves, they can be focused with large parabolic, or horn antennas similar to the Gabriel antennas shown in Figure 14–3. Unlike lower frequencies where radio waves cannot

FIGURE 14-4

Direct and Reflected Microwave Paths between Antennas

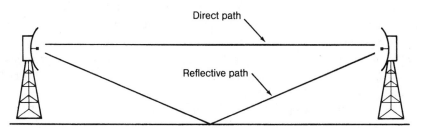

be focused narrowly enough to prevent them from radiating in all directions, microwave stations can operate in physical proximity on the same frequency without interference.

On the minus side of the ledger, microwaves have some of the undesirable characteristics of light waves, particularly at the higher frequencies. The primary problem is fading. Microwave fading is caused by multipath reflections and attenuation by heavy rain. Multipath reflections occur when the main radio wave travels a straight path between antennas, but a portion of it reflects over a second path, as Figure 14–4 shows. The reflected path is caused by some changing condition such as a temperature inversion, a heavy cloud layer, or reflection off a layer of ground fog. The reflected wave, taking a longer path, arrives at the receiving antenna slightly out of phase with the transmitted wave. The two waves added out of phase cause a drop in the received signal level. A second cause of fading is heavy rain, which absorbs part of the transmitted power at frequencies higher than about 10 GHz. The two primary causes of microwave path disruption, fading and equipment failures, are partially alleviated by diversity as described in a later section.

MICROWAVE SYSTEMS

Microwave routes are established by connecting a series of independent radio paths with repeater stations. Line-of-sight is required between the transmitting antenna and the receiving antenna for all microwave systems except those that use forward scatter techniques to transmit beyond the horizon. Repeater spacing varies with frequency, transmitter output power, antenna gain, antenna height, receiver sensitivity, number of voice frequency channels carried, free space loss of the radio path, and depth of expected fading. At the high end of the band, repeaters are sometimes spaced as close as 1 mile. At the low end of the band repeater spacings of up to 100 miles are sometimes possible, but 25 to 30 miles is more typical.

Modulation Methods

Microwave systems are modulated with either digital or with analog FM or AM signals. Most of the radio systems being installed today use digital microwave. The major advantage of digital radio results from regeneration of the signal at each repeater point. If the incoming signal is sufficiently free of interference to allow the demodulator to distinguish between 0s and 1s, digital radio provides the same high-quality, low-noise channel that T carrier provides. Unlike analog radio, which becomes progressively noisy during fades, digital radio remains quiet until it fades to a failure threshold, at which point the bit error rate (BER) becomes excessive and the radio is unusable.

Although each repeater regenerates the signal, errors are cumulative from station to station and cannot be corrected unless the radio employs forward error correction. Therefore the errors that occur in one section repeat in the next section where additional errors may occur, until finally the signal becomes unsuitable for data transmission. For voice, however, the errors have little effect. Besides the advantage of higher quality, digital microwave offers the advantage of directly interfacing T-1 carrier circuits without use of channel banks. This is particularly advantageous for transporting circuits between digital devices such as switching systems.

Bit Error Rate

The most important measure of digital microwave radio system performance is the bit error rate (BER). BER is expressed as the number of errored bits per transmitted bit, and usually is abbreviated as an exponential fraction. Specifications are often quoted at a BER of 10^{-6} which is one error per million transmitted bits. A BER of 10^{-6} is generally accepted as the highest that can be tolerated for digital data transmission over microwave. At a BER of 10^{-3} a radio is considered failed, although voice transmission can still take place at this error rate.

Diversity

To guard against the effects of equipment and path failure, microwave systems use protection, or diversity. Engineers often provide *space diversity* by spacing receiving antennas several feet apart on the same tower. This system protects against multipath fading because the wavelength of the signal is so short that the phase cancellation that occurs at one location will have little effect on an antenna located a few feet away.

Another protection system, permitted on common carrier bands, is *frequency diversity*. This system uses a separate radio channel operating at a different frequency to assume the load of a failed channel. When fades occur they tend to affect only one frequency at a time, so frequency diversity provides a high degree of path reliability. The primary disadvantages of this system are the use of the extra frequency spectrum and the cost of the additional radio equipment.

FCC rules do not permit frequency diversity in most noncommon carrier frequency bands. Therefore, many microwave systems use *hot standby* diversity. In a hot standby system, two transmitter and receiver pairs connect to the antenna, but only one system is working at a time. When the working system fails, the hot standby unit automatically assumes the circuit load. Hot standby protection is effective only against equipment failure. Hot standby cannot protect against fading and absorption, which affect the microwave path between stations.

Transfer to a protection system is initiated by the received noise level in an analog radio or by BER in a digital radio. When the noise or BER becomes excessive on a protected channel, the switch initiator sends an order to the transmitting end to switch the entire input signal to the protection channel. Technicians can initiate switches manually to clear a channel for maintenance. In any protection system, some loss of signal is experienced before the protection channel assumes the load. This signal loss is called a *hit*. Many systems can perform a *hitless* switch when a channel is manually transferred, but if equipment fails or fades, degradation will be experienced in the form of noise, excessive data errors, or both.

Protection systems protect working channels on a one-for-one or one-for-*N* basis with *N* being the number of working channels on the route. The FCC does not permit one-for-one protection where the application requires more than one radio channel because this method is wasteful of frequency spectrum. Figure 14–5 illustrates the three applications of protection—frequency diversity, space diversity, and hot standby.

Microwave Impairments

Microwave signals are subject to impairments from these sources:

◆ Equipment, antenna, and waveguide failures.
◆ Fading and distortion from multipath reflections.
◆ Absorption from rain, fog, and other atmospheric conditions.
◆ Interference from other signals.

FIGURE 14–5

Microwave Diversity Systems

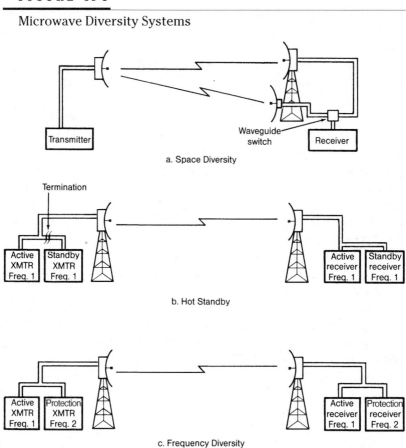

a. Space Diversity

b. Hot Standby

c. Frequency Diversity

Microwave reliability is expressed as percent availability, or uptime, which is the percentage of the time communications circuits on a channel are usable. The starting point on a microwave path calculation is to determine the number of hours of path downtime that can be tolerated in a year. For example, eight hours per year of path outage would equate to 99.91 percent availability from the following formula:

Percent Availability = 1 − (outage hours/8760 hrs. per year)

Because of path uncertainties, a satisfactory reliability level is attainable only with highly reliable equipment. Fortunately, equipment reliability has progressed to the point that equipment failures cause little downtime, and those failures that do occur can be protected by diversity. Most private microwave systems require at least 99.99 percent availability. Bear in mind that micro-wave path failures do not usually last long. An hour per year of outage caused by rain fades is more likely to occur as 60 outages of 1 minute each than as one failure of 60 minutes.

Microwave Path Analysis

Microwave path reliability is less predictable and controllable than equipment performance. The first factor to consider in laying out a microwave system is obtaining a properly analyzed and engineered path. The path designer selects repeater sites for availability of real estate, lack of interference with existing services, accessibility for maintenance, and sufficient elevation to overcome obstacles in the path.

The first step in microwave path analysis is to prepare a balance sheet of gains and losses of the radio signal between transmitter and receiver. Gains and losses are measured in decibels or dB, a concept that Appendix A explains. The dB is a measure of relative power gains and losses. Absolute measures of signal level are measured in decibels compared to one milliwatt (0 dBm). One milli-watt is equal to 1×10^{-3} watts of power. A signal of +30 dBm is equal to one watt, a signal output that is typical of many microwave transmitters. The spreadsheet in Table 14–2 shows a sample microwave path calculation. The following explains the elements that comprise the calculation and provide in-formation from which a similar spreadsheet can be constructed.

The *transmitter output power* is obtained from the manufacturer's speci-fications. For systems in the lower end of the microwave band, power is often 5 watts or more; for systems in the higher end of the spectrum power is a frac-tion of a watt. Power outputs of +10 to +30 dBm are common at 18 and 23 GHz. Remember that one watt is +30 dBm, so with the logarithmic nature of the deci-bel scale, a reduction of 10 dB is a reduction factor of 10. Therefore, +20 dBm is 0.1 watt, and +10 is 0.01 watt or 10 milliwatts.

Antenna gain can overcome the low powers in the 18 GHz to 23 GHz band. Although the industry commonly uses the term antenna gain, it is some-what of a misnomer because an antenna is a passive device that is incapable of amplifying the signal. Gain is a relative term compared to the performance of a free space mounted dipole, or *isotropic* antenna. Figure 14–6 illustrates this concept, which shows the difference between a dipole radiating equally in all directions and a microwave antenna that focuses the signal to provide a nar-rower beam consisting of a major center lobe and side lobes of lesser intensity. The amount of gain is proportional to the physical characteristics of the an-tenna, primarily its diameter. Generally, the greater the diameter of the an-

TABLE 14–2

Worksheet for Analyzing a Microwave Path

Site Name	Mt. Baldy	Three Peaks
Path length (miles)	5.2	
Frequency (GHz)	23	
Gains		
Transmitter output power (dBm)	20.5	20.5
Antenna gain	46.0	38.0
Total gains	66.5	58.5
Losses		
Free space	−138.2	−138.2
Atmospheric	−0.8	−0.8
Antenna alignment	−0.5	−0.5
Safety factor	−0.5	−0.5
Total losses	−140.0	−140.0
Unfaded receive signal level	73.5	81.5
Receiver sensitivity	74.5	74.5
Fade margin	39.0	31.0

FIGURE 14–6

Antenna Radiation Patterns

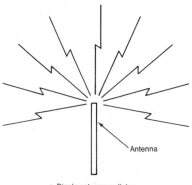

a. Dipole antenna radiates
equally in all directions.

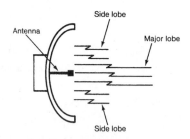

b. Horn, or parabolic, microwave
antenna concentrates signal
strength in a narrow beam
with minor side lobes.

tenna, the greater its gain. Also, for a given diameter of antenna, the gain increases as frequency increases and wavelength decreases. Because the wavelength is very short at these frequencies (1 centimeter, or slightly less than 0.5 inch, at 30 GHz), antennas with gains in the order of 40 dB or more are readily available without the high cost of both antennas and tower structures required by large diameter antennas.

Antenna gain is obtained from manufacturers' specifications. The size of the antenna is one variable that is reasonably easy to change to improve path reliability. Note that antenna gain operates in both transmitting and receiving directions. It is not necessary to choose the same gain for both ends of a microwave path.

The factor that has the most influence on path loss is *free space attenuation,* which can be calculated by the formula:

$$A = 96.6 + 20 \log P_L + 20 \log F$$

where:

A is free space attenuation in dB
P_L is path length in miles
F is frequency in Ghz.

In addition to free space attenuation, atmospheric losses are caused by absorption of the signal by oxygen molecules and water vapor in the atmosphere. This factor should not be confused with rain attenuation, which is covered later. Generally, atmospheric losses can be estimated at 0.12 dB per mile at 18 GHz and 0.16 dB per mile at 23 GHz.

The *antenna alignment factor*—usually about 0.5 dB—is a factor that designers choose to reflect the imperfect alignment of antennas. When antennas are installed, they are aligned on major radiation lobes. With time, temperature changes and tower shifting because of wind stress may cause the signal to drift slightly. This factor is added to provide a margin of safety. Besides the antenna alignment factor, other safety factors should be added to account for other imperfections. Usually another 0.5 dB of loss is added to be conservative.

Gains and losses are algebraically added to find the *unfaded received signal level.* This is the signal level that should be received at the input to the receiver in the absence of conditions such as rain that cause fade. The manufacturer supplies the *receiver sensitivity* figure as the minimum signal level that will provide a bit error rate of 10^{-6} or better. If the unfaded received signal level is added algebraically to the receiver sensitivity, the result is the *fade margin,* which is the amount of fading the signal can tolerate.

If fading did not occur, it would be easy to calculate a reliable microwave path using the above formulas. Fading occurs, however, and the major cause at frequencies above about 10 GHz is rain. At these frequencies the raindrop size is a significant fraction of the signal wavelength (wavelength is about one inch at 10 GHz). The rain rate that will attenuate the microwave signal by an amount equal to the fade margin is called the *critical rain rate*. The most important factor is not so much the amount of rain that falls, but the nature of the rain. The larger the raindrops and the more intense the rainfall, the greater the attenuation and the higher the probability of outage.

Absorption is a most significant impairment in areas of heavy rainfall with large drop size such as the Gulf Coast and southeastern United States. Conventional diversity is not effective against rain absorption because rain fading is not frequency selective. The most effective defenses are frequency diversity using a lower band such as 6 GHz, if permitted by the FCC, use of large antennas, and closely spaced repeater stations. The easiest method of obtaining rainfall data is from the microwave manufacturers, who usually can estimate the number of minutes and frequency of outage that will be caused by rain in your part of the country.

Fresnel Zone Clearance

In microwave path engineering, it is not enough to have line-of-sight communication between stations; it is also necessary to have a minimum clearance over obstacles. If insufficient clearance exists over buildings, terrain, or large bodies of water, the path will be unreliable because of reflection, or path bending.

The amount of clearance required over an obstruction is expressed in terms of *Fresnel zones*. A Fresnel zone is an imaginary elliptical zone surrounding the direct microwave beam. The first Fresnel zone is calculated by the formula:

$$FZ_1 = 72.2 \sqrt{\frac{D1 \times D2}{F \times D}}$$

where:

FZ_1 is the radius of the first Fresnel zone in feet
$D1$ is the distance from the transmitter to the reflection point in miles
$D2$ is the distance from the reflection point to the receiver in miles
F is the frequency in GHz
D is the length of the signal path in miles.

To illustrate the principle of Fresnel zone calculations, refer to Figure 14–7, in which a signal is beamed between two buildings 5.2 miles apart with an obstruction 2.1 miles from one transmitter. The first Fresnel zone is calculated to be 16.8 feet. For best results, the clearance over the obstacle should be

FIGURE 14-7

Fresnel Zone Clearance over an Obstruction

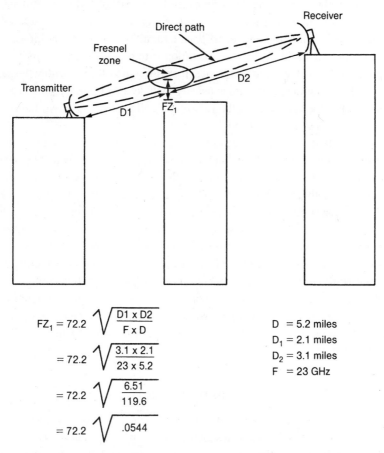

$$FZ_1 = 72.2 \sqrt{\frac{D1 \times D2}{F \times D}}$$

$$= 72.2 \sqrt{\frac{3.1 \times 2.1}{23 \times 5.2}}$$

$$= 72.2 \sqrt{\frac{6.51}{119.6}}$$

$$= 72.2 \sqrt{.0544}$$

$$= 16.8 \text{ feet}$$

D = 5.2 miles
D_1 = 2.1 miles
D_2 = 3.1 miles
F = 23 GHz

one Fresnel zone, but satisfactory results will usually be obtained if the clearance is at least 0.6 Fresnel zone, which in this case is 10 feet. If the clearance is insufficient, multipath fading will result.

Multipath Fading

Multipath fading is a source of impairment in both analog and digital microwave. It is caused by conditions that reflect a portion of the signal so both the main wave and the reflected wave arrive at the receiving antenna slightly out of phase. The phase differences between the two signals cause a reduction in the received signal level. Multipath reflections usually do not affect all frequencies within a band equally, which results in signal distortion within the received pass band. Distortion is of particular concern with digital microwave, which is susceptible to a higher BER under multipath fading conditions. One way of minimizing the effects of distortion is to use an *adaptive equalizer,* a device inserted in the receiver to cancel the effects of distortion within the passband. Digital radio specifications usually include the *dispersive fade margin,* which states the tolerance of the radio for the frequency selective fades that cause received signal distortion.

Both frequency and space diversity are effective defenses against multipath distortion. With a second receiving antenna mounted a few feet below the first on the same tower, the main and reflected paths do not affect the signal received in both antennas equally. The system selects the best of the two signals. Frequency diversity is also an effective defense against multipath distortion because of the frequency-selective nature of signal reflections. Frequency diversity is not, however, permitted for all types of service.

Other defenses against multipath distortion include an effective path profile study with proper site selection and sufficient tower height to provide adequate clearance over obstacles. Also, the use of large antennas focuses the transmitted signal more narrowly and increases the received signal level at the receiver. The larger the antenna, however, the more rigid the tower must be.

Interference

Adjacent channel and overreach interference are other microwave impairments. Overreach is caused by a signal feeding past a repeater to the receiving antenna at the next station in the route. It is eliminated by selecting a zigzag path or by using alternative frequencies between adjacent stations.

Adjacent channel interference is another potential source of trouble in a microwave system. Digital radios, particularly those using QAM modulation, are less susceptible to adjacent channel interference than PSK and FM analog radios because of the bandpass filtering used to keep the transmitter's emissions within narrow limits. Multichannel radio installations usually employ cross polarization to prevent adjacent channel interference. In this technique, channel combining networks are used to cross-polarize the waves of adjacent channels. Cross-polarization discrimination adds 20 to 30 dB of selectivity to adjacent channels.

Heterodyning versus Baseband Repeaters

Analog microwave repeaters use one of two techniques, *heterodyning* or *baseband,* to amplify the received signal for retransmission. In a baseband repeater, the signal is demodulated to the multiplex (or video) signal at every repeater point. In a heterodyne repeater, the signal is demodulated to an intermediate frequency, usually 70 MHz, and modulated or heterodyned to the transmitter output frequency. Heterodyne radio is reduced to baseband only at main repeater stations, where the baseband signal is required to drop off voice channels.

The primary advantage of baseband radio is that some carrier channel groups can be dropped off at repeater stations. Heterodyne radio has the advantage of avoiding the distortions caused by repeated modulation, demodulation, and amplification of a baseband signal. Therefore, heterodyne radio is employed for long-haul use with dropoff points only at major junctions.

Multiplex Interface

Digital microwave interfaces to multiplex equipment through either a standard or a special digital interface. Most long-haul systems marketed in the United States provide a standard DSX interface to one, two, or three DS-3 signals. Short-haul microwave generally supports some multiple of DS-1 or one DS-3 signals. These systems usually support only standard DSX-1 interfaces directly into a channel bank or PBX.

Analog microwave connects to analog multiplex through frequency modulated transmitter (FMT) and frequency modulated receiver (FMR) equipment. The multiplex baseband signal connects to the input of an FMT, which generates a frequency modulated intermediate frequency, usually 70 MHz. This signal is applied to the input of the radio and is modulated to the final rf output frequency. At the receiver, rf and if amplifiers boost the incoming signal and connect it to the input of the FMR. The output of the FMR is a baseband signal that is coupled to the multiplex equipment.

MICROWAVE ANTENNAS, WAVEGUIDES, AND TOWERS

Microwave antennas are manufactured as either parabolic dishes or horns, and range in diameter from 1 or 2 feet for short, high-frequency hops to 100 feet for earth station satellite service.

At lower frequencies, microwave antennas are fed with coaxial cable. Coaxial cable loss increases with frequency; therefore most microwave systems use waveguide for the transmission line to the antenna. Waveguide is circular or rect-

F I G U R E   14–8

Guyed Tower Supporting Microwave Antennas

Courtesy of Gabriel Electronics, Inc.

angular, with dimensions designed for the frequency range. At 18 to 23 GHz, and sometimes in lower frequency bands, the radio frequency equipment mounts directly on the antenna, which eliminates the need for waveguide.

Multiple transmitters and receivers can be coupled to the same waveguide and antenna system by *branching filters. Directional couplers* are waveguide hybrids that allow coupling of a transmitter and receiver to the same antenna. This technique often is used in repeater stations to permit using one antenna for both directions of transmission.

Antennas are mounted on rooftops, if possible. If more elevation is needed, they can be mounted on towers, as shown in Figure 14–8. Antennas must be precisely aligned. They are first oriented by eye or calculated azimuth and then adjusted to maximum received signal level. In orienting antennas, it is important to know the calculated received signal level and to ensure that the received signal is within 1 or 2 dB of that level. Without this benchmark it is possible that the antenna will be oriented on a minor signal lobe instead of the main lobe.

Manufacturers supply microwave towers in guyed and self-supporting configurations. Self-supporting towers require less space and must be designed more rigidly to support the antenna against the effects of weather. If enough land is available to accommodate down guys, a less expensive guyed tower can be used. The larger the antenna diameter, the more rigid the tower must be to prevent flexing in the wind. Tower rigidity is important because excessive flexing can disorient the antennas.

Entrance Links

The facility used to connect the final radio station in a route to the terminal equipment is the *entrance link*. The preferred way to terminate a microwave route is by mounting the radio and multiplex equipment in the same building. However, frequency congestion and path obstructions in metropolitan areas often make it necessary to terminate the radio some distance from the multiplex terminal. The entrance link links the multiplex to the radio. Entrance links operate at baseband or, for short distances, at intermediate frequencies. Lightwave is usually used for digital radio entrance links.

APPLICATIONS

With the availability of low-cost short-haul equipment, microwave technology has come within the reach of many companies and can quickly pay back the initial investment in savings of common carrier facilities. Microwave finds its most important applications in the following:

- ◆ Trunking between central offices.
- ◆ Bypass T-1 circuits from private companies to IECs.
- ◆ Studio to transmitter video links.
- ◆ Temporary or emergency restoration of facilities.
- ◆ Connecting PBXs in a metropolitan network.
- ◆ Interconnecting local area networks.
- ◆ Providing diverse routing to protect against failure of the primary circuit route.
- ◆ Crossing obstacles such as highways and rivers.
- ◆ Implementing local data communications networks.

In applying short-haul digital microwave, it is necessary to consider the following factors:

- ◆ What alternatives are available? Is microwave more cost-effective than common carrier facilities such as fiber optics and leased T-1?
- ◆ How much bandwidth is required now and for the future? The greater the amount of bandwidth, the more expensive the systems, although it is generally less expensive to purchase spare capacity with a new system than it is to add capacity later.
- ◆ What level of availability is needed to make the system feasible? With the spacing between terminals and the rainfall factor, is it possible to obtain the required availability factor with short-haul microwave?
- ◆ Is there line of sight between the terminal locations with sufficient clearance over intervening obstacles? If not, repeaters may be required. If repeaters are required, is the necessary real estate available?
- ◆ Where will the equipment be located? The most desirable location is on rooftops. If necessary, small towers can be constructed on the rooftops. Separate, ground-mounted towers are expensive and should be avoided if possible.
- ◆ What kind of specialized technical assistance will be required? Most companies require assistance with path surveys, license applications, and frequency coordination. Often, this can be supplied by the equipment vendor.

Standards

Microwave standards are set by the Federal Communications Commission in the United States and by the ITU internationally. The FCC licenses transmitters only after the equipment is type accepted. FCC rules and regulations list the operating rules for radio equipment within the United States. The EIA has established wind-loading zones in the United States for use in radio, tower, and antenna design, and several electrical and mechanical criteria for antenna and waveguide design. The Federal Aviation Administration (FAA) specifies tower lighting requirements.

Microwave equipment made by different manufacturers usually cannot be connected at the radio frequency level. Although the frequencies and number of channels are the same, proprietary alarm and maintenance signals prevent interconnection. At a repeater station, it is usually possible to interconnect baseband signals from different manufacturers because at this level they conform to standard digital signal (DS) specifications.

Evaluation Considerations

The factors of reliability, power consumption, availability, floor space, and the ability to operate under a variety of environmental conditions are important with microwave as with other telecommunications equipment. Besides these considerations, which are covered in previous chapters, the following factors also must be evaluated.

System Gain   When a microwave signal radiates into free space it is attenuated by losses that are a function of the frequency, elevation, distance between terminals, and atmospheric conditions such as rain, fog, and temperature inversions. The amount of free space loss that a system can overcome is known as the *system gain*. System gain is expressed in decibels and is a function of the output power of the transmitter and the sensitivity of the receiver. Receiver sensitivity is a measure of how low the signal level into the receiver can be while still meeting noise objectives in an analog system or BER objectives in a digital system. For example, if a microwave transmitter has an output power of +30 dBm (1 watt) and a receiver sensitivity of -70 dBm, the system gain is 100 dB.

With other factors being equal, the greater the system gain, the more valuable the system because repeaters can be spaced farther apart. Given the same repeater spacing, a microwave radio with higher system gain has a greater fade margin than one with lower system gain. System gain can be improved in some microwave systems by the addition of optional higher-power transmitters, low-noise receiver amplifiers, or both.

Spectral Efficiency   Microwave radio can be evaluated based on its efficiency in using limited radio spectrum. The FCC prescribes minimum channel loadings for a microwave before it is type accepted. Within the frequency band, the license granted by the FCC limits the maximum bandwidth. Where growth in voice frequency channels is planned, the ability to increase the channel loading is of considerable interest to avoid adding more radio channels. Spectral efficiency in both analog and digital radios is a function of the modulation method. The controlling factor is noise in analog radio and BER in digital radios.

Fade Margin   The fade margin refers to the amount of fading of the received signal level that can be tolerated before the system crashes. A crash in an analog radio is defined as the maximum noise level that the application can tolerate. In a digital microwave, fade margin is the difference between the signal level that yields a maximum permissible BER (usually 10^{-6}) and the crash level (usually 10^{-3}). Analog radios fade more gracefully than digital radios. As the received signal diminishes, the channel noise level increases in analog radio, but communication may still be usable over a margin of about 20 dB. The fade margin of a digital radio is narrow—on the order of 3 dB. Either a digital signal is very good or it is totally unusable, and the margin between the two points is small.

Protection System   The user's availability objective determines the need for protection in a microwave system. Availability is affected by equipment failures and fades. Equipment availability can be calculated from the formula:

$$Percent\ Availability\ = \frac{MTBF - MTTR(100)}{MTBF}$$

Availability as affected by fades can be determined by a microwave path engineering study. It is possible to calculate percent availability within a reasonable degree of accuracy for both fades and failures, but it is impossible to predict when failures will occur. Therefore, protection may be necessary to guard against the unpredictability of failures even though the computed availability is satisfactory.

Another factor weighing in the decision to provide diversity is the accessibility of equipment for maintenance. Some short-haul microwave is mounted in an office building where it can be accessed within a few minutes. On that basis it may be reasonable to provide spares and to forgo diversity to save money. In a system with remote repeaters, diversity usually is needed because of difficulty in reaching the site in time to meet availability objectives.

Alarm and Control and Order Wire Systems   All microwave radios should be equipped with alarm systems that provide both local and remote failure indications. An alarm system is evaluated based on how accurately the alarm is identified. Primitive systems indicate only that trouble exists, but not what it is. Sophisticated systems provide a complete remote diagnosis of radio performance. A microwave system equipped with protection and emergency power also requires a control system to switch equipment and operate the emergency engine. An order wire should be provided so technicians can talk between units for antenna lineup and maintenance.

Standard Interfaces   Digital microwave systems should be designed to connect to a standard digital signal interface such as DSX-1, DSX-2, or DSX-3. Systems designed for the operational fixed band sometimes use nonstandard interfaces such as 12 or 14 DS-1 signals. Special multiplexers are required to implement these interfaces.

Frequency Band Frequency availability often dictates the choice of microwave frequency band. Where choices are available, the primary criteria are the number of voice frequency channels required, the availability of repeater locations, and the required path reliability. As stated earlier, path reliability decreases with increasing radio frequency because of rain absorption. Reliability can be improved by decreasing the repeater spacing or increasing the antenna size.

Path Engineering A microwave path should not be attempted without an expert path survey. Several companies specialize in frequency coordination studies and path profile studies and should be consulted about a proposed route. A sites should be chosen for accessibility and availability of real estate and a reliable power source. Engineers choose tower heights to obtain the elevation dictated by the path survey. The antenna structure must support the size of antenna in a wind of predicted velocity. Wind velocities for various parts of the country are specified by EIA.

Environmental Factors Frequency stability is a consideration in evaluating microwave equipment. FCC rules specify the stability required for a microwave system, but environmental treatment may be needed to keep the system within its specifications. Air-conditioning usually is not required, but air circulation may be necessary. Heating may be required to keep the equipment above $0°$ C. Battery plants lose their capacity with decreasing temperature. Therefore, in determining the need for heating, designers should remember that battery capacity is lowest during abnormal weather conditions when power failures are most apt to occur.

Test Equipment All microwave systems require test equipment to measure frequency, bandwidth, output power, and receiver sensitivity. This equipment, which should be specified by the manufacturer, is required in addition to the test equipment needed to maintain multiplex equipment.

SELECTED MICROWAVE RADIO EQUIPMENT MANUFACTURERS

Long-Haul Microwave Transmitters and Receivers

Aydin Microwave Div.
California Microwave

Digital Microwave Co.

Ericsson, Inc.

Farinon Division, Harris Corporation

Lucent Technologies

NEC America, Inc.

Northern Telecom, Inc.

Rockwell International Network Transmission Group

Terracom Division, Loral Corporation

Short-Haul Microwave Transmitters and Receivers

Digital Microwave Co.

Ericsson, Inc.

Farinon Division, Harris Corporation

M/A-Com

Microwave Networks Corp.

NEC America, Inc.

Rockwell International Network Transmission Group

Terracom Division, Loral Corporation

Microwave Antennas, Waveguides, and Towers

Gabriel Electronics Inc.

NEC America, Inc.

Rockwell International Collins Transmission Systems Div.

Scientific-Atlanta, Inc.

15

SATELLITE COMMUNICATIONS

All the attention regarding the miracles of telecommunications technology seems to be focused on fiber optics, but satellites have a lot of life left. For one thing, they serve places that fiber cannot reach, and for another, satellites are a broadcast medium, while fiber is point-to-point. A decade ago satellites were important for handling telephone calls overseas and to remote locations. They are still important for the latter, but the oceans have been laced with undersea cable to the point that most intercontinental calls are now carried terrestrially.

Just as television has not replaced radio, fiber will not and cannot completely replace satellite. Both technologies have a range of applications. Where fiber is feasible, it clearly offers superior service, but it cannot attach to anything that moves, it cannot economically reach remote locations, and it cannot broadcast a signal simultaneously to all parts of a continent. This means there are plenty of remaining applications for satellite, and more to come.

Satellites are in the process of reinventing themselves. Telstar 1, the nations first experimental communications satellite launched in 1962, carried only 12 voice circuits in low orbit. Earth stations tracked the satellite as it moved, and before it disappeared over the horizon, the earth station switched to track the next satellite in sequence. Each satellite circled the earth in about two hours, and was visible for only a short time, sometimes less than half an hour. The low orbit proved impractical, however, because a chain of several satellites was needed to provide continuous service, and the satellite antennas required constant reaiming. AT&T, Telstar 1's owner, chose low orbit because it minimized the length of the radio signal's round-trip from earth to satellite and back, which reduced delay.

Now, low-orbiting satellites are about to make a comeback with plans announced by several groups to launch a personal communications service that blankets the earth with a network of low earth orbit satellites (LEOS). In fact, satellite service is probably the only way the PCS ideal of phone calls to any-one, anywhere, anytime can be realized in a reasonable time span. Whether it will be affordable is another issue that is discussed in Chapter 17.

Present-day communications satellites orbit the equator at a *geosynchro-nous* altitude of 22,300 miles. The equatorial orbit has the advantage of cover-ing both the Northern and Southern Hemispheres. Except the extreme polar re-gions, about one third of the earth's longitudinal surface can be covered by a single equatorial satellite. At geosynchronous orbit, the satellite travels at the same speed as the earth's rate of spin, so geostationary satellites remain at a fixed position with relation to a point on the earth. Some satellites are launched within an orbit that inclines slightly, which makes them appear to move north and south during the course of an orbit. These satellites require a moveable an-tenna to track them. From geosynchronous orbit, three satellites can theoreti-cally cover the entire earth's surface, with each satellite subtending a radio beam 17° wide. The portion of the earth's surface that a satellite illuminates is called its *footprint*.

While long-haul voice traffic may be migrating from satellites to under-sea cables, other applications are cropping up. VSAT (very small aperture ter-minal) enables users to mount small antennas on rooftops to run a multitude of applications such as point-of-sale, which need low-bandwidth facilities distrib-uted over a wide range. Communications satellites are used for global position-ing, communications with ships at sea, telemetering data from trucks in transit, and for direct broadcast television.

Satellites fall into three general categories—domestic, regional, and in-ternational. Domestic satellites carry traffic within one country. Regional sat-ellites span a geographical area, such as Europe, and international satellites are intended for traffic that is largely intercontinental. Although undersea fiber-optic systems are taking much of the international voice traffic because of their lower propagation delay, international television is still a large and growing market for satellites.

International satellite communications are controlled by the International Telecommunications Satellite Organization (INTELSAT), which is an interna-tional satellite monopoly operating under treaty among its member nations and

TABLE 15-1

Principal Communications Satellite Frequency Bands

Band	Uplink	Downlink
C	5,925–6,425 MHz	3,700–4,200 MHz
Ku	14.0–14.5 GHz	11.7–12.2 GHz
Ka	27.5–31.0 GHz	17.7–21.2 GHz

serving more than 170 countries and territories. INTELSAT operates more than 20 satellites at this writing, with 13 more scheduled by the end of the decade. Domestic satellites are owned and operated by COMSAT, AT&T, Western Union, RCA, American Satellite, and GTE.

As Table 15–1 shows, the frequencies available for communication satellites are limited. The 4 and 6 GHz C band frequencies are the most desirable from a transmission standpoint because they are the least susceptible to rain absorption. Satellites share the C band frequencies with common carrier terrestrial microwave, requiring close coordination of spacing and antenna positioning to prevent interference. Interference between satellites and between terrestrial microwave and satellites is prevented by using highly directional antennas. Currently, satellites are spaced about the equator at two degree intervals. At geosynchronous orbit each degree is equal to 450 miles, which means that satellites are spaced at 900-mile intervals. Figure 15–1 shows conceptually how a satellite is positioned in equatorial orbit.

The Ku band of frequencies has come into more general use as the C band becomes congested. Ku band frequencies are exclusive to satellites, allowing users to construct earth stations almost anywhere, even in metropolitan areas where congestion precludes placing C band earth stations. The primary disadvantage of the Ku band is rain attenuation, which results in lower reliability. With identical 2° spacing for both C and Ku bands, the hybrid satellite, which carries transponders for both bands, is becoming feasible.

Ka band satellites are becoming more feasible as the lower frequencies are used up. Ka band operates with an uplink of 27.5 to 31 GHz and a downlink of 17.7 to 21.2 GHz. Although the higher frequency of Ka band subjects the signal to a higher probability of fading, it is possible to construct satellites with smaller antennas and to use less expensive earth stations, which makes the band attractive. The Ka band frequencies are even more susceptible to attenuation. Although considerable bandwidth is available, further development is needed before these frequencies come into general use.

FIGURE 15–1

Satellites Are Positioned In Equatorial Orbit 22,300 Miles above the Earth's Surface

Courtesy AT&T Corporation

The terms *uplink* and *downlink* used in Table 15–1 refer to the earth-to-satellite and the satellite-to-earth paths respectively. The lower frequency is used from the satellite to the ground because earth station transmitting power can overcome the greater path loss of the higher frequency, but solar battery capacity limits satellite output power.

Satellites have several advantages over terrestrial communications. These include:

♦ Costs of satellite circuits are independent of distance within the coverage range of a single satellite.

♦ Impairments that accumulate on a per-hop basis on terrestrial microwave circuits are avoided with satellites because the earth-station-to-earth-station path is a single hop through a satellite repeater.

♦ Sparsely populated or inaccessible areas can be covered by a satellite signal, providing high-quality communications service to areas that are otherwise difficult or impossible to reach. The coverage is also independent of terrain and other obstacles that may block terrestrial communications.

♦ Earth stations can verify their own data transmission accuracy by listening to the return signal from the satellite.

♦ Because satellites broadcast a signal, they can reach wide areas simultaneously.

♦ Large amounts of bandwidth are available over satellite circuits, making high-speed voice, data, and video circuits available without using an expensive link to a telephone central office.

♦ The satellite signal can be brought directly to the end user, bypassing the local telephone facilities that are expensive and limit bandwidth.

♦ The multipath reflections that impair terrestrial microwave communications have little effect on satellite radio paths.

Satellites are not without limitations, however. The greatest drawback is the lack of frequencies. If higher frequencies can be developed with reliable paths, plenty of frequency spectrum is available, but atmospheric limitations may prevent their use for commercial-grade telecommunications service. Other limitations include:

♦ The delay from earth station to satellite and back is about one-quarter second, or about one-half second for an echo signal. This delay is tolerable for voice when echo cancelers are used, but the lower delay of terrestrial circuits makes them the preferable choice.

♦ Multihop satellite connections impose delay that is detrimental to voice communications and is generally avoided. Because direct satellite-to-satellite transmission is not yet feasible, multiple hops are required when the distance between earth stations exceeds the satellite's footprint.

♦ Path loss is high (about 200 dB) from earth to satellite.

♦ Rain absorption affects path loss, particularly at higher microwave frequencies.

♦ Frequency crowding in the C band is high with potential for interference between satellites and terrestrial microwave operating on the same frequency.

A satellite-to-satellite radio link is one solution to the multihop limitation, but it still lies in the realm of future technology. The delay is greater than with a single hop, but intercontinental satellite communications will be improved when this technology becomes feasible.

The rapid growth of fiber-optic systems has had an adverse effect on satellites' share of the telecommunications market, but the technology shows no signs of dying. Though the satellites' market share may be dropping, the traffic carried by communications satellites continues to increase and will do so into the future. The growth in undersea fiber-optic cables is the primary factor limiting the use of satellites for voice. Also, in the near term there is a glut of satellite capacity, but an expected increase in the type of traffic that uses the unique capabilities of satellites should absorb any excess capacity.

SATELLITE TECHNOLOGY

Satellite positions are measured by their relative longitudes east of the Greenwich meridian. For example, the Telstar 4 satellites are positioned at 271° and 263° (89° and 97° west longitude), which centers them approximately at the same longitude as New Orleans and Dallas.

A satellite circuit has five elements—two terrestrial links, an uplink, a downlink, and a satellite repeater—as shown in Figure 15–2. If the earth station mounts on the user's premises, the terrestrial links are eliminated. The satellite itself has six subsystems described below:

- ◆ Physical structure
- ◆ Transponder
- ◆ Attitude control apparatus
- ◆ Power supply
- ◆ Telemetry equipment
- ◆ Station keeping apparatus

Physical Structure

The size of communications satellites has been steadily increasing since the launch of Early Bird, the first commercial satellite, in 1965. Size is limited by the capacity of launch vehicles and by the need to carry enough solar batteries and fuel to keep the system alive for its design life of 5 to 10 years. Advances in space science are making larger satellites technically feasible. Launch vehicles can carry greater payloads, and the demonstrated ability of the space shuttle to service a satellite in flight or return it to earth for maintenance is changing design considerations that previously limited satellite size.

A large physical size is desirable. Not only must the satellite carry the radio and support equipment, but it also must provide a platform for large antennas to obtain the high gain needed to overcome the path loss between the earth station and the satellite.

Transponders

A *transponder* is a radio relay station on board the satellite. Transponders are technically complex, but their functions are identical with those of terrestrial microwave radio relay stations. The diagram in Figure 15–3 shows the major

FIGURE 15-2

A Satellite System

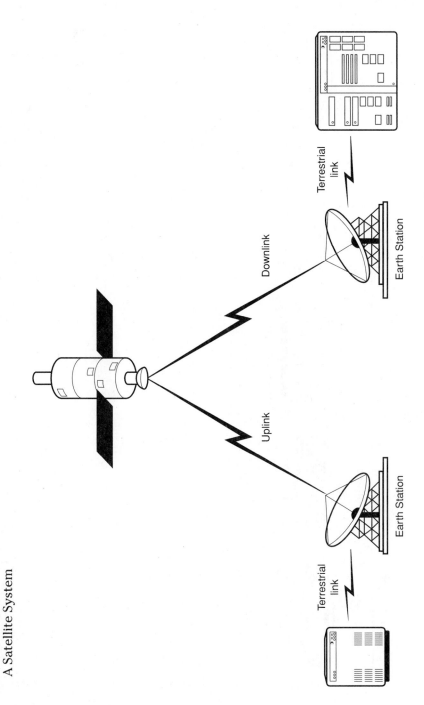

FIGURE 15-3

Components of a Transponder

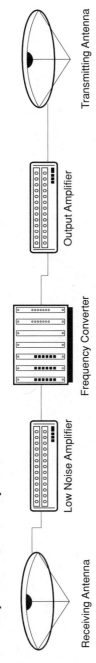

Receiving Antenna

Low Noise Amplifier

Frequency Converter

Output Amplifier

Transmitting Antenna

elements. The receiving antenna picks up the incoming signal from the earth station and amplifies it with a low noise amplifier (LNA), which boosts the received signal without adding noise. The LNA output is amplified and applied to a mixer that reduces the incoming signal to the downlink frequency. The downlink signal is applied to a high power amplifier, using a traveling wave tube (TWT) or solid state amplifier (SSA) as the output amplifier. The output signal couples to the downlink or transmitting antenna. Traveling wave tubes provide up to 10 watts of power. Solid-state amplifiers are popular because of their high reliability. Most satellites carry multiple transponders, each with a bandwidth of 36 to 72 MHz. For example, AT&T's Telstar 4 contains 48 transponders—24 in the C band and 24 in the Ku band. The output power of Telstar 4 is much higher than that of previous generations—20 watts for the C band transponders and 120 watts in the Ku band.

Both satellite and earth station antennas are cross-polarized to double the capacity of a single frequency. In some satellites, beam-focusing techniques concentrate radio frequency energy on a small spot of earth. For example, some satellites illuminate the continental United States with spots focused on Alaska, Hawaii, and Puerto Rico.

Attitude Control Apparatus

Satellites must be stabilized to prevent them from tumbling through space and to keep antennas precisely aligned toward earth. With current equipment, alignment can be maintained within 0.1°. Satellite stabilization is achieved by two methods. A *spin-stabilized* satellite rotates on its axis at about 100 RPM. The antenna is despun at the same speed to provide constant positioning and polarization toward earth. The second method is *three-axis stabilization,* which consists of a gyroscopic stabilizer inside the vehicle. Accelerometers sense any change in position in all axes, and fire positioning rockets to keep the satellite at a constant attitude.

Power Supply

Satellites are powered by solar batteries. Power is conserved by turning off unused equipment with signals from the earth. On spin-stabilized satellites, the cells mount outside the unit so that one-third of the cells always face the sun. Three-axis stabilized satellites have cells mounted on solar panels that extend like wings from the satellite body. Solar cell life is a major factor that limits the working life of a satellite. Solar bombardment gradually weakens the cell output until the power supply can no longer power the onboard equipment.

A nickel-cadmium battery supply is also kept on board most satellites to power the equipment during solar eclipses, which occur during two 45-day periods for about an hour per day. The eclipses also cause wide temperature changes that the onboard equipment must withstand.

Telemetry Equipment

A satellite contains telemetry equipment to monitor its position and attitude and to initiate correction of any deviation from its assigned station. Through telemetry equipment, the earth control station initiates changes to keep the satellite at its assigned longitude and inclination toward earth. Telemetry also monitors the received signal strength and adjusts the receiver gain to keep the uplink and downlink paths balanced.

Station-Keeping Equipment

Small rockets are installed on the vehicle to keep it on station. When the satellite drifts from position, rockets fire to return it. The tasks that keep the satellite on position are called *station-keeping* activities. The fuel required for station keeping is the other factor, with solar cell life, that limits the design life of the satellite. With future satellites, refueling from the space shuttle may become feasible, extending the design life accordingly.

EARTH STATION TECHNOLOGY

Earth stations vary from simple, inexpensive, receive-only stations that can be purchased by individual consumers, to elaborate two-way communications stations that offer commercial access to the satellite's capacity. An earth station includes microwave radio relay equipment, terminating multiplex equipment, and a satellite communications controller.

Radio Relay Equipment

The radio relay equipment used in an earth station is similar to the terrestrial microwave equipment described in Chapter 14 except that the transmitter output power is considerably higher than that of terrestrial microwave. Also, antennas up to 30 meters in diameter provide the narrow beam width required to concentrate power on the targeted satellite. Figure 15–4 is a photograph of a Scientific Atlanta earth station.

FIGURE 15-4

An Earth Station in Jakarta, Indonesia

Courtesy, Scientific Atlanta

Because the earth station's characteristics are more easily controllable than the satellite's and because power is not the problem on earth that it is in space, the earth station plays the major role in overcoming the path loss between the satellite and earth. Path loss ranges from about 197 dB at 4 GHz to about 210 dB at 12 GHz. Also, the higher the frequency, the greater the loss from rainfall absorption. Therefore the uplink always operates at the higher frequency where higher transmitter output power can overcome absorption, while the lower frequency is reserved for the downlink where large antennas and high power amplifiers are not feasible.

Antennas are adjustable to compensate for slight deviations in satellite positioning. Antennas at commercial stations are normally automatically adjusted by motor drives, while inexpensive antennas are adjusted manually as needed. Thirty-meter antennas provide an extremely narrow beam width, with half-power points 0.1° wide.

Satellite Communications Control

A satellite communications controller (SCC) apportions the satellite's bandwidth, processes signals for satellite transmission, and interconnects the earth station microwave equipment to terrestrial circuits. The SCC formats the received signals into a single integrated bit stream in a digital satellite system or combines FDM signals into a frequency modulated analog signal in an analog system.

Multiplexing

The multiplex interface of an earth station is conventional. Satellite circuits use either analog or digital modulation, with interfaces to frequency division and time division terrestrial circuits of the type described in Chapter 5.

Access Control

Satellites employ several techniques to increase the traffic carrying capacity and to provide access to that capacity. *Frequency division multiple access* (FDMA) divides the transponder capacity into multiple frequency segments between end points. One disadvantage of this system is that users are assigned a fixed amount of bandwidth that cannot be adjusted rapidly or easily assigned to other users when it is idle. Also, the guard bands between channels use part of the capacity.

Time division multiple access (TDMA) uses the concept of time sharing the total transponder capacity. Earth stations transmit only when permitted to do so by the access protocol. When the earth station receives permission to transmit, it is allotted the total bandwidth of the transponder for the duration of the station's assigned time slot. Access is controlled by a master station or by the earth station's listening to which station transmitted last and sending its burst in a preassigned sequence. Each earth station receives all transmissions but decodes only those addressed to it. TDMA provides priority to stations with more traffic to transmit by assigning those stations more time slots than it assigns to low priority stations. Therefore, a station with a growing amount of traffic can be allotted a greater share of total transmission time.

Demand assigned multiple access (DAMA) is an alternative to pre-assigned multiple access. DAMA equipment keeps a record of idle radio channels or time slots. Channels are assigned on demand by one of three methods— polling, random access with central control, and random access with distributed control. Control messages are sent over a separate terrestrial channel or contained in a control field in the transmitted frame from a TDMA station.

Signal Processing

The SCC conditions signals between the terrestrial and satellite links for transmission. The type of signal conditioning depends on the vendor and may include compression of digital voice signals, echo cancellation, forward error correction, and digital speech interpolation to avoid transmitting the silent periods of a voice signal.

SATELLITE TRANSMISSION

Much of the previous discussion is of only academic interest to those who use satellite services. However, satellite circuits and terrestrial circuits have different transmission characteristics. Users should be aware of the differences so satellite circuits can be applied where they are both technically and economically feasible.

Satellite Delay

The quarter-second delay between two earth stations is noticeable in voice communications circuits, but most people become accustomed to it and accept it as normal if the circuit is confined to one satellite hop. Data communications circuits are another matter. Throughput on circuits using a block transmission protocol such as IBM's Binary Synchronous (BSC) drops to an unacceptably low level through a satellite because a station can transmit a block only after the receiver acknowledges the preceding block. Since the transmission and acknowledgment sequence requires two round-trips, each block takes a half-second. At this rate, a maximum of only two blocks per second can be transmitted, assuming other data transmission delays such as the CPU processing time are zero. Throughput on polling circuits likewise drops because a complete poll from a host computer is an inquiry and a response, requiring two earth-station-to-earth-station links, and a half-second of propagation delay.

A satellite delay compensator can mitigate the effects of delay in data circuits, as Figure 15–5 shows. Delay compensation cannot, by itself, resolve the deficiencies of a satellite in a polling network because acknowledgments must come from the terminals themselves. In a delay compensator, the DTE communicates in its native protocol, but communication is with the delay compensator instead of the DTE at the other end of the circuit. The delay compensator buffers the transmitted block, awaiting acknowledgment from the distant end. If it receives a negative acknowledge message, indicating an errored block, the delay compensator retransmits either the errored block and all succeeding blocks (go back N) or only the errored block (selective retransmission). Figure 15–5 lists the steps the DTEs and the delay compensator use. Throughput is somewhat lower than a terrestrial circuit because the delay compensator interrupts transmission until an error is corrected. Throughput depends on error rate as it does on terrestrial circuits, although satellite circuits react more severely to a high error rate because of delays during error correction. The alternative to using a delay compensator is to change to a protocol such as HDLC or SDLC that permits multiple unacknowledged blocks. Extensive changes needed in the host computer system may make this alternative economically unfeasible.

Rain Absorption

Rain absorption has a dual effect on satellite communications: Heavy rains increase the path loss significantly, and they may change the signal polarization enough to impair the cross-polarization discrimination ability of the receiving antennas. (See Chapter 14 for an explanation of cross-polarization.) Unfortunately, the greatest impairment exists at the higher frequencies where interference is less and greater bandwidths are available. Rain absorption can be countered by these methods:

 ◆ Choosing earth station locations where heavy rain is less likely.
 ◆ Designing sufficient received signal margin into the path to enable the circuits to tolerate the effects of rain.
 ◆ Locating a diversity earth station far enough from the main station with the expectation that heavy rain storms will be localized.

Technical considerations may limit the first two options. Transmit power and antenna gain from the satellite can be increased only within limits dictated by the size of the satellite and the transmit power available. Locations with low

FIGURE 15-5

Data Transmission through a Satellite Delay Compensator

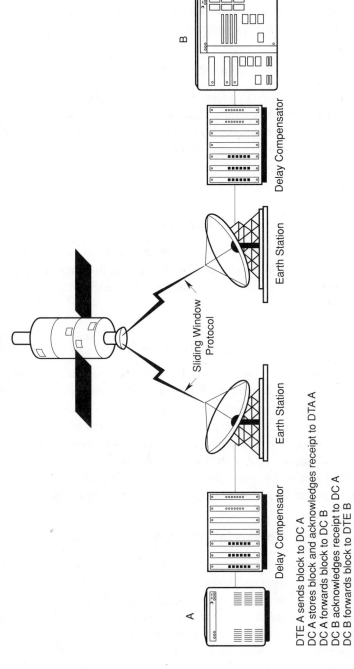

DTE A sends block to DC A
DC A stores block and acknowledges receipt to DTA A
DC A forwards block to DC B
DC B acknowledges receipt to DC A
DC B forwards block to DTE B
DTE B acknowledges receipt to DC B
DC A receives acknowledgement from DC B and removes
block from buffer

precipitation cannot always deliver service where required. These considerations mandate the use of earth station diversity at higher frequencies, which suffers the disadvantage of being costly.

Sun Transit Outage

During the spring and fall equinoxes for periods of about 10 minutes per day for six days, the sun is positioned directly behind the satellite and focuses a considerable amount of high-energy radiation directly on the earth station antenna. This solar radiation causes a high noise level that renders the circuits unusable during this time. Solutions are to route traffic through a backup satellite or to tolerate the outage.

Interference

Interference from other satellites and from terrestrial microwave stations is always a potential problem with satellite circuits. The FCC requires all proposed licensees to conduct interference studies before it grants either a satellite or a terrestrial license.

Carrier-to-Noise Ratio

Satellite transmission quality is based on carrier-to-noise ratio, which is analogous to signal-to-noise ratio measurements on terrestrial circuits. The ratio is relatively easy to improve on the uplink portion of the satellite circuit because transmitter output power and antenna gain can be increased to offset noise. On the downlink portion of a circuit, the effective isotropic radiated power (EIRP), which is a measurement of the transmitter output power that is concentrated into the downlink footprint, can be increased only within the size and power limits of the satellite or by using spot beams to concentrate signal strength.

REPRESENTATIVE SATELLITE SERVICES

In this section, four different types of satellite services are discussed to illustrate the versatility of communications satellites. Two of the services, maritime and direct broadcast television, are not feasible except through communications satellites. The third service, very small aperture terminal (VSAT), replaces conventional terrestrial communications and offers the advantage of bringing signals directly to the user without requiring the last link in a communications path—the local telephone loop—that is often expensive and bandwidth limiting.

The fourth service is aircraft-based satellite service, which GTE and COMSAT are offering on United Airlines planes. All four of these services are possible only because of the unique coverage characteristics of satellite service.

International Maritime Satellite Service (INMARSAT)

INMARSAT is an international maritime satellite service operating under the auspices of the International Maritime Organization (IMO), a United Nations agency. The INMARSAT system has a network of 17 coastal earth stations. These stations form one terminal of a circuit; the other terminal is the ship earth station. The ship earth station mounts above decks and automatically stays in position with satellite tracking equipment. INMARSAT type-accepts and regulates shipboard equipment.

INMARSAT provides the same kinds of communications services for ships at sea that land stations can access through satellite or terrestrial circuits. In the past, the principal methods of communication from ships were Telex and Morse code over high-frequency radio, which were unreliable and expensive. Now data circuits are replacing those modes of communication. Voice circuits replace the high-frequency ship-to-shore radio that often suffered from poor signal propagation reliability. In addition, services such as video and facsimile can be carried over INMARSAT. Other services that do not generally apply to land stations also can be accessed through INMARSAT. Ship locations can be monitored precisely through polling equipment. Distress calls can be received and rebroadcast to ships in the vicinity but out of radio range. Broadcasts such as storm warnings can be made to all ships in an area.

Direct Broadcast Satellite (DBS)

The services discussed to this point have been two-way communications between earth stations. A substantial demand exists for receive-only satellite services. Such services have existed for several years to transmit television signals to cable TV services such as Home Box Office, Movie Channel, and Cinemax. Many of these services are picked up by privately owned earth stations for personal use. These services are not intended for personal use, but a 1984 court ruling declared such reception to be legal, leading to a decision by many services to scramble their signals.

Unlike other satellite video services, DBS service is commercial television intended for individual reception. The 200 watts of power—considerably more than that used in most communications satellites—is needed to limit the size of receiving antennas to about 1 meter in diameter. The viewer receives

high-definition digital television signals through a special receiver and decoder. Subscription to premium programs such as movies is automatic if the receiving terminal is connected to a telephone line.

DBS had been expected to take off in this country for several years, but
not until Hughes launched its DBS-1 in 1993 was the service available. DBS-
2, launched in 1994 and DBS-3, launched in 1995, together deliver 175 channels of entertainment and informational programming to homes and businesses
equipped with the DSS system (Digital Satellite System). DSS uses a small receiving antenna that is easily concealed.

Very Small Aperture Terminal (VSAT)

VSATs are named for the size of the transmitting antennas, which are much
smaller than those used in conventional earth stations. VSAT antennas are normally 1.8 meters (6 feet) in diameter, which makes them easy to conceal on
rooftops and in areas with zoning restrictions. A VSAT network is star-con-
nected with a hub at the center and dedicated lines running to the host computer,
as shown conceptually in Figure 15–6. The hub has a larger antenna, often 4 to
11 meters in diameter aimed at the satellite. Hubs cost from $1 million to $1.5
million to construct, so only the largest organizations can justify a privately
owned hub. Usually, the VSAT vendor owns the hub, or one organization owns
it and shares it with others. Not only is a shared hub more cost-effective for most
companies, it also relieves the company of the necessity of managing the hub,
which may require one or two people per 100 nodes. Generally, a privately
owned hub is feasible when there are about 200 remote stations.

The hub controls demand assignment to the satellite and monitors and diagnoses network performance. Demand is allocated in one of four ways—pure
aloha, slotted aloha, time division multiple access (TDMA), or spread spectrum. The first three methods generally are used on Ku band, and the last on C
band. Pure aloha is an inefficient method of regulating access. Stations transmit
on a free-for-all basis and when their transmissions collide, they must retransmit. Slotted aloha is somewhat more efficient in that stations can transmit only
during allotted time slots. TDMA and spread spectrum are the most effective
ways of allocating access. VSAT provides bandwidth as high as T-1 (E-1 in
Europe), and as low as the customer needs to go. It is used for voice, video, and
data transmission.

The remote station has an antenna and a receiving unit, which is about
the size of a personal computer base unit. Figure 15–7 is a photograph of a Scientific Atlanta VSAT master station with a 7-meter antenna and a remote with
a 1.8-meter antenna. The receiving unit contains a modulator/demodulator, a

FIGURE 15-6

A VSAT System

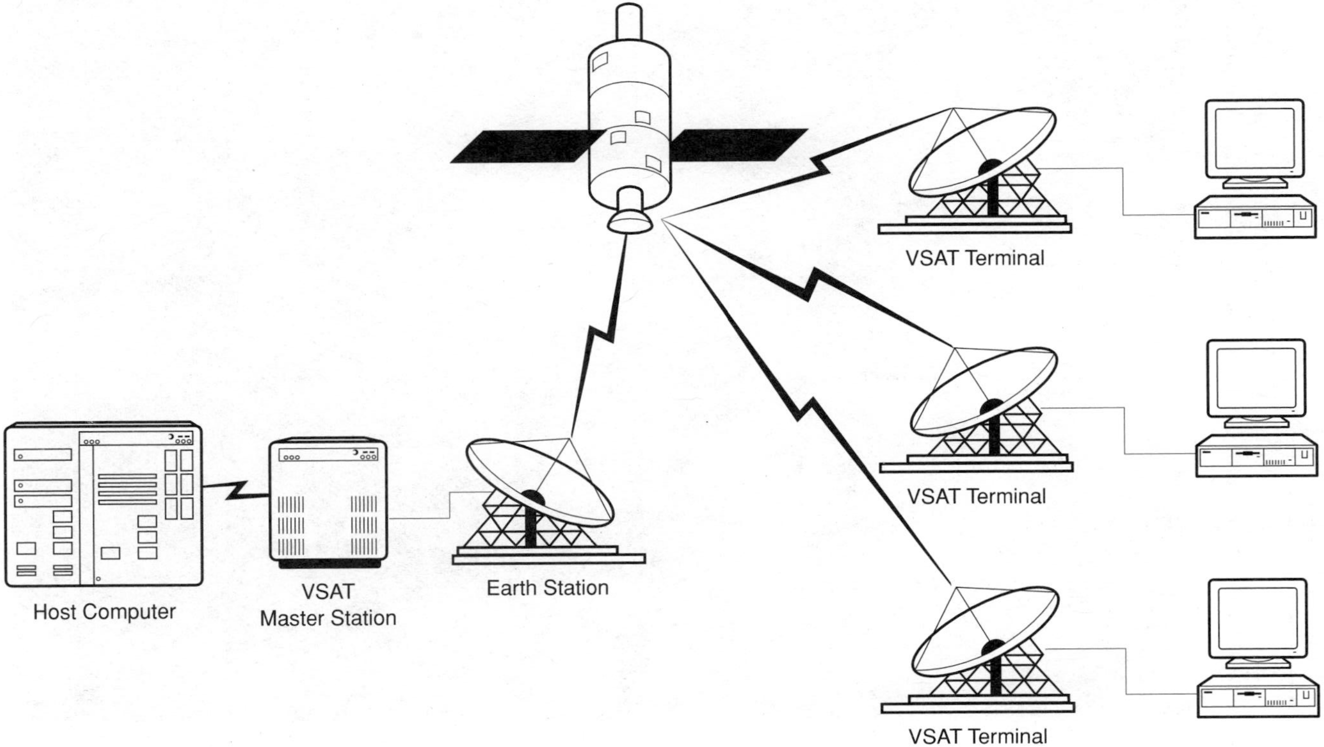

Host Computer

VSAT Master Station

Earth Station

VSAT Terminal

VSAT Terminal

VSAT Terminal

FIGURE 15–7

A Very Small Aperture (VSAT) Master Station with a 7-Meter
Antenna and a Remote Station with a 1.8-Meter Antenna Terminal

Courtesy, Scientific Atlanta

packet assembler/disassembler, and a communication controller. The remote transmitter operates with an output power of about 1 watt. The receiver uses a low noise amplifier.

The primary application for VSAT is data, although it also can carry voice and video. Typically, C band VSATs carry 9.6 kb/s data, and Ku band VSATs carry 56 kb/s data; some systems carry a full or fractional T-1 or E-1. Most applications are two-way interactive. The primary advantage of VSAT is its ability to support multiple locations. For a few locations, the terrestrial link from the host computer to the hub plus the investment in remote stations may make VSAT prohibitively expensive. As the number of remote sites increases, however, VSAT becomes more attractive.

Satellite-Based Air Telephone

COMSAT and GTE have formed a partnership that allows passengers on transoceanic flights to make telephone calls outside North America. COMSAT provides satellite telephones on more than 70 United Airlines aircraft, enabling passengers to send and receive faxes as well as telephone calls via satellite.

On United's 777 aircraft, GTE's digital service is integrated with the aircraft's interactive video system (IVS). Communication services for passengers to make phone calls and send and receive data and faxes via their laptop computers is initially available from six locations on the 777 aircraft. In a later phase of United's IVS, GTE will install its phone system at all seat locations so passengers can receive calls, conduct conference calls, and call seat-to-seat, in addition to communicating anywhere in the world from their seat location via voice, data, and fax.

APPLICATIONS

In one sense, satellite applications will diminish as terrestrial and undersea fiber-optic circuits become more plentiful and economical. Satellite services are still uniquely suited for many applications, however, and the heavy investments the major providers are making shows that they expect satellites to survive well into the future.

Standards

The FCC in the United States and ITU internationally regulate satellite communication. Satellite carriers are free to design systems to proprietary standards and objectives, but the radio frequency spectrum and satellite positioning must conform to standards set by the FCC and international organizations. Most users obtain their services from a satellite carrier and therefore are not concerned with the performance of the satellite and earth station equipment, but they are concerned with circuit performance. The carrier establishes circuit performance criteria. CCITT recommends circuit performance objectives, but compliance is voluntary.

Satellite Service Evaluation Considerations

Satellite space vehicle evaluation criteria are complex, technical, and of interest only to designers, owners, and manufacturers of satellites and onboard equipment. Therefore, this discussion omits these criteria. Likewise, common carrier earth station equipment evaluations are omitted from this discussion. Evaluation criteria discussed in Chapter 14 on microwave equipment generally apply to satellite services except that multipath fading is not a significant problem in satellite services. Also, alarm and control systems in terrestrial microwave are different from those used in satellite systems.

The following factors should be considered in evaluating satellite services and privately owned earth station equipment:

Availability

Circuit availability is a function of path and equipment reliability. To the user of capacity over a carrier-owned earth station, equipment reliability is a secondary consideration. The important issue is circuit reliability measured as percent error-free seconds in digital services and percent availability within specified noise limits for analog services.

These same availability criteria apply with privately owned earth stations, but the carrier can quote availability based only on path reliability. Equipment availability depends on MTBF and MTTR as discussed in Chapter 14 and must be included in the reliability calculation. The frequency and duration of any expected outages because of solar radiation or solar eclipse should be evaluated.

Access Method

Satellite carriers employ several techniques to increase the information-carrying capacity of the space vehicle. Techniques such as DAMA can result in congestion during peak load periods and the possibility that earth station buffer capacity can be exceeded, or access to the system blocked. Some carriers employ delta modulation or adaptive differential pulse code modulation to increase the voice circuit carrying capacity of the satellite and may thereby limit data transmission speeds. Users should determine what methods the carrier uses to apportion access, whether blockage is possible, and whether transmission performance will meet objectives.

Transmission Performance

The carrier's loss, noise, echo, envelope delay, and absolute delay objectives should be evaluated. Except for absolute delay, which cannot be reduced except by using terrestrial facilities to limit the number of satellite hops, satellite transmission evaluation should be similar to the criteria discussed in Chapter 2.

Earth Station Equipment

Earth station equipment is evaluated against the following criteria:

- ◆ Equipment reliability.
- ◆ Technical criteria, such as antenna gain, transmitter power, and receiver sensitivity, that provides a sufficiently reliable path to meet availability objectives.
- ◆ Antenna positioning and tracking equipment that is automatically or manually adjustable to compensate for positional variation in the satellite.
- ◆ Physical structure that can withstand the wind velocity and ice-loading effects for the locale.
- ◆ The availability of radome or deicing equipment to ensure operation during snow and icing conditions.

Network Management Capability

Network management is important in VSAT networks where many earth stations are under the control of a single hub. The service provider should be able to reconfigure the network rapidly from a central location. Monitoring and control equipment should be able to diagnose problems and detect degradations before hard faults occur. The network management package should collect statistics on network use and provide information for predicting when growth additions will be required.

SELECTED SATELLITE EQUIPMENT MANUFACTURERS AND SERVICE VENDORS

Earth Station Equipment

AT&T Tridom

M/A-COM DCC Inc.

NEC America Inc.

Rockwell International

Satellite Transmission Systems, Inc.

Scientific Atlanta

Satellite Transmission Services

AT&T Tridom

American Mobile Satellite Corporation

Orion Satellite

Hughes Network Services

GTE SpaceNet Corporation

VSAT Equipment

AT&T Tridom

GTE SpaceNet Corporation

Hughes Network Systems

Scientific Atlanta

16

MOBILE AND CELLULAR RADIO SYSTEMS

The history of mobile radio is short compared to other telecommunications technologies. The first documented use of mobile radio was by the Detroit police department in 1921. Mobile telephone was introduced in 1946, 25 years after the first mobile radio system went into operation. The following year the concept of cellular radio was developed in Bell Laboratories, but it wasn't practical at the time because the transistor, which had yet to be invented, was needed to condense the control unit into a reasonably-sized package. Also, the switching systems available at the time lacked the intelligence needed to control the cell sites and effect handoff from one cell to another. It wasn't until 1965 when the first electronic switching system was introduced that cellular radio became theoretically practical.

Cellular technology languished in the United States until 1974, when the FCC designated part of the UHF television spectrum between 800 and 900 MHz for a new cellular radio service. The concept of cellular radio had been studied for more than two decades, but the lack of FCC approval, a sufficiently large block of clear frequencies, and a suitable control technology impeded its advancement. Although the FCC allocated frequencies in 1974, they delayed approval of the service pending a lengthy hearing process, which included a solicitation of proposals for demonstration systems. Advanced Mobile Phone

System (AMPS), an AT&T subsidiary, installed the first cellular radio demonstration system in the United States in Chicago in 1978.

Meanwhile, conventional two-way mobile radio advanced rapidly. Police, taxicabs, utilities, farmers, and construction workers all rely heavily on conventional mobile and handheld radios. Radio is one of the enabling technologies supporting vast industries that would otherwise be impractical. The airlines, public safety, and all companies that use radio dispatch are based on access to the airways.

Citizens band radio has long been available to the public at low cost, but mobile and handheld radio connected to the PSTN was too costly for general use. As we will discuss later in this chapter, the early versions of public mobile radio shared a limited frequency resource and either manual operation or an awkward signaling arrangement. As solid-state electronics advanced, radios shrank in size, power consumption, and cost, but it was the development of cellular that turned mobile radio into a household utility. Personal communications service (PCS), which is covered in the next chapter, ultimately has the potential to untether nearly everyone from the confines of the telephone cord.

Technology has not only decreased the size of radios, but it also has found ways to pack more channels into limited frequency spectrum. Digital radio, which once required more bandwidth than its analog counterpart, now provides as much as a 20-to-1 channel advantage in the same spectrum. Spread-spectrum technology enables transceivers to use the same frequency without mutual interference, and the push to ever higher frequencies results in more directionality, which enables channel reuse with less physical separation than the lower frequencies require.

Despite cellular radio's popularity, it isn't the only technology competing for the consumer's dollar. Specialized mobile radio (SMR) has many of cellular's characteristics, but a different network architecture. SMR, originally set up as a local dispatch service, is forming into networks that are growing rapidly in competition with cellular. Roaming capability is gradually developing, enabling SMR users to enjoy the same ubiquitous telephone service that cellular provides.

This chapter discusses voice radio services of all kinds except microwave, which is covered in Chapter 14, and PCS, which, together with mobile data, is covered in Chapter 17.

CONVENTIONAL MOBILE TELEPHONE TECHNOLOGY

The term mobile radio often is used synonymously with mobile telephone. Although the two services use technology and equipment that are essentially the same, they differ in these ways:

◆ Mobile telephone uses separate transmit and receive frequencies, making full duplex operation possible. Mobile two-way radios often operate either on the same frequency in a simplex mode or on different frequencies in a half-duplex mode.

◆ Mobile telephones are connected directly to the telephone network and can be used to originate and terminate telephone calls with billing rendered directly to the mobile telephone number. Mobile radio, if connected to the telephone network, connects through a coupler to a telephone line. Billing, if any, is to the wireline telephone.

◆ Mobile telephones signal on a 10-digit dialing plan. Mobile radios use loudspeaker paging or selective signaling that does not fit into the nationwide dialing plan.

As an aid to understanding cellular radio, it is instructive to review the operation of conventional mobile telephone service. The FCC assigns 44 channels to Public Mobile Service in three ranges—35 to 44 MHz, 152 to 158 MHz, and 454 to 512 MHz. Coverage in all three bands is essentially line-of-sight with the lower frequencies providing the widest coverage. Under some propagation conditions in the 35 MHz band, coverage is so broad that mobile units frequently communicate with unintended base stations. To prevent interference, channels can be reused only with a geographical buffer of 50 to 100 miles between base stations.

Conventional mobile telephone service suffers from several drawbacks as a communications medium. First, demand greatly outstrips capacity in the limited frequency spectrum, resulting in long waiting lists for service in many parts of the country. Also, a mobile telephone channel is a large party line with the disadvantages of limited access and lack of privacy. Some parts of most serving areas have only limited coverage. When a vehicle leaves a coverage area, quality deteriorates and the conversation often must be ended and reestablished on a different channel or deferred until signal strength improves. Within the coverage area, communication is apt to be sporadic or impossible.

A metropolitan mobile telephone service area has transmitters centrally located and operating with 100 to 250 watts of output. Because of the difference between mobile and base station transmitter output power, common carriers often install receivers in more than one site to improve coverage, as Figure 16–1 shows. These receivers are called *voting receivers* because a central unit measures the relative signal-to-noise ratio of each receiver and selects the one with the best signal. This improves the power balance between the mobile, which has relatively low output and a low gain antenna, and the base station unit. Most coverage areas have several radio channels. Transceivers can shift between channels within the same band, but not between bands.

FIGURE 16-1

Diagram of Conventional Mobile Telephone Service

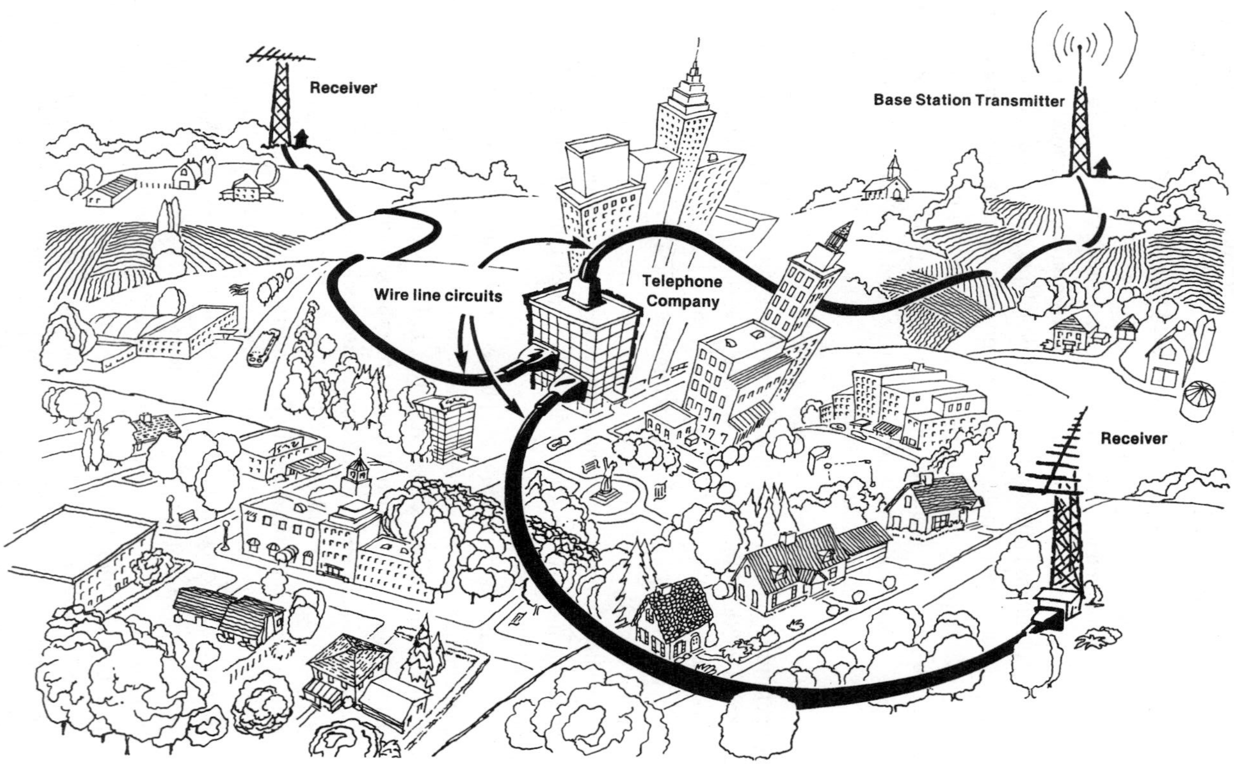

For the first 20-plus years of mobile telephone use, the LECs operated the service manually. Users placed calls by lifting the handset and keying the transmitter on momentarily to signal the operator. The operator connected and timed the call to a wireline telephone or other mobile unit. With this system the operator supervised only the wireline telephone. Mobile-to-mobile calls were manually monitored to detect the start and end of the conversation. The operator signaled the mobile telephone by multifrequency dialing. A selector inside the mobile transceiver responded to a five-digit number. To avoid the problem of frequency congestion, many users purchased multichannel sets. The greater number of channels improved the chances of finding an idle channel for outgoing service, but more channels did not improve incoming service to the mobile unit because users could be called only on the channel they monitored.

In 1964, AT&T introduced Improved Mobile Telephone Service (IMTS) to align mobile telephone service more closely with ordinary telephone service. The IMTS mobile receiver automatically seeks an idle channel and tunes the transceiver to that channel. When the user lifts the handset, the system returns dial tone, and the user dials the call like a conventional telephone. Calls from wireline to mobile units are dialed directly without operator intervention. The base station automatically selects an idle channel and signals the mobile unit over that channel. IMTS, with its idle-channel-seeking capability, improved service for users by eliminating the need for manual channel changes and by making more channels available to reduce congestion.

Roamers—users who travel between serving areas—present a particular problem for mobile telephone service providers. Mobile users have a designated home channel and can be called only while they tune that channel. When they leave their home areas, they must inform potential callers of what channel they are monitoring, or they cannot be called.

With both manual and IMTS systems, the base station configuration presents several disadvantages. The coverage area of a base station is more or less circular. The actual coverage area depends on the directionality of the antenna system and on the terrain. Obstructions are a problem with ordinary mobile telephone service. A hill some distance from the base station typically creates a radio signal shadow on the side away from the transmitter. When the user leaves the coverage area of the channel on which the call was established, the call must be terminated and reestablished on another channel.

PRIVATE MOBILE RADIO SERVICE

Mobile radio operates in one of three modes—single-frequency simplex, two-frequency simplex, and duplex. Both of the simplex modes use push-to-talk operation. When the transmitter button is in the talk position, the receiver cuts off.

In a single-frequency mode, the mobile units and base unit send and receive on the same frequency. In a two-frequency operation, the base transmits on one frequency and receives on another; the mobile units reverse the transmit and receive frequencies.

In a duplex mode, the rf carriers of both the mobile and the base are on for the duration of the session. The base station usually uses separate transmit and receive antennas, but most mobile units use the same antenna to transmit and receive. A filter separates the transmitter's rf energy from the receiving transmission line. The transmit and receive frequencies must be separated sufficiently to prevent the transmitter from desensitizing the receiver. Duplex operation provides mobile radio units with the equivalent of a wireline telephone conversation.

To improve mobile radio coverage, which is apt to be spotty in mountainous terrain, repeaters are often employed. If a session between a mobile and a base station is set up through a repeater, two sets of frequencies are used—one between the mobile and the repeater and the other between the repeater and the base station.

The base station often is mounted at a remote location to improve coverage and therefore must be remotely controlled. Control functions, including keying the transmitter, selectively calling the mobile unit, and linking the audio path between the base station and the control unit, may be carried on over land line or point-to-point radio. The siting of the base station is a complex process. Because obstructions adversely affect mobile signals, it is advantageous to mount the antenna as high as possible. To overcome the effects of fading, it is desirable to use high transmitter power. Both of these, however, must be balanced with the objective of frequency reuse. On crowded frequencies, interference from distant stations becomes a problem, and a user may capture two base stations simultaneously.

Mobile-to-mobile communication is easy to administer in a single-frequency simplex operation because the mobiles can hear each other. In a duplex operation, the mobiles can hear only the base station unless the base station retransmits the signal from mobile units. The retransmission of the mobile signal, which is called *talk-through,* permits mobiles to communicate with one another. It is necessary for the base station to monitor a mobile-to-mobile conversation and to disconnect the path when the session ends.

Mobile Unit Signaling

The simplest form of signaling a mobile unit is voice calling. The base station calls the mobile unit's identification, and the mobile unit responds if the operator is within earshot. On a crowded radio frequency, the constant squawking of the speaker can be annoying, which leads to the need for some form of selective calling.

The simplest form of selective calling relies on the receiver's squelch circuit. The squelch is the circuitry that deactivates the receiver's audio in the absence of a received carrier. Several receivers can operate on the same frequency by assigning subaudio tones to break the squelch of the desired receiver.

For a few stations, the tone-activated squelch is satisfactory, but it does not permit many users to share the same channel. In channels with more users, a selective calling system similar to that used in mobile telephone can be employed. The receiver has a selector that responds to a series of audio tones or a digital code. When the user's unit is signaled, the selector rings a bell, which also can activate an external signal such as honking a horn or turning on a flashing light.

Trunking Radio

As discussed in Chapter 35, if many people are contending for a single communication channel, the channel occupancy may be high, but service will be poor. As channels are added to a radio system, the number of calls that can be carried for a given grade of service increases dramatically. *Trunking* radio employs multiple channels to improve service to a group of users. The best example of trunking radio is a cellular system, but many private and public safety radio systems also use trunking to improve service. Specialized Mobile Radio (SMR) uses trunking radio to provide dispatch services for its customers.

A trunking system designates one channel as the calling or control channel, and all idle receivers tune to that channel. The control channel can be the next idle channel in a sequence, or it may be a channel that is designated as the control. Some loss of efficiency occurs when units must switch signaling channels, so high-usage systems, such as cellular, reach a point at which it is more efficient to have a dedicated signaling channel.

Trunking systems must resolve the occasional conflict of two stations signaling simultaneously. Two methods commonly are used—polling and contention. Both systems work the same way that channel-sharing methods in data communications systems work. In a polling system, the base station sends a continuous stream of polling messages to all mobiles on the channels. The polling messages consume signaling channel time and are therefore inefficient. In a contention system, the mobile unit listens for an idle channel before transmitting. If two mobiles transmit simultaneously, the base station recognizes the collision and informs the mobiles of it. They then back off a random time before again attempting to transmit. Cellular digital packet data (CDPD), which is discussed in Chapter 17, uses contention access.

Mobile Radio Design Objectives

Private and public mobile radio and paging systems share a common set of design objectives. The design process is not precise because of the unpredictable nature of radio waves. Obstructions and fading cause the principal disturbances. Designers of point-to-point radio systems have several tools at their disposal to compensate for the effects of disturbances. They can use high power, directional antennas, and diversity to design a reliable path. The mobile radio designer is at a disadvantage because omnidirectional antennas are needed to reach roaming users. The nature of the remote unit may make it difficult to increase power because of the resulting increase in battery drain. Also, the remote unit frequently operates in an undesirable noise environment (for example, ignition noise), and most important, the base station is attempting to communicate with a target that is constantly moving. As a result, no mobile radio system gives quality that is consistently as good as that provided by land telephones. This section discusses some techniques that designers use to generate satisfactory mobile radio service.

Wide Area Coverage

The major objective in mobile system design is to provide coverage that allows a mobile unit to move through a coverage area without loss of communication. Cellular radio, which is discussed later, is one way of accomplishing this. Another way is *quasi-synchronous* operation.

FM receivers have a tendency to be captured by the strongest signal. Quasi-synchronous, which also is called Simulcast, employs adjacent transmitters operating on frequencies that are slightly offset. The offset is small enough that the resulting beat frequency is inaudible.

A second method of achieving wide area coverage is a receiver voting system. When a mobile unit initiates or responds to a call, the receivers in the coverage area compare signal strength and determine which unit has the best signal. That unit and its associated transmitter establish communication with the mobile until it moves beyond the coverage area and captures another transmitter.

Adequate Signal Strength

Mobile units live in a hostile environment of high noise, most of which is manmade, with the predominant source being auto ignition and charging systems. Portable units often are carried inside buildings where the signal may be attenuated or other noise sources, such as elevators and industrial machinery, may interfere with the signal. These noise sources tend to be most disruptive at lower frequencies.

Another source of signal loss is fading. A primary cause of fading is a multipath signal: A signal may arrive over one path slightly out of phase with the signal over the other path, which causes a reduction in the received signal strength. A stationary user may experience a slow fade due to gradual changes in atmospheric reelection. A moving user on the edge of the coverage area is likely to experience a fast fade as the signal bounces off buildings, trees, and other obstructions. As the vehicle moves, the frequency of the fade changes. If the fade is fast enough, it can be tolerated and sounds much like a noisy signal. A fade of about 10 cycles per second has the greatest adverse effect on the user and makes communication practically impossible. A user on the fringes of the coverage area often can improve communication by stopping the vehicle and edging forward to a high-signal-strength location. A move of only a few inches can make a great difference in received signal strength.

Fading is often frequency selective. If a band of frequencies is transmitted, one range of frequencies may be subjected to heavy fading while the other suffers little or not at all. The range of frequencies that are subject to similar fading effects is called the *coherence bandwidth*. Because of the frequency-selective nature of fading, designers can use frequency diversity to establish a reliable communication path.

Since VHF and higher frequencies have a short wavelength, it is often possible to counter the effects of fading by using space diversity. In a space diversity system, antennas are mounted at a distance that reduces the probability of a similar fade striking both antennas simultaneously. In a vehicular radio, for example, one antenna might be mounted on the front fender and another on the rear.

Wave Propagation

Radio waves propagate by one of three methods—the *ground wave,* the *tropospheric wave,* and the *ionospheric,* or *sky,* wave. Each of these acts differently on different frequency ranges and has a significant effect on the propagation characteristics of the signal.

The ground wave guides radio frequencies below about 30 MHz. The signal follows the contour of the earth and diminishes with distance. Ground wave communication is effective for short distances and has little effect on VHF and higher frequencies.

The tropospheric wave is effective at VHF and higher frequencies but has little effect below 3 MHz. At microwave frequencies, the tropospheric wave can be used to communicate beyond the line of sight.

The ionospheric wave is most effective below VHF frequencies. The ionosphere reflects high frequencies in a manner that is highly frequency selective. With ionospheric reflection, signals can travel well beyond the range of the ground wave, a condition that is called *skip*. Skip conditions can result in excellent communication capability most of the way around the world with low power, but the communication path is unreliable and difficult to predict. For mobile radio skip is generally undesirable.

CELLULAR MOBILE RADIO

In 1981, the FCC authorized 666 cellular radio channels in two bands of frequencies—825 to 845 MHz and 870 to 890 MHz. The lower half of each band, called the A band, is designated for *wireline* carriers, which are defined roughly as local exchange companies. The upper half, or B band, is designated for *nonwireline* carriers, which are nontelephone company common carriers. The FCC grants licenses in both bands to serve a Cellular Geographic Serving Area (CGSA). A CGSA corresponds to a Standard Metropolitan Statistical Area (SMSA), which is a major metropolitan area defined by the Office of Management and Budget.

The demand for cellular service grew rapidly, to the point that the carriers returned to the FCC for additional frequencies. The FCC reluctantly granted an additional 10 MHz—5 MHz in each band. With the prospect of again running out of frequency spectrum, the carriers are shifting to digital cellular. Since neither the carriers nor the users can justify replacing all the existing analog equipment, cell sites are equipped with some analog and some digital transceivers. The subscriber units must be dual-mode to communicate on either analog or digital channels. Analog cellular predominates today, but over the next several years digital cellular with its greater channel capacity will replace analog.

Cellular Technology

Cellular mobile radio overcomes most of the disadvantages of conventional mobile telephone. A coverage area is divided into hexagonal *cells,* as shown in Figure 16–2.Frequencies are not duplicated in adjacent cells, which reduces interference between base stations. It also allows the carrier to reuse frequencies within the coverage area with a buffer between cells that are operating on the same band of frequencies. This technique greatly increases the number of radio channels available compared to a conventional mobile telephone system, which uses a frequency only once in a coverage area.

The general plan of cellular radio is shown in Figure 16–3. The carrier selects the number and size of cells to optimize coverage, cost, and total capacity within the serving area. FCC rules and regulations do not specify these design

FIGURE 16–2

Frequency Reuse in a Cellular Serving Area

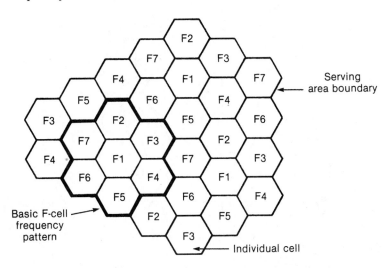

factors; they are selected by the service provider. The mobile units are *frequency agile;* that is, they can be shifted to any of the voice channels. Channel frequency assignments are shown in Table 16–1. To operate on either digital or analog channels, the mobile units also must be dual mode. A dual-mode unit responds to a digital channel first if one is available. If not, it falls back to analog.

Mobile units are equipped with processor-driven logic units that respond to incoming calls and shift to radio channels under control of the base station. Each cell site is equipped with transmitters, receivers, and control apparatus. One or more frequencies in each cell are designated for calling and control. For incoming and outgoing calls, the *cell-site controller* assigns the channel and directs a *frequency synthesizer* inside the mobile unit to shift to the appropriate frequency.

An electronic central office serves as a *mobile telephone switching office* (MTSO), and controls mobile operation within the cells. The cell-site controllers connect to the MTSO over data links for control signals, and voice channels for talking. The MTSO switches calls to other mobile units and to the local telephone system, processes data from the cell-site controllers, and records billing details. It also controls *handoff* so a mobile leaving one cell switches automatically to a channel in the next cell.

Cellular radio overcomes a major drawback of conventional mobile telephone service: the lack of supervision from the mobile unit. Cellular radio uses the control channel to supervise the mobile station. Unlike conventional mobile

FIGURE 16–3

Cellular Radio Serving Plan

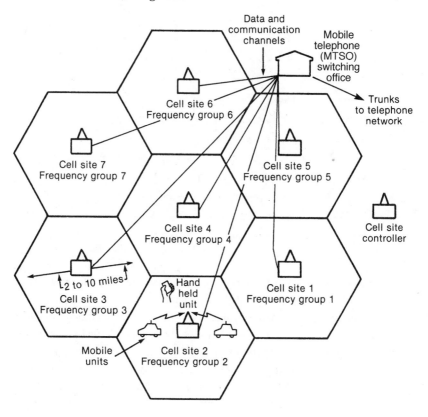

TABLE 16–1

Cellular Radio Frequency Assignments

	Transmit	Receive
A Band	824–835 MHz	869–880 MHz
	845–846.5 MHz	890–891.5 MHz
B Band	835–845 MHz	880–890 MHz
	846.5–849 MHz	891.5–894 MHz

telephone service, in which calls are timed on the basis of supervisory signals from the wireline telephone, cellular radio permits either the wireline or the mobile unit to control timing. This aids mobile-to-mobile calling, which closely approximates ordinary telephone service.

Cell-Site Operation

A cell site has one radio transmitter and two receivers per channel, the cell-site controller, an antenna system, and data links to the MTSO. The hexagon was chosen for the cell shape because it provides a practical way of covering an area without the gaps and overlaps of circular cells. As a practical matter, cell boundaries are not precise. Directional antennas can approximate the shape, but the MTSO switches a user from one cell to another based on signal strength reports from the cell-site controllers. The handoff between cells is nearly instantaneous, and users are generally unaware that it has occurred. The handoff, which takes about 0.2 seconds, has little effect on voice transmission aside from an audible click, but data errors will result from the momentary interruption. As many as 128 channels per cell can be provided, with the number of channels based on demand; most cells operate with 70 or fewer channels.

Cell sites provide coverage with the relatively low power of the cell-site transmitters. FCC rules limit cellular transmitters to 100 watts output, with higher power used only if necessary to cover large cells. At the UHF frequencies of cellular radio, transmission is line-of-sight, so careful planning is needed to define the coverage area of the individual cell while minimizing the need to realign cells in the future.

A minimum of one channel per cell is provided for control of the mobile units from the cell-site controller. The cell-site controller directs channel assignments, receives outgoing call data from the mobile unit, and pages mobile units over the control channel. When the load exceeds the capacity of one channel, separate paging and access channels are used.

The cell-site controller manages the radio channels within the cell. It receives instructions from the MTSO to turn transmitters and receivers on and off, and it supervises the calls, diagnoses trouble, and relays data messages to the MTSO and mobile units. The cell-site controller also monitors the mobile units' signal strength and reports it to the MTSO. It scans all active mobile units operating in adjacent cells and reports their signal strengths to the MTSO, which maps all working mobile units. This map determines which cell should serve a mobile unit when handoff is required.

The number of users that a single cell can support depends on traffic. As cellular radio is introduced to an area, usage is low. As the prices of portable

FIGURE 16–4

A Sectored Cell

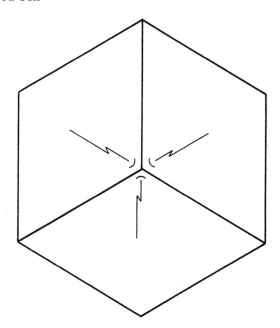

units and monthly service charges drop, the demand grows, necessitating increases in cell capacity. Cell capacity can be expanded by adding radio channels up to the maximum. When cells reach their channel capacity, they can be *sectored,* that is, subdivided into two to six sections with frequencies reused within the cells. Interference is avoided by providing directional antennas, as Figure 16–4 shows. Sectored patterns also are used near mountains, water, and other terrain obstructions to direct radio frequency energy away from areas where it is not needed.

Cells also can be split to increase capacity. One strategy for introducing cellular radio is to begin with large cells, as shown in Figure 16–5. As demand increases, a larger cell can be subdivided into smaller cells by reducing power and changing the antenna patterns. A fourth method of increasing capacity is to borrow unused channels from an adjacent cell.

Supervisory audio tones (SAT tones) prevent a mobile unit from talking on the same frequency at separate cell sites. The base station sends one of three SAT tones, and the mobile transponds it. If the SAT tone returned by a mobile unit is different from the one sent by the cell site, the MTSO will not accept the call.

FIGURE 16–5

Increasing Capacity by Splitting Cells

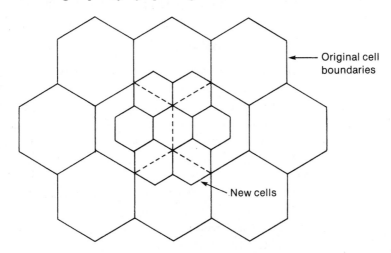

Original cell boundaries

New cells

Mobile Telephone Serving Office

The MTSO is essentially an end office switching system of the type described in Chapter 9 with a special-purpose generic program for cellular radio operation. Not all MTSOs are local switching systems; some products are designed specifically for cellular radio, but in most cases, MTSOs are digital switching systems that can be used for ordinary telephone service with a different program. The objective of most service providers is to offer cellular radio features that are essentially identical to wireline telephone features.

The MTSO links to the cell-site controller with data circuits for control purposes and with four-wire voice circuits for communication channels. When the cell-site controller receives a call from the mobile unit, the controller registers the dialed digits and passes them over the data link. The concept is similar to common channel signaling as described in Chapter 11, but X.25 protocol is used. The MTSO registers the dialed digits and switches the call to the telephone network over an intermachine trunk or to another cellular mobile unit within the system. When mobile-to-mobile calls or calls from the local telephone system are placed, the MTSO pages the mobile unit by sending messages to all cell-site controllers.

The MTSO receives reports from the cell-site controller on the signal strength of each mobile unit transmitting within the coverage area. Data is relayed to the MTSO to enable it to decide which cell is the appropriate serving cell for each active unit. The MTSO also collects statistical information about traffic volumes for allowing the system administrator to determine when to add channels. In addition, the MTSO stores usage records for generating bills.

Mobile Units

When cellular radio first was introduced, mobile units were expensive, with many units retailing for as much as $3,000. The increasing demand for cellular has resulted in a decline in prices, with many retailers giving away analog telephones provided the purchaser signs a service commitment with the carrier. Handheld units are so compact that they can easily fit into a shirt pocket or purse.

The transceiver is a sophisticated device that can tune all channels in an area. Unlike conventional mobile transceivers that use individual crystals for setting the frequency of each channel, cellular transceivers are frequency agile, using frequency synthesizers, which are circuits that generate the end frequency by multiplying from a reference frequency. When cellular theory was first examined in 1947, the science of solid-state electronics was undeveloped. Control circuitry was electromechanical and bulky and consumed considerable power. Transceivers of today are small enough to be contained in a housing the size of a telephone handset or smaller and are powered by rechargeable batteries.

The major components of a typical mobile unit are shown in the block diagram in Figure 16–6. The transmitter and receiver are coupled to the antenna through a *diplexer,* which is a device that isolates the two directions of transmission so the transmitter does not feed power into its own receiver. The frequency synthesizer generates transmit and receive frequencies under control of the logic board. The synthesizer generates a reference frequency from a highly stable oscillator and divides, filters, and multiplies it to generate the required frequency.

The most complex part of the mobile unit is the logic equipment. This system communicates with the cell-site controller over the control channel and directs the other systems in the functions of receiving and initiating calls. These functions include recognizing and responding to incoming signals, shifting the rf equipment to the working channel for establishing a call initially and during handoff, and interpreting users' service requests. The logic unit periodically scans the control channels and tunes the transceiver to the channel with the strongest signal. The user communicates with the logic unit through a control unit, which consists of the handset, dial, display unit, and other elements that emulate a conventional telephone set.

The unit also includes a power converter to supply the logic and rf equipment with the proper voltages from the battery source. FCC rules limit the

FIGURE 16–6

Block Diagram of a Cellular Mobile Radio Transceiver

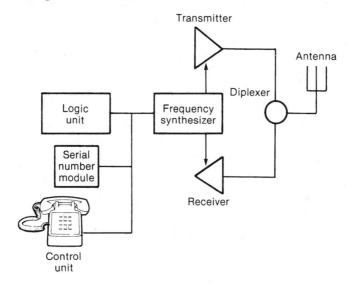

transmitter to 7 watts output, but many mobile units use 3 watts or less, and handheld units are a fraction of a watt to reduce battery drain. Battery drain is particularly important in handheld or portable units. The FCC segregates mobile units into three power classes ranging from 0.6 watts to the maximum power permitted.

Another module electronically generates the unit's 32-bit binary serial number, which theoretically prevents fraudulent or unauthorized use of a mobile unit. In practice, however, toll thieves intercept the electronic serial number and duplicate it so they can use the cellular phone to sell telephone calls. The serial number is communicated to the cell-site controller with each call for comparison with a database maintained by the MTSO. The unit's 10-digit calling number and a station class mark also are built into memory and transmitted to the cell-site controller with each outgoing call. The class mark identifies the station type and power rating.

Signal Enhancements

Some buildings are constructed with so much steel and concrete that cellular signals cannot penetrate. The cellular industry provides two solutions to the problem: booster amplifiers and microcells.

A booster amplifier amplifies the frequency range of the nearest cell site, retransmitting it inside the building. The amplifier picks up signals from hand-held units and retransmits them so they can be picked up by the cell site. This method is the least expensive alternative, but it provides poorer security. Anyone wanting to intercept cellular conversations going on inside a building has an easy time of it because the stations and frequency range are fixed.

A microcell is a low-power cell site that is dedicated to a building. An antenna system is extended throughout the building to transmit and receive low power signals. The microcell has its own set of channels, and is connected to the MTSO with a T-1 connection just like any other cell site. The microcell provides better security than a booster, at a higher cost and at a cost of additional administration. The microcell's transceivers must be administered for traffic load like any cell site. They also require the same balancing of analog and digital channels if the carrier has converted to digital.

Mobile Telephone Features

A full description of mobile telephone features is beyond the scope of this book. The following is a brief description of the most popular cellular radio mobile features. Among the most important features are those that improve safety by enabling the user to operate the system while driving.

- *Automatic Answer.* This feature allows the user to program the telephone to answer an incoming call automatically after a given number of rings.
- *Call-in-Absence Indicator.* When an incoming call is unanswered, the unit displays an indicator.
- *Call Timer.* Displays elapsed time of calls, displays accumulated time to aid in estimating billing costs, and provides a preset interval timer during a call.
- *Dialed Number Display.* The dialed number is displayed in a readout on the handset. Misdialed digits can be corrected before the number is outpulsed.
- *Last Number Dialed.* As in a conventional telephone, this feature stores the last number dialed so it can be recalled with a touch of a button.
- *Muting.* The handset cuts off with a button so the distant party cannot hear a private conversation from the mobile unit.
- *On-hook Dialing.* This feature allows the user to dial a number while the unit is on-hook. If the unit has dialed number display, the number can be pulsed into a handset and reviewed before it is sent.

♦ *Repertory Dialing*. The unit stores a list of telephone numbers that can be selected by dialing one or two digits.

♦ *Scratch Pad*. This feature stores numbers entered with the keypad in a temporary memory location.

♦ *Security Features*. An electronic lock can be programmed into the telephone so it cannot be used until the proper code is entered. Some units can be programmed to lock automatically after each use.

♦ *Self-diagnostics*. Internal diagnostics indicate trouble in transceiver and control unit to aid in rapid troubleshooting.

♦ *Signal Strength Meter*. The unit displays the strength of the received signal.

♦ *Speaker*. Some units include a speaker and remote microphone so conversations can be monitored by others in the car and to permit hands-free operation of the unit.

♦ *Special Signaling*. A *call-in-absence* indicator turns on a light when a call is received but not answered. Auxiliary signals can honk the horn or turn on the lights when a call arrives at an unattended unit.

♦ *Two-System Registration*. This feature enables the system to be registered with two telephone numbers under alternate carriers. It can be used with only one carrier at a time.

Roaming

Every cellular operator provides a home area in which normal cellular rates apply. *Roaming* is the ability of a mobile unit to move outside its normal service area. A premium charge is levied for roamers. The cellular operator must know about a roaming user to route calls to the proper service area and to know where to send the bill. Roaming service is enabled by use of Signaling System 7 between the MTSOs. The carrier may extend roaming capability throughout a wide service area by linking its switches over SS7 networks with switches of other service providers, enabling users to roam without special procedures.

When roaming outside the carrier's network, special procedures are required to place and receive calls. Callers must know the roamer access number for the service area. After the access number is reached, dial tone is provided so the cellular number can be dialed. Outgoing calls are handled normally if your serving carrier has an agreement with the other carrier. Otherwise, it may be necessary to use a credit card to place long-distance calls. If the telephone is equipped for two-service operation, it may be necessary to switch it between the A and B bands to retain full network privileges. This can occur if your home carrier is the wireline carrier in one locality, but the nonwireline carrier in another. As the SS7 network is expanded and carriers develop interconnection arrangements, roaming will become easier, but currently it requires knowing how the system operates.

Cellular Radio Services

Cellular radio duplicates the services of wireline carriers as nearly as possible. Carriers offer equal access to any long-distance carrier, to emergency numbers, and to operator services to allow users to place collect, third-number, and credit-card calls. Most carriers offer voice mail to answer calls when the telephone is off or outside the service area. An attendant service is also required so roaming users can check in when they leave one carrier's service area and enter another. Although the mobile unit automatically identifies the user, the different jurisdictions require identification and registration of the user for billing purposes.

Digital Cellular Radio

Cellular radio design has alleviated the problems of poor coverage and congested frequencies, primarily in urban areas. The principle of cell splitting, which was supposed to reduce large cells to smaller ones as traffic increased, has not proved as technically or economically feasible as expected. The cellular carriers all agree that a gradual shift from analog to digital cellular is required in order to make the best use of the frequency spectrum. They have been unable to agree, however, on which of two competing technologies will be used. McCaw Cellular (now AT&T Wireless) began deploying time division multiple access (TDMA) systems in the early 1990s. Competing carriers, including most of the wireline carriers, have either implemented or are planning to use code division multiple access (CDMA) systems. The Telecommunications Industry Association (TIA) has standardized both methods.

The two systems are not compatible with each other or with the analog method of frequency division multiple access (FDMA). To effect the transition from analog to digital, dual-mode units are required. The TDMA/CDMA controversy means that either subscriber stations must be compatible with three modulation schemes or users will be unable to roam freely or to change carriers without changing the subscriber set. The standardization of analog cellular has always been one of its major advantages. A major reason the price has dropped so dramatically is that the demand enables manufacturers to produce large quantities of a standard product.

Under the analog FDMA system a user has exclusive use of a channel in a cell site for the duration of a session. The inherent half-duplex character of voice communications, plus the frequent pauses in most conversations, wastes much airtime, which TDMA and CDMA can utilize. TDMA effectively divides each 30 kHz analog channel into three 8 kb/s segments, tripling the capacity of the spectrum. After the initial implementation, TDMA proponents expect to double the capacity of digital channels, providing a six-to-one improvement. The TDMA system is voice-only. Currently, there is no method of transmitting data over TDMA.

CDMA uses spread-spectrum techniques to multiply spectrum capacity. CDMA encodes 64 channels into 1.25 MHz of spectrum. Each channel uses an orthogonal code, with all channels transmitting across the same bandwidth. The CDMA receiver picks the code out of the appropriate signal and demodulates it. CDMA is not as susceptible to multipath fading as FDMA and TDMA. Another advantage of CDMA is its handoff method, which is a make-before-break arrangement that eliminates the signal dropout that is common with TDMA and FDMA.

RADIO PAGING

Paging is a radio application that is less sophisticated and less costly than cellular radio, but is growing at a fast pace. Developed under the centralized transmitter and receiver plan of conventional mobile telephone service, radio paging offers dial access from a wireline telephone to a pocket receiver. The readout is a beeping sound or vibration to alert the user to an incoming message. Digital pagers allow the caller to send a callback number or numeric message to a digital readout.

Several interesting advances have been made in radio paging in the past few years. The principal factor is alphanumeric paging, in which the caller can send a text message in place of the alternative, which is either beeping the user or sending a numeric message such as a callback number. To activate alphanumeric paging the caller must have a keyboard. The message is keyed in, and it displays on the pager readout. Pagers are available with one or more readout lines. By pressing a button the user scrolls the message in serial fashion across the readout if it is too long to fit in a single screen. Alphanumeric paging can reduce the number of cellular phone messages at a significantly lower cost. The main drawback is the need to have a keyboard and modem available to send the message. If only a DTMF telephone is available, the pager can operate in a numerical paging mode.

Alphanumeric paging is made easier with a paging server, which can be operated off a LAN. Any user on the network can access the server, send the message to it, and the server outdials to the paging system. Features available on available products include sending messages to E-mail, screening calls, and outdialing messages from only selected stations.

Another recent innovation is answer-back paging. When a message has been received, the recipient answers by pressing a button on the pager and the pager sends an acknowledgment to the sender. Because of the small size of the pager its transmit power is low, so the service provider must have a network of receivers throughout the coverage area. At the time of this writing the first implementations of answer-back paging are appearing on the market.

APPLICATIONS

Cellular radio is rapidly becoming a commodity, much like ordinary telephone service for those who can afford it. This section includes considerations that users of cellular radio service should evaluate, in terms of both the service itself and the mobile radio equipment.

Standards

In the United States, the FCC Rules and Regulations set forth mobile radio standards. FCC rules establish the authorized frequencies, power levels, bandwidth, frequency stability, signaling formats, and other such variables in the public mobile service. Cellular radio standards are outlined in the Cellular Mobile/Land Station Compatibility Specification issued by the FCC and EIA. Internationally, ITU-R issues mobile radio recommendations. TIA has standardized both TDMA and CDMA protocols for digital cellular.

Evaluation Criteria

Cellular mobile telephone equipment is evaluated on much the same basis as other telecommunications equipment. Reliability and the ability to obtain fast and efficient service is a paramount concern. Cost is also an important consideration. When cellular equipment was introduced, costs were high, but with the popularity of the technology, prices have dropped to the point that equipment cost is now a minor consideration. The cost of airtime, however, remains high.

Security Issues
Regular mobile radio is inherently an unsecure medium. Anyone with a receiver tuned to the mobile frequency can eavesdrop on any conversation, and there is little practical means of preventing it aside from scrambling, which is impractical on public radio systems because of the need for matched scrambling devices. Cellular radio offers inherent security that may be sufficient but still is not interception-proof. If a session takes place in one cell, it is easy for someone to intercept it. If, however, the vehicle is moving, each

time it is handed off to another cell, an eavesdropper may have some difficulty resuming reception of the conversation. The smaller the cells, the more frequent the handoff, and the less likely it is that the entire session can be monitored. A vehicle following the vehicle under observation can, however, monitor the entire session.

TDMA digital cellular is somewhat more secure than analog because the equipment for monitoring is not as readily available. Anyone with the motivation can still eavesdrop on a TDMA session. CDMA is inherently more secure than TDMA because an eavesdropper would have great difficulty intercepting the code or frequency-hopping pattern the base and mobile stations are using.

Coverage

A coverage area is one of the two or three primary considerations most users review in evaluating a mobile radio system. Coverage can best be evaluated by taking a test drive and making calls from the areas you plan to drive through, paying particular attention to the fringe areas. The carriers' coverage maps are a good way to compare alternatives. The two carriers in an area are unlikely to have identical coverage areas outside the urban area, which may make coverage the deciding factor. Note which areas are in the home area and which are in the carrier's service area, but for which a roaming charge is applied.

Ease of Roaming
For users who spend time outside the home area, the cost and difficulty of roaming are important selection criteria. Carriers that have an extensive SS7 network and interconnection agreements with other carriers make it easier and less costly to roam than more restrictive carriers.

Number of Channels
Cellular services with large numbers of cell sites are the most likely to provide satisfactory service. Large cells are likely to be sectionalized as usage increases. Sectionalization itself does not necessarily disrupt service, but the cell is apt to become crowded before the need for sectionalization is apparent. The main way of evaluating this feature is to ask other users how often they encounter a reorder signal in attempting to place calls with the carrier.

Selecting Cellular Radio Equipment
The first decision in selecting equipment is to determine whether you need vehicular or handheld equipment. As the name implies, vehicular equipment is mounted inside a vehicle. Vehicular equipment has more power output than handheld radios, and its car-mounted antenna provides more gain and therefore

better coverage than handheld units. A compromise is mounting a handheld unit where it can couple to a vehicular antenna, but still be removed when leaving the vehicle. Determine whether digital or analog cellular is the best choice. Analog station equipment is less expensive, but carriers may offer more attractive pricing plans to move to digital.

Usage Charges

Cellular radio charges are based on duration of both originating and terminating calls. Carriers charge for total airtime and add on other message charges such as roaming and long distance. Therefore, both originating and terminating calls are charged to the terminating mobile number; outgoing long-distance usage is billed twice—once for the airtime and once for the wireline long-distance service.

Evaluating Paging Equipment

Many of the same criteria apply for evaluating paging and cellular equipment. The first question is what type of service to acquire. The market offers signal-only, numeric display, and alphanumeric display. The coverage areas range from local to regional to national, with the cost increasing as the service area increases.

SELECTED MOBILE RADIO EQUIPMENT MANUFACTURERS

Cellular Central Office Equipment

Ericsson Inc., Communications Division
Lucent Technologies
NEC America Inc. Switching Systems Division
Motorola Communications & Electronics, Inc.
Northern Telecom Inc.

Cellular, Pagers, and IMTS Mobile Equipment

CIT-Alcatel, Inc.
Harris Corporation, RF Communications Group
E.F. Johnson Company
NEC America Inc. Switching Systems Division
Motorola Communications & Electronics, Inc.
M/A-COM Land Mobile Communications, Inc.
NEC America Inc., Radio & Transmission Div.

17

WIRELESS COMMUNICATIONS SYSTEMS

Wireless is one of the top growth areas in the telecommunications world today. In the last chapter we discussed cellular, paging, and other forms of mobile radio, which are two of its manifestations, but these are not what most in the industry mean when they speak of wireless. The two principal voice applications are personal communications service (PCS) and on-premise wireless. The two are similar. They use the same frequency bands and mobile units that are identical in most respects. The difference is that wireless uses unlicensed frequency spectrum, is usually privately owned, and carries no usage charges. PCS is, like cellular, publicly owned, uses licensed spectrum, and the carriers charge for usage.

The dream of not being tethered to the telephone cord has been around for many years, and spawned the cordless telephone, which is not to be confused with wireless. Wireless technology is not markedly different from cellular, but as was the case with cellular, PCS was held up by the FCC while it decided what frequency spectrum to allocate and under what conditions. The dream of PCS is to make location irrelevant to placing or receiving telephone calls. It will be many years before this ideal is realized, but unquestionably, the demand exists.

The markets for wireless and PCS are similar in many respects, but also different. Wireless is intended to be confined to a building or campus. Its customers are mobile, but not in a vehicular sense. Nurses and physicians, production personnel, managers, food service workers, technicians, maintenance personnel who move about the plant, and dozens of other such occupations need to be telephone-accessible, yet free from cords and pagers.

Once these people leave the confines of the plant, their needs don't change dramatically, but they move into the public communications arena. Cellular is one solution for mobility, but unless the building is equipped with a microcell, coverage may be a problem in heavily shielded buildings. Besides, the usage charges for extensive cellular use are hefty. Ideally, a person could have a single number that is reachable from anywhere at any time. He or she could use the phone at the desk, carry it about the plant, out into the parking lot, into the car, into an airplane, and have it work wherever the journey ends, and all of this at an affordable price.

The ideal will not be realized immediately. The handoff from wireless to PCS may not be seamless. The charge for PCS may be higher than many people are willing to pay. The ideal of a universal, transportable number will be achieved in time, but not until some technical and practical problems are solved.

This chapter discusses the emerging wireless/PCS market. As this book is written the FCC has recently concluded its auction of the PCS spectrum with companies paying large fees for licenses to provide a service, the demand for which has not yet been demonstrated. Few observers doubt that the demand exists provided the price is right. Whether the service can be made profitable will be determined as companies begin to deploy their offerings.

WIRELESS TECHNOLOGY

Several companies have been selling wireless for a number of years in the ISM (Industrial, Scientific, Medical) band, which is unlicensed spectrum in the 46–49 MHz and 902–928 MHz ranges. The 46–49 MHz band is used for cordless telephones among other things. Several manufacturers produced wireless products in the 902 MHz band while waiting for the FCC to allocate frequency spectrum. Some products are still provided in this band, but the risk of interference is high. The FCC states that users have no recourse if they are interfered with, and that they are prohibited from interfering with existing signals. This makes the ISM band a poor long-term choice for wireless.

Figure 17–1 shows the frequency spectrum that the FCC has allocated for wireless and PCS. Note that wireless is an unlicensed frequency range that fits between two licensed PCS bands. The proximity is designed to allow frequency-agile units to hop from the unlicensed to the licensed spectrum so wireless units can be used interchangeably for PCS communications. Although this

FIGURE 17-1

U.S. PCS Frequency Spectrum

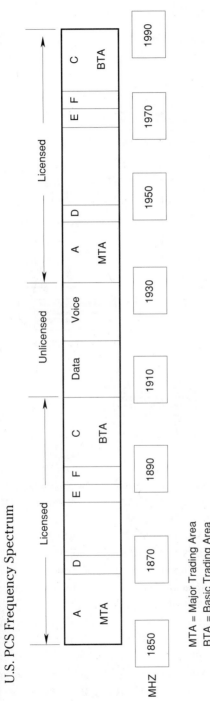

MTA = Major Trading Area
BTA = Basic Trading Area

FIGURE 17-2

Business Wireless Configuration

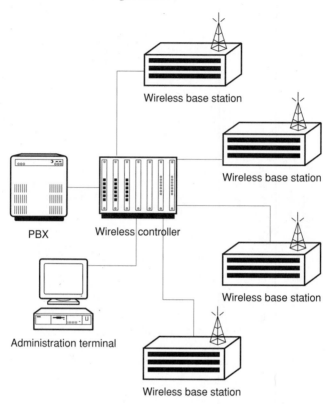

Wireless base station

Wireless base station

PBX   Wireless controller

Wireless base station

Administration terminal

Wireless base station

spectrum, like ISM, is unlicensed, it is an exclusive-use segment. The low power or wireless transmitters should limit interference, or at least make it easy to find noninterfering frequencies.

A wireless installation consists of a central controller that interfaces the office telephone system and controls a selection of remote base stations or cells. Figure 17–2 shows how the system is connected. The controller is either a standalone device that connects to analog ports on the PBX, or an integrated unit that provides proprietary station features over the radio link.

The base stations, an example of which is the Nortel Companion unit in Figure 17–3, are self-contained low-power, multichannel radio transceivers. Locations are selected throughout the building to provide satisfactory coverage. A typical base station has a maximum range of about 700 feet; less under adverse conditions. Steel and concrete in the building limit the base station

FIGURE 17–3

A Nortel Companion Wireless Base Station

COMPANION

Courtesy Nortel, Inc.

range. The base stations can be equipped with multiple radio channels, the number of which are chosen to support the number of simultaneous conversations expected. The base stations hand off to one another in a manner similar to cellular.

The portable instruments are either universal devices that emulate an analog telephone, or they are proprietary stations that work with the manufacturer's PBX. Analog stations are the least expensive, but they suffer the drawbacks of any analog telephone: Features are activated by dialing codes. Proprietary instruments offer button access to features, but the number of buttons may be limited by the physical dimensions of the instrument. Some products are designed so the portable device is the handset of the regular desk instrument. The user can pick up the handset and walk away from the instrument, making a wire-to-wireless transition.

PERSONAL COMMUNICATIONS SERVICE (PCS)

The premise of PCS is simple. Telephone numbers are associated with people, not places, and you can use the service or be reached anywhere or anytime. Of course, the telephone will provide features to handle calls when you don't want to be quite that accessible, and the completely portable telephone number won't be around until many companies have invested billions of dollars. But there is little doubt that PCS is on its way. PCS, if it meets its promise, will revolutionize the telephone system, but the cost will be enormous. Companies have already spent $7 billion to purchase licenses at the FCC's auctions, and that is only the beginning. To make the service truly ubiquitous, service providers will have to lace the continent with a network of transceivers, switches, and circuits to interconnect them. The effort will certainly stretch for more than a decade, but when PCS is complete, it will have an impact on telecommunications at least as great as the automobile and road system had on transportation, provided it can be made affordable.

The promise of PCS is improved lifestyle through a combination of easy portability and random mobility. Easy portability means the telephone instrument is small so that it fits the user comfortably. Random mobility means that subscribers can roam and use their personalized services wherever they are. For example, present nationwide paging systems approach the objective of random mobility. Except for dead spots, users can be reached easily without the caller or called party being concerned about special check-in procedures as cellular sometimes requires. A nationwide signaling network is needed to identify PCS roamers and to inform the local carrier of the subscriber's personalized services. Smartcards may enable subscribers to use any telephone on the network while keeping the system informed of their identity and preferences.

At the time of this writing PCS is little more than a concept because service providers are just beginning the monumental tasks of engineering and constructing the system. It is clear that the service will be different from cellular in several important ways. First, cellular was organized as an oligopoly with two service providers designated for each metropolitan area. In most cellular service areas the carriers are difficult to distinguish, with the possible exception of the debate on which is the preferred digital coding method. The PCS auctions were designed to inspire more competition. PCS licenses two 30 MHz channels per MTA (major trading area) and one 20 MHz plus four 10 MHz channels in the basic trading area (BTA) band, with a minimum of three competitors in each market. In addition the C and D blocks in each band are reserved for protected groups: rural telephone companies, small business, and women- and minority-owned businesses.

In theory, the additional competition should result in better coverage, innovative services, and competitive prices. PCS will have no mandatory service standards. Competition will drive the features included in carriers' service offerings.

The second difference between PCS and cellular is that the former will start as a digital service and not undergo the analog transition. The FCC rules do not specify an encoding method. TDMA and CDMA are both in contention as are at least five more encoding systems. The industry is unlikely to agree on a single method, which will result either in limiting the ability of subscribers to hop from one carrier to another, or in more expensive telephones that support multiple coding schemes.

Global PCS

PCS based on terrestrial radio has the objective of serving a region or country. More ambitious are the global PCS plans that several companies have announced. Iridium is a Motorola system using low earth orbiting satellite (LEOS) technology. Iridium, which is expected to be in service by 1998, uses a network of 66 satellites in six orbital planes. Each plane has 10 operational and one spare satellite. The satellites orbit at an altitude of 780 kilometers, which minimizes the delay problems of geosynchronous satellites. It raises the problem, however, of handoff between satellites as they move below the horizon. The earth-to-satellite link uses L band, 20/30 GHz, for communications. The satellite-to-satellite communications are carried on the Ka band.

A competing system, Teledesic, is proposed by Craig McCaw, founder of McCaw Cellular, and William Gates, one of the founders of Microsoft. This system would use a constellation of 840 to 892 satellites operating in 40 planes.

LEOS has the potential of realizing the ideal of communication anyplace and at any time, but at a cost. Airtime costs are projected at three dollars per minute, but ultimately, the cost will be set to balance a return on investment for the owners with an affordable service for the users.

WIRELESS LANS

The wired LAN is perfectly acceptable to office workers who sit at the desk all day, but many workers are mobile at least part of the day. The ideal of a wireless laptop or personal digital assistant would allow people to receive E-mail, keep their desk and portable calendars synchronized, or pop into the office file server to pick up an occasional file. All of these applications and many more are driving the need for wireless LANs. Students in a classroom are a perfect case in point. It is difficult for a teacher to predict where computer activities will be located, and the scene may shift from hour to hour. Warehouse workers, nurses, and retail clerks all need access to files from a portable computer or point-of-sale device. Nearly every retail establishment can profit from checking stock levels, preparing paperless pick slips, sending orders to the shipping department, and other such transactions that now take place with paper and pencil or telephone. Much of the communication that now requires a voice call can be eliminated or simplified with inexpensive and ubiquitous wireless data.

Also driving the need for wireless LANs is the difficulty of wiring certain buildings. Historical buildings that cannot be altered, those built of masonry, and those constructed before computers were conceived represent real wiring difficulties that the wireless LAN can overcome. Wireless LANs can be divided into three application categories: mobile/portable, building-to-building, and desktop. The applications for each of these are different, as are the alternatives that the market provides.

Wireless LANs have in the past been impeded by the lack of standards. The IEEE 802.11 task force has prepared standards operating at 1 and 2 mb/s, which should increase the number of wireless products available. The products on the market today use three different kinds of technology to fulfill the applications:

♦ Spread-spectrum radio
♦ Infrared
♦ 18 GHz microwave

Each of these has advantages and limitations for the wireless LAN.

Spread Spectrum

Spread spectrum operates on unlicensed frequency ranges in the ISM band in the frequency ranges of 902–928 MHz, 2.4–2.483 GHz, and 5.725–5.85 GHz. The FCC requires such devices to use spread-spectrum modulation with a maximum of one watt of power. Most of the wireless LAN products on the market use the 2.4 GHz band. Since the frequencies are not licensed, interference is always a possibility. Fortunately, the spread-spectrum method is robust at handling interference.

Two different methods of implementing spread spectrum are in common use in wireless LANs. In the direct sequence method the radio signal is broadcast over the entire bandwidth of the allocated spectrum. The transmitter and receiver both include a synchronized pseudo-noise generator, which the receiver uses to detect the desired signal out of the resulting jumble. Most of the early wireless LAN products use direct sequence.

The second method is frequency hopping. The transmitter and receiver are synchronized to hop between frequencies, stopping on each frequency for a few milliseconds. The amount of time per hop is called the *dwell time*. Later-generation LANs use frequency hopping, which is an excellent way of handling interference. If the equipment finds an interfering signal, it marks that portion of the spectrum as busy and skips it. Both frequency hopping and direct sequence provide excellent security. An eavesdropper would have a difficult time duplicating the pseudo noise or determining the channel hopping sequence of spread spectrum.

Unlike infrared, spread spectrum can penetrate walls to cover a broad area in a building. The main limitation is transmission speed, which, with today's technology is much slower than the speed of a wired LAN. Typical speeds do not exceed one or two mb/s. Spread spectrum is normally used either for desktop or mobile/portable applications, with the latter restricted to a narrow range such as a building or campus.

Infrared

Infrared wireless products have appeal because they do not require any form of FCC licensing. Infrared products use one of three methods of distributing signals:

- ◆ *Line-of-sight* uses infrared transceiver pairs set up in a manner similar to point-to-point microwave. This method is used for building-to-building communications.
- ◆ *Reflective infrared* bounces the infrared signal off ceilings, walls, and floors to blanket an area.
- ◆ *Scattered infrared* uses a diffused signal that also bounces off walls and ceilings to cover an area.

Scattered and reflective infrared are primarily used for desktop wireless applications. The directionality of the signal and the inability to penetrate walls generally makes infrared impractical for mobile/portable operation. Line-of-sight infrared has a wider bandwidth than spread spectrum. Reflective and scattered infrared are low-speed systems.

Microwave

Microwave, which is covered in Chapter 14, is an excellent system for point-to-point LAN links. It is not intended for portable/mobile or desktop applications.

WIRELESS DATA

Mobile and portable applications require some form of technology that allows the user to link to a remote computer or server over an intermediate network. Parcel delivery companies now use wireless data extensively. Many police departments use mobile data terminals (MDT), with which they can review arrest records and warrants without involving a dispatcher. Taxicab and service companies, and any company that dispatches personnel can save time, improve accuracy, and eliminate telephone calls with mobile data terminals. Private radio systems also use mobile terminals for such purposes as linkage between a law enforcement agency and a vehicular or law enforcement database.

The simplest and least expensive form of MDT is the alphanumeric pager. Provided the application can get by without an answer, pagers are an effective way of sending short messages, but it is slow, transmitting a limited amount of data at about 600 b/s. At the other end of the scale are terminals with full QWERTY keyboards and laptop computers equipped with rf modems.

Within a narrow range of a building or campus, wireless data can be accomplished with privately owned spread-spectrum radio. Broader ranges require some form of public network. The most common methods are dial-up over cellular, cellular digital packet data (CDPD), or using an SMR or private packet carrier.

Cellular Dial-up

While cellular appears to be, and can be, a simple method of solving the mobile data problem, some precautions must be observed. First, ordinary commercial modems may not work well with cellular, particularly at high speed. The modulation methods of these modems are complex and do not gracefully handle the vagaries of interference, fades, and signal dropout. Handoff between cells causes a momentary interruption, and may cause the connection to drop. If a file is being downloaded when the dropout occurs, it may be necessary to start over again. Furthermore, many modems are designed to operate only after they recognize dial tone, which cellular does not provide.

Two vendors, Microcom with its MNP-10 protocol, and Paradyne with its Enhanced Throughput Cellular (ETC) protocol, provide methods of addressing the problems. The MNP-10 protocol starts that handshake with the session receiver at 1,200 b/s to negotiate the connection. The protocol then gradually increases the transmission speed to reach the point of maximum throughput. ETC takes the opposite approach. It starts at a higher speed and reduces if necessary. This method of communication is shown in Figure 17–4, along with CDPD.

FIGURE 17-4

Mobile Data through Two Options: CDPD and Dial-up Cellular

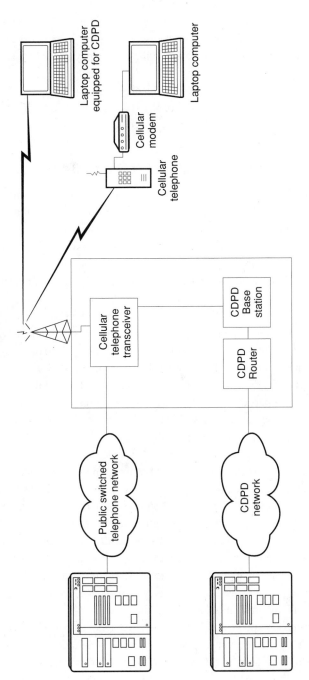

For occasional use and mobile file transfer, cellular is a good alternative, but it is too expensive for short messages. Most cellular operators levy a one-minute-per-call minimum charge, which may mean paying 30 to 50 cents for a transaction that takes only a few seconds. Also, the setup time is long compared to other alternatives. Cellular has the advantage of good coverage. In general, its applications are similar to those of the PSTN: It is good for facsimile and file transfers, but poor for short, bursty messages.

Cellular Digital Packet Data (CDPD)

A major advantage of cellular is coverage, which makes CDPD an attractive alternative. CDPD is a packet-switched data service that rides on top of cellular and uses idle analog channels. It can be added to existing cell sites at a moderate cost. Charging is by the packet or kilobyte instead of by the minute, and the long call setup time is eliminated. This makes it good for short bursty messages such as point-of-sale, dispatch, package tracking, telemetry, and E-mail. CDPD is not available in all metropolitan areas yet, but its availability is growing.

CDPD operates at 19.2 kb/s using a TCP/IP type of protocol, which raises the problem of IP addressing because the subnet is mobile. To be entirely effective for some applications, a laptop user should be able to disconnect from the LAN, travel to another location while remaining in contact with the network through a wireless connection, reconnect to the LAN at the distant location, and become part of the network again. The process is possible today, but the user needs to understand how to do it. Therefore, it is not yet feasible for the true mobile laptop or PDA application.

To implement CDPD carriers install mobile database stations (MDBS), which retrieve packets from the wireless network, and a mobile data intermediate system (MDIS), which routes them. The subscriber device is a modem and radio. Frames are picked up by the MDBS and handed off to the MDIS. Figure 17–4 shows how a signal connects through a cell site. Mobile stations use a protocol called digital sense multiple access with collision detection (DSMA/CD) for access to the network. The access method is similar to CSMA/CD, which Ethernet LANs use (Chapter 29). A station wishing to transmit listens to the outbound channel to determine if a carrier is present. If not, it transmits a packet. If so, it backs off and attempts a short time later.

The main advantage of CDPD is the coverage it can offer. The main population areas of the country are well covered for cellular, and if the carrier elects to overbuild the network with CDPD, data coverage can be equivalent. It is good for short, bursty applications, but for lengthy file transfers, dial-up application over regular cellular may be less costly.

A major drawback to CDPD is its reliance on spare analog capacity in cell sites in order to operate. At times, channels are so crowded in many locations that spare capacity is often unavailable. Since packet radio relies on readily available channels, the practice of CDPD may not be as appealing as the theory.

A key question to ask in setting up CDPD is what protocol to use. TCP/IP is a logical choice, and the carriers are generally prepared to provide IP addresses. But while TCP/IP is an excellent protocol for wired services, it isn't optimized for mobile use, particularly where a per-packet charge applies. Frequent acknowledgment packets are returned by TCP/IP, and although these are short, unless the charge is byte-oriented instead of packet-oriented, as much as one-third of the cost of a session may be taken up with acknowledgment packets. The TCP/IP protocol provides the user datagram protocol (UDP), which is a connectionless protocol, but it isn't generally robust enough for an application where the loss of link is probable. The hazards of mobile and portable communications makes dropped and out-of-sequence packets likely.

Roaming may be a problem with CDPD. Unless the carrier has equipped all cell sites with CDPD, which may not always be the case, the coverage may be narrower than regular cellular. Also, roaming to nonaffiliated areas can be a problem, ranging from lack of service to lack of an interconnection agreement.

Private Packet Carrier

Some metropolitan areas are served by private packet radio carriers. These services can be a good way to handle mobile and portable data, except that the service is not generally available everywhere. Where it is available, the coverage range may not match cellular or CDPD. The same factors must be considered in evaluating these carriers as in evaluating CDPD.

APPLICATIONS

Wireless is not a universal replacement for wired voice or LAN service. At the present time the service is experimental and expensive enough to discourage all but those who have a genuine need for wireless service. Payoff can be realized in businesses such as hospitals where nurses and physicians need to be in constant contact yet cannot be tied to a telephone. Paging can fulfill some of these needs, but some can be handled only by two-way radio.

Standards

In the United States, the FCC Rules and Regulations set forth wireless, PCS, and mobile data standards. FCC rules establish the authorized frequencies, power levels, bandwidth, frequency stability, signaling formats, and other such variables. CDPD standards were established by a consortium of major cellular carriers.

Evaluation Criteria, Wireless Voice

This section deals with evaluation criteria for wireless voice and data. PCS is not included in this section because the technology is not yet deployed, and too little is known of its services and distinguishing characteristics. The criteria discussed below are also important for selecting wireless data services.

Frequency band

Determine the frequency band that the system works in. Early products use the ISM band, which is nonexclusive to wireless, and may result in interference problems. More desirable are products that operate adjacent to the PCS band.

Coverage

Determine the coverage area of wireless cells. The narrower the coverage range, the more cells that will be required to cover a building or campus. Evaluate coverage between floors in buildings such as hospitals that may have a great deal of concrete and steel in their structure. Cells with less coverage may enable more consistent reuse of the available channels since the same frequencies can be reused in a different part of the building.

Station Sets

Analog station sets are universal and connect to any analog port on any telephone system. Proprietary sets connect to proprietary ports, and offer the advantage of button access to features. Determine what features are available and whether they match the organization's needs.

Evaluation Criteria, Wireless Data

Nature of the Application

The nature of the application is the first criterion to use in selecting wireless data. Is the application building-to-building, desktop, or mobile/portable? If the latter, what area must be covered? Is coverage required for E-mail or other types of messaging, calendar synchronization, file transfer, point-of-sale, or other application? If the application is building-to-building, what bandwidth is required? Is the distance far enough or the weather conditions such as fog frequent enough that interruption of infrared is likely?

Service Availability
For mobile/portable applications, what alternatives are available locally? Does CDPD cover the required area? Do specialized carriers offer packet radio? What do the various services cost?

Security
Can the data be intercepted easily? Is it critical? If so, is encryption available?

Robustness
How well does the protocol handle signal dropouts, fades, interference, and other such irregularities? How well does it handle long frames. How does it recover from interruptions? If it is interrupted in the middle of a file transfer, is it necessary to start over from the beginning? What kind of speed is available? Does it automatically adjust to optimize throughput?

Vendor Support
How many vendors are able to support the application in the local area? Do they have experience with wireless data? Be sure to check references.

SELECTED WIRELESS DATA EQUIPMENT MANUFACTURERS

As with the previous section, PCS manufacturers are not included in this section because of the newness of the service. This section lists some of the manufacturers of wireless data equipment.

Wireless Voice

Lucent Technologies
Nortel
Siemens Rolm
Ericsson

Wireless Remote Bridges

Cylink

Laser Communications

Motorola

Persoft

Solectek

SpreadNet

Windata

Cellular Modems

Air Communications, Inc.

Apex Data, Inc.

Compaq Computer Corp.

Data Race

Megahertz Corp.

Microcom, Inc.

Motorola UDS

Paradyne Corp.

Powertek Industries, Inc.

Racal-Datacom, Inc.

Toshiba America, Inc.

U.S. Robotics

Western Datacom

18

VIDEO SYSTEMS

For years observers talked about convergence of telecommunications and computers. That convergence is well under way, and now the entertainment industry is joining the fray. The FCC and Congress have either removed or are in the process of removing most of the restrictions on cable television (CATV) companies and LECs that in the past prevented their entering each other's lines of business. At this writing LECs can transport video, but they are prohibited from originating the information content. CATV companies can provide telephone dial tone and transport data where state utilities commissions permit it, although few have yet begun to do so. Two industries that heretofore have been heavily regulated are about to venture into new lines of business, or perhaps to merge as some companies have already tried without much success. The factor that both have in common is an information pipeline into subscribers' homes. Neither the existing twisted-pair wire that telephone companies use nor the coaxial cable that CATV companies use is the ideal medium. Both agree that fiber optics is the preferred method of carrying signals, but the cost of converting some 100 million homes to fiber is enormous.

CATV has served the country through its existence of nearly half a century. Today it is a major source of entertainment for millions of people, but the industry foresees the day when thousands of entertainment choices will be available on demand. Not all of these will be traditional movies and television programs. Besides these, cable will deliver home shopping, news sources, educational services, stock market reports, and games, just to mention a few of the possibilities. Conventional cable is handicapped by limited bandwidth and the fact that all channels are delivered to every residence. If the owner doesn't subscribe to certain services they must be trapped and filtered or scrambled to prevent their reception. For the coming multifaceted medium the industry prefers to enable subscribers to choose services from a vast storehouse and deliver only the services subscribers select. This service is called video on demand (VOD). Subscribers can dial into a database of services that may originate in a variety of sources, including the carrier that provides the backbone network. The VOD concept is shown in Figure 18–1.

Although VOD is intended primarily as a residential service, its fallout has the potential of reshaping the telecommunications industry. Video is the only technology in sight that warrants bringing broadband services into residential areas. In large metropolitan areas fiber-optics transmission is available to most businesses, but fiber has penetrated residential areas to only a limited degree. Delivering VOD requires high-speed switching, which will likely be ATM, and it requires huge servers to deliver the gigabits that compressed television signals require.

If demand for entertainment can enable carriers to justify installing fiber in residential areas, other services including telephone and data will logically ride the same medium. True competition in providing these services will drive down the costs and bring information to the home in completely different manners than it arrives today. Television sets will be digital devices that have most, if not all of the capabilities of a personal computer.

As video compression algorithms improve and the cost drops because of the economies of scale resulting from entry into household markets, videoconferencing will become the beneficiary. While videoconferencing is costly and rare today, in the future it can be expected to become the normal way of communicating. The Picturephone, which AT&T introduced in 1964, failed to attract enough interest to make it a commercially successful product at the time. Like many other product developments, however, it was merely ahead of its time. Conferencing equipment built into desktop computers will soon be a regular feature in most companies and many homes. When digital bandwidth to the home and small business becomes readily available and economical, video telephone calls will be the accepted way of communicating.

VIDEO TECHNOLOGY

At its present state of development, video is inherently an analog transmission medium because of the method of picture generation. Video signals in the United States are generated under the National Television Systems Committee

FIGURE 18-1

Video on Demand

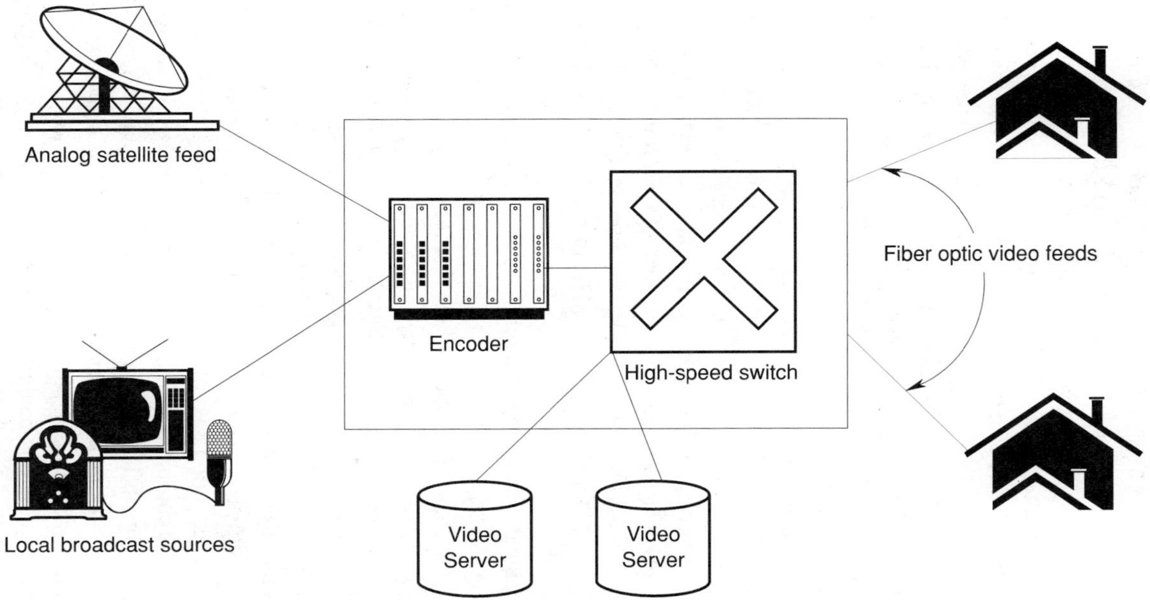

(NTSC) system. In Europe they are generated under two different and incompatible standards: PAL (phase alternate line) and SECAM (*sequential couleur avec memoire*). A video signal is formed by scanning an image with a video camera. As the camera scans the image, it creates an analog signal that varies in voltage with variations in the degree of blackness of the image. In the NTSC system, the television *raster* has 525 horizontal scans. The raster is composed of two fields of 262.5 lines each. The two fields are interlaced to form a *frame*, as Figure 18–2 shows. The frame repeats 30 times each second; the persistence of the human eye eliminates flicker. Since the two fields are interlaced, the screen is refreshed 60 times per second.

On close inspection, a video screen is revealed as a matrix of tiny dots. Each dot is called a *picture element,* abbreviated *pixel*. The resolution of a television picture is a function of the number of scan lines and pixels per frame, both of which affect the amount of bandwidth required to transmit a television signal. The NTSC system requires 4.2 MHz of bandwidth for satisfactory resolution. Because of the modulation system used and the need for guard bands between channels, the FCC assigns 6 MHz of bandwidth to television channels in the United States.

The signal resulting from each scan line varies between a black and a white voltage level, as Figure 18–3a shows. A horizontal synchronizing pulse is inserted at the beginning of each line. Frames are synchronized with vertical pulses as Figure 18–3b shows. Between frames the signal is blanked during a vertical synchronizing interval to allow the scanning trace to return to the upper left corner of the screen. Teletext services transmit information during this interval, which is known as the *vertical blanking interval.*

A color television signal has two parts: the *luminance* signal and the *chrominance* signal. A black-and-white picture has only the luminance signal, which controls the brightness of the screen in step with the sweep of the horizontal trace. The chrominance signal modulates subcarriers that are transmitted with the video signal. The color demodulator in the receiver is synchronized by a *color burst* consisting of eight cycles of a 3.58 MHz signal that is applied to the horizontal synchronizing pulse, as Figure 18–3a shows.

When no picture is being transmitted, the scanning voltage rests at the black level, and the television receiver's screen is black. Because the signal is amplitude modulated analog, any noise pulses that are higher in level than the black signal level appear on the screen as snow. A high-quality transmission medium keeps the signal level above the noise to preserve satisfactory picture quality. The degree of resolution in a television picture depends on bandwidth. Signals sent through a narrow bandwidth are fuzzy with washed-out color. The channel also must be sufficiently linear. Lack of linearity results in high-level

FIGURE 18-2

Interlaced Video Frame

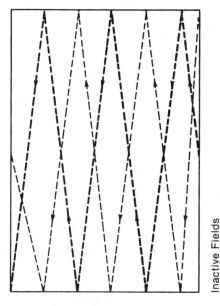

Inactive Fields
Heavy lines show retrace pattern from bottom to top of screen during vertical blanking interval. Heavy lines represent first field and light lines the second.

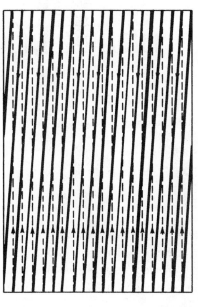

Active Fields
Heavy lines represent first field.
Light lines represent second field.
Dotted lines represent retrace lines that are blanked out.

FIGURE 18-3

Synchronizing and Blanking in a Television Signal

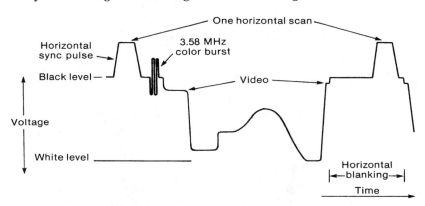

a. Voltage levels during one horizontal scan. As image is scanned, voltage varies from reference black to reference white level.

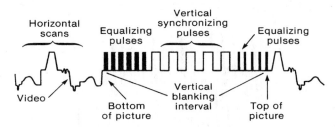

a. Voltage sychronization. Vertical blanking occurs during retrace of scanner to top of screen.

signals being amplified at a different rate than low-level signals, which affects picture contrast. Another critical requirement of the transmission medium is its envelope delay characteristic. If envelope delay is excessive, the chrominance signal arrives at the receiver out of phase with the luminance signal, and color distortion results.

The four primary criteria for assessing a video transmission medium, therefore, are noise, bandwidth, amplitude linearity, and phase linearity. The primary media used for analog video are analog microwave radio, analog co-axial cable, and, for broadcasting, free space. Analog signals also can be transmitted over fiber optics using intensity modulation or frequency modulation of a light carrier. Analog signals can be carried for a limited distance over category 5 UTP by the use of video baluns. Digital video signals can be transmitted over coaxial cable or twisted-pair wire, as well as being broadcast, but fiber optics is the preferred medium.

CABLE TELEVISION SYSTEMS

Cable television systems have three major components: headend equipment, trunk cable, and feeder and user drop equipment. Figure 18–4 is a block diagram of a CATV system. A principal limitation of CATV systems is a lack of selectivity for the end user. All channels that originate at the headend are broadcast to all stations, which means the operator must either limit the number of channels carried or block premium channels for which the user is not paying. Except for various devices to prevent unauthorized reception of pay television signals, any receiver can receive all services on the network. This is in contrast to the telephone network, which routes lines in a star configuration to each user individually.

Headend Equipment

Headend equipment, as Figure 18–5 shows, receives and generates video signals and, in two-way systems, repeats the signal from the user on the upstream channels to terminals on the downstream channels. Signals from these sources are inserted at the headend:

- ◆ Off-the-air pickup of broadcast signals, including both television and FM radio.
- ◆ Signals received over communications satellites.
- ◆ Signals received from distant locations over microwave radio relay systems.
- ◆ Locally originated signals.

The headend equipment modulates each television signal to a separate channel in the range of 50 to 500 MHz. Some companies use narrower bandwidth systems, but current systems support up to 80 channels over this frequency range, as Figure 18–6 shows. Some systems support a bandwidth of 750 MHz, and systems under development extend the bandwidth to 1 GHz. UHF television channels are remodulated into another channel within the passband. Most CATV systems use a single coaxial cable to carry signals, but some systems double their capacity by using two cables. Amplifiers and cable facilities are duplicated in a two-cable system.

FIGURE 18-4

Diagram of a CATV System

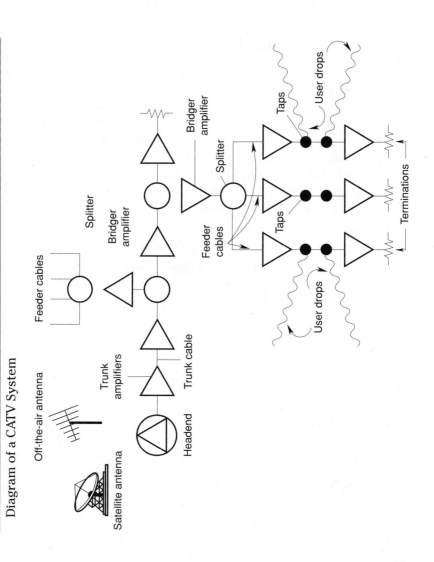

FIGURE 18-5

Headend Equipment

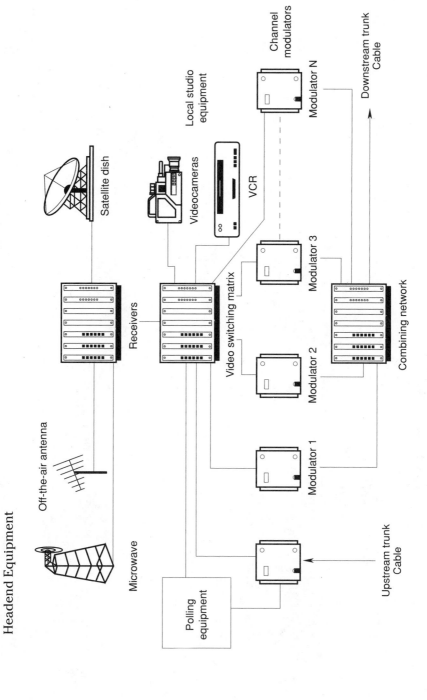

441

FIGURE 18-6

Cable Television Frequency Bands

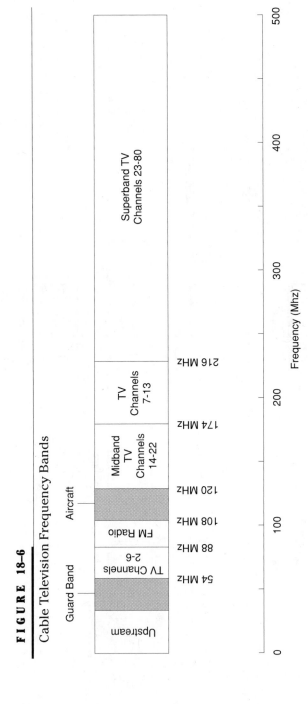

Trunk Cable Systems

Headend equipment applies the signal to a trunk to carry the signal to local distribution systems. Some systems use *hub headends* to distribute the signal. Hub headends are satellites of a master headend and have the ability to add or distribute services before sending the signal through the local feeder area. The cable between the master headend and the hubs is called a *super trunk*. Hubs may be fed by point-to-point microwave radio operating in a band designated by the FCC as Cable Television Relay Service. Increasingly, CATV companies use fiber optics for trunks.

Early CATV systems used a separate amplifier for each television channel. This technique simplified the amplifier design but restricted the practical number of channels that could be transported. Current systems use broadband amplifiers that are equalized to carry the entire bandwidth. Amplifiers have about 20 dB of gain and are placed at intervals of approximately one-third of a mile. Amplifiers known as *bridgers* split the signal to feeder cables.

Amplifiers contain automatic gain control circuitry to adjust gain as cable loss changes with temperature variations. Power is applied to amplifiers over the coaxial center conductor, with main power feed points approximately every mile. Many subscribers use CATV systems for home security and alarm systems, so continued operation during power outage is essential. To continue essential services during power outages and amplifier failures, the cable operator provides redundant amplifiers and backup battery supplies.

Trunk cable uses a high grade of coaxial cable with diameters of 0.75 to 1 inch. The cable often shares pole lines and trenches with power and telephone. The cable and amplifiers must be free of signal leakage. Because the CATV signals operate on the same frequencies as many radio services, a leaking cable can interfere with another service or vice versa. FCC regulations curtail the use of CATV in frequency bands of 108 to 136 and 225 to 400 MHz in many localities because of the possibility of interference with aeronautical navigation and communication equipment.

As with other analog transmission media, noise and distortion are cumulative through successive amplifier stages. Noise and distortion limit the serving radius of 80-channel CATV to about five miles from the headend.

Feeder and Drop System

Bridger amplifiers split feeder or distribution cable from the trunk cable. Multiple feeders are coupled with *splitters* or *directional couplers,* which match the impedance of the cables. The feeder cable is smaller and less expensive and has

F I G U R E   18–7

Two-Way Cable Frequency Splitting

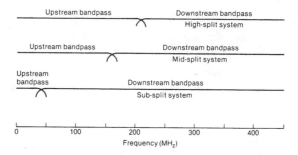

higher loss than trunk cable. Subscriber drops connect to the feeder cable through *taps,* which are passive devices that isolate the feeder cable from the drop. The tap must have enough isolation that shorts and opens at the television set do not affect other signals on the cable.

Two-Way CATV Systems

Two-way communication is available on some CATV systems, but many systems do not provide enough upstream bandwidth to make them an effective alternative for two-way service. The key to a two-way system is bidirectional amplifiers. Filters split the signal into the high band for downstream transmission and the low band for upstream transmission. Figure 18–7 shows three splitting methods. The subsplit is the most common in CATV systems with the midsplit and high-split methods often used in broadband local area networks. A guard band 15 to 20 MHz wide separates the two directions of transmission. The upstream direction shares frequencies with high-powered short-wave transmitters operating on 5 to 30 MHz frequencies, so interference from these sources is a potential problem. Cable and amplifiers must be adequately shielded to prevent interference.

Headend equipment is more complex in a two-way than in a one-way CATV system. User terminals access the upstream cable by contention or token passing, described in Chapter 29, or by being polled from the headend. The headend of a two-way system contains a computer to poll the terminals. Some systems use a transponder at the user end to receive and execute orders from the headend. For example, a polling message might instruct the transponder to read utility meters and forward the reading over the upstream channel.

VIDEO COMPRESSION

Analog video is an inexpensive and effective method of transmission, but it is wasteful of bandwidth. A video signal contains considerable redundancy. Often large portions of background do not change between frames, but conventional transmission systems transmit these anyway. Removing redundancy in an analog signal is difficult, but digital signal processing can compress a video signal into a reasonably narrow bandwidth. If a 4.2 MHz NTSC video signal is digitized with PCM, it requires a bandwidth of approximately 90 MHz. This signal can be compressed to occupy as little as 64 kb/s with today's technology, but the result falls short, even for videoconferences. At least T-1 bandwidth is needed for a satisfactory signal that is approximately equal to the quality of a home VCR, and at least two 64 kb/s channels are needed for minimally acceptable videoconferencing. Excellent quality, suitable for all but the most demanding conference applications, can be obtained on one-third of a T-1 line, or 512 kb/s.

Three public standards have been published for video compression. ITU's H.261 is intended for videoconferencing, and is discussed later in more detail. MPEG-1 and MPEG-2 are intended for broadcast or narrowcast video. MPEG is an abbreviation for Motion Picture Experts Group, which is the body that developed the standards. MPEG-1 compresses a video signal into bandwidths of up to 2 mb/s. The resolution is 288 lines per frame, which is home VCR quality. It is satisfactory for most home use including VOD if the scene doesn't have too much action. MPEG-2 compresses a high-definition television (HDTV) signal, which normally would require 25 MHz of analog bandwidth, into the 6 MHz channel allocated to broadcast television.

Video compression is achieved by eliminating redundancy and by predictive coding. The equipment that encodes and decodes the video signal is called a *codec*. Flicking by at 30 frames per second, much in a moving picture doesn't change from frame to frame. *Interframe encoding* recognizes when portions of a frame remain constant, and transmits only the changed portions. *Intraframe encoding* provides another element of compression. The picture is broken into blocks of 16 × 16 pixels. A block is transmitted only when pixels within that block have changed. Otherwise, the decoding equipment retains the previous block and forwards it to the receiver with each frame. *Predictive coding* analyzes the elements that are changing, and predicts what the next frame will be. Much in the same manner that ADPCM uses (see Chapter 5), if the transmitting and receiving codecs both use the same prediction algorithm, only changes from the prediction must be transmitted, not the complete frame. Approximately every two seconds, the entire frame is refreshed, but in intervening frames, only the changed pixels are transmitted.

Encoding systems are known as *lossless,* or *lossy.* A lossless coding system transmits information in a manner that can be restored bit-for-bit. Runlength encoding, used by facsimile (Chapter 27), is a good example. If a scan line or series of lines contain a long run of zeros (white) or ones (black), it is necessary to transmit only a short message telling the receiver how many zeros or ones to insert. If the message is shorter than the original string, compression results. This method of encoding is widely used by both data and video systems.

A lossy encoding system discards information, transmitting only enough to retain intelligibility, but not enough to ensure the integrity of the received signal. Lossy systems work well for sending still scenes, but motion can cause a tiling or smearing effect as the receiving codec attempts to catch up with the transmitter. The higher the compression and the more vigorous the motion, the greater is the smearing effect. More bandwidth improves the signal quality.

VIDEO CONFERENCING

Some companies offer videoconference facilities as a utility, with conference rooms and full video facilities available for lease. Corporations that want to reduce travel and meeting costs may provide their own videoconference facilities. Conferencing equipment is categorized as audio only, audio with graphics, freeze-frame video, and full-motion video. Videoconferencing is sometimes called *teleconferencing,* but in this book that term refers to audio-only conferences.

A videoconference facility has the following subsystems integrated into a unit:

- ◆ Audio equipment.
- ◆ Video production and control equipment.
- ◆ Graphics equipment.
- ◆ Document hard copy equipment.
- ◆ Communications.

A full description of these systems is beyond the scope of this book. We will discuss them here briefly to describe the composition of a videoconferencing facility.

Audio Equipment

Most analysts believe that audio equipment is the most important part of a videoconference facility. In large videoconferences it is often impossible to show all participants, but it is important that everyone hear and be heard clearly.

Audio equipment consists of microphones, speakers, and amplifiers placed strategically around the room. Sometimes speaker telephones are used, but with generally less satisfactory results than the audio produced by the codec. The codec robs a portion of the bandwidth to transmit the audio, so some products allow the operator to reduce the amount of audio bandwidth as a way of improving the video.

Video and Control Equipment

Video equipment consists of two or three cameras and associated control equipment. The main camera usually is mounted at the front of the room and often automatically follows the voice of the speaker. Zoom, tilt, and azimuth controls are mounted on a console, where the conference participants can control them from a panel with a joystick. A second camera mounts overhead for graphic displays. The facility sometimes includes a third mobile camera that is operated independently. A switch at the console operator's position selects the camera. Monitors placed around the room can easily be seen by the participants. Figure 18–8 shows a typical setup for a small conference room. Usually one monitor shows the picture from the distant end and another shows the picture at the near end. In single-monitor conferences the near end can usually be viewed in a window using the monitor's picture-in-picture feature.

In a videoconference, the adverse effects of smearing can be minimized by selecting the camera position. When the camera is positioned to encompass a passive group, smearing is generally not objectionable. It is most objectionable when there is considerable action or when the camera shows a close-up of the face of an individual who is talking.

Digitizing and encoding equipment compresses full-motion video or creates freeze-frames. In addition, encryption equipment may be included for security. Other equipment can freeze a full motion display for a few seconds while the participants send a graphic image over the circuit. Sometimes digital storage equipment enables participants to transmit presentation material ahead of time so graphics transmission does not waste conference time.

Graphics Equipment

Videoconference facilities may include graphics-generating equipment to construct diagrams with arrows, circles, lines, and other symbols. Some systems provide for desktop computer input so tools in the computer can be used for generating graphics.

FIGURE 18–8

A Small Videoconference Room Using Compression Labs Gallery
Equipment.

Photo courtesy of Compression Labs, Inc.

Communications

Communications facilities are audio and video circuits, with the type of facility
depending on the bandwidth required. Facilities range from voice circuits to
full DS-1 video facilities and satellite earth stations. When satellite communication facilities are used, the audio channel must be diplexed over the video
channel to keep the audio synchronized with the picture.

ISDN is an ideal medium for videoconferences. Its two 64 kb/s B channels and separate signaling channel provide enough bandwidth for an acceptable conference. BRI channels can be obtained directly from the LEC, or

through a PBX that has PRI connections to the LEC or IEC. If additional bandwidth is needed, some PBXs provide $N\times64$ capability, which provides as much bandwidth as needed up to full T-1. If $N\times64$ capability is not available in the PBX, a device known as an *inverse multiplexer* can be used to aggregate the bandwidth. An inverse multiplexer accepts multiple digital input channels and combines them into a higher-speed bit stream.

Justification for Videoconferencing Equipment

Videoconferencing is now becoming economically feasible—not just to reduce travel but as a way of doing business. Interest in videoconferencing is surging because costs are continuing to drop. Coder/decoders (codecs) that cost more than $100,000 in the mid-1980s are now available for a fraction of that amount, and prices will undoubtedly continue to drop as the volume increases.

Complementing the drop in codec costs are reductions in the costs of transmission and equipping conference rooms. Most LECs and the major IECs offer switched 56/64 kb/s services, and ISDN is now available in most parts of the country. The interexchange portion of switched 56 and ISDN service is only marginally more expensive than ordinary direct-dialed telephone service. It requires a dedicated loop to either the LEC or the IEC, which adds to the fixed cost of the service, but it is still only a fraction of what it cost a few years ago.

Portable conference room facilities, consisting of audio equipment, codec, monitor, and a camera with pan, tilt, and zoom can be purchased for about $25,000. Although this is still too high to be within the reach of casual users, it is less than half the price of a few years ago and will undoubtedly drop further as demand increases.

ITU-T Standards

A major factor that facilitates video conferencing is the ITU-T H.320 standards. The following standards fall under the H.320 umbrella:

◆ G.711, G.722, and G.728 audio compression. These standards define audio compression at bandwidths of 3.0 to 7 kHz. G.728 recommends a method of compressing 3-KHz audio into 16 kb/s. G.711 is a toll-quality audio standard. G.722 is a higher-fidelity audio standard than G.711.

◆ H.221 data formatting and framing. This standard outlines how bits are identified as video, audio, and control, and how they are fitted into frames.

◆ H.230 control and indication information. This standard defines commands for control and diagnostics.

◆ H.233 transmission confidentiality. This standard outlines methods for handling encrypted data.

◆ H.242 transmission protocols. This standard outlines call setup, transfer, and disconnect procedures.

◆ H.243 multipoint handshake. This standard defines communications between the codec and a multipoint control unit.

◆ H.261 syntax and semantics of the video bit stream. This standard defines the video coding algorithms and recommends the picture format.

◆ H.32P video telephone standards. These provisional standards recommend methods of videoconferencing over analog telephone lines.

Before the standards were developed codec manufacturers used proprietary standards, which meant that they could communicate only with codecs of the same manufacture. All codec manufacturers still have proprietary standards that, in most cases, are superior to H.261, but H.261 provides a fallback that allows otherwise incompatible systems to communicate.

ITU-T standards are known as $P{\times}64$ (pronounced P times 64). Two options are offered. The full common intermediate format (CIF) offers frames of 288 lines by 352 pixels. This is approximately half the resolution of commercial television, which is 525 lines by 480 pixels. The second alternative is one-fourth CIF, which is 144 lines by 176 pixels. The modulation method is the discreet cosine transform (DCT) algorithm. The amount of bandwidth supplied in the transmission facilities must be in multiples of 64 kb/s. Several proprietary algorithms on the market yield better quality, but as with many other ITU-T standards, the standardization process takes so long that it is difficult for standards to keep pace with advances in technology.

Desktop Video Conferencing

The videoconferencing market is likely to be revolutionized in the next few years by desktop video equipment. This equipment is contained in a standard desktop computer that has a small video camera mounted on top of the monitor. The conferencing equipment is mounted on a board that plugs into a computer expansion slot, or it is an external box that plugs into board in the computer. Some products require a BRI line, while others plug into a proprietary digital PBX port. The equipment may also include a replacement for the telephone set.

The result is an economical method of conducting a personal videoconference. Conferences are spontaneous, with no need to schedule a conference room. The addition of a picture to the call allows the parties to pick up the nonverbal content of a session by seeing expressions. The screen is generally too small and the camera angle too narrow for group conferences, but for one-to-one conferences it is excellent. Most products permit the users to share and view computer files over the network. When desktop video equipment is widely accepted, as it is likely to be over the next few years, it will be an effective tool for enhancing the quality of telephone calls.

Freeze-Frame Video

Another form of video transmission known as *freeze-frame* can be used to transmit video signals over analog voice channels. Freeze-frame equipment scans and digitizes the video signal and transmits a single frame over a digital line or over a modem-equipped analog line. Unlike compressed video, which results in a continuously varying picture, freeze-frame video presents a still picture that is refreshed periodically. The refresh rate depends on the transmission speed. For example, over a 56 kb/s line the signal is refreshed about every 15 seconds. At the receiving end the picture gradually fills the screen one line at a time from top to bottom. This waterfall effect can be eliminated by using a frame storage unit to accept the frame and relay it to the monitor after the entire frame is received.

Freeze-frame video is particularly adaptable to conferences that make extensive use of graphics. The main advantage of freeze-frame compared to compressed motion video is cost, and the gap between freeze-frame and motion is narrowing. Freeze-frame is superior for a few applications such as transmitting images, but for most applications, compressed motion video is the medium of choice.

DIGITAL TELEVISION

The future of analog television is limited. Although there is plenty of bandwidth in the UHF bands, the VHF bands, which offer the best coverage, are crowded. With MPEG-1 technology, as many as four compressed channels could be broadcast in the same frequency spectrum as one analog channel. Digital television is more likely to be delivered by satellite or terrestrial media such as fiber optics or asymmetric digital subscriber line (ADSL), a technology we will discuss in a later section. Digital television will bring the benefits that it has brought to voice: improved signal quality, reduced equipment costs, and more effective switching and multiplexing methods.

Video on Demand

A driving factor for digital television is video on demand (VOD). Today's CATV systems deliver all channels to every residence, and unwanted or unauthorized channels must be trapped out or scrambled. VOD as a concept refers to a broad spectrum of services that are delivered over the broadband medium: entertainment, information, and education services are examples of VOD services that can be ordered by dialing the service provider and arranging to have them delivered.

Although the technologies for VOD have mostly been developed, several questions remain. A major question is how the services will be delivered. Existing coaxial cable owned by the CATV companies does not lend itself well to VOD. It is analog plant, and VOD is delivered as a digital service. Digital television sets will undoubtedly be produced in quantity before long, but for now television sets are analog, which means a converter is required. Who will pay for the converters and how much they will cost has not been determined. Video servers can also be a stumbling block. The amount of data that must be delivered to fill digital pipes to thousands of simultaneous users outstrips the capabilities of today's server technologies.

Video over Fiber

A major issue is how video will be delivered to residences in the future. Fiber optics is the obvious and unanimous choice. Although the conversion will be gradual, fiber is the only terrestrial medium that has the necessary bandwidth. It also carries a hefty price tag that prevents the carriers from leaping headlong into fiber technology.

Three different schemes for deploying fiber have been proposed;

- ◆ Fiber to the node (FTTN).
- ◆ Fiber to the curb (FTTC).
- ◆ Fiber to the home (FTTH).

FTTN, which requires the least fiber, brings the video signal to a distribution point in the neighborhood. From there the signal is delivered by wire, either twisted pair, coaxial, or both. This method approximates the architecture of local telephone distribution plant today, but it requires more expensive electronics at the node. If the digital signal is converted to analog at this point it can be distributed over coax, but to do so requires additional equipment in the node.

A second alternative is distributing the signal to an interface that serves a handful of residences. This plan, FTTC, gets the signal close enough to the residence that a coaxial drop or twisted-pair wire can distribute the signal digitally. FTTC uses less nodal equipment. The third alternative, FTTH, runs fiber directly into the home. This is the technically most elegant and expensive solution, and is the one that will most likely evolve eventually.

Asymmetric Digital Subscriber Line

Everyone agrees that in the long run fiber optics is the best alternative for delivering video services to residential areas, but the cost is so high that the conversion must be gradual. Meanwhile, nearly every residence is served by twisted-pair wire, which has capability of delivering video within narrow distance and bandwidth limits. The technology is known as asymmetric digital subscriber line (ADSL). It is asymmetric because the bandwidth is greater in the downstream direction. A single cable pair delivers regular telephone service in the 0–4 kHz portion of the bandwidth. A narrow upstream channel for signaling and control is multiplexed above the voice channel, and above that is video bandwidth.

ADSL comes in two varieties: ADSL-1 and ADSL-3. ADSL-1 provides one MPEG-1 channel on subscriber loops as long as 18,000 feet. ADSL-3 provides four 1.5 mb/s MPEG-1 or one 6 mb/s MPEG-2 HDTV signals on loops as long as 9,000 feet. The loop limitation means that it cannot be used universally. It is, however, an acceptable method of video transmission from a node.

ADSL is not a long-term solution to video on demand. ADSL-1 allows only one video signal at a time, which does not meet the needs of multiset families. ADSL-3 allows multiple channels to be watched, but only as long as they are conventional TV.

Direct Broadcast Satellite Service

Direct broadcast satellite service (DBS) has finally evolved from theory to reality. Viewers have long been watching video broadcast from satellites, but that service does not fall under the FCC's definition of DBS. Most of the existing services are in the 4 GHz common carrier band, and not in the 12 GHz (Ku band) DBS band that the FCC authorized in the mid-1980s for DBS.

DBS satellites are high powered, which enables users to have small receiving antennas one or two feet in diameter. The ease with which antennas can be concealed overcomes some of the zoning restrictions that have hampered satellite service in the lower frequency bands. The new services use digital transmission, although most users convert to analog for compatibility with existing television sets. With the compression systems used, as many as 200 channels can be supported. DBS is a technically viable alternative to CATV except that it does not offer a way of receiving local channels. It offers pay-per-view video, which subscribers order with a telephone call. DBS is a good test bed for VOD because it shows the willingness of subscribers to purchase the electronic equipment and to pay for the entertainment services that DBS delivers.

High-Definition Television

The present NTSC television standard was defined in 1941 when 525-line resolution was considered excellent quality and when such technologies as large-scale integration were hardly imagined. The standard was satisfactory for its time, but it is far from the present state of the art. Larger cities are running out of channel capacity. Although not all channels are filled, co-channel interference prevents the FCC from assigning all available channels. Large television screens are becoming more the rule than the exception, and at close range the distance between scan lines is disconcerting. The 525 scan lines of broadcast television and the 4:3 width-to-height ratio of the screen, called the *aspect ratio,* place limitations on picture quality. With wide-screen movies and the growing popularity of large-screen television sets, the definition of the current scanning system is considerably less than that of the original image. HDTV will have an aspect ratio of close to 2:1 (current plans call for 16:9), which will allow wide-screen reception.

Under the urging of the FCC's Advisory Committee on Advanced Television Service (ACATS), a consortium of seven manufacturers and research institutions joined forces in 1993 to form the Digital HDTV Grand Alliance, whose goal was to produce an HDTV system for the United States. The standard is undergoing final testing at this writing. Limited HDTV broadcasts are expected to begin in 1997.

VIDEO SERVICES AND APPLICATIONS

Entertainment is likely to remain the primary driving force behind video into the future, but business and educational use of television will be increasingly important. As CATV provides a broadband information pipeline into a substantial portion of United States households, the growth of nonentertainment services is expected. The services described below are intended primarily for residences, but business applications will follow the availability of the services.

Teletext

Teletext is the transmission of information services during the vertical blanking interval of a television signal. As discussed earlier, the vertical blanking interval is the equivalent of 21 horizontal scan lines of a television signal, during which no picture information is transmitted. Teletext services transmit information such as magazines and catalogs over a television channel. An adapter decodes the information and presents it on the screen.

The British Prestel system was the first widespread application of teletext. The French have introduced teletext throughout much of the country. The service is not used widely in the United States, but if the demand develops, it can become an inexpensive way of transmitting information for little more cost than the price of a converter.

Security

Television security applications take two forms—alarm systems and closed circuit television (CCTV) for monitoring unattended areas from a central location. Many businesses use CCTV for intrusion monitoring, and it is also widely used for intraorganizational information telecasts. Alarm services have principally relied on telephone lines to relay alarms to a center, which requires a separate line or automatic dialer. The expense of these devices can be saved by routing alarms over a CATV upstream channel, but to do so requires a terminal to interface with the alarm unit. As described earlier, a computer in the headend scans the alarm terminals and forwards alarm information to a security agency as instructed by the user.

Data Communications

Many CATV companies offer two-way data communications over their systems. An rf modem converts the digital data signal to analog for application to the cable. Bandwidths up to 10 mb/s are available over systems equipped for two-way operation.

Control Systems

Two-way CATV systems offer the potential of controlling many functions in households and businesses. For example, utilities can use the system to poll remote gas, electric, and water meters to save the cost of manual meter reading. Power companies can use the system for load control. During periods of high demand, electric water heaters can be turned off and restored when reduced demand permits. A variety of household services such as appliances and environmental equipment can be remotely controlled by a computer at the headend. CATV companies themselves can use the system to register channels that viewers are watching and to bill on the basis of service consumed. They also can use the equipment to control addressable converters to unscramble a premium channel at the viewers' request.

Opinion Polling

Experiments with opinion polling over CATV have been conducted. For example, CATV has been used to enable viewers to evaluate the television program they have just finished watching. The potential of this system for allowing viewers to watch a political body in action and immediately express their opinion has great potential in a democracy, although it has not yet been used to any extent.

APPLICATIONS

Companies that had never considered videoconferencing are beginning to investigate it more closely as the economics become more compelling. The first line of justification is generally replacement for travel, but as organizations adopt video as a way of doing business, the need for economic justification will disappear. For example, the telephone and the facsimile machine no longer need to be justified; it is unthinkable to do business without them, and neither is viewed as a replacement for doing business face-to-face. The same undoubtedly will happen with video.

The most obvious video application is for meetings, but other applications will develop as costs continue to decline. For example, here are some applications that show unexpected benefits of video applications.

- ◆ A food producer has farmers bring produce to a staging area and dump it on slabs for later redeployment. Video equipment shows the production department the types of produce and quantities on hand at plants located in three different cities.
- ◆ A countywide fire and rescue system uses the CATV system to administer training to firefighting crews who must remain at their present facilities to respond to emergencies. Not only is the CATV system used for sending video, it also is used as a data communications system to provide access to the host computer and to transmit location maps from the 911 center when alarms are dispatched.
- ◆ A company has found a secondary benefit of videoconferencing. Not only are travel costs reduced, but since conference participants must schedule video facilities, it forces managers to limit time, resulting in more efficient and productive meetings.

Videoconferencing makes it economical for more people to participate directly in events. Before videoconferencing facilities were available, the company authorized only a few people to travel. With videoconferencing, more people can obtain information firsthand.

Standards

U.S. television signals are generated according to standards developed by the National Television System Committee (NTSC). Rules and standards of the FCC regulate television broadcasts and CATV. EIA specifies electrical performance standards of television signals and equipment. ITU-T establishes standards for international television transmission, recommends signal quality standards, and also specifies compression standards. The principal ITU-T standards covering videoconferencing are listed in an earlier section.

Evaluation Considerations

This section discusses evaluation considerations of videoconferencing and transmission equipment. Other video services, including CATV, are provided only as and where available and are not usually subject to choice. The exception to this is data communication over CATV facilities, which is an alternative to using the telephone network. This alternative is evaluated on criteria discussed in Chapter 31. Examples of the criteria are speed of transmission, data error rate, and cost.

Type of Transmission Facilities

The initial issue to resolve is whether full-motion, compressed motion, or freeze-frame video will fulfill the objectives. The decision largely is driven by costs, which in turn are determined by the transmission facilities available. If private facilities with bandwidths of 64 kb/s or greater are available, compressed or full-motion video is preferable unless the application can be fulfilled with still images. If available, BRI ISDN service offers ideal videoconferencing facilities. For higher bandwidths, inverse multiplexing may be required.

If compressed video is required, the following questions should be evaluated:

◆ Is the compression algorithm proprietary or does it support ITU-T standards? Is H.261 available as a fallback standard?
◆ What level of quality is needed? Is a highly compressed signal satisfactory?
◆ Does the system support still graphics?
◆ Does audio ride on the video facility?
◆ Is single-point or multipoint communication required?

Single- or Multipoint Conferences

Videoconferences are classed as point-to-point or multipoint. With terrestrial facilities, the distance and number of points served have a significant effect on transmission costs. Satellite facility costs are independent of distance and, except for earth station costs, are independent of the number of points served if the points are within the satellite footprint. If earth stations exist for other communications services, such as a companywide voice and data network, multipoint video conferences can be obtained for costs equivalent to those of point-to-point conferences.

Large companies with a significant amount of multipoint conferencing can often justify the cost of a multipoint control unit (MCU). Companies that use multipoint conferencing only occasionally can use multipoint services offered by the major IECs. The IECs offer "meet-me" conferencing in which conferees dial into a bridge. The control unit receives inputs from all locations, and sends each location the image that has seized the transmitting channel. The transmitting channel is allocated by one of three methods: under control of the conference leader, under time control in which each location gets a share of the time, or by switching in the location that is currently talking. The latter method is the most common, but it requires a disciplined approach.

The type of transmission facility also is a function of the bandwidth required. Full-motion, full-color video requires a 6 MHz analog channel or a 1.544 mb/s digital channel. With a sacrifice in clarity during motion, digital bandwidths can be reduced to as little as 64 kb/s. Freeze-frame video can be supported over narrower bandwidths. Digital transmission is usually less economical for multipoint or one-way broadcasts because of the cost of video compression equipment.

System Integration

Videoconference equipment is usually an assembly of units made by different manufacturers. To ensure compatibility, it is usually advisable to obtain equipment from a vendor who can assemble it into a complete system.

Security

The type of information being transmitted over the channel must be considered. Often, proprietary information is discussed during conferences. Both terrestrial microwave and satellite services are subject to interception; signals transmitted over fiber optics are less vulnerable. Scrambling or encryption of both video and audio signals often is warranted.

Public or Private Facilities

Private videoconference facilities have a significant advantage over public access systems. Public facilities are unavailable in many localities, which may preclude holding many videoconferences. The travel time to a public facility offsets some of the advantages of videoconference. Unless a private facility is used frequently, however, public facilities are usually the most cost-effective option..

Future Expansion

Videoconference facilities should be acquired with a view toward future expansion plans. For example, a conference facility may start with freeze-frame with plans to convert to full-motion video later. The facility should be expandable to other points if growth is foreseen.

Fixed or Portable Equipment

Portable video conference equipment is available, and some applications require it. A roll-around unit about the size of a two-drawer filing cabinet can quickly be set up for an impromptu videoconference. Unless there is a need for portability, however, the best results will be obtained with fixed equipment. Portable satellite equipment also is used in some video services—particularly one-way broadcasts to hotels and other meeting facilities.

MANUFACTURERS OF VIDEO EQUIPMENT

CATV Equipment

Reliance Comm/Tec
C-COR Electronics
Jerrold Division of General Instrument Corp.

Videoconferencing Equipment

Compression Labs, Inc.
GPT Video Systems
Lucent Technologies
NEC America Inc.
Oki America, Inc.

Picturetel Corp.

Sony Corporation of America

Videoconferencing Systems, Inc.

Vtel Corp.

Desktop Computer-Based Videoconferencing Products

Compression Labs, Inc.

Datapoint Corp.

Fujitsu Ltd.

GTE

IBM

Intel Corp.

Lucent Technologies

Mitsubishi Electronics America, Inc.

Nortel, Inc.

Novell, Inc.

Picturetel Corp.

IV

CUSTOMER PREMISES EQUIPMENT

19

STATION EQUIPMENT

The least exotic and technically sophisticated element of the telecommunications system is the ordinary telephone. Yet its importance in the design of the network should not be underestimated. Because of the enormous numbers of telephone instruments in service, much of the rest of the network is designed to keep the telephone simple, rugged, and economical. Over the more than 100-year history of telephony, the telephone set has been improved, but the fundamental principles that make it work have changed little since Alexander Graham Bell's original invention. The primary changes have been improvements in three areas: packaging to make telephones esthetically appealing and easy to use, signaling to improve the methods used to place and receive telephone calls, and transmission performance to improve the quality of the talking path between users.

This chapter discusses the various types of telephones, station protection equipment, network channel terminating equipment (NCTE), station wiring, and auxiliary devices such as recorders and dialers.

TELEPHONE SET TECHNOLOGY

The telephone is inherently a four-wire device. Transmit and receive paths must be separate to fit the user's anatomy, but they must be electrically combined to

FIGURE 19-1

Functional Diagram of a Telephone Set

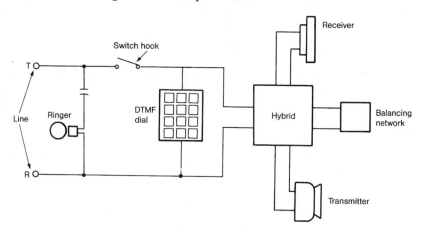

interface the two-wire loops that serve all but a small fraction of the telephone services in the country. Figure 19–1 is a functional diagram of a telephone set.

Elements of a Telephone Set

A transmitter in the telephone handset converts the user's voice into a pulsating direct current. The most common type of transmitter has a housing containing tightly packed granules of carbon that are energized by DC voltage. The voice waves striking the transmitter compact the granules, changing the amount of current that flows in proportion to the strength of the voice signal. This fluctuating current travels over metallic telephone circuits to drive the distant telephone receiver, which has coils of fine wire wound around a magnetic core. The current variations cause a diaphragm to move in step with changes in the line current. The diaphragm in the receiver and the carbon microphone in the transmitter are *transducers* that change fluctuations in sound pressure to fluctuations in electrical current, and vice versa.

Many new telephone sets substitute electronic transmitters for the carbon units that have been used for more than a century. Most telephone sets still use the carbon transmitter, however, because it is inexpensive and rugged.

The telephone set contains a hybrid coil that performs the four-wire to two-wire conversion as described in Chapter 2; it couples the two-wire line to the four-wire telephone handset. By design, the isolation between the transmitter and receiver is less than perfect. It is desirable for a small amount of the user's voice to be coupled into the receiver as *sidetone*, the feedback effect that

DTMF Dialing Frequency Combinations

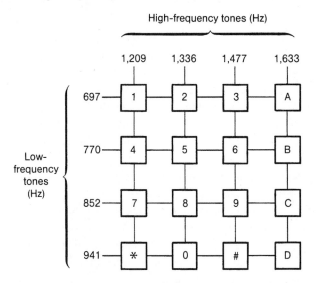

regulates the volume of the user's voice. Given too little sidetone, users tend to speak too loudly; given too much, they do not speak loudly enough.

The telephone set includes a switch hook, which isolates all the elements except the ringer from the network when the telephone is idle, or on hook. When the user lifts the receiver off hook, the switch hook connects the line to the telephone set and furnishes the power needed to energize the transmitter. When the telephone is on hook, the ringer is coupled to the line through a capacitor that prevents the DC talking current from flowing, but allows AC ringing voltage to actuate the bell. The telephone bell is an electromagnet that moves a clapper against a gong to alert the user to an incoming call. In many modern telephone sets an electronic tone ringer replaces the bell.

The dial circuit connects to the telephone line when the user lifts the receiver off hook. Dial circuits are of two types: rotary dials, which operate by interrupting the flow of line current, and tone dials, which operate by sending a combination of frequencies over the line. Tone dialing, known as dual tone multifrequency (DTMF), uses a 4 × 4 matrix of tones, as Figure 19–2 shows, to transmit pairs of frequencies to the tone receiver in the central office. Each button generates a unique pair of frequencies, which a DTMF receiver detects. Ordinary telephones send only three of the four columns of DTMF signals. The fourth column can be sent by special telephones or can be electronically generated by DTMF chips that are embedded in auxiliary telephone apparatus.

The two wires of a telephone circuit are designated as *tip* and *ring*, corresponding to the tip and ring of the cord plugs used by switchboard operators. The central office feeds negative polarity talking power over the ring side of the line. When the receiver is off hook, current flows in the line. The amount of current flow is limited by the resistance of the local loop, which depends on the wire gauge and length. For adequate transmission, at least 23 milliamps of current is needed. If too little current flows, the transmitter is insufficiently energized and the telephone set produces too little output for good transmission. If more than approximately 60 milliamps of current flows, telephone output will be uncomfortably loud for many listeners. Also, DTMF dials need at least 20 milliamps of current for reliable operation. The telephone set, the wiring on the user's premises, the local loop, and the central office equipment interact to regulate the flow of current in the line and the quality of local transmission service.

Rotary dial contacts are wired in series with the loop. When the user rotates the dial to the finger stop, a set of off-normal contacts opens the loop. When the dial is released the contacts alternately close and open to produce a string of square wave pulses. Equipment in the central office uses these pulses to operate switches that route the call.

Before the FCC opened the telephone network to connection of customer apparatus, the LECs owned all telephone sets, and because of the large numbers of sets in service, they designed the network for reliable operation with a minimum investment in station apparatus. The basic telephone set is a rugged and inexpensive device that provides satisfactory transmission over properly designed loops. If the current flowing through the loop is sufficient to provide between 23 and 60 ma. of current to the telephone set and the telephone is in good working order, satisfactory service is assured.

Caller Identification

In most states the issue of whether the LECs can offer caller identification has been settled in favor of providing the service. The LEC sends the identification digits after the first ring. Some kind of device is needed to translate the number to digital readout. Often, the circuitry is built into the telephone set itself. Several models include a name database to match the calling number with a personal directory. Auxiliary caller identification boxes are also available to connect between the line and the existing telephone set. The interface between an analog telephone set and the central office is known as analog display services interface (ADSI). This interface supports some of the interactive features that would otherwise require ISDN.

FIGURE 19–3

Diagram of a Station Protector

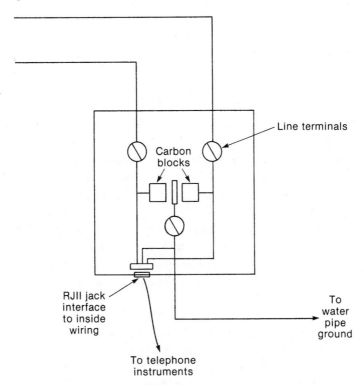

To telephone
instruments

STATION PROTECTION

Telephone circuits are occasionally subject to high voltages that could be injurious or fatal to the user without electrical protection. Lightning strikes and crosses with high-voltage power lines are mitigated with a station protector, which is diagrammed in Figure 19–3. Protectors use either an air gap or a gas tube to conduct high voltage from either side of the line to ground if hazardous voltages occur. The telephone is insulated so that any voltage that gets past the protector will not injure the user. The LEC places protectors, which also may form a demarcation point with customer-owned wiring, as shown in Figure 19–3. Protector grounds are connected to a ground rod, metallic water pipe, or other low-resistance ground.

The protector connects to the telephone set by jacketed wiring, called *inside wiring,* that is the user's responsibility to place. Inside wiring terminates on the protector on the end nearest the central office and on a connecting jack designated by the FCC as RJ-11 at the telephone end. Multiple lines terminate on a multiple-line jack such as the RJ-21X. FCC regulations require registration of telephone sets and other apparatus, including modems, PBXs, and key equipment, that connect directly to the network. Registration shows that the FCC approves apparatus for connection to the telephone network.

For more detailed information on station protection, refer to Chapter 6.

COIN TELEPHONES

The advent of the customer-owned coin operated telephone (COCOT) is a by-product of divestiture that is confusing to many users. In the first few years following the dissolution of the Bell System, many private companies saw COCOTs as a potentially lucrative business, which it is. The companies that ventured into this market with less-than-adequate equipment, however, quickly discovered what the LECs have long understood: The risks and administrative costs of coin telephones are high, and companies that enter the market without understanding the hazards can lose large amounts of money. The two major risks are fraud and vandalism. These can be combated with durable instruments and by building defenses into the telephone in the ways discussed below.

COCOTs have earned the distrust of many users—partly because of the inherent design of the telephone system and partly because of operator service providers (OSPs) that often charge more for long-distance calls than the major IECs. The courts have ruled that the LECs must permit COCOT owners to choose a primary interexchange carrier, which permits the owner of the host premises to invite OSPs to bid for the highest commissions.

It is not necessary for the owners of high-volume coin locations to own the telephones to gain commissions on long-distance calls, but for those users who do own or contemplate owning the instruments, an understanding of the features and technology is essential.

Coin Telephone Technology

A coin telephone has the following components:

- ◆ *Communication circuitry,* which is essentially identical with that of noncoin telephone sets.
- ◆ *Totalizer,* which is the device that identifies coin denominations and counts or relays the value of the money received.
- ◆ *Coin chute,* which is the physical channel that directs the coins from the coin slot through the totalizer and into the coin box.

◆ *Coin collect and control apparatus,* which controls whether coins are
   directed to the coin box or the refund chute.

◆ *Coin box,* which is the receptacle that receives and stores collected coins.

Besides the above, coin telephones may include a variety of intelligent
features that substitute for centralized telephone control.

The coin telephones operated by the LECs were, until the last few years,
devices with no local intelligence. All call rating, collect, and refund decisions
and other such functions were handled centrally. Since the central office does
not send answer supervision signals over the local loop, central office circuitry
was, and for the LECs still is, used for coin control. When a caller deposits a
coin, the coin chute holds it until the called party answers and then drops it into
the coin box. If the caller hangs up before the answer supervision signal is received, the coin is refunded. An operator or automatic apparatus rates the long-
distance call, and a human or synthesized voice announces the charge to the
caller. As the caller deposits coins, the totalizer returns to the central control
tones that announce the denomination of the coins. Since COCOTs are not connected to central coin control apparatus, intelligence in the coin telephone handles the timing, collection, and return features.

The vast majority of toll calls made from coin telephones are billed to
credit cards. Many coin telephones have credit-card readers. Some telephones
include rating apparatus and are therefore self-sufficient. Most such telephones, however, use a centralized OSP to handle the calls and collect the revenues through agreements with the credit-card companies.

Coin Telephone Features

The following are typical of features of COCOTs. The LECs also are introducing many of these same features into their telephones.

Coin Box Accounting   This feature enables the owner to determine the
amount of money in the box without counting it. This helps prevent theft but is
perhaps most important as a way of determining remotely when the box is
ready for collection.

Alarming   Many coin telephones have reporting systems that sound a local
alarm, dial a number, or both when tampering or vandalism occurs.

Remote Diagnostics   The ability to dial into a coin telephone from either a
manual or an automatic center and determine whether it is functioning properly
is an important feature for controlling maintenance costs.

Call Timing   Most LECs measure the usage on public access lines and charge the COCOT owner accordingly. This feature times the call, requests additional coin deposit when required, and cuts off the caller when the call exceeds the time limit. Some telephones have a readout that shows the amount of time remaining so callers can feed in more coins to keep the call in progress without interruption.

Call Restrictions   The call restriction feature blocks certain codes. For example, the 976 prefix that information service providers use may be restricted because of the difficulty of rating and collecting for such calls.

Voice Store and Forward   This feature enables the caller to leave a voice message that the coin phone will attempt to deliver at certain intervals. For example, a traveler could leave a message to be delivered to a busy telephone and resume his or her trip.

Database Access   Intelligent coin telephones can retain a database of telephone numbers that users can speed-dial. For example, the database might include taxi, hospital, hotel, and other such numbers. The COCOT owner may collect a fee from the called party for this service.

Facsimile Capabilities   Telephones with facsimile transmission capabilities are available in many public locations. These devices can levy a charge for facsimile service in addition to the normal long-distance charge, with the fee generally charged to a credit card.

Volume Control   The receive volume of some coin telephones can be adjusted under button control. This facility is valuable in noisy public locations.

Dialing Instruction Display   Given the complexity of operating some coin telephones, the need to access multiple IECs, the need for compatibility with different kinds of credit cards, and the requirement for the user to dial unfamiliar codes, a telephone with a display and help keys helps the caller use the device.

CORDLESS TELEPHONES

Cordless telephones are not to be confused with the wireless telephones discussed in Chapter 17. Cordless telephones have a base station that is connected to a central office line. The cordless telephone allows the user to carry the instrument within the range of the base station, which is usually limited to a few hundred feet. Wireless telephones are longer-range devices that connect to a private or public wireless network of multiple base stations. The effective range of wireless is much greater than cordless because wireless hands off from one base station to another, much as cellular phones do. Wireless telephones are frequency agile so they seek a vacant channel out of several available frequencies. Cordless telephones are set to the frequency of the base station. Except for dual-line models and channel-scanning models, they operate on a single frequency.

Cordless phones have sufficient range to cover an average residential lot. As with all radio systems, privacy can be a problem with cordless telephones. Early units were subject to interference and could be signaled by any base unit operating on the same frequency. A more serious problem is that anyone using a telephone on the same frequency can place unauthorized long-distance calls or eavesdrop on private calls.

Cordless phones operate in one of two frequency bands. Older phones operate in two channels in the 46 to 49 MHz range, with one frequency used for base-to-portable, and the other range used in the other direction. Although currently available products use the 46–49 MHz frequency range, the latest generation of cordless uses the 900 MHz band, which provides more frequencies and guards against interference. These provide excellent coverage within their design range, but coverage is limited in buildings with considerable concrete and structural steel where the building structure may attenuate radio frequencies to an unacceptable degree.

In buildings where coverage or interference is a problem, some models use spread spectrum technology in the 900 MHz band. This technology transmits signals over a range of frequencies instead of just one. The receiver digs the intended signal out of the resultant complex band of frequencies.

The new generation of telephones contains safeguards against false rings and unauthorized calls. The base-to-portable link is authenticated with a code from the portable unit so the base responds only to a unit with the correct code. This prevents unauthorized calls. The ringer in the portable unit is coded to prevent false rings. Encoders affect only the signaling and do not improve privacy. Anyone who has a telephone tuned to the same frequency can listen to the call, so extended range is not necessarily an advantage. Digital cordless telephones provide better signal clarity with less noise than analog telephones.

Cordless telephones offer a variety of features, including:

◆ Caller identification over the radio link (where it is available from the central office).
◆ Integrated answering machine with message waiting lights.
◆ Intercom and paging between the portable unit and the base station.
◆ Built-in speakerphone.

ANSWERING EQUIPMENT

Answering equipment varies from ordinary telephone answering sets to elaborate voice mail equipment that provides service similar to electronic mail. Answering sets are widely available in a variety of quality levels, and are no more difficult to install than ordinary telephones. Many units use separate cassette tapes for recorded announcements and messages from callers. Many modern units use digitized voice for the answering function, which eliminates the moving tape and reduces wear and tear on the equipment.

Other features that many users find important include:

♦ Multiple outgoing messages.
♦ Two-line capability.
♦ Selective message save and delete.
♦ Remote message retrieval.
♦ Message time/date stamp.

Because the central office does not relay answer supervision over the local loop, answering machines must include timing circuitry to determine when the calling party has hung up. Most answering machines detect the caller's voice; when a silent period of more than a specified length is detected, the machine assumes the caller has hung up, and disconnects. If a caller hangs up when the answering message is first heard, the machine may hold the line busy for a time while it completes the announcement and times out.

CONFERENCE ROOM TELEPHONES

An ordinary speakerphone is unsatisfactory for use in larger conference rooms because it may lack sensitivity for voice pickup from all parts of the room, or it may clip parts of the conversation because it operates in half-duplex mode. Half duplex means the device switches from send to receive during conversations, with the loudest talker capturing the circuit.

Conference room telephones operate in full-duplex mode. They process the voice in a manner somewhat similar to an echo canceler to enable parties to carry on a normal conversation with few or no dead spots around the room. Some units require a separate telephone for dialing, and some include a built-in dial with all other controls such as flash and mute. Conference room telephones operate behind analog telephone lines, either directly from the central office or from a PBX.

LINE TRANSFER DEVICES

Transfer devices fall into two categories: those that operate off distinctive ring from the central office, and those that answer the phone, recognize an incoming signal, and transfer the line to the appropriate terminal.

Distinctive Ring Devices

Many LECs offer distinctive ring, which provides multiple telephone numbers on a single line. Each number has a different ringing code combination. Some terminal equipment such as facsimile machines can be programmed to respond to a distinctive ring. Separate devices switch terminating equipment to the appropriate port based on the ringing signal. For example, a one-bell signal could ring the telephone, two-bell the fax, and a third combination could connect a modem to the line. The device recognizes an off-hook signal from any station and connects it to the line. Distinctive ring is a cost-effective method of sharing lines that otherwise have low usage.

Line Switcher

Another type of line-sharing device is the fax/modem switch. These devices have ports for telephone, fax, and may also have a modem port. These devices generally select ports by answering the telephone and listening for a signal from the incoming line. If a fax tone is heard the fax port is switched to the line. If a modem tone is heard a modem is switched to the line, and if no tone is heard the telephone is switched to the line. The device sends a ringing signal to the called equipment.

Some of these devices are not completely transparent to the calling party. For example, modem protocols normally operate with the receiving modem answering the line with a modem tone. This cannot work with a line switcher because it relies on the calling device to identify itself first. Also, the device returns answer supervision to the calling station regardless whether the line is ultimately answered or not. This may result in charges for long-distance calls that are not completed.

NETWORK CHANNEL TERMINATING EQUIPMENT

Network channel terminating equipment (NCTE) is any apparatus mounted on a telephone user's premises that can amplify, match impedance, or match network signaling to the signaling of the interconnected equipment.

Modems technically meet this definition, but for this discussion, NCTE is confined to devices that process signals outside the range of ordinary telephone sets. It includes the CSU and DSU equipment that terminates digital lines as discussed in Chapter 5. It also includes the customer premises end of the signaling equipment discussed in Chapter 11.

The FCC and ITU disagree on the demarcation between the network and customer premises equipment. At issue in the United States is whether NCTE is part of the network provided by the telephone company or part of the customer premises equipment provided by the user. Under ITU definition, NCTE is considered part of the network, and the LEC provides it. The FCC has ruled to the contrary. This ruling presents design and compatibility hazards that users should understand before obtaining private line services from telephone companies.

The characteristics of analog private line signaling are discussed in Chapter 11. In brief, private line signals travel over the voice network and are actuated by combinations of tones inside the voice passband. At the local loop, these signals can be carried to the user's premises as tones or converted to DC signals in the telephone central office. In most cases, DC signaling is used. Often, the cable between the central office and the user's premises has too much resistance and loss to support reliable signaling. NCTE at the user's premises amplifies the voice, boosts the DC voltage on the line, or both. Sometimes the form of the signal is altered to interface with the terminal equipment. For example, a single-frequency signaling tone may be converted to 20 Hz ringing to ring a telephone on the end of a circuit. Like any other equipment connected to the telephone network, NCTE must be registered with the FCC.

NCTE is usually constructed on plug-in circuit packs that mount in shelves. The connector on the NCTE shelf is wired to a demarcation point to meet the LEC's cable pair on the input side and to the terminal equipment on the output side. Individual shelves can be wall-mounted. Large concentrations of NCTE are usually mounted in racks or cabinets as Figure 19–4 shows.

APPLICATIONS

The market offers two categories of analog telephone sets—general-purpose sets (known in the industry as 2500 sets) and special-purpose telephones such as COCOTs, cordless sets, and answering sets. General-purpose sets are easy to apply. They are enough of a commodity that purchase can be based on price plus special features such as speed dial, hold, and speakerphone. Users should be aware of one fundamental difference in general-purpose sets with push-button dials. One type of push-button dial sends only dial pulses and therefore is not compatible with services that require DTMF pulses.

FIGURE 19–4

Bays of Tellabs Network Channel Terminating Equipment

Courtesy, Tellabs, Inc.

The price of general-purpose sets is often a clue to their quality. Many inexpensive instruments provide poor transmission quality and fail when dropped. At the high end of the scale, price usually is a function of features or decorator housings.

Since the FCC began to permit users to attach any registered device to the telephone network, the market has become flooded with special-purpose telephones. At the heart of answering machines, COCOTs, and cordless telephones is still the basic inner workings of the 2500 set, which can be evaluated by the criteria discussed in this section.

Standards

Telephone instruments and auxiliary equipment such as recorders and dialers are not constructed to any standards. The FCC sets registration criteria, but these criteria relate to potential harm to the network or personnel from hazardous voltages or to interference with other services from excessively high signal levels. The FCC also sets frequency requirements for cordless telephones and regulates the amount of electromagnetic radiation that processor-equipped devices can emit. FCC rules specify the amount of internal resistance of a telephone set but otherwise do not regulate technical performance.

EIA sets certain criteria for telephone equipment, and ITU standardizes certain aspects of the telephone set and its operation. Telephone technical standards have evolved primarily from practices of AT&T that were established when it had complete network design control. Other manufacturers have adopted most of those criteria.

Evaluation Considerations

Telephone sets, key telephone equipment, answering sets, NCTE, and all other equipment connected to the network must be registered with the FCC to guard against harm to the network. Although it is unlikely that equipment offered for customer premises will be unregistered, it should be noted that it is illegal to connect such apparatus. All telephone apparatus must be protected from hazardous voltages, as Chapters 6 and 13 discuss. The LECs, at a minimum, equip their lines with carbon block protectors. These are adequate for ordinary telephone sets, but some electronic equipment may not be adequately protected. The manufacturer's recommendations should be consulted, and if necessary, gas tube protection should be provided, as Chapter 6 explains.

Telephones

The primary consideration in obtaining a telephone should be the intended use of the instrument itself. The following criteria are important in evaluating a telephone instrument:

- ◆ *Durability and reliability.* Telephone sets are often dropped, and it is often difficult to have them repaired, so the ability of the telephone to withstand wear and tear is of prime importance.
- ◆ *Type of dial.* Specialized common carriers and other telephone-related services require a DTMF dial to enter personal identification number and call details. Some telephones with push-button dials have rotary dial output and are incompatible with these services.
- ◆ *Number of telephone lines served.* The number of telephone lines has a significant effect on whether a single-line, multiline, or key telephone system is acquired.
- ◆ *Transmission performance.* Some inexpensive telephones offer inferior transmission performance and may give unsatisfactory service. They should be evaluated before purchase.
- ◆ *Additional features.* Such features as last number redial and multiple number storage are often desirable.

Special-Feature Telephones

The garden variety telephone set has gone the way of Henry Ford's Model T. Now, telephone sets can be obtained with dozens of optional features and with auxiliary equipment such as clock radios that have nothing to do with the telephone itself. Special features are available as either parts of the telephone or as add-on adapters.

Dialers   These units store a list of telephone numbers that can be outpulsed by selecting a button. Dialers are particularly advantageous for accessing special common carriers who require 23-digit dialing for long-distance calls. Evaluation considerations include capacity, ability to handle 23-digit numbers, and ability to pause for a second dial tone.

Speaker Telephones   These units provide speaker and microphone for hands-free operation. The primary considerations are range of coverage—an office or a conference room—satisfactory voice quality, and the ability to cut off the transmitter for privacy during conversations.

Cordless Telephones   These units should include circuitry to prevent false rings and to restrict call origination to authorized telephones. The range of the base station and remote should be considered. Extended range may be an advantage in some applications, but may result in loss of privacy. Multiline operation is available and may be essential for some applications.

Memory   Telephones that store multiple digits and contain last-number redial capability are often advantageous. Some telephones visually display the number dialed and allow correction of dialed digits before outpulsing begins.

Calling Party Display   The calling number is displayed in an alphanumeric readout on the telephone instrument or on an outboard device.

Telephones for the Handicapped   Telephones with a variety of aids for handicapped users are available. These include special dials, amplified handsets, visual ringing equipment, and other such features. Of special concern are *hearing-aid compatible* telephones. Some hearing aids rely on magnetic pickup from the handset and are incompatible with some types of electronic handsets. Special telephone sets are equipped with keyboards and single-line readout for communication by the deaf. Compatibility between devices is important.

Answering Sets

Answering sets have many special features that should be considered before purchasing a unit. Among the most important features are:

◆ Battery backup for continued operation during power failures.
◆ Call counter to display the number of messages recorded.
◆ Call-monitoring capability so incoming calls can be screened over a speaker.
◆ Dual tape capability so it is unnecessary to listen to the recorded message when playing back recorded calls.
◆ Digital announcement and recording to eliminate the need for tapes.
◆ Remote control recording so the announcement can be changed from a remote location.
◆ Ring control so the number of rings before the line is answered can be adjusted. Some systems answer the telephone on the second ring if messages are present and on the fourth ring if they are not. This permits the owner to check for messages without paying for a long-distance call.
◆ Selective call erase to allow selective erasing, saving, and repeating of incoming messages.
◆ Multiple line capability so one device can answer more than one line.
◆ Synthesized voice readout so the answering machine can announce the time and date that each call was received.

Coin Telephone Application Issues

The primary concern of most readers is how to use coin telephones, not how to evaluate them for purchase. The COCOT market is growing, however, and many companies have more than an academic interest in coin telephone applications. This section discusses the principal issues to be considered in selecting and applying COCOTs.

The first concern is physical. Coin telephones should not only have the look and feel of the traditional phones used by the LECs, they also must have the durability of traditional phones. To prevent damage by vandals and theft of coin box contents, the housing must be made of a durable material. Coin box locks must be sophisticated enough to deter lock pickers. The handset cord must be armored and the caps on the handset cemented in place so the transmitter and receiver units cannot be removed. The appearance of the telephone set also is important. The familiar shape and style of the single slot coin telephone that most LECs use has been widely copied because COCOT owners have found that users prefer the look and feel of the familiar instrument.

A related issue is the instrument's ability to withstand the elements. This factor is not important in interior environments, but for outdoor installation the telephone must withstand extremes of temperatures. Cold temperatures often affect mechanical apparatus, such as totalizers and coin chutes, while hot temperatures affect the electronics.

Another key consideration is the degree of intelligence contained within the telephone. "Dumb" telephones slave off the central office and are generally used by LECs. Though the LECs have access to central office coin control apparatus, they are beginning to retrofit telephones with intelligence to handle such features as alarming and diagnostics and to meter the number of coins in the box. Intelligent telephones can prompt users and are generally locally powered, compared to dumb telephones, which are powered from the line. The amount of intelligence also is important in handling coin collection. Coin phones should be capable of recognizing call progress signals, including ringing, reorder, and busy tones, and not collecting the coin even though time has elapsed. The phone also should be able to recognize the two-tone signal of a blocked call and not collect the coin.

SELECTED TELEPHONE STATION EQUIPMENT MANUFACTURERS

Analog Telephone Instruments

American Telecommunications Corporation
GTE Business Communications Systems, Inc.
Lucent Technologies
Nortel, Inc.
Panasonic Co. Telephone Products Div.
Siemens Corporation

Cordless Telephones

Cobra/Dynascan Corp.
Lucent Technologies
Panasonic Co. Telephone Products Div.
Uniden
VTech

Telephone Answering Machines

Code-A-Phone Corporation

Dictaphone Corporation

Panasonic Co. Telephone Products Div.

Phone-Mate, Inc.

Conference Room Telephones

Lucent Technologies

NEC

Nortel

Polycom

Coin Telephones

Cointel Communications

Digitech Communications

Elcotel Telecommunications Systems, Inc.

Intellicall, Inc.

Lucent Technologies

Northern Telecom, Inc.

Omniphone

Reliance Comm/Tec R-Tec Systems

Tatung Telecom

U S Telecommunications

Network Channel Terminating Equipment

Lucent Technologies

Nortel Inc.

Proctor & Associates Co., Inc.

Pulsecom Division, Harvey Hubbell, Inc.

Telco Systems, Inc.

Tellabs Inc.

20

KEY TELEPHONE SYSTEMS

In terms of sheer numbers of systems, key telephone systems outnumber all other forms of business telephone systems. As with other forms of switching, key systems began with electromechanical equipment, which went through several evolutions before culminating in the Bell System's 1A-2 system with which nearly everyone is familiar. The beauty of 1A-2, many of which are still in use, is its simplicity. Everyone instinctively knows how to operate the telephone with its square buttons; all white except for the hold button, which is red. A steady light means the line is in use. A slow flash means the line is ringing, and a fast flash that it is on hold. For its day 1A-2 was excellent, but it has two major drawbacks. Each line requires control and talking pairs, so an unwieldy 25-pair cable is required for each six-button station; more buttons require more pairs and larger cable. A second drawback is the lack of features. Features everyone wants such as speed dial and speakerphone require add-on devices and extra cost.

Today's key systems are electronically controlled, and have features that were once available only in a PBX. In fact, many systems so closely resemble a PBX that the industry has given them the name *hybrid*. The distinctions between key system, hybrid, and PBX are not always clear. Table 20–1 shows the main factors that separate the three types of products, but bear in mind that many systems don't follow these distinctions.

T A B L E 20-1

Distinguishing Features of Different Classes of Customer Premise
Switching Systems

	Key System	PBX	Hybrid
Program	ROM	RAM	Ram or ROM
Outgoing trunk or line selection	Push line button	Dial 9	Dial 9 or push a line button
Attendant call transfer	Attendant announces over intercom	Transfer to station from attendant console	Announce or transfer from console or telephone set
Voice mail	Sometimes available	Available	Usually available
Call coverage	Not available	Available	Usually available

Further blurring the distinction between key systems and PBXs is the
trend of some manufacturers to make their key telephone instrument lines compatible with their PBX lines. A company can begin with a key system and grow
to a PBX while retaining the same instruments. A later section further amplifies
the differences between these types of systems. Chapter 21 discusses PBXs in
more detail.

KEY TELEPHONE SYSTEM TECHNOLOGY

A key system has central control equipment contained in a cabinet that is usually mounted on the wall. Some cabinets have expansion slots that contain line
and station cards; in others the number of lines and stations are fixed, and are
hard-wired in the cabinet. The central control circuitry is known as a *key service unit* (KSU). A typical key system uses from one- to three-pair cable for
each station. Electronic key systems use a microprocessor to scan incoming
lines. When the scanner detects an incoming ring, it signals the attendant. The
attendant answers an incoming call by pressing a button—the same procedure
used in electromechanical KTS. Instead of directly accessing the incoming
line, however, the telephone set sends a data message to the controller, which
connects the incoming line to the station. Calls are held by depressing the hold
button, which applies a flashing lamp signal to the line button. Figure 20–1 is
a photograph of a Nortel Norstar key system.

Electronic key telephone sets have many features that are unavailable on
electromechanical systems. For example, the Norstar display telephone shown

FIGURE 20-1

A Nortel Norstar System

Courtesy Nortel, Inc.

in Figure 20–1 includes push button access to special features that in other systems can be accessed only by dialing codes. A digital readout displays date and time, message waiting, called number, and other such messages. If the system is compatible with calling line identification, the calling number is displayed.

Key systems are rated according to the number of stations and central office lines they support. For example, a 6 × 12 system could terminate six telephone lines and 12 stations. Unlike 1A-2, which usually has only one intercom line, most key systems have multiple intercom paths for station-to-station conversations and announcing calls. Intercom lines use either the telephone handset or a speaker/microphone for the intercom talking path. The type and size of the switching matrix vary with the manufacturer. Manufacturers class larger systems supporting as many as 50 trunks and 100 lines as hybrids, but the difference between hybrids and small PBXs is not distinct. The provision of processor control allows KTSs to provide many features that are similar to PBX features.

Several manufacturers produce multiline systems that do not require a KSU. Most KSU-less systems require one pair of wires per line, which limits the size of the system to four lines or fewer. Some systems employ a special signaling arrangement and use two-pair wire—one pair for talking and one for signaling. The primary advantages of KSU-less systems are low cost and ease of installation. Anyone who knows how to install a single-line telephone can install KSU-less telephones, which makes them ideal for small offices and residences.

The primary drawbacks of KSU-less systems are limited expandability and lack of features. Since the systems have no KSU, the only features available are those contained in the telephone set itself. Most KSU-less systems also lack an intercom path, which means calls cannot be announced over an intercom as they are with most key systems.

Key Telephone System Features

All KTSs, including KSU-less systems, have in common the following features, which are the original features of 1A-2:

- ◆ *Call pickup:* the ability to access one of several lines from a telephone by pressing a line button.
- ◆ *Call hold:* the ability to press a button to place an incoming line in a holding circuit while the telephone is used for another call.
- ◆ *Supervisory signals:* lamps that show when a line is ringing, in use, or on hold.
- ◆ *Common bell:* the ringing of a single bell to indicate an incoming call.

Most electronic systems have the following additional features:

- ◆ *Automatic hold recall:* After a call has been left on hold for a specified period, the telephone emits a warning tone.
- ◆ *Conferencing:* The conferencing feature permits a station user to bridge two or more lines for a multiparty conversation.
- ◆ *Data port adapter:* A modem or facsimile machine can be connected. Without a data port adapter, data stations are unable to operate through the KTS.
- ◆ *Direct station selection:* The DSS feature, usually combined with a busy lamp field, enables the attendant to determine if the called station is busy or idle and connects the attendant to the station at the press of a single button.
- ◆ *Do not disturb:* The station user can press a button that prevents intercom calls from reaching the station and silences the bell.

◆ *Hands-free answerback:* This feature permits the station user to answer the intercom or an incoming call without picking up the handset.

◆ *Intercom:* A shared path appears on all stations. By dialing the station intercom code or pressing a DSS button, users can announce calls and hold conversations.

◆ *Last number redial:* The last number dialed can be redialed by pressing a button.

◆ *Message waiting:* A light on the telephone set shows that a message is waiting in voice mail.

◆ *Music on hold:* While a call is on hold, music or a promotional announcement is played.

◆ *Power fail transfer:* When commercial power fails, the system automatically connects the central office lines to analog station sets.

◆ *Privacy:* This feature prevents other stations from picking up a line that is in use. In some systems privacy is automatic unless the user presses a privacy release key.

◆ *Remote maintenance:* A central maintenance center can call into the system through a modem for remote trouble diagnosis.

◆ *Speed dial:* Many systems have both a system speed dial, which all users share, and station speed dial, which is activated from buttons on the telephone set.

◆ *Station display:* Proprietary telephones are equipped with readouts that may display date and time, last number dialed, elapsed time on the call, etc.

◆ *Station restriction:* Although many key systems lack station-programmable features, some systems provide different classes of service for restricting long-distance calls.

◆ *Voice call:* Stations can call other stations over the speaker so the called party does not have to lift the handset to talk to the caller.

In addition to the above features, many systems have features that were once exclusive to PBXs:

◆ *Call forwarding:* The station user can send calls to another station, on or off the system, or to voice mail.

◆ *Call park:* The attendant or a user can place a call in a parking orbit. The call is retrieved by dialing the park number, which is usually announced over a paging system.

◆ *Calling line identification:* If the local central office sends calling line identification with the call, the system transfers it to the station display.

♦ *Direct inward dialing:* Stations can be reached from the outside by dialing a seven-digit number that bypasses the attendant.

♦ *Least cost routing:* The system can choose more than one route for outgoing calls, including inserting digits such as carrier codes for placing calls over the least expensive facility.

♦ *Station message detail recording:* A port in the key service unit puts out the details of calls for connection to a call accounting system.

♦ *T-1 compatibility:* The system can interface a T-1 line directly.

♦ *Tie line:* The EKTS can be connected via tie lines to another KTS or a PBX. This feature gives the key system user access to the features of the other system.

♦ *Uniform call distribution:* Groups of stations can be associated to receive calls in round-robin order, with limited statistical information produced by the system.

♦ *Voice mail:* A station can cover to voice mail when busy or not answered.

KTSs usually include one or more intercom lines. These are used for station-to-station communication—primarily for conversations between the attendant and the called party. In large systems, however, the intercom line takes on the characteristics of the intrasystem talking paths of a PBX. Most electronic key systems provide multiple intercom paths so several intrasystem conversations can be held simultaneously. Most systems provide a built-in speaker so the intercom line can be answered without using the telephone handset. Optionally, the handset can be lifted for privacy. The number of intercom lines provided is a feature that distinguishes a PBX from a hybrid. Many hybrid systems provide a limited number of intercom paths, which limits their usefulness in systems that support a large amount of intrasystem calling. Some PBXs are nonblocking, which means enough internal switching paths are available that all stations can be talking simultaneously.

While calls can be answered from any station in many systems, a special attendant's telephone often is provided. The attendant has all the features of regular stations and also may be provided a busy lamp field (BLF) to show which stations are occupied and a direct station selection (DSS) field, which allows him or her to transfer calls to stations by pushing a button instead of dialing the station number. To support the attendant, many systems include paging. The paging system is accessed by pushing a button or dialing a code and can be divided into zones if the building is large enough to warrant it. Many systems provide for parking a call so a paged user can go to any telephone, dial a park number, and pick up an incoming call.

Computer-telephone integration is becoming an important issue in larger systems, and as software packages develop, it will be important for key systems as well (see Chapter 23). Some key systems provide an open application interface so a desktop computer can be connected either to the telephone instrument or to the KSU. For example, many office workers use a PC-based contact manager. To make effective use of the call-logging and out-dialing features of the contact manager, the user must either have an analog telephone set or a CTI interface to the key system.

KTS and Hybrids versus PBX

Although the distinction between electronic key systems, hybrids, and PBXs is not clear, if an organization requires more than 100 central office line and station ports, a PBX will undoubtedly be required because of its greater line, trunk, and intercom capacity. The upper line-size range of a key system is set by the size of the telephone instrument. When the organization has more than about 24 lines, it is impractical to terminate them all on the telephone, so the user must dial 9 to get an outside line, and the attendant must transfer incoming calls. When a key system has these pooled trunk capabilities, it is defined as a hybrid. Many products on the market can be set up in either a key system or a hybrid configuration. The main distinction is whether central office lines are pooled or terminated on telephone buttons.

Because the cost of common equipment is distributed among all stations and because the common equipment for a PBX is more expensive, in smaller sizes a key system is more economical. Between a lower range of about 30 ports and an upper range of about 100 ports, the decision as to which type of system to buy can be based on cost, features, and technical performance.

Key systems support a limited variety of trunks. Many key systems cannot support direct inward dialing, and only a few high-end systems support tie lines. Direct T-1 interface is available on some hybrids but is not available for most key systems. Some key systems optionally can interface ground start lines, and others only loop start lines (see Chapter 11).

PBXs generally support a wider variety of telephone sets, ranging from single-line 2500 sets to multiline display sets and ISDN sets. Most key systems have two or three telephone sets in their product range, with hybrids somewhere between the two. Some key systems do not support analog stations directly. To use modems, fax machines, or analog stations requires an off-premise station card or a digital-to-analog adapter. Most PBXs and some hybrids have station-programmable features, compared to key systems, in which the telephone set buttons are often fixed and available for only one function.

Another distinction between the types of systems is how the program is stored. In key systems it is always stored in some type of nonvolatile memory such as a ROM. In PBXs it is always stored in random access memory, which is lost and must be reloaded following power failure. Hybrids may have either volatile or nonvolatile memory.

Key systems usually have limited or no capability for call distribution, so users in an incoming call center must press a button to pick up calls. This results in lost time and poor customer service because calls in progress must be interrupted to answer incoming calls, and when calls are placed on hold there is no way to tell which call arrived first. Most PBXs and hybrids offer a uniform call distribution feature, which Chapter 22 discusses.

APPLICATIONS

The variety of key and hybrid systems on the market is so vast that managers must carefully evaluate their requirements before selecting a system. The following are some general rules, but readers must realize that there are many exceptions, and product lines are changing constantly, which may invalidate some of these distinctions:

- ◆ If more than 24 central office trunks are required, favor a PBX or a hybrid.
- ◆ If fewer than eight central office trunks are required, favor a key system.
- ◆ If the system will never grow beyond three lines and about eight stations, favor a KSU-less system.
- ◆ If automatic call distribution or voice processing is required, favor a PBX or a hybrid.
- ◆ If half the total system traffic is intercom, favor a PBX or, depending on size, a hybrid.

Many more criteria should be considered in choosing a system, some of which are covered in the evaluation criteria section that follows.

Standards

There are few standards for key telephone systems beyond those that govern connection to the telephone network. Manufacturers are free to define their features and method of operation in any way they choose. Most systems have a range of standard features that operate in a similar manner regardless of product.

Evaluation Criteria

The first issue that must be addressed is whether the application requires a PBX, a hybrid, or a key system. The discussion that follows assumes that a key system is required. See Chapter 21 for PBX evaluation criteria, which also can be applied to most hybrids.

Capacity

Key telephone systems should be purchased with a view toward long-term growth in central office lines and stations. Key system capacity is specified as the line and trunk capacity of the total system. For example, a 4×8 system supports four central office lines and eight stations. This figure is the capacity of the cabinet, and further expansion may be expensive or impossible. Some systems can grow by adding another cabinet, but it also may be necessary to replace the power supply and main control module. With some systems it is possible to move major components, such as line and station cards, to a larger cabinet to increase capacity.

Most key systems use plug-in circuit cards. These are less costly than wired systems, which must be purchased from the outset at their ultimate size. The number of internal or intercom call paths also should be considered.

Open Architecture

An open architecture interface is important for future computer-telephony applications that will be appearing in the next few years. Determine if the key system has such an interface, and if the standards are readily available to developers. Consider that the most popular key systems will have the greatest amount of development effort applied to them.

Cost

The initial purchase price of a key system is only part of the total lifetime cost of the system. As with all types of telecommunications apparatus, the failure rate and the cost of restoring failed equipment are critical and difficult to evaluate. The most effective way to evaluate them on a key telephone system is by reviewing the experience of other users.

Installation cost is another important factor. One factor is the method of programming the station options in the processor. Some systems provide such options as toll call restriction, system speed calling of a selected list of numbers, and other features that are contained in a database. If these features require a technician to program them, costs will be higher than for a system with features that can be user-programmed.

The least costly systems allow the user to rearrange telephones easily. Rearrangement costs are likely to be a function of the wiring plan the vendor uses when the system is installed. With some key systems ports are terminated on modular jacks so stations can be rearranged by moving modular cords. Maintenance costs may be significant over the life of the system. Cost savings are possible with systems that provide internal diagnostic capability. Some systems provide remote diagnostic capability so the vendor can diagnose the system over an ordinary telephone line. These features can offer cost savings in hybrids, but are less important in key systems.

Voice Mail

Voice mail, which was once available only in PBXs and some hybrids, is one of the most desired features among users purchasing new key systems. Most key systems are capable of voice mail support, but as discussed in Chapter 24, the degree of integration is important. Be certain that the combination of key system and voice mail can cover unanswered telephones to voice mail, light message waiting lights, transfer to an attendant, and provide after-hours answering and access to voice mail.

Centrex Compatibility

Key systems are often used behind Centrex systems, which are covered in Chapter 25. Many Centrex features, however, cannot be activated unless the key system is Centrex compatible. For example, call transfer requires a switchhook flash to get second dial tone. If you flash the switchhook on a key system, the dial tone you get is from the key system, not from the central office. To make a key system Centrex compatible, it must have a special button to flash the central office line. Many key systems are provided with buttons to make them directly compatible with Centrex features.

Number of Intercom Paths

A nonblocking switching network is one that provides as many links through the network as there are input and output ports. For example, one popular key system has capacity for 24 central office trunks, 61 stations, and 8 intercom lines. The system provides 32 transmission paths, which support calls to and from all 24 central office trunks. The eight intercom paths limit intrasystem conversations to eight pairs of stations. A nonblocking network provides enough paths for all line and trunk ports to be connected simultaneously. In this system, if all central office trunks are connected, of the remaining 37 stations, only eight pairs can be in conversation over the intercom paths. Although this system is not nonblocking, it meets an important test of having sufficient paths to handle all central office trunks and intercom lines.

ISDN Compatibility

ISDN is becoming an important factor in many locations, and is likely to become more so in the future as applications such as desktop videoconferencing develop. Consider whether ISDN compatibility is likely to be required within the life of the system, and if so, whether the system can be retrofitted to interface either BRI or PRI lines.

Power Failure Conditions

During power outages, a key system is inoperative unless the installation includes battery backup. Some systems include emergency battery supplies, while others remain inoperative until power is restored. If no backup supply is provided, the system should at least maintain its system memory until power is restored.

The system should include a power-failure transfer system that connects incoming lines to ordinary telephone sets so calls can be handled during power outages. The method of restarting the system after a power failure is also important because the method affects cost and the amount of time required to get the system restarted. Some systems use nonvolatile memory that does not lose data when power fails. Other systems reload the database from a backup tape or disk, which results in a delay before the system can be used following restoral of power. If the system makes no provision for backup power, it can be operated from an inexpensive UPS supply of the type designed for personal computers.

Wired versus Programmable Logic

Most key telephone systems use programmable logic. Older systems including 1A-2 and equivalent KTS and KSU-less systems use wired logic. The primary advantage of wired logic is simplicity. Most failures in wired logic systems are in the plug-in cards, which can be replaced by the user for minimal cost. The primary disadvantages of wired logic systems are lack of flexibility and the amount of cabling required. In stored program systems, new features can be added by changing the program, which usually is contained in a ROM. Features can be added and removed to customize stations by changing the feature database.

The most important advantage of stored program systems is the wide range of features they offer. Wired logic systems offer essentially the features of the telephone system itself plus basic key features. Other features are added with outboard equipment. Stored program systems offer features that duplicate those of more expensive and complex PBXs.

Station Equipment Interfaces

Most key telephone systems support only a proprietary station interface. There-fore, inexpensive 2500 sets cannot be used except with an off-premises extension card. With some key systems, not even the OPX card alternative is available. The lack of a single-line interface is not a disadvantage in many applications, but many station users now have modems, which require analog lines. Also, some organizations prefer to have 2500 sets in areas such as lunch rooms, warehouses, and reception areas.

An important feature for many users is upward compatibility of telephone sets and line and trunk cards across the manufacturer's entire product line. This capability reduces the cost of converting from a key system to a PBX and enables users to keep their instruments, which not only reduces cost, but also minimizes retraining.

An increasingly important feature is the ability to connect a modem or facsimile machine to a key system port. These analog devices are incompatible with proprietary station interfaces, but for many organizations, the cost of providing a dedicated line is excessive. It is possible to connect modems and facsimile machines ahead of the key system and use the same line for telephone calls, but some means must be provided to prevent telephone users from barging in on a facsimile or modem session. Several manufacturers offer adapters that permit telephones and facsimile machines or modems to share lines as discussed in Chapter 19.

Alphanumeric displays are useful additions to most key systems. A display field shows the number dialed, time of day, and station status information, such as busy or do not disturb, and in some systems the display may prompt the user in programming special features or in using features such as voice mail.

Attendant and Intercom Features

One feature that distinguishes a key system from a PBX is that in the former the attendant announces calls over an intercom path, while in the latter calls are transferred directly to the extension. The number of paths provided is important; paths are used for station-to-station communication as well as announcing calls.

Most key systems provide hands-free answer capability so a station user can answer without picking up the handset. This feature does not, however, automatically mean that speakerphone capability is available on outside calls. This often requires a special telephone set.

Many systems give the attendant the choice of announcing calls by dialing the station number or by pressing a direct station selection (DSS) key. The DSS key is usually the most effective method on small key systems and may double as a station busy lamp. If a busy lamp field is not provided, the attendant hears a busy signal or receives a busy indication on a display.

Station Features

Most key telephone sets have station speed-dial capability and a common list of system speed-dial numbers. Speakerphone capability is a standard feature on many key systems, and most systems can announce calls through a built-in speaker.

Some systems have message-waiting capability, which enables the attendant to turn on a light to show that the user has a message or lights directly from voice mail. Most systems have a privacy button, which enables the user to exclude others from the line in use or to toggle the button to permit access. A do-not-disturb button prevents others from reaching the station on the intercom, while permitting the user to make outgoing calls.

Key Service Unit versus KSU-Less Systems

Some systems provide two- or three-line capability without a KSU. For small systems these can be effective, providing the capabilities of a full key telephone system without the need for a separate central unit. KSU-less systems have disadvantages, however, which make them inappropriate for many installations. First, they have limited capacity, so they are usable only for small locations and cannot be expanded. Second, they usually lack intercom paths, on-hook voice announcing, and other features that are essential in a multiroom office.

SELECTED KEY TELEPHONE EQUIPMENT MANUFACTURERS

Key Systems with KSU

ATC

Comdial

Cortelco

Executone Information Systems

Inter-Tel

Iwatsu America

Lucent Technologies

MacroTel

Mitel

NEC America

Nortel, Inc.

Panasonic Communications

Premier Telecom Products

Tadiran
TeleConcepts
Telerad
TIE/communications, Inc.
Toshiba America
Vodavi Communications Systems

KSU-Less Systems

Comdial
Panasonic Communications
TIE/communications, Inc.
Hybrid Key/PBX
Comdial
Executone Information Systems
Hitachi America, LTD
Iwatsu America
Lucent Technologies
Mitel, Inc.
Nortel, Inc.
Tadiran Electronic Industries
TIE/communications, Inc.
Toshiba America

CHAPTER

21
PRIVATE BRANCH
EXCHANGES

Every office needs a telephone system, whether it is Centrex, key telephone, or a PBX. Most large offices with more than about 50 stations choose a PBX as the vehicle that connects stations to stations internally and connects the company to the outside world. PBXs come in a variety of sizes; 20 to 20,000 stations is a vast range, but within that range the same features and functionality can be obtained. Selecting a PBX is an important decision in most companies; one with a life of 7 to 10 years, and one where the wrong decision can adversely affect the company's costs and strategic position.

The PBX equipment on the market today is very good. Failures are rare. If a system is equipped with interruptible power it may work for its entire service life without a major failure. Since a PBX has only a few moving parts, most systems require little or no preventive maintenance. They do, however, require maintenance and administrative support, and for this reason a PBX cannot be purchased as if it were a commodity. In fact, PBXs are selected on much the same basis as large-scale computers: software, support, and strategic positioning. In a PBX much of the software is generic. All PBXs have a standard set of features that work much the same way.

If you don't need to do anything but switch telephone calls, you can choose the system that has lowest cost and adequate support, but a PBX is a strategic investment for most companies. A PBX ties your company with your customers, suppliers, the public, and other parts of the organization. The features it has and the way it is set up and administered have a significant effect on how those on the outside view your company. In this chapter we will discuss the major features of PBXs and how they are used to improve organizational effectiveness. One of the major features, automatic call distribution, is so important that it is treated in a separate chapter. ACD can be obtained in both PBXs and stand-alone systems, and also in Centrex and key systems.

Office PBXs increasingly control private voice networks. As networks evolve toward all-digital, so does the PBX. As transmission facilities increasingly become digital and as the integrated services digital network (ISDN) emerges, PBXs will evolve to the point that few, if any, analog interfaces remain.

The telephone station interface to the PBX is also rapidly evolving toward digital. Over the past few years, digital telephone sets have become cost-competitive with analog sets to the point that analog stations behind the PBX are diminishing. Analog ports are still required for such devices as modems and facsimile, but these may eventually disappear in favor of modem and facsimile pools connected to a LAN.

Even the interface to local trunks will gravitate toward digital, even before the arrival of ISDN. Most LECs now offer digital trunks, either separate two-way and direct inward dial (DID) trunks or combination trunks that can be used for either DID or outgoing service. In addition, T-1 offers the advantage of relaying answer supervision from the central office to the PBX, which eliminates the problem of inaccurate call timing that plagues call accounting systems.

The PBX is the precursor of future public network technology. ISDN, which Chapter 28 discusses, is an end-to-end digital network that supports simultaneous voice and data transmission. ISDN is evolving slowly in public networks because the costs of change are enormous and the needs are not yet developed fully, but ISDN concepts are developing rapidly in the office. Digital PBXs are the test bed of ISDN services, and are capable of most ISDN services. Most of the major switching systems on the market support primary rate interface (PRI) on the trunk side of the switch, and basic rate interface (BRI) on the line side. This chapter discusses PBX features, and concludes with a discussion of factors to consider in evaluating PBXs.

PBX TECHNOLOGY

PBX technology has progressed through three generations and, according to most manufacturers, is in the fourth. First-generation systems used wired logic and analog step-by-step or crossbar switching fabric. First-generation telephones were nonproprietary rotary dial or DTMF analog sets. If key features were required with a first generation PBX a separate key telephone system was necessary. A few first-generation systems may still exist, but they are no longer manufactured.

The second generation introduced stored-program control processors driving reed relay or PAM switching networks. Second-generation systems use either standard analog or proprietary telephones, most of which are analog sets, to control a limited number of key telephone features. Some second-generation systems are still in operation, but most of them are unable to support the North American numbering plan and either have been or soon will be replaced. The third generation, which is the first to support end-to-end digital transmission, employs PCM switching technology and both digital and analog proprietary telephones.

The fourth generation of PBXs is not clearly defined. Some products that claim to be fourth-generation systems employ LAN interfaces to provide a highway for interconnecting data devices. Some current systems use a server-type of architecture with special functions contained in servers that reside on a backbone network. Discussions of PBX generations are not important. More pertinent are the services the system is able to provide, the ease of administering it, and its capabilities of keeping up with a telecommunications technology that is moving forward at a rapid pace.

The fundamental architectures of all digital PBXs are similar. As Figure 21–1 shows, a digital PBX has a switching fabric that connects to line and trunk interface circuits. A central processor operates the generic program, which is retained in memory. The circuitry is contained on cards that slide into slots that mount in modules or cabinets. The cards plug into the PBX's backplane, which ties the lines, trunks, and central control circuits to the switching fabric and buses over which the circuit elements communicate. Although the structure of PBXs is similar, there are significant differences in products on the market and the way features are packaged and sold. Figure 21–1 shows separate line and trunk modules for clarity, but most systems have universal card slots—that is, either line or trunk cards can plug into any slot.

PBXs connect to three types of external networks: local, interexchange, and private. Also, many systems support special services such as T-1 lines and foreign exchange trunks to local calling areas in distant cities. Systems serving automated offices and data communications require interfaces to data terminals, gateway circuits, and other computer networks. Computer-telephony interfaces (CTI) connect PBXs to mainframes, minicomputers, or servers so the PBX can supply call information to the computer, and the computer can send routing instructions to the PBX. The variety of interface circuits is a key distinguishing feature among PBX generations and among products on the market.

FIGURE 21–1

Private Branch Exchange Architecture

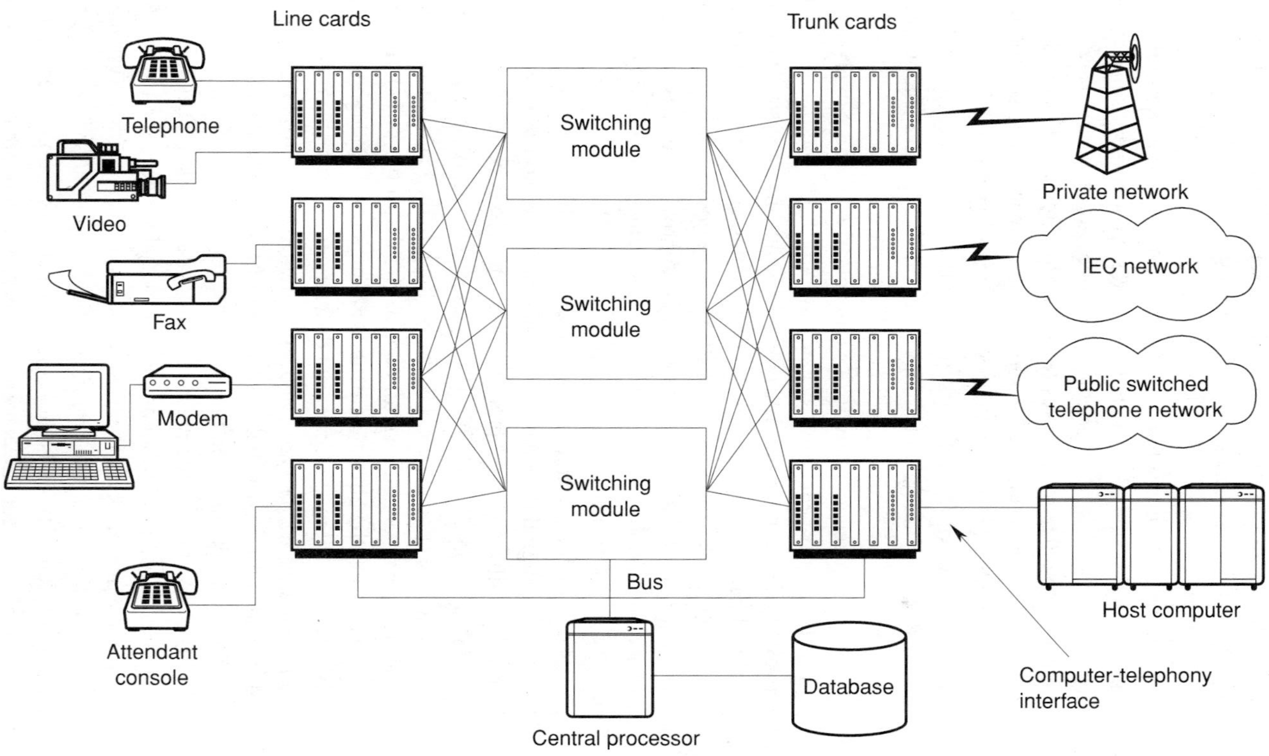

Line Interfaces

PBXs have at least two different types of line interface cards, analog and digital. Most systems also have basic rate ISDN cards. Digital line cards support proprietary telephones that work only with that manufacturer's system. Analog and ISDN cards support telephone sets that are independent of the PBX manufacturer. Although ISDN telephones should work with any manufacturer's PBX, ISDN standards do not define all of the features that the system may be capable of. Therefore, ISDN sets from the PBX manufacturer will usually provide features that other manufacturers' telephones cannot support.

Line card density, which ranges from 8 to 32 ports, is a distinguishing feature among products. High-density cards permit PBXs with a smaller cabinet size, which is usually a plus. In smaller PBXs, however, high-density cards may result in more spare ports than the owner would normally purchase. For example, if the system has 32-port cards and 33 ports are required, 64 ports must be purchased, leaving nearly half of them unused.

Another distinguishing feature is the number of cable pairs required for a proprietary telephone. All systems need only one pair for analog telephones, but some systems require two pairs for a digital telephone. The number of pairs needed is usually not an issue except in campuses and multistory office buildings where riser cable capacity is a concern.

PBX Trunk Interfaces

PBXs, like central offices, interface the outside world through trunk circuits that exchange signals with other switching systems through a variety of signaling interfaces. Analog trunk circuits mount on cards that contain from 4 to 16 trunks per card. T-1 trunk cards support 24 circuits. Some PBXs use a single type of card for T-1 or PRI; others have separate card types. Analog trunk cards support two-way central office trunks, foreign exchange lines, WATS lines, and 800 lines. A separate type of trunk card is required for direct inward dial (DID) trunks in most PBXs, although some manufacturers provide universal trunk cards.

Compatibility with central office line equipment is important for proper PBX operation. The interface standard is EIA-464, which specifies technical and performance criteria for the interface between the two types of systems. The central office interfaces the PBX with the central office's own supervision; the supervision from a distant trunk is not transferred through the line circuit to the PBX. Therefore, the PBX cannot pass answer supervision through its SMDR port to an external call-accounting system. Some LECs offer digital line and trunk connections to the central office, and these usually provide answer supervision. Supervision is also passed from the T-1 long-distance facilities of most IECs.

Signaling compatibility is an important issue in connecting a PBX to a central office. PBXs almost always use ground start trunks to prevent glare problems (Chapter 11). DID trunks are used for incoming service only, so they may be loop start from the central office, with the DID digits passed with DTMF signaling. Two-way DID trunks are normally connected to the central office as tie lines using E&M signaling. PRI trunks use the D channel for signaling, as discussed in the next section.

PBXs require an access digit, usually 9, to connect station lines to central office trunks. When the user dials 9, the PBX seizes an idle central office trunk and connects the talking path through to the station if the station is permitted off-net dialing. The station hears central office dial tone as a signal to proceed with dialing.

Integrated Services Digital Network Interface

Standard T-1 connections to the central office use the in-band bit-robbed signaling that is discussed in Chapter 5 for signaling. Since this type of signaling uses the least significant bit of each channel for signaling, the channel can support only 56 kb/s. For services such as high-speed data transfer and videoconferencing, use of the entire 64 kb/s channel is desirable. Clear channel transmission is a feature of ISDN, which most PBXs now support.

As discussed in Chapter 28, primary-rate ISDN provides 23 B (bearer) channels plus one 64 kb/s D (data) channel. Many PBXs also support the BRI interface on the line side. BRI provides two B channels (64 kb/s) and one D channel (16 kb/s signaling). PRI channels can be used in place of analog or digital central office trunks where the LEC provides the service. Most IECs also provide PRI service. A major feature of PRI is call-by-call service selection, which permits the PBX and the central office to determine for each call what type of service is needed. For example, if a PBX supports videoconferencing, multiple channels on the PRI will be needed to provide the desired degree of picture quality. The PBX and the central office set up the appropriate bandwidth by exchanging messages on the D channel.

BRI capability is needed in many PBXs to support desktop videoconferencing, which is an emerging service. BRI capability is also needed for work-at-home services, which are becoming important to avoid the need for employees to commute to the office each day.

Although ISDN is not available in all locations, and is not cost-effective in many locations in which it is available, it should be considered carefully in all new PBXs. Growth of ISDN has been impeded by a lack of services to justify its application, but that is changing. The capability of obtaining both PRI and BRI ISDN interfaces should be obtained in any new PBX being purchased today.

Tie Trunks

Organizations operating multiple PBXs often link them through tie trunks, which are intermachine trunks terminating on the trunk side of the PBX. Trunk facilities may be privately owned or obtained from IECs or LECs. They may be analog or digital, with a definite trend toward digital with the introduction of fractional T-1 tariffs. Tie trunks are generic, and can be set up between PBXs of different manufacture. Signaling is usually E&M.

If tie trunks terminate in a single location they are often accessed by dialing a digit, such as 8, which connects them to the distant PBX. Many multi-PBX organizations have a separate dialing plan for each system plus a single organizationwide dialing plan. The PBX then is programmed to provide the translations necessary to reach the distant number over the tie trunk network. This feature is called uniform dialing plan. To avoid the need for users to understand the dialing plan, many organizations use the PBX's least-cost routing system, which is discussed later, to dial the necessary codes. Users dial the number, and the PBX takes care of selecting the route and dialing any additional digits.

Special Trunks

Many PBXs have a variety of special trunks, such as T-1 lines to the IEC, foreign exchange, and 800 trunks, to provide access to lower-cost long-distance service. When several of these special trunks are connected to the PBX, it is impractical to expect users to select which trunk to use. Most PBXs offer least-cost routing features, which enable the system to select the most economical route based on the class of trunks terminated, their busy/idle status, and the station line class.

Computer-Telephony Interfaces

Chapter 23 discusses computer-telephony integration (CTI), which is a feature of growing importance in many companies. With CTI the PBX is linked to a mainframe or minicomputer, or to a LAN server with a two-way channel. The PBX provides call origination and call progress information to the computer, which in turn sends routing and call-handling instructions to the PBX. CTI is particularly important in call centers where it is used to pop up an account record on the computer screen at the same time the PBX delivers a call to the work station. CTI is also used to perform such functions as outdialing on a proprietary telephone instrument from a computer database, and to store call information such as calling number, time of day, and terminating station in the database. CTI interfaces are proprietary to the manufacturer, but published as an open interface. The physical circuit may be an open standard such as BRI, and the programming language may be a standard such as C language, but the command structure is unique in each PBX. Therefore, CTI applications must be custom designed for each product.

Remote Switching Units

Many PBXs offer remote switching systems in which groups of lines can be contained in a module that is located away from the main switch. Connection is via T-1 lines or fiber-optic cable. The remote unit typically has no standalone capability. If the umbilical back to the main unit is lost, the users in the remote are without service. Aside from this drawback, remote units have several advantages that make them worth considering:

- ◆ Only one processor and software set is needed. This is usually less expensive than maintaining separate systems.
- ◆ Administration is from a central site. All database changes are made on the central switch, with the remote automatically update.
- ◆ Wiring costs are reduced. It is often less costly to install a remote than to cable from the central site.
- ◆ Total feature transparency is achieved. Users in the remote location share the same voice mail, numbering plan, and trunks as the central site, and have access to exactly the same features. Note, however, that some systems permit terminating trunks on the remote.

PRINCIPAL PBX FEATURES

This section discusses the main features that most PBXs support. Although the features are common to most PBXs, users may find differences in how they operate, and how much they cost.

Direct Inward Dialing (DID)

DID offers station users the ability to receive calls from outside the system without going through the PBX attendant. The LEC's central office contains a software table with the location of the DID trunk group. When a call for a DID number arrives, the central office seizes a trunk and outpulses the extension number, usually with DTMF tones. The extra central office operations cause some delay on DID calls. DID is effective in reducing the load on PBX attendants. It also enables users to receive calls when the switchboard is closed. A separate group of trunks from the LEC is required. Most LECs charge a premium for DID trunks compared to normal central office trunks. Also, most LECs levy a charge for each DID number.

Voice and Data Integration in the PBX

Most organizations that are large enough to justify a T-1 line to a distant PBX have a data communications network that also can ride on the same facilities. Figures 21–2 and 21–3 show two methods of integrating voice and data at the facility level. When only single circuits are needed, the method in Figure 21–2 is economical. One or more channels of the T-1 are set aside for data by a "nailed-up" connection through the PBX. Depending on the architecture of the PBX, the data adapter is either a plug-in circuit card or an external device that gives the data circuit access to the digital channel. Any standard transmission speed up to 64 kb/s is available, although some products cannot support speeds higher than 19.2 kb/s. The connection through the PBX is either defined in software or dialed by the user.

A drop-and-insert multiplexer has the ability to split out any required amount of bandwidth to two or more destinations. It is an excellent device for sharing a T-1 line between a PBX and a data application, as Figure 21-3 shows. T-1 cards are used in the PBXs on both ends of the connection. The PBX is programmed to access as many circuits as necessary for voice, with the remainder reserved for data. The data connection of a drop-and-insert multiplexer is usually V.35, which matches a similar connection on the router.

Automatic Call Distribution

Automatic call distribution is a feature that allows PBXs to route incoming calls to a group of service positions. Typical applications are the service positions of any large organization such as airlines, utilities, catalog houses, and department stores. Incoming calls route to an agent position based on routing programmed into the PBX. Calls can be routed by the 800 number called using a service called dialed number identification system that is described below. The caller's telephone number may be delivered by the network and used to route calls, or the caller can be prompted by an automated attendant or call-prompting software in the switch to aid in identification and call routing.

When agent positions are idle, the call routes to an agent immediately. If all positions are occupied, the ACD holds calls in queue and notifies the caller

FIGURE 21-2

Connecting Data through a PBX

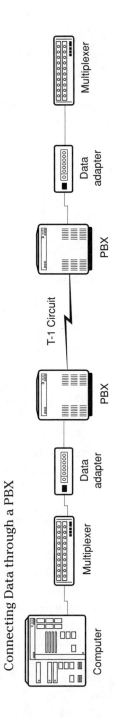

FIGURE 21-3

Sharing a T-1 Circuit with a Drop-and-Insert Multiplexer

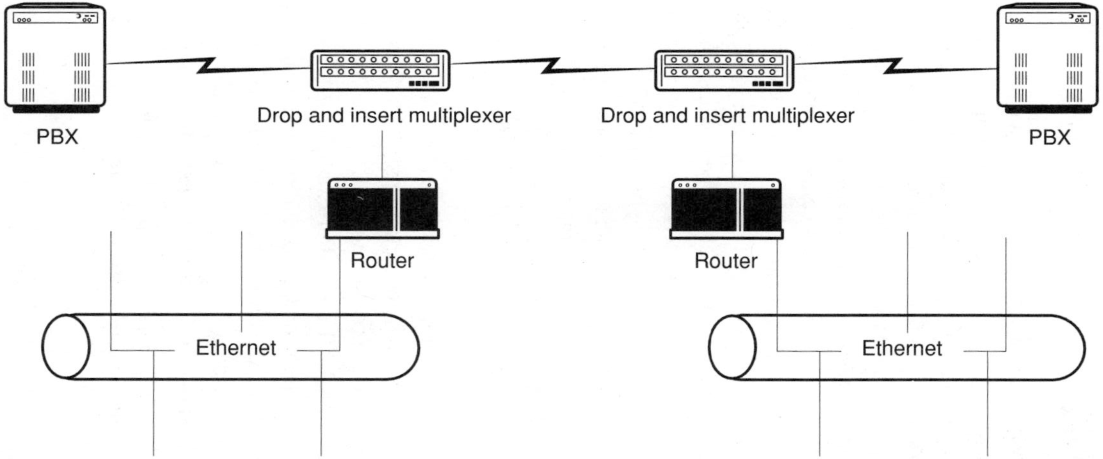

by recorded announcement that the call is being held. Calls can be overflowed to other agent groups, routed to voice mail for a callback, or handled in a variety of different ways, which are discussed in more detail in Chapter 22. ACD is one of the most important features in a PBX, and is included in more than three-fourths of the systems shipped.

Least-Cost Routing (LCR)

Most PBXs terminate a combination of public switched and private trunks on the system. For example, in addition to local trunks, the PBX may terminate T-1 lines to the IEC, foreign exchange lines, and tie trunks to another PBX. Educating users about which service to use is impractical, particularly as rates vary with time of day and terminating location, and the dialing plan varies with the carrier called. It is a reasonably simple matter, however, to program route selection into the central processor of the PBX. With LCR, sometimes called automatic route selection (ARS), the user dials the number; the system determines the least expensive route and dials the digits to complete the call over the appropriate trunk group.

The most sophisticated LCR systems can screen calls on the entire dialed number. Some less elaborate systems can screen on only three or six digits. Three-digit screening limits the PBX to routing by area code or prefix, but not both. The ability to screen on both area code and prefix is important to users on the edge of an area code boundary, where it may be less costly to use one service for nearby prefixes and another for distant prefixes in the same area code. With screening on the entire number, it is possible to allow users to dial some 900 numbers, but deny others.

A related issue is digit insertion and deletion. Some services, such as foreign exchange (FEX), may require the PBX to insert or delete an area code for correct routing. Telephone service is easiest to use if users always dial the same way regardless of the route the call takes. For example, if the PBX has FEX trunks to another area code, the user would dial the area code, but the PBX would strip it off before passing the digits forward to the FEX trunks.

Many systems also provide a warning tone when calls are about to be routed over an expensive service so the user can hang up before the call completes. Complete flexibility in route selection is an essential PBX feature that is available on most stored-program-controlled systems.

Networking Options

Most PBXs provide networking options, which allow multiple PBXs to operate as a single system. Call-processing messages pass between PBXs over a separate data channel using some form of common channel signaling. With the networking option, call-processing information, such as a station's identification and class of service, and in some systems the calling name, travel across the network to permit features to operate in a distant PBX as they do in the local system. At the present state of development, networking is possible only between systems provided by the same manufacturer, although work is currently underway to establish a networking standard..

The objective of networking is to provide complete feature transparency, which is the ability of users to have the same calling features across the network as they have at their PBX. For example, users want to be able to camp on a busy station, regardless of whether it is in their PBX or in a distant system, and they want to share a voice mail system across the network. Some features do not work across a network in some products. For example, call pickup is a feature that enables a user who hears a ringing telephone to press a button and bring the call to his or her telephone. The lack of this feature across a network is usually unimportant since users are normally in separate locations. Some companies, however, start in separate locations with separate systems and then eventually merge them. The PBXs are brought to the same equipment room and remain networked together. If features such as call pickup do not work across the network, users in one work group must be assigned to the same switch, which often requires moving people from one PBX to another.

Single-Button Feature Access

Users can access a PBX's principal features by code dialing. For example, call pickup, call hold, and call forwarding all require distinctive codes, such as *7. Code dialing has an important drawback: Users often forget the dialing codes, so they do not use the features. The solution is to assign the features to single buttons on proprietary telephone sets. If users want to pick up a call in a pickup group, for example, they need only press the call pickup button to bring the call to that telephone. The number of features that can be accessed directly depends on how many buttons are on the telephone set, which, in turn, determines the cost of the instrument. Button access to features is the most important reason for using proprietary instead of analog telephone sets.

Call Detail Recording (CDR)

This feature, sometimes known as station message detail recording (SMDR), in combination with a call accounting system provides the equivalent of a detailed toll statement for PBX users. Most businesses require call detail to control long-distance usage and to spread costs among the user departments. The CDR port forwards this information to a call-accounting system, which, as discussed in a later section, provides this capability. CDR is limited by the lack of answer supervision over a local telephone loop, so the system cannot tell whether the called station answered or not. The determination of called station answer is based on the amount of time the calling station is off hook. Because of the lack of answer supervision, the CDR output cannot be balanced precisely with central office billing detail. However, it is accurate enough for most organizations. As discussed earlier, this problem may be avoided by using digital trunks.

Voice Mail

Voice mail (see Chapter 24) is available as an optional integrated feature in some PBXs and can be added as a nonintegrated service to any PBX. When a station is busy or unattended, the caller can leave a message, which is stored digitally on a hard disk. The station user can dial an access and identification code to retrieve the message.

Some voice mail systems include automated attendant, an option that enables callers with a DTMF dial to route their own calls within the system. Incoming calls are greeted with an announcement that invites them to dial the extension number if it is known, to dial a number for extension information, or to stay on the line for an attendant. This feature saves money by decreasing the amount of work required of the attendant.

Dialed Number Identification System (DNIS)

Offered by IECs along with T-1-based 800 services, DNIS provides the equivalent of direct inward dialing for 800 calls. Incoming calls are preceded by a number that either is or can be converted by the PBX to the number the caller dialed. The DNIS feature in the PBX routes the call to the appropriate station number. DNIS enables an organization to have several 800 numbers and to route each call to a different station, UCD or ACD hunt group, voice mail, or any other location within the PBX. For example, if a company has different ACD groups for sales, service, and order inquiry, it can assign each of these groups a different 800 number and use DNIS to route the calls appropriately.

Direct Inward System Access (DISA)

The DISA feature enables callers to dial a telephone number and a password to gain access to PBX features. If the DISA number is restricted, callers can dial extension numbers or tie lines to on-net locations. If the DISA feature is unrestricted, callers can gain access to long-distance services. DISA helps reduce credit-card calls by enabling users outside the PBX to access low-cost long-distance services.

Security is an obvious problem with DISA. It is one of the most prevalent targets for toll thieves, who use it to place calls at the company's expense. The best practice with DISA is to disable it. If it must be used, managers should change the password frequently and check the call-accounting system for evidence of misuse.

N Times 64 Capability

With the growth of videoconferencing, it is often desirable to dial more bandwidth than an ordinary BRI connection provides. Conference-quality video usually requires at least 384 kb/s, which requires six 64 kb/s channels. A PBX with $N \times 64$ capability enables the user to dial as many channels of contiguous bandwidth as required.

Centralized Attendant Service

CAS enables attendants at one location to perform complete attendant functions for remote networked PBXs. Although each PBX has its own group of trunks, all calls routed to the attendant flow to the centralized location.

Power Failure Transfer

Unless a PBX is configured to run from batteries or from an uninterruptable power supply, a commercial power failure will cause the system to fail. The power failure transfer feature connects central office trunks to standard DTMF telephones. Since most PBXs require ground start trunks, provisions must be made to operate from loop start telephones. This can be accomplished by two methods: use a separate loop start-to-ground start converter or equip the telephones with a ground start button. The former method is prevalent.

The power failure transfer feature is an inexpensive and effective way to obtain minimum service during power failure conditions. Even users of systems with battery backup or UPS should consider power failure transfer to retain some service if the PBX itself fails.

Trunk Queuing

The trunk queuing feature enables a user to camp on a busy trunk group. Two queuing methods are in common use: callback queuing and hang-on queuing. With callback queuing, the user activates the feature by dialing a code or pressing a feature button and hangs up. The system calls back when a trunk is available. With hang-on queuing, the user activates the feature but remains off hook until the call completes. Some queuing features enable high-priority users to jump to the head of the queue. The system should, however, have a maximum wait, after which even low-priority users are cut through.

Restriction Features

An important feature of every PBX is its ability to restrict the calling privileges of certain stations. Even companies with an unrestricted policy normally require restricted telephones in public locations such as waiting areas and lunch rooms. The type of restriction varies with manufacturer, but it is possible with most systems to restrict incoming, outgoing, and any type of long distance. Some systems can restrict down to a specific telephone number. All restriction systems should restrict selected area codes and prefixes. Area code restriction is necessary to prevent users from dialing numbers, such as 900 numbers, for which a charge is collected.

Uniform Call Distribution

This service distributes calls evenly among a group of stations. When one or more active stations are idle, incoming calls are directed to the station that is next in line to receive a call. When all stations in the UCD group are busy, incoming calls are answered with a recording and held in queue. When a UCD station becomes idle, the call in queue the longest is directed to the station. In many UCD systems, a station user can toggle between active and inactive status by dialing a code or pressing a feature button. Compared to ACD, UCD is unsophisticated, lacking the supervisory and management features that an ACD offers. Chapter 22 discusses UCD in more detail.

Data-Switching Capability

A highly touted capability of a digital PBX is its ability to switch voice and data with equal ease. Some companies take advantage of this capability, although data switching has limitations. A terminal or desktop computer can plug into an EIA-232 port in a telephone that is so equipped. This enables the data device to access other devices that are equipped with ports, or to access a modem pool.

Data switching appeared to be an important feature of digital PBXs when they first reached the market, but it has not proved to be a popular feature, primarily because LANs have filled the role that data switching was intended for. Many companies purchase additional analog ports to provide modem capability through the PBX.

Modem Pooling

Modems are cost-effective for a few connections. If data usage is extensive, however, they become expensive because of the need for separate analog ports and modems, which together may exceed the cost of a modem pool.

A modem pool has circuit cards or external data adapters in the PBX that interface a bank of modems. When the user initiates a data call, the PBX attaches a modem and the user can dial outside the PBX as usual. A data session can be carried simultaneously with a voice session in most PBXs. The PBX requires either one or two ports per session. If an incoming data call is directed to a DID telephone number that is identified as a data device, the PBX diverts the call through the modem pool, attaches a modem, and completes the call.

Multitenant Service

PBXs that provide service to users from different organizations can use multitenant service to give each user organization the appearance of a private switch. Separate attendant consoles can be provided, and each organization can have its own group of trunks and block of numbers.

Property Management Interface

Hotels, hospitals, dormitories, and other organizations that resell service often connect the PBX to a computer to provide features such as checking room status information, disabling the telephone set from the attendant console, and determining check-in or check-out status. The PBX provides information to the computer, and accepts orders from the front desk via computer terminal.

Uniform Dialing Plan

Uniform dialing plan software in a network of PBXs enables the caller to dial an extension number and have the call completed over a tie line network without the caller's being concerned about where the extension is located. The PBX selects the route and takes care of station number translations. UDP software is effective only among PBXs of the same manufacture.

Universal Card Slots

The card slots of some PBXs are designated for a particular type of card. Therefore, it is possible that a shelf or cabinet may have vacant slots but not have any available for the type of card that is needed. Except processor and power supply cards, which usually require dedicated slots, PBXs with universal card slots can accept any type of line or trunk card in a vacant slot. This feature lends an important degree of flexibility to the system.

Wireless Capability

Many organizations have classes of users who must roam about the building. Wireless systems are just coming on the market to allow use of the telephone anywhere in a building or within a restricted range on a campus. Two types of wireless systems are available. One type plugs into analog port on the PBX, and gives the user capabilities of analog telephones. Proprietary wireless systems provide the features of digital telephones including button access to features, multiline capability, and other such features. Chapter 17 discusses wireless in more detail.

PBX Voice Features

As all PBXs are designed for voice-switching service, they have features intended for the convenience and productivity of the users. Not all the features listed below are universally available, and many systems provide features not listed. This list briefly describes the most popular voice features found in PBXs.

- The PBX can be equipped with *paging* trunks that are accessed by an attendant or dialed from a station. An option is *zone paging,* which allows the attendant to page in specific locations rather than the entire building.
- *Distinctive ringing* enables a station user to tell whether a call has originated from inside or outside the system.
- *Speed dialing* enables station users to dial other numbers by using abbreviated codes. Speed dial is available from telephone set buttons or from a system speed dial list that everyone within a speed dial group shares.
- *Integrated key telephone system features,* such as those described in Chapter 20, can be integrated into the PBX software and accessed from a nonkey telephone. Features such as call pickup, call hold, call forwarding, do not disturb, and dial-up conferencing can be provided.
- The caller's name or telephone number can be displayed on special telephones equipped with an *alphanumeric display.*

◆ *Call coverage* features allow the administrator to set up automatic coverage paths to determine how calls will route when the called station is busy, does not answer, or is in do-not-disturb status.

◆ *Forced account code dialing* is used in PBXs in which call detail must be identified by caller instead of by station number. For example, it is often used in colleges and universities where roommates share the same extension number.

◆ *Special dialing* features are provided in many systems. Besides digit dialing, some systems allow dialing by name from an integrated directory.

◆ *Executive override* allows a station to interrupt a busy line or preempt a long-distance trunk if the class of that station is higher than the class of the user.

◆ *Trunk answer any station* allows stations to answer incoming trunks when the attendant station is busy.

◆ *Portable directory number* allows a user on a networked PBX to move from one switch to another without changing the telephone number.

Attendant Features

Most PBXs have attendant consoles for incoming call answer and supervision. The following features are important for most consoles and represent only a fraction of the features available.

◆ *Camp-on* is a feature that allows an attendant to queue an incoming call to a busy station. When the station becomes idle the call is automatically completed. A related feature, *automatic callback* enables station users to camp on busy lines.

◆ *Direct station selection* (DSS) allows the attendant to call any station by pressing an illuminated button associated with the line. This feature is usually available only in small PBXs.

◆ *Automatic timed reminders* alert the attendant when a called line has not answered within a prescribed time. The attendant also can act as a central information source for directory and call assistance.

◆ *Attendant controlled conferencing* is available for multiport conference calls.

System Administration Features

System administration is a costly part of every PBX, so any features that ease the administrator's job are valuable. The following are some of the more popular features.

◆ *Automatic set relocation* allows users to move their telephones from one location to another without the need to retranslate. The administrator gives users a code and instructions to carry the set to the new location, plug it in, and dial the code. When this is complete the station translations are moved to the new port.

◆ *Network move* is a feature similar to automatic set relocation except that it works across a network, where automatic set relocation works only in the same PBX.

◆ *Ethernet connectivity* to the management terminal is a valuable feature for system managers who move around the office. The manager can go to any computer and access the system management port without dialing in from a modem.

CALL-ACCOUNTING SYSTEMS

All PBXs, most hybrids, and many key telephone systems include a call detail recorder (CDR) port that receives call details at the conclusion of each call. The call details can be printed or passed to a call-accounting system for further processing. The CDR output of most systems is of little value by itself because calls are presented in order of completion and lack rates, identification of the called number, and other such details that control of long-distance costs requires. Call-accounting systems add details to create management reports, a complete long-distance statement for each user, and departmental summaries. The primary purposes of a call-accounting system are to discourage unauthorized use and to distribute costs to users.

Most call-accounting systems on the market are software programs for personal computers. Programs for minicomputers and mainframes and several stand-alone units that use custom processors are also available, but inexpensive PCs have largely replaced them. CDR data either feeds directly into an on-line PC, or it feeds into a buffer that stores call details until it is polled. The advantage of a buffer is that it isn't necessary to tie up a PC in collecting call details, and if the power fails, the battery backup in the buffer retains the stored information.

In multi-PBX environments, a networked call-accounting system may be required. These systems use buffers or computers to collect information at remote sites and upload it to a central processor at the end of the collection interval. If long-distance calls can be placed from one PBX over trunks attached to another, a tie line reconciliation program is important. The tie line reconciliation program uses the completion time of calls to match calls that originate on one PBX and terminate on trunks connected to another.

Most PBXs can output to the CDR port any combination of long-distance, local, outgoing, and incoming calls. The amount of detail to collect is a matter of individual judgment, but remember that sufficient buffer and disk storage space must be provided to hold all the information collected.

APPLICATIONS

Nearly every business that has more than 30 to 50 stations is in the market for a PBX or its central office counterpart, Centrex (Chapter 25). PBXs are economical for some very small businesses that need features that most key systems do not provide such as restriction and least-cost routing. They are also economical for very large businesses that have PBXs using central office switching systems of a size that rivals many metropolitan public networks..

PBX Standards

Few standards exist for PBXs. The interface between a PBX and its serving local central office is standardized by EIA, and trunk interfaces follow accepted industry practices for signaling and electrical interface. The industry generally adopts the same PBX features, but the manufacturer may use a unique method of operating the feature. Analog telephones follow accepted industry signaling practice, but the loop resistance range is left to the manufacturer. Proprietary station interfaces are determined entirely by the manufacturer with little uniformity among products. With only a few exceptions, proprietary station sets intended for one PBX cannot be used in another manufacturer's system.

Evaluation Considerations

In choosing a PBX it is important that you understand exactly what you want it to do. The differences between systems are often subtle, and differences in function and support aren't apparent until you have lived with the system for several months. This makes it important to check references very carefully.

The uniqueness of every organization makes a universal PBX specification impractical. Considerations that are important in some applications will have no importance in others. Therefore, the buyer should weigh them accordingly. It is, of course, essential that the system contain the required features and that it meet the requirements for numbers of line and trunk terminations. Reliability and cost are implicit requirements in any telecommunications system and are not separately discussed.

External Interfaces

Every PBX must conform to the standard EIA-464 interface to a local telephone central office and must be registered with the FCC for network connection. In addition, interfaces such as these should be considered:

- ◆ PRI and BRI interfaces.
- ◆ EIA-232 or EIA-449 data set or workstation interface.
- ◆ Computer–telephony integration interface.
- ◆ Interface to local area networks.
- ◆ 1.544 mb/s interface to external trunk groups or to internal devices such as remote access servers.

A key consideration in evaluating a PBX is the type of terminals it supports. All PBXs have, at a minimum, a two-wire station interface to a standard analog DTMF telephone. Ordinary telephones are the least expensive terminals, and because of the quantities of stations involved in a large PBX, inability to use standard telephones can add significantly to the cost. The standard analog telephone falls short, however, as a terminal in most offices. The most effective telephone sets are integrated devices that interact with the PBX processor to operate its features.

Proprietary telephones are the most practical way of accessing integrated key telephone features. Some features tend to fall into disuse because of the difficulty of using them from standard telephones. A proprietary terminal may improve ease of use for some features, such as call pickup and hold, by using buttons to replace the switch hook flashes and special codes required with standard telephones.

These features should be considered in evaluating a PBX terminal interface:

- ◆ Proprietary or nonproprietary telephone interface.
- ◆ Number of conductors to the station.
- ◆ Station conductor loop range.
- ◆ Integrated key telephone system features.
- ◆ Message-waiting or nonmessage-waiting line card.
- ◆ Availability of BRI interface.

Universal Shelf Architecture

Universal shelf architecture permits various types of line and trunk cards to be installed in any slot. Lacking this feature, slots are dedicated to a particular type of card. It is, therefore, possible to have plenty of spare slot capacity in the PBX but have no room for cards of the desired type.

Switch Network

A key evaluation consideration is whether the switch network is blocking or nonblocking. Blocking networks are acceptable, but may require additional administrative effort to keep them in balance. Also, consider the number of busy hour call attempts the PBX is capable of supporting to determine if the processor limits the capacity of the system.

Voice and Data Integration Issues

If you have enough circuits to justify a T-1 carrier and do not need it all for voice, it is often feasible to share the T-1 between voice and data.

ISDN Compatibility Issues

ISDN is not universally available yet, but the LECs will gradually convert their central offices to ISDN over the next several years. IECs offer ISDN services now, so any company considering a new PBX must evaluate ISDN compatibility. Consider not only PRI, but also BRI so users can take advantage of desktop videoconferencing when it becomes available. Most IECs have ISDN services that require compatibility in the PBX. Generally, these services are available only over the primary rate interface.

Administrative Interface

All PBXs have some form of man–machine interface through a terminal or attached PC. The ease of use of this interface differs significantly among products. The most difficult products to use have a command-driven terminal interface. At the other end of the spectrum are systems with graphical user interfaces that allow users to make point-and-click changes.

Redundancy

Organizations that cannot tolerate PBX outages can improve reliability by purchasing redundant systems. Several levels of redundancy are available. The lowest level provides redundant processors. Higher reliability can be achieved with redundant power supplies and switching networks. Even with redundancy failures will still occur, but reliability should be much higher than with a nonredundant system.

Environmental Considerations

Most PBXs can operate without air-conditioning in an ordinary office environment. The operating temperature range should be evaluated, however, because some systems do require an air-conditioned environment. Even without air-conditioning, adequate air circulation will be required.

Database Updates

The ease of changing classes of service and telephone numbers is an important evaluation consideration. If the attendant console or an easy-to-use maintenance terminal can control these, it is possible to add, remove, and move stations and to change restrictions without using a trained technician. With a truly flexible system, station jacks are wired to line ports. A new station is added by plugging in the telephone and activating the line from an attendant or maintenance console.

Diagnostic Capability

The degree to which a PBX can diagnose its own trouble and direct a technician to the source of trouble is important in controlling maintenance expense. It also is important that a system have remote diagnostic capability so the manufacturer's technical assistance center can access the system over a dialed-up port.

Station Wiring Limits

The station loop range of both proprietary terminals and ordinary telephones must be considered in evaluating a PBX. Most proprietary terminals and those terminals requiring an EIA interface can operate only over restricted range. Range limits can be extended in some systems by using distributed switching, which moves the line circuits close to the stations.

Bandwidth Requirements

Bandwidth is of concern with systems that interface with high-speed digital lines. Digital voice PBXs may limit modem data speed to 9,600 b/s or less. With special data ports, higher speeds are supported, including, in some systems, enough bandwidth to switch a 1.544 mb/s bit stream. Consider whether $N \times 64$ capability is required to support videoconferencing.

Wireless Capability

Many organizations need wireless capability so the telephones of certain users are no longer tethered to the wall. Wireless systems that support analog telephones can be used with any PBX, but the ability to use proprietary telephones may be important.

Call-Accounting Evaluation Issues

Most PBXs today are purchased with a call-accounting system. Most systems are developed by someone other than the PBX manufacturer. The following are some criteria for selecting a call-accounting system.

Reports

The main reason for buying a call-accounting system is for its reports. Evaluate factors such as these:

◆ What kind of reports are provided? Do they meet the organization's requirements?

◆ Are custom-designed reports possible?

◆ Is it possible to link report information to an external program, such as a spreadsheet or database management system, to produce custom reports?

◆ Are traffic reports produced? If so, are they accurate?

◆ Are management reports, such as inventories, provided?

◆ What kind of manual effort is needed to produce reports? Does it require a trained operator, or can clerical people perform the month-end operations with little or no formal training?

◆ Does the manufacturer support tie line reconciliation?

Vendor Support

As with most software packages, vendor support is important for installing and maintaining the system. Evaluate the vendor's experience in supporting the package. Determine whether the vendor has people who have been specifically trained. Evaluate the amount of support the package developer has available and what it costs. Some vendors sell ongoing support packages, and where these are available, the cost-effectiveness should be evaluated.

Call Rating

Most call-accounting packages have call rating tables based on V&H (vertical and horizontal) tables. These divide the United States and Canada into a grid from which point-to-point mileage can be calculated. Tables must be updated regularly as rates change. Also, consider that many companies do not need absolute rate accuracy. To distribute costs among organizational units, precision is usually not required. Many long-distance rate plans use rates that are not distance sensitive, so V&H rating accuracy is not required. Determine facts such as these:

◆ What kind of rating tables does the manufacturer support?

◆ How frequently are tables updated?

◆ What do updates cost?

◆ What vendors' rates does the package support?

◆ How are intrastate rates calculated?

◆ Do you need to bill back with high accuracy?

Capacity

Call storage equipment is intended to maintain information on a certain number of calls. When buffer storage is full, it must be unloaded and calls processed. Usually, the system must store at least one month's worth of calls. Evaluate questions such as these:

- ◆ How much storage space is required?
- ◆ What is the capacity in number of calls, both incoming and outgoing?
- ◆ How much growth capacity is provided?
- ◆ Is storage nonvolatile so if power fails calls are not lost?

SELECTED MANUFACTURERS OF DIGITAL PBXs AND RELATED PRODUCTS

PBX Manufacturers

Cortelco

Ericsson

Excel

Executone

Fujitsu Business Communications

Harris Digital

Hitachi America

Intecom

Iwatsu

Lucent Technologies

Mitel, Inc.

NEC America

Nortel, Inc.

Panasonic

Premier Telecom Products

Redcom Laboratories

Siemens/Rolm

SRX
Summa Four
Tadiran
Telerad
Toshiba America
Vodavi

Call-Accounting Systems

Account-A-Call Corp.
Active Telemanagement
American Telecommunications
Call Management Products
Gemini Telemanagement Systems
Homisco
IntegraTRAK
ISI Infortext Systems
Lanier/Harris
Moscom
NEC Information Systems
Summa Four
Telco Research
Western Telematic
Xiox
Xtend Communications

22

AUTOMATIC CALL
DISTRIBUTION EQUIPMENT

Automatic call distribution is a major growth industry in the switching arena. Once reserved for large call centers, ACD is now part of most PBXs. Major PBX manufacturers now report that about 75 percent of their systems ship with ACD software, and stand-alone ACDs still have about one-fourth of the call center market. ACD is an inexpensive addition to most PBXs, and even some hybrids. Any business with a group of people (called *agents*) who answer incoming calls or place large numbers of outgoing calls should consider an ACD or its cousin, the predictive dialer, which is used for outbound calls.

ACDs fall into two categories: stand-alone and PBX-integrated. The former are more expensive than PBX systems and are generally effective in large call centers with sophisticated routing and reporting requirements. If the call center is a major function of a work group, a stand-alone ACD may offer features that are unavailable in a PBX. If ACD is an incidental function of a PBX that is needed for other purposes, the cost of a stand-alone system will likely be prohibitive.

Several factors have increased the importance of ACDs in the last few years. First is the tendency for more and more business to be done over the telephone. Virtually all manufacturers and software developers provide technical support, sales, and customer service over the telephone. Catalog retailing has become a major factor in many companies' marketing plans, and more business is being done through telemarketing. A call center typically has banks of 800/888 numbers with different numbers associated with different product lines or promotions. Groups of agents are equipped for access to the corporate database, and a call distribution system directs incoming calls to the appropriate agent. Telemarketing centers also may use predictive dialing equipment, a technology similar to ACD that places outgoing calls automatically and delivers connected parties to a group of agents.

The second factor involves the changing methods of delivering incoming calls. The major long-distance carriers deliver 800 calls on T-1, and even T-3. The fixed cost of T-1 lines has dropped to the point that T-1 is the preferred method of delivery for companies that have more than a handful of lines. Once a T-1 is installed, its entire 24-channel bandwidth is available, and the dialed number identification system (DNIS) option identifies the number the caller dialed so the ACD can use it to route calls to the appropriate destination.

The third factor is call distribution technology itself. A call distribution system is a marriage of telephone and computer technology used to identify callers and route them to the agents best equipped by training or availability to handle their calls. The arrival of inexpensive computers and improved tools for creating software, along with the decreasing cost of PBXs, has resulted in greatly improved call distribution capabilities. The dramatic decreases in long-distance costs that have occurred since divestiture, and improvements in distributed computing have led companies to centralize operations that once, of necessity, took place in proximity to the workforce. Now, it is no longer necessary for agents to be near paper records that can be accessed over a network.

CALL DISTRIBUTION TECHNOLOGY

An incoming call center can be set up with ordinary key telephone equipment, which is the way smaller companies handle calls to a defined work group. Calls arrive on trunk hunting lines, and an agent pushes a button to answer the call. If there are more lines than available agents, someone must interrupt a call in progress to answer it and put it on hold. If several calls are on hold, there is no easy way to know which caller has waited longest. Also, distribution of the workload depends on the action of the agents and how effectively they are supervised. Any organization with more than a few answering positions finds that the cost of some form of machine-controlled call distribution pays for itself quickly.

A uniform call distribution system (UCD), which is a standard feature of many PBXs, often improves call handling. The PBX station set is the agent telephone. The UCD routes incoming calls to the first available agent. If no agent is available, the UCD routes calls to an announcement, holds them in queue, and sends the call that arrived first to the first available agent. In most UCD systems, the caller hears only the initial announcement and listens to silence or music on hold after that. UCDs relieve agents of the need to interrupt a call in progress to answer another call and put it on hold. UCDs generally lack the ability to balance workload among agents, nor do they provide sophisticated management reports.

The stand-alone counterpart of a UCD is the call sequencer. This device may work with a PBX or key telephone system, or it may be connected directly to incoming lines. Unlike the UCD, a call sequencer does not direct calls. It alerts agents to the presence of incoming calls by lighting keys on the telephone or lighting an external beehive lamp. It answers the call, provides a delay announcement to the callers, and provides limited statistical information.

The most sophisticated device is the automatic call distributor (ACD), which is the primary focus of this chapter. ACDs provide sophisticated call-handling strategies that enable the call center to achieve its cost and service goals. They provide statistical information that can be used for balancing the staff to the load, forecasting workload, scheduling staff, and evaluating service. The differences between ACDs, UCDs, and sequencers are significant but not always apparent without analysis. Table 22–1 lists the most important differences.

An ACD, such as the Aspect CallCenter® shown in Figure 22–1, has the following major components:

◆ Switching unit.
◆ Agent positions.
◆ Supervisory and monitoring equipment.
◆ Management software.

The functions of an ACD are to answer calls, place them in priority order, route them to the appropriate position, queue them if no agents are available, provide music and announcement while callers are in queue, overflow queued calls to an alternative queue or voice mail after a prescribed interval, and collect and process call statistics.

CALL-HANDLING ELEMENTS

Every ACD call has the following elements, as Figure 22–2 shows:

◆ *Answering* the call.
◆ *Identifying* or determining who the caller is and what he or she wants.
◆ *Queuing* or holding the call for an agent if none is immediately available.

T A B L E 22–1

Comparison of Call Distribution Products

	ACD	**UCD**	**Call Sequencer**
Basis for Distributing Calls to Agents	Based on time. Usually the next call is sent to the least busy agent	Based on sequence. Usually top-down or circular hunt	Does not distribute calls. Alerts agents to incoming calls by colored lamps
Statistical Information	Provides real-time information on supervisor's terminal plus standard and custom-printed reports	Limited to line utilization and other basic reports	Provides limited reporting
Call Overflow between Groups	Programmable overflow based on variables such as time, priority, workload, etc.	Does not overflow	Overflow is not applicable
Telephone System Integration	Furnished as stand-alone or part of a PBX, hybrid, or key system	Furnished as part of a PBX, hybrid, or key system	A stand-alone device that is designed to operate with a key system

◆ *Informing,* which is keeping callers informed as to the status of the call and providing information to callers while they wait in queue.

◆ *Routing,* which is sending the call to the appropriate service agent.

◆ *Service delivery.*

◆ *Termination* of the call.

The key to successful call center operation is the sequence in which these functions are handled. If the call is identified early in the process it can be handled more intelligently than if it is identified later. The network and the call center equipment offer several identification strategies, which are covered in more detail in *The Irwin Handbook of Telecommunications Management.* Briefly, technology can assist in several ways. The caller can be identified by calling line identification (CLID) or automatic number identification (ANI). The former applies to local trunks, and the latter to 800 lines. Callers can also be identified by caller-dialed digits, such as an account number, that

FIGURE 22-1

The Aspect CallCenter® ACD

Courtesy of Aspect Telecommunications

FIGURE 22-2

Generic Call Flow Process

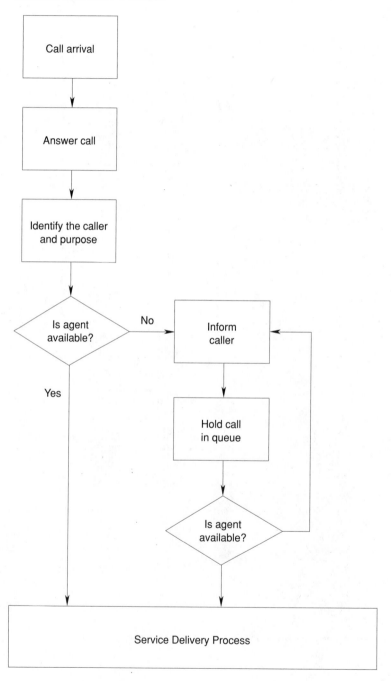

are captured in an interactive voice response unit (IVR) or a call-prompting application. Callers can be identified by giving them a special DID or 800 number to dial, with the latter captured by DNIS.

Callers can be prompted to indicate what service they want through automated attendant or IVR. Many companies provide different telephone or 800 numbers for different services. For example, one number is sales, another customer service, another is order inquiry, and so on. With early caller identification, calls can be routed much more effectively. The least effective strategy is to route the call directly to an agent without prescreening. If the agent receiving the call is incapable of providing the service, the call must be transferred, which contributes to added delay, customer annoyance, and extra cost. With early identification calls can be routed most effectively.

Service Delivery

Although service delivery is the end of the call center process, considering it first can lead to some interesting alternatives. Some services can be delivered only by a human, and in call centers where this is the case, the objective of the process is to route the call to a qualified agent with a minimum of delay. Not incidentally, another objective is to keep the agents at a comfortable level of occupancy. (Occupancy in a call center is the percentage of time that agents are busy talking on calls or wrapping up after completion.)

If callers can satisfy their requests without involving an agent, they may be willing to do some of the work themselves. The IVR, which nearly every financial institution uses, is the best example of caller-directed service delivery. Account balances and fund transfers can be handled 24 hours per day, which represents good service to customers that otherwise would have to wait for normal working hours. By thinking closely about alternatives, many forms of mechanized service delivery are possible. Here are some examples:

- ◆ Work schedules can be delivered via IVR or audiotex.
- ◆ Order status can be delivered by IVR.
- ◆ Outdialing equipment can remind patients of schedules.
- ◆ Information about job openings can be posted in an audiotex bulletin board.
- ◆ Technical service callers can be offered a trouble diagnostic tree through audiotex.

Callers should be offered a way of transferring to an agent after they have listened to the information available. For example, a job applicant who wants more detail should be able to press a digit to go to a human.

Informing

Technology can improve customer satisfaction by keeping callers informed while they wait. The most basic form is through queue announcements, which can be delivered by digital announcement systems, IVR, or even by humans who can enter the queue to provide information or entertainment. Music on hold is one form of information—it informs callers that they are still connected in queue. Some companies provide product information through a recorded source to callers while they wait.

The most effective call centers provide intelligent queue announcements, which inform callers of their queue position and expected length of wait. An external device, usually an IVR, is needed to provide intelligent queue announcements. The outboard device obtains information about queue conditions from the ACD's MIS channel, performs the necessary calculations, and reports it to the callers in conjunction with the regular queue announcement. The routing script may give the caller the opportunity to leave a callback message in voice mail if the wait becomes excessive.

Routing

The objective of an ACD is to connect a caller to an available agent who has the skills to fulfill the request. To do an effective matching job, it is evident that the system needs to know something about both the callers and the agents.

Conditional Routing
The most flexible systems permit the administrator to write a *routing script,* or *vector* as it is sometimes known, to vary call routing under different conditions. Typical conditions that can be programmed into routing scripts are length of time in queue, number of agents logged on in a queue, number of waiting calls, time of day or day of week, and other such variables. Writing a vector is similar to writing a simple computer program using if-and-then logic.

Skill-Based Routing
The most effective ACDs maintain a skills database on each agent, match the caller's needs to agents' skills, and route accordingly. The skills could be anything from language to technical knowledge. Skill-routing systems provide several levels of proficiency and give the administrator tools to set up a routing algorithm. Skill-based routing may be included in the ACD's generic program, in an IVR, or in a specialized outboard processor.

Overflow

An important function of all effective ACDs is the ability to route calls from one queue to another during overload conditions. *Timed overflow* routes calls based on the amount of time the user has waited in queue. For example, a queue might be programmed to play an opening announcement, hold the call in queue for 20 seconds, play a second announcement, and hold the call again. The system might loop through this set of instructions until a specified amount of time or number of loops has elapsed, and then route the call to another queue. To avoid routing a call into a condition of worse congestion, some ACDs provide *look-ahead routing,* in which the ACD looks at the next queue before overflowing. *Look-back routing* is an option in which the ACD checks to see if congestion has improved in the original queue, and if so, returns the call to its original position.

One feature that distinguishes an ACD from a UCD or a call sequencer is its ability to overflow calls from one queue to another. Besides length of time in queue, overflow is based on one or more of the following variables:

◆ *Number of calls waiting.* For example, a routing script might check the alternate queue and overflow if fewer than a given number of calls is waiting.
◆ *Time of day.* Calls might overflow from a center in the East to one in the West after 5:00 P.M., but not during the day.
◆ *Caller priority.* Arrival on a priority trunk group or dialing a special number might entitle the caller to different treatment than callers on nonpriority groups. Calls on more expensive trunks might be afforded priority to reduce the company's expense for 800 service.
◆ *Length of oldest waiting call.* Calls might overflow only after the oldest call in queue has been waiting more than a given number of seconds. This keeps calls in the primary queue for service, and overflows them only when the wait is excessive.

ACDs often are equipped with an automated attendant on the front end to assist in call routing and voice mail on the back end to handle overflows and give callers the option of leaving a message instead of waiting. Chapter 24 discusses these technologies. The automated attendant can be either a front-end device that is not connected with the voice mail or part of the voice mail system. Usually a call center is divided into several *splits,* or groups. When calls are queued for a group of agents, they must have some common set of characteristics, which may be identified by the automated attendant or simply by the dialed number.

When a call arrives at the head of a queue, if an agent is available the ACD routes the call directly to the agent unless the caller is forced to listen to an announcement before being routed. The call is delivered automatically to the agent's telephone set.

ACD FEATURES AND OPERATION

To be recognized by the system, agents must log on to a particular split. In some systems agents can log onto more than one split. The act of logging on does not, however, mean the agent is available to take a call. In most ACDs the agent also must press a key on the telephone set. The system identifies agents as being in one of several states. Typically, the following states are provided:

- ◆ *Available:* When an agent is available, the system can deliver the next call.
- ◆ *Busy:* The busy state indicates that the agent is currently handling a call.
- ◆ *After-call work or wrap-up:* Most ACDs permit the agent to spend a variable or fixed amount of time after each contact completing paperwork before the next call arrives.
- ◆ *Unavailable:* This state is used when the agent is temporarily away from the position, typically during breaks.

The call center supervisor usually has a terminal to monitor the status of service and load. The terminal lists agents by name, shows their current state, and displays a summary of their production statistics. In some systems the display also shows how long agents have been in their current state, which is useful for determining when wrap-up or unavailable time is excessive. The terminal also should display information about service levels.

Most ACDs also provide supervisory monitoring capability for service observing. Monitoring may be silent or accompanied by a tone that is audible to the agent but not the caller. Call monitoring is a sensitive issue, and company policy or state law may prohibit monitoring unless the agent is notified.

The agent's telephone set is important to the effectiveness of the ACD. Most PBX-integrated ACDs use one or more of the manufacturer's line of telephone sets for the agent terminal. Multibutton digital sets make it possible for the agent to perform functions such as logging in and out and changing state without dialing the special access codes that are required with single-line sets. Display sets make it possible for the system to deliver to the agent such information as the trunk group on which the call arrived, length of time the caller waited, and number of calls currently in queue. In most applications, improved agent productivity justifies the extra expense of a multiline digital display set.

FIGURE 22-3

Rockwell Spectra View® Console

Courtesy of Rockwell Telecommunications

High-end stand-alone ACDs normally are equipped with proprietary telephones like the Rockwell Spectra View® console shown in Figure 22–3. Some systems use a combined telephone and video display terminal as the agent position.

Outbound Calling

Many ACDs (also stand-alone predictive dialers) are equipped for outbound calling. A system with outbound capability dials numbers from a database and connects the called party to an agent only after dialing is complete. Some systems have answer detection capability and connect to an agent only after the called party answers. Although answering machines and voice mail sometimes fool such systems, most systems detect busy and unanswered calls and store the numbers for later retry.

The primary hazard with outcalling systems is completing a call when no agents are available. Because so many lines are busy or do not answer, and because it takes time to set up each call, the system is placing calls when there are no idle agents. If the system waits for an agent to be idle before initiating the call, the productivity of the agents will drop. Most systems use some type of predictive calling to anticipate when an agent will become available. If an agent is not available within seconds of the time the called party answers, the party perceives the call as a nuisance call and hangs up.

ACD REPORTING

A major part of an ACD's value lies in its reporting capabilities. ACD reports are either part of the generic program of the switch, or they are produced in an outboard computer that attaches to the ACD's MIS channel. Figure 22–4 shows a portion of a screen from Aspect's CustomView® program that runs under Microsoft Windows to display results. Reports produced in the ACD are not user-programmable, and are therefore less flexible than those produced in an outboard computer. Reports produced by most systems fall into the following categories:

Agent Reports   These reports provide statistics for individual agents. Included may be amount of time logged on, number of calls handled, average talking and wrap-up time per call, number and duration of outgoing calls, hold time on calls, and amount of time in an unavailable state. Supervisors can use agent reports to determine how agents perform with respect to each other, group averages, or objectives.

Group Reports   Groups, splits, or queues as they are variously known, are identifiable work groups who are assigned a particular function. Group reports show group totals and averages for the variables discussed under agent reports. They also provide information that does not apply to individual agents such as average speed of call answer, numbers of abandoned calls, average and maximum length of time to abandon, and length of longest-waiting call. Group and agent statistics together give administrators insight into service levels and information to calculate staff requirements.

Trunk Reports   Most large call centers have several trunk groups for which the ACD reports statistics. Reports such as call volume and length, number of abandons, trunk group usage, and so on, allow administrators to determine whether service or cost trends pattern to a specific trunk group.

Routing Script Reports   These reports show information such as the stage in the routing script at which calls are abandoned. These statistics can be used to evaluate the scripts' effectiveness. A high rate of abandonment at a particular point may show that the script is confusing.

FIGURE 22-4

ACO Agent Statistics Displayed by Aspect's CustomView® Software

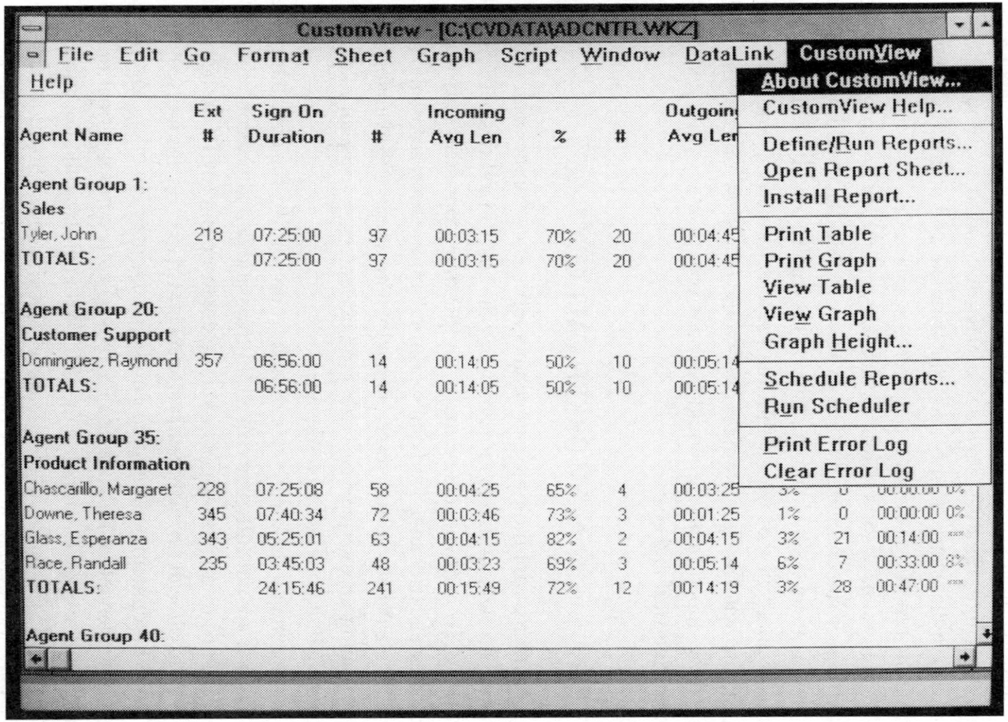

CustomView - [C:\CV\DATA\ADCNTRL.WK4]

File Edit Go Format Sheet Graph Script Window DataLink **CustomView** Help

CustomView menu:

About CustomView...

CustomView Help...

Define/Run Reports...
Open Report Sheet...
Install Report...

Print Table
Print Graph
View Table
View Graph
Graph Height...

Schedule Reports...
Run Scheduler

Print Error Log
Clear Error Log

Agent Name	Ext #	Sign On Duration	Sheet #	Incoming Avg Len	%	#	Outgoing Avg Len
Agent Group 1:							
Sales							
Tyler, John	218	07:25:00	97	00:03:15	70%	20	00:04:45
TOTALS:		07:25:00	97	00:03:15	70%	20	00:04:45
Agent Group 20:							
Customer Support							
Dominguez, Raymond	357	06:56:00	14	00:14:05	50%	10	00:05:14
TOTALS:		06:56:00	14	00:14:05	50%	10	00:05:14
Agent Group 35:							
Product Information							
Chascaillo, Margaret	228	07:25:08	58	00:04:25	65%	4	00:03:25
Downe, Theresa	345	07:40:34	72	00:03:46	73%	3	00:01:25
Glass, Esperanza	343	05:25:01	63	00:04:15	82%	2	00:04:15
Race, Randall	235	03:45:03	48	00:03:23	69%	3	00:05:14
TOTALS:		24:15:46	241	00:15:49	72%	12	00:14:19
Agent Group 40:							

Courtesy Aspect Telecommunications, Inc.

Real-Time Reporting   ACDs provide MIS channels that allow supervisors to see what is going on in real time. The screen can be switched from agent to group statistics in most systems. Group statistics show such variables as the number of calls in queue, the length of average and longest wait, number of abandoned calls, and other such variables during the current reporting period (usually 30 minutes to one hour). Agent reports show for each agent the current status (talking, available, unavailable, wrap-up, and so on), how long the agent has been in that status, number of calls handled, and number of outgoing calls during the reporting period.

Many supervisor's terminals can be programmed to show alerts in different colors or screen intensity. For example, thresholds could be set for length of time in an unavailable mode, which is normally used for relief periods. The name of an agent that was within the prescribed interval would be shown in green, one that was a few minutes over would be yellow, and one that had overstayed the upper threshold would be red. Color displays aid the supervisor in monitoring staff and costs.

NETWORKED CALL CENTERS

In a company with multiple call centers, efficiency can be achieved with networking—often enough to more than pay the cost of facilities between the centers. If ACDs are connected either with PRI or a proprietary networking interface, they can exchange load and workforce information across the D channel, switching calls across the voice channel where agents are available. An ACD experiencing an overload can check other centers, reserve an idle agent, and pass the call across the network.

The major IECs offer a call allocation service for distributing calls to ACDs that are not fully networked. In the static call allocation model, the administrator informs the IEC's signaling control point (SCP) of the percentage of calls to allocate to each center. (Refer to Chapter 11 for a discussion of an SCP.) With dynamic call allocation, the ACDs are networked together with a signaling channel, or they use the PSTN to obtain status information and communicate it over a D channel to the IEC. With call-by-call allocation, the ACD informs the SCP on a real-time basis of which center should receive the next call. This application, which is often outboard of the ACD, may be a CTI device as discussed in Chapter 23.

INTEGRATED PBX VERSUS STAND-ALONE ACD

A key question facing an ACD owner is whether to select a stand-alone or a PBX-integrated system. Both systems have their applications and advantages, and the selection should be made with the factors in this section in mind. A third choice, which we will discuss in a later section, is the central office ACD, (CO-ACD), which is on the LEC's premises.

The first factor to consider is functionality needed. ACD is a processor-intensive application, and some PBXs will lack the capacity to support a large call center. The cost of a stand-alone ACD will be two to four times the cost of a PBX-integrated ACD, so small centers that are operating on a tight budget will find it difficult to justify the cost of a stand-alone system. In any call center the cost of the equipment is only a fraction of the total cost of operating the center. If the features or productivity gains of a stand-alone system are needed, cost should not be an overriding concern.

A second question relates to the nature of the center and the need to integrate it with regular telephone features of the rest of the organization. If the call center operates as part of a larger group, and must transfer and receive calls from the rest of the organization, a PBX-integrated ACD will be easier to set up and administer. Stand-alone ACDs can be connected via tie lines to a PBX, but full networking between the two will not be available. In either case, the Achilles' heel of some stand-alone ACDs is the difficulty of transferring calls between the PBX and the ACD. In some centers the ACD agent requires two telephones, one for the PBX and one for the ACD. The ACD usually can route calls to the voice mail on the PBX, but in a nonintegrated system there is usually no way to turn on the ACD user's message waiting light.

Another question is how the call center is being deployed. If the company has an existing PBX and the call center is a new application that is being added to the company, it can almost certainly be added to the PBX more easily than acquiring a new stand-alone ACD. If the existing PBX is unsatisfactory and must be replaced, the cost per position of an integrated ACD will be less than the cost per position of a stand-alone ACD. If the PBX is satisfactory and can be retrofitted for an ACD package, this also will be less expensive than purchasing a stand-alone system. If, however, the PBX cannot be retrofitted, a stand-alone or CO-ACD should be considered.

Very large applications, including systems that require networking, often require stand-alone systems. In large applications, such as airline reservations systems, the ACD requirements may outstrip the capabilities of a PBX. Generally, stand-alone ACDs offer more processing power, more sophisticated software, and better reporting capabilities than PBX ACDs. PBXs have been increasing in processing capacity in the last few years, and networked ACD is offered by most of the major systems.

The amount of communication with non-ACD users behind a PBX is another factor that should be considered. An integrated ACD has all the features of the PBX and all the features of the ACD, which usually facilitates call transfer within the total system. If ACD and non-ACD users share central office trunks, DID trunks, and 800 lines, the PBX attendant or the DNIS feature can route calls to the ACD. If the trunks terminate directly on the ACD and there is little intermachine communication or transfer requirement, a stand-alone ACD will be effective.

OTHER CALL DISTRIBUTION ALTERNATIVES

Although the ACD is the appropriate vehicle for most call centers, other call distribution alternatives are available. Besides UCD and call sequencers, which were mentioned in the introduction to this chapter, many LECs offer ACD from the central office.

Central Office ACD

With CO-ACD agent sets and supervisory consoles are mounted on the user's premises and extended from the central office on local loops. The user's capital investment is reduced, and the LEC takes care of maintenance. If the CO-ACD is trunk-rated, the LEC applies a software restriction to limit the number of incoming trunks. If the tariff is not trunk-rated, a CO-ACD can offer the advantage of reducing trunk costs for the user. This can, however, be a disadvantage because the user may lose some control. For example, one way of handling temporary overloads is to let incoming calls ring several times before answering and queuing them. This way, 800 costs are reduced and the caller may be less critical of service because the length of time in queue is reduced. Another way of limiting calls is to choke down the number of trunks to return a busy signal to the callers. Unless the LEC offers complete customer control of the system software, some of this flexibility will be lost.

The features of a CO-ACD are similar to the features of a stand-alone unit. The advantages and disadvantages compared to customer-owned equipment are essentially the same as those of Centrex versus a PBX, as discussed in Chapter 25.

Uniform Call Distributors (UCDs)

Most PBXs and hybrids offer a uniform call distribution package as a standard or optional feature. A group of agents is defined as a UCD group. The PBX queues calls when all agents are busy, provides music or an announcement, and routes the call to the first available agent. A UCD is similar to an ACD, but it does not provide the flexible response capability of an ACD. One method of call distribution in UCDs is to route calls in sequence, starting with the agent at the head of the sequence, which means that workload is not equalized. The agent at the head of the hunt pattern receives the largest number of calls, while the agent at the end of the sequence receives calls only when all other agents are busy.

The UCD supervisory terminal is less sophisticated than with ACDs. Most UCDs use a display telephone for the supervisory terminal, so the reports and status of agents and service that an ACD provides are not available. The routing and overflowing capabilities are also less flexible with a UCD. The flexible response features discussed earlier are generally not available with a UCD. Reports are limited to what is programmed into the system and are considerably less useful than those provided by a full ACD.

On the positive side, UCDs are much less expensive than ACDs. In most PBXs the UCD software is a standard feature, and ordinary telephone sets can be used for the agent terminals. If the company does not have an extensive call center and does not require extensive reports, UCD is an inexpensive way to improve customer service. Also, the UCD can take advantage of features that the PBX provides such as voice mail.

Call Sequencers

Call sequencers are the least sophisticated call distributors. Unlike ACDs and UCDs, which deliver calls to idle agents, sequencers require the agent to press a button to select the call. Most call sequencers do not force an agent to pick up a call. Different colored lights show which call has been waiting the longest. Therefore, although customer service and productivity usually are improved by answering and holding calls automatically, there is no way to ensure that the workload is evenly distributed.

Sequencers are not integrated with the telephone system, so it is difficult to take advantage of features such as voice mail. It also may be difficult to transfer calls from a call sequencer to a PBX extension; frequently a complex sequence of switchhook flashes is required. Sequencers are most effective when the work group has other duties besides call answering. For example, a dispatch center might receive service requests from customers, make remote tests, and dispatch service people. The only portion of the job that involves answering calls is the incoming requests, which may be only a small fraction of the total process. The sequencer is valuable because it can answer calls when all agents are occupied and indicate which call has been waiting the longest.

APPLICATIONS

Selecting the correct call distribution system and applying it intelligently is critical to the success of the call center. In most applications, the arriving calls are customers or potential customers, and the objective of the organization is to treat them professionally and promptly. This section discusses some aspects of selecting and evaluating a call distribution system.

Standards

There are no call distribution equipment standards as such. External interfaces are regulated by the same standards that cover PBXs, but internal operation is governed by proprietary standards.

Evaluation Criteria

Most of the criteria listed for evaluating PBXs also apply to call distribution equipment. For example, the questions of redundant processors, backup battery supply, universal port structure, cabinet capacity, and other such criteria should be evaluated. If call distribution is part of a PBX, all the criteria discussed in Chapter 21 apply along with the criteria discussed here.

Type of Call Distributor

The first issue to resolve is whether the application requires an ACD, a UCD, or a call sequencer. If an ACD is required, a second issue is whether a stand-alone unit or one integrated with a PBX is most suitable. The following is a list of generalizations, most of which have exceptions in some product lines.

- If the office is served by a key telephone system, use a call sequencer.
- If the incoming call load is handled by a pool of people for whom answering incoming calls is only one of a list of duties, choose a call sequencer.
- If handling incoming calls is a primary duty, the office is already served by a PBX, detailed reports are not important, low cost is important, and workload equalization is unimportant, choose a UCD.
- If handling calls is a primary job, detailed reports are important, and the call center must be closely integrated with non-ACD operations in the office, choose a PBX with integrated ACD.
- If the call center is large and needs few PBX functions, choose a stand-alone ACD.

The dividing line between call distribution applications is not distinct, and product features are constantly changing. In selecting a product, it is important to match the product to the application, bearing in mind that much of the improvement achieved with a call distributor may come from changing existing procedures.

System Architecture

The architecture of most call distribution systems is similar within a particular category, but there are important differences among systems. In sequencers, the generic program is usually contained in ROM. In ACDs and UCDs it is contained in volatile memory and loaded from a disk. These criteria are important considerations selecting the architecture:

Type of Trunk Interface   Consider what types of trunks the system needs to interface. The most common types are loop start, ground start, PRI, BRI, T-1, E&M, and DID. Also consider whether the system can interface two-way trunks when both inward and out-calling are required.

Port Capacity   Consider the number of ports in the system. Port types to be included are trunk, agent, supervisory, CRT, and CTI. Also consider whether the architecture permits universal or specialized slots for ports.

Open Architecture   As Chapter 23 discusses, CTI is an important method of increasing productivity and improving call handling in a call center. Even if CTI is not planned initially, the system should provide the capability.

Traffic Capacity   ACD agent stations are designed for a much higher level of call arrivals and port occupancy than regular PBXs, and therefore consume more switch capacity. As with other switching systems, the principal evaluation criteria are expressed in terms of call completions per hour and CCS per line.

Type of Display   The type of display for both agents and supervisors can affect productivity. Color displays are less tiring for the operator, and the color can be used to display call criteria. For example, a call that has been on hold for a long time can be presented to the agent in red. Supervisory displays can show critical criteria such as low service levels in red. Supervisory graphs can be displayed with the evaluation criteria highlighted in different colors. Also consider whether the display is proprietary or whether a standard terminal or personal computer can be used. Split-screen displays permit the operator to view more than one call at a time and are particularly useful to a supervisor who monitors multiple queues.

Networking Capability   Large organizations with multiple ACDs may be interested in networking, which is the ability to connect ACDs over tie lines or PRI circuits. Networked systems should have the ability of passing call-specific information such as caller identification from one system to another.

Queuing and Routing Algorithms   The most flexible systems provide true if-then-else operators to program the treatment a call receives as it enters the queue. It is important to know how many steps can be programmed in the vector for a call. It is also important to know what criteria, such as time of day, day of week, number of calls in queue, and length of oldest waiting call can be used as the test points in the script. Determine whether the system has conditional routing and if skills-based routing is available.

Switch Architecture   The architecture of the switch is fully as important in an ACD as in any other type of switching system. Factors to considered include:

- Is the switch expandable in modular increments?
- Does the switch have built-in maintenance features that improve reliability?
- Is redundancy available? If so, what elements are duplicated?
- Does the switch use open architecture to permit easy interface with another system for enabling CTI?
- Does the switch have universal port architecture?
- How many separate queues does the system support?
- How many agents does the system support?
- How many supervisory consoles does the system support? Can more than one queue be monitored from a single terminal?

External Interfaces

Most ACDs and a few UCDs and call sequencers have interfaces to external systems. For example, consider whether the system must interface with a database on a mainframe, minicomputer, or desktop computer. Callers are given several strategies for completing their calls if the system has interfaces to voice mail, automated attendant, or an interactive voice response unit. The system may require an interface to an outbound telemarketing unit, or the outbound unit may be included as a portion of the ACD.

Features

Many of the PBX features discussed in Chapter 21 are equally important for call distributors. The following are some features that should be considered in evaluating systems.

Agent Call Access and Display   ACDs can automatically cut the call through to an agent, while some UCDs and call sequencers require agents to press a key to receive the next call. The most effective systems display for the agent such information as how many calls are waiting and, when the call is connected, how long the caller waited in queue.

Overflow Capability   Consider whether it is acceptable for callers to remain in one queue or whether they should overflow to a second queue. If overflowing is required, determine whether it can be based on length of time in queue, position in queue, trunk group over which the call arrived, caller identification, or other criteria. Also, consider whether the system provides look-ahead and look-back capability and whether the system can dynamically reassign agents to different queues to react to changes in load.

Outbound Calling Capability   Whether a feature of an ACD or of a stand-alone unit, outbound calling capability is important to companies that have telemarketing functions or other functions such as collections that require a volume of outgoing calls. The system should be able to interface with a user database. Other important features include computer-controlled pacing of agents, predictive dialing, some type of reliable detection of called party answer, and rescheduling of unanswered calls.

Wrap-up Strategy   Many applications require time for the agent to wrap up the call after completing the transaction. For example, it may be necessary to complete an order before taking the next call. ACDs should offer one or more ways to determine the duration of wrap-up:

- ◆ *Manual*. The agent presses the Available key to accept another call.
- ◆ *Forced*. The system provides a set amount of time for wrap-up, then forces the agent to available status.
- ◆ *Programmable*. The ACD supervisor can create a program to vary the amount of wrap-up time.

The strategy for handling wrap-up can have a significant effect on productivity. With the manual method, an agent can extend wrap-up time and reduce productivity. With the forced system the machine fails to recognize the variability in the amount of wrap-up time needed for different types of transactions. If the system is programmable it can vary the amount of wrap-up time allotted for each type of transaction.

Reporting Capabilities

Most companies receive as much value from the reports a call distributor creates as they do from the functionality of the unit itself. The following factors should be considered:

Record versus Status Orientation   A record-oriented system provides call status after completion. A status-oriented system provides calling information in real time. With a record-orientated system it is possible to determine how long a caller waited in queue after the transaction is finished, but not while it is in process.

Data Accumulation   ACDs have different periods of time during which they can accumulate statistical information. Hourly and subhourly information is valuable for making immediate force adjustments or changing switch parameters such as wrap-up time. Daily and monthly information are useful for load forecasting and making long-term force adjustments. Consider how the information is accumulated and displayed.

- ◆ Can information be extracted in some standard file format to analyze in a spreadsheet or database management system?
- ◆ Is information stored in a volatile medium such as random access memory, and if so, is it lost in case of power failure?
- ◆ Does the system collect information on how the call is handled in the second queue when it overflows?
- ◆ If the call is transferred or routed to give the caller an opportunity to leave a voice mail message, are the statistics continuous, or is the call treated as a fresh call and statistics counted anew?

Management Software   Many systems provide software for management analysis. These programs fall into three categories:

- ◆ *Scheduler:* This software, which may be combined with forecasting software, helps the supervisor prepare schedules. The program analyzes force requirements by hour of the day and day of the week and optimizes available staff to meet the requirements.
- ◆ *Tracker:* Tracking software dynamically reviews service levels based on the number of staff logged on and the volume of calls arriving. Force requirements are calculated based on service objectives. The

software keeps track of absences and number of agents required per hour and calculates predicted service levels based on workload and the available force.

◆ *Forecaster:* Forecasting software reviews historical data and predicts call volume, workload, and force requirements.

Transaction Audit Trail   A transaction audit trail may be an important feature for an ACD manager. The audit trail time stamps each event in the transaction from start to finish. The system identifies the agent and position handling the call and leaves a trail of the times the call was transferred or put on hold. The amount of wrap-up time is registered, and any telephone numbers, such as supervisor or wrap-up position, dialed during the transaction are recorded. If the system is equipped with DNIS or DID, the system logs the number the caller dialed. If the call fails for such reasons as inadequate facilities, excessively long wait, or poor queue management, this feature helps the supervisor diagnose the cause.

Report Types   The following reports are typically produced by the more sophisticated systems:

◆ Percent abandoned calls.
◆ Percent all trunks busy.
◆ Percent calls answered in X seconds.
◆ Percent all positions busy.
◆ Percent position occupancy.
◆ Longest waiting time in queue.
◆ Average number of calls in queue.

Consider whether the reports are produced in real time or only after the fact. Real-time reports should display on the supervisor's console while calls are in progress, although they may be updated at intervals of 10 seconds or so. Most call distributors include basic reports as part of the system's generic program. These are usually not user-programmable and seldom satisfy all users' requirements. Many call distributors provide a port to an outboard processor, which is usually a personal computer. The following questions should be considered:

◆ Are the fixed reports provided with the system sufficient? If not, does the ACD provide a port to an outboard processor?
◆ Is statistical information stored for some period, or is it lost each time the data is refreshed?

- Can the user change the reporting period—for example, from hourly to half hourly update?
- If agents shift between queues, do their production statistics follow them as individual agents, or do the statistics remain as part of the queue? Is it possible to track both?

Call Center Supervisor's Information

A major reason for acquiring a call distributor is to provide the call center supervisor with real-time information about workload and service. Some systems use a video display terminal for the supervisor's console. Low-end systems may use a display telephone or audible or visual signals or provide no information at all to inform the supervisor when certain thresholds are exceeded. The following criteria should be evaluated:

- What type of display is provided?
- Does the display alert the supervisor to critical situations with different colors, intensity, inverse video, or other means?
- If the display is variable, can the user change it to suit individual preference?
- Are thresholds programmable?
- How frequently is the information on the display refreshed? Can the user change the refresh interval?
- Is the information display programmable or fixed?
- Does the display show the supervisor how long each individual agent has been in the current state?
- Can the supervisor remotely force the agent from one state to another—for example, from wrap-up to available?
- Can the supervisor monitor calls without being detected?
- If the system provides an audible monitoring tone to the agent, does the caller hear it also?

Agent Terminals

Most call distributors will function with single-line telephones for the agent terminal. In some applications single-line sets are satisfactory, but the additional information that can be obtained from a display feature set is worth the extra cost for most call centers. The following are some criteria to use in evaluating agent terminals:

- What information is displayed on the agent's set? For example, does it show how long a call has waited in queue?

- If the agent set lacks a display, how is information such as incoming trunk group identity or the queue from which a call overflowed conveyed to the agent?
- How are agents informed in real time of critical service indicators such as waiting-time objectives exceeded?
- How do agents perform such functions as logging on and off, holding and parking calls, and changing to and from available state?
- Do the sets have enough buttons to provide push-button access to all critical features?
- How do agents transfer calls to one another and to an attached PBX?

Queue Management

The degree of flexibility the system offers in managing the way calls are routed to particular queues and the way agents are assigned to queues is fundamental to call center management. Low-end systems may have only one fixed queue and little or no ability for the administrator to reprogram the system. High-end systems have complete flexibility in changing routing to meet changes in work-load conditions. Consider the following:

- Can call routing be changed? If so, is the programming language easy to understand?
- Is a method provided for off-line testing the routing of incoming calls?
- Can the routing be changed in real time?
- If the system provides priority treatment for certain classes of callers, how is the priority recognized? How many priority classes are there?
- When a call is given priority treatment, how is the priority administered? For example, is the caller moved to the head of the queue, placed at the end of the first third, and so on?
- Can the system look ahead to evaluate congestion before overflowing to an alternate queue? If so, does the system predict waiting time in the next queue based on a dynamic evaluation as opposed to merely counting calls?
- After the system looks ahead to an alternate queue, can it look back to the primary queue?
- If a call returns to a previous queue, is it given priority treatment based on total waiting time?
- Can the supervisor remotely assign agents to another queue to relieve congestion?
- Can an agent log on to more than one queue?
- Can the queue routing be varied by time of day, day of week, and other such variables?

Incoming Call Handling

The least effective call distributors provide little flexibility in handling incoming calls. Calls are answered and placed in queue, and the caller may not hear anything until an agent is available. The most flexible systems offer callers a choice. These are some questions that should be evaluated:

♦ What does the caller hear after the initial announcement: music, promotional announcements, silence?

♦ Is a second announcement available? How many different announcements can be programmed in a routing script?

♦ Can the system vary the announcement based on time in queue or other such variable?

♦ Does the system inform callers of their position in queue?

♦ Can the caller choose to exit and leave a message in voice mail?

MANUFACTURERS OF AUTOMATIC CALL DISTRIBUTION EQUIPMENT

Stand-alone ACDs

Aspect Telecommunications

Rockwell International

Teknekron

Telecom Technologies

Call Sequencers

Automation Electronics Corp.

Dacon Electronic, Inc.

Innings Telecom

MetroTel Corp.

Viking Electronics

PBX-Integrated ACDs and Uniform Call Distributors

Virtually every PBX on the market includes UCD as a no-charge feature, and ACD as an extra-cost feature. See Chapter 21 for listing of PBX manufacturers.

CHAPTER

23

COMPUTER TELEPHONE INTEGRATION

The motivation for computer telephone integration (CTI) is not difficult to understand for anyone who has been frustrated by the lack of intelligence in telephones. The telephone is a marvel of simplicity for just one thing: placing ordinary telephone calls. Everyone grows up knowing how to use one, and for its basic purpose it is intuitive. Advance beyond the basics, and the telephone's limitations are obvious. To use a simple example, suppose you are expecting important telephone calls from your boss, your spouse, and a key customer. You have recorded a message in your voice mail that you want your spouse to listen to. You want your boss routed to a subordinate, who has important information to pass along, and you want the customer forwarded to your wireless telephone while you are on the manufacturing floor. All other calls should go to voice mail.

Instructions such as these could be given to a secretary, but if calling line identification is furnished with the call, why waste the secretary's time screening calls? Visualize a graphical user interface on your desktop computer. You click the telephone numbers of the three expected calls, and drag them into the appropriate destination. Now you are free to roam the plant, knowing that these calls will be routed correctly when they arrive.

The industry has tried to compensate for the awkward interface by putting feature buttons and alphanumeric displays on the telephone, but people tend to use only the few features they have learned, and ignore the rest. Few users know how to perform functions they use occasionally, such as setting up a multiparty conference call or transferring a caller to another station's voice mailbox. Other desirable functions are difficult or impossible on most systems. In the earlier example, you wanted to leave a message in your voice mail and allow your spouse to listen to it from outside the system. This is impossible without human assistance today, but only because the PBX has not been programmed to support it.

The desktop computer's graphical user interface (GUI) is accepted by nearly everyone as an intuitive way to operate unfamiliar features. By integrating the telephone and the computer, a GUI screen can bring to the telephone the intelligence that it lacks. With CTI, to set up a multiparty conference call you simply open a directory, click on the names of the people you want to add to the conference, and drag them across the screen to an icon representing a conference bridge. The telephone system, under control of the computer, takes care of the rest. If you want to play a voice mail message for someone in a different system, you can set up a telephone call, open a computer screen that displays messages, select the one you want, and click the play button on the screen.

Although the term CTI is relatively new, host computers and switch manufacturers have had interfaces available for several years. The costs have been high, and only the largest call centers have been able to justify them. Now, new products are diversifying the applications and bringing the cost within the reach of many businesses. Seeing new opportunities opening, hundreds of developers are working on new products that marry the computer and the telephone to make them both easier to use. The CTI industry is in its infancy, and has few international standards. Most standards have proprietary origins, but many are open and available for developers to create new applications. This chapter discusses the applications and the enabling technologies that will enable CTI to be one of the next major growth industries in telecommunications.

CTI TECHNOLOGY

As with so many aspects of telecommunications, the CTI industry offers numerous ways of accomplishing the objective. Because the different approaches to CTI are rooted in proprietary software, the major vendors tout their methods as superior to those of their competitors. As a result, prospective users find it difficult to separate hype from reality. This section explains the different approaches to CTI, and suggests where they are most effective.

To cut through the competitive claims, you must first understand your application and exactly what you want to accomplish. Then the choice of architecture

T A B L E 23–1

CTI Products of Principal PBX and Computer Manufacturers

PBX and ACD Manufacturers	Trade Name
Aspect	Application Bridge
Lucent Technologies	Adjunct Switch Applications Interface (ASAI)
Ericsson	Application Link
Fujitsu	Telecommunications Computer Services Interface
Mitel	MiTAI
NEC	Open Applications Interface
Northern Telecom	Meridian Link
Rockwell	Transaction Link
Siemens/Rolm	CallBridge CSTA
Computer Manufacturers	
Digital Equipment Co.	Computer Integrated Telephony
Hewlett Packard	Applied Computerized Telephony
IBM	CallPath Services Architecture
Tandem	Call Application Manager

will narrow quickly. With the multiple combinations of switch and computer pairs, many applications will be available using only one or two approaches, which makes the choice easy. Second, if you are starting with a modest CTI application, consider where the future might lead and attempt to match the architecture of your system with applications that are likely to be programmed for it in the future. This isn't easy to do, but most vendors are willing to discuss their future directions under a nondisclosure agreement.

Most of the differences in protocols are of interest primarily to developers. The using organization is concerned with the cost and functionality of the application, and which interface the developer uses is mostly of academic interest. As an analogy, in buying software the buyer usually doesn't care whether the developer has written it in C, COBOL, Visual Basic, Pascal, or any of dozens of other languages, provided it contains the features, the price is justified, and it meets performance expectations.

Every major switch and computer manufacturer provides some form of open application interface to PBXs. Table 23–1 lists the trade names of the major PBX and computer interfaces on the market. These interfaces accept some form of programming language, usually proprietary to the manufacturer, to enable computers and the PBX to carry on a dialog. This form of interface,

Mainframe to PBX Link

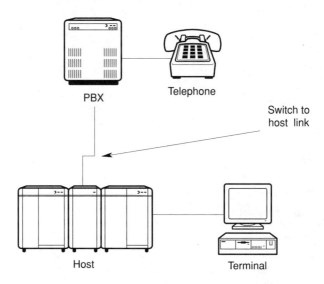

shown in Figure 23–1, has been available for several years, and it has usually been used to link mainframe computers to the PBX. Consequently, only the largest companies have employed this form of CTI.

One alternative for integrating the computer and telephone is to build the telephone into a desktop computer add-in card. Analog add-ins are easy, and have been available for several years. Digital add-in cards can either emulate a proprietary digital telephone or an ISDN telephone. Cards that interface proprietary digital ports on a switch often contain more functionality than ISDN cards because switch manufacturers have not included all the proprietary telephone functions in their ISDN interface ports.

The computer market is now shifting away from mainframe computers and toward servers and desktop computers. As a result, several important new application programming interfaces (APIs) have emerged. An API is an interface that software developers provide to enable other developers to write programs that interact with their program.

First-Party Call Control

Two terms that CTI buyers need to understand are *third-party call control* and *first-party call control*. The latter is a direct interface between the user's personal computer and the telephone system. It is called first-party or phone-oriented call control because the telephone is connected to the computer, and

FIGURE 23–2

Microsoft TAPI

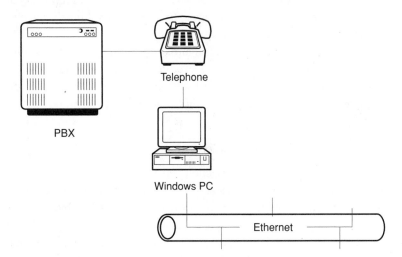

computer keyboard entries directly control call processing. With third-party, or switch-oriented, call control the user communicates with the application program, which controls the telephone system through a separate interface. First-party call control is better for small sites because less expensive hardware is needed. Switch-oriented call control is more adaptable to large sites because it isn't necessary to buy hardware and software for each desktop.

Microsoft's Telephony Applications Programming Interface (TAPI) is the industry's primary example of first-party call control. Figure 23–2 shows a typical architecture using TAPI software in the computer. TAPI is a link between a Windows-equipped PC and the telephone instrument. TAPI enables an application to set up and tear down calls, monitor progress, detect CLID, and activate features such as hold, transfer, conference, park, and pickup. It can redirect and forward calls, answer and route incoming calls, and generate and detect DTMF signals. TAPI enables multiple applications to share a single phone line. For example, voice mail and fax can both listen for incoming calls of different types on the same line. Enabling these devices to share a single telephone line allows the user to make more efficient use of the line.

TAPI is a protocol stack that operates on IBM-compatible personal computers (at this writing not on Macintosh). The interface is usually an EIA-232 connection between the telephone and the computer. The telephone can, however, be a board plugged in an expansion slot of the PC, or the telephone can plug into a jack in an expansion card.

TAPI is designed to run on the individual PC. The TAPI interface is ideal for small offices and those offices lacking Novell servers. It is independent of the telephone network type, and can interface analog, ISDN, or proprietary digital telephone ports in a PBX. A typical application is controlling the telephone from a PC screen for call logging, answering, and directory dialing.

One limitation of first-party call control is that the functions work only on certain classes of computer. For example, a function that runs under Microsoft Windows will not operate on Macintosh and vice versa. A second limitation is that telephone functions do not all work if the power is turned off on the PC.

Third-Party Call Control

In third party call control the connection between the computer and the telephone is logical, not physical. Telephony Services Application Programming Interface (TSAPI) is a third-party control interface developed by Novell and AT&T using CSTA (computer supported telecommunications application) standards. TSAPI is a coding standard, not an architecture or feature set. It is a Netware loadable module (NLM) that resides in a Novell server. The application is programmed to the TSAPI specification, and TSAPI, in turn, communicates with the PBX manufacturer's open application interface.

CSTA, upon which TSAPI is based, specifies call control services that can be used by any API. Basic call control services include establishing and tearing down calls, answering calls at a device, and activating and deactivating switch features. The features specified by CSTA include, for example, call hold, call pickup, call transfer, conferencing, and consultation hold. The server sends instructions to the switch, which returns event messages to indicate action taking place such as completed transfers, terminated and originated calls, message waiting indications, and so on.

TSAPI's main application at the present time is in call centers. Although TSAPI may run on servers other than Novell's, at this point its purpose is to enable Novell servers to control switches of multiple vendors. Separate drivers are needed for each type of PBX. Figure 23–3 shows how TSAPI fits into a Novell server. A card supporting the physical interface plugs in a server slot. For example, some products use a BRI interface.

Other Standards

Unfortunately for the industry, many developers have treated TSAPI and TAPI as mutually exclusive interfaces, but they are not. They are competing APIs that developers can choose to implement their applications. TASPI applies only to Novell-based applications, and TAPI applies only to Windows-based

FIGURE 23-3

Novell TSAPI

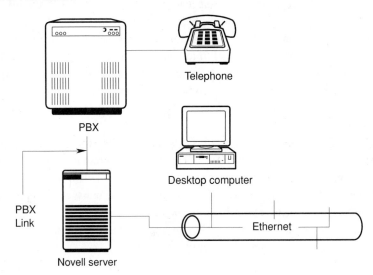

applications. Although the majority of desktop computers run Microsoft Windows and the majority of LANs use Novell servers, these limitations mean that the market has room for both interfaces. From the discussion above, it can be seen that both TAPI and TSAPI perform many of the same functions. TMAP, a program developed by Nortel, translates between the two applications so that developers can write to either interface and operate with the other.

Universal Serial Bus

PCs today come equipped with one or two serial ports, which limits the number of serial devices that can be connected. The universal serial bus (USB) is an expansion scheme that replaces the serial cards in a PC. It enables CTI by providing a high-speed serial connection to the PC's bus. As many as 63 devices can be connected to the same bus. It supports a variety of applications such as printer, plotters, modems, and other such devices. Computers manufactured from late 1986 on, may offer USB as an option

Signal Computing System Architecture

SCSA is an open software model for telephony systems. It was originated by Dialogic, which manufactures voice boards for personal computers. SCSA supports multivendor distributed applications that share a common pool of server resources. SCSA hardware consists of a digital bus supported by a switching fabric. Developers can transport and switch 64 kb/s data streams to resources in a PC.

The SCSA software model, known as telephony applications objects (TAO), defines software APIs. Because the software model is independent from the hardware model, developers can implement SCSA over different hardware models as well as over the SCSA hardware model. SCSA is a general architecture for managing real-time or time-critical resources across a network. For example, it could manage a limited pool of speech recognition or text-to-speech engines over a network. It enables voice mail developers to develop other related applications such as E-mail and fax into their platforms.

WinSock 2

WinSock 2 is a data communications protocol that does for data circuits what TAPI does for call control. WinSock 2 provides a programming interface that allows applications to become independent of both the network and the protocol by providing a uniform interface to the application. Winsock 2 supports isochronous (time-sensitive) information such as voice and video over networks. Its quality-of-service support enables an application to request a connection with a guaranteed minimum bandwidth.

Multivendor Integration Protocols

MVIP is a series of standards to integrate telephony with computer-related functions for automating communications. MVIP is a low-level protocol for hardware interconnect that enables developers to integrate different telecommunications and voice technologies in the PC. It consists of a standard bus, switching, and operating systems.

Digital Simultaneous Voice and Data

Digital simultaneous voice and data (Digital SVD) enables users to talk and exchange data simultaneously during the same session. The voice is digitized, compressed, and multiplexed with data to produce a bit stream that is transmitted over the phone line with a special 28.8 kb/s modem. Digital SVD modems are compatible with applications that presently use conventional modems. These modems facilitate such applications as desktop conferencing and image sharing over an analog telephone line.

CTI APPLICATIONS

This section discusses some of the many applications that CTI enables. The industry has only begun to develop applications. In the next few years, managers can expect to see a flood of labor- and time-saving features such as the following.

Hospitality

The earliest application of CTI is the PBX hospitality package. Although this application was widely used before the term CTI had been accepted by the industry, it illustrates the way computers and the PBX can interact to improve productivity. In a hotel (and to some degree in hospitals), interaction between the central computer and the telephone is important. When a guest checks into a hotel, the desk clerk enters name and credit information into the computer terminal. The computer interacts with the PBX to perform functions such as these

- ◆ Show the room as occupied in the PBX database, and unlock restrictions on the telephone for placing outgoing calls.
- ◆ Show the guest's name in the PBX database so it displays on telephones, enabling staff to refer to guests by name.
- ◆ Activates the guest's voice mailbox.
- ◆ Integrates chargeable call information in the computer database so it is available for inquiry to the desk or over video display in the room.

On checkout the process is reversed. The desk clerk can inform the guest of voice mail messages that have not been listened to, and transfer them to another box. Toll calls are transferred from the call-accounting system to the guest's bill. The room phone is deactivated for outgoing calls. When the room has been cleaned and is ready for occupancy, housekeeping can dial a code, which the PBX transfers to the computer as room-ready status.

Call Centers

A major application for CTI is in call centers. Nearly every call center has three major elements: the telephone system, the computer system, and the human agents. Without CTI the agent is the bridge between telephone and computer systems. The agent identifies the call, determines the purpose of the call, and pulls up the appropriate screen. Upon call termination the agent manually enters information to complete the call, including data that could be furnished through direct link to the telephone system. If the call must be transferred, the caller often must repeat information that was given to the first agent. With CTI, the system enters much of the information, and some is entered by the caller. For example, in call centers that have an IVR the caller enters the account number and the details of the transaction. If he or she must transfer to a live agent, the purpose of the call is often evident from the details of the transaction, which is still available on the screen.

The following features are provided by most call center CTI applications. The details and equipment vary with the product, but these are the most common features and benefits.

Screen Synchronization   This feature, also called "screen pop," is the most common CTI application. It delivers a call to an agent together with the customer's account screen. Screen pop is enabled by identifying the caller from the calling telephone number, which is delivered by ANI, or from a customer-dialed account number that is captured in an IVR or call prompter. When a call must be transferred to another agent the information on the original agent's screen is automatically sent to the receiving agent. This eliminates the need for the caller to repeat information. A similar feature enables more than one agent to share the same screen on a conference call.

Work Logging   This feature records the actions handled by CTI. Some products allow the agent to add information to the reports to create customized activity reports.

Terminal-Extension Correlation   This feature associates an agent terminal with ACD identification codes. It enables the computer to send calls to selected agents wherever they are sitting. It also may automatically log the agent onto both the computer and the ACD with a single entry.

Call Blending   In a call center that has both inward and outward dialing the system can automatically assign agents to inbound or outbound calls based on load. See the discussion of predictive dialers in the next section.

Expert Agent Selection   Once a caller is identified, the call can be routed to an agent who has the skills to handle the call most effectively. If the caller has a preferred agent, calls can be queued on that agent based on the routing algorithm and predicted waiting time. The call also may be routed to the agent who handled the customer's last call on the theory that this agent is familiar with the problem and requires less explanation. Expert agent routing can convey a feeling of personal service to customers who call frequently and are routed with each call to the same select group of agents.

Callback Request   This feature enables the caller to dial in a number for a callback in lieu of waiting in queue. If the caller indicates a desire for callback, the system prompts for a callback number. When an agent is available, the customer's screen is sent to the agent and the call is automatically outdialed. This feature saves the time it takes to transcribe callback requests from voice mail.

Aliasing

ANI (automatic number identification) matching is a frequently used way to identify callers and route calls. It is not, however, foolproof. Callers may call from multiple locations: home, the office, pay phones, cell phones, and so on. A list of aliases may be built in the database, but these also are not foolproof. Some ANIs may be the trunk number behind a PBX, which presents the CTI application with an impractical list of alias telephone numbers. In other cases the billing telephone number may be sent as the ANI, which makes it impossible to determine which of several customers is calling. The most effective way of identifying the caller is by capturing the account number in an IVR or call prompter.

Some CTI applications dynamically create a cross-reference file correlating customer ANIs with account numbers. A similar feature allows the agent to select the calling customer's account from a CTI screen of multiple accounts that use the same number.

Predictive Dialers

Predictive dialers are among the first of the widely accepted CTI applications. Used in telemarketing and collections, predictive dialers review the status of a group of agents and deliver calls set up and ready to talk without effort on the agent's part. The dialer selects numbers to call from a database, determines the probability that an agent will be available by the time the call is connected, and dials the number. The objective is to deliver connected calls to agents as they end the previous call, while minimizing the probability that a call will be connected before an agent is available. The system is able to recognize and re-schedule calls to busy numbers, those that don't answer, and in some products, those that terminate in voice mail or answering machines.

One version of dialer connects to the PBX or ACD via T-1 or analog station ports and transfers calls to agents with a switchhook line transfer. The most effective dialers have a CTI connection that enables agents to log in or out from a terminal, go into wrap-up or unavailable state from the telephone, and operate as part of a call-blending operation.

With call blending agents can automatically be assigned to either incoming or outgoing calls, depending on load, agent availability, and other such factors that enter into routing decisions. Call blending needs CTI to enable the predictive dialer to see agent status and workload on incoming as well as outgoing calls. Agent statistics showing total agent performance can be shown by the switch. Unless the predictive dialer and switch are connected through CTI, outgoing statistics will be separate from those the switch produces for incoming calls.

Integrated Messaging

Many products are moving toward an interchangeable and convertible in-basket. As discussed in Chapter 24, universal messaging allows people to listen to, read, and create voice mail, E-mail, and fax messages from a telephone or a computer. The office telephone system is clearly an important player. The key question is where the message center resides and how it is enabled. In the telephone-centric version of the message center, it resides in voice mail, with fax calls sent to voice mail by the switch, and E-mail messages arriving over a LAN. In the LAN-centric version, voice mail is a server on the LAN, and the universal in-basket resides in a computer. In fact, in this version, the telephone switch also becomes a server on the network. The chances are high that this architecture will eventually replace the present PBX, but for the next several years the circuit-switched PBX architecture will persevere, and conflicts and incompatibilities will remain. The universal in-basket will take a variety of different shapes depending on the owner's view of the network.

JUSTIFYING CTI

CTI applications usually require custom programming. Applications are developed to match many of the popular customer contact computer packages with the most popular PBXs, but custom-programmed databases will always require custom CTI programming. As the industry matures, off-the-shelf applications will be increasingly available.

CTI is easiest to justify in a call center, where it brings the following benefits to the customer and company:

- ◆ Customer service in call centers is improved because customers do not have to enter or speak their account number more than once, and because calls are handled more rapidly.
- ◆ Revenue can be enhanced. By capturing the calling telephone number, the company builds a database of valid telephone numbers that can be correlated with buying habits and used for telemarketing. Numbers can also be used for tracing delinquent accounts.
- ◆ Call center agents' job satisfaction is improved by relieving them of the need to handle boring and repetitive details such as asking for and entering account numbers, and waiting for response screens.
- ◆ Agent productivity improves by eliminating the keystrokes and time it takes to query the caller and enter the account number. Average talk

time is reduced and toll-free call costs are reduced because of the reduced holding time. Abandoned calls may also be reduced by making more agents available to answer calls.

◆ The calling number of abandoned calls can be captured, enabling agents to return them, improving customer satisfaction, and potentially reducing lost revenue.

CTI can often be justified by direct cost savings. Caller identification takes 15 to 20 seconds in most call centers. The shorter the agent's talk time, the larger the number of calls they handle per shift, and the easier it is to justify CTI. The cost of CTI bears little relationship to the size of the center in many cases, so large call centers can distribute the costs among more agents than small ones, and can more quickly realize the benefits. Table 23–2 shows CTI savings at 20 seconds per call for varying call lengths assuming a 7.5-hour shift, 60 percent agent occupancy, and a $20 per hour loaded agent cost. With short calls, the setup time becomes a higher percentage of total time, so CTI is easier to justify.

Also, bear in mind that the CTI industry is in its infancy. Many developers will fall by the wayside or be absorbed by their competitors. Consequently, CTI applications should be justified on the basis of a short payback.

In other cases it isn't necessary to justify CTI based on cost savings. For example, most PC users have some form of personal information manager (PIM) that contains names, addresses, telephone numbers, and other information on client and vendor contacts. With a proprietary telephone and without CTI, the PIM cannot dial telephone numbers. Also, on incoming calls CTI can automatically bring up a contact screen so you can refresh your memory about the last call. The PIM can automatically log certain details about this call such as the date and time, and the number from which the call was placed. The convenience of having such an interface is difficult to justify based on hard dollar savings, but the convenience is of tangible value.

STANDARDS

CTI is still in its infancy. Standards are available, but most of them are propriety standards that are either licensed by their developers or they have been submitted to an open industry group that now manages their future development. Many products use standard interfaces such as BRI for the link between the computer and the PBX, but the code sets are proprietary.

T A B L E 23–2

Cost Justifying CTI in a Call Center

Agent cost per hour	$20
Length of shift	7.5 hours
Agent occupancy	60%
Call setup time, seconds	20

Average Call Length, Minutes	Calls Handled per Shift	Minutes Saved with CTI	Dollars Saved per Shift with CTI
0.5	540	180	$60.00
1.0	270	90	$30.00
1.5	180	60	$20.00
2.0	135	45	$15.00
2.5	108	36	$12.00
3.0	90	30	$10.00
3.5	77	25	$8.33
4.0	67	22	$7.33
4.5	60	20	$6.67
5.0	54	18	$6.00
5.5	49	16	$5.33
6.0	45	15	$5.00
6.5	41	13	$4.33
7.0	38	12	$4.00
7.5	36	12	$4.00
8.0	33	11	$3.67
8.5	31	10	$3.33
9.0	30	10	$3.33
9.5	28	9	$3.00
10.0	27	9	$3.00

A proprietary standard isn't necessarily undesirable. For example, the personal computer industry standard architecture (ISA) was developed by IBM. Its widespread and universal acceptance as an open architecture was largely responsible for the success of the personal computer and its successors. Several major revisions such as the EISA (expanded standard industry architecture) and several successive local bus architectures have enhanced the original design. Unlike international standards that seem to move at glacial pace, proprietary standards can adapt more rapidly to technological advances. On the minus side, a proliferation of incompatible standards may be the result. Such is the case with CTI.

SELECTED DEVELOPERS OF CTI PRODUCTS

Most of the major PBX and computer manufacturers produce CTI interfaces, and many of them provide software and hardware products as well. These are listed in Table 23–1. PBX manufacturers are listed in Chapter 21, and ACD manufacturers in Chapter 22. Voice-processing equipment vendors are listed in Chapter 24. E-mail developers are listed in Chapter 26, and facsimile manufacturers in Chapter 27. This section lists a few of the hundreds of developers of specialized CTI products.

Voice Processing Boards

Brooktrout Technology
Cobotyx
Dialogic
Excel
Micom Communications
Mitel
Moscom
Rhetorix

CTI Software

Active Voice
Answer Software
Applied Voice Technology
Aristicom International
Aurora Systems
Davis Software Engineering
Dialogic
IBM
Intel
Microsoft
Natural Microsystems
Novell
Q.Sys International
Teltone

Predictive Dialers

Davox

Executone

Teltone

Information Access Technology

Predictive Dialing Systems

Rockwell

Teknekron Infoswitch

24

VOICE PROCESSING SYSTEMS

Many people have a love-hate relationship with voice processing. We love the convenience of getting voice messages when we are away from the office, and rail at the frustration of reaching only voice mail when we are in a hurry. We endure the endless prompts of miscast automated attendants, but enjoy the convenience of checking our account balance 24 hours per day. Voice-processing systems are here to stay, yet they are the most misused of telecommunications technologies. Properly designed and applied, voice-processing systems can save a great deal of time and relieve phone tag by making their users accessible while they are away from the phone, but improperly used systems generate phone tag and frustrate customers.

It is not the purpose of this chapter to discuss how to manage voice-processing technology; *The Irwin Handbook of Telecommunications Management* contains information on managing voice processing. It is worth noting, however, that voice processing is often rejected by managers who believe they risk losing business by subjecting their customers to automated attendant, voice mail, and interactive voice response. While it is true that voice processing can and does result in dissatisfied customers, the bulk of the problem lies in improper system design. Properly designed and used voice-processing systems make it easier for people to interact by enabling communications outside real time and across time zones.

In the context in which we use it in this chapter, voice processing includes the following technologies:

◆ Voice mail
◆ Automated attendant
◆ Interactive voice response (IVR)
◆ Integrated messaging
◆ Voice recognition

These technologies are listed in order of their maturity. Voice mail has become such a mainstream application that most new PBXs and many new key systems are purchased with integrated voice mail. Automated attendant, a close cousin of voice mail, enables callers (or forces them, depending on your point of view) to route themselves by selecting from a menu.

IVR carries the process a step further by enabling callers to converse with a computer using the DTMF pad on their telephones. As anyone who has designed or used such a system knows, however, the DTMF pad has shortcomings that limit its use. The triple-letter key combination does not make an ideal keyboard. Furthermore, although the number of rotary telephones is dropping, not everyone has a DTMF telephone. Obviously, there has to be a better way.

Communicating with voice mail through the keypad is frustrating when there are key combinations to remember and prompts to endure. The industry solution to this problem is integrated messaging, which brings voice, fax, and E-mail into the same personal computer platform. Using a graphical user interface, it's possible to select and handle any of these features on the same computer screen. The industry is working on media conversion techniques, which will enable users to create or retrieve messages using their choice of telephone, fax, or computer. The weak spot in media conversion today is voice recognition, which is primitive, but advancing.

Voice recognition is an up-and-coming application that can be considered now for limited use. Equipment can understand simple spoken commands, and can recognize numbers and some simple words. This makes it possible to replace automated attendant. For example, a dialog could read "for sales say 1, for customer service say 2, etc." This capability can solve the problem of directing calls for users who do not have DTMF telephones. Managers should watch voice recognition closely and be prepared to adopt it when it can help them reduce costs or improve customer service.

Even given the occasional misapplication, voice-processing technologies have enormous potential for improving customer service and cutting costs. Voice mail makes it possible to leave messages across time zones, keeping voice inflections intact and avoiding the misunderstandings that so often result from passing messages through a third party. Interactive voice response, makes it possible for people to receive information outside normal working hours and without enduring the delays that often occur during peak hours. The organization saves labor costs, employees are relieved of the mind-numbing task of repeatedly delivering the same information, and customers do not have to wait.

The automated attendant enables callers to route their own calls quickly to the appropriate department without lengthy oral exchanges, and enables the company to eliminate the cost of direct inward dialing and attendants. Everyone benefits from voice processing if the applications are chosen carefully and administered intelligently.

Integrated messaging is an excellent tool that enables users to link their desktop computers with the telephone system. With it users can handle messages more efficiently. As the technology progresses they will be able to retrieve E-mail messages by fax or voice readout, convert facsimile to text, voice readout, or E-mail, and, eventually, covert voice mail messages to any of the text forms. Many of these conversions are possible today, and lack only voice recognition to achieve universal convertibility.

This chapter discusses the elements of the five principal voice-processing technologies and describes the features available. The Applications section discusses typical uses and the precautions that must be observed in applying them. The chapter also covers digital announcers. Although these are not technically voice-processing devices, they have many of the same elements and are used behind PBXs and ACDs to deliver announcements to callers who dial a particular number or are placed in queue waiting for a service process.

VOICE MAIL

Voice mail has potential for improving internal communications in most organizations. It is no secret to anyone who has worked in an office that a high percentage of telephone calls are uncompleted because the called party is away from the desk or on the telephone, and the frustrating game of telephone tag begins. Voice mail enables people to exchange messages and often serves as a satisfactory substitute for real-time communication. This is called *asynchronous communication,* in contrast to *synchronous communication* where information exchange cannot take place unless both parties are simultaneously available. Calls can be exchanged across time zones, messages can be left and retrieved quickly when only a few minutes are available between meetings or airplanes, and the group broadcast feature enables a manager to convey information to everyone in the work group with a single call.

A voice mail system is a specialized computer that stores messages in digital form on a fixed disk. Figure 24–1 shows the Nortel Meridian Mail,

FIGURE 24–1

Nortel Meridian Mail

Courtesy of Nortel, Inc.

Voice Mail Integration with a PBX

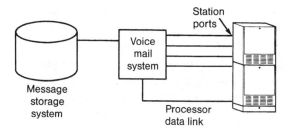

which is fully integrated with the Meridian One PBX, which occupies cabinets higher in the stack. In voice mail systems, the voice is digitized and compressed to a much slower rate than the 64 kb/s signal the PBX uses in its switching network. Messages and personal greetings are stored on a hard disk that maintains the voice mail operating system and system prompts and greetings. A processor controls the compressing, storing, retrieving, forwarding, and purging of files. Voice mail systems connect to a PBX through the PBX bus or through station ports, as shown in Figure 24–2.

Voice mail systems are grouped into three categories:

◆ Stand-alone
◆ Nonintegrated
◆ PBX-integrated

All three types share the same basic architecture, but different manufacturers design systems for different applications. Furthermore, virtually no standards for the voice mail user interface exist, and few serious attempts have been made to develop them. Therefore, the transfer of experience from system to system on the part of both users and callers is minimal.

Stand-Alone Voice Mail

In a stand-alone configuration, a PBX is unnecessary. The voice mail system can be connected directly to central office trunks or T-1 and used as a service bureau that offers voice mail services to outside callers. Service bureau voice mail systems normally have large capacity. They are accessed through the public telephone network, and the system operator charges a flat fee plus usage. Since the incoming ports are shared by all users, the system provides a way to route calls to the appropriate mailbox. The most effective method makes use of direct inward dialing or, over 800 lines, using Dialed Number Identification System (DNIS). These methods of called party identification are not always available, however. For example, calls may be trunked over private lines to a voice mail system in a distant city. In such cases, the caller may be prompted to enter a code, which may be the last four digits of the telephone number or a mailbox number that the user has printed on a business card.

Service bureau voice mail systems are excellent for users who need a few mailboxes and cannot justify the purchase of a private system. They are also effective for users who are out of the office a great deal and have no need of message-waiting lights to indicate the arrival of a call. The lack of message-waiting lights is one of the chief drawbacks of stand-alone systems for people who are regularly in the office. A second drawback may be the lack of station identification, which requires callers to know and enter the mailbox number. A third drawback is the dead-end nature of the medium. When a call enters the mailbox, the caller's only options are to leave a message or hang up.

Nonintegrated Voice Mail

Nonintegrated voice mail has many of the characteristics of a service bureau. The system is connected behind a PBX, as shown in Figure 24–2. A shared group of PBX ports is connected to the voice mail system. Users can forward their calls to voice mail, but the system cannot identify the forwarding station. Therefore, the caller is prompted to enter a mailbox number, which is usually the last three or four digits the caller dialed. A caller who dials the company's main listed number asks for a user by name and reaches an extension that has been forwarded to voice mail. If the callers hear a prompt asking for the extension number to be entered, they are confused. Users do not have message-waiting lights, so they must dial in to check for messages. Because of these drawbacks, nonintegrated systems are disappearing from the market.

Integrated Voice Mail

PBX-integrated systems integrate with a specific PBX to provide features that enhance the value of the voice mail system. A fully integrated voice mail system offers several features that require direct communication with the PBX:

◆ *Return to attendant.* A caller, upon being transferred by the system into voice mail, can transfer (escape) from voice mail to a message center or switchboard operator by dialing digits on a DTMF telephone.

◆ *Multiple greetings.* Voice mail users may have different greetings for internal versus external calls, or a different greeting when the phone is busy than when it is not answered. With time-of-day control the called party can vary call coverage and personal assistance options.

◆ *Called party recognition.* Calls can be transferred directly into voice mail when the called PBX extension is busy or does not answer. If the called party does not answer and the call forwards to an extension that is also forwarded to voice mail, the greeting of the original called party is heard.

◆ *Message-waiting indication.* When a message arrives in a user's mailbox the voice mail system and PBX activate a message-waiting light or apply stutter dial tone to remind users to retrieve messages.

◆ *Alphanumeric prompts.* The voice mail system may prompt users who have a display phone with alphanumeric instructions.

◆ *Security.* The telephone system and voice mail may interact to prevent would-be hackers from dialing invalid extension numbers to place fraudulent calls.

◆ *Internal Caller Identification.* The name of a person calling from within the system is inserted into the message header.

The first of these features allows the caller to escape from the voice mail system and leave a message with an personal attendant, such as a departmental secretary. Lacking this feature, a caller can reach only the PBX attendant.

The second feature, multiple prompts, conveys valuable information to the caller and allows the station user to treat callers more personally. If a caller hears a greeting that states the called party is on the telephone, the caller's action may be much different than if he or she hears a message stating the called party is out of the office. Furthermore, many companies are willing to have internal calls answered by voice mail but want external calls answered by an attendant.

The third feature, called-station identification, is a major flaw of many poorly integrated systems. With full integration, if calls cover to voice mail, callers always hear the greeting of the party they originally called, even if the call forwards to another station that is also forwarded to voice mail. With some systems the caller hears the greeting of someone other than the called party, which is confusing.

Message-waiting light illumination is of no concern to the caller, but greatly affects voice mail's utility to the station user. This feature turns on a message-waiting light when a message reaches the mailbox. With an electronic telephone that displays the light on a feature button, the user may have only to press the button to retrieve messages. Without the feature, the user must periodically call voice mail to check for waiting messages. This often results in delays in returning calls. For users who are rarely in the office, message-waiting light illumination is of little or no value, but for users who are frequently in the office, it is an essential feature. Some systems substitute a short burst of stutter dial tone as an alternative, which is useful for off-premise stations or telephones that lack a message-waiting lamp.

Alphanumeric prompts on display telephones are easier to use than audible prompts that many systems provide. Users can press buttons to replay, forward, delete, or save messages. Voice mail security is a matter of great concern to all companies that have it. If the proper blocks have not been installed, toll thieves transfer through voice mail to an outside line at the expense of the company. Integrated voice mail systems exchange information with the PBX processor to prevent such transfers.

Voice mail usage is enhanced by such features as internal caller identification, which inserts the calling party's name into the message header. If the system allows calls to be listened to outside the sequence in which they arrived, calls can be quickly scanned, and the most important ones handled first.

Developers use three principal methods of achieving integration. The first is through a direct data link from the voice mail processor to the PBX processor, and the second is through emulation of a display telephone. The third method is integration through a computer-telephony interface (CTI). This technology, which is discussed in Chapter 23, uses an open interface between the PBX and an outboard processor. The processor sends call-routing instructions to the PBX. The first method is faster and more efficient than the second, but it is usually available only to the PBX manufacturer or other manufacturers who pay a license fee. Anyone can reverse engineer a display set to integrate voice mail with another system, but the method is slower than the data link method. Furthermore, some features are available only through processor integration. For example, if a user has forwarded calls to a second position and that position is forwarded to voice mail, the second party's greeting may answer the call. CTI integration offers all the advantages of processor integration. Its main drawback is the expense of the interface. The extra cost may be considerable unless the interface is needed for other purposes.

To achieve integration, the PBX and voice mail system must be a matched pair. Many PBX manufacturers offer proprietary voice mail systems, but their systems are not the only ones to achieve full integration. Most voice mail service bureaus provide only nonintegrated service. It is, however, possible for the PBX and the service bureau voice mail system to be integrated over private lines, which can provide the same features as a directly attached system.

Voice Mail Capacity

Voice mail systems are sized by number of ports and hours of storage. The number of ports limits the number of callers that can be connected simultaneously. Ports are occupied while callers are listening to prompts, leaving messages, and while the called parties are retrieving messages. The number of ports required is calculated from the number of accesses and the holding time per access during the busy hour. (See Chapter 35 for an explanation of how to calculate voice mail port and storage requirements.)

Long-winded prompts, the inability to bypass prompts, and verbose greeting messages not only irritate callers but consume port and hard disk capacity. Designing the system with the correct number of ports is important. Having too many ports increases the cost of the voice mail system. Having too few restricts the ability of callers to reach voice mail and blocks users when they attempt to retrieve messages. Ports normally are added in increments of two to four at a cost of, perhaps, 10 to 20 percent of the original cost of the system.

The type of integration often affects the efficiency with which the voice mail system uses ports. A popular feature on many systems is *outcalling*, which is the ability of the voice mail system to dial the user's pager or cellular phone. This feature requires ports to handle both incoming and outgoing calls, and a problem may arise when a port is seized from both directions at the same time. This condition, which is called *glare* (see Chapter 11), causes the port to lock until both ends hang up. In a system in which the processors are linked together, glare is resolved by the processors without affecting the users. In a system integrated by display telephone emulation, it is usually necessary to provide separate incoming and outgoing ports, which increases the number of ports required.

The amount of storage required is highly variable and depends on the number of users and the number of stored messages per user. It also depends on whether disk storage capacity varies with the announcement messages and how efficiently the manufacturer packs the disk. Efficient packing algorithms compress the silent intervals so disk space is not wasted. As a rule of thumb in sizing voice mail systems, the average user takes about three minutes of storage for greetings and messages. A system serving 100 users, therefore, would require five hours of storage. Heavy users may require five minutes of storage on the average.

The voice mail system's purging algorithm also improves storage efficiency. The more effective systems inform the administrator when the disk is reaching capacity. Overage messages are manually or automatically purged after a specified time.

FIGURE 24–3

Networked Voice Mail Systems

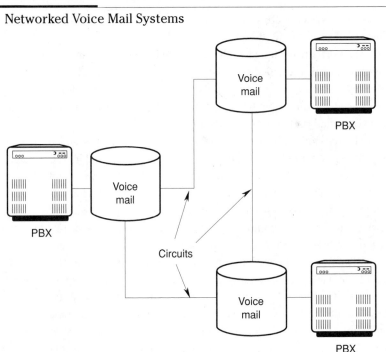

Networked Voice Mail

A large multisite operation can often bring its employees closer together with
networked voice mail. A cost-effective method of networking voice mail is to
terminate the voice mail on one PBX and connect other PBXs to the central
PBX with networking software. This software, which Chapter 21 discusses, is
an additional cost item that permits feature transparency across the network.
All voice mail functions are available to users outside the main PBX just as if
the voice mail system were attached to their PBX. The advantages of this
method extend beyond voice mail because it permits automatic callback, exten-
sion-to-extension dialing without access codes, and other features that are lost
in a tie line network.

A second method is networking the voice mail systems themselves as
shown in Figure 24–3. This method is effective when each site has many users.
Messages are stored on the local voice mail system, which reduces the tie line
traffic compared to a shared voice mail system. Networked voice mail permits
a user to have a mailbox in a distant PBX and have the messages delivered to
his or her own voice mailbox. For example, a sales manager could provide

local telephone numbers for key clients in several different cities. Managers with staffs in more than one location can maintain distribution lists and forward calls across the network.

Networked voice mail systems use analog or digital private lines or dial-up to flow messages between locations. Systems from different manufacturers can be linked through a standard known as Audio Message Interchange Service (AMIS). AMIS standards exist for both analog and digital interchange. The latter is the most effective because the digitized messages can be forwarded across the network without being converted to analog from the disk and then converted back to digital again for storage at the user's location. Note that the AMIS interface must be developed separately for each pair of PBXs, so universal networking within a company may not be possible because the interface has not been developed.

AUTOMATED ATTENDANT

The automated attendant is the most misused and maligned of the voice-processing technologies. The system answers the telephone and offers the caller a menu of choices such as "dial 1 for sales, 2 for service, 3 for engineering." A properly designed system can save time for callers, but systems with lengthy prompts and endless menus can be a source of great frustration to callers and may cause a loss of business. The automated attendant is usually a feature of a voice mail system, but the two are separable. Automated attendant functions can also be served by IVR.

Many companies prefer not to have their customer calls answered by an automated attendant, in which case it is a simple matter to establish separate trunk groups for customer and employee calls. The employee calls are answered by the automated attendant, and the customer calls by an operator. In most systems, pressing 0 returns the caller to the attendant. Most systems allow callers to bypass the prompts and route directly through to the desired function.

The simplest form of automated attendant is a substitute for direct inward dialing. The system prompts the caller to enter the extension number, if known, or to wait for an operator. This an effective tool that may reduce the extra cost of DID trunks if there is a high probability that the caller will know the extension number. When the calls are from the public, however, the extension number is less likely to be known, and the automated attendant may lengthen the average time it takes to process a call.

Name dialing can be used on most automated attendants and some IVRs. The caller dials enough digits of the last name to satisfy any ambiguity. The system responds with the called party's name, often in the person's own voice.

Large companies are likely to have several people with the same last name. The system may prompt for the first name, or it may offer a menu of choices.

The second use of automated attendant is to enable callers to route their own calls to an answering position by dialing a code from a menu of choices. The system manager must take great care in creating the menu, because it is here that callers most frequently experience frustration. If callers are offered too many choices at a menu level, they will fail to remember them and have to start over or return to the attendant. If the menu has many levels callers become confused or impatient with the delay. A good policy is to permit no more than four or five choices (plus return to the operator) at each menu level, and no more than two or, rarely, three menu levels. The system should be set up to allow callers who know the menu to dial the code immediately without waiting for the prompt. Also, if a numbering conflict does not occur, callers may be permitted to dial an extension number.

INTERACTIVE VOICE RESPONSE

Interactive voice response (IVR) is a system that prompts the user to enter information such as an account number via DTMF dialing. This information is passed to a host computer for processing, and a voice announcement unit reads the information back to the caller. Banks and credit unions use the technology to enable customers to obtain their account balances without waiting for an agent.

Besides being adopted by virtually every financial institution, IVR can be used for nearly any application where telephone service representatives receive a simple request from a caller, key it into a terminal, and read the results from the screen. The IVR enables callers to obtain the information themselves. As the first step, the typical session involves customer identification by account number and password, after which the IVR presents a menu of choices. Within the range of choices callers can send instructions to the computer or query the database. The IVR responds with audio announcements, confirming the transaction or delivering the information to the caller. One of the earliest applications was directory assistance for LECs. After receiving a request from the customer and looking up the number, the operator transfers the call to an announcement unit, which completes the transaction. LECs' intercept services are another example. When the caller reaches an intercepted number the system responds by announcing that the old number has been disconnected and reading the new.

The voice announcement technology of IVR falls into two categories. The most versatile method is voice synthesis, in which the characters coming from the computer are formed into words by a device that emulates the human larynx. The second form is a series of words stored in memory or on disk, which are triggered into the voice stream as needed. The synthesizer method is understandable, but the voice sounds accented. The stored voice method sounds natural, but the vocabulary is limited to what is stored.

IVR should be considered as more than just a voice response unit. It is an outboard processor that can perform many functions that otherwise would require computer-telephony integration. Here are examples of IVR applications:

Automated order entry and status inquiry: Callers can access databases to place an order from a catalog, check availability and price, and to check the status of pending orders.

Status verification: Callers can verify various types of information such as credit cards, employment, insurance, and other such information that can be delivered after the caller's right to access it has been confirmed. Frequent fliers, for example, can enter their account number to determine their current award status.

Time reporting and employee information: Field personnel can report time to a system that tracks attendance, provides information on accumulated leave, and other such employee information.

Dealer locator service: The IVR can prompt callers to enter their zip code for the name of the nearest dealer.

Fax on demand: The voice response unit can lead callers through a menu of document choices. When the document is selected, the system prompts for a fax number, and sends the fax immediately.

Student registration: Colleges and universities use IVR to enable students to register for classes from a DTMF telephone. Callers can use IVR to register for seminars and other events.

Appointment rescheduling: Clinic patients can reschedule their own appointments by calling into an IVR and identifying themselves by patient number. Clinics can also use the outdialing capability to remind patients of appointments.

IVRs can connect to analog ports, or they can connect through a CTI port for more versatility. The CTI connection is important when callers transfer from the IVR into a call center for additional transactions. The IVR should be able to send the caller's screen to the agent, so it is unnecessary to ask the caller for his or her account number to pull up a screen. Also, when the agent sees the screen before the transaction begins, it offers clues about the reason for the call.

With an integrated IVR, callers can be routed in ways that they may not expect. For example, a caller with a delinquent account might automatically be routed to the collections department whenever the account is accessed through the IVR.

INTEGRATED MESSAGING

Voice mail systems are rapidly taking on additional functions besides their traditional role of voice message storage and retrieval. Many voice mail systems include IVR. Other functions include fax store-and-forward, fax on demand, and fax integration with a desktop computer, which can be lumped into the category of integrated messaging. When a voice mail system is integrated with a desktop computer, usually over a LAN, the computer becomes a message center that increases the value of voice mail. With a nonintegrated system all prompting is audible. Users reach the point that they remember prompts, but the traditional voice mail system gives them no visibility as to the type or origin of messages. With a computer-integrated system all messages are listed in a window together with the type of message (E-mail, voice mail, fax, etc.), the time of arrival, and, if available, the sender's identity. The user can tell at a glance which messages are the most important and which have already been listened to. Users can drag-and-drop icons to save, forward, and delete messages. Fax messages can be displayed on the screen, filed on a computer, or sent to a printer with a few mouse clicks. E-mail messages can likewise be handled, and in time the computer will be able to translate voice mail, E-mail, and fax messages to any of the other media, making the computer a complete message-handling system.

Fax store-and-forward can be an easy way of giving everyone in the office personalized fax service. One drawback of fax today is its lack of privacy. A solution is to install a fax board in a PC and receive the messages on the PC's hard disk, but this requires additional PBX ports. Another solution is a fax server on the LAN, which is another set of equipment to administer. A third solution is a fax store-and-forward on the voice mail system. It requires additional ports and storage capacity on the voice mail, but each user administers his or her own fax system. A separate DID number can be assigned for fax, with the fax going directly to the voice mail. From there it can be handled like any voice mail message.

VOICE RECOGNITION

Pity the dilemma of the voice recognition developers. Teaching a computer to recognize voices is even more difficult than training it to recognize handwriting. Dialects, accents, vocabulary, and inflection all complicate the problem. Then there are homonyms such as *two, too,* and *to,* which can be distinguished only through context. Voice recognition takes computer power, and plenty of it, but the potential rewards are enormous.

At today's state of development a computer can be trained to recognize a wide vocabulary from a single speaker or a narrow vocabulary from the public. The latter approach has the most immediate application in telecommunications. Computers can recognize numbers with a reasonable degree of accuracy, and voice announcement equipment can repeat them back for verification.

Where a narrowly predictable range of words can be expected, voice recognition can substitute for an attendant. In a library, for example, the system could ask the caller to speak the department he or she wants. If the caller says "science" the system could prompt "do you want social science or physical science?" The answer is in a predictable range, allowing the system to carry on a dialog until it is clear where the call should go or until an attendant intervenes. Voice recognition can substitute for an attendant by asking callers to say the last name of the person they want to speak to. The result is not infallible, but the application is improving, and will get better.

The primary uses for voice recognition today are account number recognition and call routing. As the technology improves the applications will replace some of the mind-numbing tasks of today. Directory assistance is high on the list. Customer service centers can greatly multiply their effectiveness by doing a better job of screening and routing calls. For example, the voice recognition system could ask several questions that enable it to route calls to an expert. By contrast, today's expert agent applications in an ACD have limited screening capability. Callers could be asked to speak the name of a preferred agent or to say what service they want.

A powerful voice recognition application is transferring messages from a caller into an alphanumeric pager. The system should be able to accept a wide vocabulary, repeating words as they are entered, and prompting for any it does not recognize. As a fallback, the system could ask the caller to spell unfamiliar words. Although this application is not available at the time of this writing, it is one with exceptionally high payoff.

DIGITAL ANNOUNCERS

Digital announcers are the devices that play announcements over ACDs and UCDs and provide information announcements and announcements on hold. Unlike analog announcers that record messages on a tape or drum, digital announcers store messages in digitized form on chips. They are, therefore, not practical for long announcements because the cost of the device increases with the length of the message.

It is important to evaluate the application carefully before buying an announcement system. As with voice mail, the primary criteria in selecting a system are the amount of message storage and the number of channels required. It is also important to decide how the message will be changed. A permanent message such as an informational message about a company's product line probably would be recorded professionally and change infrequently. The message might even be encoded on a chip before it leaves the factory. Conversely, a school using an announcement system to distribute announcements about closures due to weather will want to record messages locally and, perhaps, from a remote location.

The control circuitry should determine when to connect the caller to the announcement. Some messages play only from the beginning; in other cases the listener can barge in on the message wherever it happens to be in a cycle. For example, if a promotional or informational message is being played, it would be appropriate to break in at only certain spots, and the message would play only once. Messages on hold might play repeatedly while the caller is on hold, or the system might vary the message depending on how long the caller waits.

Voice quality is another important consideration. As with voice mail, the higher the degree of compression, the lower the storage cost and the lower the voice quality. The best way to evaluate quality is to listen to a sample.

APPLICATIONS

Voice mail often is perceived as simply an expensive answering machine. It can be used as an answering machine, but a properly chosen and applied system can improve the effectiveness of the company's staff. The features, the most important of which are listed in Table 24–1, lend voice mail a flexibility that cannot be achieved without processor-driven or human intelligence. Its applications are too numerous to list and, in most cases, are self-evident. Some creative uses that are not so obvious are:

- ◆ A hospital offers voice mail for its patient rooms, allowing patients to receive messages while they are asleep, in surgery, and so on, and play them back at their leisure. In addition to being good for patient morale, such a system is a source of revenue for the hospital.
- ◆ A public telephone service provider allows a caller who reaches an unanswered or busy telephone the option of leaving a voice mail message for later delivery. This is a valuable service for callers who can't afford to wait.
- ◆ A hospital posts its job openings in voice mail, segregated by licensed, nonlicensed, and office occupations. Callers can listen to descriptions of the jobs available, and route themselves to the employment department to get more information.

TABLE 24-1

Common Voice Mail Features

Automated attendant: answers the telephone with a menu of choices that caller makes by pressing buttons on a DTMF telephone.

Broadcast: enables a user to send a message to multiple users in a defined group.

Bulletin board: enables the user to provide information announcements to callers.

Escape to operator: allows caller to reach a company operator or the called party's personal coverage position, usually by pressing the "O" key.

Forwarding with annotation: enables user to forward a message to another user's mailbox with an added message.

Multiple greetings: enables user to have different greetings depending on time of day or whether caller is inside or outside the system.

Outcalling: user can receive message notification on a pager or cell phone.

Respond: enables a user who has received a message from within the system to respond directly to the caller.

Voice prompts: provides both the caller and the user prompts on how to use the system's features.

◆ A food-processing plant provides guest mailboxes for its growers to inform them of recommended planting schedules and the availability of seed and fertilizer. During the harvest season, daily tonnage quotas are left in voice mail. Not only does this system eliminate calls to farmers who are away from the telephone, it also makes it possible for the processing plant to verify that the message has been retrieved.

To gain maximum benefit from voice mail, an organization must ensure that its employees do not abuse the service. The most frequent abuse is the tendency of some users to hide behind voice mail, using it to answer all calls, which they can return at their convenience. When used this way, voice mail aggravates instead of alleviates the problem of telephone tag.

A second form of abuse is the verbose greeting message. Callers are annoyed by the constant repetition of a message and detailed instructions on how to use a system that should be self-explanatory. Also, verbose greetings waste ports and disk storage. Improperly designed and applied voice mail and automated attendant systems have led to the creation of the term *voice mail jail,* which refers to the situation in which a caller is locked in the voice mail system and cannot escape to get personalized assistance. A well-designed system should be brief and clear in its instructions and should give callers a choice.

Many companies are reluctant to use voice mail with their customers because of the impersonality of the service. The first contact a company has with a new customer usually should not be through voice mail, but when the relationship is firmly cemented, voice mail can be as advantageous to a customer as it is to another employee. The key is to leave the caller in control. Many companies answer outside calls in person but give the caller the option of leaving a message in voice mail. Even if messages are taken manually, the receptionist can read them into voice mail, which is usually a more effective means of distributing messages than writing them on message slips.

Evaluation Criteria

Evaluations of voice mail, automated attendant, and audiotex systems should be based on the features outlined in Table 24–1 and on the criteria listed below, which include the most important features.

Integration with a PBX

The most important consideration in evaluating and using a voice mail system is the degree to which it integrates with the PBX. This is not to say that integration is always necessary; often, a stand-alone voice mail system is perfectly satisfactory. For most office workers, however, an integrated system provides essential features. The most sophisticated integration is available with products that use CTI integration, but the cost may be prohibitive except in companies with call centers.

Integration with Other Voice-Processing Applications

Voice processing equipment is available as an integrated unit containing voice mail, automated attendant, and IVR in the same package, or it is available as separate stand-alone units. The cost of an integrated unit is usually less than stand-alone units, but the separate systems may offer additional features and functions.

Compression Algorithm

All digital voice mail systems use some form of compressed voice technology to digitize and store messages and announcements. Part of the compression is gained by pause compression and expansion, in which the duration of a pause is coded instead of the pause itself. Voice mail systems use pause compression to speed or retard playback. If a listener wants a faster playback, the system shortens pauses; for a slower playback, it lengthens them. Also, the specific technology used for digitizing the voice affects the efficiency of the system. The more the voice is compressed, the less natural it sounds and the less storage space it occupies. Manufacturers have a choice between a natural-sounding system that takes more storage space and a more efficient system that sacrifices some intelligibility. The best way to evaluate this feature is to listen to the voice quality of several different systems and decide whether the lower cost of a highly compressed system is worth the decrease in quality.

Cost per Hour of Storage

The cost per hour of message storage is the most effective way of comparing costs of voice mail systems. The cost per hour of storage is the total time on the disk less overhead for such things as system greetings and user prompts. Cost is not, however, the only criterion for evaluating systems. It is possible to reduce the amount of overhead and increase the amount of available storage by providing only a system greeting instead of personal greetings. The personal greeting greatly improves the usability of the system because it permits users to leave messages that tell callers where they are and when they plan to return.

Port Utilization

The number of ports determines how many users can leave and retrieve messages simultaneously. Not all ports are necessarily available for full voice mail use. Some systems require dedicated ports for automated attendant. Some systems require separate ports for outgoing messages such as calls the voice mail system places to a paging or cellular radio system. Systems that integrate through display set emulation generally cannot resolve the glare situation that arises when users seize a circuit simultaneously from both ends. Therefore, such systems may require separate incoming and outgoing ports.

System Reports

System reports can be used to determine how efficiently the system is being utilized. Reports should provide information such as the following:

- ◆ Number of messages sent and received by a specific system user.
- ◆ Average length of messages by specific user or group.
- ◆ Percentage of disk space used.
- ◆ Busy hour traffic for various ports.
- ◆ Number of times all access ports are busy.
- ◆ Message aging by individual mailbox.
- ◆ Number of messages not deleted after specified time.

Personal Greeting

The personal greeting feature permits users to leave messages in their mailboxes. Although this feature uses more storage space than the system greeting, it improves user satisfaction. With a personal greeting, users can state where they are and when they will return and give callers any special routing instructions. If the user chooses not to use a personal greeting, the system should automatically provide a standard greeting.

Electronic Mail Integration
One form of electronic mail integration permits transfer of an E-mail message from a computer into the user's voice mailbox by synthesized voice. The primary advantage is that users can retrieve E-mail messages from a telephone; there is no need to have a data device to retrieve messages. This form of integration is available only from a specific computer and voice mail pair.

Networking Capability
This feature permits multiple voice mail systems to act as an integrated unit. From the system administrator's standpoint, an important issue is how to maintain distribution lists across the network. Some systems exchange messages that automatically update the other machines on the network.

Another important function of networked voice mail is how systems exchange messages. In some systems, the voice mail system can dial-up during low cost hours to exchange messages.

Security
The voice mail system must prevent callers from dialing invalid extension numbers, and thereby connecting through to trunks. The system administrator should be able to force password changes and to require passwords of a minimum length.

Evaluating Automated Attendant

In applying an automated attendant system, administrators should carefully consider its effect on callers. Although the number of people who lack DTMF dialing capability is dropping continuously, some still have rotary dials and must wait through the entire menu to reach an operator. Other callers will resent the automated attendant and may avoid businesses that use them. Some automated attendants offer a confusing array of menu choices and levels. Frequent callers usually have no problem navigating the menus, but a first-time caller may be baffled by the variety of choices. Any company considering an automated attendant will be well advised to study the application carefully, design it intelligently, test it thoroughly, and listen to the comments of callers.

The disadvantages of automated attendant notwithstanding, in many applications it makes good business sense. First, it is a good substitute for DID in a system where DID is not available, particularly during hours when the business is closed. Second, an automated attendant is often an excellent way to enable callers on 800 lines to reach an appropriate destination without an attendant. Although dialed number identification system (DNIS) is available in 800 service, not all PBXs can handle it, nor does the numbering plan allow dialing every station on a PBX.

A third application where the automated attendant is effective is with an overloaded switchboard. Instead of installing a second attendant console, the company may find that the automated attendant offers a quick solution to customer complaints of delays in answering. Remember that it isn't necessary to require callers to listen to a voice message to get the value from an automated attendant. Employees and frequent callers can be told that when the telephone is answered they can immediately dial an extension number. Other callers simply hear a short greeting and are queued to the human attendant, whose load is reduced by the callers who dial extensions directly.

Evaluating Audiotex

The audiotex feature of voice mail is a useful means of distributing information. Callers receive a menu of choices. They can select two or three levels of menu before reaching the desired information. For example, a university might disseminate class information via audiotex by listing the major courses of study—science, liberal arts, engineering—on the first menu, the field of study—biology, botany, chemistry—on the second menu level, and class—freshman, sophomore—on a third. If the menu choices are no more than the caller can easily remember, this can be an effective way of delivering information. The system should be designed to enable callers to interrupt the menu by pressing a special key such as # to repeat.

The most important criteria in evaluating audiotex are the types of host interfaces, applications development tools, and local databases supported.

Evaluating Interactive Voice Response

Many of the same criteria as voice mail can be used to evaluate IVR. A major exception is the fact that the interface between the host computer and the IVR must be programmed. So-called shrink-wrapped software is available for some applications, but most are custom programmed—often by a system integrator that provides the IVR hardware and the company's software application.

Voice quality, ease of programming, and quality of vendor support are important considerations in any type of voice processing. In addition, the following criteria should be considered with IVR:

Hardware Platform   The hardware platform will either be proprietary or based on a PC. The latter is less expensive to upgrade. Determine how many ports are available, what is the maximum capacity, and how much it costs to expand. When additional storage is required, can an industry standard hard disk be installed?

Software   Check the features that the system supports. Does the manufacturer have a good record of introducing new features to keep pace with developments on the market? What is the cost of new software releases? Has the application been programmed by a third party who makes it available for a fee, or is it necessary to train or hire an application developer? If the latter, how much does the development kit cost and how easy is it to learn? What kind of debugging tools are available?

Integration   Determine how the system interfaces to the PBX or telephone system. Is it a proprietary interface that is integrated with the PBX's processor, or is it a standard analog telephone interface? The former is more versatile, but the latter can be transported to other applications more easily. Determine how easily a caller can transfer to a live attendant. The system ideally should not require callers the reidentify themselves when transferring from IVR to an attendant.

Speech Generation Method   Does the system synthesize speech or use stored speech fragments? How natural does the speech sound? Can words or phrases unique to your operation be added easily?

Growth Capability   How many ports does the system support? Does it have the processor power to handle as many simultaneous callers as there are ports? Are you given the tools to measure and verify performance?

Reporting Capability   Does the system provide usage statistics? What form are they in? Can they easily be translated into service-related reports? Can the statistics be extracted while the system is active?

Evaluating Voice Recognition Equipment

The primary concern with voice recognition is its accuracy, which can be tested by observing the result with a variety of callers. Any system purchased today will undoubtedly be improved in the future, so determine the developer's commitment to continued research and development and find out how the updates are introduced, and at what cost.

Pay particular attention to the application. The best results will be achieved with simple applications that require recognizing a limited number of short words such as numbers, the alphabet, department names, and so on.

Evaluating Digital Announcers

Digital announcers are available as stand-alone devices that can interface to any PBX or public access line and as integrated devices that fit into a card slot in a PBX. The primary criteria in evaluating digital announcement systems are

- Voice quality.
- Storage capacity.
- Number of ports.
- Method of integration with the PBX—through the bus or through a port.
- Method of storing the announcement. Is it on RAM or PROM? How is it protected against power outage?
- Method of updating the announcement—locally, remotely, or through a professional service.

SELECTED VOICE-PROCESSING EQUIPMENT MANUFACTURERS

Voice-Processing Equipment

ABS Systems

Active Voice

Advanced Voice Technologies

Applied Voice Technology

Boston Technology

Centigram Corp.

Cobotyx Corp.

Compass Technology

Dialogic

Digital Sound

Digital Speech Systems

Ericsson Information Systems

Fujitsu Business Communications

Lanier Worldwide

Lucent Technologies

MacroTel International
MacroVoice
Microlog
Nortel, Inc.
Octel Communications
Siemens Rolm Corporation
Toshiba America
VMX
Wygant Scientific

Speech Recognition Equipment

Dialogic
Harris Corporation, Digital Telephone Systems Div.
Lernout & Hauspie
Lucent Technologies
Moscom
Natural MicroSystems
Rhetorex
Telecorp Systems
Voice Control Systems
Voice Processing Corp.

Digital Announcer Manufacturers

ATIS
Bogen Communications
Cobotyx
Code-A-Phone
Datel Electronics
Electronic Tele-Communications
Interalia
MacKenzie Laboratories
Metro Tel
Racom Products
Viking
Vodavi

CHAPTER
25
CENTREX SYSTEMS

Before the arrival of microelectronics and stored-program control PBXs, many large companies were reluctant to place PBXs on their premises. An electromechanical PBX required considerable floor space and a large electrical supply. In effect, these large PBXs were the equivalent of small central offices; in fact, many of them served more stations than dial offices in small communities. The switching technology they used—crossbar or step-by-step—was nearly identical with that used in a central office, and the maintenance requirements were high. To meet this demand for complex customer-switching systems, the LECs offer a central office-based service called *Centrex*.

Centrex blends the features of a PBX with those of ordinary business lines. A partition is established in the central office, and individual lines are run to the customer's premises. Within the partition, an array of PBX-like features is defined. Early Centrex systems operating on crossbar switches had few features; direct inward dialing (DID), direct outward dialing (DOD), automatic identification of outward dialing (AIOD), call transfer, and four-digit dialing between extensions were the most popular. As electronic central offices came into operation, features requiring intelligence in the switch were added. With electronic offices, it was possible to establish call pickup groups and provide features, such as call forwarding and speed dialing, that required a database and a processor.

Most LECs offer Centrex, including small office Centrex services, which many LECs today provide with as few as two or three lines. Most of these services no longer bear the name Centrex but go by a variety of trade names, some of which are recognizable by their inclusion of the letters *cent* somewhere in the name.

With the coming of digital central offices, many LECs began offering digital Centrex services, which more closely approximate the features offered by digital PBXs. Digital Centrex extends a digital signal from the central office to the user's premises. The digital loop permits Centrex, with a proprietary feature set, to offer single-button feature access on digital lines. By contrast, features in analog Centrex are accessed by depressing the switchhook to get a second dial tone and dialing a code or pressing a speed-dial button.

In both PBX and Centrex service, features that are accessible only through code dialing tend to fall into disuse. It is possible to assign the codes to speed-dial buttons on an analog set, but the features can be reprogrammed by users, so it is difficult to keep consistency in the feature pattern among stations on the system. Digital Centrex allows the administrator to assign buttons that cannot be changed by users.

In this chapter we will discuss the differences between Centrex and PBX and explore the applications for which each is most appropriate.

CENTREX FEATURES

In the United States, Centrex is offered almost exclusively on electronic analog and digital switching systems. Some residual Centrex systems may still be provided on crossbar switches, but the characteristics described in this section do not apply to them because crossbar systems do not have the flexibility or speed necessary to satisfy most users.

Most features of digital Centrex are identical with analog Centrex except digital Centrex integrates the telephone set with the central office line circuit. Digital telephones on premise provides push-button access to features. Stations equipped with single-line telephone DTMF sets have essentially the same features regardless whether they are served by an analog or a digital central office. Digital telephone sets can access more features, but their range is limited and cannot be extended with loop extenders and voice repeaters as can those of an analog station.

Special features, including T-1 to the IEC, tie lines, and 800 lines, can be terminated on Centrex in essentially the same manner as on a PBX. Also, Centrex switches can serve as an electronic tandem switch for a company's private network.

The following are some the major features available on Centrex:

Automatic identification of outward dialing: This feature records billable outgoing calls, allowing for departmental chargeback and tracking of unauthorized calls. It is similar to call detail recording in a PBX.

Call forward: Several call forwarding options are available to send calls from the called extension to another extension on busy, no answer, or all calls.

Call hold: Call hold permits users to put a call on hold and use the line for another call. Note that the hold button on analog sets holds the line in the set, but it is not available for another call. The hold button on a digital set or the hold feature code on either type of set holds the line in the switch so it is available for another call.

Call pickup: This enables the user to pick up calls directed to other stations that are defined as part of the user's pickup group.

Call transfer: This enables the user to transfer an incoming or outgoing call to another line. Off-system transfer allows transfer to a number outside the Centrex system.

Call waiting: Call waiting indicates to the station user that another call has arrived. The user can either answer or ignore the second call.

Class of service restrictions: This feature allows the system administrator to allow or deny station features and toll calling.

Direct inward and outward dialing: This permits station users to receive calls from outside the Centrex group and place outside calls without attendant assistance.

Distinctive ringing: This allows users to distinguish between internal and external calls.

System speed dial: Speed dial permits users to use abbreviated codes for dialing numbers.

Three-way conference: This permits users in conference with another station to add on a third party.

Note that although the capability for these features is available in the central office, LEC tariffs may impose additional charges for some of these features.

Advantages of Centrex

Centrex service provides each user the equivalent of a personal business line. A Centrex group is defined in the central office so that members of the group have a variety of PBX-like features. The following are the primary advantages of Centrex service compared to a PBX.

Reliability

Since Centrex service is furnished from a central office, the reliability is high. Central office switching systems are inherently protected against the failure of a processor or major common control equipment item. The Centrex subscriber does not have to worry about providing battery backup, duplicate processors, duplicate power supplies, or spare equipment for service restoration. The most likely cause of Centrex failure is cable trouble, which should be rare. Local central office switching systems average one hour's outage or less per 40 years in service, and even if the failure rate is higher than the average, the reliability is still higher than that of most PBXs.

Integration of Multiple Locations

To link multiple small locations with a PBX, customers must use off-premises extensions, tie lines, or a combination of both. For example, most school districts have a large central administration office and a combination of large, intermediate, and small schools. Centrex is often a less costly system for tying diverse locations together than using one or more PBXs connected with tie lines. Also, when some locations are too small to justify a PBX, they lose the features of a fully integrated system. Centrex provides uniform services to all locations, integrating them into a single system. It should be noted, however, that the range limitations of digital Centrex may preclude using digital feature sets in all locations. Also note that integrating Centrex between wire centers carries a higher tariff rate than when all stations are in the same wire center.

Reduced Capital Investment

Station equipment for a PBX costs about the same as it does with Centrex, but since the LEC owns and maintains the switching equipment, the initial capital investment required for Centrex is about half that required for a PBX. The monthly costs, however, are greater for Centrex.

Reduced Maintenance and Administrative Responsibility

The Centrex customer is relieved of maintenance and administrative responsibility except that associated with the station equipment. The LEC delivers a service and takes care of repair, record keeping, and system management. This factor is frequently overlooked by companies that underestimate the administrative work associated with owning a PBX.

Freedom from Obsolescence

PBXs have evolved through at least three and, by some counts, four generations, following similar evolutions in central offices. Centrex users have ridden through the evolution without feeling the impact of the technological change except insofar as it brought new features or required new telephone sets. Centrex may provide a relatively painless method of evolving into ISDN.

Virtually Unlimited Growth

PBXs grow in smooth increments up to existing shelf, cabinet, or system capacity. Growth beyond the capacity of one of these elements requires an investment that is sometimes substantial and sometimes requires changing the entire system. Centrex capacity is not unlimited, but if the LEC has sufficient notice, most growth requirements can be met without a major investment by the user.

Reduced Floor Space

Centrex service requires almost no floor space other than the space required for the distributing frames. This can be important in companies that have several thousand lines. In very large PBXs, the vehicle used for switching is usually a central office switch, such as the Lucent Technologies 5ESS or the Nortel SL-100, which is the PBX version of the DMS-100. Besides requiring floor space, these switches require a full-time trained staff to administer.

Short-Term Commitment

Although some LECs contract Centrex services, others offer them month to month. This can be important if future growth is uncertain or if the customer needs service for a short time while awaiting a more permanent type of service.

Centrex Drawbacks

Offsetting the advantages of Centrex are disadvantages that many organizations find outweigh the advantages.

Life Cycle Cost

The life cycle cost of a system is a composite of initial capital investment and recurring costs over the life of the investment. The cost of PBX service generally drops after the initial lease/purchase period of the equipment is over. Centrex costs continue for the life of the service and may increase with inflation. Subscriber line access charges are levied per line in a Centrex compared to a PBX, where they are levied per trunk. Centrex is usually less expensive at the outset than a PBX, but many organizations find a PBX to be less costly over the long term. The key factor in determining the break-even point between a PBX and Centrex is usually the length of time it is expected to be in service. Refer to *The Irwin Handbook of Telecommunications Management* for methods of calculating the life cycle differences between PBX and Centrex.

Features

Digital Centrex has most of the features available in a PBX. Analog Centrex has most of the important features, but they must be activated by code dialing. With either system it is difficult and costly to integrate a customer-owned voice mail or call accounting system. An integrated automatic call distributor (ACD) may be more costly or less effective in a Centrex system. Application program interfaces, which are available on some PBXs, are generally not available on Centrex, limiting the ability of a company to use services such as dialed number identification service (DNIS) and automatic number identification service or calling line identification.

Feature Costs

Though features equivalent to those in a PBX may be available with Centrex, there is often an extra monthly charge for each feature. Often the additional cost makes Centrex service noncompetitive with a PBX.

Add, Move, and Change Flexibility

Customer-controlled adds, moves, and changes are an important feature of PBXs that may be unavailable or available only on a reduced level with Centrex. With Centrex, if a terminal for making customer-controlled rearrangements is provided, the LEC often posts the changes on a batch basis. Batched changes are not posted immediately, so the changes are not effective until the next working day. With a PBX, the changes can be made instantaneously.

APPLICATIONS

This section discusses the principal factors to be considered in selecting between Centrex services and in choosing between Centrex and a PBX.

Analog Versus Digital Centrex

Most LECs provide a choice of analog or digital Centrex, although in a particular exchange only one or two wire centers may be equipped for digital Centrex. For most customers, the question whether an analog or a digital switching system provides the service is not relevant. The quality of service will be equivalent, and the use of Centrex to carry directly connected digital data will be rare. Differences in telephone sets, however, usually favor digital Centrex.

Analog Centrex is generally incapable of furnishing integrated key telephone service. The switch itself can provide functions such as call transfer, call pickup, and call hold, but the users must dial codes to activate the features. Attempts to train users to dial feature codes are rarely successful, so either the features fall into disuse or the enterprise installs key telephone equipment to provide the features.

Digital Centrex can support integrated key system features on proprietary telephone sets. This feature is the principal advantage of digital Centrex over its analog counterpart.

Feature Access

Many Centrex users apply key telephone systems behind analog Centrex to gain the advantages of button access to features. The equipment used behind Centrex must be designed to be compatible. It must, for example, provide a flash key to access central office dial tone for access to such features as call transfer.

Trunking Issues

In the past, one advantage of Centrex was the low probability of call blockage. LECs provided Centrex trunks to provide the same grade of service that the central office as a whole received. Compared to a PBX, where the number of trunks was an economic issue determined by the customer, Centrex often provided better service.

Now most LECs offer Centrex as a trunk-rated service, called network access restriction (NAR). In a trunk-rated service, the LEC interposes a software block that permits only the contracted number of incoming and outgoing calls to be connected simultaneously. Therefore, the quantity and cost of trunks required may be equivalent for both Centrex and a PBX.

Multiple Location Issues

Centrex allows an organization that spans an entire metropolitan area to function as if it were a single system. In a metropolitan area with only one wire center Centrex can eliminate the need for off-premise stations. In a multiwire center area both PBXs and Centrex require off-premises extensions, the cost of which may be identical, and in neither case is it possible to operate digital feature sets from remote locations. Some LECs offer a tariff for multiple-location Centrex, which provides the features between central offices at an additional charge plus mileage.

Ancillary Equipment Issues

Nearly half the PBXs installed today are equipped with voice mail, automated attendant, and call-accounting systems. These features are all available with Centrex, but they may be provided only as an extra cost option. Ancillary features may be charged per use by the LEC, which often makes them more costly than privately owned systems. Call-accounting information may be connected back to the customer over a remote line, or it may be provided from the LEC's automatic message accounting system and not be available on as short notice as privately owned call-accounting information.

Case History: A School District

School districts, banks, branch retail outlets, and other organizations that are geographically spread over a metropolitan area have unique communications problems that can sometimes be solved by Centrex. The school district in question served 41 schools and three administrative locations with off-premise extensions (OPXs) from a PBX located in the district administration office. The buildings are served by six different wire centers, of which four are operated by GTE, and two by US West. OPX and mileage charges resulted in costs per extension that exceeded the costs of business lines, but the convenience of four-digit dialing was deemed essential for the district.

A cost study showed the arrangement in Figure 25–1 be more economical than the OPX arrangement. One school in US West territory was the lone school in one wire center, so it was more economically left connected to the district office via OPX. The district office is connected to the serving central office with a T-1 tie line and a reduced number of DID and two-way trunks. Centrex lines are provided to all of the schools at a cost that is less than the cost of the OPX without the mileage charges. Each school has Nortel Norstar key systems that were previously connected to the OPXs, and are now connected to Centrex lines. The Norstar has flash-key compatibility, and works behind Centrex. T-1s are routed between GTE central offices to provide Centrex service to all of the schools. A T-1 tie line is run between Centrex services of the two LECs involved and from the GTE central office to the PBX. The resulting arrangement preserves four-digit dialing among all locations, and the monthly rate is approximately 20 percent lower than the OPX and mileage charges.

FIGURE 25-1

School District Centrex

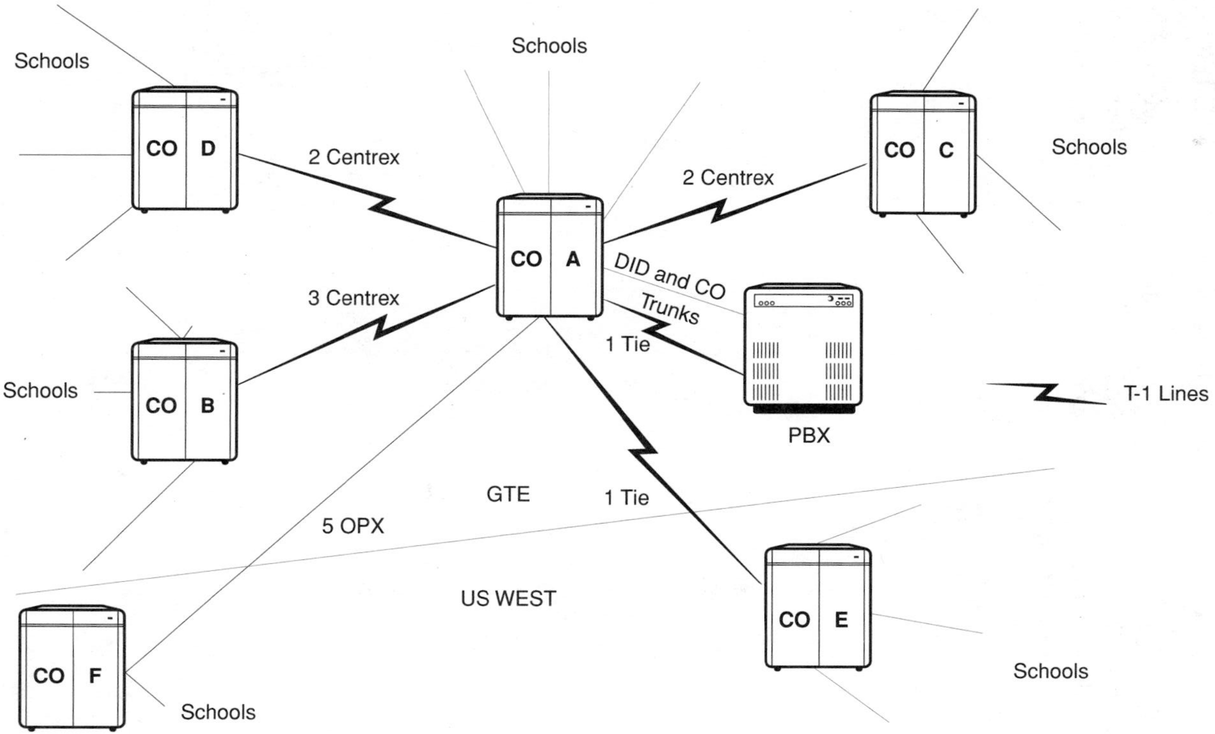

CO C

Schools

PBX

CO E

Schools

2 Centrex

DID and CO
Trunks

1 Tie

CO A

Schools

1 Tie

GTE

US WEST

T-1 Lines

2 Centrex

3 Centrex

5 OPX

CO D

Schools

CO B

Schools

CO F

Schools

CENTREX CPE EQUIPMENT MANUFACTURERS

The major central office equipment manufacturers, which are listed in Chapter 9, make the equipment that the LECs use to provide Centrex service. Most of the key telephone equipment manufacturers listed in Chapter 20 make Centrex-compatible key systems.

26

ELECTRONIC MESSAGING SYSTEMS

Messaging, which is defined as the use of computer systems to exchange messages among people, applications, and organizations, has paralleled the growth of desktop computers. When nearly every user has a terminal or computer connected to a network or host, numerous interactive applications develop that are otherwise impractical. Messages can contain any type of information such as voice, video, and files. Messaging systems are inherently asynchronous; that is, they do not require users to be simultaneously available to exchange information.

Messaging systems can be either voice or electronic, with video coming in the future. Voice-messaging systems, or voice mail as they are usually known, are commonly accepted in most companies. Computer messaging such as E-mail is used by most companies that have networked computers on a large percentage of the desktops.

The two types of messaging, voice and electronic, compete in only a narrow range of applications. Most companies use both, and, interestingly, integrated systems support each other. For example, either voice mail or E-mail can notify each other of the existence of a message on the other medium. Voice readout of E-mail messages is technically possible today, and in the future text readout of voice mail will be possible. Both types work across time zones and permit asynchronous communication, meaning the sender and receiver can communicate without being simultaneously available at the terminal device. Meanwhile, each medium has its own advantages compared to the other.

Voice mail advantages:

♦ The telephone, which is universally available, is used for retrieving messages.
♦ Addressing is simple: the 10-digit telephone number.
♦ It covers unanswered telephones without need for special training or equipment on the part of the caller.

E-mail advantages:

♦ A written record of the communication is produced.
♦ Simultaneous distribution to multiple users networkwide and across company boundaries is easy. Networking is inherent, not special as it is with voice mail.
♦ Messages can be dropped on a fax machine if the user lacks E-mail capability.
♦ E-mail can be used as the "envelope" for transferring a file to another user.
♦ Electronic messaging can tie the enterprise together with a fast, informal system that reduces the cost of mail, speeds the transfer of documents across departments and levels, and reduces the formality of the approval and review process. (Unless users apply this with discretion, this can be a disadvantage.)

This chapter discusses some of these applications and the protocols under which they operate. We will review the issues involved in implementing such applications as electronic mail, electronic data interchange (EDI), and data interchange between similar applications such as word processors. Voice messaging is covered in Chapter 24.

MESSAGING SYSTEMS

The terms messaging system and E-mail are often used interchangeably, but to be strictly accurate, E-mail is only one of the types of information that are communicated across a messaging system. Messaging is a transport system for delivering information. For example, scheduling, calendaring, forms, workflow, inventory, and all types of documents that are transported over electronic document interchange (EDI) are examples of messaging applications that can use the same transport system.

Types of Messaging Systems

Five different messaging system architectures are in use today:

- Host-based
- X.400
- UNIX computer-based
- LAN-based
- Client-server

Host-Based Messaging Systems

Most major computer manufacturers provide proprietary host-based E-mail systems. Examples are IBM's PROFS, and Digital Equipment Corporation's All-In-One. These systems are expensive, difficult to set up and administer, and depend on a mainframe or minicomputer for their operation. With the decline of mainframes in favor of servers, these systems are relatively static compared to the other alternatives. Most of the growth is in existing systems.

X.400 Messaging Systems

X.400 is an ITU standard messaging protocol, and is the common language that many proprietary systems speak. Although it is a standard protocol, it is not used in most private E-mail systems. Public E-mail systems such as those operated by the major IECs plus those operated by most international carriers use X.400.

UNIX Computer-Based Messaging Systems

E-mail comes as a standard feature of the UNIX operation system. UNIX systems can communicate with each other using Simple Message Transfer Protocol (SMTP). The addressing systems and the protocol are used in Internet E-mail, which is the means by which many private E-mail systems communicate with each other. The user interface included with UNIX is not particularly congenial, and is replaced by third-party systems in many UNIX installations.

LAN-Based Messaging Systems

LAN-based systems are inexpensive to purchase; some systems are even available in the public domain at no charge. Many systems run under graphical user interfaces, and are easier to use than host-based systems, which are often intended for ASCII terminals. LAN-based systems are easy to administer until several LANs are interconnected, and then routing and addressing may become complex.

Client-Server Messaging Systems

In a client-server system the E-mail application runs on a server and the user interface runs on the client workstation. These systems are similar to host-based systems except that users can choose their own client. In networks with mixed Macintosh and IBM-compatible computers, the client-server systems are advantageous.

Messaging Terminology

The structure of a typical computer messaging system is shown in Figure 26–1. The *user agent* (UA) is used at both ends of a mail system to create, send, receive, and manage messages. The UA is the portion of the mail system that the end user contacts directly. It can determine the capabilities of the E-mail system by the features it includes or lacks. For example, if the messaging system is capable of carrying voice clips, but the UA lacks that capability, the feature will be unavailable.

The *message transfer agent* (MTA) transfers messages between compatible systems over the *messaging backbone,* which is the network of circuits that interconnect the MTAs. It accepts messages from the UA, determines the route to the destination, and transfers to other MTAs based on the address. The MTA also determines messaging capabilities. For example, the UAs may be capable of handling voice and video clips, but if the MTA lacks the capability, the feature will not work. Messaging systems usually contain a directory, which lists the addresses of devices and users on the systems.

Message transfer between MTAs is by means of a standard protocol such as X.400 or SMTP, or a proprietary protocol such as Novell's message-handling system (MHS). The interface from the user agent to the MTA is covered in the X.400 protocol and the UNIX operating system, but Microsoft's mail application programming interface (MAPI) is becoming increasingly important.

Message transfer between incompatible MTAs must go through a *gateway,* which translates the protocols of the systems. If multiple gateways are required to translate between a multitude of incompatible systems, a *messaging switch* is used in lieu of multiple gateways.

THE X.400 MESSAGING PROTOCOL

X.400 is an ITU recommended message-handling protocol. It is implemented by most of the major IECs and international carriers as their standard. Such systems as AT&T Mail, MCI Mail, and SprintMail use X.400. The fact that they use the protocol for carrying messages across the network does not mean that

FIGURE 26-1

A Messaging System

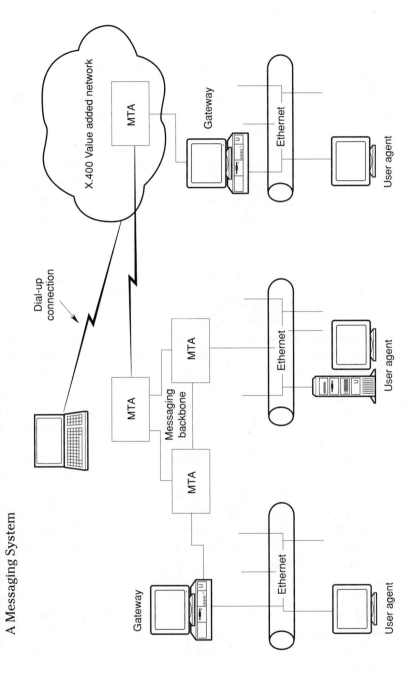

they use all portions of the protocol. For example, although X.400 includes a UA, each company is free to devise its own user interface.

The power of X.400 is procured at a sacrifice of simplicity. It is a complex system to set up and administer, which is the reason that most mail systems use their own protocol and use X.400 as a universal language across which they can exchange messages. Unlike the proprietary protocols the various messaging systems use, X.400 is an open architecture. It is impractical for LAN application, however, because of its overhead and complex addressing scheme.

Each X.400 messaging system is an independent domain, and these must be connected by agreement between the carriers. Therefore, there is no guarantee, if you are an X.400 subscriber, that you have connection to other X.400 subscribers. You will be able to send mail to them only if they have established an interconnection agreement.

X.400 Addressing

X.400 uses a multilevel hierarchical address, as illustrated in Figure 26–2. The character string can be daunting until one understands its structure. At the top level is the root, followed by country, which is a mandatory part of the address. The next level can be A or P. A is an administrative domain, usually a service provider such as AT&T Mail or MCI Mail. P stands for private domain, which large companies may use in lieu of a service provider. At the next level is organization unit (OU), which is a unique identifier referring to a company's private messaging system. Below the organization companies may identify localities and organizational units of several levels. The lowest level is the CN (common name), which can optionally be stated as given name (G) and surname (S).

The X.400 addressing system is flexible, but verbose. The protocol allows for aliasing, which can jump across directory levels to provide a shortcut address. Users are unlikely to understand the addressing well enough to create their own aliases, so expert assistance may be needed. Most effective user agents provide shortcut addresses, allowing the user to substitute a short character string for a longer address.

Other messaging systems have addressing protocols that are different from X.400. Internet, for example, has a system of user_id@hostname.domain name. The structure of IP addresses is covered in Chapter 4. SMTP addressing, which has its origin in the UNIX operating system, uses a similar structure, and is discussed later.

FIGURE 26-2

X.400 Addressing Structure

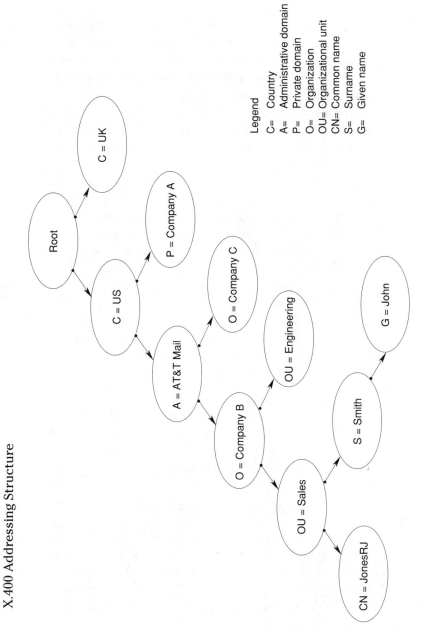

Legend
C= Country
A= Administrative domain
P= Private domain
O= Organization
OU= Organizational unit
CN= Common name
S= Surname
G= Given name

X.500 Directory Service for X.400

X.500 is a network of systems that hold information about X.400 addresses. Directory user agents (DUAs) are specialized user agents that can access directory systems agents (DSAs) in which the directory information is stored. DSAs communicate with each other using the directory access protocol (DAP) and the directory service protocol (DSP). The DAP is used for retrieving directory information. DSP is used between directories for information exchange. Users not knowing the E-mail address of another user can access the DUA much as they might call directory assistance to get a telephone number. After they obtain the address, they can store it in the E-mail application or in the central directory in an enterprise E-mail system.

X.500 was first published by the ITU in 1988, with the most recent version published in 1993. It has the capability of tying E-mail systems together through gateways regardless of vendor. Within the organization, the X.500 directory serves as a single source for storing directory information about users. This makes it easier for a company to keep updated than maintaining individual departmental post offices.

The contents of the directory are not covered by the X.500 standard. Therefore, companies can maintain any type of information desired in the database, filtering and screening to keep parts of it private. A company could, for example, publish certain E-mail addresses but keep everything else including telephone numbers and mail stops private within the company. To be X.500 compliant, a system must provide four elements:

- ◆ A directory user agent for user access.
- ◆ A directory service agent that speaks the DAP and DSP protocols.
- ◆ Basic directory functions such as information storage, retrieval, and updating.
- ◆ Security including user authentication.

SIMPLE MAIL TRANSFER PROTOCOL

SMTP is an easy and unsophisticated mail system that is used between UNIX computers. Figure 26–3 shows how UNIX computers transfer mail between each other. To send a message, the sender types the message into the UA, which passes the message to the MTA. Each computer contains a directory naming service (DNS) application, which contains the IP address for every user on the network. The MTA transfers the message to the other computer via a TCP/IP link. The link operates over a standard network such as Ethernet. The two MTAs carry on a simple dialog to establish communication. The message

FIGURE 26-3

Simple Mail Transfer Protocol

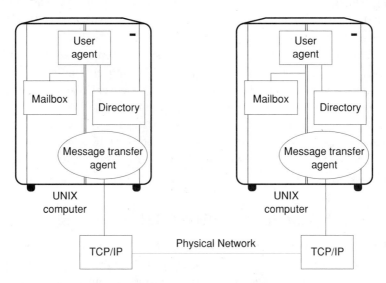

transfers to the receiving MTA, which stores it in the user's mailbox. If the addressee is unknown, the receiving MTA returns a message to that effect.

ELECTRONIC MAIL SYSTEMS

Most companies use some form of E-mail today. If the company started as a mainframe-oriented enterprise, the mail system probably began as a host-based system such as IBM's PROFS or Digital Equipment Corporation's All-In-One. As companies add LANs, the simpler forms of LAN-based E-mail emerge. Some of the more popular systems are Lotus Development Corporation's cc-Mail, Microsoft's Microsoft Mail, and Beyond, Inc.'s BeyondMail.

As E-mail becomes more a way of life in many companies, the message volume the typical worker must contend with grows, and handling becomes a problem. Intelligent E-mail systems make mail-handling decisions under user-defined criteria. Intelligent systems can make message-handling decisions such as routing, discarding, or prioritizing messages based on such criteria as who sent it, what the subject is, or where it was originated. This technique, called *rules-based messaging,* enables users to filter messages that might otherwise inundate them.

Most LAN E-mail systems provide methods for connecting their own proprietary servers, but rely on an outside service for transport to public networks. For an outside messaging backbone, three choices are available, SMTP, X.400, or MHS. An X.400 backbone maintains audit trails, which is a legal requirement when sending EDI.

Application programs such as word processing and spreadsheets can be designed to make use of messaging systems. The simplest configuration is a *mail-aware* program. It knows that a messaging system exists and how to send data over it. It does not know how to process the data. A *mail-enabled* application generates E-mail messages and uses the message transfer system to transfer information through the network. A mail-enabled application can do everything that a mail-aware program can, plus it can route, receive messages, and authenticate them.

ELECTRONIC DOCUMENT INTERCHANGE (EDI)

Global markets are changing the way we do business. To remain competitive, businesses must know their customers and respond to their needs. In international trade it takes an average of 46 documents to move products across boundaries. Traditional mail is too slow, and facsimile is impractical to authenticate for some applications, which raises the need for electronic document interchange. EDI is the intercompany exchange of legally binding trade documents. EDI enables companies to exchange a variety of business documents such as invoices, requests for proposals, and shipping and purchase orders over an electronic network. EDI assists by standardizing the format and moving documents more expeditiously.

EDI offers both cost savings and strategic benefits to the trading partners. Cost savings come from reduced labor costs, reduced stock levels that result from shorter document turnaround, and savings in telephone and postage costs. Improved response time is a major advantage. Companies can respond quickly to purchase orders, requests for quotes, and other such documents.

EDI was conceived more than 20 years ago, but its acceptance has been slow. Part of the reason has been that expensive, often mainframe-based, software was required. Now EDI can be implemented on PCs at a much lower cost than mainframe or minicomputer systems. PC-based EDI can be integrated with E-mail and its more user-friendly interface.

EDI software performs two main functions. It maps the fields on EDI documents with fields in the application software, and translates the data to and from the EDI documents. EDI applications receive and prepare documents on the screen, allowing the user to fill in the fields from the keyboard. Mapping data between fields is one of the most difficult parts of implementing EDI. It may be possible to use a translation program to remap the fields from one document to another; in the worst case it may be necessary to print out the EDI document and rekey the information into the application, which defeats much of the purpose.

EDI is based on store-and-forward messaging that can be exchanged over value-added networks (VANs) such as the major X.400 or X.25 carriers provide. The networks may offer either a store-and-forward or a store-and-retrieve class function for EDI subscribers. They may also offer document validation, security functions, and special reports. VANs may also convert protocols between the trading partners if they are incompatible. SMTP has no provisions for handling EDI, which makes X.400 a better backbone choice when using EDI.

EDI Standards

Four types of EDI standards are used:

- ◆ Proprietary.
- ◆ Noncompliant and industry-specific.
- ◆ National, such as ANSI X.12.
- ◆ International, such as EDIFACT (EDI for administration, commerce, and transport).

EDIFACT is a set of EDI standards developed under the auspices of the United Nations. As with many other standards, it is a compromise—an amalgamation of the desires of many agencies. Nor is it yet a fully formed standard. The following are examples of documents that have been standardized by EDIFACT:

- ◆ Invoice.
- ◆ Purchase order.
- ◆ Quality data message.
- ◆ International forwarding and transport message.
- ◆ Customs declaration.
- ◆ Customs response.

ANSI standard X.12 covers the structure and nature of common EDI documents, but one of the major drawbacks to EDI currently is the lack of universally accepted document standards. Some of the most common documents have been developed, but a full set of business documents has not yet been developed. Some trading partners may provide their own specialized documents, and in some cases they may redefine standard fields to suit their purposes. This makes it difficult for many suppliers or customers to communicate with other companies in the same industry.

APPLICATIONS

The typical messaging system in most companies today is a mixture of public and proprietary systems. Many company E-mail systems link to a public X.400 system such as MCI Mail or Sprint Mail, but their internal systems are proprietary, running on a LAN or mainframe. Companies may have Internet accounts, isolated UNIX pockets, LANs with stand-alone proprietary system, and accounts with one or more of the major X.400 carriers, none of which connects seamlessly to each other, and each of which uses a different addressing scheme. The existing messaging system in many companies is a hodgepodge that cannot be corrected inexpensively, but which also cannot survive indefinitely without major change.

In planning the application or restructure of a corporate E-mail system, the following considerations are important:

Adherence to standards: A messaging system must have global connectivity to be effective in maintaining communication with other organizations and other offices of the same company. The messaging system must connect to an X.400 system for connection to other companies. Gateways and X.400 carriers may suffice if the volume is low.

Manageable addressing: Multiple addresses for the same destination are not acceptable in the long run. An effective messaging system must provide a seamless connection to other systems. The addressing method should be logical to administer companywide. The messaging system should provide a user interface that provides easy ailiasing of addresses without requiring expert assistance to set up the address. Your LAN E-mail system will have a native addressing capability. It can be kept simple until the size of the organization grows to the point that duplicate names begin to crop up. This may necessitate a change in the naming convention, so adopting a standard method at the outset can save changing addresses later. The messaging system should be able to map a LAN address to an SMTP or X.400 address.

Handling conventions: Determine what should happen to misaddressed or undeliverable messages. Determine what should happen if the E-mail system cannot get a message to an X.400 or Internet within a specified time period.

External linkage: Determine how your E-mail system will be linked to the outside world. Will you carry messages in Internet, an MHS provider, or an X.400 provider? Will the access be dedicated-line access (recommended for high-volume applications) or will it use a dial-up service. How will binary messages be sent? If they are sent through SMTP, is the software multipurpose internet mail extensions (MIME) compatible, or does it automatically u u encode and u u decode the message to convert binary to seven-bit text files?

Usage information: Determine whether an audit trail through the system is needed. Is message receipting necessary? Should the system provide usage statistics for charging back to users or determining which are the high-using departments?

User interface: The user interface must be easy to use for composing, sending, receiving, and managing messages. A graphical interface in a familiar style such as Microsoft Windows or Apple Macintosh is most desirable. Users should be able to cut and paste to and from word processors, attach files easily, and move them seamlessly across the network.

Video and audio clips: The ability to move video and audio clips is becoming increasingly important in many systems. Note, however, that if this feature is enabled, storage requirements will increase, and an improved system of purging old messages may be needed.

EDI Implementation

To implement EDI, a company needs four principal elements:

User application: This is software that generates and receives EDI documents. The software may be furnished by the major partner in an EDI exchange. If not, review packages on the market, looking primarily for ease of use. Programs that operate under a graphical user interface are the easiest to use.

EDI software: This software translates the user application to EDI message formats, provides the communications protocol for accessing the network, and translates incoming EDI messages to the user application. This software may be bundled with the user application software.

EDI hardware platform: This is a computer for running the EDI software. In large companies it may be a mainframe or minicomputer. Most companies starting EDI implementation will run it on a PC.

Network for accessing the information: Most companies implementing EDI will use dial-up access to a value-added network. The trading partners store their messages in the network. The network either downloads the message to the recipient, or the recipient dials in to get the message. Companies with a large volume of messages may be directly connected to the network, or if the volume is large enough, their computers can be directly connected.

MANUFACTURERS OF ELECTRONIC MESSAGING EQUIPMENT

Electronic Data Interchange Software

Advanced Communications Systems

General Electric Information Services

Sterling Software, Inc.

Texas Instruments, Inc.

TSI International

Electronic Mail

Lotus Development Corp.

Microsoft Corporation

Banyan Systems, Inc.

Beyond, Inc.

Electronic Mail Gateways

General Electric Information Services

CompuServe, Inc.

IBM

MCI Corp.

AT&T

Novell

Sprint Corp.

X.400 Message Transfer Agents

Apple Computer, Inc.
Digital Equip Corp.
Hewlett-Packard
Retix

X.400 Value-Added Carriers

AT&T
CompuServe
MCI Communications Corp.
Sprint Corp.

CHAPTER

27

FACSIMILE SYSTEMS

Technology has resulted in enormous improvements in facsimile over the past several years. Facsimile is not new; it was invented in 1843, but it languished for more than a century before it was accepted in the business mainstream. Until international standards were developed its use was confined to a few specialized operations such as transmitting weather maps, news photos, and law enforcement mug shots. When Group 3 digital fax standards were developed in the 1980s, usage increased to the point that now it is indispensable for business, and vast numbers of individuals have fax capability because it is built into most current modems. Fax switches and distinctive ringing from the LECs make fax line sharing practical, further adding to its attractiveness.

Fax on demand (FOD) is a high-visibility application for many companies. Callers can request technical and product information from companies, and have it sent to their fax machines within minutes. Fax servers make facsimile available to everyone on the company network. Users can send and receive faxes without leaving their desk, and without the extra cost of a dedicated business line or an analog station port on the PBX.

These factors have converged to carve a permanent niche for facsimile. The technology has changed the way business operates, even more graphically than electronic mail. Either E-mail or fax can move documents quickly, but fax uses the PSTN with its universal numbering plan, where E-mail relies on convoluted addressing, lack of intersystem connectivity, and store-and-forward delays.

Fax overcomes the slowness and cost of the mail. A facsimile machine can send a letter in a fraction of a minute and for approximately the cost of a postage stamp or less, depending on how many pages are sent and whether the transmission is in the local telephone calling area. Facsimile quality isn't quite as good as the original letter, but recipients are willing to sacrifice quality for speed. A former postmaster general said, "The facsimile systems and the countless other applications of electricity to the transmission of intelligence yet to be made must eventually interfere with the transportation of letters by the slower means of post." If this statement sounds prophetic, consider that its author was Jonathan Creswell, and he was speaking in 1872.

Fax overcomes the difficult addressing and sometimes uncertain delivery of E-mail and combines it with ease of use and economy. Until the last few years, converting fax to text was difficult, but now fax received in a computer can easily be converted to text with optical character recognition (OCR) software. The quality of most fax machines is high enough that printed fax can be scanned and converted to text with OCR software.

Facsimile technology has other applications that will become more important as the technology matures. Currently, some facsimile machines can double as printers. The ITU X.400 standards make it easy to send documents from a computer to a facsimile machine. As discussed later, many electronic mail services offer the capability of sending a document from a computer to a facsimile machine through a value-added network.

Although facsimile got off to a slow start compared to other telecommunications technologies, its use has expanded to the point that it now is indispensable for many forms of record communication. This has happened because ITU standards are now universally accepted and machine prices have dropped to the point of affordability for nearly everyone.

FACSIMILE TECHNOLOGY

A facsimile machine has four major elements, as diagrammed in Figure 27–1: scanner, printer, controller, and communications facilities. The scanner sweeps across a page, segmenting it into multiple lines in much the same way that a television camera scans an image. The scanner output can be either a continuous analog signal that varies between white and black level or a digital output that converts the image to a binary code. The first facsimile machines were analog, but those earlier products have been replaced because digital fax offers better quality and faster transmission. Digital scanner output is compressed and applied directly to a digital circuit or through a modem to an analog circuit.

FIGURE 27–1

Block Diagram of a Facsimile System

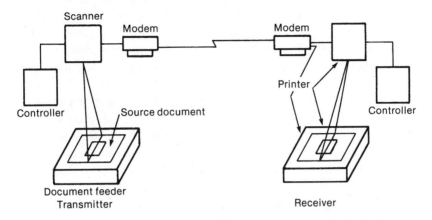

Control equipment directs the scanning rate and compresses solid expanses of black or white to reduce transmission time. At the receiving end the incoming signal is demodulated and drives a print mechanism that reproduces the incoming image on paper.

Facsimile Machine Characteristics

Facsimile equipment is categorized by modulation method, speed, resolution, and transmission rate. Digital machines produce a binary signal that is applied to the circuit through a modem. The digital transmission speed varies from 4,800 b/s to 64 kb/s. The speed of sending a page depends on circuit quality and the amount of information to be encoded, but typically a single-spaced page of text takes a minute or less. Resolution is measured in lines per inch (lpi) and varies from slightly less than 100 lpi to 400 lpi.

ITU divides facsimile standards into four groups. Group 1 and 2 are analog standards that have been discontinued. The two current standards are:

- ◆ *Group 3:* Compressed digital, 1 minute or less per page transmission time, 200 lpi resolution, 2,400 to 14,400 b/s data rate.
- ◆ *Group 4:* Compressed digital, less than 1 minute per page transmission speed, 200 to 400 lpi resolution, data rates up to 64 kb/s.

ITU sets standards for protocol, scanning rate, phasing, scans per millimeter, synchronization, and modulation method. Facsimile machines must be both phased and synchronized. Phasing is the process of starting the printer and the scanner at the same position on the page at the beginning of a transmission. Synchronization keeps the scanner and printer aligned for the duration of the transmission.

Digital fax machines break a signal into dots, or picture elements, which are analogous to the pixels in a video signal. Unlike a video signal, which varies in intensity, digital facsimile produces a binary signal that is either on (black) or off (white) for each picture element. The number of picture elements per square inch determines the resolution of a digital facsimile and the transmission time.

Transmission times vary with the density of the information on a page. Modem speeds of 9,600 b/s are standard with most digital machines. Some models, and many fax modems, are capable of 14,400 b/s transmission. As with other data signals, 9,600 b/s cannot always be transmitted reliably over the switched telephone network, which sometimes results in the transmission slowing to 4,800 b/s or less.

Group 3 facsimile uses data compression to reduce transmission time. Many documents have expanses of white or black that are compressed by a process called *run-length encoding*. Instead of transmitting a string of zeros or ones corresponding to a long stretch of white or black, the length of the run is encoded into a short data message. By using run-length encoding, a digital facsimile machine compresses data into approximately one-eighth of the number of nonencoded bits, but the amount of compression depends on the character of the document. For example, a document with a border around it cannot be compressed vertically.

Even with data compression, facsimile is a less efficient way to send text than ASCII encoding. For example, the standard pica type pitch is 10 characters per inch horizontally and 6 lines per inch vertically. To encode a character over facsimile with 200-pixels-per-inch resolution requires 660 bits, as Figure 27–2 shows. Assuming an 8:1 compression ratio, a character can be transmitted in about 80 bits. Compared to the 8 bits required to send a character in ASCII, facsimile requires ten times the transmission time. Because of this difference, it is more economical of circuit time (but often much less convenient) to transmit data in ASCII-coded form than by facsimile.

Scanners

Document scanning converts an image to binary form. The digital modulation system illustrated in Figure 27–3 uses a row of photocells, consisting of one cell per picture element and corresponding to one scan line. As the document moves through the feeder, the photocells detect light from the source and emit a 1 or 0 pulse, depending on whether the reflected light is above or below the threshold between black and white.

FIGURE 27–2

Encoding a Character with Facsimile

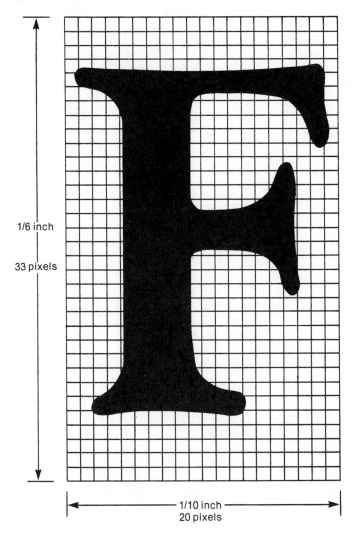

1/6 inch

33 pixels

1/10 inch
20 pixels

Printing

Facsimile machines either use plain or coated electrosensitive paper. Coated fax paper comes in a roll, and is much less desirable than plain paper fax. Its major disadvantages are that it curls up, and it is not a permanent document. Plain paper fax creates documents that have the same degree of permanence as printed output, which, in effect, it is. Coated paper deteriorates over time, so it must be

FIGURE 27-3

Digital Facsimile Scanning Process

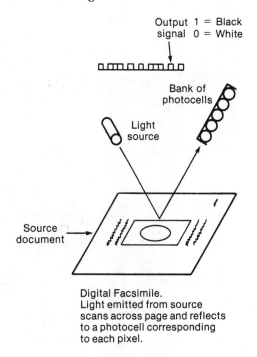

Output 1 = Black
signal 0 = White

Bank of photocells

Light source

Source document

Digital Facsimile.
Light emitted from source
scans across page and reflects
to a photocell corresponding
to each pixel.

run through a copier to make it permanent. Plain paper fax machines are more expensive, but supplies are less costly, so for high-volume applications they are the preferable method. The principal plain paper fax printing technologies are laser and ink jet. Both technologies are identical to those used in printers.

Facsimile Features

Some facsimile machines have features that make them complete document-communications centers, designed for attended or unattended operation. For example, stations can be equipped with polling features so a master can interrogate slave stations and retrieve messages from queue. In some machines the master polls the remote, after which the remote redials the master to send the document. Other machines have a feature called *reverse polling,* which enables the receiving machine to transmit a document on the initial poll. Most machines have automatic digital terminal identification capability and apply a time and date stamp to transmitted and received documents. Machines can be equipped with document feeders and stackers to enable them to send and receive documents while unattended. Machines using coated paper often include cutters to cut the document after each page. Some digital facsimile machines contain memory to store digitized messages and route them to designated addressees on either a selective or a broadcast basis. Memory also enables fax machines to receive documents when they are out of printing supplies. Most facsimile machines handle only standard letter or legal-size paper, but some machines have a larger bed for handling oversized paper.

Besides the above features, the following features are available as options on fax machines and servers:

Automatic dial directory: This feature is the same as speed dialing on a telephone. Direct speed-dialing buttons are available in some machines. In others the directory is stored in memory and is recalled from a list.

Automatic redial: When a busy signal is encountered the document can be left in the feeder. The machine continues to dial until the transmission goes through.

Custom cover sheets: This feature is common with PC fax boards and with fax servers. The system creates a cover sheet with a few key strokes by the operator and automatically fills in details such as sender's name, number of pages, return fax and telephone number, and custom graphics.

Dynamic port allocation: This feature limits fax broadcasting to certain ports so incoming ports will not be tied up with outgoing calls.

E-mail gateway: This feature is normally found only in fax servers. The server links to an electronic mail system and uses it to receive and deliver fax messages.

Group fax: This feature enables the user to send the same fax to an address list.

Message logging: The system logs both failed and correctly received messages. The date, time of day, received telephone number, and other significant information is logged. The log can be interrogated or printed automatically.

Phone book: This feature enables each user to have a personal directory of fax recipients.

Priority fax queuing: In a fax server certain stations can be designated as high priority. Their transmissions take precedence over those of lower priority.

Receive alerts: When a fax message is received, an alert pops up on the computer screen or telephone display to notify the user.

Transmission scheduling: The system can schedule faxes for delivery at night when rates are lower. This feature is particularly important when large documents are sent to multiple locations. The system also can reschedule when delivery fails for some reason such as busy or no answer.

Desktop Computer Fax Boards

Personal computer users do not have to have facsimile machines to communicate by facsimile, particularly to transmit documents that are stored in a personal computer. Two developments, PC facsimile boards and facsimile transmission over electronic mail networks, make it possible, with some limitations, to exchange documents between a personal computer and a facsimile machine.

Fax Boards and Modems

A board plugged into a vacant slot in a desktop computer or a fax feature in a modem allows the computer to emulate a facsimile machine. Fax-enabled application software can transmit a document via fax by treating the fax board or modem as a printer. The user does not have to go through any special steps to convert the document for transmission. The application software takes care of the conversion and dials the recipient without any special action on the user's part except selecting the addressee.

Desktop computer fax software offers features that are available only on high-end facsimile machines. Since the file to be transmitted is retrieved from a disk, a facsimile board can transmit a document or a list of documents to a list of different telephone numbers. With a conventional facsimile machine this is possible only with memory, which is an expensive option. The fax board can store an almost unlimited number of pages, unlike the limits on the document feeder of a conventional facsimile machine. Signatures, logos, and other graphics may be integrated from a separate file, but as discussed earlier, they are difficult to authenticate. PC facsimile is also useful as a relay device. With conventional facsimile, each time a received document is rescanned and transmitted, it loses clarity. Since a PC facsimile is received and sent from a file, it can be relayed indefinitely without loss of detail.

Although a personal computer board is a satisfactory means of transmitting fax, receiving is another matter. Not all fax boards operate in background mode, and those that do may slow down the computer while a document is being received. Received documents can be displayed on either the screen or printer. Since smaller monitors are incapable of displaying an entire page in readable form, it is necessary to scroll the document, and the resolution may be too low to read the document without expanding it. When a bit-mapped document is downloaded to a printer, the quality will be good, but the speed may be less than satisfactory. The built-in printer on a facsimile machine can print at about the speed at which the document is received. Even a laser printer attached to a desktop computer may take several times longer to print a document than a facsimile machine.

Although the fax board has many applications, it should not be considered a substitute for a facsimile machine except where cost is an issue. Although the cost is much lower than a full-featured fax machine, a fax board is less convenient for users to share, more time-consuming for transmitting graphics, and less than adequate for receiving documents. The strength of the desktop computer facsimile is in network applications. It makes it easy to send multiple documents to multiple recipients. The personal computer can receive a document, store it on a disk, and retransmit it without the loss of clarity that results from receiving and retransmitting a paper facsimile document.

Fax Servers

The fax modem makes it possible for multiple users to share modems through a fax server, which may also be a modem server. In most offices everyone uses fax, which results in users printing the fax and queuing at the fax machine to send it. Furthermore, when many outgoing faxes are being sent the number is busy to incoming callers. The solution to the busy fax machine is more lines and machines, or some form of fax store-and-forward capability. The latter is provided by LECs as a service, and it is available in fax servers and fax-enabled voice mail systems. These applications can be classified as fax networking.

Fax networking offers several advantages over stand-alone fax machines. Many of the same advantages accrue from fax boards in personal computers or fax capabilities built into modems. The following are the advantages of these methods:

- ◆ It is unnecessary to print documents before faxing them, which saves cost and time.
- ◆ The quality of received documents is higher because it is unnecessary to scan them.
- ◆ It eliminates human queues at the fax machine, and therefore increases productivity.
- ◆ Automatic delivery of received documents may be possible with one of the methods discussed later.
- ◆ The system automatically redials busy numbers and those that do not answer.
- ◆ Fax lines can be left free to answer incoming calls.
- ◆ Fax documents can be sent over the company network to file in another server, eliminating the need to go outside the system and saving transmission costs.
- ◆ Fax can originate from within fax-enabled applications. Word processors, spreadsheets, and other applications treat fax servers and modems as printers.

Fax servers have some drawbacks that limit their application. Some of the principal disadvantages of a server compared to a stand-alone fax machine are:

♦ If the document isn't already in a computer file, it must be converted with a scanner.

♦ Signatures are difficult to control and authenticate. Scanned signatures can be added to documents, but it is difficult to be certain someone other than the signer did not add it.

♦ Bit-mapped fax files are slow to print. They can be converted to text with OCR, but the conversion process is time-consuming.

♦ Automatic routing of documents is uncertain in many network applications.

Choice of modems to use with fax servers is important. Inexpensive fax modems are readily available, but they lack the features of more expensive modems. TIA/EIA has developed standards for fax modems known as Class 1 and Class 2 standards. These have not been adopted by ITU as of this writing, so many of the Class 2 features may be inoperable in international communication.

The common fax modems that are available everywhere are Class 1 modems (TIA/EIA 578). They assume that most of the transmission features are built into the application software. Class 2 modems (TIA/EIA 592) build communications features into hardware. Class 2 modems have flow control capability to enable the receiving modem to control the transmission rate. The initial handshake between the two modems establishes their ability to regulate transmission rates.

The ITU T.30 standards specify how fax handshaking takes place. Class 1 modems assume that fax timing specifications will be implemented in software. Class 2 modems handle timing from an onboard processor. The Class 2 standards provide for copy quality checking, which is absent from the Class 1 specification. These and other features make Class 2 modems preferable for heavy fax server applications, but at a higher price. Also, many of the devices the server communicates with will be unable to comply with Class 2 standards.

Inbound reception on a fax server offers special problems that stand-alone machines do not encounter. With stand-alone machines paper output is delivered manually, which may be time-consuming and cause delays. Theoretically, fax servers can deliver faxes directly to the desktop. This is accomplished by one of three methods. Most reliable is direct inward dialing, in which each user has his or her own DID fax number. This method is common with voice mail systems that support fax store-and-forward. This method is the most reliable, but it may require additional expense for DID numbers and trunks.

A second method is to scan the cover page with OCR software and pick the recipient's name out of the resulting file. This method is fine in theory, but it lacks reliability because of different ways the recipient's name may be written. Users report about 75 percent reliability with this method. The third method is using additional DTMF digits for routing the document. This method is reliable, but it requires the sender to know the receiver's personal code.

Delivering Facsimile via Electronic Mail

Most public electronic mail services offer fax delivery service. The user dials the electronic mail number, usually a local telephone number in larger metropolitan areas, identifies the addressee, and transmits the document. The electronic mail service delivers the document to the recipient's fax machine and returns a notice of delivery to the sender. The service tries several times to deliver to a busy or no-answer station before reporting nondelivery to the sender.

Electronic mail services can transmit documents with embedded graphics stored in their library. For example, a sender can furnish a logo and signature block, have them scanned and stored by the electronic mail service, and call them from storage with the transmitted document.

Group 4 Facsimile

ITU has standards for Group 4 facsimile, which is a high-speed, high-resolution digital system operating at speeds up to 64 kb/s. Most IECs offer a switched 56 kb/s service, which is an ideal medium for Group 4 facsimile. Resolution is from 200 to 400 lpi using high compression. The standard for Group 4 separates facsimile machines into three classes. All three classes support 100-pixel-per-inch resolution. Classes 2 and 3 have 300-pixel-per-inch resolution with options of 240 and 400 picture elements per inch. Table 27–1 lists the characteristics of the three classes of Group 4 machines. The quality of Group 4 fax is about as good as the quality of an office laser printer, which makes it suitable for transmitting letter-quality documents.

In addition to offering the advantages of high speed and improved resolution, Group 4 standards can ease communications between word processors. Currently, memory-to-memory data transfers are a feature of communicating word processors. This feature is known as *teletex* (not to be confused with teletext, which is the transmission of information during the vertical blanking interval of a video signal). Most manufacturers now use proprietary protocols that are incompatible with the protocols of other equipment. Group 4 facsimile standards make it possible to integrate facsimile and communicating word

T A B L E 27–1

CCITT Group 4 Facsimile Characteristics

Service	Class		
	1	2	3
Facsimile	Transmit/receive	Transmit/receive	Transmit/receive
Teletex		Receive	Create/transmit/receive
Mixed mode		Receive	Create/transmit/receive
Resolution:			
Standard	200	200/300	200/300
Optional	240/300/400	240/400	240/400

processors. To overcome the inherent disadvantages of each type of system, Class 2 and 3 machines send textual information in alphanumeric form and graphic information in facsimile form. Terminals capable of this form of communication are called *mixed mode*. Page memory is required for memory-to-memory transmission.

Group 4 facsimile standards are developed around the ISO open systems interconnection model for data communications. See Chapter 4 for a description of the OSI model. Currently, Group 4 facsimile is not widely used for several reasons:

◆ Dial-up 56 kb/s circuits are not available to many companies. As ISDN becomes more common, the popularity of Group 4 fax should increase.

◆ Group 4 machines cost several times as much as Group 3 machines.

◆ Many documents now transmitted by facsimile do not need the higher resolution of Group 4. Business culture will change to adopt Group 4 quality, which approaches that of a laser printer, when machines are more widely used.

Facsimile Line-Sharing Devices

It is awkward to receive fax messages if the machine is not connected to a dedicated telephone line. Without a dedicated line, someone must answer the telephone and on hearing facsimile tones, manually initiate the handshake sequence with the sending machine. Several devices on the market enable the fax machine to share the telephone line with voice. Some devices answer the telephone with synthesized voice that instructs the caller to press a DTMF key to direct the call to a person. Otherwise, the device connects to the fax machine to initiate a facsimile session.

Some line-sharing devices monitor the line for a voice signal from the calling end. If no voice is heard, the incoming line switches to the facsimile port. If no tones are heard, it transmits a voice message and monitors for voice. If a voice response is heard, it switches the call to the voice port. Other devices monitor the line for facsimile tones, and switch the line to voice if no tones are heard from the sending end. For residences and smaller businesses, a line-sharing device can save money on dedicated telephone lines.

A more effective method is distinctive ringing, which most LECs offer, and which many fax machines support. Distinctive ringing assigns more than one telephone number to the same line, with each number assigned a different ringing code. A decoding box recognizes the ring and switches it to telephone, fax, or modem as appropriate.

APPLICATIONS

Virtually every business and governmental organization has and uses fax. Its prevalence makes it reliable for many applications that previously relied on the mail. One of the most effective applications is fax on demand (FOD), which is a combination voice and fax service. FOD has become almost obligatory for business-to-business customer service operations. A high percentage of callers to many such operations are requesting technical or marketing information that can easily be delivered by fax. A typical FOD dialog leads callers through a menu of choices, followed by a request for the caller's fax number. Within minutes the FOD application retrieves the document from the database, seizes an outgoing circuit, and sends the document to the caller. A well-designed FOD application allows callers to obtain information 24 hours per day without human assistance.

The telecommunications aspects of FOD are not complex. FOD is an option in some voice mail systems, or it can run in a desktop computer that is either stand-alone or connected to local exchange trunks. Call centers can make effective use of FOD. Calls arrive in the call center, where an automated attendant offers callers an FOD option. If the caller chooses FOD the call is transferred over an analog port to the FOD server. The server may either contain the fax documents on its own hard disk, or it can be networked with a file server.

One precaution that must be observed in FOD is to design the system to prevent a new variety of fraud and personal harassment. If a caller wants to harass someone, he dials an FOD application, usually over an 800 number, and orders documents sent to a voice telephone number. The FOD device dials the number, which fails. Unless the program has been written to prevent it, the FOD may dial the number repeatedly, trying to deliver a fax document, and running up long distance-bills and annoying the called party in the process. The FOD software must be programmed to recognize and prevent such attempts.

Standards

The principal source of facsimile standards is ITU, which sets the standards to which Group 3 and 4 facsimile machines adhere. ITU's T.30 specification covers handshaking between fax machines, and the T.4 protocol defines document encoding. TIA/EIA standards discussed earlier cover Class 1 and Class 2 fax modems used stand-alone and in servers. ITU standards deal only with the protocols and line signals exchanged between machines. Manufacturers' specifications control other features intended to integrate facsimile into a network. Differences in storage, polling, machine identification, and other features may result in incompatibility with some machine functions, even among machines conforming to the standards of one ITU group. Fortunately, incompatibility between facsimile machines is rare.

Evaluation Criteria

The criteria discussed below apply primarily to the telecommunications aspects of facsimile. A discussion of the technical requirements and features of facsimile machines is beyond the scope of this book.

Transmission Facilities

Facsimile transmission facilities should be evaluated and selected on the same basis as voice and data circuits are evaluated. Digital facsimile can be transmitted over either analog or digital circuits, which should meet the same requirements as any other data communication service applied to the telephone network or to a public data network.

Compatibility

When special features such as halftone transmission, networking, and polling are required, the systems should be from the same manufacturer or fully tested with systems of other manufacturers. Compatibility problems between machines for basic sending and receiving is generally not a problem.

Document Characteristics

The primary factors in determining which group of facsimile equipment to select are the document volume and resolution required. Plain-paper fax offers superior quality compared to coated paper. Of the plain-paper devices, laser printers offer better quality than ink jet machines, although the difference is unimportant in most companies.

Many machines offer a high-resolution mode, which produces quality close to that of a letter-quality printer. If copy quality is important, a high-resolution machine should be selected. The need for halftones in documents also should be considered. Facsimile machines vary widely in their ability to handle halftones, with the level of gray scale varying from 0 to 64 shades of gray.

Labor-saving features such as automatic document feed, paper cutter, automatic dial and answer, document storage, and document routing should be considered. If confidential information is being transmitted, encryption should be considered.

Document Memory

Most high-end fax machines offer memory for document storage. This feature is useful for unattended operation. If the machine runs out of paper, received documents can be stored in memory. Multipage documents can be sent without fear of paper jams. Documents can be sent to address lists that are recalled from memory. Transmission time is often reduced because the machine receives into memory so that transmission is not paced by the speed of the printer.

SELECTED FACSIMILE EQUIPMENT MANUFACTURERS

Fax modem boards and external fax modems are so common that they have become a commodity. Products from any of the major modem manufacturers are comparable in many respects. Many even use the same chip set to implement fax in addition to modem capability in the same device.

Manufacturers of Facsimile Machines

Canon USA

Dex Business Systems, Inc.

Fujitsu

Hewlett-Packard Co.

Hitachi America

Konica

Lanier

Minolta

Mita

Murata

Panasonic

Pitney Bowes

Ricoh Corp.

Sanyo Business Systems

Savin

Sharp Electronics

Toshiba

Xerox Corporation

Manufacturers of Personal Computer Facsimile Boards

Brooktrout Technology, Inc.

Dialogic

GammaLink, Inc.

Manufacturers of Facsimile Servers

Biscom

Castelle

Delrina

Devcom

Extended Systems

Ibex Technologies

LANsource Technologies

Multi-Technology Systems, Inc.

Optus Software

Rightfax

T4 Systems

V

TELECOMMUNICATION NETWORKS

THE INTEGRATED SERVICES DIGITAL NETWORK

Many telecommunications technologies have caught on quickly and gone from introduction to universal acceptance in a short time. Fiber optics, LANs, satellites, and ATM all found or are finding their niche rapidly, but not so with ISDN. Under development for more than two decades, ISDN is far from fully deployed, and no one is predicting when or even if it will be. The LECs provide ISDN in a high percentage of the wire centers in the country, but availability does not mean that users can order an ISDN line with the same degree of ease that they order analog lines. Users have to understand something of the technology to make it work, and even after it does work, the ability to place end-to-end digital calls anywhere in the world is far from assured.

Despite its gradual introduction, ISDN is here and is beginning to catch on. The main impediment in the past has been the lack of a compelling application. The attraction of end-to-end digital connections sounds good, but the plain analog telephone still has a lot of life for making phone calls, which is what most of us do. Furthermore, ISDNs were proprietary until as recently as 1992, when National ISDN-1 was introduced.

Now the need for which ISDN is the fulfillment seems to be emerging. One such application is desktop videoconferencing, which operates nicely on ISDN's digital channels. Another major trend is telecommuting. As more and more incentives develop for workers to spend at least part of the workweek at home, ISDN can be an economical way of retaining a link to the office at reasonable speed. A related need is remote LAN access, which enables people to dial into access servers from off premises. Analog lines are a poor match for the graphical user interfaces that most programs use. Another driving force is the rapid growth of Internet. High-bandwidth services such as the Worldwide Web demand high-speed access. V.34 modems at 28.8 kb/s provide respectable speed, but they can't compete with ISDN's digital channels, which operate at an aggregate speed of 128 kb/s.

One reason ISDN has been slow to arrive is the enormous investment it requires. LECs have a huge investment in analog switching, which still has plenty of service life left for regular telephone calls. The LECs are reluctant to invest in digital systems with ISDN capability until the demand exists. As replacement of these systems, many of which are approaching 30 years of age, is justified, they will be replaced with digital switching systems that can support ISDN, and the service will become more widely available.

One motivation for ISDN is that today's telecommunications networks give users little control over their options. Networks are either circuit switched, packet switched, or private. Separate local loops are provided for every service; telephone circuits have two-wire loops, data circuits usually have four-wire loops, other special services such as alarm circuits have either two- or four-wire loops, and all services can be rearranged only with the participation of the LEC. Although the internal networks of the LECs and IECs are largely digital, users do not realize the benefits of end-to-end digital connectivity because of the analog local loops and analog switching systems.

Both voice and data circuits can have either a digital or an analog interface, but the interface and terminating equipment are far from uniform. Public data networks have different interfaces from those of the telephone network, and video networks such as CATV have yet another type of interface. Furthermore, the networks are incapable of handling information interchangeably. Analog voice networks are slow and inefficient at handling data, and low-speed data networks are ineffective for voice transmission. ISDN can be the answer to all of these deficiencies.

INTEGRATED SERVICES DIGITAL NETWORK TECHNOLOGY

ISDN lines come in two varieties, basic rate interface (BRI) and primary rate interface (PRI). BRI consists of two 64 kb/s B (bearer) channels plus one 16 kb/s D (data) channel. In ISDN shorthand the interface is called 2B+D. The D channel is used for signaling between the central office switch and terminating equipment, which could be a telephone set, personal computer, videoconferencing set, or other device. The B channels are used for any kind of service including voice, data, and video. BRI is provided by most LECs and as a lineside option of most major PBXs. The applications behind the PBX and the customer premises are essentially the same. A special station set is required for ISDN, or, as shown in Figure 28–1, ordinary station equipment can be installed behind a terminal adapter (TA). The station equipment can be a telephone set, a card in a key telephone system, a card in a PC, or a direct interface into a Group 4 fax machine or video codec.

A PRI interface is a 24-channel T-1 carrier with one channel reserved for signaling, yielding a 23B+D channel. A PRI can plug into any device designed to be PRI-compatible, including PBXs, routers, T-1 multiplexers, central office switches, tandem switches, or computers. The equipment can select 64 kb/s channels singly, in pairs, or, with some systems, in an $N \times 64$ configuration. $N \times 64$ means contiguous bandwidth equal to any quantity of 64 kb/s channels. For example, 384 kb/s is a popular bandwidth for conference-quality video, and is defined as an HO channel. The LECs provide dial tone over PRIs, and the major IECs also provide their services over PRIs. The separate data channel allows communication between the IEC's switch and the PBX so channels can be switched at will to outgoing, 800, 900, video, data, or any other such service that can be delivered over T-1.

Where LECs have priced ISDN service attractively, PRI service is less expensive than analog trunks, in addition to which it offers the following advantages:

◆ Hardware costs are reduced in the PBX. In most PBXs a PRI card costs about the same as an eight-port analog trunk card, and uses one-third the number of slots.

◆ ISDN trunks with their call-by-call service selection provide listed directory number, outgoing, DID, and other services without the need for special trunk groups. Depending on the size of the system, trunk requirements can be reduced substantially.

◆ Transmission performance is enhanced. Digital trunks can be operated with no loss and imperceptible noise. By contrast the loss and noise of analog trunks increase with the distance from the central office.

◆ ISDN trunks can be provided over self-healing networks, reducing the vulnerability to outage.

◆ Trunks can be added up to the 23-trunk capacity of a PRI with no wiring work or hardware additions on the customer's premises.

FIGURE 28-1

ISDN Architecture

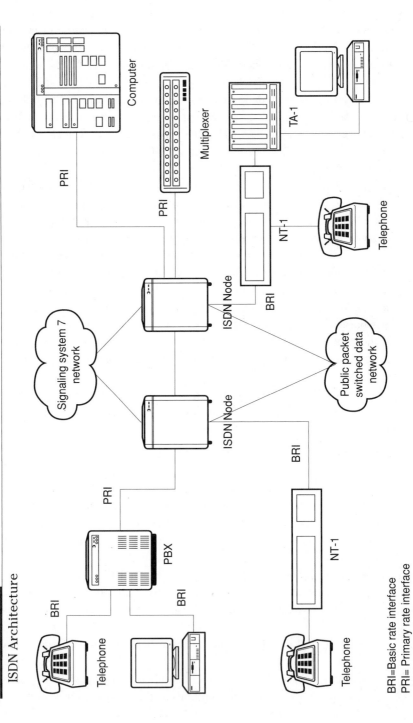

BRI=Basic rate interface
PRI= Primary rate interface
NT-1= Network termination 1
TA1= Terminal adapter

The offsetting disadvantages are minimal. The signaling channel takes a substantial fraction of a T-1's bandwidth, but most carriers provide *nonfacility associated signaling* (NFAS), which permits multiple PRIs to share a single signaling channel. NFAS is an effective way to improve channel utilization, but if the T-1 carrying the signaling channel fails, access to all channels may be lost. A second disadvantage is the inability to use power fail transfer on PBX trunks.

One benefit of connecting a PBX to an ISDN is call-by-call service selection. Different types of calls require different configurations, which the PBX and central office set up in response to signals received over the D channel. For example, an ordinary telephone call takes one channel, incoming or outgoing. If it is a video call, two channels are usually required. A data call may take one or two channels, depending on how the equipment sets up the call. ISDN can assign services to any channel in a trunk group. This eliminates the need for special circuits such as switched 56 that are used for a narrow range of purposes.

Although PRI is a good substitute for analog trunks for ordinary telephone service, it is far from universally available. Most LECs have equipped only their major wire centers with ISDN. ISDN access through the LEC to the IEC or to other LECs may be unavailable. In wire centers with multiple switching systems, ISDN is frequently available only in one system, which may mean a number change will be required to use ISDN service. The key advantage of end-to-end digital connectivity is an ideal that may be realized in the future, but cannot be depended on until the service becomes more widely available.

Whether an actual cost reduction will result from ISDN depends on the LECs' pricing policies. To implement the service, LECs must invest enormous sums in improving local loops and replacing or upgrading switching systems. Furthermore, not all users need the services ISDN can provide. Residential customers can profit from having only one circuit to carry a second telephone line, but many users do not need end-to-end digital service or call-by-call service selection. Many new services that ISDN makes possible are desirable, but many residential customers will not be willing to pay for them until new services such as video telephones become common.

One advantage of ISDN is network intelligence, which allows users to instruct the network to respond differently according to time of day, day of week, or identity of the calling party. Incoming calls can be treated with the same kind of discrimination the callers would receive if they arrived in person. For example, nuisance calls can be turned away, priority callers can be shunted to trained specialists, and callers can leave voice or data messages when it is unnecessary to speak in person with someone at the receiving end. Since the calling party's identification is transmitted with the signaling message, the user has the opportunity to handle the call in a variety of ways, either manually or under processor control. The call can be selectively forwarded, rejected, sent to an answering point, or asked to hold. The central office can deliver a distinctive ring to the called party's premises, which has tremendous potential for eliminating annoyance calls and for selectively handling important calls. Most of these services can be provided by analog electronic switching systems, however, so it isn't necessary to subscribe to ISDN to obtain the service. These features fall under the umbrella of Custom Local Area Switching Services (CLASS), which Chapter 9 covers in more detail.

ISDN ARCHITECTURE

The ISDN network architecture is based on standards set by ITU, with standards in the United States largely driven by Bellcore. ISDN supports any combination of voice, data, and video services over a unified network. ISDN standards are based on the ISO open systems interconnect model. They specify physical, data link, and network layer protocols for the physical interface, and electrical characteristics for the network. The standards specify how information is encoded and how supplementary services such as calling features are provided. As with present telecommunications networks, ISDN has a local and an interexchange element. An LEC usually provides the local element, and an IEC furnishes the interexchange element.

The objectives of ISDN are:

◆ To provide end-to-end digital connectivity.
◆ To gain the economies of digital transmission, switching, and signaling.
◆ To provide users with direct control over their telecommunications services.
◆ To provide a universal network interface for voice and data.

ISDN Standards

Figure 28–2 shows the major ITU standards that have been set and how they relate to the OSI model. The physical layer specifies the movement of bits over the physical medium. The data link layer uses the distributed link access procedure (LAPD), which permits multiple terminal devices to communicate with higher-level devices in ISDN. The Level 3 protocol, Q.931, is the signaling protocol that provides for call setup, supervision, and disconnection.

F I G U R E 28–2

ISDN Standards Related to the OSI Model

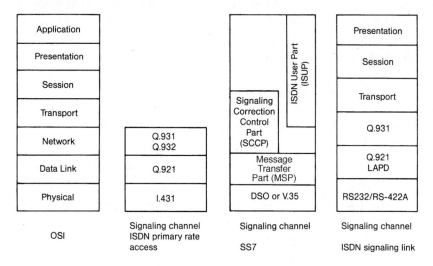

Network Terminations

Equipment connects to ISDN over network termination equipment designated as NT-1 and NT-2. NT-1 provides functions dealing with physical and electrical termination of the network, corresponding to the physical layer of the OSI reference model. Devices that combine the services of both NT-1 and NT-2 are called NT-12. The NT-1 functions are:

- ◆ Termination of the two-wire transmission line and conversion to four-wire.
- ◆ Monitoring performance and maintenance functions.
- ◆ Timing the loop.
- ◆ Termination of the four-wire user interface and conversion to two-wire.

NT-2 terminations, which may be built into a PBX, multiplexer, local area network, or terminal controller, perform the data link and network layer functions of the OSI model.

Terminal equipment that is BRI-compatible can plug directly into an NT-1 interface. In ISDN terminology it is known as TE-1. TE-2 equipment is not BRI-compatible, and must plug into a terminal adapter (TA). Terminal adapters are required for non-ISDN voice terminals and equipment with non-ISDN interfaces such as EIA-232-D, EIA-449, X.21, and V.35.

Basic rate service permits as many as eight terminal devices to be connected to a passive bus, as Figure 28–3 shows. The passive bus is a four-wire circuit—one pair for transmit and one for receive. Since basic rate is limited to two B channels, only two of the devices connected to the passive bus can be active simultaneously, but the D channel could be used for data communications from other devices on the bus.

ISDN Interfaces

Five points of demarcation have been defined in ISDN standards, as Figure 28–4 shows.

- ◆ The R interface is a link between non-ISDN equipment and an ISDN terminal adapter.
- ◆ The S interface connects ISDN terminals to NT-2 and NT-12 devices.
- ◆ The T interface connects NT-2 and NT-1 devices.
- ◆ The U interface connects NT-1 and NT-12 devices to the public network.
- ◆ The V interface, located in the ISDN node, separates the line termination equipment from the exchange termination equipment.

The U-V connection is the ISDN access line and replaces the local loop of pre-ISDN services. It is a single twisted-pair metallic line with a maximum length of 6,500 meters. NT-1 and the ISDN node obtain a full-duplex connection by using a technique called *echo cancellation*. The transmitting power of the four-wire input to the NT-1 splits between the line and an equalizing network in the NT-1. An electronic filter determines whether a line signal is original data or an echo caused by a mismatch between the line and the network. Echoes are canceled out so only the original signal remains.

APPLICATIONS

The primary issues surrounding ISDN are cost and availability. Where the service is both available and cost-effective, managers will find little reason not to use it. Cost must be examined closely before reaching a conclusion. Even if the cost is greater than an equivalent number of analog lines, the two-way nature of ISDN means that fewer trunks will be needed for the same grade of service. Chapter 35 explains how to determine the number of lines needed to achieve a desired grade of service.

Anyone who is selecting a new PBX, or even a key system, should consider ISDN-compatibility. Applications are emerging that require the digital

Connection of Devices to the ISDN Basic Rate Service Bus

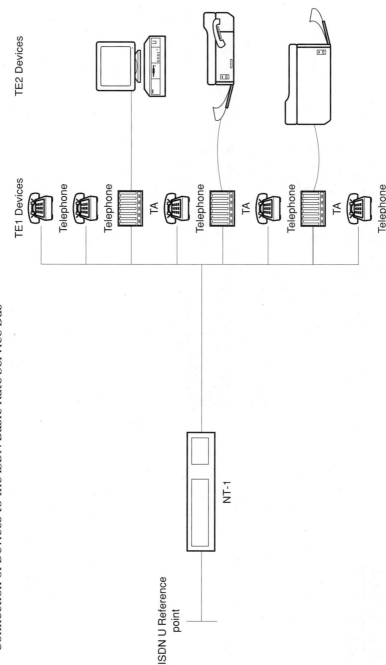

FIGURE 28–4

ISDN Demarcation Points

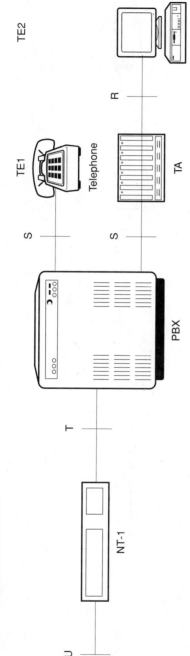

connectivity of ISDN, and as the service becomes more ubiquitous, the applications such as these will develop:

◆ Videoconferencing, primarily desktop devices.
◆ High-speed access to remote databases such as the various on-line services and Internet.
◆ High speed remote access to LANs.
◆ High-speed image applications such as Group 4 facsimile.
◆ Second line in the home applications driven by the development of telecommuting.

Many LECs offer attractive ISDN tariff rates where facilities permit. Note, however, that in many cases one switching system in a wire center is equipped for ISDN, which means that a number change may be needed to take advantage of the service. The major IECs provide PRI as an alternative to the T-1 connections over which they offer bulk outgoing and incoming services. With call-by-call service selection the channels can be allotted to any service, which increases utilization and reduces costs.

Standards

Most of the important ISDN standards have been completed and accepted by ITU, and published in North America as NI-1 and NI-2 ISDN. In the United States, ISDN standardization work is handled by ANSI's T1S1 subcommittee.

ISDN standards promulgated by ITU are grouped into the following categories:

◆ I.100 series. ISDN general concepts, methods, structure, and terminology.
◆ I.200 series. ISDN service aspects.
◆ I.300 series. ISDN network aspects.
◆ I.400 series. ISDN user-network interface aspects.
◆ I.500 series. Internetwork interfaces.
◆ I.600 series. Maintenance principles.

Appendix D lists the primary ISDN standards.

A new ISDN standard being prepared as this book is written will give users greater control of ISDN bandwidth. The standard, known as bandwidth allocation control protocol (BACP), lets users set thresholds so high bandwidth applications such as videoconferencing use both B channels when needed, while using and paying for only one channel for lower-speed applications.

SELECTED ISDN EQUIPMENT MANUFACTURERS

Customer Premises Equipment

Virtually all of the PBX manufacturers listed in Chapter 21 provide PRI compatibility, and most offer BRI compatibility. Most of the router manufacturers listed in Chapter 30 also offer PRI compatibility. In addition, the following specialized manufacturers offer ISDN customer premises equipment:

Adtran

Exceltech

Forum Communication Systems

Gandalf Systems Corp.

Intel

ISDN*TEX

Link Technology

Primary Rate Inc.

Teknekron

Teleos Communications, Inc.

Telerad Telecommunications

Tone Commander

Trillium

Tylink

Central Office Equipment

Ericsson

Fujitsu Network Switching

Lucent Technologies

NEC

Northern Telecom

Siemens Stromberg Carlson

29

LOCAL AREA NETWORK PRINCIPLES

Just as offices can no longer function without desktop computers, computers multiply their value when they are connected to a local area network. Without a LAN people share files by passing floppy disks between machines with the result that no one is quite sure which disk contains the latest version of a file. Furthermore, it wastes time to interrupt others to borrow a file, and many files are too large to fit on a floppy disk. LANs also make it easy to share expensive peripherals such as printers, plotters, and pools of faxes and modems.

LANs bring other benefits as well. They make productivity-enhancing features such as electronic mail and calendar available to all users. They help administrators enforce uniformity, and they tie remote offices together so far-flung companies can operate as if everyone was in the same building. Compared to centralized computers, LANs offer scalability. You can add computing power in small increments compared to a mainframe or minicomputer where adding processing power usually means a major change. Also the variety of application software is a big factor in favor of PCs. LANs have become the glue that binds the office together and connects it to other offices.

LANs have reached their state of development today because an effective set of standards makes it possible for hardware and software developers to design to known interfaces. In this chapter we will discuss these standards and how the principal access protocols work.

When the Institute of Electrical and Electronic Engineers (IEEE) began developing LAN standards in its 802 committee in 1980, no one could foresee the impact of desktop computers. IBM had not announced its personal computer, the availability of which sparked an explosion in desktop computing. Fueled by ever-faster processors, cheap memory, and excellent software, desktop computers are now firmly entrenched, and the LAN provides their connectivity.

Local area networks began with modest objectives: sharing files, expensive peripherals such as printers and plotters, and software applications. It wasn't so easy to see additional requirements that have since emerged, including access to mainframe computers and connectivity to WANs. It also wasn't clear that desktop processing power and storage would become so inexpensive that desktop systems would replace many mainframes, and that bandwidth requirements for LANs would increase accordingly.

The networked desktop computer today is the rule rather than the exception that it was a few years ago. LANs are shared-media systems, which provide the workstation with access to the full bandwidth of the network for a portion of the available time. Shared-media LANs work well over a short range. They are intended to be confined to a building or, at most, a campus. Just as desktop computer users discovered their drawbacks as stand-alone devices, LAN users quickly discovered a need to communicate with other LANs. To accomplish this, remote bridges and routers were developed, which are examined in the next chapter.

By definition, a LAN is a network dedicated to a single organization, limited in range, and connected by a common communication technology. This definition has important implications. Because the network is private, it can be specialized for a function. Security may be less critical than in wide area networks, and because range is limited, a LAN can operate at high speeds without incurring the high costs of broadband transmission. Although LANs started out as narrow-range systems, their reach has expanded now to the point that wide area networks increasingly are networks of interconnected LANs.

LOCAL AREA NETWORK TECHNOLOGY

A LAN has the following characteristics:

- ◆ High speed that permits users to transfer data at speeds approaching or exceeding the rate of transfer from a directly attached hard disk.
- ◆ A restricted range—usually two kilometers or less.
- ◆ An access protocol that permits stations to share a common transmission medium.
- ◆ A network operating system that permits stations to address file and print servers as if they were directly attached.

Personal computers, printers, and other devices that connect directly to a LAN do so through a *network interface card* (NIC). The original version of Ethernet used thick coaxial cable, so some of the functions of the NIC were contained in a separate transceiver, but most current types of LAN combine the functions in a single card. The combined functions of the NIC and transceiver are these:

- Provides a physical interface to the transmission medium.
- Monitors the busy/idle status of the network.
- Buffers the speed of the attached device to the speed of the network.
- Converts the protocol of the attached device to the network protocol.
- Assembles the transmitted data stream into packets for transmission on the network and restores the data stream at the receiving end.
- Recovers from collisions that result from simultaneous transmissions.

LANs can be classified according to four criteria, which this section discusses:

- Topology
- Access method
- Modulation method
- Transmission medium

Topology

Network topology is the pattern of interconnection of the network nodes. LANs use the same topologies as global and metropolitan networks: star, bus, ring, and branching tree, but rarely mesh. The most common topology is the bus, in which terminals connect to a single circuit, as in Figure 29–1a. Messages or packets are broadcast simultaneously to all devices on the bus. Most networks that use coaxial cable as the transmission medium use a bus topology.

Star networks, which are illustrated in Figure 29–1b, are the preferred topology in virtually all LANs that use twisted-pair wire or fiber optics as the transmission medium. The EIA/TIA 568 wiring standards specify star wiring. The wire from the device is connected to a hub at a central point. Multiple hubs often are interconnected to form a network of multiple stars. Electrically, the star network is identical to the bus. Note, however, that token ring, which is configured as a star, is wired as a ring.

Branching tree networks, illustrated in Figure 29–1c, are often used in broadband LANs that employ cable television technology. The branching tree is electrically identical to the bus except that its branches are connected through properly designed impedance-matching devices. In a practical broadband LAN

FIGURE 29-1

Local Area Network Topologies

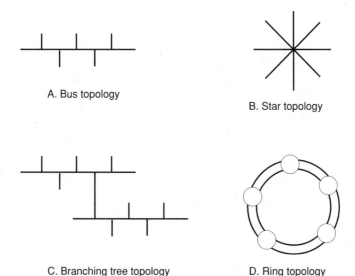

A. Bus topology

B. Star topology

C. Branching tree topology

D. Ring topology

the transmit and receive directions of transmission are full duplex, occupying either separate cables or separate frequencies on a single cable.

The star, branching tree, and bus topologies function identically in a LAN: A station with a message to send gains access to the network and broadcasts a signal that all stations receive. The addressee retains the message; all other stations discard it.

In a ring topology, illustrated in Figure 29–1d, all stations are connected in series, and the signal is transmitted one bit at a time. Each station receives the signal, regenerates it, and transmits it to the next station in the ring. Bits flow in only one direction. The addressee copies the message, but it continues to circulate until it returns to the sending station, which is the only station entitled to remove it from the ring. Other stations act as repeaters that pass the message but do not retain it.

Access Method

A key distinguishing feature of LANs is the method of providing the stations access to the network. In a circuit-switched network, stations gain access by signaling over the network and transmitting an address to a central controller. The controller determines the destination and sets up a path or circuit between the sender and receiver. Because the network has multiple paths, stations cannot interfere with one another after a session is established. By contrast, a shared-media LAN has only one path to handle high-speed data. The total capacity of the path, however, exceeds the transmission speed of any station, so stations are usually unaware that they are sharing the medium. Stations are given exclusive access to the entire network for long enough to send a packet of data or a message. LAN access methods are classified as contention or noncontention.

Contention Access

A *contention* network can be visualized as a large party line with all stations vying for access. In contention networks, control is distributed among all stations. When a station has a message to send, it listens to the network and, if it is idle, sends a packet of data.

It is not always possible, however, for a station to determine when the network is idle. A finite time is required for a signal to transit the length of the transmission medium. In LANs pulses typically travel at about three-fourths of the speed of light. Therefore, as Figure 29–2 shows, a station at one end of a LAN may begin to transmit without realizing that a station at the other end of the network has also begun to transmit. When simultaneous transmissions occur, the two signals collide, and are mutilated.

During the time it takes a pulse to travel from the sending station to the furthest stations on the network, known as the *collision window,* stations are blinded to potential collisions. In one kilometer of coaxial cable the collision window is approximately 5 microseconds wide. Because of potential collisions, contention networks are restricted in diameter; the wider the network the longer the collision window. The practical limitation in contention LANs operating at a data rate of 10 mb/s is about two kilometers. The 802.3 standards specify a maximum length of 500 meters for a single coaxial segment, with up to five segments connected through a maximum of four repeaters.

The most common system for managing access and collisions in a contention network is known as *carrier sense multiple access with collision detection* (CSMA/CD). CSMA/CD, which is used in Ethernet and IEEE 802.3, is a listen-before-transmit protocol. A station wishing to transmit monitors the network to determine whether any traffic is present. If the network is idle, it begins to transmit. If two stations transmit simultaneously, their packets collide. The first station hearing the collision transmits a jamming signal, and when the two transmitting stations hear it they immediately cease to transmit. If an entire packet was transmitted before a collision was detected, the collision would mutilate both signals and valuable network time would be wasted in retransmission.

The procedures that stations follow when a collision occurs are called their *backoff algorithm.* If stations attempted to reaccess the network immediately

FIGURE 29-2

Collisions in a Contention Network

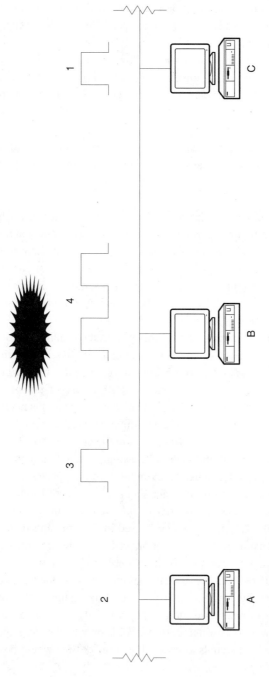

1. Station C begins to transmit.
2. Station A listens to network, but signal from C has not arrived.
3. Station A transmits.
4. Signals from A and C collide.
5. Station B detects the collision and transmits a jamming signal.
6. Stations A and C back off and wait a random time before retransmitting.

following a collision, repeated collisions between the same two stations would occur. To prevent repeated collisions, the protocol causes stations to wait a random time before the next attempt.

Noncontention Access

CSMA/CD is known as a *statistical* access method, relying on the probability that its stations will get enough share of the network to send their traffic in a timely manner. During heavy load periods access may be delayed, so CSMA/CD is not satisfactory for applications that rely on predictable network access.

A noncontention system called *token passing* introduces a form of control that overcomes the drawbacks of the free-for-all system used by CSMA/CD. A token is a unique combination of bits that circulates through the network following a predetermined route. When a station has data to send, it captures the token, transmits its message, and replaces the token on the network. Token passing is a *deterministic* system. If a station has traffic equal to or higher in priority than other traffic on the network, the control mechanism will allocate it a portion of the network's capacity.

The advantages of control are purchased at the price of greater complexity. One of the stations in a token network must be equipped to initiate recovery action if the token is lost or mutilated, which can occur if a station fails or loses power at the time it possesses the token. Other functions required of the control station include the removal of persistently circulating packets, removal of duplicate tokens, control of priority, and addition and removal of stations. Further complicating the process is the need for a recovery routine if the control station fails. To avoid the need for a single control station, all stations are equipped with the logic to assume control if necessary. Because of this greater complexity, token passing NICs are more expensive than contention NICs.

Ring and bus topologies predominate in token networks. In a token ring, which is illustrated in Figure 29–3, each station receives each message and repeats it to the next station in turn. Sequencing is automatic; it always follows the same route in the same direction around the ring. As shown in Figure 29–3, although token ring networks are wired as a ring, the wire is configured as a star. Two pairs of wire terminate in a multistation access unit (MAU) in the center of the network. The MAU routes the token from port to port, and bypasses a port if its station is inoperative.

In a token bus network, messages are broadcast to all stations simultaneously, but control follows a logical ring sequence, as illustrated in Figure 29–4. When a station acquires the token, it is permitted to broadcast a message, but the token can be passed to any other station without regard to its physical position on the network.

FIGURE 29-3

Token Ring Network

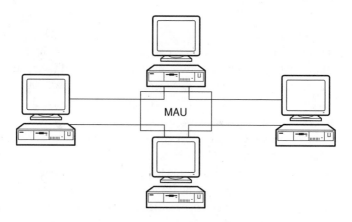

Modulation Methods

LANs use one of two methods of imposing a data signal on the transmission medium. In the first, known as *baseband,* the signal is pulsed directly on the transmission medium in the form of high-speed square wave pulses of DC voltage. *Broadband* systems use cable television (CATV) technology to divide the transmission medium into frequency bands or channels. Each broadband channel can be multiplexed to carry data, voice, or video. Broadband networks are used in a few specialized applications, but the vast majority of LANs use baseband modulation.

Baseband and broadband networks accept identical data streams from the terminal, but they differ in the network access unit. In a baseband thick coaxial cable system, the NIC is coupled to a transceiver, which is a simple cable driver that matches the impedance of the cable and transmits pulses at the data transfer rate. In thin net and twisted-pair systems, the transceiver is built into the NIC. In a broadband network, the NIC plugs into a *radio frequency modem,* which modulates the data to an assigned rf channel.

Baseband

The primary advantage of baseband is its simplicity. No tuned circuits or radio frequency apparatus is required. A baseband system has no active components aside from the NICs, hubs, and, in thick Ethernet systems, external transceivers. Only the cable is common to the network, making baseband less vulnerable to failure than broadband, which contains amplifiers and other active components.

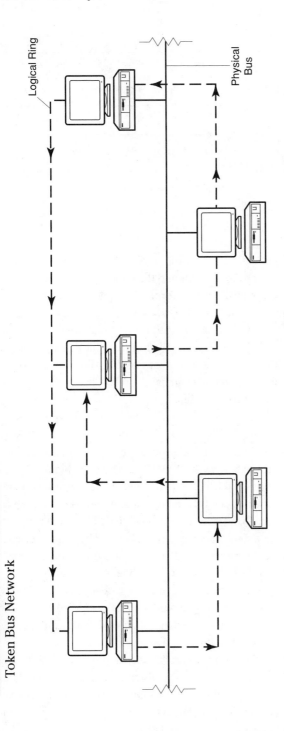

FIGURE 29-4

Token Bus Network

FIGURE 29–5

CATV Frequency Allocations

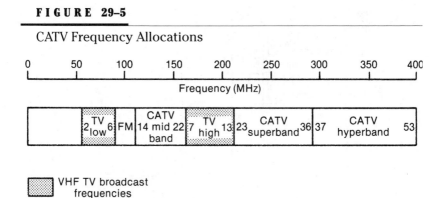

VHF TV broadcast
frequencies

A baseband network consists of workstations, which contain NICs plugged into an expansion slot or built into the motherboard. The NICs accept a data stream from the application and form it into packets that are pulsed directly on the transmission medium. The transmission medium, discussed in a later section, can be unshielded or shielded twisted-pair copper wire, coaxial cable, fiber-optic cable, or wireless. In fiber-optic cable, data pulses drive a light transmitter, which turns a laser or light-emitting diode on and off corresponding to the 0s and 1s of the data signal. Wireless uses infrared or spread spectrum radio signals to carry the signal.

Broadband

Broadband networks use a coaxial cable and amplifier system capable of passing frequencies from about 5 MHz to 400 MHz, as shown in Figure 29–5. Television channels each occupy 6 MHz, with the total cable supporting more than 60 one-way channels, which can be used for a LAN, video, or voice. The primary advantage of broadband over baseband LANs is their greater capacity. The equivalent of several baseband networks is derived by using multiple subcarriers for increased LAN channels, video, or in some cases, voice. Broadband LANs should not be confused with the use of the term broadband to describe high-speed transmission facilities. Chapter 32 discusses broadband networks such as ATM, SMDS, and other high-speed technologies. These technologies use baseband modulation at high speeds to obtain the bandwidth needed for specialized applications such as imaging and multimedia.

Unlike baseband, where signals are broadcast in both directions simultaneously, broadband is inherently a one-way system because of its amplifiers. Bidirectional amplifiers are available, but the transmitting and receiving signals must be separated to obtain bidirectional transmission. The reverse direction is handled either by sending on one cable and receiving on another or by splitting the sending and receiving signals into two different frequencies. The first method is called a *dual-cable* system, and the second a *single-cable* system. *Headend equipment* couples the transmit cable to the receive cable in a dual-cable system and shifts the transmit frequency to the receive frequency in a single-cable system. Headend equipment in a single cable system and amplifiers in all broadband systems are active elements; a failure can interrupt the network.

Devices in a broadband network connect to the transmission medium through radio frequency (rf) modems that contain a transceiver tuned to the network transmit and receive frequencies. Two types of rf modems are available. *Fixed-frequency modems* are tuned to a single frequency. *Frequency agile* modems can be shifted under direction of a central controller that connects stations by selecting an idle channel, directing the two modems to the channel, and dropping out of the connection.

Baseband and broadband LANs are similar in most respects except for the frequency separation in a broadband network and differing methods of collision detection. Collisions are detected on a direct-current basis in a baseband network, but because broadband networks are incapable of passing DC, they employ a different method of collision detection. A common technique is for the sending station to listen for transmissions mutilated by collision. Another system of collision detection is the bit comparison method in which a series of bits is transmitted to acquire the network. If a collision occurs, the first section detecting the collision transmits a jamming signal on a separate channel. Throughput is reduced slightly by the increased overhead and the added length of the doubled cable.

When LANs were first developed, broadband appeared as if it would be an important method of implementing them. Since then, the simplicity of baseband LANs, primarily those using unshielded twisted-pair wire (UTP), has eliminated broadband LANs for all but a few specialized applications.

Transmission Media

All of the transmission media used in other networks—twisted-pair wire, coaxial cable, fiber optics, radio, and infrared—are employed in LANs. Radio and infrared are used for special applications; the other three for general LAN application. The choice of transmission medium is usually dictated by the application. Because of differing characteristics the choice of system may be driven by the transmission medium required. The principal factors to consider are:

◆ Presence of electromagnetic interference (EMI).
◆ Network throughput.
◆ Bandwidth required.

◆ Network diameter.
◆ Multiple device access.
◆ Cost.
◆ Security.

Twisted-Pair Wire

In the early LAN designs UTP was considered to lack the bandwidth and noise immunity needed for reliable operation over a reasonable distance. Recently, however, structured cable systems using precisely manufactured and carefully installed components have been standardized by EIA and TIA. Category 5 UTP has enough bandwidth to handle up to 155 mb/s, which enables it to carry FDDI and ATM to the desktop. As a result, UTP has become the default medium. The IEEE designation for Ethernet running on UTP is 10-Base-T.

The primary advantages of twisted-pair wire are cost and ease of installation. Wire is readily available from many vendors and can be installed by trained personnel with simple and inexpensive hand tools. It has enough bandwidth to handle data speeds of up to 155 mb/s for distances of up to 100 meters. See Chapter 7 for a discussion of structured wiring systems that support high-speed LANs. Wire is available in multiple twisted-pair cable, both shielded and unshielded, and in flat ribbons that can be installed under carpet. It is durable and capable of withstanding considerable abuse without damage, and with its sheath intact, it is impervious to weather.

Industry standard RJ-45 jacks and patch cords are used to connect the NIC to the transmission medium. Many NICs have two or three types of adapter on the card so the workstation can connect to UTP, thin net, or to thick net through an attachment unit interface (AUI) connector.

Coaxial Cable

Coaxial cable, or "coax," is a good transmission medium for some LANs. It is inexpensive, has wide bandwidth, and can be installed by moderately skilled workers. Coax can support both high-speed data and video, and because it is widely used for cable television (CATV), it is readily available at moderate cost.

Coaxial cable has one or more center conductors surrounded by a shield of flexible braid or semirigid copper or aluminum tube, with an outer jacket of PVC or Teflon®. When properly installed, the conductor is shielded from EMI and is reasonably impervious to weather. Special precautions are required to avoid unwanted effects in installing coaxial cables. In baseband networks, cables must be grounded in only one place; precautions are required to insulate

FIGURE 29-6

Thin Ethernet Daisy Chains between Computers

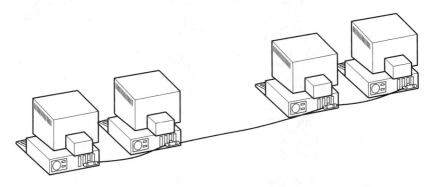

connectors from ground at unwanted places. Branching points in broadband coax must be equipped with splitters and directional couplers to avoid impedance irregularities. The bend radius of coax must be sufficiently wide to prevent kinking, which can cause an impedance irregularity.

Coax can be tapped with little difficulty, which is advantageous when adding stations to a LAN without interrupting service. This means, however, that communications on the network are not entirely secure from unauthorized access. Refer to Chapter 18 for further discussion of CATV components.

The earliest versions of Ethernet, now known as 10-Base-5, operate on thick coaxial cable. Segments are limited to 500 meters in length. Transceivers mount on the cable and connect to the network interface card through the attachment unit interface (AUI). This method of node attachment is effective for interconnecting large-scale computers, but it is difficult to install in an office environment. The cable can be placed in suspended ceilings or in the wiring troughs of modular furniture, but it is difficult to administer, so that it has been replaced by fiber optics in most cases. The AUI-to-transceiver cable is limited in length to 50 meters.

Some of thick Ethernet's deficiencies are resolved with thin Ethernet, which works on RG-58 cable. This cable is about the thickness of a pencil, and is easier to install. Thin Ethernet, also known as 10-Base-2, is daisy-chained from station to station, as shown in Figure 29–6. Thin Ethernet segments are limited to 185 meters in length, not 200 meters as its 10-Base-2 designation would imply. The cable terminates directly on a BNC connector, which mounts on the NIC. A T connector is used to daisy-chain the cable from one station to the next, with a terminator placed on the end stations.

Thin Ethernet is acceptable in an open work area where cable can be run easily from station to station. In an area with fixed walls, the cable must be looped down the wall and back up again to connect from office to office. The 185-meter segment length can be reached quickly in such an environment. Thin Ethernet also has the disadvantage of being difficult to troubleshoot. If the cable is broken, all the stations downstream (away from the server) are isolated.

Fiber Optics

Fiber-optic cable with its wide bandwidth can support data speeds far higher than those needed by most LANs. Fiber can be applied in three configurations, as illustrated in Figure 29–7:

- ◆ 10-Base-FL, a fiber link segment.
- ◆ 10-Base-FP, a star topology using a passive optical coupler at the hub.
- ◆ 10-Base-FB, which are fiber-optic synchronous links.

Fiber optics is the primary transmission medium that is used with fiber distributed data interface (FDDI) covered in Chapter 32. FDDI will also run on UTP, where it is sometimes called CDDI (copper distributed data interface). Refer to Chapter 13 for additional information on lightwave.

Radio

As discussed in Chapter 17, spread-spectrum radio is used for wireless LANs where bandwidth requirements are not great. Spread spectrum is an inherently secure mechanism for releasing stations from the confines of a mounting cord. For portable applications such as personal digital assistants, spread-spectrum radio is an effective medium that can penetrate walls and floors without the need to string wire. It is not, however, robust enough at this stage of development to replace wired media.

Microwave radio is inherently a point-to-point medium, and as such is useful for linking LANs. Microwaves travel in a straight line, so intermediate stations can be linked only if they are on the path of the radio beam. Radio is useful where right-of-way is a problem, as in crossing obstructions and spanning moderate distances. It is also useful in connecting LANs.

Among its limitations, radio is not easily secured. It is impossible to prevent unauthorized detection of data signals over a microwave path, so when security is important, encryption is required. Frequency allocations are coordinated by the Federal Communications Commission and may be difficult to obtain in crowded urban areas. Also, microwave is expensive to purchase, requires trained

FIGURE 29-7

Fiber-Optic Links

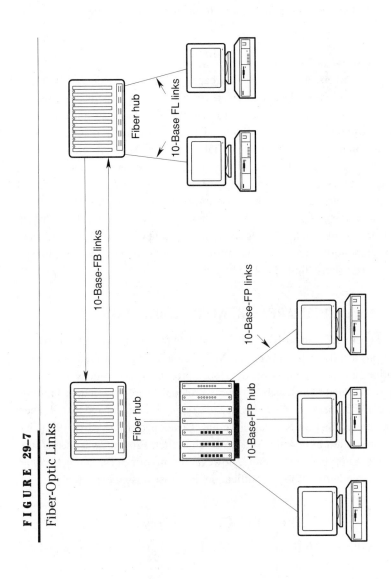

technicians to install and maintain, and is susceptible to interference from outside sources. Nevertheless, it is an economical way of interconnecting LANs, particularly where obstructions make it impossible to obtain right-of-way for fiber optics. Refer to Chapter 14 for additional information on microwave.

Light

Optical transceivers, as discussed in Chapter 17, are available for the same kinds of applications as described above for radio. Point-to-point systems use infrared light transceivers operating over short line-of-sight distances such as crossing a street between two buildings. Distances are limited, and transmission is not completely reliable because light beams can be interrupted by influences such as fog and dust. Its application is limited to short distances where other alternatives are prohibitively expensive.

Some wireless LAN products use infrared light to connect stations to a hub. Light is transmitted from the workstation to a centrally located infrared transceiver mounted on the ceiling or, as discussed in Chapter 17, light is scattered throughout the coverage area. Infrared cannot penetrate walls, so its applications are strictly limited to line of sight.

LOCAL AREA NETWORK STANDARDS

Local area network standards originated in much the same way that other communications standards have been set. Manufacturers experimented with communications and access methods, developed proprietary techniques, and gradually demonstrated their feasibility. Early protocols were proprietary, limiting the compatibility between the network and existing equipment and that of other manufacturers. Ethernet is a case in point. Developed in the early 1970s by Xerox Corporation in its Palo Alto Research Center, Ethernet was offered for licensing at a nominal cost. Rarely, however, do proprietary systems become adopted as standards without modification. Ethernet was no exception.

The IEEE 802 Committee

In 1980, the Institute of Electrical and Electronic Engineers (IEEE) formed the 802 committee, which was charged with developing LAN standards. A few years earlier, Digital Equipment Company, Intel, and Xerox had collaborated to produce Ethernet, a contention protocol. Ethernet was offered to the 802 committee as a potential standard. Several companies objected to a contention protocol as the sole standard, however, so eventually IEEE settled on the three standards that will be discussed in this chapter. The 802 committee's objectives were to establish standards for the physical and data link connections between devices. The following requirements were established:

◆ Existing data communications standards were to be incorporated into the IEEE standard as much as possible.

◆ The network was intended for light industrial and commercial use.

◆ The maximum network diameter was set at two kilometers.

◆ The data speed on the network was to be between 1 mb/s and 20 mb/s.

◆ The network standard was to be independent of the transmission medium.

◆ The failure of any device on the network was not to disrupt the entire network.

◆ There was to be no more than one undetected error per year on the network.

The committee concluded that Ethernet would not suffice as a single standard because of the potential of blockage under heavy load conditions. Therefore, the committee adopted three incompatible standards. For light duty, a bus contention network, 802.3, similar but not identical to Ethernet, was selected. For applications where assurance of network access is needed, token passing bus (802.4) and ring (802.5) standards were selected. All LAN protocols are connectionless, which means that frames are launched onto the transmission medium as unacknowledged packets. Table 29–1 lists the 802 standards, which have expanded significantly since the initial project.

The 802 standards are developed around layers 1 and 2 of the OSI protocols (see Chapter 4) and do not include all the functions of a complete network. The missing functions are provided by the network operating system (NOS), which operates between the user application and the logical link control layer of the 802 standards. The NOS controls access to the network through rights and permissions that are a function of the user's account. The NOS handles the following functions, which are discussed in more detail in a later section:

◆ Controls and regulates access to the network's resources, including disk space and printers.

◆ Controls security, including rights and permissions to access files and directories.

◆ Contains network utilities for setting up user accounts, granting rights to files, controlling passwords and log-in scripts, setting up printers, and so on.

◆ Connects the user applications to the underlying transmission medium and access control.

TABLE 29-1

802 Local Area Network Standards

802.1	Overview document containing the reference model, tutorial, and glossary
802.2	Logical link control
802.3	Contention bus standard, 10-Base-5 (Thicknet)
802.3A	Contention bus standard, 10-Base-2 (Thin net)
802.3B	Broadband contention bus standard, 10-Broad-36
802.3D	Fiber optic interrepeater link (FOIRL)
802.3E	Contention bus standard, 1-Base-5 (Starlan)
802.3I	Twisted-pair standard, 10-Base-T
802.3J	Contention bus standard for fiber optics, 10-Base-F
802.3U	100 mb/s contention bus standard, 100-Base-T
802.4	Token bus standard
802.5	Token ring standard
802.5B	Token ring standard 4 mb/s over unshielded twisted pair
802.F	Token ring standard 16 mb/s operation
802.6	Metropolitan area network DQDB
802.7	Broadband LAN recommended practices
802.8	Fiber-optic contention network practices
802.9A	Integrated voice and data LAN
802.10	Interoperable LAN Security
802.11	Proposed wireless LAN standard
802.12	Proposed contention bus standard 100-Base-VG AnyLAN

Note: This table lists only the major standards in the 802 series. Each standard has numerous subparts, many of which are omitted for clarity.

 ◆ Detects and corrects errors and recovers from network failures.
 ◆ Manages the transfer of data across the network.

The layered protocol structure of the 802 standards means that any NOS can operate with any of the 802 standards by changing the NIC and software drivers. This architecture provides a great deal of flexibility and interoperability among applications and different manufacturers' products.

The IEEE 802.3 CSMA/CD Standard

The 802.3 standard is a CSMA/CD network intended for commercial or light industrial use. The specification supports baseband and broadband coaxial cable, twisted-pair wire, baseband fiber, and wireless. Although the terms 802.3 and Ethernet are often used interchangeably, there are differences between the two protocols. Both use CSMA/CD, but the frame structure is somewhat

T A B L E 29–2

802.3 Network Standards

	Transmission Medium	Maximum Segment Length (Meters)	Connections per Segment
10-Base-5	RG-8 50 ohm coax	500	100
10-Base-2	RG-58 72 ohm coax	185	30
10-Base-T	Unshielded twisted-pair wire	100	NA
10-Base-FL	Multimode 50/125 fiber	2,000	NA

different, and the transmission media they support are not identical. Ethernet specifies only a 50 ohm coaxial cable medium; 802.3 supports 50 ohm coax, unshielded twisted pair (UTP), fiber optics, and wireless. Despite the differences, the Ethernet term is used by the industry (and in this book) synonymously with 802.3.

The 802.3 standards are identified by a three-part designation that specifies the data rate, modulation method, and, except for twisted-pair wire, the maximum segment length. Twisted-pair segments terminate in hubs, with the maximum length from the workstation to the hub, including patch cords, set as 100 meters. Table 29–1 shows the shorthand designations for the standard and proposed 802 standards. Table 29–2 shows the essential characteristics of the coaxial, UTP, and fiber-optic standards.

Figure 29–8 illustrates the elements of 802.3. The link layer is divided into two sublayers—the logical link control (LLC) and the media access control (MAC)—which together correspond to the data link layer in the OSI model. The 802.3 standard interacts with higher layers for error recovery and network control. The interface between the media access sublayer and the LLC transmits and receives frames and provides status information to forward to higher levels for error recovery. The interface between the media access and the physical layers includes signals for framing, detecting and recovering from collisions, and passing serial bit streams between the two layers.

The network is composed of cable segments a maximum of 500 meters (1,640 feet) long—the greatest distance that can be spanned efficiently at the maximum signaling rate of 20 mb/s. As many as five segments can be interconnected through a maximum of four repeaters. Figure 29–9 shows one method of connecting segments. The design rules specify that a signal between two stations cannot traverse more than four repeaters. The repeaters sense carriers from both cable segments to which they are connected and also detect and

F I G U R E   29–8

IEEE 802 Standard Protocol Stack

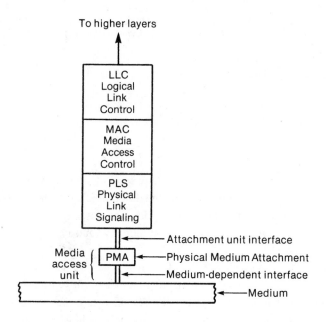

avoid collisions. When a repeater detects a collision in one segment, it transmits a jamming signal to both segments to which it is connected.

Two pairs of UTP are used for 10-Base-T, one to transmit and one to receive. During transmission the device continues to listen to the receive pair for collisions. Throughput in a contention network cannot reach the wire speed because upper-layer protocols send acknowledgment packets, collisions cause retransmissions, and frames cannot space themselves perfectly without colliding.

The 802.3 frame, which Figure 29–10 shows, must always be at least 64 octets long, and no more than 1,500 octets in length. The reason for the frame lengths relates to the collision detection algorithm. If the frames are too short, a collision could escape undetected because the frame could have completed transmission before the collision could be reported back to the transmitting station. This would require higher-layer protocols to compensate for the errors caused by the collision. Therefore, the frame includes a variable-length pad field to build out the frame length if necessary.

FIGURE 29-9

A Five-Segment Ethernet

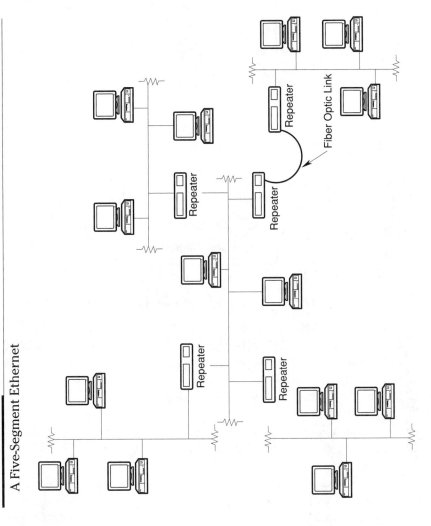

FIGURE 29–10

802.3 Frame Format

Preamble (7)
Start frame delimiter (1)
Destination address (2 or 6)
Source address (2 or 6)
Length (2)
Data field (0-1500)
Pad (0-46)
Frame check sequence (4)

The IEEE 802.4 Token Bus Standard

A token bus LAN, illustrated in Figure 29–4, uses the same topology as CSMA/CD, but control flows in a logical ring. Although messages are broadcast as with CSMA/CD, control passes in sequence from station to station by means of a circulating token. Each station is programmed with the address of the preceding and succeeding stations, and is programmed to recover if one station goes off-line or fails.

Token passing allows a wider physical network diameter than CSMA/CD. The diameter can range from 1,280 meters (4,200 feet) to 7,600 meters (25,000 feet) depending on cable grade.

The MAC in a token bus performs many of the same functions that it does in CSMA/CD, such as address recognition and frame encapsulation, but several functions are added to accomplish the more complex control. The primary functions of the MAC are to determine when its station has the right to access the medium, to recognize the presence of a token, and to determine when and how to pass the token to the next station. The MAC must be capable of initializing or resetting the network. It must be able to recognize when a token has been lost and to regenerate it when necessary. It also must be able to control the addition of a new station to the network and to recognize when a succeeding station has failed.

On the surface, token passing does not appear complicated, and if all goes well, the protocol has little work to do. Each MAC is programmed with the address of its successor and predecessor stations. When it passes the token to its successor, it listens for the successor's transmission. If the successor fails to transmit, the MAC sends a second token and again listens for a response. If it hears no response, it assumes the next station has failed and transmits a message asking which station follows. Each MAC on the network compares its predecessor station number with the number contained in the "who follows" message. The station that follows the failed station responds to the message, and the failed station is bypassed. A similar process is required for a station to reinsert itself in the network.

The primary use for the token bus LAN is industrial applications. The manufacturing automation protocol (MAP) is the principal product using the 802.4 token bus. The protocol, which has no application in the office, is covered in books listed in the bibliography.

The IEEE 802.5 Token Ring Standard

The token ring LAN, illustrated in Figure 29–3, is both a logical and a topological ring. Each station is a repeater, enabling greater diameter than bus networks. A token ring network is wired as a ring in a star topology, with a hub known as a multistation access unit (MAU) at its center. MAUs are either passive or active devices that couple the twisted-pair wire of the side legs to the central ring. MAUs can be chained to broaden the scope of the ring. If the ring becomes overloaded, it is split by breaking the tie between MAUs and segmenting a single ring into two or more rings. Because each node repeats the data stream, failure of a node could disrupt the network. Therefore, the MAUs are equipped with trunk-coupling units to bypass a failed station automatically.

Tokens, which are a three-octet fragment, contain a priority indicator. When a token circulates through a station that has traffic of a priority equal to or greater than the priority designator in the token, that station can seize the token and send priority traffic until a timer within its MAC, known as the *token holding timer,* expires. When the THT expires, the station generates a new token and passes it to the next station. In this manner, the network ensures that traffic always is transmitted up to capacity and that low-priority traffic is deferred.

One station on the ring is designated as the active monitor (AM) to supervise the network. The AM controls error recovery, detects the absence of a token or valid frames of data, and detects a persistently circulating token or frame. The AM sets an indicator on each frame and checks the indicator to be sure a frame circulates only once. Although only one station is designated as the AM, all stations contain its logic. If the AM fails, the station first detecting the failure assumes the role.

T A B L E 29–3

Token Ring Wiring Types

Wire Designation	Wire Type	Number of Pairs	Use
Type 1	STP	2	Ring and lobe
Type 2	STP	2 data, 4 voice	Ring and lobe
Type 3	UTP	4	Ring and lobe
Type 5	Fiber optic	100 micron	Backbone
Type 6	Stranded	2	Patch cable
Type 8	Flat	2	Under carpet
Type 9	STP	2	Short ring and lobe

A token ring has three rules that are simple in concept but complex to execute in the NICs:

♦ A station can transmit a frame only when it possesses the token.

♦ All stations copy the frame, but only the addressee retains it, putting it back on the ring as it is received.

♦ Only the sending station (or the AM if the sending station should fail) is permitted to remove the frame.

The 802.5 protocol, like 802.3, does not correct errors. When any receiving station detects an error in a frame, it sets an error flag, which the sending station detects almost immediately. Upon detecting the error flag, the sending station begins to resend the frame, which can commence before the last of the errored frame is received.

Token ring runs at 4 mb/s and 16 mb/s on six different wiring types, which are listed in Table 29–3. When the network was initially designed, it required shielded twisted-pair wire (STP), which is significantly more costly and more difficult to install than UTP. As wire quality improved, IBM, which designed token ring, supported the use of UTP on 4 mb/s, but required STP on the 16 mb/s LAN. Now UTP is supported for both 4 and 16 mb/s, but STP is required for the backbone.

Token ring is a more robust network than Ethernet, but it is also more expensive. The NICs are more costly, and the MAUs are more expensive than Ethernet hubs. The cost of the installation can be reduced considerably by using the UTP alternative. Category 4 wiring (see Chapter 7) is specifically designed to support token ring. Most companies install category 5, however, because it also supports FDDI, which is an upward migration path. Token ring is capable of greater throughput than Ethernet because of its more disciplined way of allocating network access. Where Ethernet is capable of about 60 percent utilization (throughput of about 6 mb/s), token ring can approach 90 percent utilization. Most installations of token ring are in companies that use IBM hardware, while most other installations use Ethernet.

The 802.6 Metropolitan Area Network

The limited speed and range capabilities of LANs spawned the need for a standard network that can transmit data at speeds of 100 mb/s or more over a range approximating the size of a metropolitan area. The 802.6 metropolitan area network, which Chapter 32 discusses, fulfills this requirement. Unlike LANs, which are intended for private use, the 802.6 network is intended for shared use over public rights-of-way.

FAST ETHERNET

Token ring networks have the option of 4 and 16 mb/s network speeds, with a path for upgrading to FDDI if a higher data rate is needed. Standard Ethernet is fixed at a 10 mb/s data rate with throughput limited to about 6 mb/s in normal operations. These limits are dropping, however, as a spate of fast Ethernet alternatives enter the market. At the time of this writing the 802 committee is in various stages of considering the alternatives, and it isn't certain that all of them will survive, but it is certain that 100 mb/s Ethernet will become an important force in the LAN market. Although FDDI is an alternative, it is significantly more expensive than the fast Ethernet LANs, some of which command only a small cost increment over conventional Ethernet.

The alternatives, which are listed in Table 29–4, all use twisted-pair wire. Other than that, they have little in common.

100-Base-T

This network uses the same protocol as standard Ethernet, but operates at 10 times the speed. It was adopted by IEEE in 1995 as 802.3U. Two different varieties are proposed, 100-Base-T4 and 100-Base-TX. The attraction of the latter alternative is its simplicity. The protocols and the packets are the same as standard Ethernet. Dual-speed Ethernet cards are readily available, and dual-speed hubs are becoming available. These make upgrade to 100 mb/s easy, provided the cable infrastructure supports the increased speed. Any wire installed according to EIA/TIA 568 standards will support 100-Base-T except for the reduced segment length discussed below.

T A B L E 29–4

Fast Ethernet Alternatives

	Speed	Cable Type	Number of Pairs	Node-to-Hub Distance Limit	Number of Hps
100-Base-TX	100 mb/s	Category 5, Category 3, Fiber	2	100 meters	2
100-Base-T4	100 mb/s	Category 3, Fiber	4	100 meters	2
VG AnyLAN	100 mb/s	Category 3, Category 5, Fiber	4	Cat. 3: 200 meters Cat. 5: 100 meters	4
Full-Duplex Ethernet	20 mb/s	Category 3, Category 5 Fiber	2	100 meters	4
IsoEthernet	16.144 mb/s	Category 3, Category 5	2	100 meters	4

The 100-Base-T4 protocol is also attractive, although unlike standard Ethernet, which uses two of the four pairs in a category 3 wire run, 100-Base-T4 uses all four pairs. Companies that installed nonstandard wire runs will have to upgrade the wire to use this alternative.

One drawback of this alternative is its reduced network diameter. Where standard Ethernet supports a total diameter of 2.5 km, the 100-Base-T alternatives have a 100-meter repeater-to-node limit for UTP, with a limit of two hops per network.

100VG AnyLAN

The VG in this protocol stands for voice grade. This method uses four pairs of category 3 wire to provide 100 mb/s service. It does not use the standard Ethernet protocol. Instead, it uses a polling process that eliminates collisions. The hubs poll the workstations in the order in which they connected to see if they have traffic to send. Nodes respond with an indication of normal or priority traffic.

VG carries both Ethernet and token ring frame types, and offers an upgrade path from either type of network. Because of the polling protocol, the network diameter is not limited as it is with 10-Base-T.

The protocol is supported by IBM, Lucent Technologies, and Hewlett-Packard, but whether it will become the accepted 803.12 standard has not yet been determined.

Full-Duplex Ethernet

In its standard implementation, Ethernet is a half-duplex protocol. Since the original transmission medium was coaxial cable, full-duplex operation at baseband was impossible with the standard contention access method. With UTP, however, which uses separate wire pairs for transmit and receive, full-duplex operation is feasible if the traffic is run through a switch (Chapter 30). The switch provides a separate segment for each station on the network, and since there is one segment per station, collisions are eliminated.

The value of full-duplex Ethernet comes when the application is full-duplex. In networks that support such functions as word processing and spreadsheets, full-duplex offers little or no advantage because traffic is mostly one-way between workstation and server. In networks that support heavy database use where files are constantly being saved and retrieved and the amount of traffic is approximately equal in both directions, full-duplex can come close to doubling the basic speed.

Although full-duplex Ethernet is not an accepted standard at this time, numerous proprietary products are on the market. Since the protocol is largely identical with standard Ethernet, the risk of buying a nonstandard product is not high.

Isochronous Ethernet

A major disadvantage of standard Ethernet is its inability to handle time-sensitive traffic such as voice or video. One proposed solution to this is isochronous Ethernet (isoENET), which combines standard 10-Base-T with 6.144 mb/s isochronous channels to provide a total of 16 mb/s of bandwidth. At the time of this writing IEEE is considering isoENET as the 803.9A standard. Through the use of switching, this bandwidth can be made available to every user. The 6.144 mb/s of isochronous bandwidth can be subdivided into 96 ISDN B channels and one D channel of 64 kb/s.

Ethernet runs on a 10 mb/s channel known as the ISDN P channel. The P channel uses the standard 802.3 frame structure and CSMA/CD access algorithm. The 6.144 mb/s bandwidth occupies an ISDN C channel. It uses the same 8,000-frame-per-second clocking mechanism of T-1 carrier. IsoENET is compatible with standard 802.3 networks, but to access the isochronous channels, special station adapters are required. Circuits are set up and torn down using the Q.931 signaling protocol of ISDN.

NETWORK OPERATING SYSTEMS

By themselves, the 802 networks implement only the first two layers of the OSI model, and are incapable of complete communications. The higher protocol layers, which are needed to complete the network, are implemented in the network operating system (NOS). The following are the primary functions of the NOS:

- ◆ Capture calls to the computer's operating system from the application program and convert them to network operating system calls.
- ◆ Manage the hard disk in the file server to maximize the efficiency of information transfer between the network and the server.
- ◆ Manage security on the network, permitting users to offer their files for shared access and restrict them from unauthorized access.
- ◆ Designate shared resources as if they were directly attached to the users' personal computers.
- ◆ Provide tools with which the network administrator can manage the network.

The concepts of redirection and virtual resources are important to understanding any NOS. The NOS interacts with the computer's operating system. In the process of logging onto the network the users' log-in scripts define virtual disk drives and printer ports. Virtual drives and ports act as if they were installed as hardware, but they actually exist on a server. For example, a PC might be equipped with one hardware line printer port, defined as LPT1. The NOS allows the administrator to set the computer up with LPT2, which does not exist in hardware. When the application program sends a document to LPT2, the NOS intercepts the document and redirects it to the network printer. LPT1 could also be redirected, say to another printer, in which case it would be unavailable as a hardware port as long as the computer was logged on the network. If the computer was used as a stand-alone device, the hardware port would be available as usual.

File service works in the same manner. Most NOSs define the F drive as a path to the file server's disk. The file server then behaves as if it was directly attached to the workstation. When the application program makes a file call, the NOS redirects it to the file server over the network.

To simplify the task of reaching various directories, the NOS allows you to establish virtual drives represented by any letter from G to Z. For example, many LAN administrators set up directory space for each user. A virtual drive letter such as P for personal is set up in the log-in script as the path to each user's personal directory. After the user logs on with his or her log-in name, the P drive then leads directly to the personal directory.

NOSs can be classified as peer-to-peer or server-centric. A peer network enables all users to offer their resources for sharing. A server network concentrates the resources in one or more servers. Nothing prevents a peer network from using dedicated servers. If a workstation is not occupied, it can be designated as a server, offering its resources as print or file services, to other stations on the network.

Peer-to-Peer Networks

Peer networks enable users to share directories, disk space, printers, or other resources that are attached to their computers. If a directory is marked for sharing, other users have access to all the files it contains. If a printer is marked for sharing, print jobs are spooled from the network to that printer. Peer network operating systems work well in small offices that do not have regular network management or a great concern for security. Users must, however, be trained to observe network discipline. For example, if users reboot or turn off their computers while other stations are accessing a file or using a printer, the data or print job are likely to be corrupted. Normal file shutdown procedures inform users when others are attached to their computer, so if procedures are followed the results are satisfactory.

Enforcing security on a peer network may be difficult. If all files are stored on a server, the network administrator can prevent users from accessing files by marking the directory as unshared. With some peer networks the entire directory is either sharable or not, in which case it is impossible to allow some users rights to access files while denying them to others.

Network statistics, which enable the administrator to check the amount of activity, collisions and other such load indicators are generally not provided by a peer NOS even if one workstation is dedicated as a file server. Although some companies operate peer networks successfully with numerous workstations (roughly more than 20), most networks of this size will find it preferable to use a server. Unless a file server is used on a peer network, the probability of data loss is high because no one is responsible for backing up all files. Without a dedicated server, it is difficult to be sure where the latest version of files is stored because users can copy a file from another user's disk, modify it, and save it to their own hard disk. Peer network operating systems are intended for small offices that cannot justify the cost of a server NOS.

Server-Centric Network Operating Systems

The server-centric network has various service functions such as file, print, fax, modem pool, and remote access centralized in one or more servers.

A server NOS has significantly more administrative features than a peer NOS. The following are some of the administrative features that typical operating systems provide:

Control of File and Directory Access   Users are given rights to access files. Typical rights include:

◆ Who is authorized to access what files and with what level of rights.
◆ What shared resources are available and to what group of users.
◆ How security is managed to prevent unauthorized access and damage to files.
◆ What administrative tools are available to evaluate network performance, control access to the network, and add, move, and change stations.
◆ What other networks are accessible and how access is controlled.
◆ What maintenance, statistical, and troubleshooting tools are available to alert managers to impending problems and assist in restoral when they occur.
◆ What utility programs are made available to the users and administrator.

The administrator can grant or revoke rights to directories or individual files. Files and directories can be hidden to conceal their presence from users who lack the appropriate rights.

User Groups   Users can be assigned as groups of users who have a common set of interests. Members can send messages, the supervisor can assign rights to selected files and directories, users can share exclusive use of a common printer, and so on.

Security Administration   The administrator can assign and control passwords, user IDs and other means of regulating security. The administrator can force passwords of a particular length, and can force users to change passwords as needed.

Administer Log-in Scripts   Log-in scripts can be established for every user. These define virtual drives, set up port redirection for printers, send messages to the users, and with other commands allow the administrator to otherwise customize configurations for users and groups.

Printer Administration   The network administrator can identify stations as printer control stations. These stations can delete or move print jobs in queue, establish or change print priorities, pause the printer to change forms, and other such tasks concerned with printer management.

Administrative Tools   Many local area network users underestimate the amount of administrative effort it takes to keep a network operating. The network administrator is defined in software as the person who has the right to modify and control the rights of other users. In most networks, the rights approximate the following list, which is ordered by the degree of control the right provides, with the highest rights listed first. Each right has the rights of succeeding but not of preceding levels of authority:

◆ Hidden: The presence of the file or directory is itself concealed from unauthorized users.
◆ Parental: Has full control over any file in the directory.
◆ Private: Only users with parental rights can read files.
◆ Modify: Can change any file in the directory.
◆ Read/write: Can read any file or write any file in the directory but cannot modify existing files.
◆ Read only: Can read files in the directory but cannot add a file.

The operating system permits managers to create a tree-structured directory structure on the server. Files are contained in directories and subdirectories; the network administrator can regulate rights at any level from a file up to the entire directory.

The operating system also provides statistical information that enables the administrator to isolate trouble and reconfigure the network as necessary. For example, the administrator needs to know the volume of traffic on the network and the frequency with which users encounter delays. Contention networks should show the frequency of collision. The operating system should inform the administrator of factors such as the number of cache hits that affect the operating efficiency of the file server.

Utility Programs   Most network operating systems also provide a set of utilities for performing the same sorts of functions that a user expects on a single-user operating system. Utility programs enable users to list directories, copy files, and perform other such functions. The network administrator has utilities to add and remove users, establish rights, change the classifications of files, and oversee the activities of the users. In most networks, administrators have utilities that allow them to create menus to insulate users from the operating system's command language.

OTHER LAN APPLICATION ISSUES

The foregoing factors are the principal issues involved in selecting and applying LAN technology. Several other issues must be considered, however, when deciding which product to purchase. These issues are discussed in this section.

Network Management

In larger networks consider the availability of a network management network system. Components installed on the network should be SNMP-compatible. More details on network management are provided in Chapter 37.

Internetworking

Most multisite companies connect their LANs with an internet. Internetworking raises several issues that affect the choice of NOS. Some peer protocols do not support TCP/IP, some protocols cannot be routed, and some network protocols are not supported by many routers. Refer to Chapter 30 for additional discussions on routing, and Chapter 33 for further information on internetworking.

Infrastructure Planning

The default transmission medium in LANs today is UTP. In some specialized situations thick or thin coax may be used, but 10-Base-T or 16 mb/s token ring running over UTP constitutes a majority of networks.

Companies that occupy multiple floors of a building or have multiple departments will probably segment the LAN using bridges or routers. The architecture of the system should be planned in advance to be certain that the infrastructure has been built to accommodate the necessary hardware. Planning is especially important when a structured wiring system is being installed. It is always less expensive to install additional capacity in the horizontal and backbone wiring paths at the time of initial wiring than it is to add it later.

The minimum of two horizontal wiring paths specified by EAI/TIA 568 is not enough for many companies. It is difficult to look far enough in the future to predict bandwidth requirements, but fiber optics in the horizontal distribution system will probably be needed in most companies. Installing dark fiber at the time of twisted-pair installation saves the labor cost of adding it later.

Backbone Architecture

LAN architecture is flexible, and as discussed in Chapters 30 and 33, it can often be rearranged by changing the equipment if the proper infrastructure is in place. In planning a LAN, determine whether a backbone such as FDDI will be used to link segments, or whether the segments will connect in a collapsed backbone. The choice effects the number of fibers in the backbone. Consider whether the company needs a virtual LAN architecture.

Network Speed and Throughput

Throughput, or rate of transfer of information between stations, is an important issue with LANs as with any other network. LANs have high data transmission speeds, generally ranging between 10 and 16 mb/s, with FDDI and fast Ethernet networks operating at 100 mb/s. Transmission speed should not be confused with throughput, however, which may be a fraction of the transmission speed. Throughput is limited by several factors in a LAN:

♦ Data transmission speed of the network.
♦ Overhead bits used by the network protocol.
♦ Time spent in collision and error recovery.
♦ Bandwidth of the transmission medium.
♦ Diameter of the network.

Throughput is predictable in token ring networks but is difficult to predict in contention LANs. In contention networks, throughput can be determined by a computer simulation or experimentally by loading the network to see how response time is affected. Although the network itself may have a high throughput, communication may be slowed because of characteristics of the file server, which is the principal device other stations wish to communicate with. Factors affecting file server efficiency are discussed in Chapter 30.

Throughput can be increased by using a faster protocol. LAN protocols operating at 100 mb/s are either available today, or are under active consideration. As the price of the hardware drops and as bandwidth demands increase, these faster protocols will replace standard Ethernet as the default network protocol.

Network Size or Diameter

All LANs have a limited diameter, which can be overcome with ancillary devices such as bridges, routers, and gateways. Designers must be careful in designing networks not to exceed the maximum diameter. Remember that the limiting factor is measured in cable feet, not in point-to-point distance. Designers must take into account routing that may add to network diameter. Diameter can be extended with repeaters. Be careful to observe the design rule that states that no more than four repeaters can be connected between any two stations.

Virtual LANs

The theory of LAN development is that a network may start as one or more large segments. As the network use grows, the network is subdivided into segments by bridging or routing. As long as the users on the segments remain in the same physical proximity, this method of segmentation works well. If a user moves to a location that is served by a different LAN segment, the benefits of segmentation may be lost because traffic from that station flows over both segments as well as the backbone. Furthermore, unless the hub offers port switching, hub ports may be unused because they are dedicated to a segment, and there may not be enough users physically located near enough to use the excess capacity.

The solution to this dilemma is known as a *virtual LAN*. Stations in a virtual LAN are assigned to ports in a port-switching hub, which connects to a backbone network through a router. Traffic from the stations in a virtual LAN flows through the routers and the backbone, but does not overload segments to which the member does not belong. The concept is discussed in more detail in Chapter 30.

Fault Tolerance

A fault-tolerant LAN is one that can handle irregularities in network operation while allowing users to continue processing or, at worst, to terminate their operation without losing data. Network irregularities fall into three categories, each of which may require a different recovery strategy: *faults,* which are software or hardware defects; *errors,* which are incorrect data; and *failures,* which are breakdowns of network components. End users do not distinguish between these three categories; their concern is the continued operation of the network.

Fault-tolerant LANs employ a combination of hardware and software, usually consisting of the following elements:

◆ An uninterruptable power supply to protect against AC power failure or at least permit a graceful shutdown.
◆ A duplicate file allocation table (FAT) kept on the disk.

- ◆ Software that logs what users were doing at the time of a crash and saves their files. For example, Novell fault-tolerant software provides a transaction log that helps bring a failed system back to the starting point.
- ◆ Redundant hardware, such as multiple disk drives that mirror each other so the second drive takes over when the first fails, mirroring servers, duplicated bridges, and redundant cabling.
- ◆ Applications software that stores information between saves.
- ◆ Careful backup procedures.

A key to fault tolerance is a network management system that alerts the administrator to impending problems by detecting minor faults before they grow into major problems. All the systems comprising fault tolerance come at a price, so the degree of fault tolerance a network is likely to have is a function of the willingness of management to pay for it.

CHAPTER
30
LOCAL AREA NETWORK EQUIPMENT

With LAN protocols, access methods, and topologies covered in Chapter 29, in this chapter we turn to equipment that makes up single and multisegment LANs and LAN internets, a topic that will be covered in more detail in Chapter 33. Excellent equipment is readily available for assembling one of the many LAN configurations. No single configuration is universally best. In planning a LAN you need to understand the issues, the alternatives, and the objectives and choose the architecture accordingly. The task is not difficult in small LANs with up to two or three dozen workstations, but as the LAN expands and branches off-site the issues become complex. Unless the appropriate equipment is selected and properly configured, performance will suffer. Managing a complex LAN requires information of the type that a management system such as simple network management protocol (SNMP) provides, a topic we will visit in Chapter 37.

As it turns out, the arguments of the 1980s about whether Ethernet or token ring was the best protocol were largely irrelevant. Although token ring has a performance edge, in most offices it makes little difference which access method is used, so the choice usually defaults to Ethernet. The discussions about thick net, thin net, or twisted pair have been settled in favor of UTP for all but a few specialized applications. The broadband/baseband argument has resolved itself in favor of baseband except in those applications where a broadband cable is in place or is needed for video.

Now attention has shifted to higher layers in the protocol stack, which raises issues such as these:

♦ Performance of the network operating system.
♦ Sectionalization of the network to improve performance.
♦ Extension of the network range limits.
♦ Performance of the file server.

The industry uses the term *system integration* to describe the process of bringing together software and devices from multiple sources and causing them to operate as a unit. Network managers have three choices in the matter of system integration: turn the project over to the vendor, who usually can furnish all the components; contract with an independent system integrator; or become their own system integrator. This chapter discusses the equipment-related issues that must be addressed no matter which path is chosen. To achieve satisfactory performance from your local network, you will need to gather information and address issues such as these:

♦ How large will the network be? Determine the number of workstations at the network's immediate and ultimate size.
♦ What applications will the network run? Pay close attention to database, imaging, and multimedia applications, which can impose a large load on the network. Word processing and spreadsheet, on the other hand, load the network only when users are retrieving or saving files.
♦ Where will software be stored? If on workstations, large workstation disks are required; otherwise, a larger server hard disk is needed.
♦ Where will workstations be located? Multiple locations require bridging and routing.
♦ What protocols will the network operate? Identify requirements for protocol conversion.
♦ What network operating system (NOS) will be used?
♦ How will the network will be managed? Include such issues as file backup, trouble isolation and repair, and administration of adds, moves, and changes.
♦ What vendors have the resources to engineer, install, and support the network?

So many variables are involved in network design and implementation that it is impossible to generalize. The equipment considerations for a small office with a single-segment network are significantly different from those for a campus environment or for a multilocation company. In this chapter we will discuss the major families of equipment that are available and the differences between products. The purpose of this chapter is to give you an understanding of the issues surrounding equipment selection and to provide information that will help you select firms with the expertise to develop the network.

SERVERS

The network usually includes one or more *servers,* which fill the following functions:

> *File servers* enable users to store files in a central location. The file server may contain allocated disk space for users, and it may regulate their access to shared space and files. The filer server contains the network operating system (NOS), and may also fulfill one or more of the other server functions on the network.
>
> *Print servers* connect one or more printers to the network and regulate printing jobs. Print servers determine priority, send jobs to the appropriate printer, and enable the operator to manage print resources through NOS utilities.
>
> *Terminal servers* connect nonintelligent terminals and asynchronous ports to the network.
>
> *Fax servers* connect users to a pool of facsimile devices for sending and receiving faxes.
>
> *Modem servers* connect users to a modem pool. The modem and fax server function makes it unnecessary for each user to have his or her own fax card or modem.
>
> *Remote access servers* enable users outside the network to dial in to access network resources as if they were directly attached. The access server may also function as an outbound modem pool.

File Servers

The file server is the kingpin of any server-centric network. It serves these major functions:

- ◆ Provides storage facilities for user files.
- ◆ Provides storage facilities for application programs.
- ◆ Provides facilities for sharing common resources such as disk space and printers.
- ◆ Provides, in server-centric LANs, a residence for the network operating system.

Peripherals are not attached to the network only through the file server. As Figure 30–1 shows, peripherals may be attached in three ways: through the file server, through a workstation, or directly to the network itself. Workstation attachments have a place for specialized devices such as plotters that are used primarily by the workstation operator. They also are effective in smaller networks where the administrator can ensure that the station user makes the peripheral available for sharing, but in larger networks workstation attachments may create administrative problems.

Direct attachment to the LAN is completely satisfactory but is not available with all NOSs and all printers. If direct attachment is available, it is the preferable method, offering the highest speed and fewest administrative problems of the alternatives. Server attachment is feasible with most server-centric networks, but it may operate more slowly than direct attachment.

The file server in a LAN is treated as a virtual drive on the users' desktop computers. A virtual drive is one that appears to be directly attached but is shared with other users. The network operating system maps the drive to the user's personal computer, intercepts calls from the personal computer's operating system, and directs them to the file server.

Factors Affecting File Server Performance

The greatest source of LAN vulnerability is the file server. Failures can result in potentially disastrous file and productivity loss. Techniques for guarding against data loss are discussed in the Chapter 29 discussion of fault-tolerant networks. This section discusses the design and administrative factors that affect file server efficiency.

Network Data Rate   In every network, some factor limits throughput, and the data rate may be the limiting factor. The data rate is not the same as the data transfer rate or throughput; the latter is often no more than one-third of the data rate because of overhead and collision recovery time. Often network inefficiencies are caused by a factor other than the data rate, but with other factors equal, a faster network will provide better response time to the users.

Number and Activity of Users   With other factors equal, the greater the number of users and the greater their activity, the slower the network's response time will be. The effect is more pronounced in a contention network, but file servers attached to deterministic networks will experience greater demand with more users and respond less efficiently to service requests.

FIGURE 30-1

LAN Configuration Showing Different Methods of Peripheral Attachment

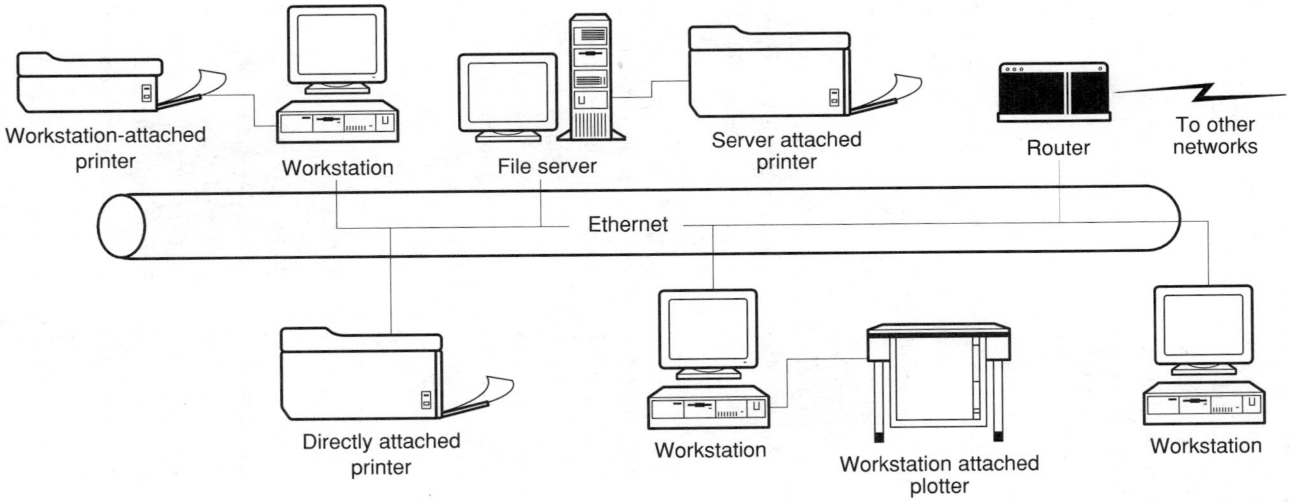

Hard Drive Access Time   Access time is a function of how rapidly the disk moves to the sectors where data is stored. The access time of a hard disk is composed of two factors: *seek time,* which is the time it takes for the read head to move to the proper track, and *rotation time,* which is the time it takes for the disk to rotate to the appropriate sector. Also, the design of the hard disk controller affects access time. The shorter the access time, the more efficient the file server will be. Generally, access times greater than about 12–15 milliseconds should be avoided in LANs with more than a few users.

File Server Memory   In addition to housing operating system and application software, file servers use memory to execute read and write commands and to buffer print data. It is better to err on the side of providing too much RAM than too little because a shortage of memory will adversely affect file server efficiency. The network operating system uses RAM for *caching* to improve network efficiency. When a user issues a read instruction to the disk, the operating system reads more data than necessary on the probability that the next read operation can be served from RAM rather than from the disk. Caching, which requires RAM, reduces the frequency of disk access, and therefore improves response time.

Network Software Efficiency   Network operating system vendors are quick to point out differences in efficiency between their products and those of their competitors. The network operating system, which the next section discusses, is probably the most difficult for a LAN owner to evaluate because it is difficult to construct tests that match reality and because organizations use networks in so many different ways. The NOS provides network administrators with numerous tools for tuning the network.

Print Servers

Many printers can be connected directly to the network, which eliminates the need for a print server. Printers that are not network-compatible are connected through a print server or, if the NOS permits, to a workstation. A print server is a computer that has enough ports to host the printers. Parallel printers must be collocated with the server. Serial printers can be located any place in a building or a campus by using line drivers if the distance exceeds the limits of a serial port.

Printers can also be attached to workstations as shared devices. Some NOSs provide for printer sharing through the workstation. If the network uses a server-centric NOS that does not permit sharing printers through the workstation, peer network operating systems and some desktop computer operating systems can be operated with the NOS to enable users to share printers.

Terminal Servers

Terminals, being nonprogrammable devices, cannot be connected directly to a LAN except through a terminal server. A terminal server is a protocol converter that accepts ASCII input from terminals, packetizes it, and outputs it on the network. It accepts characters from asynchronous terminals or ports, buffers them, packetizes them, and inserts them on the network in an Ethernet frame. It recognizes the addresses of its attached ports, breaks down the packets, and distributes a data stream to the appropriate port. The concept of a terminal server is similar to that of a statistical multiplexer, using Ethernet as the transmission medium.

As discussed in Chapter 29, connecting an asynchronous device directly to a contention network is inadvisable because each character is individually packetized. If a host echoes the character, each keystroke generates two packets that must be padded to the minimum length. An Ethernet can support several users manually keyboarding, but the safest course is to use a terminal server that stores and packetizes keystrokes. Figure 30–2 shows a terminal server connecting to asynchronous ports from a host computer to a LAN. This method is used if the host is not network-compatible.

Fax Servers

A fax server gives all users the services of a fax machine at their desks without the need to put a fax-modem card in each PC and provide analog ports off the PBX. The fax server provides a pool of fax cards in a central server. The server connects to an Ethernet port on one side and multiple business lines or analog PBX boards on the output side. Users can have as many simultaneous sessions as there are cards in the server.

Outgoing calls are easy with a fax server. Most products have a graphical user interface, which enables the user to click on a fax icon to set up a session across the network to a fax card. Application software operates with the server to choose an idle card and set up the session through the PBX or the business lines.

Incoming calls are more difficult. Some systems are compatible with DID. The PBX detects the DID number dialed, reads it over a group of lines to the fax-server, and passes the DID digits to the server so it knows which workstation to send the call to. If DID is not available, calls are sent to a common pool and distributed on a conventional basis.

FIGURE 30-2

Terminal and Host Connections to a LAN through Terminal Servers

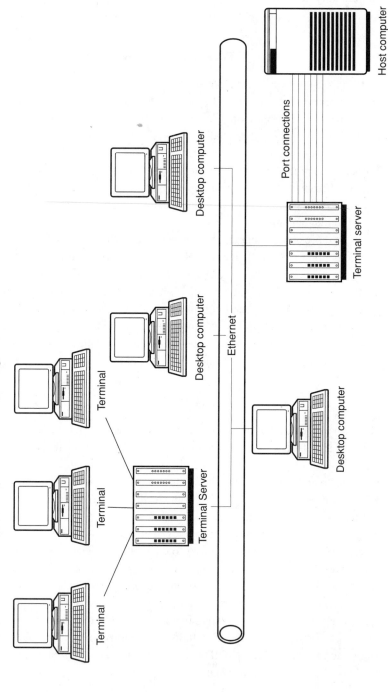

Remote Access Server

People who travel or work at home need access to files and services on the LAN. Options for remote access to LANs, in the order of descending cost, are remote access servers, dial-up bridges and routers, remote control software, and remote access capabilities of some NOSs such as Microsoft Windows NT Server.

Except for the speed of the telephone line the remote access server provides the same functionality as a direct connection. Remote access servers fall into two categories: remote control and remote node. Remote control software enables users to operate as if they were sitting at a keyboard of a computer attached to the LAN. After satisfying the log-in and security requirements, users see exactly the same screens and prompts that they see with a directly attached computer. Remote control can be installed on stand-alone computers, or it is available in banks of computers that are racked to provide multiple channels. If the company has a mixture of Macintosh and IBM-compatible computers, different devices will be required in the pool. The main advantage of remote control is that users have a familiar interface. However, graphical user interfaces such as Microsoft Windows are high overhead, so applications may run slowly on a telephone line, even with V.34 modems. The throughput is generally acceptable with ISDN lines, particularly when both B channels are used.

Remote node systems can further be divided into two types: dial-up bridge/router and modem connections. The dial-up bridge, operates like a remote bridge so the dial-in station is, in effect, a LAN segment connected by a telephone line. The modem alternative uses point-to-point protocol (see Chapter 4) or synchronous line interface protocol (SLIP) to establish a connection between the remote station and the LAN. Software running on a remote computer enables the user to log on as if the station was directly attached. Remote node systems are normally independent of the type of computer dialing in. Either Macintosh or IBM-compatible devices can use the ports interchangeably.

Remote access servers reside on the corporate LAN and allow remote users to be fully functioning nodes, subject only to the speed of the interconnecting circuit. Most remote access servers also provide modem pool service for outgoing calls. Remote dial-up bridges and routers are paired with a matching unit at the central site so workers can operate as if they were attached to the LAN. Remote control software is the least expensive, but its performance is not as good in graphics intensive applications.

The least costly method of remote access is built into the NOS. The file server hosts one or more modems. Client software on the distant end pairs with host software to enable properly authenticated users to access the network exactly as if they were directly attached.

LAN SEGMENT EQUIPMENT

Many LANs, perhaps a majority of the LANs in existence, consist only of workstations, network interface cards (NICs), hubs, a server, and a network operating system. The *segment* or *subnet,* as it is called in a multisegment LAN, is common to all LANs, and the equipment chosen has a large effect on user satisfaction.

Network Interface Cards

The choice of NIC can have a large effect on network performance. It is tempting to buy on price alone, but more expensive cards offer features, such as self-configuring, that can be repaid in reduced administrative costs. Network performance is affected by the speed of the NICs in both the server and the workstations. If the server has a high-speed bus such as PCI, a NIC that uses the auxiliary bus will be faster than one that fits an ISA bus alone. Server performance can also be improved in some cases by using high-speed or full-duplex cards or by using cards that plug into a 32-bit bus.

The network interface card (NIC) plugs into an expansion slot or PCM-CIA (personal computer memory card international association) connector on the workstation. The functions of the interface card are:

- *Buffering* the speed of the network to the speed of the device.
- *Packetizing and depacketizing* the information. The NIC accepts a data stream from the device and converts it to a network packet. Incoming data packets are converted to a continuous data stream and presented to the device.
- *Parallel/serial conversion.* The NIC plugs into the parallel bus in the workstation and converts data into the serial form that the network requires.
- *Encoding and decoding.* Many LANs use a scheme such as Manchester coding for pulsing the data on the network. The NIC converts the coding on the computer bus to that required by the network.
- *Access* to the transmission medium. The NIC checks the busy/idle status of a contention network or grabs the token in a token network.
- *Address detection.* The NIC checks incoming packets to determine if it is the addressee.

NICs are specific to the type of transmission medium, and to the network access method. Ethernet cards are available with one or more of the three common interface connectors: RJ-45 for 10-Base-T, BNC for thin net,

FIGURE 30–3

A Synoptics 5000 LAN Wiring Concentrator

Courtesy Bay Networks, Inc.

and attachment unit interface (AUI) for transceiver connections. Token ring cards are unique to the two transmission rates, 4 and 16 mb/s, and to shielded and unshielded wire connections.

Hubs

Hubs come in two varieties, stackable, as or modular wiring concentrators, as shown in Figure 30–3. The latter type holds plug-in modules that support different access protocols. Modules are available for Ethernet, token ring, and AppleTalk. The hub backplane may be segmented and provide for plug-in bridges or routers to connect the segments. Some hubs support switching modules and FDDI or switching backplanes. The modular hub is more versatile and also more expensive than the stackable hub.

Stackable hubs have a fixed number of ports; 8, 12, 16, 24, 36, and 48 are common port multiples. To expand the number of ports, additional hubs are cabled to the primary hub. Although the term *stackable* implies shelf-mounting, many stackable hubs are equipped for rack mounting. Hubs are interconnected with twisted-pair wire or fiber optics. If hubs are fiber connectable, it is through an FOIRL module that plugs into a connector in the chassis.

The modular wiring concentrator hub consists of several individual components. The chassis consists of a framework that contains multiple card slots. The card slots hold different types of modules. Depending on the type of hub, individual modules may support Ethernet, token ring, AppleTalk, router, bridging, switching, FOIRL, and network management. The card slots are connected by a backplane that serves to connect the modules together.

LAN segmentation is different between the two types of hub. Stackable hubs require external devices. Wiring concentrators may have bridging capability built in, or it may be added in some models with plug-in modules. Figure 30–4 shows three different methods of fitting hubs into the enterprise network environment. These methods, the distributed backbone, collapsed backbone, and switched backbone, are discussed in more detail in Chapter 33.

Port switching is a valuable feature of enterprise hubs. With standard hubs users are moved between segments by unplugging the computer from one port and moving it to another. The port switching feature allows the administrator to assign a port to any segment regardless where it appears in hardware. Lacking port switching, all of the ports in a module have to be assigned to the same LAN segment. Port switching has two advantages. First, it improves port utilization. Without the feature some ports will be unused because the segment a hub serves does not have enough stations to use all the available ports. The second value of port switching is to implement *virtual LANs* (VLANs). A VLAN is one composed of stations that are independent of physical location. Switching allows the administrator to connect a station to any LAN segment in the hub. With port switching, ports can span multiple segments, and in some products, multiple hubs. Port switching is usually confined to modular hubs, although some high-end stackables also offer the feature.

Switching backplanes come in two versions. The *physical layer* switching backplane permits switching users from one LAN to another without moving the wire to another port. Any port can be assigned from the management terminal to any LAN served by the hub. The *MAC layer* switch is a software

FIGURE 30–4

Alternatives for Applying Hubs in the Enterprise Network

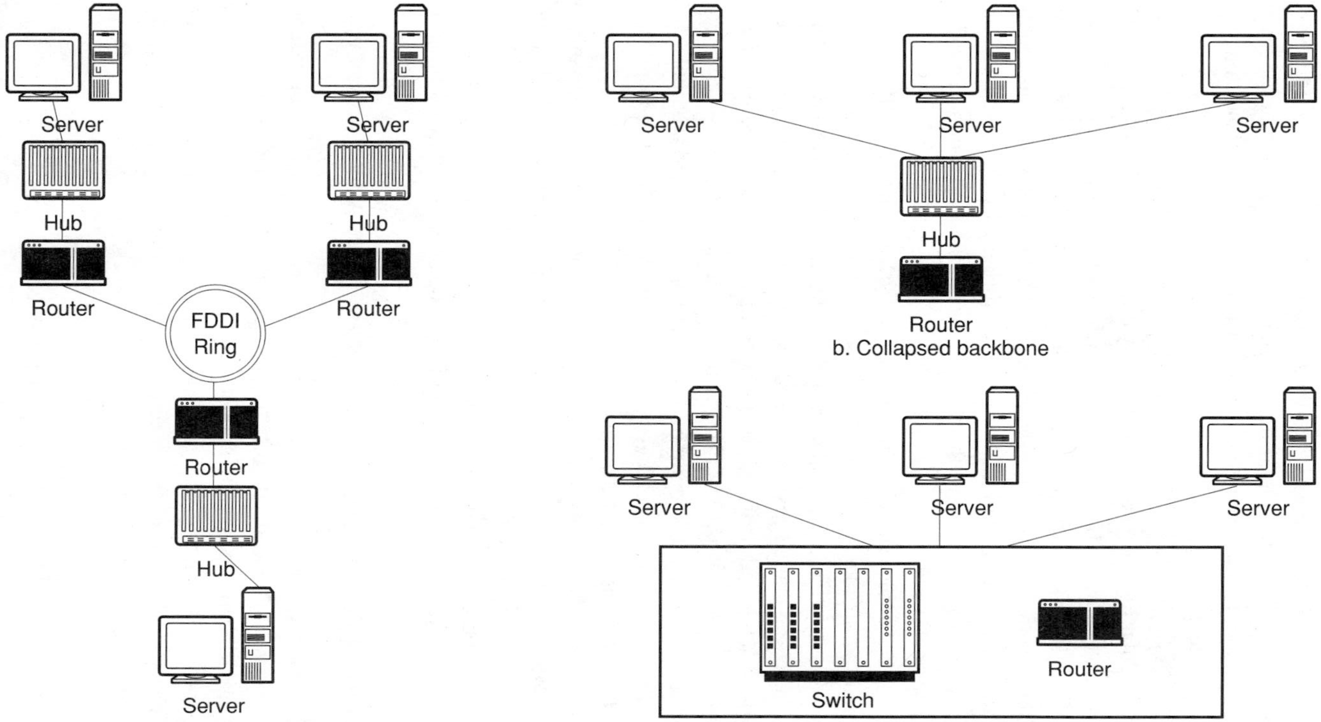

Server

Server

Server

Hub

Router

b. Collapsed backbone

Server

Server

Server

Router

Switch

c. Enterprise hub

Server

Hub

Router

FDDI
Ring

Router

Hub

Router

Server

Hub

Router

Server

a. Distributed backbone

application that allows switching users from one segment to another by packet routing. Users can be assigned their own segment connected to a switch port, or segments can be shared. Backplane speed is an important consideration. Some modular hubs have multimegabit-per-second backplanes that enable one hub to support multiple LANs simultaneously.

As with NICs, hubs supporting the fast Ethernet protocols are available. In modular hubs separate modules may be available to support fast Ethernet. In stackable hubs the hub itself is designed to support single or dual speeds.

Network management is an important hub feature. Managed hubs can shut off defective ports or isolate ports that have a defect such as a jabbering or unresponsive workstation. Remote monitoring (RMON) support is available with some hubs, making the degree of compliance an important factor. See Chapter 37 for discussion of RMON.

The choice of hubs is easy for some companies and difficult for others. Small companies and branch offices, including virtually all single-segment networks, use stackable hubs because of their lower cost. Modular hubs have a high getting-started cost because of the cost of the card cage and power supply. On the other end of the scale, large companies with enterprise networks will almost invariably use modular wiring concentrators because of their greater capacity and ability to support multiple network media and protocols. Also, their ability to support switching, bridging, and routing in the hub make modular wiring concentrators the preferred option.

Between size extremes, hub selection is not easy. Companies that are growing rapidly and with no capacity limit in sight will generally prefer modular hubs. Companies that are growing more slowly, and particularly those with one protocol and access medium, will find stackable hubs to be less expensive and to have growth capability comparable to many modular hubs.

REPEATERS, BRIDGES, ROUTERS, GATEWAYS, AND SWITCHES

When LANs outgrow the span of a single segment, they can be extended with a *repeater*. If the capacity of a single segment is exceeded, they are broken into multiple segments that are connected by a *bridge, switch, router,* or a *gateway* to form an internetwork. Figure 30–5 shows the relationship of each type of device to the OSI model. This section discusses the building blocks and the considerations in their choice.

Repeaters

As signals travel along the transmission medium they are attenuated, and must be regenerated by a repeater. A repeater operates at the physical level, and can

FIGURE 30–5

Repeaters, Bridges, Routers, and Gateways Related to the OSI Model

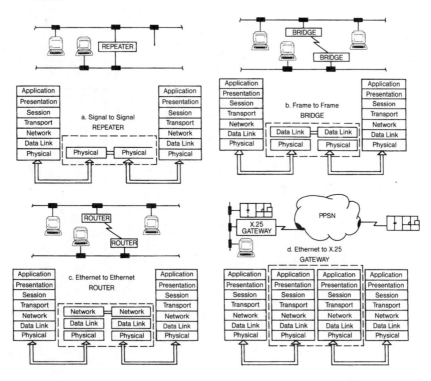

detect collisions. It has no processing ability. The only function of the repeater is to regenerate the bit stream. Its purpose is to extend the diameter of the network by linking segments.

Bridges

One drawback of conventional Ethernet is its method of growth. Network usage typically starts low, but as high-bandwidth applications are added, performance begins to deteriorate. The solution is to identify communities of users and break the LAN into segments using a bridge, as Figure 30–6 shows. Bridges are relatively inexpensive devices that are independent of the network protocol. A bridge fits between two network segments and reads the MAC layer addresses of packets on both segments. If the destination of a frame is the same side of the bridge as its origin, the bridge ignores it (*filtering*), but if the address is on the other segment the bridge lets it across (*forwarding*). A bridge is, therefore, an

FIGURE 30-6

Ethernet Segments Connected with a Bridge

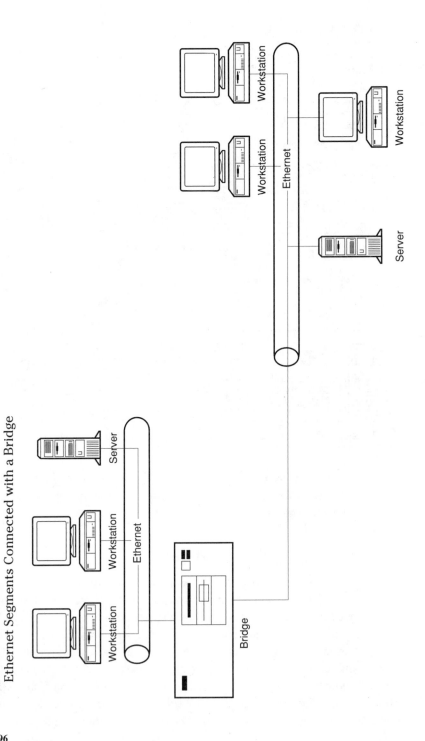

appropriate device for dividing an overloaded network into two segments. Note, however, that unless the segment being divided has distinct communities of interest, segmentation is ineffective. For example, if the segment has one server and all the traffic is directed toward that one device, breaking it into two segments with users still accessing the same server will accomplish nothing.

Bridges are protocol independent. They ignore all information above the data link layer, so they can pass higher-level protocols such as TCP/IP and IPX. When a bridge is first put in operation it sends broadcast messages to learn the addresses on the segments to which it is attached. By recording the responses it builds an address table so it knows which frames belong on which side of the network. If a node moves from one subnetwork to another, the bridge automatically discovers the change and updates its table. One feature of a bridge is that different ports can be configured for different types of media. For example, you can bridge a twisted-pair network to coaxial cable or to a fiber-optic backbone.

Remote bridges are installed in pairs with a telecommunications circuit linking the two halves, as Figure 30–7 shows. Except for the slow-speed telecommunications circuit between the halves, a remote bridge operates exactly like a regular bridge. Remote bridges usually have the ability to compress data to improve throughput. Compression of from 2:1 to as much as 7:1 are possible, depending on the type of data being transmitted. Remote bridges contain buffers to hold excess frames when the capacity of the connecting circuit is exceeded. The buffer size is an important factor because if the telecommunications circuit is congested, the bridge has no choice but to discard frames.

Bridging is of two types; *transparent bridging* and *source routing*. In a transparent bridge the only information used to make the bridging decision is the packet's source and destination address. The bridge ignores all other packet information. Ethernet-to-Ethernet bridges use the transparent bridging technique.

Source routing bridges, which are often used in token ring networks, are protocol dependent, and are therefore slower than transparent bridges. The source routing algorithm allows the source to specify the route a packet will take to reach the destination. To learn the route, the source sends a route discovery packet with only the destination address. As the packet travels through the network the bridges that handle it append routing information to the MAC layer. When the destination station receives the packet it returns it to the destination complete with routing information.

A bridge is a potential failure point that can disrupt a network that lacks backup protection. Data link protocols do not provide for alternate routing, but it is still possible to run two bridges in parallel provided one is active and the other is standby. The bridges negotiate with each other to determine which is designated as primary and carries all traffic unless it fails, in which case the

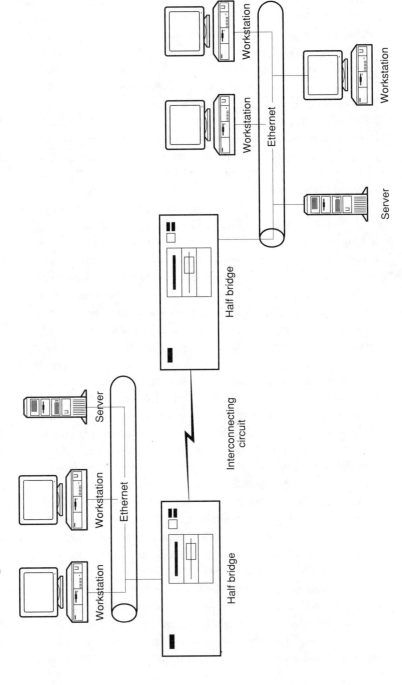

FIGURE 30-7

Ethernet Segments Connected with a Remote Bridge

secondary bridge takes over. The IEEE 802.1 *spanning tree* algorithm is used to allow multiple bridges to communicate with each other and ensure that only one route is active at a time.

The industry tendency is to build more intelligence into bridges. Some products that are sold as bridges provide functions of higher-level devices such as a routers and gateways. A bridge equipped for alternate routing is called a *brouter*. Also available are bridges that support multiple links and prioritize traffic. For example, some devices can block longer packets such as file transfer during periods of heavy traffic.

Compared to routers, which are discussed later, bridges have the following strengths:

- ◆ They are protocol independent. They can pass higher-level protocols of all types.
- ◆ They are less expensive.
- ◆ They have higher throughput.
- ◆ They require less effort to start up and to manage.

Limiting their use for many application, bridges have the following weaknesses:

- ◆ They are subject to broadcast storms that flood a network with unwanted traffic.
- ◆ They lack the intelligence of higher-layer devices, so they are unable to filter specific types of packets or prevent unauthorized traffic from reaching a segment.

Switches

In effect, switches are fast multiport bridges that switch one port to another long enough to pass a packet. Each port on the switch supports the full wire speed of the network, so if a station is directly connected to a port, it has the equivalent of a dedicated segment. A switch is an economical way to deload a network. Since ports are switched together, collisions between segments are eliminated, which increases the total network throughput. A switch port can be connected to a single station such as a server, or to a multistation network segment. If a segment is connected to the port, collisions are not eliminated in the segment, but only in the path between the source and destination ports of the switch. Although the most common type of switch is the Ethernet switch, token ring switches are also available, but the broadcast scheme of Ethernet is more adaptable to switching than is token passing.

Switching is sometimes built into hubs, but Ethernet switches are not to be confused with port-switching hubs. As discussed earlier, port-switching hubs allow network managers to move users from one segment to another without reconfiguring the hub. When a port is assigned to a segment, it remains connected with all other users in the segment. When a station or segment is connected to a port on an Ethernet switch, the port is isolated from all other ports until the switch reads a MAC address intended for another port, whereupon both ports are connected together for the duration of one packet.

Switching technology uses either hardware or software to route frames. Hardware switches use application-specific integrated circuits (ASICs) as the switching element. Software switches use a high-speed processor such as a RISC processor to route frames between ports.

Switches are also distinguished by the way they connect frames. A *cut-through* switch makes the connection from the incoming to the outgoing port as soon as it reads the address. A *buffered* or *store-and-forward* switch reads the entire frame and forwards it only after it determines that the frame is valid. A cut-through switch may forward invalid frames such as broadcast storms or those mutilated by collision. Buffered switches have somewhat greater latency than cut-through switches, but they have the ability to discard invalid frames.

Some switches are compatible with both conventional and fast Ethernet. Fast Ethernet may be a desirable option even if it will not be used initially because the network could be upgraded to fast Ethernet or it might be desirable to use fast Ethernet or full duplex on the server port to eliminate bottlenecks.

Switches have the following strengths:

♦ They are a fast and economical way to resolve network congestion. A switch is less expensive than other alternatives such as FDDI or ATM.

♦ The network can be reconfigured while retaining its present topology, cabling, NOS, and NICs.

♦ They have low latency and a high filtering and forwarding rate compared to other alternatives.

♦ They are less difficult to configure than routers.

♦ Switches establish point-to-point connections between nodes, which makes it easy to move users among subnets or to form virtual LANs.

Switches have the following drawbacks:

♦ They make it difficult to measure, identify, and manage traffic. Traffic flow is not visible as it is with bridges and routers. New network management tools will probably be required.

♦ Under heavy load conditions some switches may drop packets.

♦ Compared to routers they lack the ability to filter out or firewall unwanted or unauthorized traffic.

FIGURE 30–8

Token Ring Networks Connected by Routers

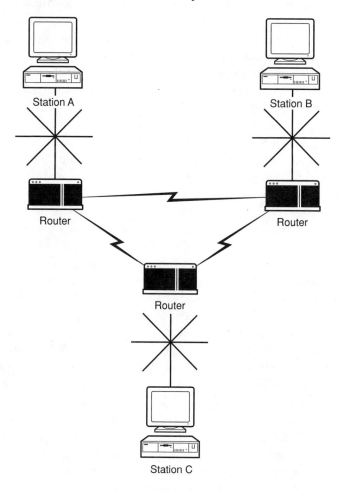

Station A

Station B

Router

Router

Router

Station C

Routers

A router works at the network layer of the OSI stack, which enables it to perform the functions of a bridge, plus routing. This gives it the capability of choosing alternate routes to the destination, but at the same time it is protocol dependent. Therefore, routers are chosen to support the specific protocols the network uses. Routing is important when multiple segments are connected in such a way that there is more than one possible path by which a station can reach another station on the network. Figure 30–8 shows three token ring networks interconnected by routers. Station A can reach station B by the direct route or via the third ring, which both A's and B's network have in common.

Source routing enables the source to specify the route that a packet should follow to its destination. Source routing requires the originating station to map the network with the location of addressees and routers. Packets originated by the source are transmitted to the destination with routing information.

A basic difference between a bridge and a router is that the router knows the location of the destination address. A bridge knows only whether the address is local or not. Furthermore, a router knows all the paths to the destination. It can consider such factors as congestion, cost of the route, and other such information that a bridge cannot.

A single-protocol router can handle only one protocol; a multiprotocol router can handle more than one. Routers may have to segment packets to put them on the intervening network. For example, if routers are connected across a packet-switching network that has a maximum packet size of 100 bytes, the router would segment the packets to make them fit.

Router performance is measured by packets transferred per second, the filtering rate, and the forwarding rate. Multiprotocol routers are configured to support protocols such as TCP/IP, DECnet, AppleTalk, IPX, etc., but routers do not convert protocols or allow different protocols to communicate with one another. Routers can keep statistics on traffic in the network, and assist in managing it. Figure 30–9 is a photograph of a Wellfleet backbone router.

Before shopping for routers it's important to have the network architecture selected. A collapsed backbone architecture (see Chapter 33) requires a single router with multiple ports and high packet-forwarding capacity. A distributed backbone requires smaller routers, fewer ports, and more devices.

The primary benchmark of router performance is its packet-forwarding rate. This states the number of packets per second it can forward from input to output ports. Although the vendors' specifications don't normally indicate it, the packet-forwarding capability will depend on packet size, and may depend on how many protocols are being supported. Routers can handle more aggregate data throughput with large packets than with small because each packet forwarded requires reading the packet header, which consumes time. To send the same number of bits with multiple small packets compared to a single large one, more processing is required and more delay results.

Routers offer the following strengths in connecting networks:

◆ They can make routing decisions based on more criteria than address alone.
◆ They can make alternate routing decisions based on network congestion and other such conditions.
◆ They can create firewalls to block traffic between unauthorized networks.

FIGURE 30-9

A Wellfleet Backbone Router

Courtesy of Bay Networks, Inc.

Compared to other alternatives, routers have the following weaknesses:

◆ Routers are complex to install, configure, and manage.
◆ They may have a lower packet-filtering and -forwarding rate than bridges and switches because of the greater amount of processing required.
◆ Routing table exchanges among routers may add to network congestion.

◆ Since they are protocol dependent, routers may be unable to handle some protocols on your network without reconfiguration. Furthermore, not all protocols can be routed.

Gateways

The fifth device for linking networks is the gateway, which spans all seven layers of the OSI protocol model. A gateway is designed to link incompatible networks. For example, a gateway could link Ethernet to an SNA network. A gateway is a protocol converter that must be specific to the network pairs it is intended to link. Gateways typically handle three different protocols: source network, destination network, and transmission path protocols.

SNA gateways are available for most LANs, which permits stations on the LAN to function as if they were terminals behind a cluster controller. Gateways are protocol-specific devices that link dissimilar networks, so they are designed for specific protocol pairs. Since they work at all seven layers of the OSI protocol stack, the activity of the gateway is processor-intensive, and the device can become a bottleneck. All the criteria in selecting routers also apply to selecting gateways.

APPLICATIONS

The applications for local area networks are as varied as the organizations they serve. This section discusses some of the criteria used in selecting LAN equipment and presents a case history that illustrates the variety of configurations that LAN equipment can assume. LAN standards are discussed in Chapter 29.

Case History: A School District Network

A large suburban school district with 43 schools and several administrative buildings initiated a project to bring network technology down to the classroom level. The schools use a combination of Macintosh and IBM-compatible devices. The district started with approximately 3,000 existing computers, many of which were not network-compatible. The district plans to increase this number to about 10,000 computers within the third year of operation. The schools are linked by two CATV channels that use a token passing protocol for data communications. One channel is assigned to elementary schools and the other to the middle and high schools.

The applications on the network are instructional software, electronic mail, Internet access, and access to the district's automated library system. All computers are equipped with general-purpose works software, which provides spreadsheet, word processing, and database. Teachers also have access to student records, which, together with the library system, run on a DEC mini-computer.

The architecture chosen is shown in Figure 30–10. Each classroom is wired with four category 5 UTP drops, which are installed in pairs in two classroom locations. Each school has a main distributing frame that serves the front office plus some classrooms. Each school has one or more intermediate distributing frames that serve the remaining classrooms plus special-purpose rooms such as libraries, gymnasium, teacher's workroom, counselors' rooms, and so on. IDF locations are chosen to balance the cost of wire against the cost of additional electronics. Drops average about 150 feet in length. This distance allows the school to distribute video on the shorter category 5 wire runs.

The IDFs are connected to the MDF with three types of cable: multimode fiber for connecting Ethernet hubs, 50-pair category 2 wire for telephone, and RG-11 coaxial cable for video. Hubs and patch panels are installed in relay racks in each IDF and MDF. A typical IDF is shown in Figure 30–11. Each classroom is supported with two 10-Base-T ports. Eight-port mini-hubs are installed in each classroom. The mini-hubs provide ample port capacity for less money than installing additional hubs in the MDFs and IDFs and providing additional category 5 wire runs.

A remote access server in the administration building enables students and teachers to dial in from home for Internet access and, where permitted, for access to on-line files. It also provides dial-out modem pool access for authorized users.

All classrooms can reach applications in the administration building such as mechanized library, Internet access, and the remote access server over the backbone CATV network. The limited bandwidth of the backbone makes it necessary to provide file service capacity in each school.

This network is a good example of balancing cost with functionality. In a school district the budget is typically tight, and while the network is important, it is not mission-critical. Therefore, some features that would be detrimental to operations in a business can be tolerated in a school. The backbone bandwidth is insufficient for a commercial network of this size, but the school has fewer shared files than an organization with an equivalent number of computers.

Application Criteria

This chapter has discussed the primary criteria that users consider in selecting a network. The following are the most important considerations in deciding among the many alternatives on the market.

FIGURE 30-10

School District Network

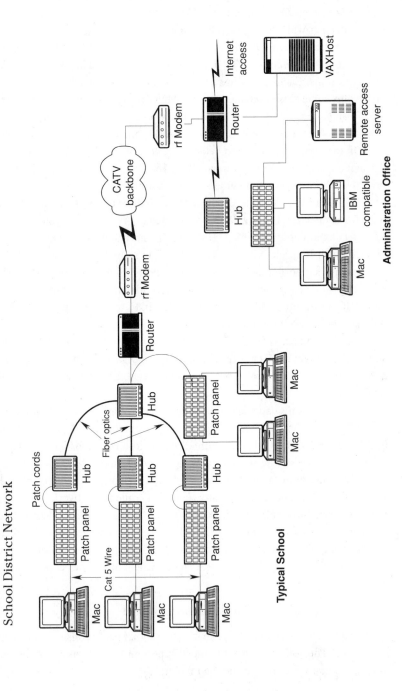

Typical School

Administration Office

FIGURE 30–11

An Intermediate Distributing Frame

Photo by Author

Preferred Computer Vendor

Companies that use IBM equipment and software should consider the token ring network because it is directly supported by IBM. Companies that use Digital Equipment computers will favor Ethernet. Other computer manufacturers may support either or both networks, but the predominant network for most manufacturers is Ethernet.

Wiring

Although it is possible to operate a LAN successfully on existing wiring that may not be intended for data applications, anytime a new building is constructed or an existing building is remodeled, the wiring should be upgraded to EIA/TIA 568 standards. Category 5 wiring should be installed for data at every workstation. With a properly designed and installed system, the wiring will support present and any future networks that have been proposed up to now. If the present wiring system is not designed for data, it should be replaced as part of the job of installing a LAN.

Network Management

Small networks of a few workstations do not need centralized network management, but when the size of the network expands to encompass multiple rooms, floors, and buildings, a network management system is required. Devices should be compatible with SNMP down to, and possibly including, the NIC. Consider whether the system supports RMON and version 2 of SNMP.

Access Protocol

When LANs were first introduced, there was a common belief that contention protocols would not provide enough throughput to support applications that required guarantees of data delivery. Experience has shown, however, that CSMA/CD networks are as effective in most applications as token passing, and the access protocol argument has largely disappeared. The most important reason for using token passing is that the application or manufacturer supports it.

Vendor Support

The choice of LAN will frequently be dictated by the degree of support offered by the vendor. Unless someone in the organization is equipped to become the systems integrator, it is usually necessary to have assurance of continued local support from the vendor. The following support features should be evaluated:

  ◆ *Implementation and installation assistance.* The design and
    engineering of LANs is specialized enough that vendor support will
    usually be required to implement a system. The vendor should have
    the resources to install the operating system and debug the software.

◆ *Maintenance and administration support.* When a LAN fails, immediate and competent support is needed. Most failures will be of the transmission medium. Difficulties with the network operating system will be the next most frequent. The vendor should employ enough technicians to cover absences and resignations. The vendor also should have the necessary test equipment to diagnose troubles with the transmission medium and the operating system. The vendor should be an authorized dealer who offers warranty support on both hardware and software.

◆ *System integration capabilities.* Most networks do not come out of the box ready to install. It may be necessary to apply cable from one vendor, network interface cards from another vendor, and personal computers from a third. Also, most LANs require integration with existing applications programs and interfacing with hardware of diverse manufacture. Unless an organization has internal capabilities for integrating the network, it will be necessary to obtain the service from the vendor or a contractor.

Costs

LAN costs vary widely and change frequently enough that it is risky to generalize about per-station costs. Costs ranging from $25 for network interface cards to more than $2,000 per device for FDDI are quoted, but it is essential to determine total costs before acquiring a network. The following cost factors should be considered:

◆ Design and engineering of the network, including the cost of collecting usage data for sizing it.

◆ Purchase price of the equipment, including spare parts, delivery, and taxes.

◆ Purchase price of new devices required because of incompatibilities.

◆ Installation costs, including labor, building and conduit rearrangements, and special permits and licenses.

◆ Software right-to-use fees, including both the operating system and upgrading applications software to operate on a network.

◆ Cost of growth when the system exceeds its capacity.

◆ Transition costs, including cutover from the old network, if any, training of users and operators, and preparation of new forms and passwords.

◆ Purchase of special test equipment, such as protocol analyzers, necessary to maintain the network (unless the vendor maintains the network).

◆ Documentation of the network, so repairs will not be delayed by lack of information.

◆ Maintenance costs, including the cost of finding and repairing trouble and lost production time during outages.

◆ Costs of periodic hardware and software upgrades.

◆ Administration costs, including usage monitoring, service monitoring, and interpretation of network statistics.

Traffic Characteristics

The volume, character, and growth rate of data traffic are important factors to consider in selecting a network. The ultimate size of the network must be considered so it can be segmented as it approaches capacity. When predicting future requirements, it is valuable to have a network that includes the ability to gather statistics on current usage. Some network operating systems provide usage information, which is used to expand the network and assess its health.

Bridges, routers, and gateways are potential bottlenecks in networks. It is important to understand the volume of traffic crossing these devices and to pick the device to handle the required traffic. Capacities are usually stated in packets per second. The load devices are required to carry will depend on the demands of the application.

Reliability

The initial cost of a network often pales in significance compared to the cost of outages. The cost of lost production time can mount rapidly when people are depending on a failed network for their productivity. Networks should be as nearly invulnerable to the failure of a single element as possible. Where common equipment such as amplifiers, repeaters, and head end equipment exists, spares and duplicates should be retained. Most important, qualified repair forces must be available within a short time of failure.

When a network element or the total network fails, the more rapidly it can be restored to service, the more valuable the network. Some systems have internal diagnostics that aid in rapid trouble isolation and restoral. The network also should be designed for fault isolation. For example, a ring network should be designed to identify which node has failed. It should be designed for bypass of a failed node, and the media access controller or network control center should provide alarms indicating a loss of received signal to aid in rapid fault isolation.

Security

Both contention and token networks allow access to all traffic by all stations on the network. Although the stations are programmed to ignore messages that are not addressed to them, the potential of unauthorized reception exists. For example, a protocol analyzer can see all messages. Where security is important, it may be necessary to select a network with additional security provisions such as encryption. The transmission medium is also an important element of security. Twisted-pair wire is easy to tap. Radio transmissions can be easily intercepted. Fiber-optic cable is difficult to tap, and coaxial cable lies somewhere between fiber optics and twisted-pair wire on the ease-of-tapping spectrum. Firewall security through a router is required for networks that connect with public networks such as Internet.

Throughput and Response Time

Ideally, a LAN should not impose response delays on the attached devices. The choice of operating system and the characteristics of the file server are the most important variables affecting throughput. For minimum delay, the file server must have a 486 or Pentium® processor, running at high speed, say 100 MHz or higher. The file server should have plenty of RAM for print buffering and disk caching. The speed of the network will also affect throughput.

Network Diameter

Distance limitations may dictate the choice of a LAN. When the network diameter exceeds the design limitations of the network, it must be segregated through a repeater or a bridge. To obtain the maximum diameter, a high-speed medium such as fiber optics may be used.

EQUIPMENT EVALUATION CRITERIA

The first step in implementing a LAN is to determine as accurately as possible how many users the network will support, where they are located, and what applications they will use. Determine what protocols the network must run. Determine how the network will be segmented and interconnected. As discussed in Chapter 33, larger networks will be developed with internetworking.

This section discusses factors in selecting the equipment that goes into a typical LAN.

Evaluation Criteria: File Servers

Both regular personal computers and special purpose computers can be used for file servers. The principal criteria in selecting servers include:

Processor Type and Operating Speed   Small networks using low-demand applications such as word processing and spreadsheet will find slower processors such as 80386 and 80486 are adequate for file servers provided

enough memory is provided. High-end specialized servers using Pentium®
and higher processors operating at 100 mb/s or more will be needed for
large networks, particularly those using high-demand applications such as
database. Companies that have a minicomputer may elect to add server software to it.

Amount of RAM   In general, the more RAM in the server the better. Consider 16 mb to be a minimum, with amounts up to the capacity of the motherboard desirable.

Reliability   A server crash can mean disaster for the work group, which
makes this factor the most important to evaluate. Unfortunately, it is also the
most elusive. The reason is that several components may form the weakest link,
with the hard disk the most vulnerable. Request comparative statistics from the
manufacturer, and check experience and references carefully.

Fault Tolerance   If the NOS supports it, servers can be made fault tolerant
by duplexing or mirroring hard disk drives. A UPS supply should always be
provided to protect against power failures.

Evaluation Criteria: Remote Access Servers

Number of Ports   Servers come in cabinets with ports and, in some cases,
modem cards installed. When the port capacity is exceeded cabinets must be
added. Question how the network is expanded when the port capacity is
reached. Can cabinets be appended or are they administered as separate independent devices? What is the maximum port speed supported? Does it support
basic rate ISDN?

System Administration   Can the system be set up from any workstation?
Is specialized client software required? If so, what is involved in setting it up?

Compatibility   What protocols does the system support? Be certain that it
is transparent to any protocol you use. Also, be certain it is compatible with the
LAN protocol you plan to use.

Workstation Support   Is the system capable of supporting both Macintosh
and IBM-compatible computers? If not, how are incoming calls recognized and
routed to the appropriate port?

Dial-in/Dial-out Capability Does the system have the capability of both receiving calls and allowing users on the network to place outgoing modem calls? Is the procedure intuitive?

Security Any remote access server is a target for hackers, so security measures must be provided. The system should provide a password for getting into the network, after which the user can use his or her own network password to access functions. Does the system allow the network supervisor to change passwords? Can the network supervisor require a password of particular length and with special characters? Are passwords case-sensitive? Does the system disconnect after a programmable number of ineffective log-on attempts?

Evaluation Criteria: Hubs

The first question in selecting hubs is whether to purchase stackable hubs or modular wiring concentrators. The choice is sometimes determined by the protocol and transmission medium. Some products require different modules for each transmission medium, while others provide multiple connectors. Stackable hubs normally do not support multiple protocols. To connect, and perhaps to bridge Ethernet, token ring, and AppleTalk, a wiring concentrator with different modules is required.

Manageability Managed hubs support the SNMP protocol, which enables them to perform such functions as detecting and isolating defective ports, counting packets, determining busy stations, and other such functions that are discussed in more detail in Chapter 37. Determine whether the hub supports RMON. Determine how much traffic is generated by the network management system, and whether an external port is available to diagnose troubles through dial-up when the network is down.

Expandability and Scalability The hub must provide sufficient slots or expansion cabinets to enable it to support projected growth. Determine how many slots the chassis has. Consider whether the card slots are universal. Dedicated card slots may limit the growth capability of the chassis. Determine the number of ports added per growth increment. Is it necessary to add more ports than will be needed just to accommodate addition of one more station?

Fault Tolerance Hubs that provide card slots for modules should provide for hot-swapping cards. Lacking this feature, it is necessary to turn down the hub and all stations attached to it to change modules. Some types of hubs provide redundancy of active elements and the power supply to increase reliability. Determine if the backplane is active or passive. Active backplanes are more susceptible to failure.

Protocols Supported   The most effective hubs for offices that use multiple protocols are those that support and bridge different protocols. Determine whether the hub supports switching and emerging protocols such as fast Ethernet, 100 VG AnyLAN, isoEthernet, and so on.

Switching Capability   Intelligent hubs with a switching backplane are becoming increasingly important for support of virtual LANs (Chapter 32). In switching hubs the bandwidth of the backplane is an important consideration.

Evaluation Criteria: Network Interface Cards

Network interface cards are specific to the transmission medium, but they are standardized to such a degree that cards from any vendor can be used with any NOS provided the NOS or NIC manufacturer provides a driver. Drivers are software routines that reside on the workstation, and couple it to the network's MAC layer. The drivers are loaded in the workstation's start-up routine. For example, portions of the drivers in IBM-compatible computers using MS-DOS operating system load the drivers through the CONFIG.SYS and AUTOEXEC.BAT files. Compatibility with the operating system should be tested before purchasing cards in quantity.

Hardware Compatibility   Some cards have settable DMA, memory addresses, and interrupts. Other cards choose these automatically, but they are no guarantee that conflicts will not arise. Check the range of interrupts available. In some workstations all the interrupts below 9 are occupied, which means that the NIC must support higher interrupts. It may also be necessary to reserve areas of high memory to avoid memory address conflicts.

Ease of Installation   Some cards come with the software stored in flash RAM, which reduces the setup time. Self-configuring cards can locate vacant interrupts and memory addresses, and set them automatically, which reduces setup time. Check the manufacturer's and vendor's technical support. The manufacturer should have technical support available on the telephone during normal business hours. It should also provide a BBS for downloading new drivers.

Fast Ethernet Support   Some cards support only 10-Base-T, but many cards have a thin net BNC connector as well, and some cards also include an attachment unit interface (AUI). Some NICs support one of the fast Ethernet protocols in addition to standard 802.3. As discussed in Chapter 29, at least two competing protocols, 100-Base-T, and 100VG-AnyLAN cards, are available, either as single-protocol cards or in combination with standard 10-Base-T.

SNMP Compatibility   If you plan to use a network management system check to be sure the card is SNMP-compatible. If the management information base (MIB) is not built into the card you will not be able to diagnose troubles to the workstation.

Evaluation Criteria: Bridges

Buffer Size   If the link between two halves of a remote bridge is congested, how much data can the bridge store before it begins dropping frames?

Filtering   Does the bridge have the ability to filter frames destined for specific addresses? What is the filtering rate?

Forwarding   What is the rate at which the bridge forwards frames to the other segment?

Ease of Setup   Consider how easy it is to change the filtering setup, the maximum frame size, and the speed of the WAN link. Also, can compression easily be disabled for testing?

Benchmarks   Check the bridge against competitors for such variables as frame filtering and forwarding, and size of buffer.

SNMP Support   Is the system SNMP compatible? Does it support SNMP Version 2? Is it RMON compatible?

Evaluation Criteria: Switches

Before applying a switch, it is necessary to know where the traffic is going. If the majority of the traffic is going to a server, for example, the port from the switch to the server can be a choke point. The solution may lie in using multiple ports or a higher-speed port between the switch and the server.

The first question to consider is the type of switch you need. Switches fall into three size ranges in increasing order of port size and complexity: desktop, work-group, and backbone. Desktop devices are inexpensive with approximately 24 ports plus one high-speed port for the server connection. All switching and filtering decisions are based on the MAC address. Work-group switches have a larger number of ports, and support multiple addresses per port. They have the ability to contain broadcast traffic, and generally have more sophisticated network management capability than desktop devices. Backbone switches are used to connect networks or LAN segments. They have a high-speed backplane and support several thousand MAC addresses per switch. They also can route packets and do more complex filtering than lower range products.

Quantity of Ports   How many ports does the system support? Can the system support wire speed bridging on all ports simultaneously? If not, what happens to excess frames?

Latency   How much delay is there between ports?

Packet Forwarding   Does the switch support cut-through or store-and-forward? At what forwarding rate does it begin dropping packets? What is the total forwarding bandwidth?

Filtering Capability   Can the switch filter all errored frames? Does it provide destination address filtering?

Fast Ethernet Compatibility   Is the system compatible with fast Ethernet or other protocols such as 100VG AnyLAN? Does it support full-duplex Ethernet?

SNMP Support   Is the system SNMP compatible? Does it support SNMP Version 2? Is it RMON compatible?

Virtual LAN Support   Does the switch support VLAN? Is it interoperable with products from other manufacturers?

Evaluation Criteria: Routers

Begin router selection by evaluating the manufacturer's record and the protocols the router supports. Be certain the router is compatible with the LAN and WAN protocols you plan to use, and that it has the necessary interface capability. For example, if frame relay will be used as the WAN, be certain that the router supports frame relay and that it has interface cards capable of the speed you plan to use.

Fault Tolerance   Mission-critical applications require fault-tolerant routers with redundant processors and power supplies. Check to be certain that cards are hot-swappable, meaning they can be changed without powering down the system.

Scalability   How well can the router meet the needs of both a high-end and a low-end network? Does it grow from low to high gracefully, or does it require a complete changeout at some growth point?

Ease of Installation   The configuration should be supported by setup menus that are easy to follow. SNMP compatibility is a must, and it should be possible to administer the router remotely with a local dial-in port. In a multi-router stack, is it necessary to configure each router individually, or can configuration files be downloaded from other devices in the stack? Can devices be configured on the fly without requiring network downtime during reconfiguration?

Routing Protocol   Most routers support routing information protocol (RIP). Many also support open shortest path first (OSPF) protocol.

Performance Benchmarks   Check the forwarding and filtering rate, the dropout rate, which is the rate at which packets are lost at the full forwarding rate of the router, and the amount of delay or latency that can be expected. Check how different traffic mixes affect throughput. Check performance in real-world conditions such as different protocols, different packet sizes, and two-way traffic,

Management   Is the router manageable through SNMP? Does it have direct terminal connection via EIA-232 ports? Is remote dial-up feasible? This is particularly important in remote offices.

SELECTED MANUFACTURERS OF LOCAL AREA NETWORK EQUIPMENT

File Servers

AST Research, Inc.

Compaq Computer Corp.

Data General Corp.

Dell Computer Corp.

Digital Equipment Corp.

Hewlett-Packard Co.

IBM

Hub Manufacturers

3Com Corp.

ADC Fibermux Corp.

Alantec Corp.

Allied Telesyn, Inc.

Asante Technologies, Inc.

Bay Networks/Synoptics

Bytex Corp.

Cabletron Systems, Inc.

Chipcom Corp.

Cray Communications

Digital Equipment Corp.

Fibronics International, Inc.

Gandalf Technologies, Inc.

Hewlett-Packard

IBM

Intellicom Inc.

Lannet Data Communications

Plexcom

Proteon, Inc.

RAD Data Communications

Racal-Datacom, Inc.

Standard Microsystems Corp.

UB Networks

Whittaker Communications

Xyplex, Inc.

Bridge and Router Manufacturers

3 COM

ADC Fibermux

Ascom Timeplex, Inc.

Bay Networks Wellfleet

Chipcom Corp.

Cisco Systems, Inc.

Digital Equipment Corp.

Gandalf Systems Corp.

General DataComm, Inc.

Hewlett-Packard Co.

Hughes Network Systems

IBM

Microcom, Inc.

Network Equipment Technologies, Inc.

Newbridge Networks

Penril DataComm Networks, Inc.

Proteon, Inc.

Retix

Ungermann-Bass, Inc.

Xyplex, Inc.

Ethernet and Token Ring Switches

3Com Corp.

Alantec

Bay Networks Synoptics

Cabletron Systems

Centillion Networks, Inc.

Chipcom

Cisco Systems, Inc.

Data Switch Corp.

Digital Equipment Corp.

Fibronics

Fore Systems, Inc.

Grand Junction Networks, Inc.

Hewlett-Packard

IBM

Kalapana, Inc.

Lannet Data Communications

Network Peripherals, Inc.

Proteon

Retix

Standard Microsystems Corp.

UB Networks

Whittaker Communications, Inc.

Xyplex, Inc.

Fast Ethernet Products

3Com

Alantec

Bay Networks

Cisco

Fore Systems

Grand Junction

Hewlett-Packard

Hughes LAN Systems

IBM

UB Networks

Remote Access Servers

3 COM

Digital Equipment Corp.

IBM

Microcom, Inc.

Shiva Corp.

Telebit Corp.

Xyplex, Inc.

31

WIDE AREA DATA NETWORKS

Wide area network architectures are shifting radically. The architectures of legacy networks were developed at a time of voice-grade analog circuits running on facilities with an error rate that was several orders of magnitude higher than today's fiber optics. Conventional networks are characterized by fixed-bandwidth point-to-point circuits, and single applications. Protocols are proprietary, and equipment sources may be limited to the network developer. Communications are controlled by the host, and direct communications among peers may be impossible. Terminals on a legacy network can run the applications supported by the host computer, but over the past decade the dumb terminal has largely been replaced by desktop computers that have an unlimited source of application software. The host connection is no longer the coaxial cable or EIA-232 connections of a terminal network; these have been replaced by LANs. The hierarchical networks of the past are evolving into nonhierarchical or flat networks driven by the following trends:

- ◆ Personal computers are replacing dumb terminals.
- ◆ Workstations have processing power greater than mainframe computers had a few years ago.
- ◆ Most personal computers are networked, with a trend toward linking LANs with an internet.

◆ Applications such as imaging and CAD/CAM demand greater bandwidths.

◆ An abundance of low-error-rate high-speed digital fiber-optic facilities results in reduced transmission costs.

◆ Emerging standards such as ATM provide new data transmission alternatives.

◆ Processing is evolving from centralized to distributed facilities.

◆ Compression technology squeezes voice, video, and data in ever smaller bandwidths.

Even though many networks are evolving toward broadband, voice-grade data circuits will remain for years to come because some applications do not require greater bandwidth. For example, the bandwidth requirements for automatic teller machines and point-of-sale terminals are so low that dozens of them can be supported on a single voice-grade circuit.

The network architecture of interconnected LANs is completely different from that of wide area terminal networks. Many companies are in a transition involving both legacy networks and LAN internets, which raises a special problem for network managers. An easy and expensive solution is to leave the two types of networks separate. The logical solution is to combine networks, but then issues of handling multiple protocols are raised. A complete examination of such issues is beyond the scope of this book, but we will briefly discuss the alternatives.

New networks are constructed on the enterprise network model shown in Figure 31–1. This model assumes that users can choose applications, the terminal devices on which they run, and that they can communicate any place in the network provided they have permission. The circuits are multilocation, and, within limits, able to deliver bandwidth on demand. Applications reside on servers that may be distributed throughout the network and accessed by any authorized station. Circuits are high-quality and digital, with at least 56 kb/s of bandwidth—more if needed. Peers can communicate freely, and error correction is left to the end devices.

Although the enterprise network on the above model is emerging, legacy wide area networks have not disappeared, and are likely to survive for as long as they meet the needs of the applications. In this chapter we will discuss both conventional and newer networks. This chapter will focus on facilities and common carrier alternatives that are used for both legacy networks and LAN internets up to T-1 bandwidth. Discussions of the protocols are reserved for other chapters: Chapter 4 discusses data protocols and Chapter 32 discusses broadband protocols such as FDDI, ATM, and SMDS. Chapter 33 discusses LAN internets, which connect LANs over the wide area. In this chapter we will

FIGURE 31-1

The Enterprise Network Permits Any Desktop Device to Connect to Any Data Source

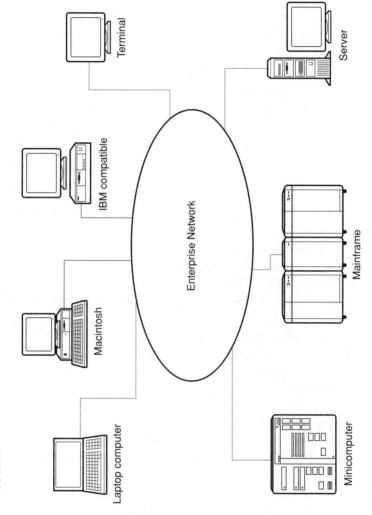

discuss the alternatives for multiplexing voice-grade circuits and the different types of public data networks that offer an alternative to fixed circuits.

DATA NETWORK FACILITIES

The data communications designer has several key decisions to make in selecting network facilities. This section discusses the primary network choices the designer must make in implementing a data communication network. Decision points such as these must be considered:

- ◆ Will facilities be privately owned, leased, or a combination of both?
- ◆ If facilities are leased, will a single vendor furnish the circuits?
- ◆ Are digital or analog facilities required?
- ◆ Will facilities be terrestrial, satellite, or a combination?
- ◆ Does the application require switched or dedicated facilities?
- ◆ Is the application inherently point-to-point or multipoint? Full duplex or half duplex?
- ◆ Is line conditioning required?
- ◆ Is there an opportunity to share bandwidth with other applications such as compressed voice and video?
- ◆ How will the network be managed?

Private or Public Ownership

Private ownership is the rule with local area data networks, but in wide area networks the cost of right of way usually precludes private ownership. Wide area networks are feasible for private ownership by only the largest companies. Most networks today are evolving toward a combination of private and public ownership. Such networks are one form of the hybrid networks discussed in Chapter 34.

Digital or Analog

Digital versus analog decisions are mostly resolved in favor of digital circuits. Tariff offerings such as fractional T-1 are driving the network from analog to digital, so designers who choose analog facilities should do so with the knowledge that it is an interim step toward an all-digital network.

Common Carrier or Value-Added Carrier

A common carrier delivers data communications circuits to an interface point on the user's premises. The carrier transports the signal but does not process the data. A *value-added carrier* not only transports data but also may process it or add other services such as store-and-forward, error correction, and authentication. The carrier also may provide other message-processing services such as filing, electronic mail, electronic data interchange, and message logging and receipting. The value-added carrier furnishes the user a dial-up or dedicated interface and provides the equivalent of a private network over shared facilities.

Switched or Dedicated Facilities

The nature of the application determines whether it requires a switched or dedicated network service. If multiple users communicate over distances greater than a few miles and send a few short messages, switched services tend to be most effective. If messages are long and the number of points limited, dedicated or private line services are most economical. Four types of switched services can be obtained.

1. *Circuit switching* connects channels through a centralized switching system. The public switched telephone network is an example of a circuit-switched network. Its primary advantage is worldwide access to any location with telephone service. Another advantage is that messages cannot arrive out of sequence because the circuit is intact from end to end. Its disadvantages are cost and limited bandwidth. As the LECs deploy ISDN, bandwidths will increase, and as the network evolves toward fiber-optic facilities in the local loop, errors will decrease.

2. *Message switching,* or store-and-forward switching, is a service that accepts a message from a user, stores it, and forwards it to its destination later. The storage time may be so short that forwarding is almost instantaneous, or messages may be stored for longer periods while a receiving terminal is temporarily unavailable or while awaiting more favorable rates.

The primary advantage of store-and-forward switching is that the sender and receiver do not need to be on-line simultaneously. If the receiving device is unavailable, the network can queue messages and release the originating device. If instantaneous delivery is not important, the store-and-forward technique can make maximum use of circuit capacity. Its primary disadvantages are the added cost of storage facilities in the switching device and the longer response time compared to circuit or packet switching.

3. *Packet switching* controls the flow of packets of information through a network by routing algorithms contained in each node. Stations interface with the packet nodes on a dedicated or dial-up basis and deliver preaddressed packets to the node, which routes them through the network to the destination.

Packet switching is flexible. During temporary overloads or circuit outages, service can be maintained by the dynamic routing capability of the network. Packet switching is also good for overseas applications because many network vendors have interconnection agreements that permit delivering packets worldwide. Its primary disadvantages are its cost and the latency that packet nodes introduce. We will discuss two variations of packet switching in this chapter: X.25 packet switching and frame relay.

4. *Cell switching* is an emerging technology that is discussed in more detail in Chapter 32. Messages are broken into 53-byte cells and routed through the network over a path that is set up for the duration of the session. Cell switching, or ATM, is capable of providing bandwidth on demand.

Terrestrial or Satellite Circuits

Communications satellites offer a cost-effective alternative to terrestrial circuits for distances of 1,000 miles or more and to multiple destinations over shorter distances. Because the tariff rates of terrestrial circuits are distance based, terrestrial circuits are less expensive over shorter routes unless the network has many terminal locations. Beyond a break-even point, satellite circuits are less expensive because their cost is independent of distance within the coverage field of a single satellite. Satellite circuits are also the most effective way of data transmission for mobile applications such as ships at sea and long-haul transportation.

Line Conditioning

As Chapter 2 discusses, analog voice channels have limitations that impair high-speed data. Two types of line conditioning, designated as types C and D, are available from common carriers. Type C conditioning minimizes the effects of amplitude distortion and envelope delay distortion. Conditioning levels are designated as C1, C2, C3, C4, and C5 in increasing order of control over distortion. Type D conditioning controls the amount of harmonic distortion on a data channel and controls noise to tighter limits than C conditioning. See Chapter 2 for a description of these impairments.

Circuit Sharing

Most data applications do not use the full bandwidth of a circuit, so circuits can be multiplexed with a variety of methods. As discussed later, multidrop circuits are polled by the host. Multiplexers enable multiple devices to share the same circuit. By using drop-and-insert multiplexers on T-1 lines, voice and data can share the same transmission medium.

Point-to-Point Network Facilities

Point-to-point circuits can be obtained through dial-up or dedicated connections. They can be analog or digital, with digital dedicated circuits replacing analog in most applications. Circuits are billed in three elements, as shown in Figure 31–2. The local access channels are obtained from the LEC or an AAC,

Billing Elements of an Interexchange Leased Circuit

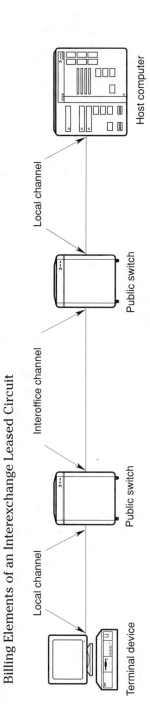

Terminal device

Local channel

Public switch

Interoffice channel

Public switch

Local channel

Host computer

727

and the interoffice channel is obtained from an IEC. Normally, the IEC obtains the local channel, bills the circuit as a single entity, and accepts end-to-end responsibility for clearing trouble. The cost of the IOC portion of the circuit is distance sensitive. The cost of the local access channel is not distance sensitive within a wire center, but between wire centers a mileage charge applies.

Dial-up Circuits

The public switched telephone network carries a significant portion of the data that is transported in the world. Circuit switching isn't an ideal way of handling data, but it has one major advantage: It is available nearly everywhere in the world with a universal numbering plan. Wherever telephones are found, data can be transported with respectable speed, reasonable cost, and easy setup. Dial-up data is effective under the following conditions:

◆ Data is exchanged among multiple terminating points.
◆ The application does not require an on-line connection.
◆ The use of data is occasional for limited periods each day.
◆ The time required to set up a data connection is not a limiting factor.

Facsimile is a data application that fits the above conditions perfectly. As a result, nearly all facsimile is sent over the PSTN because of its universal availability. The same is true of the countless dial-up sessions into Internet and public databases. Circuit switching is not ideal for these types of sessions. The transmissions are largely one-way, so bandwidth is wasted in one direction while transmission is taking place in the other. Ideally, data would be sent over a data network with switched virtual circuits, but such a network with ubiquitous connections does not yet exist. Therefore, although the PSTN may be less than ideal, nothing else can take its place for the moment.

Dial-up data has become a great deal more effective in the last few years with the introduction of fast modems with data compression and error correction. V.32 *bis* modems running at 14.4 kb/s have become a commodity. V.34 modems running at 28.8 kb/s with data compression and error correction are attractively priced. The handshake for setting speed and other variables is practically automatic, which makes dial-up an attractive option for many applications.

Switched 56 kb/s Service

The major IECs and LECs offer switched 56 kb/s services, which allow users to set up 56 kb/s connections between locations equipped for the service. Switched 56 is intended for applications that need a digital connection for a time too short to justify the use of a dedicated channel—generally three or fewer hours per day. Examples are videoconferences, high-speed facsimile transmission, graphics, and part-time extensions to existing digital networks. As with other switched services, switched 56 charges are based on usage time and carry a rate slightly higher than an ordinary voice connection.

Point-to-Point Analog Facilities

In the past analog facilities and modems were the default private circuit, but with the introduction of fractional T-1 services, networks are rapidly converting to digital. Analog private lines have a nominal bandwidth of 4 kHz, with a usable bandwidth of approximately 300 to 3,300 Hz. The error rate should be in the order of 10^{-5} or better.

Point-to-Point Digital Facilities

Digital facilities are available in a variety of configurations from common carriers. AT&T has offered Dataphone Digital Service® (DDS) for many years. Similar types of service are available from other carriers. Digital circuit speeds of 2.4, 4.8, 9.6, 19.2, and 56 kb/s are common. The user can multiplex signals to lower speeds if desired. DDS service objectives are 99.99 percent error-free seconds and 99.96 percent availability. The carriers transport most digital circuits on lightwave and extend service to the end user over four-wire nonloaded cable facilities furnished by the LECs. Increasingly, the IECs deliver digital services over T-1 facilities that the customer obtains for both voice and data services. Figure 31–3 shows how a T-1 can provide entrance facilities for both voice and digital data.

DDS uses a bipolar signaling format that requires the user's data signal to be converted from the usual unipolar output of terminal equipment. A data service unit (DSU) located on the user's premises does the conversion. If the user's equipment can accept a bipolar signal and provide timing recovery, the data signal is coupled to a channel service unit (CSU). Both units provide loopback facilities, so the local cable can be tested by looping the transmit and receive pairs together. The signal is fully synchronized from end to end. A DDS hub office concentrates data signals from multiple users and connects them to the long-haul network. The hub is also a testing point.

T-1 and Fractional T-1

Most IECs and LECs offer bulk digital T-1 transmission facilities at prices that are more attractive than those of multiple analog lines. The major interexchange carriers and some LECs also offer the fractional T-1 services. Fractional T-1 is economical up to some crossover point with full T-1, after which a full T-1 is more cost-effective. For example, AT&T's ACCUNET® Spectrum of Digital Services (ASDS) offers digital transmission at speeds ranging from

FIGURE 31-3

Sharing T-1 between Voice and Data

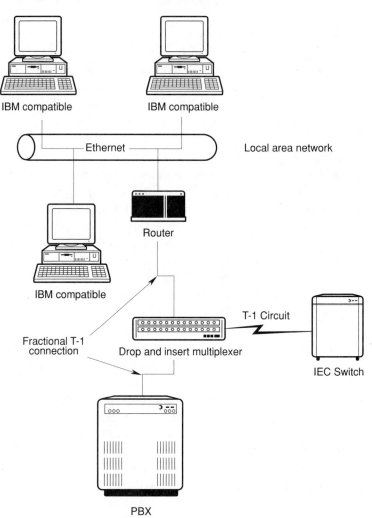

9.6, 56, or 64 kb/s up to 768 kb/s in 64 kb/s increments. Fractional T-1 can support analog service as well as digital. Multidrop bridging is also available. This type of service has replaced analog 3002 circuits in most cases. A *fan-out* option multiplexes up to five 9.6 kb/s circuits onto one 56 kb/s fractional T-1 circuit. The local access portion of T-1 can be delivered by LECs and AACs over fiber optic or copper facilities.

If the local access circuit permits, T-1 and fractional T-1 can be offered as clear channel 64 kb/s service. Some carriers provide central office multiplexing and service protection measures such as diversity routing and routing exclusively over fiber-optics facilities.

T-3 and Fractional T-3

Where multiple T-1 circuits are needed between two points, T-3 or fractional T-3 become economical. T-3 service is a full 28 DS-1s operating at 45 mb/s. Fractional T-3 is at submultiples of T-1. For example, AT&T's ACCUNET® Fractional T45 service offers 3, 4, 5, and 7 DS-1s. The interoffice channel of fractional T-3 must be central-office-routed over the same DS-3, or the DS-1s may arrive at slightly different times. Local channels may be routed over microwave or fiber-optic facilities provided by the customer or an access carrier.

MULTIDROP NETWORKS

Point-to-point circuits are cost-effective when there is enough traffic on the network to justify the cost of a dedicated circuit between two devices. Where the traffic flows in bursts or short transmissions, some method of sharing the circuit among multiple devices is needed. Such a method, used in IBM's SNA network, is *polling*. If a polling protocol is used, a multidrop circuit is often the choice. As discussed later, however, SNA, which represents the most widespread use of polling, can be applied to packet-switching and frame relay circuits. The choice of the polling protocol does not, therefore, necessarily dictate the use of multi-drop circuits.

The advantage of multidrop is in the ability of multiple devices to share the same backbone circuits. For example, a bank that has multiple automatic teller machines in an area can obtain local loops to the machines and bridge them in the central office to share a single circuit to the *front-end processor,* which is a computer equipped for telecommunications. The front-end processor's role is to relieve the host computer of teleprocessing chores. Each station is assigned an address. The host polls the stations by sending short polling messages to the controller. If the controller has no traffic from any of its attached terminals, it responds with a negative acknowledgment message. If it has traffic, it responds by sending a block of data, which the host acknowledges. Before sending data to the distant devices, which are usually terminals or printers, the host sends a short message to determine whether the device is ready to receive. If it is ready, the host then sends a block of data.

Multidrop networks are designed as full duplex or half duplex. In half-duplex networks, the modem reverses after a poll or response. In full-duplex networks, the devices can send data in both directions simultaneously. Polling is an efficient way of sharing a common data circuit, but it has high overhead compared to other alternatives. The overhead of sending polling messages, returning negative acknowledgments, and reversing the modems consumes a substantial portion of the circuit time. Throughput can be improved by using *hub polling*. In hub polling, when a station receives a poll, it passes its traffic to the host and passes the polling message to the next station in line. Hub polling is more complex than *roll call* polling and is not as widely used.

IBM Systems Network Architecture

The most prominent example of multidrop architecture is IBM's Systems Network Architecture. SNA is a tree-structured hierarchical architecture, in which a mainframe computer serves as the network host. The boundaries described by the host computer, front-end processors, and cluster controllers and terminals are called the network's *domain*. Figure 31–4 is a diagram of the logical and physical elements in SNA. SNA establishes a logical path between network nodes and routes each message with addressing information contained in the protocol. The SNA data link protocol is synchronous data link control (SDLC).

Access Method
The access method provides access to applications in the host computer and controls the flow of data between application programs and the network. The most common access methods are advanced communications function/virtual telecommunications access method (ACF/VTAM) and ACF/telecommunications communication access method (ACF/TCAM). These are normally abbreviated VTAM and TCAM respectively. VTAM gives an application more direct network control than does TCAM, which isolates the application from the network environment.

Network Addressable Units
The major components in the network are called Network Addressable Units (NAUs). SNA defines four types:

- Type 1—Terminals
- Type 2—Controllers
- Type 4—Front-End Processors
- Type 5—Hosts

FIGURE 31-4

Physical and Logical View of IBM Systems Network Architecture

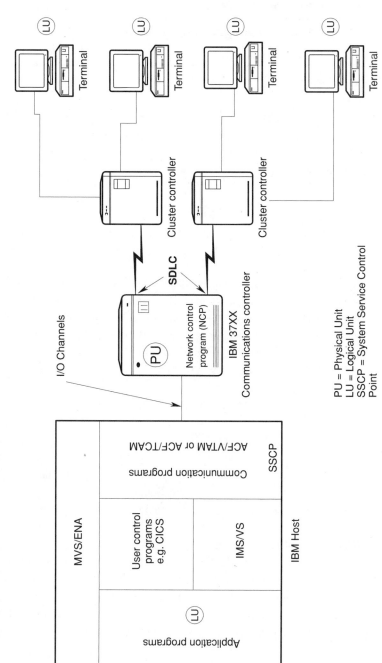

733

FIGURE 31-5

Synchronous Data Transmission (IBM SDLC Frame)

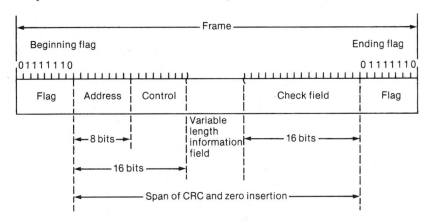

The host NAU is categorized as a system service control point (SSCP). Each network contains at least one SSCP, which resides in an IBM mainframe computer. The SSCP exercises network control, establishing routes and interconnections between logical units. The end user interfaces the network through a logical unit (LU). The LU, generally a terminal or a personal computer, is the user's link to the network. The next higher unit in the hierarchy is a physical unit (PU). Although its name implies that it is a piece of hardware, a PU is a control program executed in software or firmware.

Network Control Program

The network control program (NCP) resides in the front-end processor. Its purpose is to control information flow in the network. It polls the attached controllers, handles error detection and correction, establishes circuits under control of the SSCP, and other functions that deload the host computer.

SNA's Layered Architecture

SNA is defined in layers roughly analogous to the layers in ISO's OSI model. SNA was first announced in 1974 and is the basis for much of the OSI model, but it differs from OSI in several significant respects.

Level 1, physical, is not included as part of the SNA architecture. The physical interface for analog voice-grade circuits is ITU V.24 and V.31. The digital interface is X.21.

Level 2, data link control, uses the synchronous data link control (SDLC) protocol. Figure 31-5 shows the SDLC frame, which has six octets of overhead. The first octet is a flag to establish the start of the frame. This is followed by a one-octet address and a one-octet control field. Next is a variable length data field followed by a two-octet cyclical redundancy check field and an ending flag. The control field contains the number of packets received to allow SDLC to acknowledge multiple packets simultaneously. SDLC permits up to 128 unacknowledged packets, which makes it suitable for satellite transmission. This layer corresponds closely to ISO's data link layer and the LAPB protocol used in X.25 networks.

Level 3, path control, is responsible for establishing data paths through the network. It carries addressing, mapping, and message sequencing information. At the start of a session, the path control layer establishes a virtual route, which is the sequence of nodes forming a path between the terminating points. The circuits between the nodes are formed into transmission groups, which are groups of circuits having identical characteristics—speed, delay, error rate, and so on. The path control layer is also responsible for address translation. Through this layer, LUs can address other LUs by terminating address without being concerned with the entire detailed address of the other terminal. This layer is also responsible for flow control, protecting the network's resources by delaying traffic that would cause congestion. The path control layer also *segments* and *blocks* messages. Segmenting is the process of breaking long messages into manageable size pieces so errors do not cause excessive retransmission. Blocking is the reverse—combining short messages so the network's resources are not consumed by small messages of uneconomical size.

Level 4, transmission control, is responsible for pacing. At the beginning of a session the LUs exchange information about factors, such as transmission speed and buffer size, that affect their ability to receive information. The pacing function prevents an LU from sending more data than the receiving LU can accept. Through this layer, SNA also provides other functions such as encryption, message sequencing, and flow control.

Level 5, data flow control, conditions messages for transmission by *chaining* and *bracketing.* Chaining is the process of grouping messages with one-way transmission requirements, and bracketing is grouping messages for two-way transmission.

Level 6, function management data services, has three primary purposes. Configuration service activates and deactivates internodal links. Network operator services is the interface through which the network operator sends commands and receives responses. The management services function is used in testing and troubleshooting the network.

Level 7, NAU services, is responsible for formatting data between display devices such as printers and CRTs. It performs some functions of the ISO presentation layer, including data compression and compaction. It also synchronizes transmissions. SNA lacks an applications layer as such, but IBM has defined standards that allow for document interchange and display between SNA devices. Document interchange architecture (DIA) can be thought of as the envelope in which documents travel. DIA standards cover editing, printing, and displaying documents. The document itself is defined by document content architecture (DCA), which is analogous to the letter within the envelope. The purpose of the DIA/DCA combination is to make it possible for business machines to transmit documents with formatting commands such as tabs, indents, margins, and other format information intact. Documents containing graphic information are defined by graphic codepoint definition (GCD), which defines the placement of graphic symbols on printers and screens.

Peer-to-Peer Communications

A drawback of SNA in the past was the requirement that all data flow through the host. This condition was reasonable when terminals lacked intelligence, but as the terminal of choice evolved from dumb to intelligent, it became undesirable to have the host control every session between intelligent devices. PU Type 2 cluster controllers could support only one SDLC link and could not communicate among themselves.

IBM developed a cluster controller modification known as PU 2.1, which enabled two controllers to be linked across an SDLC or dial-up connection without requiring a path through the PU type 4 communications controller. Although PU 2.1 supports the physical connection, it does not provide all the logical functions necessary for peer-to-peer communications exclusive of the host computer. To enable device-to-device communications, IBM introduced the LU 6.2 advanced program-to-program communications (APPC) protocol. LU 6.2 does away with the SNA master/slave relationship between devices and, instead, permits communication between peers. Either device can manage the session, establishing and terminating communications and initiating session error recovery procedures without the involvement of an SSCP. APPC permits direct PC to mainframe communications, which enables the PC to transfer files without consuming excessive mainframe processing power.

PACKET SWITCHING

Unlike circuit switched networks, which provide a circuit between end points for the exclusive use of two or more stations, packet networks support *virtual circuits,* which share many characteristics with switched circuits. The difference is that the circuits are time-shared rather than dedicated to the connection. As Figure 31–6 shows, a packet network has multiple nodes that are accessed

X.25 Packet Network Showing Access Options

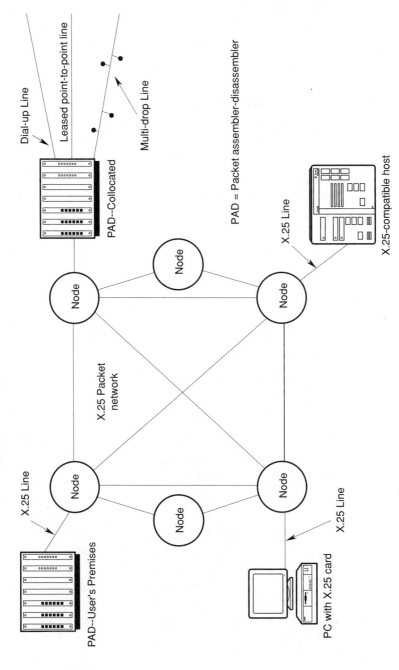

through dedicated or dialed connections from the end user. The nodes control access to the network and route packets to their destinations over a backbone of high-speed data circuits.

Access to public data networks is provided by one of three methods:

◆ A dedicated X.25 link between the user's host computer and the data network.
◆ A dedicated link between the data network and a PAD on the user's premises.
◆ Dedicated or dial-up access over the telephone network into a PAD provided by the network vendor.

In the first option, the user's host computer performs the PAD functions. The second option requires either a PAD provided by the vendor on the user's premises or a user-owned PAD that the vendor certifies is compatible with the network.

The third option, dial-up access, is the least complex and is the only method economically feasible for small users. It does, however, have several disadvantages. The first problem is the loss of end-to-end error checking and correction. Modems with a built-in error correcting protocol are an effective method of error correction.

The packet assembler/disassembler (PAD) creates a packet when one of three events occurs:

◆ A predetermined number of bytes is received.
◆ A specified time elapses.
◆ A particular bit sequence occurs.

Packet networks are effective in both public and private implementations. The primary advantages of packet switching are:

◆ *Ready availability:* Most computer manufacturers support the X.25 protocol.
◆ *Reliability:* Alternate paths between packet switches minimize the effect of a switch or circuit failure.
◆ *Ease of crossing international boundaries:* Public data networks cover the major countries in the world. Time-consuming circuit setups are not required to begin sending data.
◆ *Economy of multiple sites:* Since costs are usage-based, small sites that often cannot justify fixed private lines can justify a connection to the nearest node.

FIGURE 31–7

Level 2 Frame Enclosing X.25 Packet

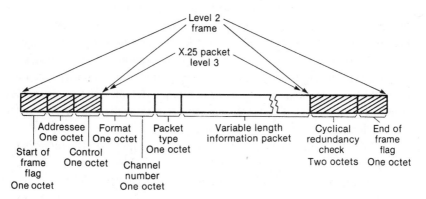

Disadvantages are:

- *Latency:* Packet switches are subject to both packetizing and switching delays; the more nodes on the network, the longer the delay.
- *Packet overhead:* The X.25 protocol adds headers that reduce throughput.
- *Probabilistic performance:* The response time of a packet network depends on load. During heavy load periods, response time deteriorates.

Packet-Switching Nodes

The packet-switching nodes are processors interconnected by backbone circuits. High-speed digital facilities are usually employed between nodes. Data flows through the network in packets consisting of an information field sandwiched between header and trailer records. Figure 31–7 shows the packet used by ITU's X.25 protocol. Note in the figure that *octet* is used to denote an eight-bit byte. The X.25 packet is enclosed in a frame consisting of a one-octet flag having a distinctive pattern that is not repeated in the data field. The second octet is an address code that permits up to 255 addresses on a data link. The third field is a control octet that sequences messages and sends supervisory commands. The X.25 packet has three format and control octets and an information field that contains the user data. The final three octets of the trailer are a 16-bit cyclical redundancy check field (see Chapter 3) and an end-of-frame flag.

Packet Assembly and Disassembly

A packet assembler/disassembler slices the message into packets. The PAD communicates with the packet network using a packet network protocol, X.25, which is a ITU protocol recommendation that describes the interface to a packet-switching node. The packet network uses the address field of the packet to route it to the next node on the way to the destination. Each node hands off the packet following the network's routing algorithm until it reaches the final node. At the terminating node, the switch sequences the packets and passes them off to the PAD. The PAD strips the data from the header and trailer records and reassembles it into a completed message.

Error checking takes place in each link in the network. If a block is received in error, the node rejects it and requests a replacement block. Because errors require resending blocks and because blocks can take different paths to their destinations, it is possible for blocks to arrive at the destination out of sequence. The receiving node buffers the message and delivers the data blocks in the proper sequence.

In many ways packet networks are similar to message switching or store-and-forward networks, but with the following differences:

◆ Packet-switching networks are intended for real-time operation. Message switching networks store messages for later delivery. Although the time is often short, it may be a substantial fraction of a minute.

◆ Message networks typically retain file copies of messages for a given period. Packet networks deliver the messages and clear them from their buffers.

◆ Message networks transport the message as a unit. Packet networks slice the message into shorter blocks and reassemble them at the receiving end.

A special type of message known as a *datagram* is available in some packet networks. A datagram is a single packet that flows through the network to its destination without acknowledgment. An alternative to the datagram is the *fast select* message, which is a single packet and response. A typical application for fast select messages is the credit-checking terminal that transmits the details of a transaction from a point-of-sale terminal and receives an acknowledgment from a credit agency's database.

The network designer specifies packet size to optimize throughput. Because each packet has a fixed-length header and trailer record, short packets reduce throughput because time must be spent transmitting overhead bits in the header and trailer. On the other hand, long packets reduce throughput because the switching node cannot forward the packet until it receives all bits, which increases buffer requirements at the node. Also, the time spent in retransmitting errored packets is greater if the packet length is longer. Most packet networks operate with a packet length of 128 to 256 octets.

Virtual Circuits

Packet networks establish two kinds of virtual circuits, switched and permanent. *Permanent virtual circuits* are the packet network equivalent of a dedicated voice circuit. A path between users is established, and all packets take the same route through the network. With a *switched virtual circuit,* the network path is established with each session.

Packets consist of two types, data and control. *Control packets,* which contain information to show the status of the session, are analogous to signaling in a circuit-switched network. For example, a call setup packet would be used to establish the initial connection to the terminating device, which would return answer packets. The network uses control packets to interrupt calls in progress, disconnect, show acceptance of reversed charges, and other functions that operators and supervisory signals control on telephone networks. Switched virtual circuit operations use these control packets to establish a session. In permanent virtual circuit operation, the path is preestablished and no separate packets are needed to connect and disconnect the circuit.

X.25 Protocol

X.25 is an example of an important protocol built on the OSI model. X.25 specifies the interface between DTE and a packet-switched network. It forms a network from the physical, link, and network layers of the OSI model. The physical layer interface is the X.21 standard. Another version of the standard, X.21 *bis,* is nearly identical with EIA-232-C and is more commonly used.

The link layer uses a derivation of HDLC called balanced link access procedure (LAPB) to control errors, packet transfer, and to establish the data link. The network layer establishes logical channels and virtual circuits between the PAD and the network. The X.75 protocol recommends the interface for gateway circuits between packet networks.

Value-Added Networks

Public data networks, also known as *value-added networks,* provide an alternative to the telephone network for long-haul data communications. The term "value added" derives from processing functions that are added to the usual network functions of data transport and switching. The value-added services include such features as error checking and correction, code conversion, speed conversion, and storage.

Public Packet-Switched Data Networks

Packet-switching service can be obtained with private network equipment or through a public data network such as Sprint's SprintNet. Several other networks offer packet-switching service, and most larger LECs provide packet switching within their LATAs. Because of the nature of the applications, most users require interLATA connections. These can be provided by the user as private lines, or the user can obtain a connection to a long-haul packet network for the interLATA connection.

Public packet-switching networks have developed more rapidly in Europe, where it is more difficult to obtain private network facilities from the postal telephone and telegraph agencies. Public data networks in the United States can often transport data overseas by interconnecting through a gateway to a data network in another country.

FRAME RELAY

X.25 has several drawbacks that have led many networks to move to frame relay. X.25 was developed when error rates were high: Analog circuits with error rates of 10^{-5} or 10^{-6} were common. Fiber-optics circuits deliver error performance of at least 10^{-9}, and often better. X.25 link-by-link error checking and correction imposes excessive latency that is unneeded in high-quality circuits. X.25 value-added networks charge by the kilopacket. The huge quantities of data that flow across an internet would render X.25 prohibitively expensive. X.25 networks provide access speeds of up to 56 kb/s, which is slow for interconnecting LANs. Frame relay offers access speeds of up to 1.544 mb/s in North America, and up to 2.048 mb/s in Europe.

Frame relay has an architecture similar to packet switching, but a different data-handling and pricing structure. Frame relay is a connection-oriented service that leaves error detection and correction to the end devices, which are frame relay access devices (FRADs) or routers. Unlike X.25, the pricing structure is not based on the number of packets transferred. Frame relay has three pricing elements:

◆ *Committed information rate (CIR):* This is the throughput the carrier guarantees will be transported.

◆ *Port speed:* This is the speed of the access port into the carrier's network. It is in multiples of 64 kb/s.

◆ *Access circuit:* This is the cost of the access circuit provided by the LEC or AAC. It ranges from 56 kb/s or multiples thereof up to T-1.

The difference between the CIR and port speed is the key to frame relay's method of operation. If the carrier's backbone capacity permits, the network will transport data up to the port speed. This makes the service ideal for applications with bursty data because the network can carry the average data the applications require while handling short-term bursts. Some LEC frame relay offerings do not impose a CIR choke. They always carry data at the port speed so that the network is, in effect, a high-speed data switch.

Customers contract with the carrier for permanent virtual circuits between end points. A typical network might resemble the one in Figure 31–8. This type of network is typical of a headquarters with several branch offices. A network such as this is frequently used for E-mail and occasional file transfers. The branch offices use 56 kb/s access circuits with a low CIR; 16 kb/s is common, but some branches with higher traffic volume or priority would use a higher CIR. Some carriers offer a zero CIR, which can be acceptable for light applications such as E-mail. The access circuit and port speed at the headquarters location would be higher than the speeds at the branches. A 256 kb/s CIR would support several branch offices. Typically, a frame relay network costs from 25 to 50 percent less than an equivalent dedicated digital network. The cost difference depends on tariffs, distance of the nodes from the carrier's frame relay POP, and span of the network. The wider the network's span, the more attractive frame relay becomes because it is not distance sensitive.

Frame relay is a robust service. The most likely point of failure is in the access circuits. Once the traffic reaches the carrier's backbone network, disruption is unlikely. To get the same degree of protection in a dedicated network would require a full mesh architecture, which is too costly for many companies to justify. If all the traffic is destined for a single headquarters location, the access circuit and port speed for that location will need higher bandwidth and port speed than satellite locations. If satellite locations need to communicate with one another, they can communicate through the central location or they can set up virtual circuits between themselves. For light and occasional traffic, communicating through the central site is the most economical.

The major LECs offer frame relay in their serving areas. While court restrictions on providing long-distance exist, LEC frame relay must connect to an IEC to bridge LATA boundaries. Their service areas may be further curtailed by exchange boundaries with independent telephone companies. Some LECs and IECs have worked out network-to-network interface (NNI) arrangements to

FIGURE 31-8

A Frame Relay Network

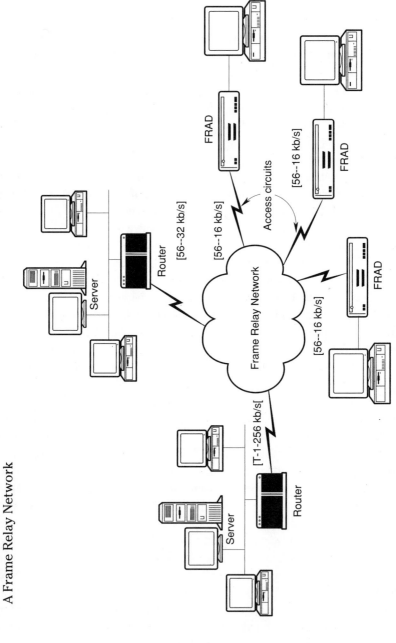

Access circuits and committed information rates are shown in brackets [56-16 kb/s].

F I G U R E   31–9

Frame Relay Frame Format

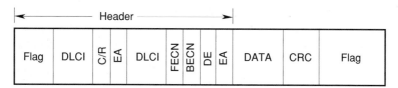

DLCI = Data link connection identifier
EA = Address extension bit
C/R = Command/response bit
FECN = Forward explicit congestion notification
BECN = Backward explicit congestion notification
CRC = Cyclical redundancy check

make the service area boundaries transparent to the customer. In other cases dedicated circuit extensions across exchange boundaries may be required. Most frame relay services offer both dedicated and dial-up access.

The Frame Relay Protocol

Frame relay is a connection-oriented service with a variable-length packet that can range as high as 4,000 octets. Figure 31–9 shows the frame structure used by frame relay. Each frame has an 11-bit address field known as the data link connection identifier (DLCI), which supplies the virtual circuit number. If the DLCI is defined for a link, the frame is forwarded over the permanent virtual circuit. Otherwise, it is discarded. The protocol uses the frame check sequence block to review frame integrity. If it is in error, it is discarded.

Congestion Control

The frame relay protocol allows the carriers to mark any frames over the CIR as discard eligible. If the network becomes congested, the carrier buffers frames up to its buffer capacity. After the buffers are full, it can discard frames, which the routers must detect and retransmit. A partial solution is flow control, which both the frame relay switch and the router must support. The frame relay protocol includes forward explicit congestion notification (FECN) and backward explicit congestion notification (BECN) as a flow control mechanism, but not all carriers and routers support FECN/BECN. As backbone networks become more heavily loaded, packet loss may become a problem.

Virtual Circuits

Today frame relay services offer only permanent virtual circuits. Sometime in the future the Frame Relay Forum intends to introduce switched virtual circuits (SVCs), which can provide the equivalent of dial-up service for data networks. SVCs will allow users to dial their own connections to any other user connected to the same frame relay network. NNIs between networks would allow users to connect to frame relay customers of competing networks.

VERY SMALL APERTURE TERMINAL

VSAT is an excellent medium for a widely dispersed operation. Its pricing is not distance sensitive, and it is particularly effective in remote locations that are not close to a frame relay point-of-presence. A typical application is point-of-sale with widely dispersed terminals, many of which are located in rural areas and small towns where a service such as frame relay is not cost-effective because of the access circuit cost. Another application for which VSAT is admirably suited is telemetering from mobile devices such as trucks, ships, and trains.

Figure 31–10 shows a typical VSAT arrangement. As discussed in Chapter 15, the VSAT terminal is a small device with a one- or two-meter antenna. Transponder space is leased from the satellite provider or obtained from the hub provider. Large companies can justify the cost of the earth station and hub. Smaller companies will lease capacity from a service provider. Added to the cost of the transponder is a terrestrial extension from the hub to the host computer. VSAT bandwidth can range from as low as 1,200 b/s to T-1 speeds.

With all else equal, terrestrial circuits are more effective for data than satellite circuits. At longer distances, however, the greater cost of terrestrial circuits often offsets the disadvantages of a satellite. The primary disadvantage of a satellite circuit is the round-trip propagation delay, which is approximately 0.5 seconds. Some protocols such as IBM's bisync will not operate well with this much delay. Other protocols function with reduced throughput because of error retransmission time. Satellite delay compensators can alleviate some protocol problems, but they add latency. IBM's SDLC allows the protocol to acknowledge as many as 128 packets at a time, which enables it to operate effectively on satellite circuits.

APPLICATIONS

Data network applications can be separated into the following general types:

FIGURE 31-10

VSAT Network

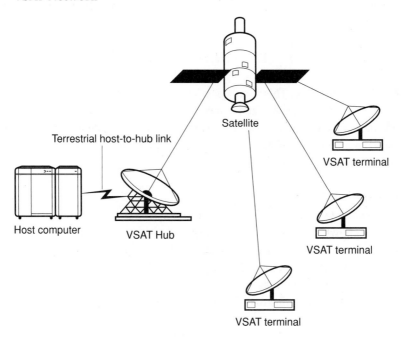

Inquiry/Response   This is typical of information services where a short inquiry generates a lengthy response from the host. Because the data flow is greater in one direction than in the other, half-duplex facilities generally offer the greatest throughput. Either dedicated or dial-up facilities can be used depending on two primary factors, cost and setup time. If sessions are set up occasionally, setup time is not a significant factor, but if many sessions are established each day, the time required to dial the connection may mandate a dedicated circuit.

Applications that are typical of inquiry/response are airline reservations and on-line database sessions. The operator keys a few characters into the terminal, and the host computer responds with a lengthy message that might be confirmation of a reservation, a printed ticket, or an information dump.

Conversational   This mode, typical of terminal-to-terminal communication, is characterized by short messages that are of approximately equal length in both directions. Throughput is improved by using full-duplex operation. Conversational mode is typical of LAN connectivity via remote bridges or routers. Users log on to remote file servers and send approximately equal amounts of data in each direction when files are retrieved and periodically saved.

Bulk Data Transfer   This is typical of applications such as mainframe-to-mainframe communications where large files are passed, often at high speed, in only one direction. This method is often used when a local processor collects information during the day and makes daily updates of a master file such as an inventory on the host. Bulk data transfer is usually a half-duplex operation because large amounts of data flow in one direction with the line reversed periodically to return an acknowledgment.

Remote Job Entry   This is typical of applications in which terminals send information to a host. The bulk of the transmission is from the terminal with a short acknowledgment from the host. Half-duplex circuits may be the most effective form of transmission because the bulk of the information flows from remote to host. Dedicated lines are almost invariably needed for this kind of application. Many remote terminals, each of which is used only occasionally, share a higher-speed line to the host.

Multiprotocol Networking with SNA

Most corporate networks today incorporate multiple protocols in their network environment. For example, LANs linked over a backbone network using TCP/IP often must coexist with SNA. If these networks are separated, the result is costly duplication. The most cost-effective solution is to run a multiprotocol network. Several different strategies can be employed, including the following:

◆ Circuit integration at the physical layer; for example, through time division multiplexers.
◆ SNA encapsulation in a higher-layer protocol such as X.25 or IP.
◆ Use of multiprotocol routers.
◆ Use of IBM's Multiprotocol Transport Network.
◆ Transporting integrated data over frame relay.

The latter solution is generally effective if frame relay is used for LAN interconnection. Like SNA, frame relay is a connection-oriented service. The protocols can be built into the 37XX front-end processor.

Standards

ITU-T sets international data network standards, with supporting standards set by ANSI, EIA, and major equipment vendors whose products take on the character of de facto standards. For example, in data communications, IBM's Systems Network Architecture (SNA) is so widely used as to constitute a de facto standard. The primary ITU standards that affect data communications networks are included in Appendix B.

Evaluation Considerations

The criteria used to evaluate data networks differ significantly from those used to evaluate voice networks. For example, the short length of many data messages makes setup time, which is of little concern in voice networks, an important factor. Also, error considerations are important in data networks. Circuit noise that is merely annoying in a voice network may render the channel unusable for data. Also, because many data networks' billing is not distance sensitive and because billing is based on volume rather than connect time, cost evaluations are significantly different for the two types of network.

Private Line Services

Digital or Analog Facilities   The trend in both metropolitan and long-haul circuits is toward the use of digital facilities. Digital facilities have the additional advantage of providing improved performance. The carrier can monitor the bit error rate performance of backbone circuits and take corrective action when it exceeds the advertised limits. Also, as such circuits are inherently full-duplex four-wire circuits and have no modems, the time consumed in modem reversals and modem failures is eliminated.

Reliability and Availability   Data circuit reliability is the frequency of circuit failure expressed as mean time between failures (MTBF). A related factor is circuit availability, which is the percentage of time the circuit is available to the user. Availability depends on how frequently the circuit fails and how long it takes to repair it. The average length of time to repair a circuit is expressed as mean time to repair (MTTR). The formula for determining availability is:

$$\frac{(MTBF - MTTR) \times 100}{MTBF}$$

For example, a circuit with an MTBF of 1,000 hours and an MTTR of 2 hours would have an availability of:

$$\frac{(1,000-2) \times 100}{1,000} = 99.8\%$$

It is important to reach with the supplier an understanding of the conditions under which a circuit is considered failed. When the circuit is totally inoperative, a failure condition clearly exists, but when a high error rate impairs the circuit, it is less clear whether the service is usable. The error rate in a data circuit is usually expressed as a ratio of error bits to transmitted bits. For example, a data circuit with an error rate of 1×10^{-5} will have one bit in error for every 100,000 bits transmitted. Reliability and error rate have a significant effect on throughput. Most error correction systems initiate retransmission of a block, and retransmission of blocks reduces throughput.

Costs   Cost comparisons between public data networks are difficult to make because of differences in the way data is handled. Cost depends on how the network handles data and renders bills for usage. The geographic area to be covered has a significant effect on the cost of public data network services. Costs are higher in low-density areas. With dial access, the cost of measured local telephone service or long-distance charges to the node when none is available in the locality must be considered.

Session Setup Time   Setup time is critical to most data applications. When using dial access over a public data network, setup time is significant—often longer than message transmission time. Dedicated access to a public data or frame relay network eliminates the dialing, answer, and authentication routines, greatly reducing call setup time. The time it takes to establish a session through the network to the terminating station remains a significant factor and is comparable whether dial or dedicated access to the public data network is used.

Line Conditioning   High-speed analog private line data transmission facilities may require conditioning. Type C conditioning improves the attenuation distortion and envelope delay distortion in the facility. Type D conditioning also improves noise performance and harmonic distortion of the circuit. Some types of modems equipped with adaptive equalization may not require conditioning, but other modems will require conditioned lines at 9,600 b/s. Now that fiber-optic circuits comprise most of the interexchange network, an analog circuit may be completely digital except the local loops. In such circuits, conditioning may be unnecessary.

Frame Relay and X.25 Services

Features Supported Data communications features should be examined and compared to the services available from the different data communications network alternatives. Features to be considered include:

- *Virtual circuit or datagram service.* Users with very short messages may require a datagram or fast select service.
- *Type of message delivery.* Consider whether message delivery is to be automatic or delayed awaiting a busy or unattended terminal.
- *Message storage or electronic mail services* may be offered by the network or a value-added service on the network.
- *Multidestination message service.* Consider whether it is important to broadcast messages to many stations simultaneously.
- *Billing service.* Consider whether detailed call accounting is required or whether message charges are bulked to a user number.
- *Security.* Networks should offer password security and also should offer encryption and a private storage facility that can be unlocked only with an additional private code.
- *Closed user groups.* These are private networks within the network that are designated for the exclusive use of users who gain access only with proper authentication. They are used either for terminal-to-terminal communication or for privately accessed store-and-forward service.
- *Protocol conversion.* Communication between terminals using unlike protocols may be supported by the network.
- *Disconnect of idle stations* should be provided.
- *Abbreviated or mnemonic addressing* may be provided, with the system generating the data network number from a simplified address.

Access Circuit and Port Speed Determine the required speed of the access circuit and port speed into the carrier's network. Determine if 56/64 kb/s service offers enough bandwidth or if T-1 or fractional T-1 is required at each location. Determine if access can be shared with some other service routed to the same carrier.

Network-to-Network Connections Some of the major IECs and LECs have signed NNI agreements that makes local access to IEC frame relay networks more economical. For example, a company with both inter- and intra-LATA connections on the same network can often obtain local access circuits from the LEC's frame relay network at a lower cost than using dedicated line extensions.

Point-of-Presence The location of the carrier's POP is of concern to designers. In locations without a POP in the same city, the cost of the local access circuit can be high enough that frame relay is not cost-effective. If international service is required, determine what countries the carrier covers.

Committed Information Rate Selection of the CIR is one of the most important factors in determining the success of frame relay. If the wrong choice is made initially, the carrier can change CIR in a short interval. Review the expected maximum data throughput requirement of your network and the times of day that bursts of data are likely to occur. Review how the carrier handles bursts over the CIR. Determine whether they buffer or discard packets when congestion occurs.

Network Information A major advantage of frame relay over fixed networks is the amount of network information that the carrier provides. Determine what reports are available, how often they are produced, and how they are obtained. For example, does the carrier provide data on line over the frame relay network?

Access Method Determine whether frame relay access can be shared over existing T-1 lines, or if access can be obtained from LECs or AACs. Is dial-up access required in some locations, and if so, is it available from the carrier? Is X.25 access available? Determine whether a router or FRAD will be used as the access switch.

SELECTED VENDORS OF DATA NETWORK SERVICES

Packet-Switched Network and Value-Added Services

AT&T

Cable & Wireless

CompuServe Network Services

Sprint SprintNet

MCI Communications

Frame Relay Services

The following are the major carriers offering interLATA frame relay service. In addition, most major LECs offer frame relay within the LATA.

AT&T

British Telecom

Cable & Wireless

CompuServe Network Services

MCI

Sprint

Worldcom, Inc.

VSAT Services

American Mobile Satellite Corp.

Hughes

MCI

Orionnet

Dedicated Network Services

AT&T

Cable & Wireless

MCI Communications

Sprint

Worldcom, Inc.

Switched Services

AT&T

Cable & Wireless

MCI Communications

Sprint

32

BROADBAND NETWORKS

Many forces are converging to drive the demand for greater communications bandwidth. When voice communications originate from the telephone and data from a terminal, bandwidth demands are modest. Digital leased lines and multiplexed voice-grade circuits, which have expanded from 4 kHz to 64 kHz with ISDN, can carry all the traffic that a roomful of people can generate from the keyboard; but keyboards and terminals as a data source are becoming the exception rather than the rule. For the price of a 1970s electric typewriter, users can purchase desktop computers with the power of a 1980s supercomputer. These have the ability to generate enormous quantities of data, and with such applications as imaging, CAD/CAM, desktop videoconferencing, and E-mail with voice and video clips, traffic loads are at once huge and unpredictable. Network managers have the choice of squelching the bandwidth-hungry applications or expanding the network to accommodate them.

Today's networks are largely composed of fixed-bandwidth circuits, ranging from voice grade to T-3 (45 mb/s). When the demand imposed by the application exceeds the bandwidth available, something has to give. About the only alternative is to back up the data at the source, where the user sees flow control as a delay in the application's response. At other times the circuit is idle and bandwidth is wasted, even though applications on adjacent circuits may be experiencing delays. Fixed-bandwidth circuits are acceptable for many applications, but emerging services have a high ratio of peak-to-average data flow. For example, a physician examining an X ray may demand 10 megabits or more of data while the image is being downloaded to the display, but demand drops to zero while the image is being examined.

Contrast this to voice and videoconferencing. Voice is inherently half duplex; that is, one party transmits while the other listens. Videoconferencing is full duplex with both ends of the conference sending data simultaneously. Today's circuit-switched network is fine for these two applications, which are normally short duration sessions to widely distributed destinations. The bandwidth requirements are fixed, but the applications have minimal tolerance for delay, and no need to correct bit errors. If voice and video are segmented into short packets, the service works fine if the packets flow in a steady stream. If packets are delayed or lost, however, the result is jerky video or distorted voice.

Some data applications, such as facsimile, lend themselves nicely to the dial-up network. Other applications, such as access to information service providers, use the dial network as a matter of convenience, but would find other network forms preferable if they were available at reasonable cost. Still other applications, such as on-line access to a host computer, inherently require dedicated facilities.

Dedicated facilities are satisfactory for data applications that have reasonably constant bandwidth requirements. If the load is predictable, fixed-bandwidth circuits are satisfactory, provided they terminate at a single destination. If the bandwidth requirements are variable, you must pay a penalty, either in slow response during high-bandwidth periods, or in wasted circuit time during low-bandwidth periods. If one device must communicate with a variety of destinations, the setup time of dial-up circuits is a handicap. ISDN was expected to solve some of the problems. With SS7 signaling, setup time is faster, and its two B channels can provide appreciable bandwidth for some applications, but ISDN still suffers from being a fixed-bandwidth circuit-switched service. It is unsatisfactory for services such as multimedia and imaging, which require variable bandwidth on demand. For these services, broadband ISDN (B-ISDN) is the industry's answer. B-ISDN uses ATM as a switching and multiplexing method.

The term broadband covers a gamut of alternatives for handling high-bandwidth traffic. The industry does not have a clear definition for broadband. ATM clearly qualifies as a broadband technology, but its speeds range from 25 to 1,200 mb/s. At the low end it isn't as fast as fast Ethernet protocols. These local area network products generally aren't classified as broadband even though their 100 mb/s speed matches FDDI, which is considered a broadband backbone protocol.

The picture is further confused by lumping together services and protocols. For example, switched multimegabit data service (SMDS) and ATM are both lumped under the broadband umbrella, but SMDS is a service that happens to use the IEEE 802.6 protocol. SMDS could, and someday probably will, use ATM's connectionless option, although 802.6 and ATM are designed to interoperate, so both protocols may survive.

A key issue in broadband is how far into the network the protocol penetrates. ATM is the one protocol that can be used end-to-end without conversion. The signal can originate in a desktop card, traverse the network, and terminate on a distant desktop without undergoing a protocol conversion. This distinguishes it from the fast Ethernet protocols, which are bound by distance limitations and must ride a transport protocol to traverse a fixed-bandwidth public network. It is also distinguished from FDDI, which is distance-limited, although it spans a much greater diameter than Ethernet. SMDS is generally limited to the metropolitan area, and is not intended to go to the desktop.

Plans are in the works to haul Ethernet traffic over ATM using LAN emulation, which is effective mainly because it enables companies to squeeze a few more years of life out of their legacy customer premise equipment, while using ATM in the backbone and long-haul arena. The other factor prolonging the life of legacy equipment is that the vast majority of desktop applications today do not need ATM's bandwidth, and won't for years to come. But the growth of new applications is limited only by the inventive genius of technologists, and new applications tend to consume more and more bandwidth, leaving little doubt that broadband will be imperative for most companies in the future.

Many broadband protocols and services have been proposed, but some are destined to fall by the wayside as others build momentum. This chapter will focus on three alternatives: FDDI, because currently it is the most fully developed; SMDS, because it is the LECs' broadband vehicle and has reasonable availability; and ATM, because it enjoys the broadest base of support. Virtually every networking company in North America has announced its intention to develop ATM products and services, but at this writing the standards are not fully developed. Other standards are being proposed to supplement or even replace some of the broadband standards. Several vendors have launched a proposed Gigabit Ethernet standard for broadband data transfer. At the time of this writing the standard is just being proposed, and any serious attempts at adoption will likely be a few years away.

FIBER DISTRIBUTED DATA INTERFACE

Fiber-distributed data interface (FDDI) is a standard for a 100 mb/s network that operates on intensity-modulated 62.5/125 micron multimode fiber in the 1,300 nanometer wavelength window. The FDDI specification also can be met by 50/125, 80/125, and 100/140 micron fiber, single-mode fiber, and category 5 UTP wire. The UTP application is sometimes called copper-distributed data interface (CDDI), although the standard is called twisted-pair physical medium dependent (TP-PMD). FDDI operates over counter-rotating token rings; one ring is designated as primary, and the other as secondary.

The FDDI standard specifies two classes of stations. Dual attachment stations (DAS) connect to both rings, while single attachment stations (SAS) connect only to the primary ring through a wiring concentrator. In addition, concentrators, which are FDDI devices that can support non-FDDI stations, can also be single- or dual-attachment. The dual ring appearance of DAS stations permits double the throughput since the station can send on both rings simultaneously, but the second ring is usually reserved for backup. The FDDI network supports three types of networks (see Figure 32–1):

◆ Front-end networks. These are networks connecting workstations through a concentrator to a host computer or other peripherals over the FDDI network.
◆ Back-end networks. These allow connections from a host computer to peripherals such as high-speed disks and printers to be connected over FDDI to replace parallel bus connections.
◆ Backbone networks. These are connections between the main nodes on the network.

The FDDI specification permits a maximum of 500 nodes with no more than two kilometers between attachments. The total end-to-end diameter of the network cannot exceed 200 kilometers. The dual-ring architecture provides an effective measure of protection. If a link or a station fails, the stations go into an automatic bypass mode to route around the failure. Stations on either side of the break loop the primary ring to the secondary ring to form a single ring of twice the diameter. The possibility of a failed station or link must be considered when designing the network to stay within the interstation and total length limitations.

FDDI operates much like 802.5 token ring with some important exceptions besides the obvious difference in speed. First, multiple frames can circulate simultaneously on an FDDI network. When a station completes sending a frame, it reinserts the token on the network. A second station on the ring can

FIGURE 32-1

FDDI Topology

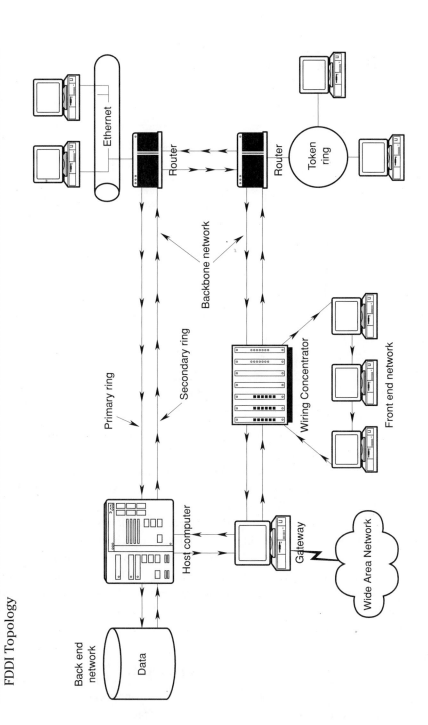

FDDI Protocol Layers

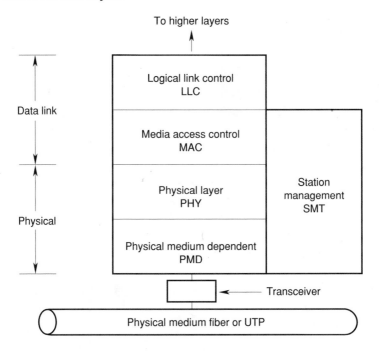

seize the token and send a frame while the first frame is still making the trip back to the originating station. As the frames circulate, each station checks for errors, and if it detects one, sets an error indicator. The network protocol does not, however, attempt to correct errors. It sends an error indication to higher-level protocols to resolve.

Other differences are the dual ring configuration of FDDI, while token ring supports only a single ring. Another difference is in the line-coding format. Token ring uses differential Manchester coding, while FDDI supports a five-bit encoding system that is discussed later. The FDDI protocol includes a reliability specification, while token ring provides none. Clocking on 802.5 is centralized, while in FDDI each station has a stable autonomous clock that synchronizes to incoming data.

The FDDI Protocol

The FDDI protocol fits into the OSI model in a manner closely paralleling the 802 protocols. Figure 32–2 shows the two-layer protocol with its sublayers that

T A B L E 32–1

FDDI 4B/5B Code

Hexadecimal	4-Bit Binary	5-Bit Binary
0	0000	11110
1	0001	01001
2	0010	10100
3	0011	10101
4	0100	01010
5	0101	01011
6	0110	01110
7	0111	01111
8	1000	10010
9	1001	10011
A	1010	10110
B	1011	10111
C	1100	11010
D	1101	11011
E	1110	11100
F	1111	11101

connect the physical ring to the higher protocol layers. The station management (SMT) handles management of the FDDI ring. Functions include fault detection and reconfiguration, insertion and removal of stations from the ring, neighbor identification, and traffic statistics and monitoring.

The physical layer uses a four-bit out of five-bit (4B/5B) coding scheme. The code, shown in Table 32–1, is encoded on the ring using a nonreturn to zero inverted (NRZI) signal, in which a transition between on and off in the light wave represents a 1, and no transition represents a 0. The 100 mb/s signal is therefore coded into a line signal of 125 megabaud. With the five-bit code, there are at least two transitions in each five-bit code, and never more than three 0s in sequence, which maintains clocking on the ring. Each station provides its own clocking in FDDI, in contrast to token ring, in which the active monitor provides a master clock.

The protocol supports a mixture of bursty and continuous stream traffic by defining two types of traffic: synchronous and asynchronous. Each station is allocated part of the capacity of the ring. During a station's allocated transmission time the frames it sends are referred to as synchronous frames. Frames using nonallocated or unused times are referred to as asynchronous.

The MAC layer of the protocol defines a maximum token rotation time (TRT), which measures the time between successive receipts of the token. When the ring is initialized each station bids for a target token rotation time (TTRT). The value of the TTRT establishes the amount of bandwidth the station can use per rotation of the token. The value in the station's token holding timer (THT) determines how long it can transmit synchronous traffic before relinquishing the token. If the token arrives before its expected TRT, it indicates that upstream stations have not used their total allocation, so a station can transmit asynchronous traffic up to the value of THT.

If the token fails to arrive after an interval determined by the protocol, a station initiates a claim token mode, which regenerates the token. If a station does not see its claim token frame return, it assumes that a ring failure has occurred. If the ring fails, the stations enter a beacon mode that is used to isolate the failure. In the beacon mode, a station sends a continuous string of beacon frames until it receives a beacon frame from an upstream neighbor. When a station receives an upstream beacon frame, it quits sending its own beacon frames, and begins repeating frames from the neighbor. All stations repeat this process until the only station left beaconing is the one immediately downstream from the fault. That station connects the primary ring to the secondary ring, a process known as a *wrap*. When the network wraps, the two rings are initialized as a single ring, and traffic resumes. The self-healing process in FDDI ensures a high degree of reliability and effectively insulates most stations from loss of service if the ring or a station fails.

FDDI-II

At the time FDDI was developed, it was envisioned as a metropolitan area network protocol, which would make voice and video transmission a desirable enhancement. As discussed above, however, the potential for delays in packet networks make them unacceptable for isochronous traffic. To overcome this limitation in FDDI, a proposed standard, FDDI-II, divides the 100 mb/s bandwidth into separate voice and data segments. As many as 16 segments of 6.144 mb/s each could be allocated for voice or nonpacketized data. Designers chose this bandwidth because it could carry four North American or three European T-1 systems. The voice portion of the bandwidth is transmitted in serial format, while the data portion follows the normal FDDI protocol.

Although FDDI-II is not completely dead, at this writing it is not being actively pursued by any standards organizations, and will probably be abandoned. The primary use for FDDI has proved to be in backbone LAN applications, which do not require voice and video capability.

SWITCHED MULTIMEGABIT DATA SERVICE

SMDS is a high-speed connectionless data service that is deployed by LECs and others for linking applications within a metropolitan area. The SMDS concept was developed by Bellcore, using portions of the IEEE 802.6 metropolitan area network (MAN) protocol. SMDS is a service, not a protocol in itself, so it can use any transport mechanism, including ATM. In fact, as discussed later, ATM provides a connectionless class of service option that is capable of supporting SMDS. The major objective of SMDS is to provide data with the any-to-any connectivity that we get from telephone or fax service. The major difference between SMDS and other services such as frame relay and ATM is that permanent virtual circuits are eliminated. Wideband data connectivity is provided at a generally attractive price. Most LECs charge a flat rate price per month, with no additional cost for distance or usage. SMDS speeds range from 1.7 to 34 mb/s, the latter being the effective throughput of a T-3 circuit after the overhead bits are eliminated. Access to SMDS is generally via an SMDS-compliant router or through host computers equipped with SMDS adapters. T-1, fractional T-3 or full T-3 are used as access circuits.

SMDS supports the most common protocols including OSI, IPX, SNA, and AppleTalk, plus providing multicast addressing. SMDS maintains a database of addresses that are validated to communicate with receiving stations. This ensures that receiving sites get messages only from valid points of origin, which improves security. Its similarity to telephone service is a major advantage because with a connectionless service like SMDS you can reach any device that will accept the transmission. SMDS is, however, far from ubiquitous, so partners who wish to communicate must subscribe to the service, which is not available everywhere in ex-Bell companies, and seldom in independent telephone companies.

The principal application for SMDS is LAN interconnection, although it can be used for any data transport. It is attractive for companies with multiple sites that are interconnected with T-1. To illustrate, assume that as in Figure 32–3 a company has five sites. To connect these with a full mesh network as in A requires $N \times N - 1$ or 20 connecting circuits. To connect them with SMDS as in B requires five access circuits. Furthermore, if SMDS switches are located in the same wire center as the terminal points, the mileage charges typical of T-1 circuits are eliminated. Both frame relay and ATM offer the same type of connectivity, but they require permanent virtual circuits for each pair of nodes, which may make them economically unattractive for full mesh connectivity. For uses such as Internet access, frame relay has the edge because of its lower access speed, which makes it more attractive for smaller sites. Some LECs, however, are offering 56/64 kb/s access to SMDS, which competes favorably with frame relay for low-speed access.

FIGURE 32-3

Full Mesh Connectivity with SMDS Reduces Access Circuit
Requirements

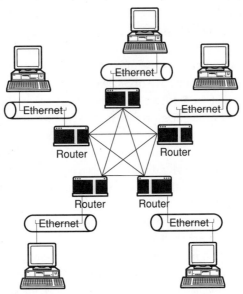

A. LANs connected with full mesh connectivity

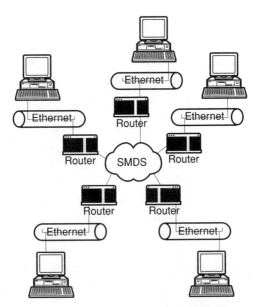

B. LANs connected through SMDS

In summary, SMDS offers the following services and advantages:

◆ High speed, low delay, connectionless data transport providing bandwidth on demand.

◆ Robustness, because data can take the least congested route to the destination.

◆ Any-to-any or full mesh connectivity, sometimes called dial tone for data without incurring the extra cost of permanent virtual circuits. ITU E.164 addressing similar to standard telephone numbers is used.

◆ Multicasting or group addressing, which enables users to send traffic to multiple points.

◆ Support for multiple protocols, including TCP/IP, IPX, AppleTalk, DECnet, SNA, and OSI.

◆ Network management capability.

◆ Security and privacy provided by call blocking, validation, and screening.

◆ Scalability—you can keep pace with network growth. To add a node you pay only the port connection charge.

SMDS Service Characteristics

SMDS services are unique with each LEC. Although Bellcore developed the service characteristics, pricing and service features are developed by each LEC, so the services discussed here are typical. Readers can expect local variations.

SMDS is designed to operate over a dual-bus fiber-optic network using the 802.6 protocol, which is also known as dual queued dual bus (DQDB). The protocol, which is discussed later, was developed in Australia to be a robust, low-latency protocol. Figure 32–4 shows a typical SMDS network. The SMDS switches are located in LEC central offices, with fiber-optic access circuits operating in a dual bus arrangement to the subscribers. Multiple subscribers are bridged across the dual bus arrangement, as discussed in the next section.

The backbone switching system is a high-speed packet switch. The protocol places a limit on the amount of sustained information that the subscriber can send across the subscriber network interface to the switching system. SMDS uses the term *sustained information rate* (SIR) as the maximum guaranteed rate at which data can transit the network. SIR is similar to the committed information rate concept discussed in Chapter 31 under frame relay. SMDS supports five classes of service with SIRs running from four to 34 mb/s. As with frame relay and ATM, the subscriber can send bursts of data up to the speed of the access circuit, which is T-1 or T-3, but the access class limits the average rate of information that can be sent. The switch contains a credit manager that keeps track of the amount of data sent across the network and com-

FIGURE 32-4

SMDS Architecture

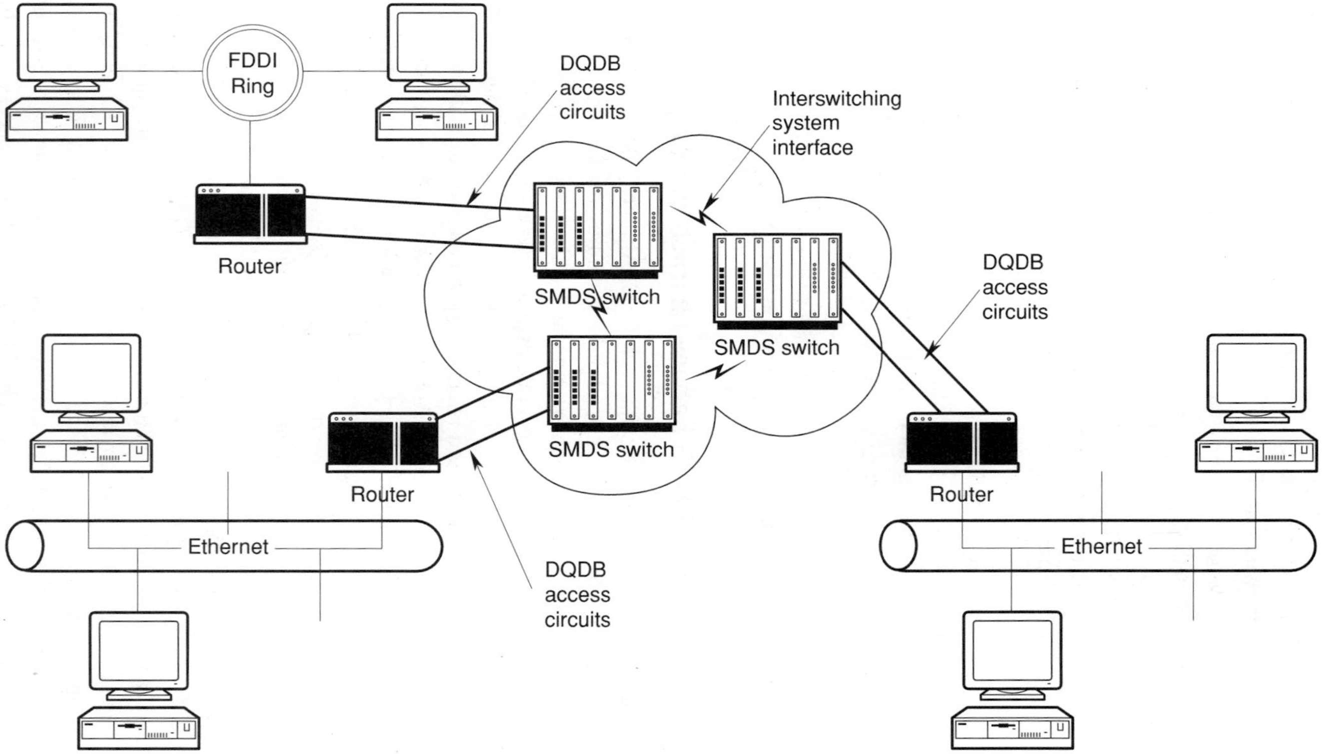

pares it to the amount permitted by the access class. If the subscriber has a credit the traffic is accepted; if it doesn't have credit the traffic is rejected.

SMDS has a three-tier architecture. The switching system consists of SMDS-compatible high-speed packet switches. The delivery system is made up of subscriber network interfaces, and the third tier, the access control system, enables subscribers to connect to the switching system. The level 3 protocol data unit accepts packets up to 9,188 octets in length. These are segmented into a level 2 PDU, which uses 53-byte cells. The cells cross the network to the destination, where they are reassembled. Since the protocol is connectionless, the cells do not follow a predefined path through the network, so a user in one site can dial up a link to a user in another site without establishing a virtual circuit. The nodes are constructed with side legs into the subscriber's premises. Traffic always passes on LEC premises, but traffic belonging to one subscriber never passes through another subscriber's premises.

The SMDS cell structure is similar to ATM, which is described later, except the cells contain an address in the header, which is necessary in a connectionless system. The connection-oriented ATM, by contrast, uses a virtual path and virtual connection identifier instead of addresses. The address fields in the SMDS header use a 10-digit number following the North American numbering plan.

The 802.6 DQDB Protocol

The 802.6 architecture, shown in Figure 32–5, is similar to FDDI in that it uses two counterrotating rings, which permits full-duplex communication between any of the nodes. Each node has two attachments to each bus. One attachment reads bus slots and the other writes bus slots. Busses are managed by a head-end, which generates slots for use by the downstream nodes. A logical break, at which clocking is introduced, is located between two of the nodes. The network is self-healing if the fiber is cut. As shown in Figure 32–6, if the fiber breaks between two of the nodes, the logical break shifts to the point of failure and the ring closes to form the logical break at the point of the physical break.

A frame generator at the master station emits 125 microsecond frames, which is the length of a T-1 frame. Each frame can contain a fixed number of fixed-length time slots. The number of slots depends on the bit rate of the bus, which, in turn, depends on the transmission medium. In a free-standing configuration the network contains its own synchronization. When connected to a public network, however, the network must derive its synchronization from the public network.

Although the dual-ring architecture of DQDB appears to be a pair of rings, it is a logically looped dual bus with each node appearing on each bus.

FIGURE 32–5

802.6 Metropolitan Area Network Architecture

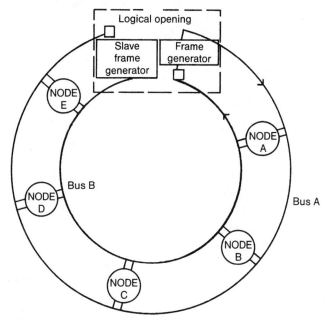

FIGURE 32–6

The 802.6 MAN Shifts Logical Break to Point of Failure to Close Ring

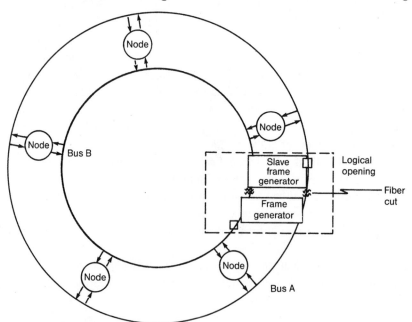

F I G U R E   32–7

Queued Arbitrated Access to the 802.6 Bus

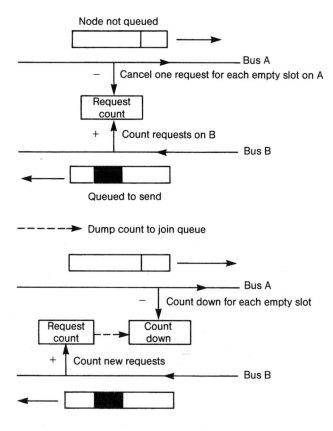

Usually the transmission medium is fiber optics, but the standard permits the use of coaxial cable. Twisted-pair wire does not have enough bandwidth for the backbone network, but it can be used for the access network.

Isochronous services such as digitized voice and video must be transmitted across the network with minimum delay. DQDB has two classes of service, prearbitrated (PA), and queued arbitrated (QA). PA service is for voice and video, which require a fixed amount of bandwidth. QA provides service on demand for bursty applications such as data transmission.

DQDB uses an ingenious method of allocating QA access to the bus. Each node is equipped with a request counter and a packet countdown, as Figure 32–7 shows. When a node has a packet ready for transmission it transmits a request upstream to the headend. As the request passes the upstream nodes, each node increments its request counter by one, so each node knows at any time what its place in queue is based on the number in its request counter. As

T A B L E 32–2

ATM Physical Transports

25 mb/s UTP channel
45 mb/s DS-3
100 mb/s FDDI
155 mb/s fiber channel
155 mb/s UTP channel
155 mb/s SONET
622 mb/s fiber channel
622 mb/s SONET
1,200 mb/s fiber channel
1,200 mb/s SONET

empty slots flow downstream, each node decrements its request counter, knowing that these slots will be filled by downstream nodes with unfilled requests. Each node has a record, therefore, of how many slots were requested and how many were filled by passing slots intended for downstream stations. If a node's request counter is set at n, when the nth slot goes by, its counter has reached zero, so it can send on the next empty slot.

With this method of allocating bandwidth, upstream locations have a better chance to seize empty slots than downstream locations. To avoid this problem, the protocol forces stations to pass empty slots, depending on their physical location. This scheduling method provides a high degree of efficiency. Slots are never wasted while a station has traffic to send, and no station can monopolize the network.

ASYNCHRONOUS TRANSFER MODE

ATM is a combination switching and multiplexing protocol that is rapidly developing as the broadband networking standard. Even though standards are not complete, few observers doubt that it will be gradually accepted over the next few years. It is as close to being a universally accepted protocol as anything that exists in the world today. Virtually all major manufacturers concur that ATM is the service of choice as a switching and multiplexing protocol, and many proprietary ATM implementations are available. Standards are being developed for a variety of media. Table 32–2 lists the different speeds and media for which ATM is developed or under development.

ATM is a cell relay protocol. Information is segmented into short data blocks of 48 octets with a five-octet header, making a total cell length of 53 octets. At the receiving end cells are reassembled into the original bit stream, a process that is known as segmentation and reassembly (SAR). ATM is connection-oriented service. Cells are routed through the network based on a virtual channel identifier (VCI), which is a field in the cell header. Another field, the virtual path identifier (VPI), together with the VCI identifies the virtual circuit by which the ATM switches route the call from source to destination. Figure 32–8 shows the topology of a conceptual ATM network.

Rationale for the 53-Octet Cell

The objective of any data circuit is to maximize throughput. In conventional data circuits, if the data block is too short, the overhead bits in header and trailer records become significant as a percentage of total bits in the packet, which reduces efficiency. On the other hand, if the data block is too long, excessive circuit time is consumed in retransmitting errored packets. In most circuits, the lower the error rate, the longer the data block that can be set. It would seem logical that a protocol that is designed to run over low-error-rate fiber-optic circuits would have a long data block, not a short one. So why does ATM use such short data blocks and have a header overhead that is approximately 10 percent of the total cell length?

The reason lies in the nature of the information that ATM is required to carry. Like frame relay, the ATM protocol is designed without error detection and correction. An exception is in the header, which we will discuss later. The protocol can discard cells under certain overload conditions, and when cell header errors exceed a threshold. Data applications, which are carrying on an end-to-end error detection and correction dialog, are slowed somewhat by cell loss, but otherwise are unaffected. Voice and video, however, have no need for error correction, so lost cells are not restored. A digitized voice or video signal operates at 8,000 octets per second, so the occasional loss of 48 octets is such a small fraction of one second that it is hardly noticeable. The loss of a long data block, however, would be detrimental to isochronous communications. The 48-octet data block was chosen as a compromise between members of the ATM Forum, one group of which wanted 64 octets and the other 32 octets as the cell length, so they split the difference.

ATM Protocol Layers

Like all modern protocols, ATM is a layered protocol, but greatly simplified compared to others. Figure 32–9 shows the logical layers of ATM. User applications communicate with the ATM adaptation layer (AAL). The AAL is

FIGURE 32-8

ATM Topology

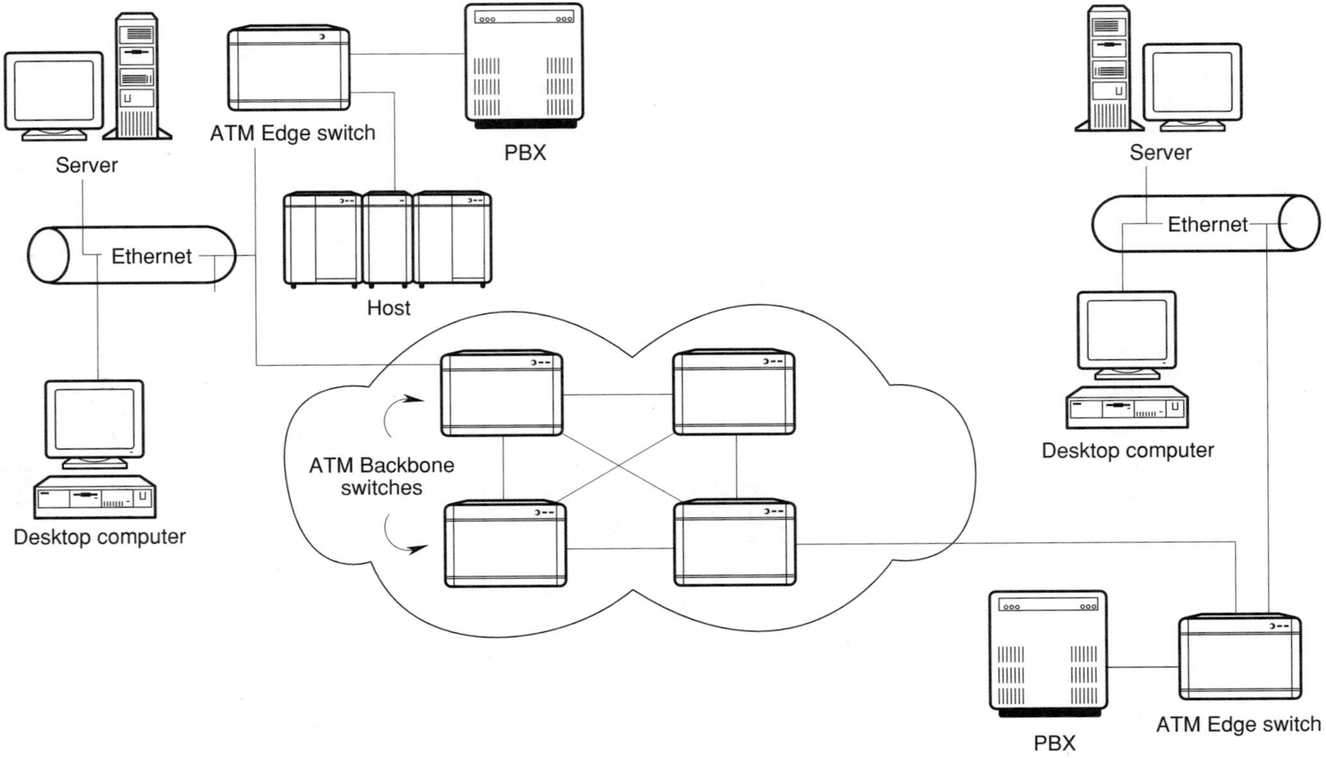

ATM's Layered Architecture

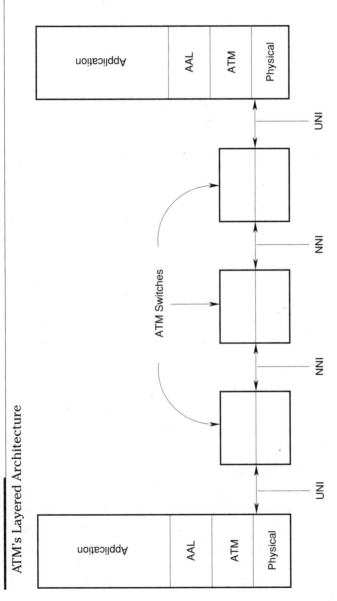

AAL = ATM adaption layer
ATM = ATM layer
UNI = user network interface
NNI = network to network interface

divided into two sublayers, the SAR and the convergence. The SAR is responsible for segmentation and reassembly of the user's data stream. The convergence sublayer protocols are different for the various types of information such as voice, video, and data. The AAL supports five different classes of traffic:

- ◆ Class A traffic is constant-bit-rate, connection-oriented traffic such as video. Timing between the source and destination is required.
- ◆ Class B traffic is variable-bit-rate connection-oriented traffic such as voice. Timing between the source and destination is required.
- ◆ Class C traffic is variable-bit-rate connection-oriented traffic such as bursty data, where a timing relationship between source and destination is not required.
- ◆ Class D traffic is variable-bit-rate connectionless traffic such as datagram services. Timing between the source and destination is not required.
- ◆ Class X allows user-defined traffic and timing relationships.

The protocol treats the different classes of traffic differently, which is the key to ATM's ability to handle mixed applications more effectively than other protocols. Voice and video receive constant delay, compared to Class C data traffic, which does not require timing between source and destination. The various classes of service use different protocol data units (PDUs), with different-sized data blocks. Fields are robbed from the data block to perform such functions as sequencing, time stamping, and cyclical redundancy check of the data block. As discussed later, the header is always checked for errors.

The ATM layer moves traffic from the AAL to the switch. The user connects to the network through the user network interface (UNI). Two types of UNI are defined. A public UNI defines the interface between the user and a public ATM switch, and a private UNI defines the interface between the user and a private ATM switch. ATM switches interconnect through network-to-network interfaces (NNI).

ATM offers two classes of circuit: permanent virtual circuit (PVC) and switched virtual circuit (SVC). The distinction between the two is similar to the distinction between a voice private line and a dial-up connection. A private line, and likewise a PVC, is set up, or "provisioned," by the carrier. If the users want to make changes, they place a service order with the carrier and wait until the connection is completed in software by the carrier. An SVC is, in effect, dialed by the user. The user establishes a service agreement with the carrier, and after that can set up a virtual circuit to other destinations by signaling.

ATM Switching Architectures

The ATM protocol does not specify how switching is to be done. The method is left to the developer, who has several alternatives for the switching fabric. The switching fabric is the means by which inputs are connected to outputs. Analog circuit switching, for example, uses relays to make the connection, while digital circuit switches connect inputs and outputs together during a time slot interval. To reduce latency, ATM switches rely on hardware switching to the maximum degree possible. Although hardware switching is less flexible, it is faster. The predominant ATM switching architectures are shared memory, shared access bus, and the self-routing or banyan switch.

Shared-memory switches connect input and output circuits through a large memory module. A shared-access bus ties the input and output circuits to a single high-speed bus. If the speed of the bus is higher than the combined speed of the input circuits, cells can coexist without collision. Input circuits put cells on the bus with the address of the output port. All ports read the cell addresses, but only the destination port copies it.

A banyan switch is a two-stage device that takes its name from the many branches of the banyan tree. The device switches a full cell at a time. The header finds a path through the switch, and the path remains intact for the duration of the cell, after which it is torn down and reused. The header directs the packet through each of the bidirectional switching stages. A 1 in the header causes the switch to connect to the upper path, and a 0 to the lower. The remainder of the cell follows the header through the path. Figure 32–10 shows a three-stage banyan switch, which can handle a three-bit address. If two cells converge on the same output, one is buffered and sent through later. A banyan switch is fast and therefore ideally suited to switching the high speeds of ATM. It is also inexpensive and can be implemented easily in large-scale integration.

ATM Call Processing

Calls are established under ATM with a setup message that contains a call reference number, addresses of called and calling parties, traffic characteristics, and a quality of service indicator. The destination returns a call-proceeding message that contains the same call reference number plus a VPI/VCI identifier. A series of setup and call-proceeding messages are exchanged while the network determines such matters as whether the called party is willing to accept the call. Public networks use an addressing system of up to 15 digits following E.164 standards. Private networks use a 20-octet address modeled after OSI network service access point addressing.

FIGURE 32–10

A Banyan Switch

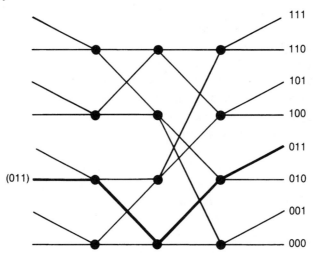

Cells flow through an ATM network based on the VCI and VPI identifiers contained in the header, which is shown in Figure 32–11. A virtual path can be thought of as bundle of virtual channels, with each bundle having the same end points. To avoid long setup time by the carrier, the user can contract for a virtual path between end points, after which virtual channels can be set up within the path without placing service orders with the carrier.

The GFC (generic flow control) field, which is currently undefined, will be used for flow control on the UNI interface. It is not used with NNI. The payload type (PT) indicator identifies the type of traffic the cell contains. This field is also used to carry congestion information to the receiving end of the connection. The cell loss priority indicator notifies the network if the cell is subject to being discarded. Cells that are transmitted in violation of the traffic management contract or cells with a low quality of service can be discarded.

The header error control (HEC) field in the header is a combination cyclical redundancy check and forward error correction field. If the header experiences a single bit error, the HEC field can correct it. In case of multiple bit errors, the cell is discarded. Data applications detect the cell loss with end-to-end error correction. Voice and video applications do not detect the lost cell, and are minimally affected by it.

FIGURE 32–11

ATM Header

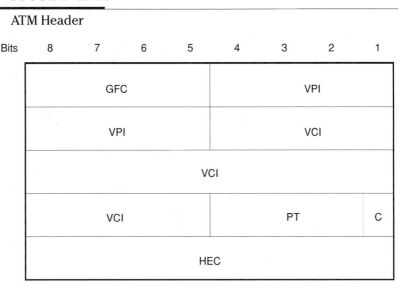

GFC = generic flow control
VPI = virtual path indentifier
VCI = virtual channel identifier
PT = payload type
C = cell loss priority
HEC = header error control

LAN Emulation

A great deal of today's communications take place over conventional LANs, and these will not soon be changed in favor of ATM to the desktop. For ATM to succeed, therefore, it must enable LAN devices to communicate over an ATM network. LAN and ATM protocols have vast differences. LANs use variable packet lengths, the shortest of which is still much longer than ATM's cells. LANs are connectionless with long addresses; ATM is connection-oriented with path and connection indicators in lieu of addresses. The task of LAN emulation is to make the two protocols coexist without involving the user in delays or forcing a change of network interface cards. These services are enabled by using a LAN emulation client (which is a different definition for LEC than we have been using).

The LEC software presents a MAC layer interface to the LLC layer, as shown in Figure 32–12. LAN emulation software resides in any device such as a server or router that connects the LAN to ATM. To make the connection, the

F I G U R E   32–12

ATM LAN Emulation

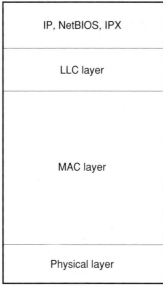 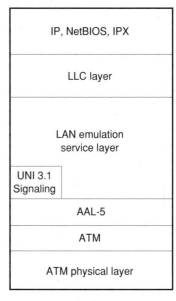

LAN Layers   ATM LAN
                              Emulation Layers

LEC must know the address of the destination ATM device. Address registration is done through a LAN emulation server (LES). If the LES cannot resolve the destination address, it sends a multicast packet to a broadcast server, which connects to all stations on the network.

ATM Access Modes

ATM is available in several different modes. Most of the major IECs and many LECs have announced ATM support. To use the service customers must access the network by one of several methods. One method is a dedicated access line, which could be T-1, T-3, or one of the levels of SONET. With this access method the customer furnishes data in a continuous bit stream. The carrier's ATM node does the segmenting and desegmenting.

A second access method is via private ATM network. With this access method the customer delivers and receives cells, and provides its own segmentation and desegmentation. An ATM network can also be fed from other sources such as frame relay or SMDS.

Advantages of ATM

One major advantage ATM brings over other alternatives is its scalability. No other protocol can operate at a wide range of speeds, nor can any other alternative be used effectively in a local, metropolitan, and wide area network. ATM's classes of service make it effective for voice, video, and data communications, which have widely different requirements. The switching fabric itself can be implemented in hardware without software control, which decreases the latency that is common in other switching methods.

Conventional networks, both circuit switched and packet switched, have deficiencies that ATM is designed to solve. The following lists the major reasons many companies are considering ATM for their enterprise networks.

Quality of Service   ATM is one of the few network protocols that can offer quality of service. ATM ensures quality of service by rejecting connections that would congest the link, and marking the cell loss bit for cells that violate the traffic management contract.

Mismatch between LAN and WAN Speeds   Local area networks operate at 10 mb/s or higher speeds. Although the throughput of such LANs is typically 30 to 40 percent of the data rate, when LANs are interconnected, information moves across the WAN at a greatly reduced speed. In metropolitan networks some LECs offer transparent LAN service, but this kind of bandwidth is prohibitive in wide area networks.

LAN Capacity   Legacy LANs operate at 10 to 16 mb/s. Second-generation LANs, including FDDI, 100-Base-T, and 100-Base-VG, raise the capacity to 100 mb/s. For speeds beyond 100 mb/s, ATM is an effective alternative.

Multiapplication Networks   Voice, video, and data do not coexist comfortably in today's networks. ATM is designed to be transparent to the type of service the network is supporting.

Connectivity   Voice and video today use the circuit-switched network for universal connectivity, but many data applications do not work well with circuit switching. ATM is designed to provide the equivalent of circuit switching's ubiquitous connectivity.

Low Latency   ATM has low delay through the network because it does no error checking, its switching is done in hardware, and during high congestion periods it drops cells to prevent congestion.

Ease of Rearrangement   Conventional networks require extensive involvement of the carrier's designers, technicians, and circuit assigners to develop new fixed circuits. When switched virtual circuits are available in ATM, customers will be able to rearrange their own networks and add sites with little involvement from the common carrier.

APPLICATIONS

Fiber-Distributed Data Interface

FDDI has carved a niche for itself as a backbone protocol. It is widely used for linking LAN segments through routers in a private internet, as we will discuss in Chapter 33. FDDI is theoretically a LAN alternative, but its major drawback is the cost of adapter cards, which make it unlikely to compete effectively with fast Ethernet to the desktop. In the backbone its major competitor is Ethernet switching, which is less expensive. Fast Ethernet cards are on the market at a fraction of the cost of FDDI, but they fall far short of FDDI's span of 200 km.

As a campus backbone, FDDI is currently the best alternative available. In the future it is likely to be displaced by ATM when that technology becomes more mature. FDDI is a shared-access medium, which means that bandwidth available to any station diminishes as the number of stations increases. Its frame-based structure makes it easy to map to Ethernet and token ring packets. By contrast, ATM does not map well to frame-based technologies, necessitating the use of LAN emulation.

Besides its span, FDDI's primary advantage is its maturity. It has been available since it received ANSI approval in 1988, and is a proven and stable technology. Its dual-fiber ring architecture makes it a robust backbone that can survive fiber cuts and station loss. Running on fiber, FDDI is immune to electromagnetic interference, which may affect copper wire alternatives in some industrial applications.

Switched Multimegabit Data Service

The primary application for SMDS is LAN interconnection. As the FCC and courts free the LECs from intraLATA restrictions, SMDS may become more prominent over a wider range. Its main drawback is lack of universal availability.

Where SMDS is available, it can be a cost-effective way of connecting LANs or high-speed computer connections. Its major advantage is its ability to deliver traffic between sites in a manner similar to dialed connections on the telephone network. A major unknown factor is the impact that ATM will have on SMDS. ATM may replace DQDB in the metropolitan network, or SMDS may interconnect with ATM carriers for longer hauls. Such uncertainties should not affect the use of SMDS, however, because the investment to enable companies to use SMDS is modest and easily recoverable in the next few years of use.

Asynchronous Transfer Mode

For the next few years ATM will have only a narrow range of applications. The organizations most apt to need it are those with multiple applications over the same wide area network. Companies that can justify T-3 networks now have inefficient use of the bandwidth because of the nature of circuit switching and fixed bandwidth data, which tend to occupy such networks. ATM enables such companies to multiplex multiple applications onto the same bandwidth, making use of facilities that otherwise would be wasted. The economics of ATM are not as compelling for voice and video, however, as they are for data, which means that the first applications of ATM will be in the data arena. At the time of this writing, work on voice and video standards is just beginning, which means that practical mixed-media applications will not be widely deployed before 1998 or 1999.

Companies that are contemplating a shift to ATM sometime in the future are advised to take certain steps now to position themselves:

◆ Bear in mind that ATM is not a good substitute technology for today's services. It is a technology that enables new applications today, with a future migration path for voice.
◆ Recognize the applications that live most comfortably with ATM and stay in tune with plans to shift to them.
◆ Engage in early and limited trials to reduce the learning curve.
◆ Use similar bandwidth-on-demand technologies such as frame relay and SMDS to become familiar with the operational characteristics.
◆ Set realistic expectations for the technologies.
◆ Be certain that the premise wiring system is designed to support high-speed technologies.
◆ Monitor developments in carrier services and ATM hardware and software.

SELECTED MANUFACTURERS OF BROADBAND EQUIPMENT

FDDI Products

Bay Networks

Cabletron

Cisco Systems

Computer Network Technology

Cray Communications

Digital Equipment Corp.

IBM

Madge Networks

Network Peripherals

Optical Data Systems

Rockwell Network Systems

Sun Microsystems

Xyplex

SMDS Network Interface Products

3Com Corporation

Advanced Computer Communications

Ascom Timeplex

Bay Networks, Inc.

Cascade Communications Corp.

Cisco Systems, Inc.

Computer Network Technology, Inc.

Hewlett-Packard Co.

IBM

Lucent Technologies

Network Systems Corp.

Proteon, Inc.

UB Networks

ATM Manufacturers

Large ATM Network Switches
Fujitsu

General DataComm

NEC America

Lucent Technologies

Nortel

Newbridge Networks

ATM Enterprise Switches
Bay Networks

Cabletron Systems

Cisco Systems

Digital Equipment Corp.

Fore Systems

General DataComm

IBM

NEC America

Network Equipment Technologies

Newbridge Networks

Nortel

StrataCom

UB Networks

The Internet, which was a dim concept to most people only a few years ago, has become a household word. Schoolchildren access information worldwide on the Internet, businesses use it to keep in touch with customers and branch offices, families use it as a source of entertainment; Internet is reshaping society in a major way. This chapter is not, however, about the Internet, it is about internets, the LAN interconnections that have become the glue binding together departments, branch offices, and work-at-home employees. In earlier chapters we have discussed the building blocks: the LANs, routers, bridges, switches, hubs, and other devices that, together with the protocols discussed in Chapter 4, can be used to assemble a LAN internet. This chapter discusses how these are connected to form an internet.

The older networks, assembled from fixed circuits, modems, controllers, multiplexers, and the like, were better behaved than today's internets. The traffic volumes were predictable within a reasonable range, and the origins and destinations were more or less fixed. Design algorithms made the process of network configuration routine, and network performance could be modeled mathematically.

Internets, like the LANs they connect, don't behave so predictably. It's impossible to predict when a user somewhere on the network will decide to move a multimegabit file somewhere else. It's also difficult to determine when relationships will change and what effect the changes will have on traffic patterns. This leads to the need for network probes, protocol analyzers, and network management systems, which are the subjects of Chapters 36 and 37.

On the brighter side, however, just as internets need more flexibility, they are easier to reconfigure than the older hierarchical networks. Network management tools provide more visibility into the network than older systems did. The old paradigms about circuit types and cost are also changing to simplify things. Fixed analog and digital circuit costs increase with bandwidth and distance. Frame relay and ATM are distance insensitive (except for the access circuits) and provide variable bandwidth within the limits of the access ports.

This chapter discusses internet architectures and the issues surrounding their choice. Internets have the following objectives:

◆ Provide adequate bandwidth in a scalable fashion between nodes to meet the demands of internodal traffic.
◆ Provide multiple paths so the network is robust enough to survive individual circuit failures.
◆ Maintain a high level of network availability.
◆ Prevent unauthorized stations from accessing the network.
◆ Keep facilities at a high level of utilization consistent with service level and affordable cost.
◆ Provide a flexible structure that is easy to administer, maintain, and troubleshoot.
◆ Preserve investment in existing resources such as NICs, hubs, and other devices.
◆ Obtain information that can be used for evaluating service and sizing and reconfiguring the network.

As with all networks the results are affected by the architecture, the quality of the equipment, the administrative structure, and the accuracy of the information that went into the design. The design, in turn, is heavily influenced by the applications. The last three chapters have been building up to this point. Chapter 30 discussed internetworking equipment, Chapter 31 discussed conventional wide area network circuits, and Chapter 32 discussed broadband circuit alternatives. In addition, Chapter 4 discussed TCP/IP, the protocol that ties the internet together. In this chapter, we will focus on bringing these elements together into an internet design.

THE INTERNET DESIGN PROBLEM

When LANs first rose to prominence, the applications were, within reasonable limits, predictable. Applications such as word processing, database, and spreadsheets communicate with the file and print server. By knowing something of the users, the amount of traffic could be estimated and the size of the segment could be regulated accordingly.

Conventional database applications were, and remain, a wild card in network design. If the database application runs on the workstation, the file server merely delivers the database across the network to the workstation where the actual work of file searches and updates is done. A few stations working in this mode can overload the network. The solution is a client server type of application in which the client, which runs on the workstation, requests the search, but the search is actually done on the server. The server delivers the results of the search to the client, sending only a few kilobits instead of megabit-sized files. With a client-server database, the network again returns to predictability—until peer-to-peer applications emerge.

Peer applications such as desktop videoconferencing again throw the network into a chaotic situation for the network manager. When any groups of workstations can begin to communicate within and between segments, the network load increases and the route is unpredictable. Furthermore, stations that were once generating a modest traffic volume can suddenly begin dumping multimegabit traffic on the network. Not only is the amount of bandwidth required by these stations important, they also need a predictable grade of service. A few discarded or delayed packets can be tolerated in conventional data applications—the user sees them as delay, which is tolerable, within limits. Delay impairs time-sensitive applications such as video, however, to the point of unsuitability.

Some of the chaos can be controlled. Network designers can place servers strategically so their traffic remains on their segment and stays off the backbone. Other applications, however, E-mail for example, are inherently centralized for a work group or even the enterprise. In its conventional mode E-mail is modest in terms of bandwidth demands, but new E-mail packages permit users to add voice and video clips, which suddenly consume bandwidth in an unprecedented and unpredictable manner. The same is happening to other docile applications such as word processing and spreadsheets, which now can be annotated with voice notes. Even when the database is tamed with a client-server architecture, the addition of images can make even simple screens consume vast amounts of bandwidth. In Chapter 32 we discussed the broadband facilities that enable the network to handle these bandwidths. In this chapter we will discuss the architectures and equipment that feed these networks.

INTERNET ARCHITECTURES

When the collision lights begin to wink too often in an Ethernet or if the network begins to show signs of congestion such as slow response time, a logical solution is to segment the network, a process that requires finding the high users and what devices they communicate with. Segmenting isn't always an effective strategy, however, because everyone on a segment may be aiming for the same server, and breaking the network in two doesn't reduce traffic. A handful of users may be accessing the server heavily and contributing to its congestion, a situation that isn't easily solved by installing a bridge. One approach is to bump the network speed to 100 mb/s using FDDI, ATM, or one of the fast Ethernet products, but this can be expensive because it requires replacing the NICs and hubs and in some cases the cabling. The fastest and least expensive solution may be to use an Ethernet switch, which we will discuss later.

Segmentation with Bridges

Segmentation with inexpensive bridges, as shown in Figure 33–1, works on small networks, but bridges have limitations. As the network is further segmented, segments handling transit traffic can become overloaded. The only way a device on Segment A can communicate with a device on Segment C, for example, is to transit Segment B, which adds to the load on B. A bridge can be added between Segments A and C, but that provides two potential paths between them, a situation that bridges cannot handle because they lack routing capability. The spanning tree algorithm allows the network administrator to define two paths across bridges to provide redundancy, but only one path must be active with the other on standby. In the spanning tree algorithm, bridges exchange information to establish a subnet that contains no loops but which links the LANs. If one bridge fails the standby bridge takes over. Token ring networks often use source routing, in which a route discovery process is used to develop a single path through the network. With source routing the bridges exchange messages to establish a route from source to destination.

Segmentation with Routers

A typical solution for bridges' shortcomings is to substitute routers. These devices, operating at the network layer, contain route information in addition to addresses. With routers connected between all three segments, as shown in Figure 33–2, Segment A can reach Segment C by either of the two paths. As the network continues to grow, however, the router connections become complex.

F I G U R E 33-1

Intersegment Bridging

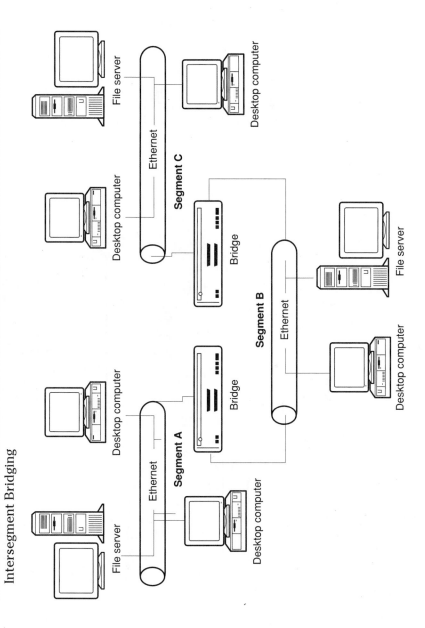

FIGURE 33-2

Intersegment Routing

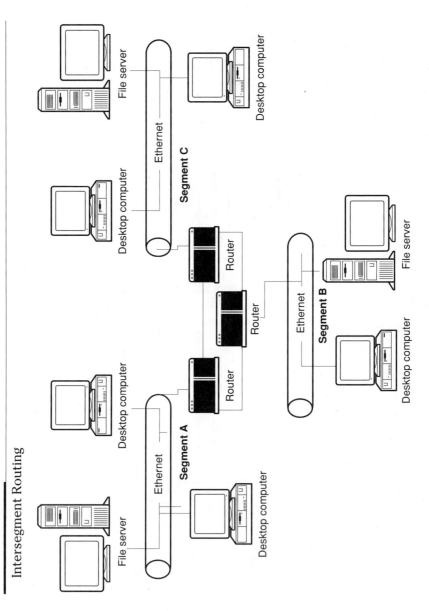

If they use public networks for the connection, they can be expensive as well. In a simple configuration such as Figure 33–2 only three circuits are required for complete connectivity. As routers are added, however, the number of circuits grows, which means that one or more routers must be configured to handle transit traffic. A good solution, as discussed in Chapter 31, is to use frame relay. Each router then has a single direct connection into the carrier's frame relay network.

If the network consists of multiple segments carrying a significant amount of traffic, the routers may be connected using a high-speed backbone such as FDDI or ATM. The routers are designed with Ethernet or token ring connections on the front, and a high-speed connection on the backbone.

If the physical layout is such that all three routers can be collocated, instead of using separate devices connected to circuits, the network can be configured using a multiport router to form a *collapsed backbone*. Figure 33–3 shows a collapsed backbone in which all the segments attach to a single router, with the router's backplane acting as the backbone. The collapsed backbone introduces a single point of failure, which may be mitigated by equipping routers with redundancy.

Segmentation with Switches

The network managers in many companies must cope with frequent rearrangements. Organizations may split and centers of interests may shift, but the station users' locations do not change. Conversely, users may move, but their community of interest does not change, which means more load on the router backbone. Port-switching hubs make it possible to assign users to any segment regardless of location. A port-switching hub is a chassis that has a backplane with multiple segments. Any port can be assigned to any segment, which offers the advantage of improved port utilization. Without port-switching, if all users in a single card in the hub must be assigned to the same segment, some ports will necessarily go unused. With port-switching hubs, a port can be assigned to any segment, which improves port utilization. The downside to this segmentation is that the more segments are created, the more routers or bridges are needed to interconnect them.

An increasingly important variation is the Ethernet switch, which is, in effect, a multiport bridge. It reads the destination MAC addresses of incoming frames, determines which segment the node resides on, and forwards the frame to the appropriate port. If the address of a frame is on the same segment, the Ethernet switch ignores it. If the switch doesn't know where the destination address is, it forwards the frame to all ports and learns the addresses as it goes. As

F I G U R E 33-3

Collapsed Backbone Internet

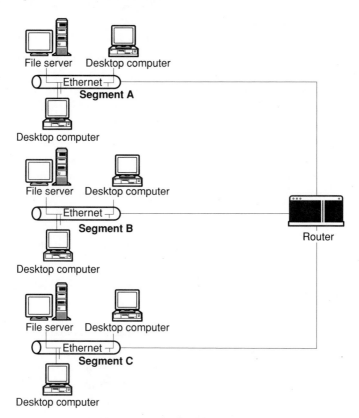

Figure 33–4 shows, the switch ports can carry traffic from a segment, or stations can have exclusive ports if they need the bandwidth. In the extreme case each device on the network can have a full 10 mb/s of bandwidth, with collisions virtually eliminated by the switch.

The switching fabric is usually some type of shared memory. Unlike conventional bridges, which read and store the entire frame before forwarding it, some Ethernet switches use a cut-through technique to speed throughput. As soon as the switch has read the destination address, it connects the frame through to the destination port so the frame header is leaving the switch before the CRC enters it. As a result, the switch does no integrity checking of the frame, which means that invalid frames such as runts and jabbers are propagated through the network. Buffered switches read the entire frame, and connect it through after they have verified its validity. Buffered switches filter out

FIGURE 33–4

Switched Ethernet

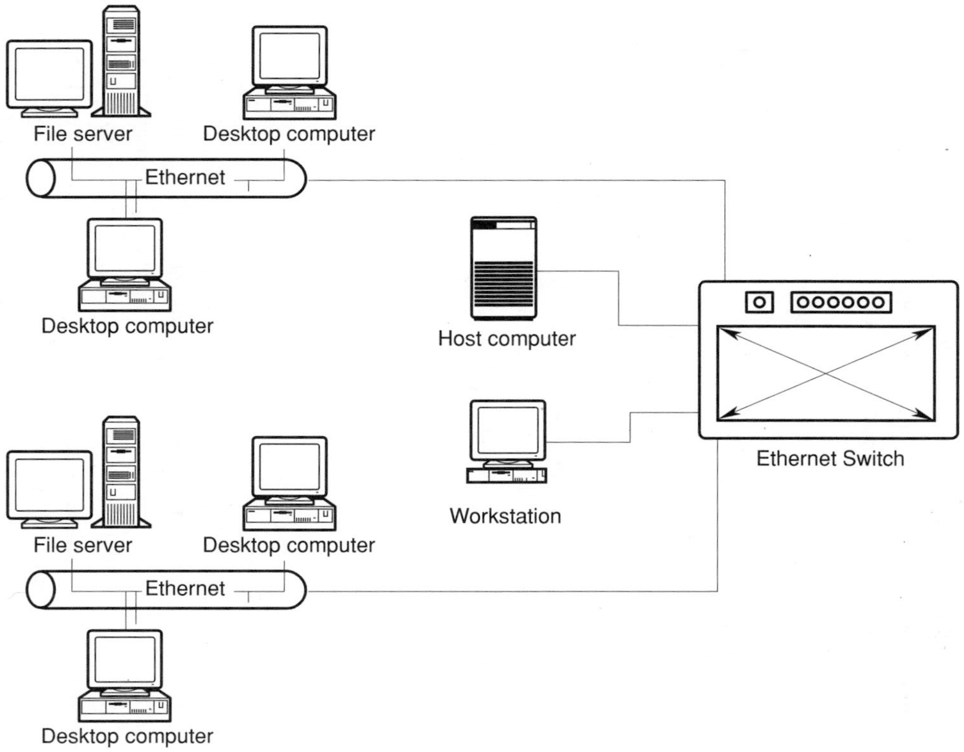

invalid frames, but at the price of lower throughput. Absent invalid frames, the cut through technique substantially reduces latency, but it can propagate bad packets and collisions through the network.

A conventional Ethernet switch opens the way for the virtual LAN. A virtual LAN provides each user with a connection to a switch hub, which enables users to be assigned to the same work group without regard to their physical location. The network manager defines the LAN segment by grouping a number of ports together as a logical unit. Users can move physically without the need to change IP addresses. As ATM becomes available, its LAN emulation client (LEC) option will allow it to serve as the central switch.

Switching is not confined to Ethernet. Token ring switches, while less common than Ethernet switches, are also available, and offer the same advantages.

BACKBONE NETWORKS

As the network grows, the amount of traffic between LAN segments increases to the point that a backbone network is needed. Backbones can be constructed from high-speed shared-media network such as FDDI, or they can be compiled from switching products such as Ethernet and token ring switches or ATM. In this section we will examine the ways of deploying a backbone network and the pros and cons of the different alternatives.

Distributed Router Backbone

As networks grow, a common design is to install a high-speed backbone. FDDI is a popular protocol for the purpose, with ATM following on rapidly. Figure 33–5 shows the layout of Ethernets connected by an FDDI backbone. In a simple network such as the one shown in the figure, this architecture works well. It is robust: The failure of a single router has minimal impact on the network, provided the FDDI ring bypasses the failed device. Its main drawback is that traffic between segments passes through at least two routers. The routers must convert the backbone protocol to Ethernet for every packet that crosses the backbone, which takes a finite period of time. The latency of two routers is usually acceptable, but as the network expands into multiple rings, the number of routers increases, as does latency.

A second drawback of this architecture is the difficulty of rearranging stations. If a station moves from Segment A to Segment B, a change of IP address is needed. The virtual LAN concept does not work well with this architecture because traffic on the backbone increases. Even though 100 mb/s FDDI

FIGURE 33-5

Distributed Router Backbone

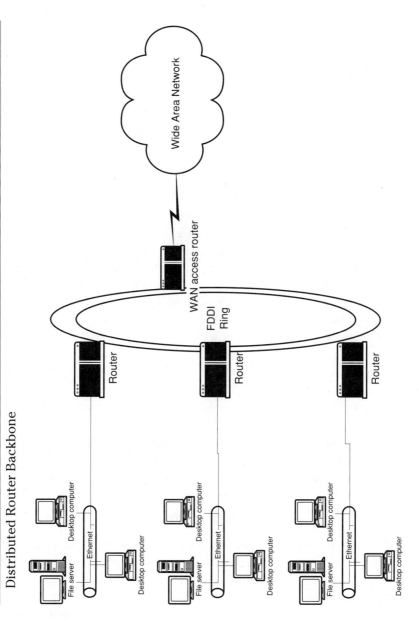

has considerable bandwidth, overloads with some applications are not inconceivable. Substituting an ATM backbone for FDDI increases the bandwidth to 155 mb/s or more, but current ATM devices are significantly more expensive than FDDI, which in itself is not cheap.

A third drawback is the lack of scalability. As more segments are added, the load on the backbone increases to the point that parallel backbones are required. Also, the cost of multiple routers is often higher than the cost of a single high-speed device. Multiple routers also increase network management complexity. With routers distributed throughout the building, additional effort is required to monitor status, distribute software upgrades, keep routing tables updated, and other such administrative chores.

Collapsed Backbone

The latency problems caused by traversing multiple routers can be solved with a collapsed backbone, as shown in Figure 33–3, but at the expense of a more powerful router. The LAN segments are brought to multiple ports in a high-speed router, usually over fiber optics. This configuration is less expensive than an FDDI backbone because the expense of the FDDI nodes is eliminated. It is faster than the distributed router architecture because the Ethernet-to-FDDI protocol conversions are eliminated. Management is easier on this type of network because only a single device must be monitored.

It is not as robust as an FDDI backbone, however, because a router failure can disrupt the entire network. By contrast, the self-healing nature of FDDI makes it less likely that a single failure will do more than isolate a single segment. Availability can be improved by using redundant processors and power supplies. As with the multirouter backbone, the collapsed backbone does not lend itself well to a virtual LAN. The backplane bandwidth is enough in many high-performance routers, but moving stations logically between segments requires changing the IP address.

Switched Backbone

If a frame switch is substituted for the router in Figure 33–3, the switched network shown in Figure 33–4 results. Each port on the network has a full 10 mb/s of bandwidth, which can be dedicated to a segment or a station as the need dictates. Collisions are eliminated, and a significant increase in capacity for moderate cost is the result. Stations can be assigned to any LAN segment to create a virtual network, which simplifies rearrangements. The performance of such a network is excellent. The switch backplane is constructed with plenty of bandwidth to handle that required of all the ports transmitting simultaneously. This architecture is excellent for peer-to-peer traffic such as videoconferencing, but if all the traffic is sent to a server, the bandwidth of the server port may not be enough to carry the traffic volume. The solution may be a port supporting high-speed Ethernet.

Despite its economy and bandwidth advantages, switching introduces some challenges for the network manager. The main drawback is network management. Network management systems (Chapter 37) can see individual segments, but systems to monitor all segments simultaneously are not developed at this writing. Virtual LANs, for all their advantages, are not a standard application, so interoperability between products may be limited.

APPLICATIONS

The trade press has been predicting that switching will ultimately replace routing as the preferred means of connecting internets. In the long run, this prediction is undoubtedly true. All major vendors are supporting ATM as the next generation of switching technology. As its price comes down in the next few years, it may well replace routing, but in the near term, routing has an important role in enterprise networks, and this role is not likely to be displaced soon. As Chapter 31 discusses, routers have capabilities that cannot be matched in bridges, which switches are. Among these are:

◆ Routers can administer network security and create firewalls against unwanted intrusion.

◆ Routers can control traffic flow, including broadcast and stray packets. Switches, on the other hand, tend to propagate such packets through the network.

◆ Routers provide LAN-to-LAN connections in both the local and wide area.

◆ Routers do a better job of filtering protocols.

◆ Routers can provide dynamic rerouting.

For the next few years, corporate internets are likely to employ combinations of routing and switching. Switching is an excellent way of solving immediate bandwidth problems, using routing to segment the network for reasons other than just bandwidth improvement—security, for example. Routing increases network complexity, while switching reduces it, so apply routers where the additional complexity is worth adding. Switches don't do any processing, but routers do, so have they greater latency, but this can be controlled by judicious placement of switches. In the next generation of products, routing capability will be embedded in devices such as servers and switches.

The key to any network development is to ensure that the design is driven by business needs, not technology. Technology is important only insofar as it assists business in meeting its goals. In deciding on which technology to implement, consider the following:

- ◆ Understand the timing and technical requirements of new applications such as desktop video and what effect they will have on the network.
- ◆ Understand the availability of new networking technologies such as ATM and the timing and method for introducing them.
- ◆ Get experience with the new technologies through controlled introduction trials and by using such services as frame relay as a prelude to ATM.
- ◆ Plan changes in the network infrastructure. Migrate at your own pace.
- ◆ Carefully evaluate suppliers' capabilities and standards adherence.
- ◆ Focus solutions on known and standards-based products.

For information on manufacturers of internetworking equipment, refer to the lists at the end of Chapters 30, 31, and 32.

34

ENTERPRISE NETWORKS

Private networks bring many benefits to organization that can justify them. The obvious reason for developing a network is cost saving, although reductions in long-distance rates over the last few years have made the public network more cost-effective than private networks unless call volumes between locations is high. A major reason for a private network is to draw the organization more closely together. Dialing extension numbers somehow seems more unified than dialing a seven- or ten-digit number. It's also easier to transfer calls across a network than it is to use the PSTN. Networks are sometimes established to allow users in remote PBXs to share low-cost dedicated facilities to the long-distance carrier. If T-1 facilities can be shared with data, the economics are often more compelling.

Private circuits are sometimes installed to share other resources. For example, voice mail can be shared across a network, or multiple voice mail systems can be networked to enable widely distributed users to set up closed user groups, forward voice mail messages, and retrieve messages from another office. The reasons for establishing a private voice network are often not solely economic; they relate more to the company's preferred method of operation.

The structure and economics of a private voice network are determined by the proximity of the switches. Switches in the same metropolitan area are usually linked by T-1. Analog tie lines are rare within most metropolitan areas because the economics of T-1 are so compelling that only a few channels are needed to break even with analog tie lines. In the interexchange market fractional T-1 or full T-1 are the medium of choice. As discussed in Chapter 35, a small number of tie lines is not effective because of high blockage. At least eight to ten tie lines are needed to reach a critical mass. If traffic volumes are not high enough to reach that point, the PSTN or virtual networks are likely to be more cost-effective.

With wide area voice networks voice compression multiplexers may be cost-effective. Compression multiplexers can apply multiple voice channels to a single 64 kb/s circuit. A typical voice compression multiplexer can provide a 9.6 kb/s digital data channel plus four or five voice channels over a single DS-0 circuit. They can be an economical way of providing tie lines at some reduction in voice quality.

The key word for any private network designer is flexibility. It is difficult to foresee what products and services will emerge in the highly competitive market that telecommunications has become, but the most effective network managers will avoid locking themselves into a single vendor or a particular architecture. The devices on today's and tomorrow's networks are intelligent and are continually getting smarter. Coupled with inexpensive circuits, networks are changing the social fabric of the world as it becomes feasible to move information instead of people.

WHY PRIVATE NETWORKS?

This chapter brings together the building blocks that previous chapters have covered and integrates them in a discussion of the shapes private networks assume. Companies that have never considered a network beyond a few data circuits to tie remote terminals to the corporate mainframe are considering more extensive networks. The following are some of the benefits companies realize from private networks:

Integrate the Company More Tightly   Human endeavor revolves around communication, and the more personalized the communication, the more effective the organization. Multilocation companies can be more closely knit if they have easy access to voice communication. Meetings can be made more productive with videoconferencing and presentation graphics equipment. As desktop videoconferencing becomes more universal, private networks will enable people to hold impromptu conferences and exchange or share files easily. As LANs are interconnected, workers can access remote file servers as easily as servers on their own subnet.

Tie the Company to Its Customers   The strategic use of telecommunications to integrate a company's business with that of its major customers has been well documented. By giving customers direct access to the company's database through the telecommunications network, companies have intertwined their businesses closely with their customers' businesses, making it easier for the customers to do business and more difficult for them to draw apart.

Tie the Company to Its Major Suppliers   Businesses can become more competitive by tying their ordering procedures with those of their major suppliers using such processes as electronic data interchange (EDI). Costs drop as inventories shift from purchaser to supplier and the time between manufacture of subcomponents and delivery of completed products is reduced.

Integrate Voice and Data Communications   The single-purpose networks of the past are giving way to multipurpose networks. T-1 has become the default method of connecting networks, and it is usually effective to merge voice and data circuits when networks are developed. The merger is particularly effective in the loop to the IEC. The major IECs are making T-1 based long-distance service increasingly attractive. The same T-1 circuit that delivers switched voice service also can carry the local loops of data services.

Enterprise Networks

The term industry increasingly uses to describe the network discussed here is the *enterprise network*. An enterprise network, which Chapter 31 discusses, extends to the desktop, where it can support a variety of devices regardless of the application or the operating system. The enterprise network recognizes that users' personal preferences dictate what kind of workstation they have. Instead of converting Apple Macintosh users to Microsoft Windows or vice versa, it is more effective to use the network to do the conversion. Instead of concerning users with routes and protocols, the network enables them to access servers as virtual drives on their workstations wherever they are located. Client-server applications are becoming more prominent. The client runs on any type of system, and the server delivers data in a format the client can understand.

The enterprise network is also multivendor. The telecommunications market increasingly is composed of niche players who happen to produce a very good device, which might be a bridge, a router, or a network operating system, that fills a particular need better than any competing product from the major manufacturers. To remain with one vendor in today's market is to pay a premium in cost or a penalty in functionality, so companies are avoiding single-vendor solutions.

The globalization of business means the enterprise network is multilocation and even multinational. The strategic implications of the network also
mean that it is likely to be multicompany. The multilocation/multicompany
network is difficult to control. As companies do business electronically with
their strategic partners, conflicts arise in protocols, governmental regulations,
and standards. The enterprise network ties the parts together as if the design
and architecture were unified.

VIRTUAL PRIVATE NETWORKS

The voice private network question is greatly affected by virtual networks offered by the major IECs. A virtual private network is one that operates as if it
is composed of voice private circuits, but it actually is part of the IEC's
switched network. AT&T's virtual network is Software Defined Network
(SDN), MCI's is V Net, and Sprint's is Virtual Private Network (VPN). Figure
34–1 is a diagram of AT&T's SDN architecture. The network architecture of
SDN is similar to that of the other major IECs except that terminology may be
somewhat different. The network elements are connected by Signaling System
7 (Chapter 11), which is an out-of-band packet switching system. The following is a brief description of the major network elements:

The action control point (ACP) is a digital switching system. The switch
receives call setup requests and forwards a message to the NCP
requesting instructions on how to handle the call.

The network control point (NCP) is a database of subscriber information.
It screens all calls made on the network to determine how to route the
call. It checks for restrictions and service classifications such as forced
account code dialing.

The network services complex (NSC) stores and plays announcements
under direction of the NCP.

The service management system (SMS) is a database that is used to
update the NCP. Some information can be entered by the customer; other
information is entered only by AT&T.

The Software Defined Network control center (SDNCC) is the
centralized maintenance and support center that surveils the network.

One advantage of a private network is the reduction in long-distance
charges that result from bypassing LECs' access charges for both the originating and the terminating end of a call. A virtual network also provides this

FIGURE 34–1

Architecture of AT&T's Software Defined Network

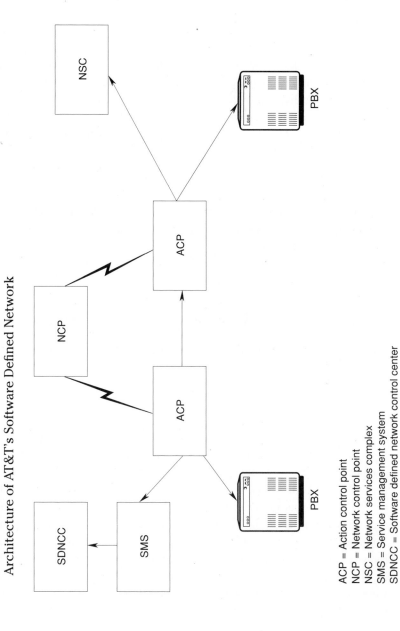

ACP = Action control point
NCP = Network control point
NSC = Network services complex
SMS = Service management system
SDNCC = Software defined network control center

capability. Access is dedicated (on-net) or switched (off-net). Calls placed over the network are rated in three categories: on-net to on-net, on-net to off-net, or off-net to off-net. The on-net portion of calls does not incur LEC access charges, which reduces the cost of the call.

Virtual networks are economical for large companies that have considerable amount of on-net calling. Most of the features of a dedicated private network can be provided. For example, locations can call each other with an abbreviated dialing plan, calls can be restricted from selected area or country codes, and other dialing privileges can be applied based on trunk group or location. Special billing arrangements are provided. Call detail furnished on-line or on CD/ROM enables the company to analyze long-distance costs in a variety of ways.

A virtual network should be considered by any company that has the following characteristics:

◆ Long-distance usage in excess of about 200,000 minutes a month.
◆ Multiple locations, at least one of which is large enough to justify one or more T-1 access lines.
◆ The organization needs tie line services such as extension number dialing, but lacks the volume to justify a dedicated tie line network.

BUILDING BLOCKS OF THE ENTERPRISE NETWORK

This section discusses the elements of an enterprise network. These have been discussed in earlier chapters and are presented here with applications to show how they fit as an integrated whole.

Terminal Equipment

Figure 34–2 shows the evolution of terminal equipment interfaces to a host computer. Many legacy networks resemble Figure 34–2a: A host computer superintends a network of dumb terminals. The terminals connect through a cluster controller or multiplexer to the host, which contains the database and manages the network. The dumb terminal is rapidly being replaced by the personal computer—at first emulating the terminal and then operating as a peer, as shown in Figure 34-2b. Even with terminal emulation, gateways, which are less expensive and more responsive, replace the cluster controller. Local area networks, usually using twisted-pair wire, replace the coaxial and EIA-232 wiring to controllers and multiplexers.

FIGURE 34-2

Evolution of Terminal Equipment Interfaces to a Host Computer

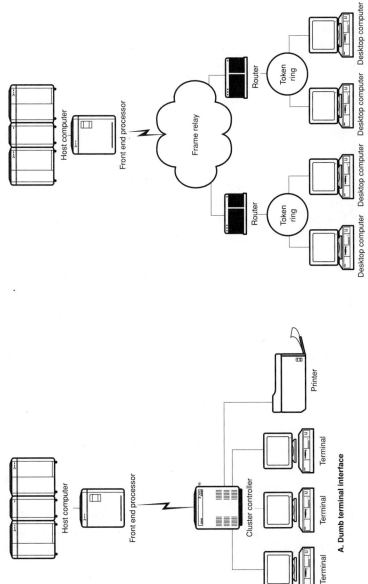

A. Dumb terminal interface

B. Desktop computer interface

Local Area Networks

The high-growth area of private networks today is the LAN, and that growth is expected to continue. The basic building blocks—the network interface card, transmission medium, servers, network operating system, and routers—are becoming so common as to be practically commodities. Interest is high and expected to remain so for devices such as bridges, routers, and gateways that interconnect LANs over the facilities discussed in following sections.

Circuits

The circuit building block of the network of the past was the voice-grade circuit. With conditioning it supports data, and with signaling it supports voice. The limited bandwidth of the voice-grade circuit gave rise to DDS, a fully synchronized digital service operating at speeds up to 56 kb/s. Based on the bit-robbed signaling of a T-1 backbone, DDS is expensive and incapable of providing 64 kb/s clear channel circuits. As the demand for greater bandwidths increased, the major IECs provided T-1 and fractional T-1 facilities and, increasingly, are delivering T-3 and fractional T-3. The trend clearly is toward providing circuits in bulk. A T-1 can be leased for the price of six or seven voice-grade circuits; a T-3 can be obtained for the price of the same number of T-1s.

Fractional T-1 now holds the limelight, not so much because companies don't need a full T-1, which many don't, but because it is the migration path away from analog services that carriers have chosen. Anyone designing a network today should evaluate fractional T-1, which is superior to voice-grade analog circuits except for two things: It isn't universally available, and it may not be suitable for multi drop bridging. At the time of this writing, fractional T-1 is largely a point-to-point service between major metropolitan areas, but that limitation will inevitably disappear. Some LECs offer fractional T-1, but others offer digital service only in DS-0, DS-1, and DS-3 increments.

Common Carrier Switched Facilities

IECs and LECs offer strong incentives to remain on the public switched networks. Dedicated circuits are effective for high-volume voice and most data applications, but every enterprise network makes some use of the PSTN. One of the theories behind divestiture was that competition would drive down long-distance costs, and that has proved to be true. Costs are nearing the bottom and in some cases have started to rise, however, because IECs' costs and the access charges they must pay to the LECs for the local network support prices on the downside.

In the past, switched long-distance networks offered two alternatives: WATS for the heavy users and direct distance dialing for everyone else. Now, WATS has disappeared except for a few isolated instances. T-1 services are replacing it for large users, and discounted long-distance is cost-effective for all but the smallest users, who will remain on message telephone service. T-1 access is particularly attractive for larger companies because the service charge is low, the usage charges are low, and the T-1 can be justified by a combination of services. T-1 lines can support outbound, inbound, data, ISDN and switched 56, which companies use for videoconferencing, Group 4 facsimile, and other wideband services.

Companies obtain local switched services from the LECs as ISDN, direct inward dial, and central office trunks. For data communications, frame relay is a popular service. Packet services such as SprintNet and the intraLATA X.25 services of many LECs are available.

Premises Switching Systems

The PBX is the most familiar kind of circuit switch in private networks. Larger networks use tandem switches, but most private networks use all or part of a PBX for the purpose. Common carrier switching services also are available and gaining increased attention. The most familiar type is the Centrex services that most LECs offer. With few exceptions, Centrex systems can support the tie lines, T-1 long-distance services, and special trunks that PBXs support.

Although they are not switching services in the strictest sense of the word, digital crossconnect services are offered by many LECs and IECs. These services do not switch one call at a time but reroute individual circuits or bandwidth on demand.

Facility Termination Equipment

Private facilities must be terminated in equipment that provides testing access, conditions the signal to meet the line protocol, and divides the bandwidth among the users. Digital facilities terminate in a channel service unit (CSU) that converts the bipolar line signal to the T-1 format. Individual channels are derived by terminating the line in channel banks or T-1 multiplexers, as Figure 34–3 shows. Circuits also are terminated on customer premises in digital crossconnect systems.

F I G U R E 34–3

T-1 Line Termination Options

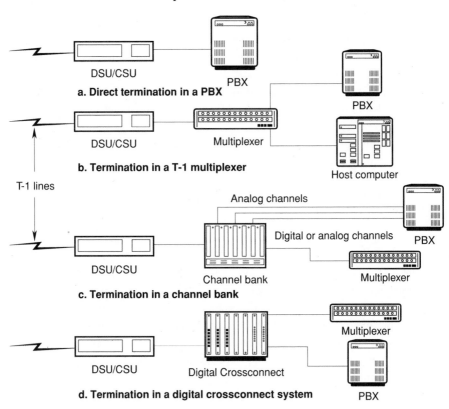

Time division and statistical multiplexers divide both analog and digital circuits, and increasingly the voice/data multiplexer is used to combine voice and data on the same digital facility. Where it is necessary to separate channels on a T-1 system, a drop-and-insert multiplexer can divide and combine the T-1 routes. Figure 34–4 illustrates the use of drop-and-insert multiplexers.

Although the use of analog circuits is declining, families of analog network channel terminating equipment (NCTE) are still used. These devices include repeaters, signaling systems, and other devices designed to amplify, convert, and condition the line. The shift from analog has not displaced the modem, a device that continues to be used in quantity, with special emphasis on high-speed dial-up modems.

FIGURE 34–4

Using a Drop-and-Insert Multiplexer to Share a T-1 Line

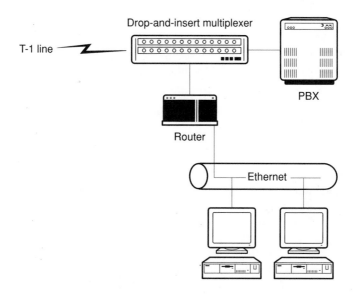

PRIVATE NETWORK DEVELOPMENT ISSUES

This overview of the building blocks of telecommunications networks shows that there is no shortage of options. In fact, network designers are faced with an abundance of options. This book and chapter discuss some of the principal design issues that managers must consider in implementing networks.

The Hybrid Network

Networks of today are not composed of any pure form of facilities or owner-ship. These "hybrid" networks have most or all of the following characteristics:

- ◆ *Multivendor:* In terms of circuits, equipment, and perhaps even management, the modern network involves many vendors.
- ◆ *Multiapplication:* Networks carry all of a company's applications— voice, data, video, text, graphics, and electronic mail—over the same transmission medium and possibly through the same switches.
- ◆ *Multiprotocol:* It is difficult to use a single protocol to support an enterprise network because of its multivendor characteristics. Protocol conversions or multiprotocol routers are the rule for more elaborate networks.

◆ *Circuit or packet switched:* The design rules are changing. In the past, packet switching was avoided for voice, and circuit switching was avoided for most data. Today's hybrid network may have a circuit-switched PBX feeding voice and data over an ATM backbone. Some products are available for carrying voice over frame relay.

◆ *Private or public:* Even the largest private networks still find it necessary to use public facilities for some applications.

Security

More and more private networks connect to the Internet, which raises security concerns for every network manager. Everyone knows and many have experienced the hackers who find it a challenge to invade private networks. An even more subtle threat to security are the network's users, who are authorized access to the network itself but who attempt to obtain access to unauthorized files. Network security involves the following issues:

◆ *Physical security:* Network and computer equipment and the circuits that connect them must be physically secure. Equipment rooms and wiring closets must be kept locked, and the keys under control. Fire prevention precautions must be taken. The facilities should be kept clean and free of debris.

◆ *Terminal security:* Access to the network must be controlled. Dial-up circuits should use a system such as dial-back or a hardware security device to prevent unauthorized access. Passwords must be controlled and revised periodically. Terminals and computers should be kept physically secure, and the keyboards locked if possible.

◆ *Disaster recovery:* Every network should have a plan for restoring service in case common carrier services fail or major equipment is lost because of fire, earthquake, sabotage, or other disaster.

◆ *Data security:* It is impossible to prevent unauthorized access to many types of telecommunications circuits, particularly those that are carried over radio. An organization's telecommunications plan must include methods of preventing unauthorized people from obtaining access to the information. Often, this requires encryption of data and scrambling of voice or video.

Network Intelligence

Networks composed of dedicated facilities tend to have static configurations because of the delays and high cost of facility rearrangements. Static networks, however, fail to meet the need for information flow in most modern organizations and contribute to low utilization of facilities. Network intelligence allows an organization to reconfigure the network based on instantaneous service demands. Products to accomplish this objective are based on digital circuit switches or on a digital crossconnect system that operates under some form of network management system. A key issue is whether intelligence is on the user's premises or at the common carrier's facility. In either case, the intelligent network provides users with a greater degree of control.

In an intelligent network, user services home on a service node that directs digital bandwidth where it is needed. Bit compression multiplex equipment compresses the bit stream to make the most effective use of digital facilities. The digital crossconnect system routes traffic to dedicated or switched services as needed. The network control system located on the user's premises dynamically monitors load and service and changes the network configuration in response to demand. For example, an airline reservation system extending across several time zones can be reconfigured to move calls to different answering centers as the load shifts during the day. Also, an intelligent network can give the airline the capability of offering priority treatment to their best customers when all positions in the nearest reservation center are occupied. For example, a call from a customer identified as a frequent flier could be shifted over the intelligent network to the opposite end of the country while less important customers wait in queue at the local ACD.

Network intelligence is most effective with all-digital circuits where bandwidth can be reallocated according to demand. Digital circuits that normally are used for individual voice channels can be rerouted during off-peak hours to a computer center for high-speed data transmission or reallocated to a videoconference center. The availability of low-cost bulk digital facilities has a significant impact on the demand for network intelligence.

The growth of network intelligence greatly improves the utility of information resources and demands a higher level of knowledge to use the network effectively. Users will have greater flexibility and control and will undoubtedly have to employ computer-based tools to make the maximum use of the network.

Future Compatibility

Network products and services are changing so rapidly that it is difficult to be sure a current design will be compatible with the future shape of the network. ATM will be an important part of many networks in the future.

Services that demand high bandwidth are here now and will gain importance in the future. Some will have a strong impact, and others may fizzle. The key to designing a network is to remain flexible—not locked into any single technology that will limit the organization's ability to follow the shifting telecommunications environment in the future.

On-Premises Distribution

Debates on the best method for distributing information on the user's premises have raged for several years. Some services are suited to coaxial cable. Others can be served on twisted-pair wire, but then the question of whether shielded or unshielded is best must be answered. Arguments can be made favoring all three media. For the most part the choice is UTP, but companies planning for the future must also decide how fiber optics fits into the distribution plan. FDDI is available, but it is too expensive to use for ordinary office applications now. But what of the future? Will FDDI or another technology replace the present token ring and Ethernet networks? Many experts contend that FDDI is not fast enough for the network of the future, and there are even some present applications for which it is not fast enough. The relative importance of these factors is, of course, different for every company, so there are no principles to suggest except that the applications must be thoroughly understood before equipment is chosen.

Vendor Dependence or Independence

In the past, most of the components of the network were likely to be furnished by one vendor, who also probably furnished the mainframe computer at its headend. Network designers must determine whether a past vendor preference will be continued into the future. The penalty for not doing so is the risk of incompatibility and difficulties in testing and clearing trouble. The penalty for remaining dependent on one vendor, however, may be a loss of performance. No vendor has a monopoly on technology, and niche players are more apt to exhibit superior performance in one family of products because their developmental efforts are more concentrated.

Network Management Issues

Chapters 36 and 37 discuss principles of testing and managing networks. The hierarchical networks of the past had a significant advantage over the peer-to-peer networks of the present and future: They were easier to manage. Vendor-specific network management products make it possible to look into the network's components and diagnose and sometimes clear trouble. As the network becomes multivendor, these management capabilities diminish.

National, International or Proprietary Standards?

The ideal route to follow in developing a network would be to use only products that meet an international standard. As the standard develops, production costs decline, and prices drop with them. Most companies, however, will find it effective to deviate from the ideal simply because standards take too long to develop. If the payback period is short, it is often desirable to use proprietary standards to gain an immediate advantage. The course to follow depends on the company's tolerance for uncertainty.

How to Plan Networks

Many managers today face a dilemma. Control of computing budgets is moving from the management information department to the end users. Users purchase computers today as they purchased office machines in the past: They are justified on an individual basis. The arrival of stand-alone computers almost inevitably leads to a demand for networking, and the network manager may find it almost impossible to plan because he or she lacks control over the applications. Organizations that have control over equipment standards are in the best position to plan the network. If the information in desktop devices is of any value, someone also must plan for such factors as security, regular data backup, and network capacity.

APPLICATIONS

With the trend toward obtaining digital circuits in bulk—as either full or fractional T-1—the most cost-effective networks are those that integrate different applications at the transmission level. Devices such as PBXs, T-1 multiplexers, drop-and-insert multiplexers, and digital crossconnect systems are the means of integrating the applications onto the circuit backbone. Developing a network generally involves the following:

◆ *Identify the applications:* Present and future applications, including voice, data, video, facsimile, imaging, and all other foreseeable communications services, should be identified. It is not enough to consider only present applications. Knowledge of future plans and expected growth is essential.

◆ *Identify locations to serve:* The geographic location of all points on the network must be identified. Although some locations are obviously too small to justify dedicated voice circuits, such locations often require data and may have enough volume to justify equipment such as voice-data multiplexers.

◆ *Determine traffic volume:* The amount of traffic, both terminating and originating, should be identified at each location. Determine the volume, type, and length of data transactions from such sources as routers, multiplexers, and front-end processors. Determine the quantity of voice traffic from sources such as common carrier bills, traffic usage recorders, and call-accounting systems. Identify both on-net and off-net traffic. It is usually useful to create a matrix of traffic volumes and costs between on-net locations.

◆ *Determine network type:* Each application will have an optimum network type to support it. For example, short-range, high-speed data applications are usually best served by a local area network. Geographically dispersed LANs with a common interest can be linked by routers and remote bridges.

◆ *Develop network topology:* The topology of the network is based on the application, using techniques discussed in Chapter 35. Costs of alternative transmission methods are calculated, and where the volume and cost of traffic are enough to justify private circuits or a public network such as a virtual network, these are added to the design. Optimize the design by trying different combinations of circuits and by selecting alternative concentration points.

◆ *Determine how the network will be managed:* Most networks use SNMP and a proprietary network management system to oversee the network. See Chapter 37 for further information on selecting and applying a network management system.

35

NETWORK DESIGN PRINCIPLES

Designing a telephone network is somewhat analogous to connecting a stereo or personal computer system. You begin with a variety of components, each of which has a particular purpose and certain characteristics. Rules must be followed, but within the guidelines the components can be assembled in many ways to achieve the desired result. Telecommunications system designers are not concerned with design in the sense of creating the components. Instead, designers deal with such factors as these:

- How many circuits—trunks, lines, voice mail ports, DTMF registers, and so on—are required?
- What are the interfaces between the circuits—tip and ring, EIA-232, E&M, and so on?
- What are the capacities of the component in Hz, bits per second, and so on?
- In what topology are the components assembled—star, ring, point-to-point, and so on?
- What type of circuit—digital or analog—will be used?

Telecommunications system design is beyond the scope of this book, but an understanding of several principles is essential to understanding telecommunications networks. This chapter presents the vocabulary and the basic principles of network design. This information, with the circuit design tables contained in Appendix E, supplies enough information to enable you to find how many circuits to provide for an objective level of service if the traffic load is known. *The Irwin Handbook of Telecommunications Management* or any of the design books listed in the bibliography provide more detailed explanations.

Integrating switching systems and trunks into a network requires that the designer determine the number of trunks and the amount of shared network equipment needed to reach a reasonable balance between service and costs. The telecommunications industry calls this function *network design* or *traffic engineering*. Designers base trunk group size and shared equipment quantities on the probability of occurrence of some value of offered traffic load. When the load is less than the network capacity, the unused capacity wastes money. When demand exceeds the designed load, service is affected by ineffective attempts and delays, and lost revenues and unproductive employee time waste money. The designer's job is to balance cost and service.

Telecommunications traffic engineering is similar in many respects to highway traffic engineering. In highway engineering, the traffic capacity depends on the number of lanes. Each circuit in a group has a given capacity and is analogous to a lane on a highway. It is impossible in either a highway or a circuit group to achieve full utilization. The objective is to keep the lanes reasonably full without impeding traffic. The amount of load offered to the highway or circuit group varies with time of day, day of the week, and season of the year. Within limits, these variations are predictable. The network is designed for anticipated peaks—called the *busy hour* in network design terms. When the offered traffic load exceeds the designed capacity, blockage results.

The design is a composite of the following information about the character of the network:

◆ Network owner's *grade of service* objectives.
◆ Anticipated *load* measured in number of call attempts and call holding time distributed by hourly, daily, and seasonal variations.
◆ *Behavior* of users in placing and holding calls.
◆ *Capacity* of the network elements—trunks, ports, switching network, common equipment, and processors.

THE NETWORK DESIGN PROBLEM

The essential problem in designing a telecommunications network is to find how much equipment and trunking is required to reach an objective balance between service and cost. The process used to reach this balance is somewhat complex and requires special formulas, software tools, tables, and training.

F I G U R E 35–1

Hourly Variations in Call Volume for a Typical Telephone Central Office

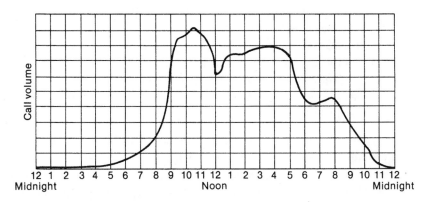

This chapter explains only the concepts and provides examples in the Applications section to show how to reach the cost-service balance.

Network design is the process of predicting future demand based on past results, evaluating the capacity of equipment and facilities, and providing the correct amount of capacity, in the proper configuration, in time to meet service objectives. The primary complication in network design is how to provide the right amount of equipment and facilities to meet a constantly fluctuating demand. In any part of the network, demand fluctuates from minute to minute as users originate and terminate calls. Hourly fluctuations also occur, as Figure 35–1 shows, because of changes in usage as the business day peaks and wanes during breaks and lunch hours. Also, demand varies by season of year, by class of service, and by type of call—local or long haul.

QUEUING THEORY

The most common design method involves modeling the network according to principles of queuing theory, which describes how customers or users behave in a queue. Three variables are considered in network design. The first variable is the *arrival* or *input process* that describes the way users array themselves as they arrive to request service. Examples are arrivals of users at a group of DTMF receivers to begin dialing or at a group of trunks to a distant office. The second variable is the *service process,* which describes the way servers handle the users when they leave the queue and enter the service-providing mechanism. The third variable is the *queue discipline,* which is the way users behave when they encounter blockage in the network. The network is designed by observing how users behave and selecting the appropriate design formula. Three disciplines or reactions to blockage are possible:

- *Blocked calls held (BCH):* When users encounter blockage, they immediately redial and reenter the queue.
- *Blocked calls cleared (BCC):* When users encounter blockage, they wait for some time before redialing.
- *Blocked calls delayed (BCD):* When users encounter blockage, the service mechanism holds them in queue until capacity to serve them is available.

Traffic engineers apply different formulas or tables corresponding to their assumption about how users behave when blockage occurs. Service systems are grouped into two categories—*loss systems* and *delay systems.* In a loss system, when users encounter blockage they are turned away. An example is the "fast busy" tone that signals that all trunks are busy. In a delay system, the system holds the user in queue until a server is available. An example is the queue for an idle DTMF receiver. When DTMF receivers are all busy, users do not receive dial tone, but if they wait, dial tone will be provided.

Traffic Load

In a given hour the load on any part of the network is expressed as the product of the number of call attempts and the average holding time of all attempts. For example, if a circuit experienced six call attempts that averaged 600 seconds (10 minutes) each, the group would have carried 3,600 call-seconds of load. To express the load in more convenient terms, traffic engineers divide the number of call-seconds by 100 and express the result as *hundreds of call seconds,* abbreviated as *CCS.* Since there are 3,600 seconds in an hour, a load of 36 CCS represents 100 percent occupancy of a single circuit for one hour.

Traffic loads are also expressed in *Erlangs,* units named for A. K. Erlang, a Danish mathematician. One Erlang is equal to 36 CCS; both represent full occupancy of a circuit for one hour. Designers can choose to use either unit. CCS is generally more convenient for small units of traffic. Most measuring devices, such as the traffic usage registers in a PBX, use CCS as the unit. Erlangs are usually more convenient when demand is expressed in hours or minutes because it is easier to convert to Erlangs than to CCS.

It is important to distinguish between the *carried* and *offered* loads of a network. The difference between the two is the ineffective attempts that the network did not carry because of blockage or failures. The offered load can be estimated from the carried load, but it is impossible to determine accurately.

FIGURE 35–2

Waiting Time as a Function of Circuit Occupancy

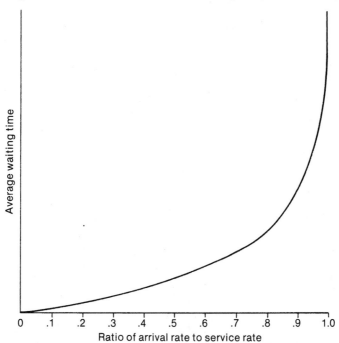

When people encounter blockage, they tend to generate additional attempts. When the blockage is removed, the total number of attempts drops.

One hundred percent occupancy in a circuit group is unachievable in the real world because of variations in timing and duration of access attempts. Calls do not align themselves neatly so that when one terminates, another is waiting to occupy the vacated capacity. Calls can be queued on a trunk group to improve utilization, but even with queuing the full 36 CCS capacity of a circuit cannot be reached. The reason for this can be seen in the queuing formula:

$$\text{Average waiting time} = \frac{\text{Average arrival rate}}{\text{Service rate} \times (\text{Service rate} - \text{Arrival rate})}$$

When the service rate and arrival rate are equal, as they would be at 100 percent occupancy, the denominator of the equation is 0, which means the waiting time will be infinite. Figure 35–2 illustrates the relationship between occupancy and length of queue. Network design becomes a task of determining how long the queue can be allowed to extend before the cost of delays outweighs the cost of adding capacity. It is evident, therefore, that network design requires a service objective, of which more will be said later.

FIGURE 35-3

Poisson Distribution of Call Arrivals

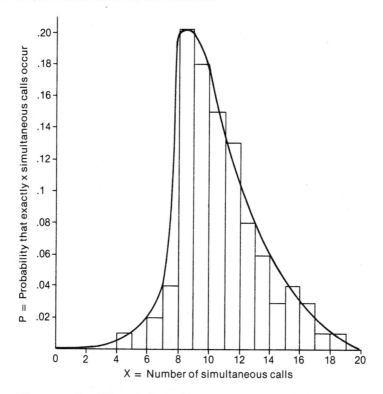

The unpredictability of users further complicates the network design problem. Users vary widely in the number of calls they attempt per hour and the length of time they hold a circuit. Unless the network blocks them, users place calls at random. That is, the attempts and holding time of any user are independent of activities of other users. Users are far from uniform in their behavior. Some dial faster than others; some frequently dial a few digits and hang up (called *partial dial*); some redial immediately when a reorder or busy is encountered, while others wait for a time before redialing. If we observe this randomness in user behavior, it begins to fall into a pattern that can be used to predict how load in a network element will be distributed.

To illustrate how random behavior is used in network design, assume that we make many observations of the habits of customers attempting to access a group of DTMF receivers. With enough observations, it becomes possible to predict the probability that a given number of attempts will occur in the busy hour. Probability is stated as a decimal number between 0 and 1; the sum of the probabilities always equals 1.0. If we plot probabilities in a bar chart such as Figure 35-3, a pattern begins to develop. Countless observations have

Exponential Distribution of Service Times

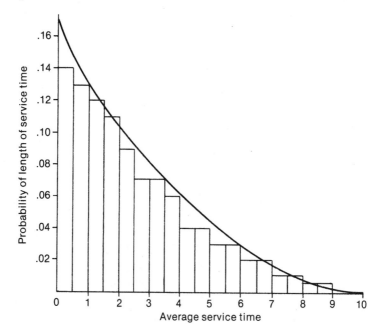

shown that arrivals tend to array themselves according to the curve shown by the solid line in Figure 35–3. This curve can be described by a formula known as *Poisson* distribution, so named after the French mathematician S. D. Poisson. Although Poisson distribution is not a perfect match for the distribution of incoming service arrivals, its accuracy is sufficient for network design.

With a good estimate of patterns of call attempts, the second question is how long the average holding time of the group of DTMF registers will be. If we plot holding times, they tend to follow the exponential curve shown by the solid line in Figure 35–4.

These distributions of attempts and holding time are modeled by tables or software that designers select according to the disposition of blocked calls. Assuming the arrival rate is random, we choose the traffic formula according to the behavior of users in the queue. The Erlang B formula assumes blocked calls are cleared; that is, when users encounter blockage they do not immediately reenter the system. The Poisson formula assumes blocked calls are held. They are not actually held, but instead, users immediately redial when they encounter blockage. For a given grade of service, the Poisson tables require slightly more trunks than Erlang B. Erlang C tables are used for the blocked calls delayed or queued assumption.

FIGURE 35-5

Load/Service Curve of Typical Common Control Equipment

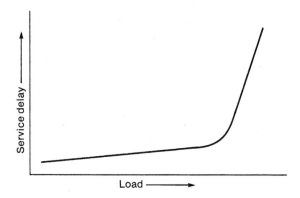

It is important to understand that traffic formulas are valid only if the attempts are random. Several things can affect randomness. A national or local emergency can drive the number of attempts far beyond the capacity of the network. This causes blockage and results in many retrials, which in turn generates more attempts. Most common control switching equipment exhibits a load-service response curve similar to that shown in Figure 35–5. With a gradually increasing load, service, as measured in amount of delay, follows a slope that is almost flat until a critical point is reached. At that point service degenerates rapidly, and the network, for all practical purposes, collapses. Networks are protected from overload by *flow control,* which is a series of procedures, described in a later section, to keep additional traffic off the network when excessive congestion will result.

It is also important to understand that in a common control network, overloading one critical element can cause the entire network to collapse. For example, if a central office with ample trunks and switching capacity has too few DTMF receivers, the trunk and switching capacity will be underused because users will not receive dial tone, and therefore will be unable to access the trunks. Because designers select the quantity of equipment to handle a given amount of usage, *suppression* in one portion of the network makes it appear that other parts of the network have excess capacity. When the cause of suppression is removed the true demand becomes apparent.

Common carriers, particularly those operating in a competitive environment, are well aware that blockage can result in loss of customers. Therefore, most common carriers design to avoid blockage in all but a few attempts. Blockage is often greater in private networks, however, because of the attempt to control communications costs by underproviding network capacity. Private networks usually can afford to provide a lower grade of service than public networks. If carried too far, however, the risk is great that the randomness of attempts will be lost, service will be poor, measurements will be invalid, and productivity will deteriorate.

Busy Hour Determination

Since networks must handle peak loads, a designer needs to know the heaviest load periods, called the busy hour. The busy hour is not a single hour, but rather is a composite network design point, leveled to represent the design peak. A common factor for engineering switching systems is the 10-high-day (10HD) busy period. This factor is determined by averaging the amount of traffic in the busiest hour of the 10 days during the year when the highest traffic load is carried. PBX managers often use the average bouncing busy hour (ABBH) as the busy hour for sizing trunk groups. The ABBH is the average of the daily busy hour over the study period, which is usually one week.

The busy hour for the network as a whole is not necessarily the busy hour for all circuit groups or all equipment. Each group is likely to have its own busy hour because of the varying traffic flow between nodes, particularly when they are in different time zones. Unless the designer chooses these load peaks carefully as design criteria, congestion in some parts of the network will result.

Grade of Service

The service grade in a loss system such as a trunk group is expressed as the probability of blockage. Designers size trunk groups by using tables or computer programs that express blockage as a decimal number. For example, a P.01 grade of service means that a call has a 99 percent chance of finding a vacant circuit and a 1 percent chance of being blocked. Traffic tables used for sizing circuit groups are indexed by grade of service; therefore, selecting a grade of service objective is the starting point in designing a network.

The grade of service for a delay system such as access to service circuits is expressed in terms of the percent of calls that encounter a delay higher than the objective. For example, the dial tone delay objective is often expressed as "no more than 1.5 percent of the attempts will be delayed more than 3 seconds."

It must be understood that a network has several elements connected in tandem, each of which has a possibility of blockage. For example, after a call is dialed, it must contend for a path through the switching network, next for a trunk to the destination, then for a path through the terminating switching network. As each of these elements has its own probability of blockage, the probability of completing a call is the sum of the individual probabilities.

This additive nature of blockage probability can result in a network design that is wasteful of capacity if it is not carefully controlled. For example, if a circuit group is designed to a P.005 grade of service (0.5 percent blockage probability), but incoming calls encounter a terminating switching network with a high degree of blockage, a considerable amount of trunk capacity will be wasted in carrying calls that cannot be completed because of blockage in the final link of the chain. This waste of circuit capacity is not detected by traffic load measurements, because measures of attempts and holding time do not discriminate between successful and unsuccessful calls.

Traffic Measurements

The most difficult task in network design is obtaining accurate load data. With accurate data a skilled designer can design a network that meets service objectives. In public networks with a clientele that remains constant, the load can be predicted with reasonable accuracy. The number of call attempts and holding time can be predicted, and change occurs gradually enough that it can be accommodated with minor adjustments in capacity. When major fluctuations in load occur, however, it is sometimes impossible to adjust capacity quickly enough, and users experience slow dial tone or blocked calls.

The best predictor of traffic load is a historical analysis of past usage, but in many networks historical information is unavailable for predicting the traffic load. When an organization first establishes a new private network, the only source of information may be records of long-distance calls billed by the LEC and IEC. The detailed bills provided by the long-distance carriers can be used to predict future demand by observing past calling patterns. Historical information is a good predictor of the future if the conditions that generated the original demand remain unchanged. When changed conditions affect demand, however, the original design may be rendered invalid and require modification.

Traffic usage equipment measures usage either with an external device attached to the circuit for measuring attempts and holding time or in software registers assigned to groups of circuits and equipment items. Measurements are produced in raw number form and must be processed before the results can be applied to network design. For example, assume that a group of circuits is connected between two switching systems. Traffic usage recorder readings express the load in CCS. The designer consults traffic tables derived from the Poisson or Erlang formulas to determine the number of circuits needed to fill the demand for an objective grade of service. Table 35–1 is an example of a typical

TABLE 35–1

Partial Poisson Traffic Table

	Carried Traffic Load in CCS		
Trunks	P.02	P.05	P.10
1	0.4	1.9	3.8
2	5.4	12.9	19.1
3	1.6	29.4	39.6
4	30	49	63
5	46	71	88
6	64	94	113
7	84	118	140
8	105	143	168
9	126	169	195
10	149	195	224
20	399	477	523
30	675	778	836
40	964	1,088	1,157
50	1,261	1,403	1,482

Steps in using traffic tables:
1. Choose the appropriate queuing discipline.
2. Choose the objective grade of service.
3. Locate the load in CCS in the proper column.
4. Read the number of trunks required from the first column.

table and shows how it is used to determine the required number of circuits. Poisson and Erlang B tables are included for up to 100 circuits in Appendix E.

If the data in Table 35–1 is converted to call-carrying capacity in CCS per circuit, the curve shown in Figure 35–6 is obtained. This curve shows an important factor in network design: Large circuit groups are much more efficient in their per circuit traffic carrying ability than small groups, because large groups have less idle circuit time for a given grade of service.

Often, usage data sufficient to predict demand accurately is unavailable. For example, it may be known that an organization change or a circuit routing change will affect demand on a trunk group between systems. Without valid measurements, the designer must estimate circuit numbers based on experience or rules of thumb until measurements can be made. Usage measurements show only the load that was carried. Besides usage it is important to measure ineffective attempts, the number of calls queued, and length of time in queue (if queuing is used) to derive a valid indication of the true demand.

FIGURE 35–6

Circuit Capacity as a Function of Size of Circuit Group

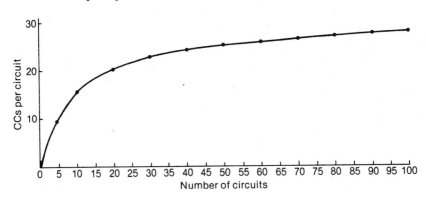

A network can be visualized as a black box consisting of sources and dispositions (also called *sinks*) of calls, as Figure 35–7 shows. Every attempt must be accounted for by its possible dispositions. The network administrator must determine whether the service provided by dispositions meets the organization's cost and service objectives. The combination of all calls—including intramachine, those terminating on a tone trunk such as busy or reorder, off-net local calls, and toll calls—comprise the total load on the switching network. The various ports must be sized to fit the offered load, or blockage will result. The network design task becomes one of computing the numbers of circuits and pieces of equipment needed to fit the possible call dispositions.

Alternate Routing

One possible disposition of a call, as Figure 35–7 shows, is overflow to an alternate route. Alternate routing is one of several techniques used to maintain circuit occupancy at a high level. The decision whether to use alternate routing is based on cost. For example, assume that a network consists of three nodes, as in Figure 35–8. The circuits between A and C are designed for a high level of occupancy and are called *high-usage* circuits. When the A–C trunk group is blocked, calls route through the tandem switch B over a *final route*. Different design criteria must be used on final and high-usage trunk groups. On high-usage groups an Erlang B table is used to size the group because blocked calls are released (overflowed to a final group). For example, it may be economical to have as much as 10 percent of the traffic overflow to the final group, so the P.10 column of the Erlang B table would be used. On final groups the Poisson table is used at a higher grade of service.

FIGURE 35–7

Sources and Dispositions of Network Load

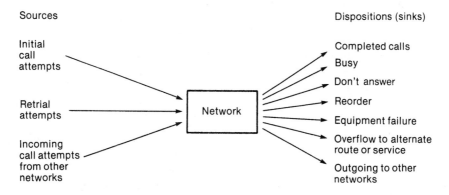

FIGURE 35–8

High-Usage and Final Routes in a Three-Node Network

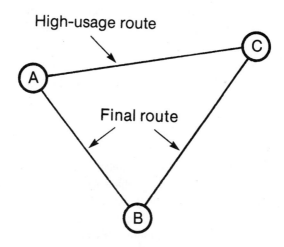

Simulation

The techniques discussed so far for determining demand and capacity use mathematical modeling to calculate required capacity given an objective grade of service and estimated demand. Modeling is a valid way of designing a network if the demand is random and if it follows a known distribution of arrivals and holding time. Also, modeling is an inexpensive way of designing

F I G U R E 35–9

Distribution of Holding Time Probability in a Circuit-Switched Data Network

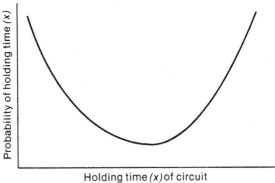

Holding time *(x)* of circuit

a network. Although computer design tools are useful in modeling, manual design using traffic tables is equally valid and can be done by a trained person with little apparatus beyond a book of tables and a hand calculator.

The modeling technique falls apart, however, when demand is not random and fails to follow predictable arrival and service rates. As shown previously, this occurs during high blockage conditions. It is impossible to compute what happens to service when a network is blocked. Therefore, a design is valid only within the limits prescribed by the original assumptions. In addition, the modeling technique is often unable to describe the load when the network handles a significant amount of data traffic. Data terminals and computers behave entirely differently than people using voice communications.

The holding time of data terminals tends to follow the probability distribution shown in Figure 35–9. Many computer calls are established only long enough to send one page or less of text, which at 9,600 b/s takes about two seconds—much less than the average telephone call. Other circuits used for bulk data transfer may have holding times much longer than average telephone calls—on the order of 30 minutes or more. Also, the data busy hour may be different from the telephone busy hour. For example, workers may dial their electronic mailboxes immediately upon returning from lunch, imposing on the system a high momentary load that is unlike that imposed by voice traffic.

Where this randomness and lack of uniform distribution occur, simulation can be employed to find how costs will be affected by service or capacity changes. A simulation program treats the network as a black box and varies the parameters to show the designer the costs and effects on service. Unlike modeling, simulation requires an elaborate program and a trained operator to produce valid designs. Data from traffic measurements is still required to operate the program, but simulation differs from modeling in that service results can be observed outside the limits of the modeling formulas.

The chief limitation on any network design is the validity of observations about users. Also, this behavior rarely remains constant. The smaller the network, the more difficult it is to predict behavior because small perturbations tend to have a large effect. For example, in a small private network a reorganization can change the calling patterns of the users, and blockage may occur where previously capacity was ample.

Network Topology

Choice of topology, which is the pattern of interconnection of circuits and nodes in the network, is another element of network design. Chapter 3 discusses the principal topologies. In both voice and data networks, all nodes can be afforded an equal access level, or they can be configured hierarchically. Private networks also can be ordered hierarchically with high-usage trunks between low-level nodes and final routing through a higher-level node. The chief advantage of a hierarchical network is in the ability to conserve circuits by concentrating traffic in shared final circuit groups where insufficient traffic exists to justify high-usage groups.

DATA NETWORK DESIGN

The data network designer has many more alternatives than the voice network designer has. The building blocks of a voice network are generally limited to switches and circuits. Circuits are obtained individually or in bulk, and in the latter case multiplexers may be required. The grade of service in a voice network is usually expressed as percentage of blockage.

Data networks, on the other hand, use a combination of devices, including routers, bridges, multiplexers, concentrators, front-end processors, cluster controllers, modems, and switches, to develop a network. The grade of service in a data network usually is expressed as response time, which is the time between the issuance of a request to the host computer and the arrival of the first character of the response at the terminal.

An important factor in data network design is the location of concentration points. Figure 35–10 shows two different ways of interconnecting multiple points on a circuit. The network design task is to minimize the cost of circuits, modems, and concentrators while keeping throughput at an acceptable level. In a large multipoint network, the number of possible configurations is

FIGURE 35–10

Two Possible Network Topologies: The Design Task Is to Optimize
Cost and Service

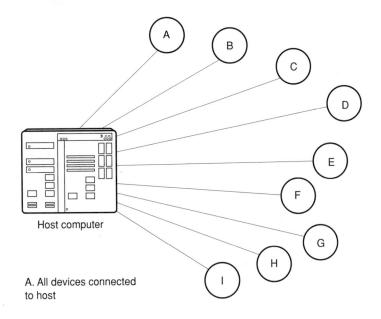

A. All devices connected
to host

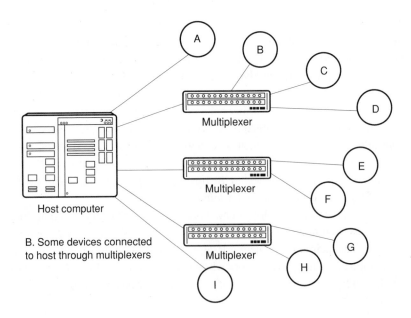

B. Some devices connected
to host through multiplexers

substantial. Network designers use one of several empirical algorithms in reaching an optimum configuration. Two such algorithms are:

◆ *Add Algorithm*. All sites are initially assumed to be connected to the host. The designer chooses a concentrator location and calculates the cost of connecting each site to the concentrator. Additional concentrator locations are chosen and sites moved from the host or other concentrators until adding concentrators no longer improves cost.

◆ *Drop Algorithm*. The designer chooses several provisional concentrator locations and calculates the cost of connecting devices. Concentrators are then dropped and devices reassigned to other concentrators or to the host. If the total cost increases, the concentrator is restored; otherwise it is dropped.

Neither approach is necessarily superior. In complex networks with many nodes, different answers may be obtained from the different approaches. The solution is likely to be dictated by other variables, such as location of administrative headquarters, availability of technical support, and floor space. The task of selecting multiplexer or concentrator locations is eliminated when using frame relay, which is one of its advantages.

Closely related to the location of concentration points is network topology, which refers to the configuration in connecting circuits. The topologies shown in Figure 35–11 are usually a function of the network access method. Circuit-switched networks are usually deployed in a star or hierarchical configuration. Packet-switched networks normally employ a mesh topology, while polled networks employ a tree or bus topology. The ring topology is most commonly applied in local area networks that use a token passing access method.

Many of the principles used in voice network design are applicable to data network design. Queuing theory is used to design data concentrator and statistical multiplexer networks. Other shared data equipment such as dial-up ports into a computer and pooled modems can be designed by measuring usage and comparing it to capacity determined from traffic tables.

Other types of data networks, however, have no counterparts in voice networks. Two examples are polled-multidrop and packet-switched data networks. Like voice networks, these can be sized by modeling or simulation—using different techniques.

A multidrop network is a typical application. Response time is expressed as the interval between the time a request is sent to the CPU and the time the first character of the response is received. A generalized response time model

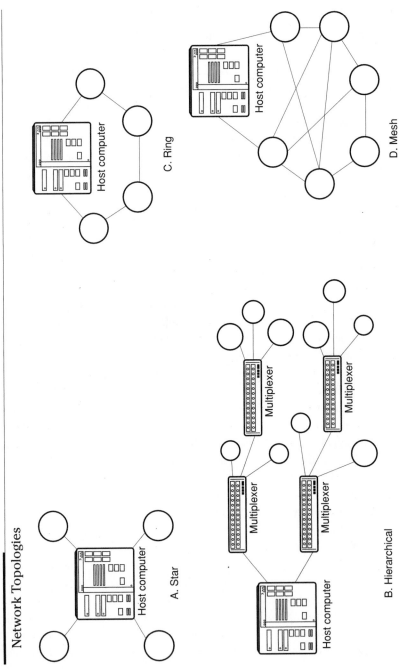

FIGURE 35-11

Network Topologies

A. Star

Host computer

B. Hierarchical

Host computer

Multiplexer

Multiplexer

Multiplexer

Multiplexer

C. Ring

Host computer

D. Mesh

Host computer

FIGURE 35-12

Multidrop Polled Network Generalized Response Time Model

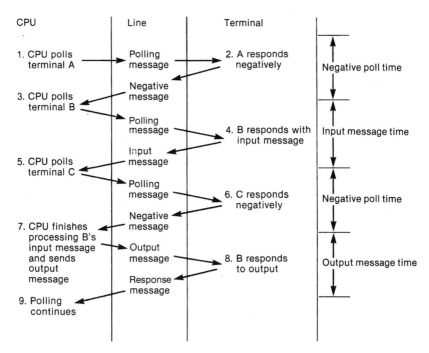

is shown in Figure 35–12. A terminal in a polled network either sends a block of data or returns a negative response to indicate that it has no data to send. The terminal response time of a network depends on these factors:

- ◆ CPU response time.
- ◆ Transmission speed.
- ◆ Error rate.
- ◆ Data block size.
- ◆ Number of overhead bits—NAK messages, CRC, headers, and so on.
- ◆ Modem turnaround time (for a half-duplex circuit).
- ◆ Propagation speed of the transmission medium.
- ◆ Protocol error recovery method.

If these factors are known, network throughput and terminal response time can be calculated.

Packet-switched networks are designed with similar criteria. The network throughput is related to transmission speed, block length, error rate, the number of overhead bits, propagation speed, and the network's packet routing algorithm. Throughput can be increased by using an efficient algorithm. The primary algorithms are:

◆ *Flooding*. The node transmits packets on every route except the one they arrived on.
◆ *Static*. Incoming packets are transmitted according to a fixed routing table.
◆ *Centralized*. A network control center optimizes the route based on load and congestion reports from the nodes.
◆ *Isolated*. Nodes adjust their routing tables using their knowledge of network load and congestion.
◆ *Distributed*. Nodes adjust their routing tables by exchanging information about network load and congestion.

Local area networks are a specialized form of packet-switching network that use design criteria similar to those used for long-haul packet networks. Contention networks present a unique design problem because not only are the other criteria of transmission speed, block length, error rate, and protocol important, but the frequency of collisions presents an additional factor that is difficult to model. Generalized design criteria are impossible to specify because of variations in the method of implementing contention networks. Such networks usually are sized by the experience of the designer. If overloads develop, the designer sectionalizes the network with the segments linked by a bridge that keeps traffic on its own segment unless it is addressed to a node on the other segment.

Token passing networks with their deterministic access method are easier to design. Given the characteristics of the input data and the number, length, and frequency of messages, throughput for any terminal becomes a function of network transmission speed, error rate, and the priority of the individual terminal. With all local networks, the manufacturer's instructions should be followed for design.

Like voice networks, data networks require flow control to prevent congestion. The network access nodes queue incoming messages and allow them on the network up to the capacity limits, holding the remainder in a buffer or stopping them at the source. The physical layer protocol provides a method of flow control by actuating the clear-to-send (CTS) lead of the interface. To stop a terminal from overloading the network, its control node turns off the CTS signal until congestion has cleared, thereby holding the message in the terminal. Similarly, a receiving device can stop a transmitting terminal from overrunning its buffer capacity by sending an X OFF character. When it can receive data again, it sends an X ON character.

NETWORK ADMINISTRATION

A network is a dynamic thing. The original premises on which it was designed never remain static, which means the network must be monitored continually and adjusted when change is indicated by the results. The process of monitoring and adjusting the network is called *network administration.*

Network Administration Tools

Network administration requires skills and tools to keep the network in the proper cost/service balance. The first requirement is a current and valid report of the demand on all network elements. These reports, as previously discussed, must include attempts, usage, and ineffective attempts on every circuit and equipment group in the network.

Next, the administrator must have a full understanding of the network itself. Current records of circuits and equipment, including circuit identification, end points, and capacity, should be maintained. A network administrator must have a comprehensive knowledge of how the network functions, what the service objectives are, and what the capacity of each element is. The administrator also must have information on common carrier services and rates. When the service results indicate that capacity adjustments are needed, the administrator must add or drop circuits to retain the best cost/service balance. This requires knowledge of common carrier tariffs and the cost of other alternatives.

Network administration also requires knowledge of the status of circuits and apparatus. Although the administrator may not be directly responsible for maintenance, knowledge of trouble frequency and history is essential for diagnosing service results and timing adjustments of capacity. Status records should show, preferably in real time, all cases of equipment and circuits out of service. The length of outage should be monitored carefully so excessive clearing times can be reported to maintenance personnel or the common carrier.

When the administrator observes blockage beyond planned levels, he or she should administer controls to relieve the blockage. The tools for relieving blockage include these:

◆ Additional capacity can be provided. This may require temporarily removing restrictions on overflow to other networks.
◆ Some code groups can be blocked. This may require the ability to block codes in an originating system to keep congestion caused by ineffective attempts off the network.

◆ Circuit groups can be rerouted temporarily. It may be necessary to cancel alternate routing or to revise the rerouting tables in some systems temporarily to relieve congested systems or circuit groups.

◆ Trunk directionalization can be applied. Two-way trunks can be temporarily converted to one-way trunks to allow a congested system to place outgoing calls while insulating it from excessive incoming traffic.

Managing flow controls such as these requires that the administrator have the necessary skills and understand the network well enough to know where and how to apply controls to relieve blockage. The feasibility of applying these controls depends on the complexity of the network. In complex networks, mechanized assistance may be required.

Automatic Network Controls

Administration of a network composed of stored program control switching systems that are designed for mechanized network management can be simplified by applying automatic controls. Mechanized network management requires a central computer with a map of the total network and two-way data links to the network nodes. The network control system monitors load and transmits orders to the nodes to relieve congestion. Such systems are complex, expensive, and warranted only for networks composed of multiple nodes and large numbers of trunks.

APPLICATIONS

Network design is a complex topic that is beyond the scope of this book. This section presents typical design problems and shows how the tables in Appendix E are used to solve them. For additional examples and more information on how to apply these techniques, readers are referred to *The Irwin Handbook of Telecommunications Management.*

Determining Trunk Quantities

Most PBXs contain traffic usage measuring equipment that states usage in CCS. Assume that management wants no more than 1 percent of the incoming or outgoing calls in a two-way trunk group to be blocked. Also, assume that the trunk group contains 15 circuits and the PBX's traffic usage equipment shows that the average bouncing busy hour traffic load was 324 CCS. Refer to the Erlang B traffic tables in Appendix E. Look at the row containing 15 trunks, and follow across the table to the column to find the load figure nearest 324 CCS. At 1 percent blockage, 15 trunks can carry 292 CCS, so it is evident that we have too few trunks. At 3 percent blockage, 15 trunks can carry 347 CCS, so the actual blockage is just under 3 percent. The exact amount is not important. If we add one trunk, we will be able to carry 319 CCS at 1 percent blockage, which is just under the objective. To carry the full 324 CCS, 17 trunks are required, so we must add two trunks.

Often, the amount of traffic carried during the busy hour is unknown. Designers must, therefore, use rules of thumb to reach a starting point for calculating circuit quantities. One rule of thumb states that during the busy hour for an organization working eight hours per day, approximately 17 percent of the traffic is carried during the busy hour. If a long-distance bill shows, for example, that 100 hours of traffic were carried during a month with 20 working days, 5 hours (or 5 Erlangs) of traffic were carried per day. If 17 percent was carried during the busy hour, the busy hour was approximately 0.85 Erlangs of traffic, which Appendix E shows could be carried by four trunks at 1 percent blockage.

Another rule of thumb often used by designers who have no usage data is that the average business station uses six CCS of traffic during the busy hour. From knowledge of the organization, this is broken down into incoming, outgoing, and intrasystem traffic. For example, a telemarketing organization would have a high portion of incoming and outgoing traffic compared to a city or county government, which would have high intrasystem traffic.

Designers are also faced with deciding which tables to use. When data is not precise, most designers use Erlang B tables. Common carriers, who have accurate measuring equipment and collect data regularly, use Erlang B for high-usage trunks and Poisson tables for final trunk groups. Erlang C tables are used for queuing situations such as automatic call distributors.

Determining Numbers of Voice Mail Ports

Managers who are installing voice mail for the first time are faced with the question of how many ports and how much storage to provide. Most voice mail systems furnish information that can be used to measure service, but these are no help in initially sizing the system.

Studies have shown that the average voice mail user uses about 3 minutes of storage capacity per day. If a system has 100 users, it needs 300 minutes, or 5 hours, of capacity. If 17 percent of this occurs during the busy hour, 0.85 Erlangs of port capacity are needed, which requires four ports. It may be advisable to provide more capacity, but this process provides a starting point.

Determining Service Positions in an Automatic Call Distributor

An ACD manager is always faced with the necessity of deciding how many service positions to staff at any time. Most ACDs provide load and service information that the manager can use to balance load and service. Erlang C tables are used to evaluate service.

To illustrate the process, assume that ACD data indicates that the busy hour traffic load is 2.0 Erlangs and that the average holding time per call is 3.7 minutes. Also, assume that the ACD manager has an objective of having no more than 10 percent of the calls delayed.

The Erlang C table in Appendix E (Column N) for 2 Erlangs of load (Column A) gives a range of from three to nine servers or agents. To stay within the objective of 10 percent or less of the calls delayed, Column P_d shows that five servers are required. (Note that four servers would block 17.4 percent of the calls.) To find the average delay for all calls, multiply the average holding time by Column D1. In this case the result is:

$$3.7 \text{ minutes} \times .02 = 0.074 \text{ minutes} = 4.4 \text{ seconds.}$$

The average delay for all calls tells us little about how long the delayed calls are delayed. To find this factor, multiply the average holding time by Column D2. The result is:

$$3.7 \text{ minutes} \times .333 = 1.23 \text{ minutes.}$$

The remaining columns show the probability that calls will be delayed longer than a specific time. For example, the factor .0333 is shown in the column headed .2. This means there is a 3.3 percent probability that calls will be delayed longer than 20 percent of the holding time, or 0.74 minutes.

Standards

Network design and administration are not covered by standards. Instead, networks are designed and administered to cost and service objectives that are achieved by applying network design principles. The bibliography lists publications that describe these principles more fully.

36

NETWORK TESTING PRINCIPLES

As networks change, testing strategies must follow. In traditional analog networks managers can concentrate on circuit and protocol tests, but in broadband networks and LAN internets with all digital circuits, different testing strategies are needed. To do an effective troubleshooting job on an internet, an analyst needs to know such things as which device is originating the most traffic, what route the traffic is taking, what protocols are being used, and what time of day peak loads are occurring. Some of this information can be determined with a network management system, which we will discuss in Chapter 37, but network management isn't the whole answer. A network management system may collect and display statistics and network maps, turn down defective devices, and monitor network segments for errors and other irregularities, but analysis with portable test equipment is required in almost every internet.

An effective maintenance strategy always starts with trained personnel who know how the network and its protocols function and how it looks when all is well. An investment in test equipment is wasted unless technicians know how to use it to advantage.

Some degree of testing capability is essential for most telecommunications networks. Even if the test is as simple as a check at the common carrier's demarcation point to determine whether trouble is in company or carrier facilities, the ability to make these tests can pay dividends in reduced maintenance costs. Companies with complex networks find that testing capability is essential, not only to control costs but to restore failed service quickly.

Telecommunications network testing has two primary objectives:

♦ To establish benchmarks that serve as references or to confirm that design objectives have been achieved.
♦ To locate faulty network elements by sectionalizing and isolating defective equipment.

The first category of tests is usually called acceptance or proof of performance. These are conducted to establish a database that later can be the basis for fault-locating tests. The second category of tests usually does not require the depth and sophistication of the first. In an analog circuit, for example, it is often sufficient to measure a single variable such as circuit loss when searching for a defective element. When the cause of excessive loss is found, the tester may also locate the source of poor frequency response or excessive noise. Therefore, the tests used for routine circuit verification can be reduced to single frequency measurements, which in turn can be automated to survey a complex network rapidly and reliably.

Network reliability has increased dramatically over the years in spite of the ever increasing complexity of the network. Nevertheless, every element of a telecommunications system is subject to failure, and when a circuit or service is in trouble, it is often difficult to find what portion of the network is at fault. Service irregularities and end-to-end tests can reveal the presence of a fault, but the defective element can be identified only by testing to sectionalize the trouble.

As we evolve into an integrated all-digital network, testing is simplified in comparison with older analog networks. A bit stream originates on the user's premises and is carried over the network to the distant end without crossing physically wired interfaces. The logical interfaces, on the other hand, are often more difficult to troubleshoot because technicians are dealing with intangibles. With today's networks, testing is complicated by several factors:

♦ Network elements are obtained from multiple vendors.
♦ Trouble must be sectionalized by testing to interfaces between vendors.
♦ The responsibility for impairments such as high noise and data errors often is unclear, and vendors are not quick to claim responsibility.
♦ Incompatibility at interfaces may arise under some conditions, and lacking interface standards, the user may be left to negotiate the solution between vendors.

Until low-cost processors became available, network testing was almost entirely manual. Tests were designed specifically for a particular class of equipment, and the testing principles were essentially the same whether the test was manual or automatic. For example, trunk-testing devices stepped through circuits, performing loss, noise, and supervision tests exactly as a technician would do them. Now, devices such as protocol analyzers help technicians locate the source of logical malfunctions by such techniques as setting traps, emulating devices, and providing expert assistance. Technicians can multiply their effectiveness manyfold by using sophisticated equipment, but only if they understand the intricacies of how the protocol operates.

Transmission and switching systems require specialized test equipment to perform general tests and some tests that are unique to the manufacturer. For example, two types of tests are required on microwave radio—system performance and service. FCC-required system performance tests include frequency and bandwidth measurements and are similar for both analog and digital microwave. However, service criteria for the two types of microwave is different. Analog microwave service is closely related to its channel noise performance; the primary service indicator of digital microwave is its error rate.

A fundamental principle in designing a network is that it must include a plan for testing, sectionalizing, and clearing trouble. It is sometimes possible to obtain network services from a vendor that assumes full end-to-end testing and maintenance responsibility, but this may be more expensive for many organizations than the alternative of providing that service in-house. In any event, it is rare that an organization's total communications needs can be supplied by a single vendor that assumes full responsibility for performance, which means that the responsibility falls on telecommunications managers. This chapter describes the principles of testing the major components of a telecommunications network.

TEST ACCESS METHODS

A common problem for all types of circuit tests is how to obtain test access to the circuit. Access is obtained by one of four methods:

- ◆ Manual access through jacks, test points, or distributing frames.
- ◆ Switched access.
- ◆ Permanently wired test equipment.
- ◆ Probes that are connected to circuits under test or built into circuit elements.

Manual access methods include jacks and terminal strips that allow direct connection of test equipment to the circuit conductors. The primary drawbacks of manual access methods are that they are labor intensive and often result in delays while a technician travels to a remote location. Switched-access methods provide circuitry for connecting remote test equipment to a circuit from a distant location. Switched circuits are often accessible through the switching system. Dedicated circuits may be connected through a separate switching matrix that connects the transmission path to collocated test equipment. Test equipment also may be inserted into a circuit or designed into the terminating equipment. For example, most modems provide lights to show circuit status and many provide a low-speed channel for performing tests while the circuit is in operation. Internetworking equipment such as routers and hubs usually provides logical probes that monitor operations, collect statistics, and tally mutilated packets.

ANALOG CIRCUIT TESTING PRINCIPLES

Certain tests are common to all elements of the network. The testing equipment may vary widely, but the principles are identical. The tests discussed in this section are applied to voice frequency, video, and analog data circuits and, where indicated, also may be applied to broadband analog transmission facilities. Analog data circuits require all the tests described in this section, but many impairments that cause trouble on data circuits are undetectable when the circuit is used for voice. The following discussion points out differences between data and voice tests.

Loss Measurements

Loss (or gain) measurements are made by injecting a signal source into the input of a circuit and reading the result at the output. Voice frequency measurements are made at a nominal frequency of 1,000 Hz; 1,004 Hz is actually used to prevent interference with digital transmission equipment. The frequency source, or *oscillator,* generates a pure audio tone. The signal is applied across the input of a circuit at a test level point and measured at the output, as shown in Figure 36–1. The difference between the two readings is the loss or gain of the circuit. This same principle is applied in measuring loss on analog radio and carrier systems. High-frequency signal sources and level measuring sets are used to measure loss at baseband or at carrier or radio frequencies.

In addition to single-frequency loss measurements, the gain-frequency or attenuation distortion characteristic of analog circuits is of interest. Attenuation distortion is a variation in loss at the audio frequencies within a circuit passband. It is measured by sending and receiving tones across the audio passband or by sweeping the circuit with a signal that varies continually in frequency. A *swept* channel can be displayed on a cathode-ray tube to present a visual display of the

FIGURE 36-1

Transmission Measurement on a Circuit between TLP

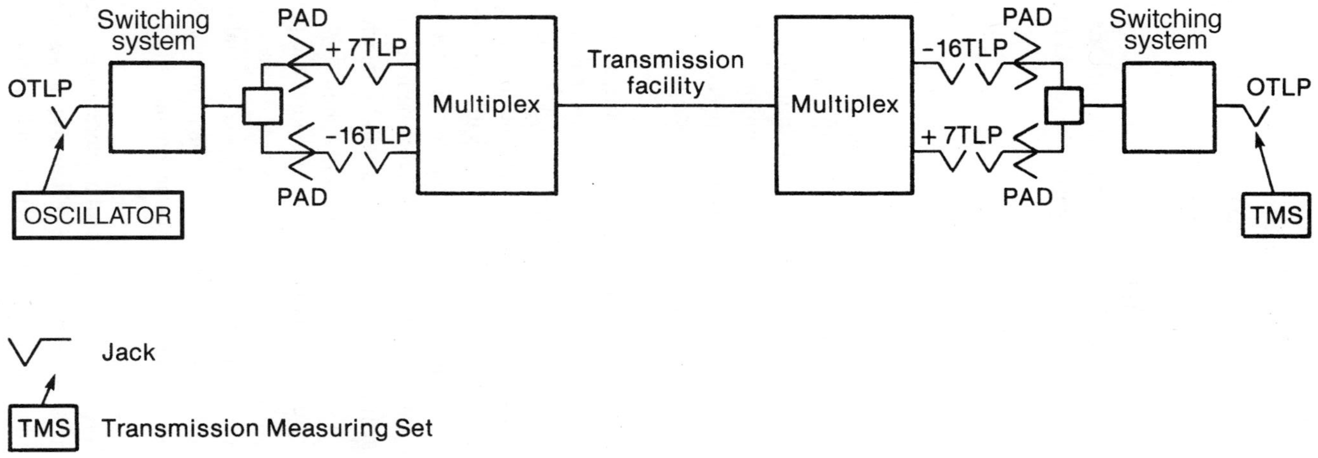

circuit passband. Similar tests are made at carrier and radio frequencies to examine the linearity of a broadband facility. Spectrum occupancy and the presence of extraneous or high-level frequencies are readily determined with a spectrum analyzer, a test instrument that displays the frequency domain of a signal. These types of test are particularly valuable on analog video and CATV circuits because the entire spectrum can be viewed at once.

Transmission level measurements typically are expressed as decibels related to one milliwatt (dBm), as explained in Chapter 2. To ensure accurate results, test equipment must be calibrated by comparing the test set to a reference frequency and level standard.

Noise Measurements

As explained in Chapter 2, noise is expressed in dB compared to a reference noise level of -90 dBm (0dBrn). Noise measurements are made with a measuring set that reads the noise power through a weighting filter and registers it on a digital or meter readout. Voice frequency circuits normally are measured through a C message filter, which approximates the human perception of the interfering effect of noise on a telephone conversation. Special service and program lines are measured through flat filters, which weight all frequencies equally within the pass band.

When power is applied to a circuit, noise may increase because the greater loading reacts with nonlinearities in the circuit to increase the intermodulation noise. This effect is measured by injecting a single frequency into the circuit at the sending end and removing it with a filter at the receiving end so that only the intermodulation products remain. Circuits that are equipped with companders exhibit low noise in the idle state because the receiving end expander has no signal and consequently reduces the volume level of its output. To obtain a realistic measurement of the noise that will be interfering with a live conversation it is necessary to place a test tone of appropriate level on the circuit to activate the compressor and expander combination and permit a useful assessment of the circuit's noise performance. The test tone is removed at the receiving end by a narrow-band filter so that only the residual noise under approximately active conditions is measured. When the residual noise is measured through a C message-weighted filter by this technique, it is designated as C-notched noise.

Impulse noise measurements are of particular interest in evaluating a circuit for data transmission. A common source of impulse noise is electromechanical relay operations that induce a sharp spike of noise into a circuit. Impulse noise has little effect on voice communication, but it can be devastating

FIGURE 36-2

Phase Jitter

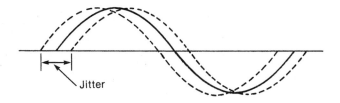

Jitter

to data transmission. An impulse noise measuring set establishes a threshold level and counts the number of impulses that exceed the threshold. The set also includes a timer so impulses above reference level can be measured over a fixed time period. As long-haul circuits migrate to fiber optics, and electromechanical switching systems are replaced with digital switches, impulse noise diminishes as a problem. In some rural areas, however, transmission facilities are still analog and impulse noise impairs data transmission, particularly at high speeds.

Envelope Delay

Envelope delay measures the difference in propagation speed of the various frequencies within the audio pass band. It is measured with an envelope delay measuring set, which applies a pair of frequencies at the originating end of the circuit and registers the relative delay of each frequency at the receiver as the test signals move through the transmission band. Envelope delay affects high-speed data but has no discernible effect on voice transmission.

Return Loss

Return loss measurements determine the amount of energy returned from a distant impedance irregularity such as the mismatch between a two-wire circuit and the network on the balancing port of a hybrid. Return loss measurements are made over a band of frequencies between 500 and 2,500 Hz by transmitting a white noise signal source on the circuit as described in Chapter 2.

Phase Jitter

Phase jitter is any variation in the phase of a signal, as illustrated in Figure 36-2. Jitter is measured with a special test set that detects phase variations in a steady-state tone injected at one end of a circuit and measured at the other.

Peak-to-Average Ratio

A peak-to-average ratio (P/AR) test gives an effective index of the quality of an analog circuit for data transmission. A P/AR transmitter sends a repetitive pulse consisting of a complex combination of signals. The P/AR receiver measures the envelope of the received signal and indexes the circuit quality on a scale of 0 to 100. The P/AR measurement provides a composite indicator of circuit quality.

Harmonic Distortion

As described in Chapter 2, a harmonic is a multiple of the fundamental frequency applied to a circuit. For reliable data communication, the second harmonic must be at least 25 dB lower than the fundamental frequency, and the third harmonic 28 dB lower than the fundamental. Harmonic distortion is measured with a special test set that reads the amount of second and third harmonic distortion directly.

Subscriber Loop Measurements

As Chapter 6 discusses, the subscriber loop is the part of a telecommunications circuit most susceptible to transmission impairment. Tests on subscriber loops can be grouped into three categories: manual tests from a local test desk attached to a switching system, automatic tests through a switching system, and manual tests from the user's premises or intermediate points on the cable to the central office. Subscriber loop tests differ from trunk tests in that full loss and noise measurements on a loop require manual or remotely controlled tests from the user's end of the circuit. Equipment to perform remote measurements can be justified only in locations with large concentrations of high-cost circuits. Because such tests are labor intensive, they normally are made only to locate the cause of repeated trouble.

Local Test Desks

A local test desk (LTD) is a manually operated system that accesses a cable pair through the switching system or over a trunk to the main distributing frame. The latter connection requires manually placing a device called a *test shoe* at the main distributing frame to access the cable pair directly. Many local loops are inaccessible through switching systems because they are dedicated to special services. These circuits may be tested from an LTD through an MDF shoe or through switched-access connectors and special service testing apparatus as

FIGURE 36–3

Common Cable Faults

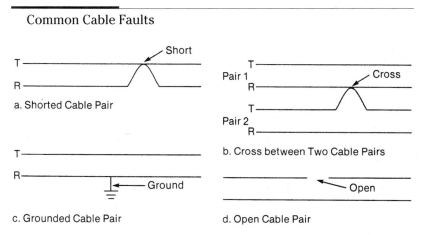

a. Shorted Cable Pair

b. Cross between Two Cable Pairs

c. Grounded Cable Pair

d. Open Cable Pair

described later. The principal faults that occur in local cable pairs are shorts, crosses, grounds, and opens, as Figure 36–3 shows. Crosses and grounds cause a high level of noise on the cable pair and often result in unwanted voltage (called foreign EMF) from the central office battery of the interfering pair. Crosses and grounds are often the result of wet cable, which causes current flow between conductors. If users complain of noise or crosstalk, wet cable is frequently the cause.

Figure 36–4 shows a diagram of a properly functioning circuit and its access from an LTD. The LTD accesses the line through a circuit in the switching system that connects the LTD to the line without ringing the telephone. The LTD evaluates the circuit by measuring capacitance between the two conductors of a cable pair, and from each conductor to ground. Because the pair consists of two parallel conductors separated by an insulator, the conductors form the two plates of a capacitor. When test voltage is applied, the meter on the LTD registers the amount of current flowing in the line as the capacitor charges. When the line reaches full charge, current ceases to flow and the meter returns to zero.

An experienced test board operator or automatic test apparatus can diagnose the condition of the line from the amount of capacitance kick to the meter. Shorted and open lines kick only a small amount. Properly functioning lines kick to a greater degree, with the amount of kick proportional to the length of the cable pair and the number of telephone sets installed on the line (the measurement charges the capacitor in the telephone ringer when the cable pair is charged, so more ringers increase the amount of capacitance).

FIGURE 36-4

Local Test Desk Cable-Testing Circuit

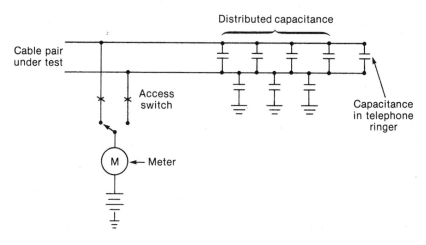

Foreign EMF is detected by using the LTD voltmeter to measure the battery from each side of the line to ground. When the line is connected to the testing circuit, the central office battery is removed. Any voltage observed is coming from an interfering source such as a cross with a line that is connected to central office battery. When water enters a cable, it often provides a conductive path permitting foreign EMF to reach many lines simultaneously.

The LTD also can make loss measurements on the line. Loss measurements require someone at the distant end of the circuit. Noise measurements can be made at the central office end of a circuit, but because the noise signal is attenuated by the loss of the cable pair, noise measurements made at only the central office end of a circuit do not fully express the interfering effect of the noise.

Automatic Testing

Automatic test equipment accesses local loops through the switching system to perform tests similar to LTD tests. The least complex type of automatic subscriber loop test system is the line insulation test (LIT), which has been used in central offices for many years. An LIT machine steps through each line in a central office, accessing the line through the switching system and applying to each line tests similar to those applied by the LTD. LIT machines look for shorted and grounded cable pairs and for foreign EMF. The results of the tests are printed.

LIT machines are capable only of qualitative tests and offer few clues to the nature and location of the trouble. More sophisticated automatic test equipment also accesses the subscriber loop through the switching system. It can profile the impedance of the subscriber loop and determine more accurately what and where the trouble is. A mechanized line-testing system functions by storing the electrical characteristics of normal lines and those with various faults in its database. A remote test unit is accessed manually through a console or driven automatically by a computer to perform routine measurements.

Manual Loop Tests

Local test desks and mechanized line-testing equipment are limited in their ability to locate certain types of cable faults. Open and wet cable pairs are among the most difficult faults to locate and often require measuring interactively with a technician in the field. The time domain reflectometer (TDR) locates trouble with a high degree of accuracy in all types of cable, including coaxial cable and fiber optics. It uses the same principle in cable with which radar operates in free space. The TDR sends a pulse on the line. Any irregularity in the cable returns a reflected pulse that is displayed on a cathode-ray tube calibrated in distance to the fault.

TDRs are excellent devices for locating all types of impedance irregularities, but their cost prevents their widespread use for less complex testing. Shorted and open cable pairs can be located by making precise resistance and capacitance measurements to a fault. Electronic instruments for these measurements are less expensive than TDRs and locate trouble with a satisfactory degree of accuracy.

Subscriber loop loss and noise measurements must be made from the user's premises to be accurate. Specialized test sets are available to measure the three variables that affect subscriber loop transmission—loss, noise, and loop current. Loss measurements are made by dialing a test signal supply in the central office. Noise measurements are made by dialing a termination, or *quiet line,* in the central office. Current measurements are made by measuring the off-hook current that would be drawn by a telephone set.

Network Interface Devices

Test equipment located in the central office is generally unable to distinguish between troubles located in outside cable plant and troubles in the customer premises' wiring and equipment. To aid in sectionalizing trouble, network interface devices (NIDs) are available and are sometimes installed at the interface between the customer's wiring and the telephone company's equipment. By applying voltage or an actuating tone from the LTD, the NID opens the line at the interface. Some types of NID also short the cable pair so tests can be made from the central office to the interface. With the NID actuated, if the trouble observed by the LTD remains, it is evidence that the fault is in the loop facilities. If the trouble disappears, the fault is in the customer premises' wiring or equipment. NIDs are not universally applied because most ordinary telephone services do not experience trouble often enough to justify the cost of the NID. On data circuits, many data modems are equipped with loop-around capability that performs a similar function.

Trunk Transmission Measurements

The voice frequency measurements described earlier are of critical importance on all trunks. Transmission measurements are made either manually or automatically between TLPs, and adjustments are made by changing fixed-loss pads or adjusting amplifier gains.

Manual Switched-Circuit Test Systems

Circuit access for manual testing is obtained through jacks wired to the circuit, by access through the switching system, by removing jumper wires at a cross-connect point, or by switched access connectors. Both portable and fixed test equipment measures transmission variables and supervision. Supervision tests, which Chapter 10 discusses, are made on the signaling leads. These tests detect and register the status of supervisory leads under various conditions of circuit operation.

Manual tests are made either to a manual test board at the distant end or to responders. As described in Chapter 10, trunks may be equipped with a variety of test lines that are accessed by dialing special codes over the trunk. A typical test line is the 105, which permits two-way loss and noise measurements from an office equipped with a remote office test line (ROTL) and responder.

Automatic Switched-Circuit Test Systems

In offices equipped with large numbers of circuits, the most economical way of testing is with automatic test equipment that conducts the tests under computer control. Figure 36–5 is a diagram of automatic circuit test equipment of the type discussed in Chapter 10. A computer-driven device actuates a ROTL, which communicates with a test line at the distant end. A full range of transmission and supervision tests can be made with such a system. The results are stored in memory and printed out. Trunks exceeding design limits are automatically taken out of service.

FIGURE 36-5

Automatic Remote Trunk Testing System

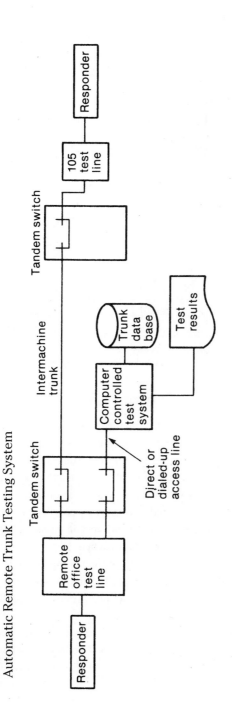

851

FIGURE 36–6

Switched-Access Remote Testing

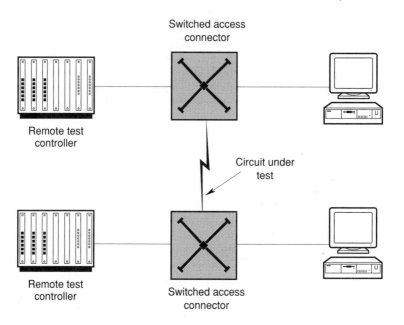

Tests on Special Service Trunks

Tests on special service lines cannot be made with the test equipment described in this section because they are not accessible through a switching system. Manual testing is particularly difficult in multipoint private lines because of the number of technicians needed to sectionalize trouble. In locations with large concentrations of special services, switched-access systems, illustrated in Figure 36–6, can be justified. Circuits are wired through crosspoints that monitor the circuit or open it to sectionalize trouble. Testing terminations and signal sources can be connected to the circuit through switched-access connectors. The test console, which is typically located centrally for a company or region, is connected to a near-end testing unit. Each remote location is equipped with a matching test unit, and the two units communicate over a dedicated or dialed access line.

Switched-access connectors can provide access to circuits the same as jacks. Connectors are available to operate two, four, or six wires and allow the operator to monitor, split, test, and busy-out connections. Circuits also can be wired to enable patching hot standby spare equipment or circuits. Most systems also provide computer-supported operational functions such as logging trouble, recording circuit outage time, and maintaining trouble histories.

With a switched-access testing system, a technician can obtain remote access to all points that are equipped. For example, if a multipoint circuit is singing, the technician can remotely terminate the legs of the circuit until the one causing the trouble is found. Circuit lineup tests can be made by performing two-way transmission measurements to test equipment that is accessed through the switched-access connector.

DIGITAL CIRCUIT TESTING

Digital circuit testing is less complex than analog testing because the impairments are fewer. Impairments such as loss, noise, envelope delay, gain-frequency distortion, and poor return loss are effectively nonexistent on digital circuits. When problems occur with the transmission medium the circuit is likely to be failed, not impaired.

The principal factor of concern in a digital circuit is the error rate. The error rate can be measured with a bit error rate tester (BERT), which is a hand-held device that monitors the line looking for errors from a source that is generating a known bit pattern. Such tests require the line to be out of service. BERT tests are frequently made by both common carriers and field technicians on T-1 lines.

With T-1 lines using extended superframe, the bit error rate can be monitored while the line is in service. As discussed in Chapter 5, ESF lines multiplex an 8,000 b/s framing channel to provide six-bit cyclical redundancy checking on the data. A 4,000 b/s facility data link is used for end-to-end diagnostics, network control, and maintenance functions such as forcing loop-back of a failed channel. Most BERT testers are capable of monitoring the Fe channel to provide in-service testing. Also not to be overlooked is the capability built into CSUs that are capable of monitoring the Fe channel. Such CSUs can send diagnostic information to a printer, or by equipping them with a modem, technicians can dial in to retrieve data from the storage buffer. Both test sets and CSUs can monitor bipolar line violations, which are two consecutive pulses of the same polarity.

Increasingly, digital circuits contain information in their overhead channels that testers can use to diagnose circuit trouble. For example, the Hewlett-Packard SONET test set shown in Figure 36–7 is a portable unit that is used for field testing. The results can be displayed on a large screen in either text or graphics format.

A Hewlett-Packard SONET Test Set

Courtesy Hewlett-Packard Co.

DATA CIRCUIT TESTING

Although nonconditioned data networks and voice networks share the same voice frequency facilities, data networks are more complex to test than voice networks. Voice network users can give a qualitative analysis of what the trouble is. Data network troubles are apt to be reported as slow response time, with no clue to whether the trouble is high error rate, CPU problems, noise, or momentary interruptions. Also, data circuits are subject to incompatibilities such as protocol and addressing faults that can be caused by troubles in DCE, DTE, or software.

Tests are applied to data circuits for one of three purposes: to resolve specific trouble reports, to monitor the circuit for proper operation, or to prevent trouble by detecting incipient faults with a preventive maintenance program. Many data network problems are found in the user's equipment—the software, the interface between the DTE and DCE, or a hardware element. Because each data network has a custom design, it is imperative that the manager diagnose the trouble as fully as possible before referring it to a vendor. Such analysis will save time and money and will solve many problems without the help of an outside vendor.

Interface Tests

Many test sets are available to test the EIA-232 or equivalent interface. The test set plugs between the DCE and the DTE and provides access points to the principal signaling and communication leads. The status and polarity of the leads are often displayed with colored lamps. Switches are provided to reconfigure the interface. A breakout box provides access for connecting test probes and injecting test signals.

Loop-back Tests

A loop-back test on a full-duplex circuit is an effective way of locating faults and impairments in a data circuit. Figure 36–8 shows the different points at which a data circuit can be looped. Many modems contain integral loop-back capability. If not, circuits can be looped with an adapter plug. Tests are performed either by sending a phrase that uses all letters of the alphabet, such as "fox" (the quick brown fox jumped over the lazy dog's back 1234567890), or by sending a standard test pattern and monitoring for errors with a BERT. Many modems also include built-in bit error rate testing capability. By looping the circuit at progressively further points, the element causing the complaint can be identified.

Although loop-back tests are useful in locating hard faults, some impairments such as data errors, phase jitter, and envelope delay are cumulative over the length of a circuit. Therefore, the results of a loop-back test must be tempered with the knowledge that the amount of impairment will be doubled because the length of the circuit is doubled. Such tests are more effectively made end-to-end.

Protocol Analyzers

Protocol analyzers are devices that are either inserted in or bridged on the digital portion of a data communications line to provide a character-by-character analysis of the data signal. Protocol analyzers typically include several digital test functions in the same test set. Many analyzers measure bit error rate, block error rate, and percent error-free (or errored) seconds. These variables are useful for detecting the character of noise in a data circuit. For example, if a circuit has a high bit error rate but a low block error rate, it indicates that errors are coming in bursts with error-free intermediate periods. A low bit error rate with a high block error rate indicates that errors are more equally spaced.

FIGURE 36-8

Modem Loop-back Paths

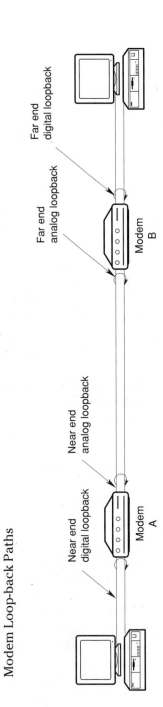

Protocol analyzers operate in a monitor or simulation mode. In the monitor mode the test set is a passive observer of the bit stream between two devices. In the simulation mode, the circuit is opened and the test set simulates circuit elements. Test sets can simulate terminals, modems, CPUs, and other such devices. Among the features commonly included is a terminal exerciser to facilitate diagnosing terminal troubles by sending data messages into a terminal. Some systems contain a polling generator to simulate the CPU in polling a multidrop line. Most units include some form of storage so an error sequence can be captured for off-line diagnosis. Programmable units allow the operator to set triggers or test sequences for trapping error conditions. Many such devices can remember test sequences so they can be recalled without reprogramming.

Local area networks and internets can be tested with LAN probes or portable protocol analyzers. A LAN probe connects to a network segment, capturing statistics, and reporting the results back to a network management system, either when polled or in response to a triggering event. The probe is typically mounted permanently on the segment, although it can be moved. Remote monitoring (RMON) is discussed in Chapter 37.

LAN protocol analyzers can be moved from segment to segment to capture information that can be used for monitoring network performance problems. At the low end is software built into a laptop computer or installed in a computer permanently attached to the segment. This is an inexpensive testing method, but the device may not be able to keep up with traffic on the network. Midrange devices have a combination of hardware and software that gives them more processing capability, but with limited filtering and data capture capability. High-end protocol analyzers are specialized devices that not only capture data but may have built in analytical software. These devices often have a separate processor for data capture.

Protocol analyzers are essential for in-depth troubleshooting of LANs and LAN internets. They can capture all the information flowing across the network, or they can be programmed to filter certain types of packets. They also can compile statistical information to provide a view of what is going on in the network. For example, in a multiprotocol network the analyzer can display a distribution of traffic by protocol type. This information helps in eliminating some devices as a source of overload. For example, if a network carrying a combination of IP, IPX, and AppleTalk traffic shows signs of overload, the tester needs to know which stations are originating the bulk of the traffic. By displaying a line graph or pie chart of traffic distribution, the technician knows where to start looking. For example, if the bulk of the traffic is IP, devices originating IPX and AppleTalk can be eliminated as a source of the problem.

Protocol analyzers may also have expert analysis support built in. Besides capturing and presenting data, they provide the user with an analysis of the information and suggestions on its meaning. Analyzers can be mounted on the network and programmed to send alert messages called *traps* to SNMP workstations when triggering events occur.

Baselining

An excellent technique for supporting network troubleshooting is baselining. When the network is operating normally, baseline information is captured and retained for later comparison. For example, network utilization is a key indicator in Ethernet. If a utilization snapshot is taken at regular intervals it can be plotted on a chart to show normal performance. Later, if users begin to complain of slow response, subsequent measurements can show time in which overloads are occurring. By capturing addresses, the analyzer can help pinpoint which devices are causing the problem.

APPLICATIONS

Anyone who has reviewed the advertisements for testing systems and equipment is aware that the market offers an abundance of options. Any organization that owns or is planning to develop a telecommunications network must attend to testing strategy at the outset. After the overall strategy is developed, individual test systems can be selected.

In general, the more sophisticated and expensive the test equipment, the higher the skill level the technician must have, or the more elaborate the software must be to obtain and interpret the results. Equipment should match the level of communications expertise within the organization. It is a waste of money to purchase sophisticated equipment that is beyond the capabilities of the personnel, and it is also shortsighted to buy simple equipment when complex equipment can rapidly pay for itself in the hands of an experienced technician. As networks become more mission-critical, the costs of downtime can rapidly exceed the cost of test equipment.

Standards

Standard-setting agencies issue standards on testing methods and procedures but generally do not produce test equipment standards. Instead, manufacturers design test equipment to their specifications to conform to the standards of the circuits under test. Purchasers should look for both international and proprietary standards in test sets. For example, a LAN protocol analyzer that lacks the capability of detecting both IP and IPX packets would have limited usefulness.

Evaluation Criteria

Accuracy

Accuracy and stability are of concern in all testing equipment and systems. This is of particular importance with analog test equipment, which must be held to precise level and frequency standards. Improperly calibrated test equipment and the failure to match the impedance of test equipment to the circuit are frequent causes of inaccuracy in measuring circuits and setting net loss. Every testing program must, therefore, include a procedure to ensure test equipment accuracy, and regular calibration against a standard that is traceable to the National Bureau of Standards.

Portability

Test equipment is produced in three levels of portability: handheld, portable, and fixed. Portable test equipment is packaged in cases for mobility but is sometimes heavy enough that it is not easily moved. Fixed test equipment is mounted in relay racks and is used in test centers where circuits are accessed through jacks or switched access connectors. The type of equipment selected for an application is based on the need for portability and the number of functions included in a single package. Handheld test equipment generally is as accurate as portable or fixed equipment, but several units may be needed to perform the functions that are contained in one package with larger equipment.

Analog versus Digital Tests

On analog data circuits, tests can be made between either the analog or the digital side of modems. Digital tests are of little value in finding totally failed circuit conditions and of no value in voice frequency circuit tests. Analog tests are useful only on dedicated circuits or in verifying the condition of a circuit up to the point of interface with a common carrier.

Analog test sets are available to measure most transmission variables. Measurements include attenuation distortion, intermodulation distortion, steady state and impulse noise, peak-to-average ratio, envelope delay, and phase jitter. Test sets that combine all these measurements in the same unit are more flexible and more expensive than single-purpose units.

Centralized versus Distributed Testing

As network complexity grows, the usefulness of centralized testing becomes more apparent. From a central location where circuit status is continually monitored, reports of congestion and blockage can be most efficiently handled. The primary concern in determining whether to centralize is the availability of switched-access connections to the circuits under test. If only jack access is provided, centralized testing is useful only on circuits terminating in the central location. In general, the larger and more complex the network, the greater the benefit from centralized testing. Also, the larger the network, the greater the benefit of automated testing.

Protocol Flexibility

The cost of protocol test equipment is proportional to its flexibility in testing various data protocols. In selecting this type of test set, present and planned protocols should be examined. The test equipment acquired should have the necessary capability without the cost of unneeded features. Programmable test sets have the greatest flexibility in implementing new protocols.

Security

A critical feature of any remote testing system is its provision for preventing unauthorized access. Because these systems enable monitoring and testing of operating circuits, it is important that unauthorized access be prevented. The most secure form of access is the use of dedicated circuits between the test console and the remote units, but over long distances, dedicated access is uneconomical. Access to long-haul facilities is usually provided over dial-up units. Where dial-up circuits are used, the telephone number of the remote units is difficult to keep secret, so means must be provided to prevent unauthorized access. A complex handshake between the master and the remote unit may deter anyone who lacks knowledge of the protocol. Passwords are also useful but far from foolproof. The most effective method is to use a dialer at the remote to dial the master back from the remote.

Evaluating Protocol Analyzers

Reading Filtering and Capture Capability

To be effective, the analyzer must have the processing power to read the addresses of the packets going by on the network segment, determine the packet type, and capture the ones needed for the analysis while filtering out unwanted packets. The unit should be capable of counting packets, runts, jabbers, and other types of traffic. The system should display statistics in real time.

Protocols Supported

Be certain that the analyzer can recognize and analyze all types of protocols the network carries.

SNMP Compatibility
The analyzer should be capable of initiating SNMP trap messages and responding to GET messages from the management workstation.

Diagnostic Support
Low-end analyzers display information but leave interpretation to the user. High-end analyzers include some diagnostic capability to aid the user in interpreting data and detecting problems.

User Interface
Graphical displays are important for viewing trends and different statistical compilations. In addition, the system should be capable of building and displaying charts and tables.

Physical Interface
The analyzer should be capable of direct interface to the most popular networks. Adapters may be required for some interfaces, but these detract from usability.

Download Capability
The system should be capable of downloading information to a standard PC so it can be captured in a spreadsheet or other medium.

Protocol Decodes
For each protocol supported, the system should be capable of decoding and displaying header information in human-readable form.

Locate High Users
The system should be capable of finding which stations are producing the greatest amount of traffic. The number of stations so screened should be programmable by user.

Node Discovery
The system should be capable of finding all nodes on the network and listing their hardware and network addresses.

SELECTED TESTING SYSTEMS AND EQUIPMENT MANUFACTURERS

Circuit-Testing Equipment

Adtech

Ameritec

Ando Corp.

Digitech

Fluke Mfg. Co., Inc.

Hekimian Laboratories, Inc.

Hewlett-Packard Co.

GN Navtel, Inc.

Scientific-Atlanta, Inc.

Siemens Corporation

Tektronix, Inc.

Telecommunications Techniques

Wandel & Goltermann, Inc.

Wide Area Network Data Test Equipment and Protocol Analyzers

Ameritec

Ando

Azure Technologies

Comtest International

Digilog

Digitech Industries, Inc.

Frederick Engineering

GN Navtel, Inc.

Hewlett-Packard Co.

International Data Sciences

Network General

Scientific-Atlanta, Inc.

Siemens Corporation

Tekelec

Telenex

Telecommunications Techniques Corp.

Wandel & Goltermann, Inc.

Local Area and Internetworking Testing Equipment

Azure Technologies

Digilog

Digitech

GN Navtel, Inc.

Fluke Mfg. Co., Inc.

Hewlett-Packard Co.

Network General

Tekelec

Telecommunications Techniques Corp.

Wandel & Goltermann, Inc.

37

NETWORK MANAGEMENT

As mission-critical operations migrate from mainframes to LANs and distributed servers, the need for a comprehensive network management system becomes compelling, and at the same time becomes more difficult. Mainframe manufacturers have long provided proprietary network management for their networks and equipment, but interoperability was, and remains, rare. A company with equipment from multiple vendors has to settle for multiple network management systems with separate management workstations for each. The arrival of new protocols such as ATM and switched Ethernet further complicates the picture. With regular Ethernet, a management probe can monitor an entire segment, but with switching each workstation becomes its own segment, requiring a probe per station. Distributed communication systems do not map well to the older network management systems, which are hierarchically structured.

As networks become more complex and skilled labor to maintain them climbs in cost and shrinks in supply, it becomes attractive to mechanize network management to the greatest degree feasible. Network equipment can support automation to an ever increasing degree. Management agents built into such devices as hubs, routers, channel banks, multiplexers, and even modems can report status and accept orders to reconfigure themselves. As the equipment becomes capable of reporting status and accepting orders, it becomes feasible to control the network from computers. Humans are needed to make decisions that cannot easily be formulated into yes and no choices, but computers can react faster and weigh and discard alternatives at a speed that humans cannot match.

As the science of artificial intelligence develops, it will support the needs of network managers. The uniqueness of every network makes it difficult to adopt standard rules and procedures, but some of the expertise of managers who know how the network is to function and the relative importance of its different elements can be captured in an artificial intelligence program and used to expand the abilities of the staff.

Local area networks present a special management challenge because they are so closely integrated with the end users' operations. The requirements for managing a LAN are not a great deal different from the management of a data center. This means the following functions, which are typical of data centers, must be provided:

◆ Capacity planning.
◆ Change management.
◆ Disaster planning and recovery.
◆ Fault management.
◆ Power conditioning.
◆ Security management.
◆ Service management.
◆ Storage medium backup and recovery.

The proprietary network management systems of the past are giving way to open systems. Simple network management protocol (SNMP) and common management information protocol (CMIP) are the two predominant nonproprietary network management systems in existence today. SNMP is based on TCP/IP, and CMIP on OSI. SNMP is supported by all major manufacturers in most of their products. It is inexpensive to implement, but it has deficiencies that limit its effectiveness. Replacements, however, have been slow in coming. Version 2 of SNMP (SNMPv2) has been under discussion in the Internet Engineering Task Force since 1993. At this writing development has been temporarily curtailed, which means further delays in standardization. CMIP is even slower to gain acceptance because of its complexity. Its primary use to date has been in common carrier networks where the additional complexity is accepted in exchange for its versatility.

This book does not attempt to explain the administrative aspects of network management. For information on how to use and administer network management products, refer to the companion text, *The Irwin Handbook of Telecommunications Management*. This book discusses the technical aspects of network management, including how representative protocols operate and how the managed devices are configured.

NETWORK MANAGEMENT AND CONTROL

Network management is essentially a specialized client-server application that filters and correlates alarms, alerts, and statistics to either make or assist humans in making decisions that maximize network performance. *Technical control* is a term often applied to centralized network management and control systems that monitor status and manage capacity in large networks. These systems include provisions for accessing data circuits by jacks or computer-controlled switched access similar to that described in Chapter 36. Besides providing testing capability, technical control centers include alarm reporting, trouble history, and, usually, a mechanized inventory of circuit equipment. Regardless of the type of network management system, network control center operations can be divided into the following classifications:

◆ *Configuration management:* Retains records and, where possible, configures network equipment remotely. Retains a complete record of users, assignments, equipment, and other records needed to administer the telecommunications system. The function discovers nodes on the network and detects changes in configuration and operational status.

◆ *Accounting management:* Tracks vendor bills and distributes costs to organizational units relative to resource usage.

◆ *Fault management:* Receives reports from users, diagnoses trouble, corrects trouble, and restores service to the users. Fault management also detects disorders or deterioration before users report trouble.

◆ *Performance management:* Monitors service levels and measures response time, throughput, error rate, availability, and other measures of user satisfaction. Also collects network statistics such as packet quantities, runts, jabbers, and other trouble indications.

◆ *Security management:* Ensures that network and files are accessible only to authorized personnel. Assigns passwords and user numbers and detects unauthorized attempts to penetrate the network. Controls access through authorization and authentication.

Generically, a network management system consists of managed devices connected to a management workstation over the managed network. The heart of the system is network management software that resides on a management workstation. The workstation can be a PC running management software under Microsoft Windows, or in high-end systems it may be a UNIX-based workstation with a RISC processor running an application such as Hewlett-Packard's OpenView. Figure 37–1 shows a network diagram from an Open View workstation. Technically, both PC and workstation devices are often called the manager, but this nomenclature is easily confused with the humans

FIGURE 37-1

A Network Diagram from Hewlett-Packard OpenView

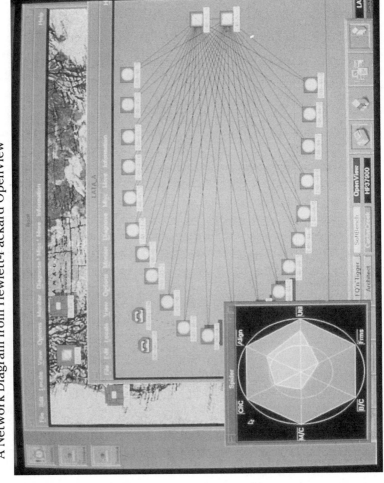

Courtesy Hewlett-Packard Co.

that run the system. In this chapter the manager is the human administrator of the network management system, and the management workstation, whether a PC or a workstation, is the hardware and software that support the manager.

Each managed device contains an *agent,* which is software that communicates with the management workstation. The agent collects information about its environment, responds to management workstation commands, and provides that information to the management workstation, either when polled or in response to an event. Management workstations are capable of communicating with agents, drawing network maps, and forming the interface between the managed devices and the operator. The workstation software stores and presents network information for the use of the manager. In most cases the management workstation sends requests to the agents and receives responses over the managed network, but when the network is down, it may be necessary to access certain devices over the dial network. As a result, some devices allow access to the agent over a dial-up connection.

The network management protocol includes a set of rules known as the *structure of management information* (SMI). The SMI defines relationships between management elements, organizes the network management data, and assigns identifiers to the variables.

Network devices often contain internal statistics that can be used to monitor the configuration, health, and activity in the network. For example, a device may contain static information about itself, such as its defined type; operational status such as up, down, or testing; and it may count statistics such as frames sent, received, and discarded as errors. This information, may be stored in tables, counters, or as switch settings. This logical base of information is called a management information base (MIB). The MIB determines what the agent collects and stores—for example, packets sent and received, errored packets, and so on. Each MIB consists of a set of *managed objects*. For example, system description, packet counts, and IP addresses are all examples of managed objects. A managed device may contain multiple managed objects. Figure 37–2 shows a schematic view of a network management system.

The above structure is common to most types of network management systems. SNMP is the preferred network management method with LANs, but many WANs still retain a proprietary network management system, and many common carriers use CMIP.

SIMPLE NETWORK MANAGEMENT PROTOCOL

SNMP is a protocol for the exchange of information or objects. SNMP is developed and maintained by the Internet Engineering Task Force. It was

FIGURE 37-2

Elements of a Network Management System

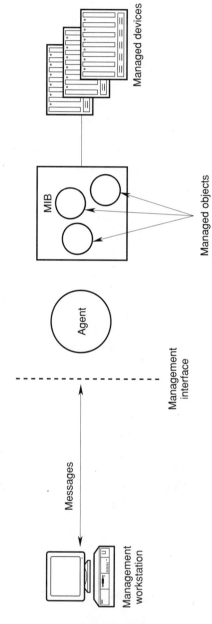

developed with the objective of being a fast and easy network management system to implement, and it has achieved that objective admirably. SNMP can perform the following operations:

◆ Identify devices
◆ Aggregate traffic measurement
◆ Control devices
◆ Detect unreachable devices

SNMP uses the user defined protocol (UDP) as its transport mechanism. UDP is a connectionless counterpart of TCP, either of which can be used as the transport mechanism for IP. Network management systems use two techniques for obtaining information from the managed devices: polling and interrupts. SNMP supports both methods. A management workstation polls agents for information that they have collected such as performance statistics and status information. Management agents wait to be polled in all cases except for messages known as *traps,* which they send in response to thresholds and events. A trap message might, for example, be the number of error packets during a specified interval. Trap messages are simple in many managed devices, which means the management workstation must poll to get the additional information needed to interpret the trap. Polling is one of the major drawbacks of SNMP. As the size of the network grows the amount of capacity devoted to polling overhead increases. The usual response is to increase the polling interval, which limits the timeliness of information.

A key issue in network management is fault correlation. When multiple alarms are received, the manager must determine which is the major fault, and which are sympathetic alarms that other devices initiate as a result of the major fault.

MIB-I from the first implementation of SNMP includes information such as the following:

◆ The number and type of interfaces the device has.
◆ The IP address of each interface.
◆ Packet and error counts.
◆ System description of the managed device.

SNMP's MIBs are defined in an English-like text using abstract system notation 1 (ASN.1) syntax. The MIB represents or describes the managed device, containing static information such as the vintage of the managed device, or dynamic information such as the number of packets handled. MIBs are defined with a minimum of computation. Computations are done at the management workstation where processing power resides. MIBs consist of basic information defined by the standard, plus proprietary extensions that most manufacturers add. These proprietary additions limit the management system's ability to collect and digest information in a multivendor network.

The SNMP protocol provides for five message types:

- *Get request* retrieves specific MIB objects.
- *Get response* sends the value of specific MIB objects in response to a get request.
- *Get next request* is used to traverse the MIB tree or to get the next sequential MIB object.
- *Set* allows the management workstation to modify a MIB object to a new value.
- *Trap* messages are sent from the managed device to the management workstation in response to some triggering event or threshold.

Figure 37–3 shows how the SNMP protocol operates. The managed device responds to commands from the network management station with a get response. When it needs to report an event in response to a trigger, it initiates a trap message to the workstation. Trap types include the following:

- *Cold start:* The device has done a complete reboot, which may result in reconfiguration.
- *Warm start:* The device has done a warm reboot, which retains the existing configuration.
- *Link down:* A link connected to the device is inoperative.
- *Link up:* A previously failed link has been restored.
- *Authentication failure:* A workstation attempting to communicate with the device has failed to authenticate itself properly.
- *EGP neighbor loss:* A device linked with the exterior gateway protocol has been lost.

The protocol uses an identifier called a *community string* in combination with IP addresses to authenticate set and get requests. The community string is not encrypted, and is easy to duplicate, which leaves SNMP vulnerable to security violations. Any management workstation could intercept messages, duplicate them, and use them to send its own messages to a managed device. The security weakness in the system is one of the chief weaknesses that led to the proposal of SNMP version 2.

Each managed device contains agent software. The agent receives commands from the network management system, executes the request, and returns a response. It may also initiate a trap message when an alarm or event occurs. A *proxy agent* is one that does not reside in the same system as that which holds

FIGURE 37–3

SNMP Command Protocol

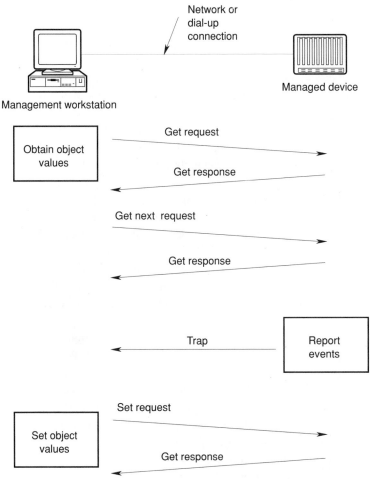

the MIB data. For example, a proxy agent can be configured to enable older non-SNMP devices to interface to an SNMP network management system. The proxy agent acts as a protocol translator to talk to the managed device and convert it to SNMP. Managers have an objective of managing the entire network from a single console, which may mean converting all devices on the WAN to SNMP. This can be done with proxy agents, but proxy agents often do not implement all the information in the proprietary protocol. Furthermore, proxy agents may not implement all the SNMP functions.

MIB-II

MIB-II was devised to augment and provide information that was omitted from MIB-I. It is organized into the following groups:

- The *system* group is required for every device. It includes basic system information that enables nodes to identify and describe themselves. A management station can poll a device to extract its system information.
- The *interfaces* group describes the configuration and status of any type of interface to the managed device. Interfaces could include any type of network such as frame relay, X.25, Ethernet, FDDI, ISDN, or any other network type. The MIB provides information about the status of the interface and pertinent data such as traffic statistics and error counts.
- The *address translation* group maps the IP address to the physical address of the managed device. A table may be created manually or by using a protocol such as address resolution protocol (ARP).
- The *internet* protocol group provides configuration and management information for hosts and routers. It contains such information as the default time-to-live counter by which misrouted IP datagrams are deleted. It includes IP routing, address translation, and forwarding tables. It also collects statistical information on IP traffic and errors.
- The *internet control message protocol (ICMP)* group provides information back to the source about unreachable destinations, redirected messages, time-out information, and invalid information in IP headers. ICMP provides special service requests and responses such as echo request that forms the ping function, which allows the workstation to determine the operational status of a device.
- The *transmission control protocol group* enables the workstation to detect TCP variables such as traffic and error statistics and TCP connection statistics. The group allows the network management station to view active TCP connections to see which applications are being accessed.
- The *user datagram protocol* group enables the management station to view UDP traffic statistics and to determine which UDP services are active.
- The *exterior gateway protocol* group provides information such as message counts and the identity of EGP neighbors.
- The *SNMP* group keeps count of SNMP variables such as the number of traps and get and set responses that occur.

Remote Monitoring MIB

RMON is an SNMP MIB that enables a network management workstation to monitor remote devices much in the same way a protocol analyzer would be used locally. The management workstation can communicate with RMON over TCP/IP to tabulate statistics in a flexible manner. Networks using protocols other than IP cannot use RMON. RMON allows probes installed on the LAN segment to collect as many as nine types of information:

1. *Statistics* measures such variables as numbers of packets, octets, broadcasts, collisions, errors, and distribution of packet sizes. These variables are accumulated since the start of the monitoring session.

2. *History* collects statistics based on user-defined sampling intervals.

3. *Host* discovers what hosts are active on the network and tracks statistics for each of them.

4. *Host Top N* selects the hosts that had the largest traffic or error counts based on statistics from the host group.

5. *Alarm* allows managers to set alarm thresholds based on absolute or delta values. Alarms trigger other actions through the events group.

6. *Events* operates with alarms to define an action that will be taken when the condition occurs. The event may write a log entry or send a trap message.

7. *Matrix* logs statistics by pairs of nodes.

8. *Filter* allows the manager to define the criteria that triggers an event.

9. *Capture* stores captured packet data for protocol analysis.

Although RMON is not quite as versatile as a local protocol analyzer (Chapter 36), it provides much more complete information than SNMP does by itself. Note, however, that RMON compliance does not mean that all nine categories are implemented, so it pays to inquire which categories a product supports.

SNMP Version 2

SNMP has numerous weaknesses that have led to proposals for SNMPv2. Chief among these is its rudimentary security provisions. The community string serves as a password in each protocol data unit. A hacker monitoring the network with a protocol analyzer would be able to intercept SNMP messages, determine the community string, and communicate with agents to wreak mischief. For example, a hacker might send a message to a mission-critical device such as a hub or router telling it to disable its ports or shut itself down. As a result, many network managers disable the set command to prevent malicious interference.

SNMPv2 introduces security measures, which also increase its complexity. The SNMPv2 message consists of an outer wrapper that contains security information. The community string gives way to a concept known as *parties,* which are any two elements that wish to communicate. The parties can communicate on a nonsecure basis, or they can use authentication, encryption, or both. Authentication is a protocol known as the digest authentication protocol. The source and destination computers compute a unique string of check digits to identify themselves.

Authentication validates messages, but they can still be intercepted. If the network manager wants completely secure communication, the protocol calls for encryption using the data encryption standard (DES).

The SNMPv2 inner protocol data unit supports the five original commands from SNMP Version 1, plus two new operations: inform-request, and get-bulk-request. Inform-request enables management workstations to pass information between themselves. Inform-request is similar to a trap message in that the network management workstation sends the message without being polled. Unlike trap messages, however, the receiving station responds with a confirmation so the sender can be certain the message was received. Inform-request messages can be more complex than the trap messages ordinary devices send. Since the management workstation has intelligence, it can receive, digest, and report complex events that may be summarization of many events sent from the managed devices.

A further deficiency with Version 1 is its inability to retrieve large blocks of data, such as a large router table, without multiple requests. If the agent is unable to respond to the entire get request, it responds with nothing. The get-bulk request enables the management workstation to retrieve a collection of variables; perhaps an entire table.

SNMPv2 adds several other enhancements. Here are some of the differences between Versions 1 and 2:

◆ The word "get" is dropped from responses. Instead of responding to a get request with "get response" the station simply returns "response."

◆ A manager-to-manager MIB is added to enable management workstations to exchange information.

◆ SNMP can be mapped to a variety of different transport protocols in addition to UDP.
◆ The data types in MIBs are expanded.
◆ MIB definitions allow the vendor to specify which of the MIB variables it supports.

A major problem with SNMPv2 is that to implement it all devices must be updated to the new version, which can be expensive if the upgrade is available, which it often is not. Second, the management workstations themselves must be updated to SNMPv2. Proxy agents can be used to translate between versions if they are available. Another alternative is to use a bilingual network management workstation that supports both SNMP 1 and 2.

Most manufacturers expand the standard MIB to include the controllable elements embedded in their equipment. When obtaining equipment from another vendor, the only functions available may be those in the standard MIB. Without a proxy agent the vendor-specific information may be lost. SNMPv2 was first proposed in 1993, but at the time of this writing it had not yet been adopted.

Desktop Management Interface

Another problem with SNMP is that it extends only to the network interface card, and not down to the level of the computer itself. DMI is a protocol from the Desktop Management Task Force that is designed to act as a management framework for PC products. The objective is to do for desktop systems what SNMP did for network devices. It provides an interface between desktop components such as application software and peripherals and SNMP agents.

Within the DMI structure is the management information format (MIF), which provides a format for tracking the following elements:

◆ Processor performance.
◆ Motherboard.
◆ Physical and logical memory.
◆ Basic input/output system (BIOS).
◆ Serial and parallel ports.

Application program interfaces translate information about the computer configuration and performance into a format that can be read by SNMP management workstations. Currently, few desktop devices support DMI, but in the future it should become an important tool for managers attempting to control a diverse network of computers and applications.

COMMON MANAGEMENT INFORMATION PROTOCOL

CMIP is the other contender for the title of a universal standard network management protocol, but like the contention between OSI and TCP/IP for the network architecture standard, it is losing out to SNMP. The principal reason is that while SNMP is alive and well and supported by nearly every manufacturer in North America, CMIP is bogged down in complexity, at least as far as non-common carrier networks are concerned. CMIP maps a MIB to each of the OSI layers, as Figure 37-4 shows.

The functions defined so far for CMIP far outstrip SNMP's limited functions. They include:

◆ Access control
◆ Accounting meter
◆ Alarm reporting
◆ Event reporting
◆ Log control
◆ Object management
◆ Relationship management
◆ Security audit trail
◆ Security-alarm reporting
◆ State management
◆ Summarization
◆ Test management
◆ Workload monitoring

Although its complexity has held its development back so far, CMIP is an international standard that will undoubtedly grow in the future. One factor that is expected to push CMIP into the mainstream is the expansion of ATM, which is too complex to be managed by a protocol as basic as SNMP. Some of the major advantages of CMIP over SNMP include the following:

◆ Unlike SNMP, which manages devices, CMIP manages relationships between devices.
◆ CMIP uses a connection-oriented transmission medium. With SNMP's datagram transmission method data can be lost without the sender being notified.
◆ CMIP has more comprehensive automatic event notification. It has a larger number of alarm indications.
◆ Polling is reduced or eliminated with CMIP.
◆ Improved event filtering reduces the number of event messages (corresponding to SNMP's traps) that are sent to the management workstation.

OSI Network Management

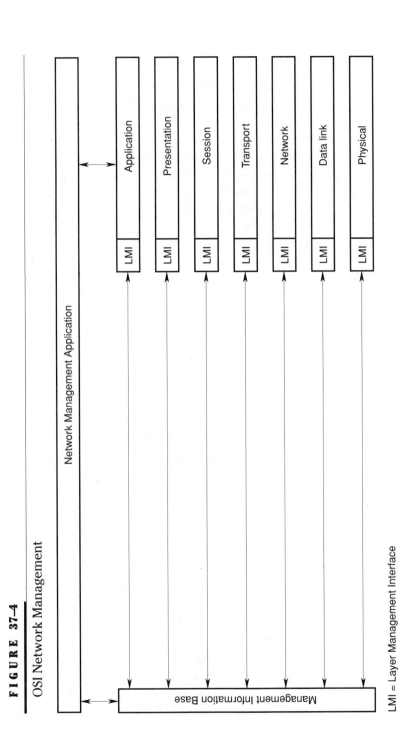

Network Management Application

Application

Presentation

Session

Transport

Network

Data link

Physical

LMI

LMI

LMI

LMI

LMI

LMI

LMI

Management Information Base

LMI = Layer Management Interface

CUSTOMER NETWORK MANAGEMENT

The major IECs are just beginning to offer CNM to their customers. CNM gives users the ability to access information on usage, accounting, fault, and performance on a near real-time basis. Through a CNM interface, customers can order new services and reconfigure existing ones in less time than it takes to order them through regular channels. Network managers can use the service to determine if their facilities are being used efficiently, and also to determine just what they have in the way of service. Without CNM, phone bills are about the only source of information on what services a company has. Extracting information on private lines, frame relay circuits, access circuits, and the like from bills is often a daunting task, and getting the information from the carrier is difficult. CNM enables the user to extract the information from the carrier's database without going through conventional channels.

CNM is a MIB that enables the service to work through network management systems. Some network management systems are available with a CNM interface, but the lack of standards may make it difficult to obtain the desired result immediately. The initial implementations of the service for most users will likely be through vendor-provided application software.

APPLICATIONS

Single-segment networks and networks that reside within a single building can be managed effectively without a network management system, but when these boundaries extend into other buildings and other cities, network management becomes vital. Ideally, managers would have a single system that manages the entire network from a single group of consoles, but that is rarely possible today except when all equipment is from a single manufacturer. Managers are faced with conflicting alternatives. Proprietary network management systems are available for proprietary networks, but they cannot be expanded to encompass LANs. Simple management systems are available for LANs, but they lack security, may overload the network with overhead traffic, and they are not easily extensible to proprietary WAN architectures. More secure and robust systems are becoming available, but these are not backward compatible with legacy equipment, and they increase the complexity and resources needed to manage the network.

Faced with these alternatives, most mangers will be forced to live with network management systems that are less than ideal for the next several years. As networks migrate into ATM, management will take on a different flavor than it has today, but the problems will not diminish. To minimize management difficulties today, the best approach is to obtain all equipment from a single vendor, or at least to require interoperability among the equipment you purchase. That too, however, is an ideal that few networks can realize in practice. As a result, network management will remain one of the major challenges that managers face.

Centralized versus Decentralized Network Management

Hard-and-fast rules about centralization or decentralization of a network management system cannot be stated. The benefits of centralization depend on the character of the network, the types of services being carried, the penalty for outages, the availability of trained people to administer the system at remote locations, and the nature of the organization that owns the network. If centralization can be justified, it is usually the most effective method of managing a network because diagnosing network trouble requires information that often can be analyzed more meaningfully from a central site. The people on the spot, however, are usually the best equipped to take corrective action when troubles occur. Some of the most complex networks in the world, the telephone networks, are administered locally with central sites monitoring traffic flow and dealing with congestion. The issue of centralization is one that must be dealt with as part of the fundamental network design and reexamined as new services and equipment make it feasible to change the basic plan.

A parallel issue to that of centralization is whether testing will be done manually or automatically. As networks gain intelligence, automatic testing becomes more the rule than the exception. The network must be large enough, however, to justify the cost of automatic testing before it can be considered. Equipment to do automatic tests is advancing rapidly, and network management strategies should be reexamined periodically in the light of new developments.

Multiple Vendor Issues

With the demise of the end-to-end service responsibility of the LECs, network users increasingly must obtain their equipment from multiple vendors. Although this offers opportunities for cost saving, it thrusts a much greater responsibility on the network manager to monitor service and develop techniques for dealing with multiple vendors. Compatibility problems become the user's responsibility—a responsibility that can be exercised best by preparing precise procurement requirements and specifications when acquiring equipment and services.

An allied issue is the degree of internal network management expertise that an organization develops. Although it is possible to turn the problem of network administration over to an outside contractor, to do so is to incur both a risk and an expense. The risk and the expense may be preferable to developing internal resources, but this is a decision that should be made only after an analysis of the alternative of developing internal staff.

Organizational Considerations

Many companies have not yet aligned their internal organizations with the realities of the new telecommunications networks. In many companies data-processing people administer the data network, and a separate staff administers the voice network. The information resource that both support may be managed by yet a third group. In the future the integration of voice and data networks is inevitable for most large organizations. Though the two may be separated at the source, bulk circuit procurement is more economical and flexible than obtaining individual circuits. When failures occur, a single organizational unit will be the most effective in dealing with the problems of restoring services and rerouting high-priority circuits over alternate facilities. In most organizations, the most effective structure will separate the information-generating entities from the information-transporting entities. As this is contrary to the way most companies are organized, this issue should be dealt with as the character of the network becomes more integrated.

Another issue that must be dealt with is flexibility of network planning. Changing tariffs and rates of long-haul carriers, access charges, and measured local service of local telephone companies make it essential that managers continually reexamine network plans. Plans should be flexible enough to enable the organization to react quickly as changes in tariffs and grades of service occur.

Standards

As discussed earlier, two standards, ISO's common management information protocol and the IETF's simple network management protocol, are the two major standards in existence today.

Evaluation Criteria

As networks grow increasingly complex, network management systems likewise grow in complexity. Also, as networks are continually changing, network management systems must have the flexibility to accommodate the growth and rearrangement of the network without becoming so complicated that only experts can administer them. Network management can be simplified by using computers, and as with any mechanized system the user interface is essential to keeping it understandable. The primary issues in evaluating a network management system are include the following.

Interoperability

Ideally, the system should operate with equipment from several different manufacturers. In practice, manufacturers include functions in their MIB implementations that may reduce interoperability with network management systems from other manufacturers to only basic functions.

Multiprotocol Support

The most effective systems are able to operate over the common transport protocols.

Security

The system should provide adequate security to prevent unauthorized persons from deactivating equipment, intercepting confidential information, duplicating commands, or other such potentially harmful functions.

Ease of Configuration

The administrator should be able to configure the key elements in the network from a management workstation. The workstation should be capable of performing all the desirable functions without requiring a visit to the managed device to set switches, check light status, and other items of status and configuration.

Scalability

As the network grows the management system should grow with it without overloading the network with additional management overhead traffic.

MIB Definitions

The management workstation should provide MIB definitions on demand.

Out-of-Band Management

In addition to in-band management, the system should be accessible over the dial network to aid in diagnosing and restoring troubles during circuit failure conditions.

Alarm Correlation

The system should aid the manager in determining which of multiple alarms is the primary fault, and which are sympathetic alarms. For example, a hardware alarm should be diagnosed as the cause of a group of circuit failures. The system should aid the operators in determining appropriate action for alleviating symptoms.

Manager-to-Manager Capability

The system should provide for management workstations to communicate with one another. Subordinate workstations should be able to summarize and condense information, and report it to workstations higher in the hierarchy.

Platform Performance

The platform on which the management workstation runs must be powerful enough to handle the volume of traffic and overhead. Microsoft Windows–based workstations are less powerful and the software is not as complete as that running on UNIX-based workstations with RISC processors.

Mapping Capability

The management workstation should be able to interrogate all devices on the network and compile a network map showing information such as IP addresses, system status, and alarms in color. The network layout records should be readily accessible and easily understood.

Output Data

The system should provide output data summarized and sorted for analysis or should provide a port to an external system to accomplish the same objective. A complete trouble and event log should be provided.

SELECTED NETWORK MANAGEMENT SYSTEMS MANUFACTURERS

Network Management Systems

AT&T
BM Networks
Cabletron
Cisco

Hewlett-Packard

IBM

Lucent Technologies

Network Managers

SNMP Research

Sunsoft

UB Networks

Unisys Corp.

Digital Equipment Corp.

Local Area Network Management Equipment

Armon Networking, Inc.

Axon Networks, Inc.

Hewlett-Packard Co.

IBM

Intel Corp.

Network Application Technology, Inc.

Network General Corp.

Novell

ON Technology

Racal-Datacom

Solcom Systems, Inc.

Wandel & Golterman Technologies, Inc.

CHAPTER

38

FUTURE DEVELOPMENTS IN TELECOMMUNICATIONS

Through the first hundred years of its history the shape of the North American telecommunications network changed at a snail's pace compared to today. Almon B. Strowger patented the first automatic switch in 1891, but 50 years later, at the opening of World War II, a large number of manual telephone exchanges remained. The war interrupted the conversion of the domestic telephone network to dial, and many manual exchanges still remained more than 20 years after the war's end, just when electronic switching was introduced. The first electronic central office was installed in 1965, and the transition away from electromechanical offices was more rapid, but still required nearly 30 years.

The invention of the vacuum tube made carrier telephony feasible, but it required the transistor and integrated circuitry to make digital telephony what it has become today. By contrast, fiber optics, one of the major enabling technologies, revolutionized transmission in less than a decade.

The future of telecommunications becomes more unpredictable with every passing year. In the decades before 1982 when AT&T controlled the nation's telecommunications, new developments originated in the laboratories. After a technologies were thoroughly proven, they were subjected to a long product development cycle and underwent lengthy field trials before reaching general use. Now, the telecommunications market is similar to the computer industry, where new products and services are introduced so rapidly that even the experts can't keep pace.

The future of telecommunications looks dazzling. Fueled by the same techniques that are expanding computer applications and bringing prices down, telecommunications and computers together are improving productivity and making applications possible that were only a dream a few years ago. Human ingenuity is boundless in its ability to examine the way people work and develop new applications to improve the process. The transition to new ways of doing things isn't always easy. We adapt certain methods and styles to work around the technical obstacles, and when the obstacles are removed some of the old ways persist.

Meetings are a good case in point. Technology is advancing to the point that face-to-face meetings could be eliminated. Groupware makes it possible for people linked by computers and networks to work jointly on projects. Desktop videoconferencing is on the verge of becoming inexpensive enough that even some of the nonverbal cues that a face-to-face meeting requires can be restored. Although the technology is available, the shift will be gradual as people adapt to new ways.

It is easy to look back and see the technologies that have driven these fundamental shifts. Local area networks and the personal computer have reshaped the office in ways that would have been difficult to predict two decades ago. Document quality and variety have risen as, not coincidentally, has the quantity. Internetworking devices have brought dispersed organizations together and sparked electronic mail as a way of enabling instant communication and document transfer. Facsimile has eliminated the need to wait for the mail to move important documents. We have reached the point that unless there is a compelling need for appearance, we fax documents instead of mailing them. Assisted by cheap long distance, facsimile is usually cheaper than the mail.

More of these fundamental forces are on the horizon. In fact, many of them are available today, but they have not yet made an impact. Broadband communications, exemplified by ATM, have been available for some time, but haven't affected more than a small segment of the workplace. It seems clear that the initial impact of ATM will be on data in the backbone network, and will extend to the desktop and to voice and video later. Less clear is the impact ATM will have on other technologies. FDDI-II seems destined to fall by the wayside, and SMDS may suffer a similar fate. It is clear that the applications driving the need for a broadband switched service are coming, and that ATM seems to have the momentum and support of enough major companies to ensure that it will play the enabling role.

Social as well as technical forces are extending the reach of the traditional office. Telecommuting is a growing trend and one that seems likely to continue as companies face mandates to help relieve traffic congestion. Telecommunications makes it possible for people to choose where they work and live, so at least in some occupations the fixed office environment may give way to a dispersed office, at least part of which is in the home. This, in turn, will drive the need for broadband facilities. As the carriers move fiber optics into residential areas, a trend that will presumably be driven by entertainment, facilities for broadband communication will become available although the cost is impossible to predict.

Predicting changes of the future telecommunications system is a risky proposition. No one can predict the rate of technological development, but several clear trends will shape the network of the future. Some of these are:

◆ Processor speeds will continue to increase, and prices will continue to drop, at least as measured by MIPs per dollar. This will spawn new applications in voice processing, multimedia, imaging, and other bandwidth-hungry services.

◆ Competition, which already has reshaped the network significantly, will continue to have an enormous impact. The local network is the current battleground with little to slow competition's progress.

◆ The future of regulation, which is competition's recourse, is in the hands of Congress and the courts, and the outcome is anything but certain. The 1996 telecommunications legislation will undoubtedly reshape the network as companies jockey for new positions.

◆ Broadband technologies, in particular asynchronous transfer mode, will be key in the next few years. They will emerge as the current technologies no longer provide the bandwidth and switching speed that new applications require.

◆ Telecommuting will gain in popularity for some occupations.

◆ Wireless technology will affect cellular service and will bring about new services as PCS providers begin to offer service.

◆ Voice recognition technology will advance, and with it new applications will assist companies in providing a higher quality of customer support.

The telecommunications industry is poised on the threshold of dramatic change that will reshape its services over the next few years. This chapter is more a projection than a prediction. In it, we will look at some of the fundamental forces reshaping the telecommunications industry and discuss the impact they are likely to have during the next few years. We are specifically excluding technologies such as photonic switching and superconductivity, which have yet to emerge from the laboratories and carve a niche for themselves.

MEETING BANDWIDTH DEMANDS

A big unknown in the future of telecommunications is how quickly ATM will develop; that it will develop seems beyond question. All of the major players are behind ATM as the future switching and multiplexing vehicle. They are not unanimous, however, as to whether the initial emphasis will be in the WAN or the LAN.

We believe the next spurt of LAN growth will use one of the fast Ethernet technologies, which will further widen the gap between LAN and WAN bandwidths. Although the carriers have plenty of backbone capacity and the ability to expand it inexpensively, end user rates are still high. The expansion of distributed processing and the need to link LANs at ever increasing speeds means companies need more bandwidth in their backbone networks. Fixed-bandwidth facilities such as T-1 and T-3 provide excess capacity some of the time and insufficient capacity at other times. Major companies will begin using private ATM switches to improve utilization of their backbone networks, and public ATM services where they are cost-effective. The large IECs will begin to migrate their circuit-switched networks onto ATM, but the conventional circuit-switched network will still be clearly in evidence well into the 21st century.

Unlike the middle of the 20th century when advances into electronic switching were fueled by a demand-pull environment, ATM switching in the closing years of the century is in a technology-push situation. Except for common carriers and a few organizations that need the vast amount of bandwidth that ATM offers, most current applications are satisfied by the conventional fixed-bandwidth network. The situation is not like LAN development in the early 1980s. At the time IEEE began work on 802 standards, the IBM PC had not been introduced. LAN development followed slowly, but once it caught on, demand soared. Something similar is likely to happen to ATM.

Pricing is a key and largely unresolved issue with ATM. The various classes of carriers, LECs, IECs, AACs, and CATV companies, have invested huge sums in fiber-optic facilities. Most major customers in the United States can be served directly by SONET-based fiber optics, which is the ideal transport medium for ATM. Increasingly, fiber-optic facilities are being extended into residential areas, where the driving application is assumed to be video on demand. With video justifying the need for bandwidth into the subscriber's home, a plethora of other services becomes possible, including the LECs' cash cow, local dial tone service. As competition ramps up in the local service arena, prices of basic telephone service are likely to drop. With ATM, a local telephone call is technically no different than video on demand, except that it needs much less bandwidth. The vast difference in the number of bytes of a video session compared to a telephone call lies at the heart of the pricing complexity as discussed in the next section.

VIDEO ON DEMAND

Video on demand is the service that many observers believe will justify the cost of extending fiber optics to the residence. To make VOD work, some form of switching is needed. Most plans assume ATM will be the switching medium. The use of ATM raises some interesting economic questions. If VOD is to compete with other entertainment alternatives that subscribers have, it obviously must be cost-effective. To illustrate, assume that the cost of renting a video tape of a first-run movie, including the cost and inconvenience of picking it up and returning it, is five dollars. Whatever the cost, it establishes a threshold that consumers will be willing to pay for VOD.

Assume that a digitized movie runs two hours, and that its effective bit rate is 1.5 mb/s. In the course of the movie, 10.8 gigabits will have been transmitted at an effective cost of 0.05 cents per megabit. By contrast, if voice can be digitized at 10 kb/s, and a long-distance call costs 10 cents per minute, the effective cost per megabit is 17 cents. One characteristic of ATM is that bits are carried indiscriminately. The technology doesn't know or care whether voice, data, or video is being transferred. If the subscriber's video converter can also handle voice and data, which is a trivial technical challenge, the cost of those services will drop to a fraction of their present level.

If VOD is to survive, it must be cost-effective, but making it cost-effective has the effect of driving down the costs of other types of switched services. This is good news for consumers, but it cuts deeply into the revenues of companies that have built their businesses on today's prices. Of course, regulation can keep the prices of telephone and data calls high, but that means suppressing competition, which is contrary to current trends.

The technical challenges of ATM are speeding toward solution, but it may turn out that the greater challenges are political and economic. ATM isn't intended as a replacement for the public switched telephone network, but as voice, video, and data become inextricably mixed at the source, the replacement is inevitable in the long run. The result will likely be dramatic realignment in the pricing of services.

EFFECTS OF COMPETITION

For decades, the local network was visualized as a utility like the water system. It was against public interest, the theory went, for more than one LEC to serve an area because the duplication of facilities raised the cost of providing service and placed an undue burden on the public rights of way. That theory may still hold in some parts of the world, but it is discredited in the United States. Most urban homes have, or easily could have, two entrances now: telephone and CATV. The two have been restrained by regulation from trodding on each other's territory, but with the passage of the Communications Act of 1996, those restraints have been lifted, and the boundaries will dissolve. Some technical obstacles such as local number portability remain, but these can be solved by more computer power, although at what cost is unclear. Just as 800 portability was a major issue in the past, local number portability is a current issue, the solution to which will affect the shape of the local network.

The shape of the local architecture is also unclear, although there can be little doubt that it will eventually evolve into fiber-optic transmission of voice, video, entertainment services, games, and a plethora of other services that consumers will purchase if they can be made affordable.

LECs and CATV operators are not the only players in the local exchange market. Companies such as AT&T, MCI, and Sprint have invested heavily in PCS and have made it clear that they intend to compete for local exchange business. The result, for the local exchange customer, can be only good. Local rates have been pumped artificially high by lack of a feasible alternative. As the alternatives develop, rates are bound to decrease, and both the quality and diversity of services will improve.

Mergers and alliances can also be expected to reshape the local network. Nothing in the 1982 consent decree prohibits the ex-Bell LECs from merging, and at this writing, two pairs of them have announced their plans. Southwestern Bell Corp. will mege with Pacific Bell, and Bell Atlantic with Nynex. The next few years may see mergers among more of the seven regional companies and the independents, with cable companies thrown in to boot.

The alternate access carriers also present potential competition, not only for transport services but also for switching in the local exchange network. Their current networks now cover areas of heavy business concentration, but in combination with other players or by themselves, they will help reshape the local network.

High-definition television and "video dial tone" are related issues that affect the shape of the local network. Cable companies will begin to offer exchange services in some areas, and as competition heats up the LECs will offer video services. The result is likely to be a broadband pipe into many homes in affluent, urban neighborhoods. This raises numerous issues such as who will serve the less affluent neighborhoods and rural areas, and how basic telephone service can be kept affordable. PCS is a potential solution, but it is unlikely to reach the low-profit areas or be less expensive than wired telephone service. In fact, consumers can expect to pay more for PCS calls for the convenience of number portability.

PBX ARCHITECTURES

Many industry observers have been predicting the death of PBX for the last several years, but it still shows every sign of vitality. There is little doubt that the PBX as we know it will evolve significantly in the next few years, at least in some manufacturers' product lines. A station instrument may lose features with the intelligence transferred to the desktop computer. This move can enhance its usefulness, since hardly anyone knows how to use all the features of a proprietary telephone anyway. As features such as desktop conferencing migrate to the computer, the telephone may merely be a handset attachment in an interface card. Switching functions may move to ATM, or be assigned to servers that reside on the same network as the stations. Several manufacturers are working on a switching system that consists of multiple, specialized servers linked by a high-speed LAN. This architecture can support multimedia more effectively than the present fixed-bandwidth digital interface ports.

The architecture of the PBX may change over the next several years, but the traditional circuit-switched PBX will survive well beyond the turn of the century. Many applications require nothing more than voice communication and will not change at any time soon. Hospital patient rooms, guest rooms in all but the upscale hotels, student rooms in universities, public-area telephones in most companies, and dozens of other applications are used for placing only voice calls. The only thing that would propel a transition to a LAN-based switching architecture would be a cost advantage, which is not predictable in the near term.

Computer telephony integration will offload many of the functions of the PBX to outboard processors. Initiatives by major manufacturers such as Microsoft and Novell are leading numerous developers to produce CTI products. Although the quantity of applications won't equal the flood of software products inspired by inexpensive desktop computers, the facts remain that everyone has a telephone and the user interface is deficient. The next few years should bring hundreds of new CTI products, not just for call centers but also for PBXs, key systems, and ordinary telephones. Will the products be a computer with a telephone inside, or a telephone with a computer inside? We can expect both kinds of products.

CTI will also augment the call center. Functions that are considered leading edge today will become commonplace tomorrow. Screen pop is just the beginning of CTI applications for the call center. Personalized treatment for callers will be enhanced by caller recognition and call routing based on callers' personal preferences. Voice-processing adjuncts, including speech recognition, will aid the call center in determining who the callers are and what they want. Computers will also assist callers in fulfilling their requests without human assistance.

SPEECH RECOGNITION

Speech recognition is apt to have a significant effect on the way companies do business over the next few years. Faster computers, better operating systems, and better voice recognition algorithms are moving this technology ahead at a rapid pace. Some applications such as the voice-driven word processor will have more to do with personal productivity and working styles than with telecommunications. Affecting telecommunications, however, will be major changes in automated attendants and the possibility of replacing many conventional console attendant duties by enabling callers to access the company directory and transfer to extensions by voice command. Many such products are available today. The results aren't flawless, but the potential demand for future products is enormous.

Today's DTMF keypad is a poor substitute for a keyboard. It is slow, limited in scope of coverage, and requires eye contact for its operation. Speech recognition overcomes all of these difficulties and can make the telephone (or microphone) a universal input device. The ability to convert speech to text enables the universal mailbox, which allows an unrestricted exchange among E-mail, voice mail, and facsimile messages. Telephone operator and console attendant functions will be revolutionized. The challenge managers face is in preventing the functions from being objectionably dehumanized.

When systems reach the point of recognizing a large vocabulary from a wide variety of speakers, numerous applications will be possible. Applications that can have a large effect on telecommunications include:

- ◆ Automated attendant replacement.
- ◆ Replacement of directory operators.
- ◆ Voice-driven commands to perform operations such as conferencing, outdialing, transferring, and so on.

WIRELESS

The radio spectrum is a marvelous and underutilized resource. Technologists are discovering how to cram an increasing amount of information into a limited amount of spectrum. This enables more efficient user of cellular frequencies, and equally important, enables personal communications service (PCS) to develop. Wireless also enables the mobile data terminal, which solves numerous problems such as portable and desktop calendars that are often out of sync, and the ability to retrieve a file without the worry of cabling, ports, and protocols. It solves some of the problems of connecting workstation users to LANs, particularly in buildings that are difficult to wire.

Wireless PBX stations will likely have a significant impact in the future. Many people such as health care workers, retailers, manufacturing personnel, and others who work on their feet most of the day have learned to work around the confines of the telephone cord. Wireless will change the working styles and probably improve the productivity of such people.

Wireless data can have similar effect on workers. The keyboard-equipped mobile data terminal has application in law enforcement, dispatch operations, and any class of workers who carry a laptop to meetings. The wireless personal digital assistant will have a large impact on working styles and productivity if the service is cost-effective.

The transition from wired to wireless will not happen overnight, and many years will pass before copper wires are eliminated, if they ever are. Being tied to a telephone cord doesn't matter for many people, but for those who must roam, the implications of wireless are important. Professions such as medicine, retail, education, construction, and other occupations that are currently able to receive calls only in fixed locations that they may occupy for short intervals during the day will be changed by easy portability. Whatever form it takes, PCS will have a significant impact on the way we work and live. Whether the change is a convenience or an intrusion will depend on how the cultures of those professions adapt.

PCS may someday achieve the objective of the universal portable telephone number. It may make location irrelevant in placing and receiving calls. At issue, however, is the digital encoding algorithm that PCS will use. Incompatible CDMA and TDMA systems may give rise to separate PCS networks, which may detract from the anytime, anywhere objective. Also yet to be determined is the impact of low earth orbiting satellite PCS systems.

Even deskbound occupations may change. Leisure time may take on a new complexion if communication portability is so easy that it becomes expected. Without doubt, as PCS emerges, our culture will change in ways that we do not yet understand.

Affordability issues aside, wireless is apt to play an important role in future communications. Cellular has demonstrated that users are willing to pay for the convenience of mobile telephone service. Cellular so far has not introduced any innovative services (as distinguished from the technology, which is extremely innovative.) In fact, cellular is plain old telephone service without wires. PCS may become cellular roaming without the difficulties, but the government-mandated competition in PCS may lead to value-enhancing services that surpass what is available with wired telephone service, including ISDN today.

LONG-DISTANCE TRENDS

The future in domestic long-distance service looks bright for large and small users alike. International long-distance costs are improving, but the gap between domestic and international cost is widening. The most important trend in long distance is the fact that distance is becoming irrelevant. Many domestic pricing plans offer a flat-rate cost for interstate long distance. Often, cross-country calls cost less than intrastate calls to a neighboring city.

Another favorable trend is the deregulation of intrastate calls by state utility commissions. State rules that reserved intrastate calls to the LEC are gradually being eliminated, leading the LECs to offer competitive pricing plans. As the LECs venture into interLATA long distance, pricing distinctions between inter- and intrastate calls will disappear. The anomalies of the past that resulted in higher intrastate pricing were not cost based; they resulted from state regulators' attempts to subsidize local rates by pushing long distance rates artificially high. As competition increases in the local network, these conditions will disappear.

International costs remain high despite the fact that fiber-optic transmission facilities have reduced the carriers' costs. Much of the reason lies in the noncompetitive nature of the telecommunications market in most countries. Several sources, however, are acting to push international costs down. The first is privatization of the telecommunications network in many first-world countries. Governments are gradually realizing that their antiquated regulations harm their economic development efforts vis-à-vis other countries.

A second force driving rates down is the competitively charged atmosphere in the United States. The imbalance between costs of calls originating in the United States compared to the same route originating in other countries has spawned a new international dial-back service. Users all over the world are discovering that it is often cheaper to place a call to the United States, where a dial-back service connects calls to both the calling and called parties at a cost lower than users would pay for a direct connection. The dial-back industry will not survive indefinitely, but it performs a valuable service in helping to drive international calling costs down to a level more commensurate with the cost of providing the service.

ISDN

For years, ISDN has been the wild card in telecommunications. The LECs have taken a toe-in-the-water approach to providing ISDN, but it seems finally to have carved a niche for itself. In all likelihood, ISDN will remain a niche player for the next several years. The vast majority of telephone systems in use today are not ISDN-compatible, and cannot be made so. Of those that can be upgraded, the cost often outweighs the benefits.

In ISDN's favor are the many software developers who are creating new applications that use ISDN's features. As attractive as many of these are, most small businesses and residences cannot justify the cost. Therefore, conversion to ISDN will wait for the normal system replacement cycle, which typically has an interval of 5 to 10 years. As systems are replaced, many companies will require ISDN compatibility, but the transition time is likely to be long. Even companies who need ISDN for an application such as videoconferencing can satisfy the requirement with individual ISDN lines that do not go through the existing switch.

Access to Internet and other information service providers can be an interesting application for ISDN and will contribute to its growth. In many locations, however, frame relay offered by the LEC is a feasible alternative for accessing the service provider.

ISDN has always suffered from three fatal flaws: cost, the lack of a compelling application, and the lack of universal connectivity. In some LECs the monthly cost issue has been resolved in favor of ISDN, but in others it demands a premium. In LECs where the cost of ISDN is higher than analog services, ISDN will continue to languish. In LECs where it is lower, it should gain a respectable market share, although the terminal equipment cost remains high.

The second drawback, the lack of a driving application, is gradually being resolved, but most users are surviving nicely with analog service. Desktop videoconferencing is likely to become the application that will inspire the service's future growth.

The third issue, lack of universal connectivity, is likely to remain as an impediment for years to come. Users cannot complete an end-to-end digital call without specific knowledge of the terminating end's capabilities. This limits ISDN to fulfilling specific functions, while the majority of users stay with analog service.

In the interexchange network ISDN is a viable service for large companies. Such companies tend to have applications such as desktop video that need the connectivity and call-by-call service selection that ISDN offers. ISDN is also valuable in call centers for call routing and caller identification.

Over the next few years ISDN should increase in popularity, but it will remain far short of the universal acceptance enjoyed by analog telephone service. Eventually, the companies that today gain the most from its application may migrate away from ISDN to broadband services as they become more readily available.

VIDEOCONFERENCING

Videoconferencing is an excellent example of the convergence of computers and communications. The increase in computer processing power and the attendant reduced costs, plus improved and economical communications facilities, are driving video from a narrowly restricted conference room application to the desktop. As prices drop, the use of video will become more common. Just as facsimile evolved from a range of applications to becoming a mainstream utility, something similar will happen to videoconferencing. With it will come a host of cultural and technological changes.

INTERNET

The long-predicted merger of telecommunications and the computer is becoming a reality. Nowhere is it better illustrated than the Internet, which has leapt into public consciousness over the past few years. Where communicating ends and computing begins is irrelevant to users. They are concerned only with the ability to access information wherever it resides, and to communicate with others effortlessly, with the network making distance and protocol irrelevant.

The Internet has emerged in the last few years as one of the major forces shaping telecommunications. The momentum behind Internet will ensure its role for the future. Many key issues remain to be solved. Among them are funding, security, control of objectionable and obscene matter, and the impact of high-bandwidth applications such as voice messages and video clips. The original concept of the Internet as a means of open information interchange among government, universities, and contractors has been swamped by the deluge of the World Wide Web. Access to the Internet is viewed as a right in many businesses. It is also becoming essential for businesses in keeping in touch with their publics and customers. All of this leads to increased demand for bandwidth. Dial-up access is suitable for SOHO (small office/home office), but larger businesses need direct connectivity, which inevitably leads to security problems.

The so-called information superhighway has received considerable publicity from the government. Many states and municipalities are undertaking ISH studies or building networks. The relationship between Internet and ISH is unclear. It is also unclear whether ISH will be publicly owned and funded, what shape it will take, or even whether it will ultimately evolve as anything more than separate, loosely interconnected networks. It is clear that Internet will continue to thrive because it has been a source of both business utility and entertainment. Any company that is developing network plans must include provision for Internet connectivity.

A P P E N D I X   A

Principles of Electricity Applied to Telecommunications

Although it is possible to gain an appreciation of telecommunications with little or no technical background, the technology is based on the applied science of electronics. Without some understanding of the principles, the reader is apt to be confused by some concepts. A complete understanding of communications technology cannot be developed without understanding the mathematics involved, some of it complex. A working knowledge of the concepts presented in this book, however, can be gained with no more than elementary mathematics and some fundamental principles of electrical theory. For those readers who lack understanding of electricity, this appendix is an overview of the basic principles of electricity as used in telephony. This appendix also explains most of the terminology used in basic electricity. An understanding of the terminology begins with the units of measure. These are multiplied or divided by factors ranging from one to one billion. For those who are unfamiliar with electrical units, Table A–1 lists the ones most frequently encountered.

ELECTRICITY AND MAGNETISM

The characteristics of permanent magnets are familiar to all who have experimented with magnetized iron bars. In their natural state, electrons in ferrous metals array themselves in disorderly patterns and have no attracting force. When the material is magnetized the electrons align themselves neatly, creating the power to attract and repel other elements. The opposite ends of magnetized material are called its *poles.* Anyone who has experimented with magnets knows that like poles repel and opposite poles attract, and that either pole attracts some metals, but not others. Metals such as iron and its alloys exhibit strong magnetic properties while others such as copper and aluminum cannot be magnetized.

Relays and Solenoids

Permanently magnetized materials have application in telecommunications; for example, loudspeakers and the receiver in an ordinary telephone set contain permanent magnets. A more important application of magnetism in telecommunications is the *electromagnet,* a device that becomes magnetized when ex-

TABLE A-1

Common Units of Electrical Measurements

	Prefix	Abbreviation	Frequency	Power	Current	Resistance	Voltage	Other	Data
1×10^{12}	Tera	t	Terahertz						Terabit
1×10^9	Giga	g	Gigahertz (gHz)						Gigabit (gb)
1×10^6	Mega	Meg or M	Megahertz (mHz)	Megawatt		Megohm	Megavolt		Megabit
1×10^3	Kilo	K	Kilohertz (kHz)	Kilowatt (kw)		Kilohm	Kilovolt		Kilobit (kb)
1			Hertz (Hz)	Watt (w)	Ampere (amp or a)	Ohm (Ω)	Volt (v)		bit
1/10	Deci	d						Decibel (dB)	
$1/10^{-3}$	Milli	m		Milliwatt (mw)	Milliamp (ma)	Milliohm (mΩ)	Millivolt (mv)		
$1/10^{-6}$	Micro	μ		Microwatt (μw)	Microamp (μa)		Microvolt (μv)	Microfarad Microhenry	
$1/10^{-9}$	Pico	p					Picovolt (pv)	Picofarad	

FIGURE A–1

Schematic Diagram of a Relay

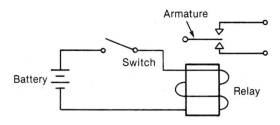

ternal current is applied, and nonmagnetized when it is removed. The switches in electromechanical telephone central offices use this principle. Although solid-state electronic circuits have replaced relays in most telecommunications apparatus, relays remain in service in electrical equipment from automobiles to power substations, and are important to understanding telecommunications.

A relay is shown schematically in Figure A–1. When the coil surrounding the relay's core is energized by closing a switch to the battery, the core attracts the armature, and the movement closes or opens contacts. Relays control large electric currents with a small current flowing through the winding. For example, the starter solenoid in an automobile allows the ignition switch, which is a low-current device, to control the large amount of current needed to connect the starter to the battery. Relays often are made with multiple sets of contacts so that a single source can control current to multiple paths. A relay is a binary device; that is, its coil and contacts are either open or closed, corresponding to the zeros and ones of logic circuitry. These principles are used in chaining relays to form logic circuits in electromechanical central offices.

Electric Current and Voltage

When an electric source is applied to a circuit by closing a switch, *current* begins to flow. A circuit is composed of three variables, current, *voltage,* and *resistance.*

- ◆ Current is the quantity of electricity flowing in a circuit. The unit of current is the *ampere* or "amp." Its symbol in circuits and formulas is I.
- ◆ Voltage (sometimes called electromagnetic force, or EMF) is the pressure forcing current to flow. The unit of voltage is the *volt.* Its symbol is E.
- ◆ Resistance is the opposition to flow of current. The unit of resistance is the *ohm.* Its symbol is R.

F I G U R E   A–2

Current Flow in a Resistive Circuit

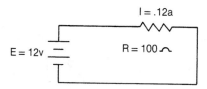

These three variables are interrelated by Ohm's law, which states that the amount of current flowing in an electric circuit is directly proportional to the voltage and inversely proportional to the resistance. Stated as a formula, Ohm's law is:

$$I = \frac{E}{R}$$

This simple formula is the basis for understanding much about the behavior of electricity. To illustrate with a simple example, assume the circuit in Figure A–2. A 12-volt battery such as that used in automobiles is feeding current to a 100-ohm resistance such as a light bulb. In this circuit, 12 volts/100 ohms, or 120 milliamps of current flows.

Power

Because current and voltage are inversely related and may vary with changing circuit conditions, neither is an adequate measure of the power consumed. The power in a circuit is the product of the current and voltage, and is measured in *watts*. For example, the circuit in Figure A–2 consumes 12 volts × .12 amps = 1.44 watts of power. The measurement of power usually is combined with the length of time the current flows, and is expressed in kilowatt hours (abbreviated KWH). One KWH is equal to 1,000 watts of power being supplied for one hour.

The Decibel

The power in telecommunications circuits is so low that it is usually measured in milliwatts. The milliwatt is an effective way of expressing how much power is supplied to a circuit, but it is not a convenient way to express differences in power between circuits or between two points on the same circuit. Voice frequency circuits are designed around the human ear, which has a logarithmic

FIGURE A–3

Chart of Power and Voltage Ratios versus Decibels

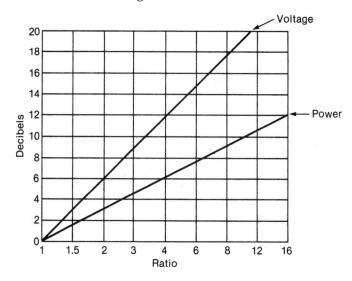

response to changes in power. In telephony the *decibel* (dB), which is a logarithmic rather than a linear measurement, is used as a measure of relative power between circuits or transmission level points. A change in level of 1 dB is barely perceptible under ideal conditions. The value of dB corresponding to a power ratio is expressed as:

$$dB = 10 \log \frac{P_2}{P_1}$$

The dB also can express voltage and current ratios if the impedance, which will be discussed in a later section, is the same for both values of voltage or current. The dB ratio between voltage and current is:

$$dB = 20 \log \frac{V_2}{V_1}$$

$$dB = 20 \log \frac{I_2}{I_1}$$

Figure A–3 is a chart showing the ratios between power, voltage, and current plotted as a function of decibels. Note that the horizontal scale is logarithmic. Also note that increases or reductions of 3 dB results in doubling or halving the power in a circuit. This ratio is handy to remember when evaluating power differences. The corresponding figure for doubling or halving voltage and current is 6 dB.

FIGURE A–4

Series and Parallel Resistance

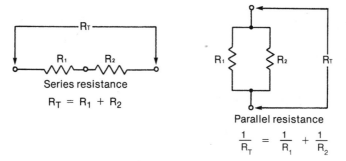

Series resistance
$$R_T = R_1 + R_2$$

Parallel resistance
$$\frac{1}{R_T} = \frac{1}{R_1} + \frac{1}{R_2}$$

Series and Parallel Resistance

Figure A–4 shows resistors connected in series and parallel. In a series circuit the total resistance is the sum of the values of the individual resistors. In a parallel circuit current divides between the resistors. If the resistors are of equal value the current divides equally; if they are unequal a greater current flows through the smaller resistance.

The formula for calculating the total resistance of series resistors is:

$$R_T = R_1 + R_2 + R_3 \ \cdot \ \cdot \ \cdot$$

The formula for calculating the total resistance of parallel resistors is

$$R_T = \frac{1}{R_1} + \frac{1}{R_2} + \frac{1}{R_3} \ \cdot \ \cdot \ \cdot$$

DIRECT AND ALTERNATING CURRENT

So far we have been discussing only the flow of direct current (DC) in a circuit. In a DC circuit the source or battery supplies voltage with fixed *polarity*. The polarity in a battery corresponds to the poles in an electromagnet, and is designated as positive (+) or negative (-). All telecommunications apparatus is powered by a DC source. However, the signals it carries and the power source that charges its batteries or powers its converters come from commercial alternating current (AC).

The polarity from an AC source is constantly reversing. If voltage is measured against time the result is a *sine wave,* as in Figure A–5. The sine wave is so named because it describes the shape of the wave that results from plotting the sine of the angles from 0 to 360 degrees.

FIGURE A–5

Alternating Current Sine Wave

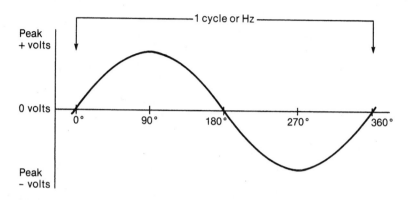

TABLE A–2

Frequencies and Wavelengths of Radio Frequencies

Frequency	Wavelength (Meters)	Frequency Class	Abbreviation
30 kHz	10,000	Very low	VLF
300 kHz	1,000	Low	LF
3,000 kHz	100	Medium	MF
30 mHz	10	High	HF
300 mHz	1	Very high	VHF
3,000 mHz	0.1	Ultra high	UHF
30,000 mHz	0.01	Super high	SHF

In AC circuit analysis, we are concerned not only with the magnitude or voltage of the source, but also with the *frequency* of its reversals. A complete cycle carries the voltage from its zero starting point through one cycle to peak positive, back through zero to peak negative, and back to zero again. The unit of measurement is the Hertz (Hz). One Hz is equivalent to one cycle. The distance between corresponding points on a cycle is called its *wavelength,* which is inversely proportional to frequency. Table A–2 shows the frequency and corresponding wavelengths of the radio frequency spectrum.

Another property of AC is *phase,* which describes the relationship between the zero-crossing points of signals. Figure A–6 shows two voltages that are 90 degrees out of phase with each other. Phase is measured in degrees, as

FIGURE A-6

Phase Relationship between Two Sine Waves

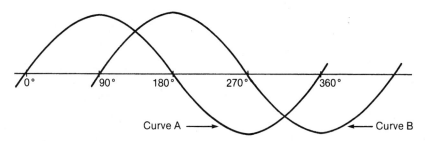

illustrated in the figure. A full cycle describes a 360 degree arc. The two signals shown are out of phase, with Curve B lagging Curve A by 90 degrees.

AC follows Ohm's law in a circuit composed only of resistance. Because the voltage in an AC circuit varies continually, the current flow in such a circuit is proportional to the *root mean square* (RMS) voltage, which is .707 of the peak voltage. RMS voltage is normally used in describing AC; for example, the 120 volts of electric house current actually has a peak value of 170 volts.

A sine wave has a single fundamental frequency. Voice signals, on the other hand, are a complex composite of several fundamental tones rapidly varying in both frequency and amplitude. Because of the limited passband of a voice frequency telecommunications channel, higher and lower frequencies are cut off, but enough frequencies remain to ensure intelligibility. A digital signal, however, is not a sine wave. Instead, it takes the shape of a square wave, as in Figure A–7.

If a square wave is examined, it is found to consist of a fundamental frequency and numerous *harmonics,* which are multiples of the fundamental frequency. Figure A–7 shows the derivation of a square wave from the fundamental frequency and its harmonics. The harmonics consist of high frequency components, many of which are filtered out by a telephone channel. As Figure A–8 shows, the attenuation in a cable pair is generally limited, but as loading is applied, as described in Chapter 2, the cutoff frequency becomes sharper. The filters in amplifiers and multiplex equipment are sharper yet, approximating the curve shown in Figure A–9.

When a square wave signal passes through a voice channel, the high-frequency components are filtered out. The signal is reduced to its fundamental frequency and is shaped like a sine wave. The degree of filtering in a voice channel is in direct proportion to the frequency of the square wave (or speed of

FIGURE A-7

Derivation of a Square Wave from Its Harmonics

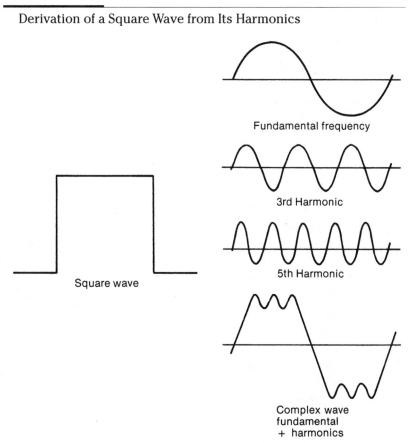

Fundamental frequency

3rd Harmonic

5th Harmonic

Square wave

Complex wave
fundamental
+ harmonics

a data signal), and the distance the signal travels. This filtering effect makes it necessary to use modems to pass data signals over voice frequency channels.

INDUCTANCE AND CAPACITANCE

All circuits also contain two more variables: capacitance, which is the property of storage of an electric charge, and inductance, which is the property of an electric force field built up around a conductor. Although inductance and capacitance are present in all circuits, their effects are slight in many circuits and can be ignored. In other circuits, however, they are introduced deliberately to produce an intended effect.

FIGURE A-8

Frequency Response of Loaded and Nonloaded Voice Cable

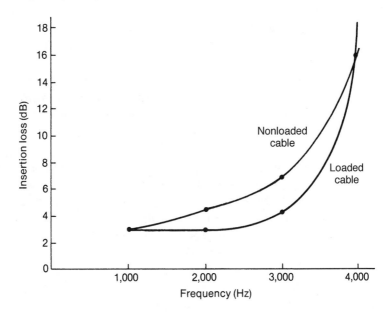

FIGURE A-9

Frequency Response of a Typical Telephone Channel

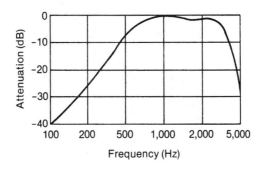

Capacitance

The capacitance effect occurs when two plates of conducting material are separated by an insulator called a *dielectric.* Common dielectrics are air, mica, ceramics, and plastics. Capacitance has the property of blocking the flow of DC, but permitting some AC to flow. Capacitors are constructed with fixed values or with movable plates so the amount of capacitance is variable.

The unit of capacitance is the *farad,* although the farad is so large that capacitors used in telecommunications equipment are measured in microfarads or picofarads. The amount of capacitance is proportional to the amount of area of the conducting plates and the insulating properties or *dielectric constant* of the insulator.

AC does not flow through a capacitor without some opposition, called the *reactance* of a capacitor. For a capacitor of a given size, its reactance is inversely proportional to the AC frequency of the current flowing in the circuit. Capacitors are used in any electronic circuit where it is desirable to block the flow of DC while permitting the flow of AC, or to permit higher frequencies to pass while attenuating lower frequencies.

Of great pertinence to telecommunications is the fact that capacitance occurs naturally whenever two conductors parallel one another. The capacitance effect occurs in a cable pair where the two wires form the plates of a capacitor and the insulation forms the dielectric. In a voice frequency circuit, some current flows between the two wires, attenuating the higher frequencies more than the low. The capacitance effect causes the shoulders of a square wave to become rounded as the high-frequency components are attenuated.

When capacitors are connected in parallel, the effect is directly additive. For example, if two 1.0 mf capacitors are connected in parallel, the resulting capacitance is 2.0 mf. When they are connected in series, the total capacitance is reduced. The formula for calculating the total capacitance of capacitors connected in series is

$$C_T = C_1 + C_2 + C_3 \ . \ . \ .$$

The formula for calculating the total capacitance of parallel capacitors is

$$C_T = \frac{1}{C_1} + \frac{1}{C_2} + \frac{1}{C_3} \ . \ . \ .$$

Inductance

An *inductor* is formed by winding a conductor into a coil. The amount of inductance is a function of the number of turns, the length and diameter of the coil, and the material used in the core of the coil. Many coils are wound with air cores, but the inductance of an air core coil can be increased by using magnetic material such as iron for its core. Inductors made with a moveable core inside the winding have a variable amount of inductance.

When current flows through a wire, lines of force are built up around the wire. The field created by DC current is steady and unvarying, but when AC flows through a wire, the lines of force are constantly building up and collapsing. These lines of force impede the flow of AC. The effect of inductance on current flow is the opposite of the effects of capacitance: The flow of AC is impeded by an inductor, while DC passes with little effect. The unit of inductance is the *henry,* or in smaller coils, the millihenry or microhenry. The higher the frequency of an AC signal, the higher the *inductive reactance* of the coil.

The paralleling wires of a cable pair present some inductive reactance, but the effect is outweighed by the much greater effects of capacitive reactance. To counter capacitive reactance, inductance is often deliberately introduced into telephone circuits. For example, inductors known as *load coils* are connected in series with the two wires of long subscriber loops to counteract the effects of capacitive reactance and reduce the loss of the loop, as shown in Figure A–8. Inductors behave in the same way as resistors when connected in series and parallel; that is, paralleling inductors reduces inductance, and adding them in series increases the inductance.

Impedance

The algebraic sum of inductive and capacitive reactance effects is known as the *impedance* of a circuit. Impedance in a circuit describes the opposition to the flow of current, and varies with the frequency of an AC signal. Mathematically, the impedance of a circuit is the ratio of voltage to current. In a purely resistive circuit, impedance is independent of frequency, but in a reactive circuit, impedance varies with frequency.

When capacitive reactance and inductive reactance are equal to each other, the circuit is said to be in *resonance.* At its resonant frequency, a circuit offers minimum opposition to current flow. The principles of resonance are used in electronics to tune circuits to a desired frequency. When a small amount of energy is added to a resonant circuit and some output is fed back into the input, the circuit *oscillates* at its resonant frequency. Figure A–10 illustrates the concept of oscillation in a parallel resonant circuit. Oscillators are widely used in telecommunications to generate audio tones and radio frequencies.

Oscillator Circuit

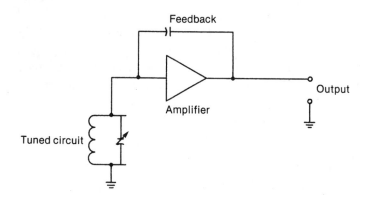

TRANSFORMERS

When a coil is moved into the electrical field caused by the rising and collapsing lines of force surrounding another coil that is fed by an AC source, a portion of the energy couples from the first coil into the second. This effect, shown in Figure A–11, is known as *mutual inductance* or the *transformer* effect. The transformer windings connected to the source are known as the primary, and those connected to the load, the secondary. The amount of voltage induced into the secondary is a function of how closely coupled the two windings are, the frequency of the AC source, and the ratio of turns between the primary and secondary windings. If the secondary consists of more turns than the primary, the voltage is stepped up; with fewer turns in the secondary the voltage is stepped down.

Many transformers have multiple windings in the secondary to create several voltages from a single source, but of course, the total power in the secondary windings cannot exceed the power of the primary. For example, if a transformer that draws one amp of current at 120 volts in the primary has a 1:2 turns ratio, the voltage in the secondary is 240 volts, but no more than 0.5 amps of current can be supplied by the secondary winding. Actually, the power supplied in the secondary is somewhat less because the transformer is not 100 percent efficient.

Transformers are used widely in telecommunications, where they are often called *repeat coils*. Not only do transformers convert AC power to the voltages used to charge batteries and to power apparatus, they also are used as impedance-matching devices.

FIGURE A–11

Transformer

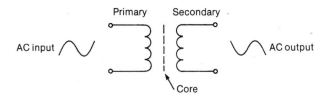

When two circuits are interconnected, the maximum transfer of power occurs when their impedances are exactly matched. Telephone circuits are designed with characteristic impedances of 600 ohms or 900 ohms. These impedances were chosen because of the characteristic impedances of wire transmission lines. The characteristic impedance of equipment used in amplifiers and multiplex is often much higher than the 600 or 900 ohms of telephone circuits. Therefore, wherever equipment connects to external telephone circuits the impedances are matched by repeat coils or other matching circuits that are beyond the scope of this discussion.

All users of telecommunications services must be alert to the hazards of mismatched impedances. Wherever a mismatch occurs, part of the signal reflects toward the source, and a reduced transfer of energy results. Impedance mismatches are the source of echo, unwanted oscillations, and excessive loss. It is important in telecommunications not to connect circuits without the use of impedance-matching devices.

FILTERS

A *filter* is any device that rejects a frequency or band of frequencies while allowing other frequencies to pass. Capacitors and inductors, as we have seen, make effective filters with opposite effects. A capacitor presents high impedance to low-frequency signals, blocks DC entirely, and allows high-frequency signals to pass with little or no attenuation. Inductors, on the other hand, offer little resistance to the flow of DC, but high resistance to AC. As a practical matter, an instantaneous high impedance is offered to AC by a capacitor until an initial charge is established. Similarly, an initial high impedance is offered to the flow of DC by an inductor until the lines of force build up and collapse. These effects are used in pulse-generating circuits, but in filters where the flow of current is steady, this effect can be ignored.

Bandpass Filter

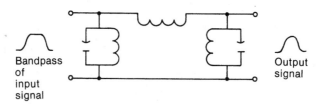

Bandpass of input signal

Output signal

   Capacitors and inductors are used in filter networks such that shown in Figure A–12. As shown in the figure, if a broad band of frequencies is applied to the input of the circuit, the upper and lower frequencies are attenuated while the mid-band is passed. Although such a bandpass is adequate where it is unnecessary to reject the high and low frequencies entirely, in many telecommunications applications this "leak-through" of signal power is unacceptable. For example, if two analog channels share the same medium and both have response curves similar to those shown in the output of Figure A–12, the overlapping passbands would result in audible crosstalk, which is clearly undesirable. For most telecommunications circuits, filters with steep-skirted response curves and a passband with little amplitude distortion are required. This is accomplished by inserting piezoelectric crystals in the filter, resulting in a passband curve with square skirts.

RADIO

The principles of radio transmission are fundamental to understanding telecommunications. Not only is radio widely used for carrying voice channels, and for mobile telephones, the same principles are also used in analog multiplex. An analog carrier system resembles a multichannel radio except the signal is low powered and is not radiated into free space.

Transmitters

Tuned or resonant circuits are at the heart of every radio. A tuned circuit is a type of filter in which the capacitance and inductance are tuned to a resonant frequency and pass only a very narrow band of frequencies. As we discussed earlier, when amplification is added to a tuned circuit and a portion of the output is fed back into the input of the amplifier, the amplifier oscillates. Oscillators are

Block Diagram of a Radio Transmitter

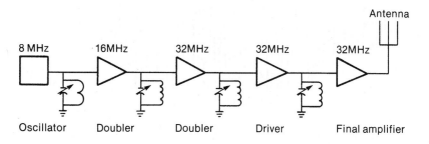

used to generate radio frequencies (rf). Piezoelectric crystals are often employed in oscillator circuits to ensure frequency stability and accuracy. The output of the oscillator is a sine wave of a fundamental frequency and is often rich in harmonic frequencies as well.

Harmonic frequencies are used in circuits called *frequency multipliers.* In the block diagram of Figure A–13 an oscillator and a chain of frequency multipliers raise the fundamental frequency to the desired rf output frequency. Low-frequency oscillators are used in radio because it is easier to control the stability at low frequencies than at high.

Frequency multiplier stages employ tuned circuits to select the desired harmonic. For example, in Figure A–13 the first-stage frequency doubler is tuned to the second harmonic of the 8 MHz oscillator to select an output frequency of 16 MHz.

The output of the multipliers is connected to a *driver* that amplifies the signal to the higher level required by the final rf amplifier. The final amplifier boosts the signal to the desired output level. The output may range from less than a watt in handheld cellular or PCS transmitters to a megawatt or more in high-power broadcast transmitters.

Modulation

The transmitter described in the last section produces only a single high-powered radio frequency wave known as a *carrier*. The carrier contains no intelligence. Radio telegraph transmitters carry information by interrupting the carrier with a coded signal of dots and dashes. This type of modulation is known as *continuous wave* (cw).

FIGURE A–14

Amplitude Modulation

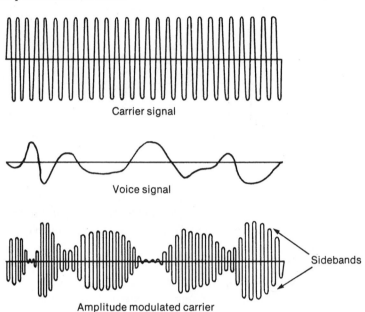

Carrier signal

Voice signal

Sidebands

Amplitude modulated carrier

Amplitude Modulation

Voice communication is far more essential to telecommunications than cw, which is disappearing as a means of communication. A voice signal is impressed on an rf carrier by a process called *modulation*. The simplest form is called *amplitude modulation* (AM). An AM modulator consists of several stages of audio amplification that are coupled to an rf amplifier through a transformer. The resultant signal is shown in Figure A–14.

Single Sideband

When amplitude modulation occurs, four frequencies result; the original voice frequency, the carrier frequency, the sum of the two frequencies, and the difference between the two frequencies. The sum and difference frequencies are called *sidebands*. In an AM signal all the information is contained in either of the two sidebands. The carrier contributes nothing to communication, and the two sidebands are redundant. Moreover, 75 percent of the signal power is contained in the carrier and the redundant sideband. A large improvement in efficiency is obtained by using *single sideband* (ssb) telephony.

FIGURE A–15

Mixer

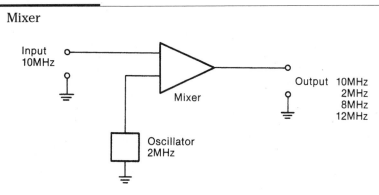

In an ssb transmitter the carrier is suppressed in a circuit called a *bal-anced modulator*. The output of this modulator consists of the upper and lower sidebands, only one of which is needed. The unwanted sideband is eliminated with a filter. The carrier suppression and filtering are done in low-level stages of the transmitter where little power-handling capacity is needed. After filtering, the ssb signal is boosted to the desired output power by the rf amplifier.

Frequency Modulation

Telecommunications apparatus also makes wide use of *frequency modulation* (FM) in radio, and to a limited degree, in multiplex systems. In an FM transmitter an rf signal is generated by an oscillator. With no modulating voice signal the carrier rests at its center frequency. The modulating signal shifts the carrier above and below its center frequency in proportion to the frequency and amplitude of the modulating signal. The result is a broadband signal of varying frequencies.

FM passes a wideband signal with a great deal of linearity. Noise, which tends to affect the amplitude of a signal, can be eliminated in the receiver by filtering the received signal through limiting amplifiers that chop off the noise peaks. The result is a low noise output with wide bandwidth. FM is widely used in mobile and microwave radio, but it is rarely used in analog multiplex systems.

Heterodyning

The transmitter in Figure A–13 uses frequency multipliers to generate the desired transmitting frequency. Both transmitters and receivers also use an effect called *heterodyning* to raise or lower the fundamental frequency. Figure A–15 is a block diagram that illustrates the principle. As discussed in the modulation

FIGURE A–16

Block Diagram of a Superheterodyne Radio Receiver

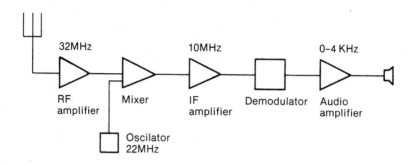

section, when two frequencies are applied to a mixer, the output consists of the two original frequencies, the sum of the two frequencies, and the difference between the frequencies. Tuned circuits select the desired frequency.

Heterodyning is used in many microwave repeaters to change the frequency of the received signal to a different transmit frequency. Most receivers also use heterodyning to change an incoming signal to a fixed intermediate frequency, as we discuss in the next section.

Receivers

A block diagram of a typical radio receiver using *superheterodyne* technology is shown in Figure A–16. The signal from the antenna is boosted by an rf amplifier and coupled to a mixer. A signal from an oscillator is coupled into the other mixer port. The selected output is a fixed *intermediate frequency* (if) that is coupled to succeeding if amplifier stages. The superheterodyne technique improves selectivity. Intermediate frequency amplifier stages have steep-skirted filters to reject unwanted frequencies.

The superheterodyne technique is used in virtually all receivers, ranging from simple broadcast receivers to microwave radios. The intermediate frequency is chosen to be high enough to pass the entire range of desired frequencies. Broadcast band radios, which are tuned selectively to only one voice channel at a time, typically use a 455 kHz if, FM radios use 10.7 mHz, and most microwave systems use 70 mHz as the if. An intermediate frequency this high is required to handle the bandwidth of a microwave system in which bandwidths of 10 or 20 mHz are common.

The demodulator stage in a receiver selects the audio output from the if stages. In a broadcast receiver only a simple device such as a diode is needed

FIGURE A–17

Three Types of Radio Wave Propagation

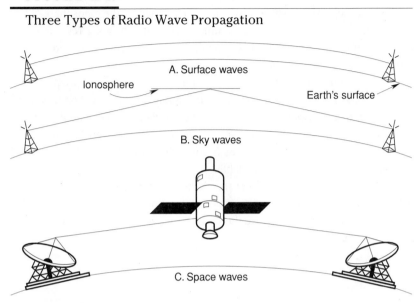

to detect the audio envelope from the AM signal. In single sideband receivers a frequency identical to the original suppressed carrier frequency must be injected into the detector by an oscillator. In FM receivers the detector is a linear circuit known as a *discriminator* that translates the frequency excursions into a signal identical to the original modulating frequencies.

Radio Wave Propagation

As shown in Figure A–17, radio waves propagate in three different ways. Lower frequencies, from about 30 kHz to 3 MHz, propagate via *surface waves.* The radio signal hugs the surface of the earth, and may travel for hundreds or even thousands of miles.

From 3 MHz to 30 MHz, waves propagate as surface waves for some distance, but they also propagate as *sky waves,* which are reflected by an ionized layer of the atmosphere known as the *ionosphere*. Propagation conditions are always changing in the ionosphere. Sky waves are affected by such factors as sunspots and weather conditions, to the point that they are not a reliable and consistent means of communications. When conditions are favorable, worldwide communications are possible over these frequencies, but when conditions are unfavorable, only the ground wave can be used.

Frequencies from 30 MHz to 30 GHz travel by means of *space waves;* that is, by line of sight. These waves are not affected by the ionosphere, which means they can escape the earth's atmosphere without being reflected. This makes them ideal for satellite communications. Inside the atmosphere these frequencies are used for line-of-sight communications.

The boundaries of these frequency ranges are only approximate. Everyone has experienced long-range communications on the AM broadcast band, which sits in the middle of the low frequency range. Other people have received television signals, which are all above 50 MHz, well beyond line of sight. Some atmospheric reflections occur at these frequencies, but communications over them are not dependable.

This overview of electrical theory has only brushed the surface of the technology. Readers who require more information are advised to consult one of the many manuals on electric theory that are available in most bookstores.

A P P E N D I X   B

Principal Voice and Data Standards of the International Telecommunications Union

E.160 Definitions Relating to National and International Numbering Plans

E.161 Arrangements of Digits, Letters, and Symbols on Telephones and Other Devices That Can Be Used for Gaining Access to a Telephone Network

E.164 Numbering Plan for the ISDN Era

E.301 Impact of Non-Voice Applications on the Telephone Network

E.450 Facsimile Quality of Service on PSTN—General Aspects

E.600 Terms and Definitions of Traffic Engineering

E.750 Introduction to the E.750-Series of Recommendations on Traffic Engineering Aspects of Mobile Networks

E.751 Reference Connections for Traffic Engineering of Land Mobile Networks

E.770 Land Mobile and Fixed Network Interconnection Traffic Grade of Service Concept

E.771 Network Grade of Service Parameters and Target Values for Circuit-Switched Land Mobile Services

E.486 Accessibility for 64 kbit/s Circuit Switched International End-to-End ISDN Connection Types

F.140 Point-to-Multipoint Telecommunication Service via Satellite

F.160 General Operational Provisions for the International Public Facsimile Services

F.180 General Operational Provisions for the International Public Facsimile Service between Subscribers' Stations (Telefax)

F.182 Operational Provisions for the International Public Facsimile Service between Subscribers' Stations with Group 3 Facsimile Machines (Telefax 3)

F.182 Operational Provisions for the International Public Facsimile Service between Subscriber Stations with Group 4 Facsimile Machines (Telefax 4)

F.300 Videotex Service

F.400/X.400 Message Handling Services: Message Handling System and Service Overview

Interfaces

G.704 Synchronous Frame Structures Used at Primary and Secondary Hierarchical Levels

G.706 Frame Alignment and CRC Procedures Relating to Basic Frame Structures Defined in Rec. G.704

G.707 Synchronous Digital Hierarchy Bit Rates

G.708 Network Node Interface for the Synchronous Digital Hierarchy

G.709 Synchronous Multiplexing Structure

G.726 40, 32, 24, 16 Kbit/s Adaptive Differential Pulse Code Modulation (ADPCM)

G.728 Coding of Speech at 16 kbit/s Using Low-Delay Code Excited Linear Prediction (LD-CELP)

G.736 Characteristics of a Synchronous Digital Multiplex Equipment Operating at 2048 kbit/s

G.772 Protected Monitoring Points Provided on Digital Transmission Systems

G.773 Protocol Suites for Q Interfaces for Management of Transmission Systems

G.774 Synchronous Digital Hierarchy (SDH) Management Information Model for the Network Element View

G.781 Structure of Recommendations on Equipment for the Synchronous Digital Hierarchy (SDH)

G.782 Types and General Characteristics of Synchronous Digital Hierarchy (SDH) Multiplexing Equipment

G.783 Characteristics of Synchronous Digital Hierarchy (SDH) Multiplexing Equipment Functional Blocks

G.784 Synchronous Digital Hierarchy (SDH) Management

G.797 Characteristics of a Flexible Multiplexer in a Plesiochronous Digital Hierarchy Environment

G.803 Architectures of Transport Networks Based on the Synchronous Digital Hierarchy (SDH)

G.823 The Control of Jitter and Wander within Digital Networks Which Are Based on the 2048 kbit/s Hierarchy

G.824 The Control of Jitter and Wander within Digital Networks Which Are Based on the 1544 kbit/s

G.825 The Control of Jitter and Wander within Digital Networks Which Are Based on the Synchronous Digital Hierarchy (SDH)

G.831 Management Capabilities of Transport Networks Based on the Synchronous Digital Hierarchy (SDH)

G.911 Parameters and Calculation Methodologies for Reliability and Availability of Fibre Optic Systems

G.955 Digital Line Systems Based on the 1544 kbit/s and the 2048 kbit/s Hierarchy on Optical Fibre Cables

G.957 Optical Interfaces for Equipments and Systems Relating to the Synchronous Digital Hierarchy

G.958 Digital Line Systems Based on the Synchronous Digital Hierarchy for Use on Optical Fibre Cables

G.960 Access Digital Section for ISDN Basic Rate Access

G.961 Digital Transmission System on Metallic Local Lines for ISDN Basic Rate Access

G.962 Access Digital Section for ISDN Primary Rate at 2048 kbit/s

G.963 Access Digital Section for ISDN Primary Rate at 1544 kbit/s

G.971 General Features of Optical Fibre Submarine Cable Systems

G.972 Definition of Terms Relevant to Optical Fibre Submarine Cable Systems

H.120 Codec for Videoconferencing Using Primary Digital Group Transmission

H.200 Framework for Recommendations for Audiovisual Services

H.221 Frame Structure for a 64 to 1920 Kbit/s Channel in Audiovisual Teleservices

H.230 Frame Synchronous Control and Indication Signals for Audiovisual Systems

H.231 Multipoint Control Units for Audiovisual Systems Using Digital Channels up to 2 Mbit/s

H.233 Confidentiality System for Audiovisual Services

H.242 System for Establishing Communication between Audiovisual Terminals Using Digital Channels Up to 2 Mbit/s

H.243 Procedures for Establishing Communication between Three or More Audiovisual Terminals Using Digital Channels Up To 2 Mbit/s

H.261 Video CODEC for Audiovisual Services at P x 64 Kbit/s

H.320 Narrow-band Visual Telephone Systems and Terminal Equipment

H.331 Broadcasting Type Audiovisual Multipoint Systems and Terminal Equipment

I.112 Vocabulary of Terms for ISDNs

I.114 Vocabulary of Terms for Universal Personal Telecommunication

I.120 Integrated Services Digital Networks (ISDNs)

I.121 Broadband Aspects of ISDN

I.122 Framework for Frame Mode Bearer Services

I.140 Attribute Technique for the Characterization of Telecommunication Services Supported by an ISDN and Network Capabilities of an ISDN

I.150 B-ISDN ATM Functional Characteristics

I.210 Principles of Telecommunications Services Supported by an ISDN and the Means to Describe Them

I.211 B-ISDN Service Aspects

I.221 Common Specific Characteristics of Services

I.231.9 Circuit-Mode 64 kbit/s 8 KHz Structured Multi-use Bearer Service Category

I.212.3 User Signalling Bearer Service Category (USBS)

I.233 Frame Mode Bearer Services 91/10

I.310 ISDN Network Functional Principles

I.311 B-ISDN General Network Aspects

I.321 B-ISDN Protocol Reference Model and Its Application

I.325 Reference Configurations for ISDN Connection Types

I.327 B-ISDN Functional Architecture

I.333 Terminal Selection in ISDN

I.350 General Aspects of Quality of Service and Network Performance in Digital Networks, Including ISDNs

I.352 Network Performance Objectives for Connection Processing Delays in an ISDN

I.353 Reference Events for Defining ISDN Performance Parameters

I.354 Network Performance Objectives for Packet Mode Communication in an ISDN

I.355 ISDN 64 kbit/s Connection Type Availability Performance

I.361 B-ISDN ATM Layer Specification

I.362 B-ISDN ATM Adaptation Layer (AAL) Functional Description

I.363 B-ISDN ATM Adaptation Layer (AAL) Specification

I.364 Support of Broadband Connectionless Data Service on B-ISDN

I.370 Congestion Management for the ISDN Frame Relaying Bearer Service

L.15 Optical Local Distribution Networks—Factors to be Considered for Their Construction

L.16 Conductive Plastic Material (CPM) as Protective Covering for Metal Cable Sheaths

M.60 Maintenance Terminology and Definitions

M.1045 Preliminary Exchange of Information for the Provision of International Leased Circuits

M.1340 Performance Allocations and Limits for International Data Transmission Links and Systems

M.1385 Maintenance of International Leased Circuits That Are Supported by International Data Transmission Systems

M.3010 Principles for a Telecommunications Management Network

M.4100 Maintenance of Common Channel Signalling System No. 7

N.60 Nominal Amplitude of Video Signals at Video Interconnection Points

N.62 Tests to Be Made during the Line-up Period That Precedes a Television Transmission

N.67 Monitoring Television Transmissions—Use of the Field Blanking Interval

N.86 Line-up and Service Commissioning of International Videoconference Systems Operating at Transmission Bit Rates of 1544 and 2048 kbit/s

N.90 Maintenance of International Videoconference Systems Operating at Transmission Bit Rates of 1544 and 2048 kbit/s

O.133 Equipment for Measuring the Performance of PCM Encoders and Decoders

P.10 Vocabulary of Terms on Telephone Transmission Quality and Telephone Sets

P.11 Effect of Transmission Impairments

P.31 Transmission Characteristics for Digital Telephones

P.34 Transmission Characteristics of Hands-Free Telephones

P.37 Coupling Hearing Aids to Telephone Set

P.38 Transmission Characteristics of Operator Telephone Systems (OTS)

P.56 Objective Measurement of Active Speech Level

P.62 Measurements on Subscribers' Telephone Equipment

P.64 Determination of Sensitivity/Frequency Characteristics of Local Telephone Systems

P.65 Objective Instrumentation for the Determination of Loudness Ratings

P.66 Methods for Evaluating the Transmission Performance of Digital Telephone Sets

P.78 Subjective Testing Method for Determination of Loudness Ratings in Accordance with Recommendation P.76

P.79 Calculation of Loudness Ratings for Telephone Sets

P.80 Methods for Subjective Determination of Transmission Quality

P.83 Subjective Performance Assessment of Telephone-Band and Wideband Digital Codecs

P.84 Subjective Listening Test Method for Evaluating Digital Circuit Multiplication and Packetized Voice Systems

Q.115 Control of Echo Suppressors—Control of Echo Suppressors and Echo Cancellers

Q.141 Signal Code for Line Signalling—Clause 2 Line Signalling

Q.513 Digital Exchange Interfaces for Operations, Administration and Maintenance

Q.521 Digital Exchange Functions

Q.541 Digital Exchange Design Objectives—General

Q.542 Digital Exchange Design Objectives—Operations and Maintenance

Q.543 Digital Exchange Performance Design Objectives

Q.554 Transmission Characteristics at Digital Interfaces of Digital Exchanges

Q.601 Interworking of Signalling Systems—General

Q.602 Interworking of Signalling Systems—Introduction

Q.604 Interworking of Signalling Systems—Information Analysis Tables

Q.614 Interworking of Signalling Systems—Logic Procedures for Incoming Signalling System No. 7 (TUP)

Q.617 Interworking of Signalling Systems-Logic Procedures for Incoming Signalling System No. 7 (ISUP)

Q.624 Interworking of Signalling Systems—Logic Procedures for Outgoing Signalling Systems No. 7 (TUP)

Q.627 Interworking of Signalling Systems—Logic Procedures for

Outgoing Signalling Systems No. 7 (ISUP)

Q.646 Interworking of Signalling Systems—Logic Procedures for Interworking of Signalling System No. 5 to Signalling System No. 7 (ISUP)

Q.656 Interworking of Signalling Systems—Logic Procedures for Interworking of Signalling System No. 6 to Signalling System No. 7 (ISUP)

Q.667 Interworking of Signalling Systems—Logic Procedures for Interworking of Signalling System No. 7 (TUP) to Signalling System No. 7 (ISUP)

Q.675 Interworking of Signalling Systems—Logic Procedures for Interworking of Signalling System RI to Signalling System No. 7 (ISUP)

Q.686 Interworking of Signalling Systems—Logic Procedures for Interworking of Signalling System R2 to Signalling System No. 7 (ISUP)

Q.690 Interworking of Signalling Systems—Logic Procedures for Interworking of Signalling System No. 7 (ISUP) to No. 5

Q.691 Interworking of Signalling Systems—Logic Procedures for Interworking of Signalling System No. 7 (ISUP) to No. 6

Q.692 Interworking of Signalling Systems—Logic Procedures for Interworking of Signalling System No. 7 (ISUP) to No. 7 (TUP)

Q.694 Interworking of Signalling Systems—Logic Procedures for Interworking of Signalling System No. 7 (ISUP) to RI

Q.695 Interworking of Signalling Systems—Logic Procedures for Interworking of Signalling System No. 7 (ISUP) to R2

Q.700 Introduction to CCITT Signalling System No. 7

Q.701 Functional Description of the Message Transfer Part (MTP) of Signalling System No. 7

Q.703 Signalling System No. 7—Signalling Link

Q.704 Signalling Network Functions and Messages

Q.705 Signalling System No. 7—Signalling Network Structure

Q.706 Signalling System No. 7—Message Transfer Part Signalling Performance

Q.708 Numbering of International Signalling Point Codes

Q.709 Signalling System No. 7—Hypothetical Signaling Reference Connection

Q.711 Signalling System No. 7—Functional Description of the Signalling Connection Control Part

Q.761 Functional Description of the ISDN User Part of Signalling System No. 7

Q.762 General Function of Messages and Signals of the ISDN User Part of Signalling System No. 7.

Q.763 Formats and Codes

Q.764 Signalling System No. 7 ISDN User Part Signalling Procedures

Q.766 Performance Objectives in the Integrated Services Digital Network Application

Q.767 Application of the ISDN User Part of SS No. 7 for the International ISDN Interconnections

Q.771 Signalling System No. 7—Functional Description of Transaction Capabilities

Q.772 Signalling System No. 7—Transaction Capabilities Information Element Definitions

Q.773 Signalling System No. 7—Transaction Capabilities Formats and Encoding

Q.774 Signalling System No. 7—Transaction Capabilities Procedures

Q.775 Guidelines for Using Transaction Capabilities

Q.780 Signalling System No. 7—Test Specification—General Description

Q.781 Signalling System No. 7—MTP Level 2 Test Specification

Q.782 Signalling System No. 7—MTP Level 3 Test Specification

Q.782 (D) MTP Level 3 Test Specification

Q.786 SCCP Test Specification

Q.787 Transaction Capabilities (TC) Test Specification

Q.850 Usage of the Cause and Location in the Digital Subscriber Signalling System No. I and the Signalling System No. 7 ISDN User Part

Q.920 Digital Subscriber Signalling System No. I (DSSI)—ISDN User-Network Interface Data Link Layer—General Aspects

Q.921 (D) ISDN User-Network Interface—Data Link Layer Specification

Q.921 Bis Abstract Test Suite for LAPD Conformance Testing

Q.922 ISDN Data Link Layer Specification for Frame Mode Bearer Services

Q.930 Digital Subscriber Signalling System No. I (DSS 1)—ISDN User-Network Interface Layer 3—General Aspects

Q.931 Digital Subscriber Signalling System No. I (DSS 1) ISDN User-Network Interface Layer 3 Specification for Basic Call Control

Q.931 (D) ISDN User-Network Interface Layer 3 Specification for Basic Call Control

Q.932 Digital Subscriber Signalling System No. I (DSS 1)—Generic Procedures for the Control of ISDN Supplementary Services

Q.932 (D) Generic Procedures for the Control of ISDN Supplementary Services

Q.933 Digital Subscriber Signalling Systems No. I (DSS 1) Signalling Specification for Frame Mode Basic Call Control

Q.939 Digital Subscriber Signalling System No. I (DSS 1)—Typical DSS 1 Service Indicator Codings for ISDN Telecommunications Services

Q.941 Digital Subscriber Signalling System No. I (DSS 1)—ISDN User-Network Interface Protocol Profile for Management

Q.950 Digital Subscriber Signalling System No. I (DSS 1)—Supplementary Services Protocols, Structure and General Principles

Q.951 Stage 3 Description for Number Identification Supplementary Services Using DSS I—Clause 3—Calling Line Identification Presentation (CLIP). Clause 4—Calling Line Identification Restriction (CLIR). Clause 5—Connected Line Identification Presentation (COLP). Clause 6—Calling Line Identification Restriction (COLR).

Q.952 Stage 3 Service Description for Call Offering Supplementary Services Using DSS I—Diversion Supplementary Services

Q.953.2 Stage 3 Description for Call Completion Supplementary Services Using DSS 1. Clause 2—Call Hold

Q.954 Stage 3 Description for Multiparty Supplementary Services Using DSS I Clause I Conference Calling. Clause 2—Three Party Service

Q.955 Stage 3 Description for Community of Interest Supplementary Services Using DSS I. Clause 3—Multi-Level Precedence and Preemption (MLPP)

Q.957 Stage 3 Description for Additional Information Transfer Supplementary Services Using DSS I— Clause 3—User-To-User Signalling (UUS)

Q.1200 Q-Series Intelligent Network Recommendation Structure

Q.1201 (D) Principles of Intelligent Network Architecture (Same as 1.312)

Q.1203 (D) IN Global Functional Plane Architecture (Same as 1.329)

Q.1204 Intelligent Network Distributed Functional Plane Architecture

Q.1205 Intelligent Network Physical Plane Architecture

Q.1208 General Aspects of the Intelligent Network Application Protocol

Q.1211 Introduction to Intelligent Network Capability Set 1

Q.1213 Global Functional Plane for Intelligent Network

Q.1214 Distributed Functional Plane for Intelligent Network CS-1

Q.1215 Physical Plane for Intelligent Network CS-1

Q.1218 Interface Recommendation for Intelligent Network CS-1

Q.1290 Glossary of Terms Used in the Definition of Intelligent Networks

Q.1400 Architecture Framework for the Development of Signalling and OA&M Protocols Using OSI Concepts

T.4 Standardization of Group 3 Facsimile Apparatus for Document Transmission

T.30 Procedures for Document Facsimile Transmission in the General Switched Telephone Network

T.52 Non-Latin Coded Character Sets for Telematic Services

T.82 Information Technology—Coded Representation of Picture and Audio Information—Progressive Bi-Level Image Compression

T.102 Syntax-Based Videotex End-to-End Protocols for the Circuit Mode ISDN

T.125 Multipoint Communication Service Protocol Specification

T.417 Information Technology—Open Document Architecture (ODA) and Interchange Format: Raster Graphics Content Architecture

T.418 Information Technology—Open Document Architecture (ODA) and Interchange Format: Geometric Graphics Content Architecture

U.1 Signalling Conditions to be Applied in the International Telex Service

U.7 Numbering Schemes for Automatic Switching Networks

U.15 Interworking Rules for International Signalling Systems According to Recommendations U.1, U.11, and U.12

V.10 Electrical Characteristics for Unbalanced Double-Current Interchange Circuits Operating at Data Signalling Rates Nominally up to 100 kbit/s

V.11 Electrical Characteristics for Balanced Double-Current Interchange Circuits Operating at Signalling Rates up to 10 Mbit/s

V.a3 Simulated Carrier Control

V.14 Transmission of Start-Stop Characters over Synchronous Bearer Channels

V.17 A 2-Wire Modem for Facsimile Application with Rates up to 14400 Bit/s

V.24 List of Definitions for Interchange Circuits between Data Terminal Equipment (DTE) and Data Circuit-Terminating Equipment (DCE)

V.28 Electrical Characteristics for Unbalanced Double-Current Interchange Circuits

V.32 A Family of 2-Wire, Duplex Modems Operating at Data Signalling Rates of up to 9600 bit/s for Use on the General Switched Telephone Network and on Leased Telephone-type Circuits

V.38 A 48/56/64 kbit/s Data Circuit Terminating Equipment Standardized for Use on Digital Point-to-Point Leased Circuits

V.42 Error Correcting Procedures for DCEs Using Asynchronous-to-Synchronous Conversion

V.110 Support of Data Terminal Equipments with V-Series Type Interfaces by an Integrated Services Digital Network

V.120 Support by an ISDN of Data Terminal Equipment with V-Series Type Interfaces with Provision for Statistical Multiplexing

X.1 International User Classes of Service in, and Categories of Access to, Public Data Networks and Integrated Services Digital Networks (ISDNs)

X.2 International Data Transmission Services and Optional User Facilities in Public Data Networks and ISDNs

X.3 Packet Assembly/Disassembly Facility (PAD) in a Public Data Network

X.6 Multicast Service Definition

X.7 Technical Characteristics of Data Transmission Services

X.10 Categories of Access for Data Terminal Equipment (DTE) to Public Data Transmission Services

X.21 Interface between Data Terminal Equipment and Data Circuit-Terminating Equipment for Synchronous Operation on Public Data Networks

X.25 Interface between Data Terminal Equipment (DTE) and Data Circuit-Terminating Equipment (DCE) for Terminals Operating in the Packet Mode and Connected to Public Data Networks by Dedicated Circuit

X.28 DTE/DCE Interface for a Start-Stop Mode Data Terminal Equipment Accessing the Packet Assembly/Disassembly Facility (PAD) in a Public Data Network Situated in the Same Country

X.29 Procedures for the Exchange of Control Information and User Data Between a Packet Assembly/Disassembly (PAD) Facility and a Packet Mode DTE or another PAD

X.30 Support of X.2 1, X.21 bis and X.20 bis Based Data Terminal Equipments (DTEs) by an Integrated Services Digital Network (ISDN)

X.31 Support of Packet Mode Terminal Equipment by an ISDN

X.32 Interface Between Data Terminal Equipment (DTE) and Data Circuit-Terminating Equipment (DCE) for Terminals Operating in the Packet Mode and Accessing a Packet Switched Public Data Network through a Public Switched Telephone Network or an Integrated Services Digital Network or a Circuit Switched Public Data Network

X.53 Numbering of Channels on International Multiplex Links at 64 kbit/s

X.75 Packet Switched Signalling System Between Public Networks Providing Data Transmission Services

X.96 Call Progress Signals In Public Data Networks

X.121 International Numbering Plan for Public Data Networks

X.214 Information Technology—Open Systems Interconnection Transport Service Definition

X.218 Reliable Transfer: Model and Service Definition

X.220 Use of X.200-Series Protocols in CCITT Applications

X.227 Connection-Oriented Protocol Specification for the Association Control Service Element

X.233 Information Technology—Protocol for Providing the Connectionless-Mode Network Service: Protocol Specification

X.264 Transport Protocol Identification Mechanism

X.301 Description of the General Arrangements for Call Control within a Subnetwork and between Subnetworks for the Provision of Data Transmission Services

X.340 General Arrangements for Internetworking between a Packet Switched Public Data Network (PSPDN) and the International Telex Network

X.435 Message Handling Systems—EDI Messaging System— Companion to F.435

X.500 (D) Information Technology—Open Systems Interconnection—
The Directory—Overview of Concepts, Models and Services

X.501 (D) Information Technology—Open Systems Interconnection—
The Directory—The Models

X.509 (D) Information Technology—Open Systems Interconnection—
The Directory—Authentication Framework

X.511 (D) Open Systems Interconnection Information Technology—
The Directory—Abstract Service Definition

X.518 (D) Information Technology—Open Systems Interconnection—
The Directory—Procedures for Distributed Operation 92/05

X.519 (D) Information Technology—Open Systems Interconnection—
The Directory—Protocol Specifications

X.520 (D) Information Technology—Open Systems Interconnection—
The Directory—Selected Attribute Types

X.521 (D) Information Technology—Open Systems Interconnection—
The Directory—Selected Object Classes

X.525 (D) Information Technology—Open Systems Interconnection—
The Directory—Replication

X.720 Information Technology—Open Systems Interconnection—
Structure of Management Information—Management Information
Model

X.721 Information Technology—Open Systems Interconnection—
Structure of Management Information—Definition of Management
Information

X.722 Information Technology—Open Systems Interconnection—
Structure of Management Information—Guidelines for the Definition of
Managed Objects

X.723 Information Technology—Open Systems Interconnection—
Structure of Management Information: Generic Management
Information

X.733 Information Technology—Open Systems Interconnection—
Systems Management—Alarm Reporting Function

X.734 Information Technology—Open Systems Interconnection—
Systems Management—Event Report Management Function

X.745 Information Technology—Open Systems Interconnection—
Systems Management—Test Management Function

A P P E N D I X   C

Telecommunications Manufacturers and Vendors

This appendix lists many of the North American companies that manufacture equipment and supply products and services to the telecommunications industry. Readers are cautioned that telephone numbers in this appendix may be unreliable because of area code and telephone number changes.

3COM Corporation Santa Clara, CA 408-764-5000

3M Dynatel Systems Austin, TX 800-426-8699

3M Telecom Systems Division Austin, TX 512-984-1800

Active Voice Seattle, WA 206-441-4700

ADC Kentrox Portland, OR 800-733-5511 503-643-1681

ADC Telecommunications Minneapolis, MN 800-366-3891

ADP Autonet Dayton, NJ 609-395-5076

Adtech, Inc. Honolulu, HI 808-734-3300

Adtran Huntsville, AL 205-971-8000

Advanced Communications Systems North Olmstead, OH 800-223-5424

Advanced Computer Communications Cupertino, CA 408-366-9600

Advanced Voice Technologies Nashville, TN 800-237-3914

Air Communications, Inc. Sunnyvale, CA 408-749-9883

Alantec San Jose, CA 408-955-9000

Alcoa Fujikura LTD Duncan, SC 800-866-3977

Allied Telesyn Mountain View, CA 800-424-4284 415-964-2771

Alpha Wire Elizabeth, NJ 201-925-8000

American Power Conversion West Kingston, RI 401-789-5735

American Telecommunications Corp. Charlottesville, VA 804-978-2200

Ameritec Corp. Covina, CA 818-915-5441

AMP, Inc. Harrisburg, PA 800-722-1111

Amphenol Corporation Sidney, NY 800-944-6446

Amphenol Fiber Optics Products Lisle, IL 708-960-1010

Analytic Systems Surrey, BC 604-543-7378

Ando Corp. Rockville, MD 301-294-3365

Andrew Corp. Orland Park, IL 708-349-3300

Anritsu Wiltron Morgan Hill, CA 408-776-8300

Answer Software Plano, TX 214-612-5101

Antel Optronics, Inc. Richardson, TX 214-690-5200

Apex Data, Inc. Pleasanton, CA 510-416-5656

Apple Computer, Inc. Cuptertino, CA 408-996-1010

Applied Voice Technology Kirkland, WA 206-820-6000

AR Division of Telenex Springfield, VA 703-644-9190

Aristicom International Alameda, CA 510-748-1553

Armon Networking, Inc. Camarillo, CA 805-388-5566

Asante Technologies, Inc. San Jose, CA 408-435-8401

Ascom Timeplex, Inc. Woodcliff Lake, NJ 201-391-1111

Associated Business Systems (ABS) Bricktown, NJ 908-206-0808

AST Research, Inc. Irvine, CA 800-876-4278

AT&T Basking Ridge, NJ 800-325-7466

AT&T Global Business Communications Systems Basking Ridge, NJ 908-953-4364

AT&T Network Cable Systems Morristown, NJ 201-606-2000

AT&T Network Cable Systems Morristown, NJ 800-344-0223

Atis Atlanta, GA 404-664-4744

Atlantic Research Corporation Alexandria, VA 703-642-4000

Aurora Systems Action, MA 508-263-4141

Axon Networks, Inc. Newton, MA 617-630-9600

Azure Technologies, Inc. Hopkinton, MA 508-435-3800

Banyan Systems Westboro, MA 508-898-1000

Bay Networks, Inc. Billerica, MA 508-670-8888

BBL Industries Atlanta, GA 404-449-7740

Belden Electronic Wire and Cable Richmond, IN 317-983-5200

Bellcore Piscataway, NJ 800-521-CORE 908-699-5800

Berk-Tek New Holland, PA 717-354-6200

Best Power Technology, Inc. Necedah, WI 608-565-7200

Beyond, Inc. Cambridge, MA 800-845-8511

Biddle Instruments Blue Bell, PA 215-646-9200

Bogen Communications Ramsey, NJ 201-934-8500

Boston Technology Wakefield, MA 617-246-9000

Brand-Rex Co. Willimantic, CT 203-456-8000

Brooktrout Technology Needham, MA 617-449-4100

Bytex Corp. Westboro, MA 508-366-0040

Cable & Wireless Vienna, VA 703-790-5300

Cabletron Systems East Rochester, NH 603-332-9400

Canoga Perkins Chatsworth, CA 818-718-6300

Canstar Markham, Ontario 905-946-7600

Cascade Communications Corp. Westford, MA 508-692-2600

Castelle, Inc. Santa Clara, CA 800-289-7555

Centigram Communications San Jose, CA 408-944-0250

Centillion Networks, Inc. Mountain View, CA 415-969-6700

Chipcom Corp. Southborough, MA 508-460-8900

Cisco Systems, Inc. San Jose, CA 408-526-4000

Citel Miami, FL 800-248-3548

Clary Dallas, TX 800-442-5279

Coastcom Alameda, CA 510-523-6000

Cobotyx Danbury, CT 800-288-6342

Code-A-Phone Clackamas, OR 503-655-8940

Codex Corp. Mansfield, MA 617-364-2000

Comdial Corporation Charlottesville, VA 804-347-1432 804-978-2200

CommScope, Inc. Claremont, NC 704-459-5000

Compaq Computer Corp. Houston, TX 713-370-0670

Compass Technology Sarasota, FL 813-371-8000

Compression Labs, Inc. San Jose, CA 408-922-5416

CompuServe, Inc. Columbus, OH 614-457-8699

Computer Network Technology Cambridge, MA 617-661-6262

ConferTech Westminster, CO 303-633-3000

Consultronics Concord, Ontario 416-738-3741

Cook Electric Division of Northern Telecom Morton Grove, IL 312-967-6600

Corning, Inc. Corning, NY 607-974-7813

Cortelco Memphis, TN 800-866-8880 901-365-7774

Cray Communications Annapolis Junctions, MD 800-FOR-CRAY

Cylink Sunnyvale, CA 800-533-3958 408-735-5800

Data General Corp. Westborough, MA 800-328-2436

Data Race San Antonio, TX 210-558-1900

Data Switch Corp. Shelton, CT 203-926-1801

Dataprobe, Inc. Paramus, NJ 201-967-9300

Datel Electronics Minneapolis, MN 612-721-6778

Davis Software Engineering Dallas, TX 214-746-5210

Davox Westpond, MA 508-952-0200

Dell Computer Corp. Austin, TX 512-338-4400

Devcom Mid-America, Inc. Oak Brook, IL 708-574-3600

Dialogic Parsippany, NJ 201-993-3000

DiDon Fiberoptics, Inc. Berkeley, CA 510-528-0427

Digilog/CXR Telecom Montgomeryville, PA 215-628-4530

Digital Equipment Corp. Maynard, MA 508-493-5111

Digital Microwave Corp. San Jose, CA 408-943-0777

Digital Products Saint John, New Brunswick 506-635-1057

Digital Sound Carpinteria, CA 805-566-2000

Digital Techniques Allen, TX 800-634-4976

Digitech Industries Danbury, CT 203-797-2676

Diversified Technology Largo, FL 813-535-6007

DSC Communications Corp. Plano, TX 214-519-3000

Eagle Telephonics, Inc. Hauppauge, NY 516-273-6700

Edify Santa Clara, CA 408-982-2000

Electrodata, Inc. Bedford Heights, OH 800-441-6336

Electronic Tele-Communications Waukesha, WI 414-542-5600

Ericsson Inc. Communications Division Garden Grove, CA 714-895-3962

E-TEK Dynamics, Inc. San Jose, CA 408-432-6300

Excel Sagamore Beach, MA 508-833-1144

Exceltech Yankton, SD 605-665-5811

Executone Darien, CT 203-655-6500

Exide Electronics Raleigh, NC 919-872-3020

Extended Systems, Inc. Boise, ID 800-235-7576

Fibermux Corp Chatsworth, CA 818-709-6000

Fiberoptic Switch, Inc. Norwalk, CT 203-838-7509

Fibersense & Signals, Inc. Concord, ON 905-669-0665

Fibertron Fullerton, CA 714-871-3344

Fluke Everett, WA 206-347-6100

Fore Systems, Inc. Warrendale, PA 412-772-6600

Forum Communication Systems Richardson, TX 214-680-0700

Frederick Engineering Columbia, MD 410-290-9000

Fuijitsu Danbury, CT 203-796-5400

Fujitsu America, Inc. Telecommunications Div. Phoenix, AZ 800-553-3263

Fujitsu Network Transmission Systems Richardson, TX 214-690-6000

GAI-Tronics Mohnton, PA 610-777-1374

Gandalf Systems Corp. Delran, NJ 800-937-1010

Geist Lincoln, NE 402-474-3400

Gemini Telemanagement Systems Palo Alto, CA 800-487-3210

General Cable Company South Plainfield, NJ 908-412-3906

General DataComm, Inc. Danbury, CT 800-777-4005 203-574-1118

General Electric Information Services Rockwell, MD 800-433-3683

Genesis Electronics Folsom, CA 916-985-4050

GN Navtel Norcross, GA 800-262-8835 404-446-2665

Gordon Kapes Skokie, IL 708-676-1750

Gould, Inc. Fiber Optics Div. Millersville, MD 410-987-5600

GPT Video Systems Stamford, CT 203-348-6600

Grand Junction Networks, Inc. Fremont, CA 510-252-0726

Granger Associates Santa Clara, CA 408-954-5000

Grass Valley Group, Inc. Grass Valley, CA 916-478-3000

Graybar Electric Co. Clayton, MO 314-727-3900

Harris Corporation, Digital Telephone Systems Div. Novato, CA 415-892-1394

Harris Farinon San Carlos, CA 415-594-3000

Harris/Dracon Division Camarillo, CA 805-987-9511

Hekimian Laboratories Rockville, MD 301-590-3600

Hewlett-Packard Co. Palo Alto, CA 415-857-1501

Hewlett-Packard Network Test Division Santa Clara, CA 800-452-4844

Hitachi Norcross, GA 404-446-8820

Homisco Melrose, MA 617-665-1997

Hubbell Premise Wiring, Inc. Stonington, CT 203-535-8326

Hughes LAN Systems Mountain View, CA 415-966-7300

Ibex Technologies Placerville, CA 916-621-4342

IBM Corporation Armonk, NY 914-765-1900

INET Richardson, TX 800-969-4638

Information Access Technology Salt Lake City, UT 801-265-8800

Innovative Technology Roswell, GA 404-998-9970

Intecom, Inc. Dallas TX 214-447-8473

Intellect Network Systems Dallas, TX 214-640-4180

Intellicom Inc. Chatsworth, CA 818-407-3900

Intellisystems Chatsworth, CA 818-341-7000

Intellivoice Farmington Hills, MI 313-488-0180

Interalia Eden Prairie, MN 612-942-6088

International Data Sciences Warwick, RI 401-737-9900

Inter-Tel Chandler, AZ 602-961-9000

ISDN*TEK San Gregorino, CA 415-712-3200

Isotec Darien CT 203-655-6500

Iwatsu America Carlstadt, NJ 201-935-8580

Jerrold Communications Hatboro, PA 215-674-4800

Kalapana, Inc. Sunnyvale, CA 408-749-1600

Krone, Inc. Englewood, CO 303-790-2619

Lanier Worldwide Atlanta, GA 800-708-7088

Lannet Cata Communications Irvine, CA 800-778-7427

LANsource Technologies Toronto, Ontario 800-677-2727

Laser Communications Lancaster, PA 717-394-8634

Laser Precision Corp Utica, NY 315-797-4449

Lernout & Hauspie Woburn, MA 617-932-4118

Leviton Telcom Bothell, WA 800-722-2082

Liebert Columbus, OH 614-888-0246

LightScan Advanced Technologies Penacook, NH 603-753-6362

Link Technology Holland, PA 215-357-3354

Lotus Development Corp. Mountainview, CA 800-448-2500

Mackenzie Laboratories Glendora, CA 800-423-4147

MacroTel Boca Raton, FL 800-826-1627

MacroVoice Boca Raton, FL 407-994-9781 800-622-7689

Madge Networks, Inc. San Jose, CA 408-955-0700

MCI Telecommunications Corporation Washington, DC 202-872-1600

Megahertz Corp. Salt Lake City, UT 801-272-6000

Metro Tel Jericho, NY 516-937-3420

Micom Systems, Inc. Chatsworth, CA 213-998-8844

Microcom, Inc. Norwood, MA 617-551-1000

Microsoft Corporation Redmond, WA 206-882-8080

Microtest Phoenix, AZ 602-971-6464

Minuteman Carrollton, TX 800-238-7272

Mitel, Inc. Boca Raton, FL 305-994-8500

Mitsubishi Electronics America, Inc. Santa Clara, CA 408-732-6928

MOD-TAP Harvard, MA 508-772-5630

Mohawk/CDT Leominister, MA 508-537-9961

Moscom Pittsford, NY 716-381-6000

Motorola UDS Huntsville, AL 205-430-8000

Motorola Schaumberg, IL 800-426-1212

Multi-Technology Systems, Inc. Mounds View, MN 800-328-9717

Natural MicroSystems Natick, MA 508-650-1300

NEC America Business Systems Sales Div. Melville, NY 516-753-7000

NEC America Irving, TX 800-TEAM-NEC

Network Application Technology, Inc. Campbell, CA 408-370-4300

Network Communications Eden Prairie, MN 612-944-8559

Network Equipment Technologies Redwood City, CA 415-366-4400

Network General Corp. Menlo Park, CA 415-473-2000

Network Managers, Inc. North Chelmsford, MA 508-251-4111

Network Peripherals, Inc. Milpitas, CA 408-321-7300

Network Systems Corp. Minneapolis, MN 612-424-4888

Newbridge Herndon, VA 800-343-3600

Newton Instrument Company Burner, NC 919-575-6426

Nextel Communications, Inc. Sacramento, CA 916-568-4400

Nextest Communications Products, Inc. Oakbrook Terrace, IL 800-888-0180

Northern Telecom, Inc. Cable Group Morton Grove, IL 708-967-6600

Northern Telecom, Inc. (Nortel) Richardson, TX 800-NORTHERN 214-437-8000

Novell, Inc. Orem, UT 801-226-8202

Octel Milpitas, CA 408-321-2000

Oki America, Inc. Hackensack, NJ 201-646-0011

ON Technology Cambridge, MA 617-374-1400

Optelecom, Inc. Gaithersburg, MD 301-840-2121

Optical Cable Corporation Roanoke, VA 703-265-0690

Optical Data Systems, Inc. Richardson, TX 214-234-6400

Opto-Electronics, Inc. Oakvill, ON 416-827-6214

Optus Software, Inc. Somerset, NJ 908-271-9568

Pacific Netcom, Inc. Portland, OR 503-292-0050

Panamax San Rafael, CA 415-499-3900

Panasonic Secaucus, NJ 201-392-4405

Panduit Tinley Park, IL 708-532-1800

Paradyne Corporation Largo, FL 800-482-3333 813-530-2287

Penril Datacomm Networks Gaithersburg, MD 301-921-8600

Persoft Madison, WI 608-273-6000

Phoenix Microsystems Huntsville, AL 205-721-1200

Photon Kinetics, Inc. Beaverton, OR 503-644-1960

PictureTel Corp Danvers, MA 508-762-5198

Plantronics Santa Cruz, CA 800-544-4660 408-426-5868

Plexcom Simi Valley, CA 805-522-3333

Polycom San Jose, CA 800-POLYCOM

Porta Systems Syosset, NY 516-364-9300

Powertel Industries, Inc. Englewood, CO 303-680-9400

Predictive Dialing Systems East Meadow, NY 800-677-1100

Preformed Line Products Cleveland, OH 216-461-5200

Premier Telecom Products Industrial Airport, KS 913-791-7000

Primary Rate, Inc. Salem, NH 508-533-4170

Proctor & Associates Redmond, WA 206-881-7000

Progressive Computing Oak Brook, IL 708-574-3399

Proteon, Inc. Westborough, MA 508-898-2800

Q.Sys International Cincinnati, OH 513-745-8078

Quality Power Systems Billerica, MA 508-670-9292

Racal Datacomm, Inc. Boxborough, MA 800-RACAL-55 508-263-9929

Racom Products Cleveland, OH 800-722-6664

RAD Data Communications Mahwah, NJ 201-529-1100

Redcom Laboratories Victor, NY 716-924-7550

Reliance Comm/Tech Cleveland, OH 216-266-5300

Retix Santa Monica, CA 310-828-3400

Rhetorix Campbell, CA 408-370-0881

RIFOCS Corp. Camarillo, CA 805-389-9800

Rightfax Tucson, AZ 520-327-1357

Rockwell Corp., Switching Systems Div. Downers Grove, IL 312-852-5700

Rockwell Network Systems Santa Barbara, CA 805-968-4262

Rycom Instruments, Inc. Raytown, MO 816-353-2100

Samsung Telecommunications America Deerfield Beach, FL 305-426-4100

Saunders Telecom Santa Fe Springs, CA 800-927-3595

Scientific-Atlanta Inc. Transmission Systems Div. Norcross, GA 404-903-5000

Securicom Valencia, CA 805-294-9121

Security Dynamics Cambridge, MA 617-547-7820

Shure Brothers Evanston, IL 708-866-2200

Siecor Hickory, NC 704-327-5000

Siemens Stromberg Carlson Boca Raton, FL 407-955-5000

Siemens/Rolm Communications, Inc. Santa Clara, CA 408-492-2000

Siemon Company Watertown,CT 203-274-2523

Simplex Wire and Cable Corp. Newington, NH 603-436-6100

SMC Happauge, NY 516-435-6000

SNMP Research, Inc. Knoxville, TN 615-573-1434

Sola Elk Grove Village, IL 800-289-7652

Solcom Systems, Inc. Reston, VA 703-758-6722

Solectek San Diego, CA 619-450-1220

Sony Corp. Of America, Inc. Montvale, NJ 201-930-7194

SpreadNet Dallas, TX 214-247-5021

Sprint Atlanta, GA 404-859-6742

Standard Microsystems Corp. Hauppage, NY 516-273-3100

Standard Wire and Cable Co. Ranch Dominguez, CA 310-609-1811

Sterling Software, Inc. Columbus, OH 614-793-7000

Stratacom, Inc. San Jose, CA 408-294-7600

Sumitomo Electric Fiber Optics Corp. Research Triangle Park, NC 919-541-8100

Summa Four Manchester, NH 603-625-4050

Sunsoft, Inc. Mountain View, CA 415-960-1300

Synoptics Communications/Bay Networks Mountain View, CA 415-960-1100

Syntellect Phoenix, AZ 602-789-2800

Systron-Donner Microwave Instruments Division Sylmar, CA 818-362-9900

T4 Systems, Inc. Little Rock AR 800-233-1526

Tadiran Electronic Industries, Inc. Clearwater, FL 813-536-3222

Tau-Tron Westford, MA 508-392-3133

Tekelec Calabasas, CA 818-880-5656

Teknekron Ft. Worth, TX 817-267-3025

Tektronix, Inc. Wilsonville, OR 800-547-8949

Telco Research Nashville, TN 615-872-9000

Telco Systems, Inc. Fiber Optics Norwood, MA 617-551-0300

Telco Systems, Inc. Fremont, CA 510-490-3111

Telebit Chelmsford, MA 800-989-8888

Telecommunications Techniques Corp. Germantown, MD 301-353-1550

TeleConcepts Newington, CT 203-666-5666

Telecorp Systems Atlanta, GA 404-587-0700

Teleos Communications, Inc. Eatontown, NJ 908-544-6432

Tellabs Inc. Lisle, IL 708-969-8800

Telrad Telecommunications Woodbury, NY 516-921-8300

Teltone Corp. Bothell, WA 800-426-3926 206-487-1515

Teradyne Deerfield, IL 708-940-9000

Texas Instruments, Inc. Attleboro, MA 508-699-3851

Texas Instruments, Inc. Dallas, TX 214-575-6320

TIE/communications, Inc. Shelton, CT 203-929-7373

Tone Commander Redmond, WA 206-883-3600

Toshiba Irvine, CA 800-222-5805 714-583-3000

Trillium Los Angeles, CA 310-479-0500

Triplett Bluffton, OH 419-358-5015

Tripp Lite Chicago, IL 312-329-1777

TSI International Wilton, CT 800-338-4194

Tylink Norton, MA 508-285-0033

Tymnet, Inc. San Jose, CA 408-946-4900

UB Networks Santa Clara, CA 408-496-0111

Unisys Corp. Blue Bell, PA 610-993-3081

US Robotics, Inc. Skokie, IL 708-982-5001

Verilink San Jose, CA 408-945-1199

Videoconferencing Systems, Inc. Norcross, GA 404-242-7566

Viking Electronics Hudson, WI 715-386-9961

VMX San Jose, CA 800-284-4VMX

Vodavi Communications Systems Scottsdale, AZ 800-843-4863

Voice Control Systems Dallas, TX 214-386-0300

Voice Processing Corp. Cambridge, MA 617-494-0100

Vtel Corp. Austin, TX 512-314-2636

Wandel & Goltermann Research Triangle Park, NC 919-941-5730

Wellfleet/Bay Networks Billerica, MA 508-670-8888

Western Datacom Cleveland, OH 216-835-1510

Western Telematic Irvine, CA 714-586-9950

Whittaker Communications Santa Clara, CA 408-565-6000

Wilcom Laconia, NH 800-222-1898

Wiltel Tulsa, OK 918-588-5773

Windata Northboro, MA 508-393-3330

Wiremold Co. West Hartford, CT 203-233-6521

Wye Technologies Annapolis, MD 410-268-1770

Wygant Scientific Portland, OR 503-227-6901 800-NUVOICE

Xyplex, Inc. Littleton, MA 508-952-4700

A P P E N D I X   D

Sources of Additional Technical Information
Standards Institutions, Trade Associations, and Trade Publications

STANDARDS INSTITUTIONS AND TRADE ASSOCIATIONS

American National Standards Institute (ANSI)
1430 Broadway
New York, NY 10018
212-642-4900

American Society for Testing and Materials (ASTM)
1916 Race Street
Philadelphia, PA 19103
215-299-5400

Bellcore Customer Service
60 New England Avenue, Room IB252
Piscataway, NJ 08854-4196
201-699-5800

Canadian Standards Association (CSA)
178 Rexdale Blvd.
Rexdale, Toronto, Ontario
Canada M9W lR3
416-747-4363

Electronic Industry Association (EIA)
2001 Pennsylvania Avenue NW
Washington, DC 20006
202-457-4900

Federal and Military Specifications
U.S. Department of Commerce National Technical Information Service
(NTIS)
5285 Port Royal Road Springfield, VA 22161
Federal Communications Commission (FCC)
Washington, DC 20554
301-725-1585

Institute of Electrical and Electronic Engineers, Inc. (IEEE)
IEEE Service Center
445 Hoes Ln.
PO Box 1331
Piscataway, NJ 08855-1331
201-981-0060

IEEE Communications Society
345 East 47th St.
New York, NY 10017
212-705-7018

International Electrotechnical Commission (IEC)
Sales Department
PO Box 131
3 rue de Varembe 1211 Geneva 20 Switzerland +41 22 34 0150
NOTE: Also obtainable from ANSI
International Organization for Standardization (ISO)
1, Rue de Varembe
Case Postale 56
CH-1211 Geneva 20
Switzerland
+41 22 34 12 40
NOTE: Also obtainable from ANSI
National Electrical Manufacturers Association (NEMA)
2101 L Street
Washington, D.C. 20037
202-457-8400

National Fire Protection Association (NFPA)
Batterymarch Park
Quincy, MA 02269
617-770-3000

National ISDN Users Forum (NIUF)
NIUF Secretariat
c/o NIST
Bldg 223, Room B364
Gaithersburg, MD 28099
301-926-9675

North American Association of Telecommunications Dealers (NATD)
25 Wearimus Ave.
Ho Ho Kus NJ 07423
201-444-5006

Society of Telecommunications Consultants (STC)
800-STC-7670

Telecommunications Industries Association (TIA)
2001 Pennsylvania Avenue NW
Washington, DC 20006
202-457-4934

Underwriters Laboratories, Inc. (UL)
333 Pfingsten Road
Northbrook, IL 60062
312-272-8800

United States Telephone Association (USTA)
900 19th Statistics. MW, Suite 800
Washington, DC 20006
202-835-3100

TRADE PUBLICATIONS

Business Communications Review 950 York Rd., Hinsdale, IL 60521
800-227-1234
Cabling Installation and Maintenance PO Box 2139, Tulsa, OK 74101
800-331-4463
Call Center Magazine 1265 Industrial Highway, Southampton, PA
18966 800-677-3435
Communications News Harcourt Brace Jovanovich, 124 S.W. 1st St.,
Geneva IL 60134 312-232-1401
Communications News 2504 North Tamiami Trail, Nokomis, FL 34275
Communications Week CMP Publications, Inc. 600 Community Dr.,
Manhasset, NY 11030 516-365-4600
Computer Telephony 12 W 21 St., New York, NY 10010 212-691-8215
Data Communications McGraw-Hill, Inc. 1221 Avenue of the Americas,
New York, NY 10020 212-512-2000

Datapro Reports on Telecommunications
  Communications Networking Services
  Voice Networking Publications
  Managing Voice Networks
600 Delran Parkway, PO Box 1066, Delran, NJ 08075 800-328-2778

Fiberoptic Product News 301 Gibraltar Dr., Box 650, Morris Plains, NJ 07950 201-292-5100

IEEE Communications IEEE Publishing Services, 345 East 47th St., New York, NY 10017-2394 212-705-7018

LAN: The Network Solutions Magazine 600 Harrison St., San Francisco, CA 94107 415-905-2200

LAN Times 1900 O'Farrell St., Suite 200, San Mateo, CA 94403 415-513-6800

Lightwave 235 Bear Hill Rd., Waltham, MA 02154 617-890-2700

Netware Solutions 10711 Burnet Rd., Ste 305, Austin, TX 78758 512-873-7761

Network World 161 Worcester Rd., Framingham, MA 01701 508-875-6400

Networking Management PennWell Publishing Co., 1421 South Sheridan, Tulsa, OK 74112 918-831-9424

Telecommunications 685 Canton St., Norwood MA 02062 617-769-9750

Telecommunications Reports 1333 H St. NW, #200 West, Washington, DC 20005 202-842-3022

Teleconnect 12 West 21 St., New York, NY 10010 212-691-8215

Telephony Magazine Telephony Publishing Corporation, 55 E Jackson Blvd., Chicago, IL 60604 312-922-2435

Voice Processing 34700 Coast Highway, Ste. 309, Capistrano Beach, CA 92624 714-493-2434

APPENDIX E

Network Design Tables

TABLE E-1

Erlang B Traffic Table

Trunks	P.01 Erlangs	CCS	P.03 Erlangs	CCS	P.05 Erlangs	CCS	P.10 Erlangs	CCS
1	0.01	0.4	0.03	1.1	0.05	1.8	0.11	4
2	0.15	5.4	0.28	10.1	0.38	13.7	0.60	21.6
3	0.46	16.6	0.75	26.9	0.90	32.4	1.27	45.7
4	0.87	31.3	1.26	45.4	1.52	54.7	2.05	73.8
5	1.36	49	1.88	67.7	2.22	79.9	2.89	104
6	1.91	68.8	2.54	91.4	2.97	107	3.75	135
7	2.50	90	3.25	117	3.75	135	4.67	168
8	3.14	113	4.00	144	4.53	163	5.61	202
9	3.78	136	4.75	171	5.36	193	6.56	236
10	4.47	161	5.53	199	6.22	224	7.50	270
11	5.17	186	6.33	228	7.08	255	8.50	306
12	5.89	212	7.14	257	7.94	286	9.47	341
13	6.61	238	7.97	287	8.83	318	10.47	377
14	7.36	265	8.81	317	9.72	350	11.47	413
15	8.11	292	9.64	347	10.64	383	12.48	449
16	8.86	319	10.50	378	11.53	415	13.50	486
17	9.64	347	11.36	409	12.47	449	14.53	523
18	10.44	376	12.25	441	13.39	482	15.56	560
19	11.22	404	13.11	472	14.31	515	16.58	597
20	12.03	433	14.00	504	15.25	549	17.61	634
21	12.83	462	14.89	536	16.19	583	18.64	671
22	13.64	491	15.78	568	17.14	617	19.69	709
23	14.47	521	16.67	600	18.08	651	20.78	748
24	15.28	550	17.58	633	19.03	685	21.78	784
25	16.11	580	18.47	665	20.00	720	22.83	822
26	16.97	611	19.39	698	20.94	754	23.89	860
27	17.81	641	20.31	731	21.89	788	24.94	898
28	18.64	671	21.22	764	22.86	823	26.00	936
29	19.50	702	22.14	797	23.83	858	27.06	974
30	20.33	732	23.06	830	24.81	893	28.11	1012
31	21.19	763	24.00	864	25.78	928	29.17	1050
32	22.06	794	24.92	897	26.75	963	30.22	1088
33	22.92	825	25.83	930	27.72	998	31.31	1127

TABLE E-1

Erlang B Traffic Table—*(Continued)*

Trunks	P.01 Erlangs	CCS	P.03 Erlangs	CCS	P.05 Erlangs	CCS	P.10 Erlangs	CCS
34	23.78	856	26.78	964	28.69	1033	32.36	1165
35	24.64	887	27.72	998	29.67	1068	33.42	1203
36	25.50	918	28.64	1031	30.67	1104	34.22	1232
37	26.39	950	29.58	1065	31.64	1139	35.58	1281
38	27.25	981	30.50	1098	32.64	1175	36.64	1319
39	28.14	1013	31.44	1132	33.61	1210	37.72	1358
40	29.00	1044	32.39	1166	34.61	1246	38.78	1396
41	29.89	1076	33.33	1200	35.58	1281	39.86	1435
42	30.78	1108	34.28	1234	36.58	1317	40.94	1474
43	31.67	1140	35.25	1269	37.58	1353	42.00	1512
44	32.53	1171	36.19	1303	38.56	1388	43.08	1551
45	33.42	1203	37.11	1336	39.56	1424	44.17	1590
46	34.33	1236	38.11	1372	40.53	1459	45.25	1629
47	35.22	1268	39.06	1406	41.53	1495	46.33	1668
48	36.11	1300	40.00	1440	42.53	1531	47.39	1706
49	37.00	1332	40.97	1475	43.53	1567	48.47	1745
50	37.89	1364	41.92	1509	44.53	1603	49.56	1784
51	38.81	1397	42.89	1544	45.50	1638	50.61	1822
52	39.69	1429	43.89	1580	46.50	1674	51.69	1861
53	40.61	1462	44.81	1613	47.50	1710	52.81	1901
54	41.50	1494	45.81	1649	48.50	1746	53.89	1940
55	42.39	1526	46.69	1681	49.50	1782	55.00	1980
56	43.31	1559	47.69	1717	50.50	1818	56.11	2020
57	44.19	1591	48.69	1753	51.50	1854	57.11	2056
58	45.11	1624	49.61	1786	52.61	1894	58.19	2095
59	46.00	1656	50.61	1822	53.61	1930	59.31	2135
60	46.89	1688	51.61	1858	54.61	1966	60.39	2174
61	47.89	1724	52.50	1890	55.61	2002	61.50	2214
62	48.81	1757	53.50	1926	56.61	2038	62.61	2254
63	49.69	1789	54.50	1962	57.61	2074	63.69	2293
64	50.61	1822	55.39	1994	58.61	2110	64.81	2333
65	51.50	1854	56.39	2030	59.61	2146	65.81	2369
66	52.39	1886	57.39	2066	60.61	2182	66.89	2408
67	53.40	1922	58.39	2102	61.61	2218	68.00	2448
68	54.31	1955	59.31	2135	62.61	2254	68.00	2448
69	55.19	1987	60.31	2171	63.69	2293	70.19	2527
70	56.11	2020	61.31	2207	64.69	2329	71.31	2567

TABLE E-1

Erlang B Traffic Table—*(Concluded)*

Trunks	P.01 Erlangs	CCS	P.03 Erlangs	CCS	P.05 Erlangs	CCS	P.10 Erlangs	CCS
71	57.00	2052	62.31	2243	65.69	2365	72.39	2606
72	58.00	2088	63.19	2275	66.69	2401	73.50	2646
73	58.89	2120	64.19	2311	67.69	2437	74.61	2686
74	59.81	2153	65.19	2347	68.69	2473	75.61	2722
75	60.69	2185	66.19	2383	69.69	2509	76.69	2761
76	61.69	2221	67.19	2419	70.81	2549	77.81	2801
77	62.61	2254	68.11	2452	71.81	2585	78.89	2840
78	63.50	2286	69.11	2488	72.81	2621	80.00	2880
79	64.39	2318	70.11	2524	73.81	2657	81.11	2920
80	65.39	2354	71.11	2560	74.81	2693	82.19	2959
81	66.31	2387	72.11	2596	75.81	2729	83.31	2999
82	67.19	2419	73.00	2628	76.89	2768	84.39	3038
83	68.19	2455	74.00	2664	77.89	2804	85.50	3078
84	69.11	2488	75.00	2700	78.89	2840	86.61	3118
85	70.00	2520	76.00	2736	79.89	2876	87.69	3157
86	70.89	2552	77.00	2772	80.89	2912	88.81	3197
87	71.89	2588	78.00	2808	82.00	2952	89.89	3236
88	72.81	2621	78.89	2840	83.00	2988	91.00	3276
89	73.69	2653	79.89	2876	84.00	3024	92.11	3316
90	74.69	2689	80.89	2912	85.00	3060	93.11	3352
91	75.61	2722	81.89	2948	86.00	3096	94.19	3391
92	76.61	2758	82.89	2984	87.11	3136	95.31	3431
93	77.50	2790	83.89	3020	88.11	3172	96.39	3470
94	78.39	2822	84.89	3056	89.11	3208	97.50	3510
95	79.39	2858	85.89	3092	90.11	3244	98.61	3550
96	80.31	2891	86.81	3125	91.11	3280	99.69	3589
97	81.19	2923	87.81	3161	92.19	3319	100.81	3629
98	82.19	2959	88.81	3197	93.19	3355	101.89	3668
99	83.11	2992	89.81	3233	94.19	3391	103.00	3708
100	84.11	3028	90.81	3269	95.19	3427	104.11	3748

TABLE E-2

Poisson Traffic Table

Trunks	P.01		P.03		P.05		P.10	
	Erlangs	CCS	Erlangs	CCS	Erlangs	CCS	Erlangs	CCS
1	0.01	0.4	0.03	1.1	0.05	1.9	0.11	3.8
2	0.15	5.4	0.27	9.7	0.36	12.9	0.53	19.1
3	0.44	15.7	0.67	24	0.82	29.4	1.10	39.6
4	0.82	29.6	1.16	41.6	1.36	49.1	1.75	63
5	1.28	46.1	1.71	61.6	1.97	70.9	2.44	88
6	1.79	64.4	2.30	82.8	2.61	94.1	3.14	113
7	2.33	83.9	2.92	105	3.28	118	3.89	140
8	2.92	105	3.58	129	3.97	143	4.67	168
9	3.50	126	4.25	153	4.69	169	5.42	195
10	4.14	149	4.94	178	5.42	195	6.22	224
11	4.78	172	5.67	204	6.17	222	7.03	253
12	5.42	195	6.39	230	6.92	249	7.83	282
13	6.11	220	7.11	256	7.69	277	8.64	311
14	6.78	244	7.86	283	8.47	305	9.47	341
15	7.47	269	8.61	310	9.25	333	10.28	370
16	8.17	294	9.36	337	10.06	362	11.14	401
17	8.89	320	10.14	365	10.83	390	11.97	431
18	9.61	346	10.89	392	11.64	419	12.83	462
19	10.36	373	11.67	420	12.44	448	13.67	492
20	11.08	399	12.47	449	13.25	477	14.53	523
21	11.83	426	13.28	478	14.08	507	15.39	554
22	12.58	453	14.08	507	14.89	536	16.25	585
23	13.33	480	14.89	536	15.72	566	17.11	616
24	14.08	507	15.67	564	16.56	596	17.97	647
25	14.86	535	16.47	593	17.39	626	18.83	678
26	15.61	562	17.31	623	18.22	656	19.72	710
27	16.39	590	18.11	652	19.06	686	20.58	741
28	17.17	618	18.94	682	19.92	717	21.47	773
29	17.97	647	19.75	711	20.75	747	22.36	805
30	18.75	675	20.58	741	21.61	778	23.22	836
31	19.53	703	21.42	771	22.47	809	24.11	868
32	20.33	732	22.25	801	23.33	840	25.00	900
33	21.11	760	23.08	831	24.19	871	25.89	932
34	21.92	789	23.92	861	25.06	902	26.78	964
35	22.72	818	24.75	891	25.92	933	27.67	996

TABLE E–2

Poisson Traffic Table—*(Continued)*

Trunks	P.01 Erlangs	CCS	P.03 Erlangs	CCS	P.05 Erlangs	CCS	P.10 Erlangs	CCS
36	23.53	847	25.61	922	26.78	964	28.56	1028
37	24.33	876	26.44	952	27.64	995	29.44	1060
38	25.14	905	27.28	982	28.50	1026	30.33	1092
39	25.97	935	28.14	1013	29.36	1057	31.25	1125
40	26.78	964	28.97	1043	30.22	1088	32.14	1157
41	27.58	993	29.83	1074	31.11	1120	33.06	1190
42	28.42	1023	30.67	1104	31.97	1151	33.94	1222
43	29.22	1052	31.53	1135	32.83	1182	34.86	1255
44	30.06	1082	32.39	1166	33.72	1214	35.75	1287
45	30.89	1112	33.25	1197	34.61	1246	36.67	1320
46	31.72	1142	34.11	1228	35.47	1277	37.56	1352
47	32.53	1171	34.97	1259	36.36	1309	38.47	1385
48	33.36	1201	35.86	1291	37.22	1340	39.36	1417
49	34.19	1231	36.72	1322	38.11	1372	40.28	1450
50	35.03	1261	37.58	1353	38.97	1403	41.17	1482
51	35.86	1291	38.44	1384	39.86	1435	42.08	1515
52	36.72	1322	39.33	1416	40.75	1467	43.00	1548
53	37.56	1352	40.19	1447	41.64	1499	43.92	1581
54	38.39	1382	41.06	1478	42.53	1531	44.83	1614
55	39.22	1412	41.92	1509	43.42	1563	45.72	1646
56	40.08	1443	42.81	1541	44.31	1595	46.64	1679
57	40.92	1473	43.67	1572	45.19	1627	47.56	1712
58	41.78	1504	44.56	1604	46.08	1659	48.47	1745
59	42.61	1534	45.42	1635	46.97	1691	49.39	1778
60	43.47	1565	46.31	1667	47.86	1723	50.31	1811
61	44.31	1595	47.17	1698	48.75	1755	51.22	1844
62	45.17	1626	48.06	1730	49.64	1787	52.14	1877
63	46.03	1657	48.94	1762	50.53	1819	53.06	1910
64	46.86	1687	49.83	1794	51.42	1851	53.97	1943
65	47.72	1718	50.69	1825	52.33	1884	54.89	1976
66	48.58	1749	51.58	1857	53.22	1916	55.81	2009
67	49.44	1780	52.47	1889	54.11	1948	56.72	2042
68	50.31	1811	53.36	1921	55.03	1981	57.67	2076

TABLE E-2

Poisson Traffic Table—*(Concluded)*

Trunks	Erlangs	P.01 CCS	Erlangs	P.03 CCS	Erlangs	P.05 CCS	Erlangs	P.10 CCS
69	51.17	1842	54.25	1953	55.92	2013	58.58	2109
70	52.03	1873	55.14	1985	56.83	2046	59.50	2142
71	52.89	1904	56.03	2017	57.72	2078	60.42	2175
72	53.75	1935	56.89	2048	58.64	2111	61.36	2209
73	54.61	1966	57.78	2080	59.53	2143	62.28	2242
74	55.47	1997	58.67	2112	60.44	2176	63.22	2276
75	56.33	2028	59.58	2145	61.33	2208	64.14	2309
76	57.17	2058	60.44	2176	62.25	2241	65.06	2342
77	58.08	2091	61.36	2209	63.17	2274	66.00	2376
78	58.94	2122	62.25	2241	64.06	2306	66.94	2410
79	59.81	2153	63.14	2273	64.97	2339	67.86	2443
80	60.67	2184	64.03	2305	65.89	2372	68.81	2477
81	61.53	2215	64.92	2337	66.81	2405	69.72	2510
82	62.42	2247	65.83	2370	67.69	2437	70.64	2543
83	63.28	2278	66.72	2402	68.61	2470	71.58	2577
84	64.17	2310	67.64	2435	69.53	2503	72.50	2610
85	65.03	2341	68.53	2467	70.44	2536	73.44	2644
86	65.92	2373	69.42	2499	71.36	2569	74.39	2678
87	66.78	2404	70.33	2532	72.25	2601	75.31	2711
88	67.67	2436	71.22	2564	73.17	2634	76.25	2745
89	68.53	2467	72.11	2596	74.08	2667	77.17	2778
90	69.42	2499	73.03	2629	75.00	2700	78.11	2812
91	70.28	2530	73.92	2661	75.92	2733	79.06	2846
92	71.17	2562	74.83	2694	76.83	2766	80.00	2880
93	72.06	2594	75.72	2726	77.72	2798	80.92	2913
94	72.92	2625	76.64	2759	78.64	2831	81.86	2947
95	73.81	2657	77.53	2791	79.56	2864	82.81	2981
96	74.69	2689	78.44	2824	80.47	2897	83.72	3014
97	75.58	2721	79.36	2857	81.39	2930	84.67	3048
98	76.44	2752	80.25	2889	82.31	2963	85.61	3082
99	77.33	2784	81.14	2921	83.22	2996	86.56	3116
100	78.22	2816	82.06	2954	84.14	3029	87.47	3149

TABLE E–3

Erlang C Table

					Probability of Delay (All Calls) of Time†						
A	N	P_d	D1	D2	.2	.4	.6	.8	1	2	3
.05	1	.0500	.053	1.05	.041	.034	.028	.023	.019	.007	.003
	2	.0012	.001	.513	.001	.001					
.10	1	.1000	.111	1.11	.084	.070	0.58	.049	.041	.017	.007
	2	.0048	.003	.526	.003	.002	.002	.001	.001		
	3	.0002		.345							
.15	1	.1500	.176	1.18	.127	.107	.090	.076	.064	.027	.012
	2	.0105	.006	.541	.007	.005	.003	.002	.002		
	3	.0005		.351							
.20	1	.2000	.250	1.25	.170	.145	.124	.105	.090	.040	.018
	2	.0182	.010	.556	.013	.009	.006	.004	.003		
	3	.0012		.357	.001						
	4	.0001		.263							
.25	1	.2500	.333	1.33	.215	.185	.159	.137	.118	.056	.026
	2	.0278	.016	.571	.020	.014	.010	.007	.005	.001	
	3	.0022	.001	.364	.001	.001					
	4	.0001		.267							
.30	1	.3000	.429	1.43	.261	.227	.197	.171	.149	.074	.037
	2	.0391	.023	.588	.028	.020	.014	.010	.007	.001	
	3	.0037	.001	.370	.002	.001	.001				
	4	.0003		.270							
.35	1	.3500	.538	1.54	.307	.270	.237	.208	.183	.095	.050
	2	.0521	.032	.606	.037	.027	.019	.014	.010	.002	
	3	.0057	.002	.377	.003	.002	.001	.001			
	4	.0005		.274							
.40	1	.4000	.667	1.67	.355	.315	.279	.248	.220	.120	.066
	2	.0667	.042	.625	.048	.035	.026	.019	.013	.003	.001
	3	.0082	.003	.385	.005	.002	.001	.001			
	4	.0008		.278							
	5	.0001		.217							
.45	1	.4500	.818	1.82	.403	.361	.324	.290	.260	.150	.086
	2	.0827	.053	.645	.061	.044	.033	.024	.018	.004	.001
	3	.0114	.004	.392	.007	.004	.002	.001	.001		
	4	.0012		.282	.0001						
	5	.0001		.220							

A = Offered load in Erlangs
N = Number of trunks (servers) required
P_d = Probability that a call will be delayed

D1 = Average delay of all calls
D2 = Average delay of delayed calls

TABLE E-3

Erlang C Table—*(Continued)*

A	N	P$_d$	D1	D2	Probability of Delay (All Calls) of Time†						
					.2	.4	.6	.8	1	2	3
.50	1	.5000	1.00	2.00	.452	.409	.370	.335	.303	.184	.112
	2	.1000	.067	.667	.074	.055	.041	.030	.022	.005	.001
	3	.0152	.006	.400	.009	.006	.003	.002	.001		
	4	.0018	.001	.286	.001						
	5	.0002		.222							
.55	1	.5500	1.22	2.22	.503	.459	.420	.384	.351	.224	.143
	2	.1186	.082	.690	.089	.066	.050	.037	.028	.007	.002
	3	.0196	.008	.408	.012	.007	.004	.003	.002		
	4	.0026	.001	.290	.001	.001					
	5	.0003		.225							
.60	1	.6000	1.50	2.50	.554	.511	.472	.436	.402	.270	.181
	2	.1385	.099	.714	.105	.079	.060	.045	.034	.008	.002
	3	.0247	.010	.417	.015	.009	.006	.004	.002		
	4	.0035	.001	.294	.002	.001					
	5	.0004		.227							
.65	1	.6500	1.86	2.86	.606	.565	.527	.491	.458	.323	.227
	2	.1594	.118	.741	.122	.093	.071	.054	.041	.011	.003
	3	.0304	.013	.426	.019	.032	.007	.005	.003		
	4	.0046	.001	.299	.002	.001	.001				
	5	.0006		.230							
	6	.0001		.187							
.70	1	.7000	2.33	3.33	.659	.621	.585	.551	.519	.384	.285
	2	.1815	.140	.769	.140	.108	.083	.064	.049	.013	.004
	3	.0369	.016	.435	.023	.015	.009	.006	.004		
	4	.0060	.002	.303	.003	.002	.001				
	5	.0008		.233							
	6	.0001		.189							
.75	1	.7500	3.00	4.00	.713	.679	.646	.614	.584	.455	.354
	2	.2045	.164	.800	.159	.124	.097	.075	.059	.017	.005
	3	.0441	.020	.444	.028	.018	.011	.007	.005		
	4	.0077	.002	.308	.004	.002	.001	.001			
	5	.0011		.235							
	6	.0001		.190							

A = Offered load in Erlangs

N = Number of trunks (servers) required

P$_d$ = Probability that a call will be delayed

D1 = Average delay of all calls

D2 = Average delay of delayed calls

TABLE E–3

Erlang C Table—*(Continued)*

					Probability of Delay (All Calls) of Time†						
A	N	P_d	D1	D2	.2	.4	.6	.8	1	2	3
.80	1	.8000	4.00	5.00	.769	.738	.710	.682	.655	.536	.439
	2	.2286	.190	.833	.180	.141	.111	.088	.069	.021	.006
	3	.0520	.024	.455	.034	.022	.014	.009	.006	.001	
	4	.0096	.003	.312	.005	.003	.001	.001			
	5	.0015		.238	.001						
	6	.0002		.192							
.85	1	.3500	5.67	6.67	.825	.800	.777	.754	.732	.630	.542
	2	.2535	.220	.870	.201	.160	.127	.101	.080	.025	.008
	3	.0607	.028	.465	.039	.026	.017	.011	.007	.001	
	4	.0118	.004	.317	.006	.003	.002	.001	.001		
	5	.0019		.241	.001						
	6	.0003		.194							
.90	1	.9000	9.00	10.0	.882	.865	.848	.831	.814	.737	.667
	2	.2793	.254	.909	.224	.180	.144	.116	.093	.031	.010
	3	.0700	.033	.476	.046	.030	.020	.013	.009	.001	
	4	.0143	.005	.323	.008	004	.002	.001	.001		
	5	.0024	.001	.244	.001						
	6	.0004		.196							
.95	1	.9500	19.0	20.0	.941	.931	.922	.913	.904	.860	.818
	2	.3059	.291	.952	.248	.201	.163	.132	.107	.037	.013
	3	.0801	.039	.488	.053	.035	.023	.016	.010	.001	
	4	.0172	.006	.328	.009	.005	.003	.001	.001		
	5	.0031	.001	.247	.001						
	6	.0005		.198							
	7	.0001		.165							
1.0	2	.3333	.333	1.00	.273	.223	.183	.150	.123	.045	.017
	3	.0909	.045	.500	.061	.041	.027	.018	.012	.002	
	4	.0204	.007	.333	.011	.006	.003	.002	.001		
	5	.0038	.001	.250	.002	.001					
	6	.0006		.200							
	7	.0001		.167							

A = Offered load in Erlangs
N = Number of trunks (servers) required
P_d = Probability that a call will be delayed

D1 = Average delay of all calls
D2 = Average delay of delayed calls

TABLE E–3

Erlang C Table—*(Continued)*

					Probability of Delay (All Calls) of Time†						
A	N	P_d	D1	D2	.2	.4	.6	.8	1	2	3
1.1	2	.3903	.434	1.11	.326	.272	.227	.190	.159	.065	.026
	3	.1146	.060	.526	.078	.054	.037	.025	.017	.003	
	4	.0279	.010	.345	.016	.009	.005	.003	.002		
	5	.0057	.001	.256	.003	.001	.001				
	6	.0010		.204							
	7	.0002		.169							
1.2	2	.4500	.562	1.25	.383	.327	.278	.237	.202	.091	.041
	3	.1412	.078	.556	.098	.069	.048	.033	.023	.004	.001
	4	.370	.013	.357	.021	.012	.007	.004	.002		
	5	.0082	.002	.263	.004	.002	.001				
	6	.0016		.208	.001						
	7	.0003		.172							
1.3	2	.5121	.732	1.43	.445	.387	.336	.293	.254	.126	.063
	3	.1704	.100	.588	.121	.085	.061	.044	.031	.006	.001
	4	.0478	.018	.370	.028	.016	.009	.006	.003		
	5	.0114	.003	.270	.005	.003	.001	.001			
	6	.0023		.213	.001						
	7	.0004		.175							
	8	.0001		.149							
1.4	2	.5765	.961	1.67	.511	.453	.402	.357	.316	.174	.095
	3	.2024	.126	.625	.147	.107	.077	.056	.041	.008	.002
	4	.0603	.023	.385	.036	.021	.013	.008	.004		
	5	.0153	.004	.278	.007	.004	.002	.001			
	6	.0034	.001	.217	.001	.001	.001				
	7	.0006		.179							
	8	.0001									
1.5	2	.6429	1.29	2.00	.582	.526	.476	.431	.390	.236	.143
	3	.2368	.158	.667	.175	.130	.096	.071	.053	.012	.003
	4	.0746	.030	.400	.045	.027	.017	.010	.006	.001	
	5	.0201	.006	.286	.010	.005	.002	.001	.001		
	6	.0047	.001	.222	.002	.001					
	7	.0010		.182							
	8	.0002		.154							

A = Offered load in Erlangs
N = Number of trunks (servers) required
P_d = Probability that a call will be delayed

D1 = Average delay of all calls
D2 = Average delay of delayed calls

TABLE E–3

Erlang C Table—*(Continued)*

| | | | | Probability of Delay (All Calls) of Time† | | | | | | |
A	N	P_d	D1	D2	.2	.4	.6	.8	1	2	3
1.6	2	.7111	1.78	2.50	.656	.606	.559	.516	.477	.320	.214
	3	.2738	.196	.714	.207	.156	.118	.089	.068	.017	.004
	4	.0907	.038	.417	.056	.035	.021	.013	.008	.001	
	5	.0259	.008	.294	.013	.007	.003	.002	.001		
	6	.0064	.001	.227	.003	.001					
	7	.0014		.185							
	8	.0003		.156							
1.7	2	.7811	2.60	3.33	.736	.693	.652	.614	.579	.429	.318
	3	.3131	.241	.769	.241	.186	.144	.111	.085	.023	.006
	4	.1087	.047	.435	.069	.043	.027	.017	.011	.001	
	5	.0326	.010	.303	.017	.009	.005	.002	.001		
	6	.0085	.002	.233	.004	.002	.001				
	7	.0020		.189	.001						
	8	.0004		.159							
	9	.0001		.137							
1.8	2	.8526	4.26	5.00	.819	.787	.756	.727	.698	.572	.468
	3	.3547	.296	.833	.279	.220	.173	.136	.107	.032	.010
	4	.1285	.058	.455	.083	.053	.034	.022	.014	.002	
	5	.0405	.013	.312	.021	.011	.006	.003	.002		
	6	.0111	.003	.238	.005	.002	.001				
	7	.0027	.001	.192	.001						
	8	.0006		.161							
	9	.0001		.139							
1.9	2	.9256	9.26	10.0	.907	.889	.872	.854	.838	.758	.686
	3	.3985	.362	.909	.320	.257	.206	.165	.133	.044	.015
	4	.1503	.072	.476	.099	.065	.043	.028	.018	.002	
	5	.0495	.016	.323	.027	.014	.008	.004	.002		
	6	.0143	.003	.244	.006	.003	.001	.001			
	7	.0036	.001	.196	.001						
2.0	3	.4444	.444	1.00	.364	.298	.244	.200	.164	.060	.022
	4	.1739	.087	.500	.117	.078	.052	.035	.024	.003	
	5	.0597	.020	.333	.033	.018	.010	.005	.003		
	6	.0180	.005	.250	.008	.004	.002	.001			
	7	.0048	.001	.200	.002	.001					
	8	.0011		.167							
	9	.0002		.143							

A = Offered load in Erlangs
N = Number of trunks (servers) required
P_d = Probability that a call will be delayed

D1 = Average delay of all calls
D2 = Average delay of delayed calls

TABLE E-3

Erlang C Table—(Continued)

A	N	P_d	D1	D2	.2	.4	.6	.8	1	2	3

Header: **Probability of Delay (All Calls) of Time†** spans columns .2 through 3.

A	N	P_d	D1	D2	.2	.4	.6	.8	1	2	3
2.1	3	.4923	.547	1.11	.411	.343	.287	.240	.200	.081	.033
	4	.1994	.105	.526	.136	.093	.064	.044	.030	.004	.001
	5	.0712	.025	.345	.040	.022	.012	.007	.004		
	6	.0224	.006	.256	.010	.005	.002	.001			
	7	.0062	.001	.204	.002	.001					
	8	.0016		.169							
	9	.0003		.145							
	10	.0001		.127							
2.2	3	.5422	.678	1.25	.462	.394	.335	.286	.244	.109	.049
	4	.2268	.126	.556	.158	.110	.077	.054	.037	.006	.001
	5	.0839	.030	.357	.048	.027	.016	.009	.005		
	6	.0275	.007	.263	.013	.006	.003	.001	.001		
	7	.0080	.002	.208	.003	.001					
	8	.0021		.172	.001						
	9	.0005		.147							
	10	.0001		.128							
2.3	3	.5938	.848	1.43	.516	.449	.390	.339	.295	.146	.073
	4	.2560	.151	.588	.182	.130	.092	.066	.047	.009	.002
	5	.0980	.036	.370	.057	.033	.019	.011	.007		
	6	.0333	.009	.270	.016	.008	.004	.002	.001		
	7	.0101	.002	.213	.004	.002	.001				
	8	.0027		.175	.001						
	9	.0007		.149							
	10	.0001		.130							
2.4	3	.6472	1.08	1.67	.574	.509	.452	.400	.355	.195	.107
	4	.2870	.179	.625	.208	.151	.110	.080	.058	.012	.002
	5	.1135	.044	.385	.040	.024	.014	.008	.001		
	6	.0400	.011	.278	.019	.009	.005	.002	.001		
	7	.0126	.003	.217	.005	.002	.001				
	8	.0035	.001	.179	.001						
	9	.0009		.152							
	10	.0002		.132							

A = Offered load in Erlangs
N = Number of trunks (servers) required
P_d = Probability that a call will be delayed

D1 = Average delay of all calls
D2 = Average delay of delayed calls

TABLE E-3

Erlang C Table—*(Continued)*

					Probability of Delay (All Calls) of Time†						
A	N	P_d	D1	D2	.2	.4	.6	.8	1	2	3
2.5	3	.7022	1.40	2.00	.635	.575	.520	.471	.426	.258	.157
	4	.3199	.213	.667	.237	.176	.130	.096	.071	.016	.004
	5	.1304	.052	.400	.079	.048	.029	.018	.011	.001	
	6	.0474	.014	.286	.024	.012	.006	.003	.001		
	7	.0154	.003	.222	.006	.003	.001				
	8	.0043	.001	.182	.002	.001					
	9	.0012		.154							
	10	.0003		.133							
	11	.0001		.118							
2.6	3	.7589	1.90	2.50	.701	.647	.597	.551	.509	.341	.229
	4	.3544	.253	.714	.268	.202	.153	.116	.087	.022	.005
	5	.1487	.062	.417	.092	.057	.035	.022	.013	.001	
	6	.0558	.016	.294	.028	.014	.007	.004	.002		
	7	.0188	.004	.227	.008	.003	.001	.001			
	8	.0057	.001	.185	.002	.001					
	9	.0016		.156							
	10	.0004		.135							
	11	.0001		.119							
2.7	3	.8171	2.72	3.33	.769	.725	.682	.643	.605	.448	.332
	4	.3907	.301	.769	.301	.232	.179	.138	.106	.029	.008
	5	.1684	.073	.435	.106	.067	.042	.017	.002		
	6	.0652	.020	.303	.034	.017	.009	.005	.002		
	7	.0227	.005	.233	.010	.004	.002	.001			
	8	.0071	.001	.189	.002	.001					
	9	.0020		.159	.001						
	10	.0005		.137							
	11	.0001		.120							
2.8	3	.8767	4.38	5.00	.842	.309	.778	.747	.718	.588	.481
	4	.4287	.357	.833	.337	.263	.209	.164	.129	.039	.012
	5	.1895	.086	.455	.122	.079	.051	.033	.021	.002	
	6	.0755	.024	.312	.040	.021	.011	.006	.003		
	7	.0271	.006	.238	.012	.005	.002	.001			
	8	.0088	.002	.192	.003	.001					
	9	.0026		.161	.001						

A = Offered load in Erlangs   D1 = Average delay of all calls
N = Number of trunks (servers) required   D2 = Average delay of delayed calls
P_d = Probability that a call will be delayed

TABLE E-3

Erlang C Table—*(Continued)*

A	N	P_d	D1	D2	Probability of Delay (All Calls) of Time†						
					.2	.4	.6	.8	1	2	3
2.9	3	.9377	9.38	10.0	.919	.901	.883	.866	.848	.768	.695
	4	.4682	.426	.909	.376	.302	.242	.194	.156	.052	.017
	5	.2121	.101	.476	.139	.092	.060	.040	.026	.003	
	6	.0868	.028	.323	.047	.025	.014	.007	.004		
	7	.0320	.008	.244	.014	.006	.003	.001	.001		
	8	.0107	.002	.196	.004	.001	.001				
	9	.0032	.001	.164	.001						
3.0	4	.5094	.509	1.00	.461	.417	.377	.341	.309	.241	.187
	5	.2362	.118	.500	.193	.158	.130	.106	.087	.053	.032
	6	.0991	.033	.333	.073	.054	.040	.030	.022	.010	.005
	7	.0376	.009	.250	.025	.017	.011	.008	.005	.002	.001
	8	.0129	.003	.200	.008	.005	.003	.002	.001		
	9	.0040	.001	.167	.001	.001					
3.1	4	.5522	.614	1.11	.505	.461	.422	.385	.352	.281	.225
	5	2616	.138	.526	.216	.179	.148	.122	.101	.063	.039
	6	.1126	.039	.345	.084	.063	.047	.035	.026	.013	.006
	7	.0439	011	.256	.030	.020	.014	.009	.006	.002	.001
	8	.0155	.003	.204	.009	.006	.004	.002	.001		
	9	.0050	.001	.169	.003	.002	.001				
3.2	4	.5964	.746	1.25	.551	.508	.469	.433	.400	.327	.268
	5	.2886	.160	.556	.241	.201	.168	.140	.117	.075	.048
	6	.1271	.045	.357	.096	.073	.055	.041	.031	.016	.008
	7	.0509	.013	.263	.035	.024	.016	.011	.008	.003	.001
	8	.0185	.004	.208	.011	.007	.004	.003	.002	001	
	9	.0061	.011	.172	.003	.002	.001	.001			
3.3	4	.6422	.917	1.43	.599	.558	.521	.485	.453	.380	.319
	5	.3169	.186	.588	.267	.226	.190	.161	.135	.089	.058
	6	.1427	.053	.370	.109	.083	.063	.048	.037	.019	.010
	7	.0585	.016	.270	.040	.028	.019	.013	.009	.004	.001
	8	.0219	.005	.213	.014	.009	.005	.003	.002	.001	
	9	.0074	.001	.175	.004	.002	.001	.001			
	10	.0023		.149	.001	.001					

A = Offered load in Erlangs
N = Number of trunks (servers) required
P_d = Probability that a call will be delayed

D1 = Average delay of all calls
D2 = Average delay of delayed calls

TABLE E–3

Erlang C Table—*(Continued)*

					Probability of Delay (All Calls) of Time†						
A	N	P_d	D1	D2	.2	.4	.6	.8	1	2	3
3.4	4	.6893	1.15	1.67	.649	.611	.576	.542	.511	.440	.378
	5	.3467	.217	.625	.295	.262	.215	.183	.156	.104	.070
	6	.1595	.061	.385	.123	.095	.073	.056	.043	.023	.012
	7	.0670	.019	.278	.047	.033	.023	.016	.011	.005	.002
	8	.0256	.006	.217	.016	.010	.006	.004	.003	.001	
	9	.0090	.002	.179	.005	.003	.002	.001	.001		
	10	.0029		.152	.001	.001					
3.5	4	.7379	1.48	2.00	.702	.668	.635	.604	.575	.507	.448
	5	.3778	.252	.667	.325	.280	.241	.207	.178	.123	.084
	6	.1775	.071	.400	.138	.108	.084	.065	.051	.027	.015
	7	.0762	.022	.286	.054	.038	.027	.019	.013	.006	.002
	8	.0299	.007	.222	.022	.014	.009	.006	004	.001	
	9	.0107	.002	.182	.007	.004	.003	.001	.001		
	10	.0035	.00l	.154	.002	.001	.001				
	11	.0011		.133	.001						
3.6	4	.7878	1.97	2.50	.757	.727	.699	.671	.645	.584	.528
	5	.4104	.293	.714	.357	.310	.270	.234	.204	.144	.101
	6	.1966	.082	.417	.153	.122	.096	.075	.059	.032	.018
	7	.0862	.025	.294	.061	.044	.031	.022	.016	.007	.003
	8	.0346	.008	.227	.022	.014	.009	.006	.004	.001	
	9	.0127	.002	.185	.007	.004	.003	.002	.001		
	10	.0043	.001	.156	.002	.001	.001				
3.7	4	.8390	2.80	3.33	.814	.790	.767	.744	.722	.670	.622
	5	.4443	.342	.769	.390	.343	.301	.264	.232		
	8	.0521	.013	.244	.035	.023	.015	.010	.007	.002	.001
	9	.0205	.004	.196	.012	.007	.004	.003	.002		
	10	.0074	.001	.164	.004	.002	.001	.001			
	11	.0025		.141	.001	.001					
3.8	4	.8914	4.46	5.00	.874	.856	.840	.823	.807	.767	.730
	5	.4796	.400	.833	.425	.377	.355	.297	.263	.195	.144
	6	.2383	.108	.455	.191	.153	.123	.099	.079	.046	.026
	7	.1089	.034	.312	.079	.057	.042	.030	.022	.010	.004
	8	.0457	.011	.238	.030	.020	.013	.009	.006	.002	.001
	9	.0176	.003	.192	.010	.006	.004	.002	.001		
	10	.0062	.001	.161	.003	.002	.001	.001			
	11	.0029		.139	.001						

A = Offered load in Erlangs
N = Number of trunks (servers) required
P_d = Probability that a call will be delayed

D1 = Average delay of all calls
D2 = Average delay of delayed calls

TABLE E–3

Erlang C Table—*(Continued)*

A	N	P_d	D1	D2	.2	.4	.6	.8	1	2	3
							Probability of Delay (All Calls) of Time†				
3.9	4	.9451	9.45	10.0	.936	.926	.917	.908	.899	.877	.855
	5	.5162	.469	.909	.462	.414	.371	.332	.298	.226	.172
	6	.2609	.124	.476	.212	.271	.139	.113	.091	.058	.032
	7	.1215	.039	.323	.089	.065	048	.035	.026	.012	.005
	8	.0521	.013	.244	.035	.023	.015	.010	.007	.002	.001
	9	.0205	.004	.196	.012	.007	.004	.003	.002		
	10	.0074	.001	.164	.004	.002	.001	.001			
	11	.0025		.141	.001	.001					
4.0	5	.5541	.334	1.00	.501	.454	.410	.371	.336	.262	.204
	6	.2848	.142	.500	.233	.191	.156	.128	.105	.064	.039
	7	.1351	.045	.333	.100	.074	.053	.041	.030	.014	.007
	8	.0590	.015	.250	.040	.027	.018	.012	.008	.003	.001
	9	.0238	.205	.200	.014	.009	.005	.003	.002	.002	
	10	.0088	.001	.167	.005	.003	.001	.001			
	11	.0030		.143	.002	.001					
4.1	5	.5933	.659	1.11	.542	.496	.453	.414	.378	.302	.241
	6	.3098	.263	.526	.256	.212	.176	.145	.120	.075	.046
	7	.1496	.052	.343	.112	.084	.063	.047	.035	.017	.008
	8	.0667	.017	.256	.045	.031	.021	.014	.009	.004	.001
	9	.0274	.006	.204	.017	.010	.006	.004	.002	.001	
	10	.0104	002	.169	.006	003	.002	.001	.001		
	11	.0036	.001	.145	.002	.001					
	12	.0012		.127	.001						
4.2	5	.6338	.792	1.25	.585	.540	.499	.460	.425	.348	.285
	6	.3360	.187	.556	.281	.234	.196	.164	.137	.087	.056
	7	.1651	.059	.357	.125	.094	.071	.054	.041	.020	.010
	8	.0749	.020	.263	.051	.035	.024	.016	.011	.004	.002
	9	.0314	.007	.208	.019	.012	.007	.005	.003	.001	
	10	.0122	.002	.172	.007	.004	.002	.001	001		
	11	.0044	.001	.147	.002	.001	.001				
	12	.0015		.128	001						

A = Offered load in Erlangs
N = Number of trunks (servers) required
P_d = Probability that a call will be delayed

D1 = Average delay of all calls
D2 = Average delay of delayed calls

TABLE E-3

Erlang C Table—*(Concluded)*

A	N	P_d	D1	D2	.2	.4	.6	.8	1	2	3
					\multicolumn{7}{}{*Probability of Delay (All Calls) of Time†*}						
4.3	5	.6755	.965	1.43	.630	.587	.548	.511	.476	.400	.335
	6	.3634	.214	.588	.307	.259	.218	.184	.155	.102	.066
	7	.1815	.067	.370	.139	.106	.081	.062	.047	.024	.012
	8	.0839	.023	.270	.058	.040	.028	.019	.013	.005	.002
	9	.0358	.008	.213	.022	.014	.009	.005	.003	.001	
	10	.0142	.002	.175	.008	.005	.003	.001	.001		
	11	.0052	.001	.149	.003	.001	.001				
	12	.0018		.130	.001						
4.4	5	.7184	1.20	1.67	.667	.637	.600	.565	.532	.458	.394
	6	.3919	.245	.625	.334	.285	.243	.207	.176	.118	.079
	7	.1988	.076	.385	.153	.118	.091	.070	.054	.028	.015
	8	.0935	.026	.278	.065	.046	.032	.022	.015	.006	.003
	9	.0407	.009	.217	.026	.016	.010	.006	.004	.001	
	10	.0164	.003	.179	.009	.005	.003	.002	.001		
	11	.0061	.001	.152	.003	.002	.001				
	12	.0021		.132	.001						
4.5	5	.7625	1.52	2.00	.725	.690	.656	.625	.594	.524	.462
	6	.4217	.281	.667	.363	.312	.269	.231	.199	.137	.094
	7	.2172	.087	.400	.169	.132	.103	.080	.062	.033	.018
	8	.1039	.030	.286	.073	.052	.036	.026	.018	.008	.003
	9	.0460	.010	.222	.029	.019	.012	.008	.005	.002	.001
	10	.0189	.003	.182	.011	.006	.004	.002	.001		
	11	.0072	.001	.154	.004	.002	.001	.001			
	12	.0026		.133	.001	.001					

A = Offered load in Erlangs
N = Number of trunks (servers) required
P_d = Probability that a call will be delayed

D1 = Average delay of all calls
D2 = Average delay of delayed calls

Domestic and International Dialing Codes

NORTH AMERICAN AREA CODES IN ALPHABETIC ORDER

Alabama	205	Connecticut	860
Alabama	334	Delaware	302
Alaska	907	District of Columbia	202
Alberta	403	Florida	305
Arizona	520	Florida	352
Arizona	602	Florida	407
Arkansas	501	Florida	813
Bermuda	441	Florida	904
British Columbia	250	Florida	941
British Columbia	604	Florida	954
California	209	Georgia	404
California	213	Georgia	706
California	310	Georgia	770
California	408	Georgia	912
California	415	Hawaii	808
California	510	Idaho	208
California	562	Illinois	217
California	619	Illinois	309
California	707	Illinois	312
California	714	Illinois	618
California	805	Illinois	630
California	818	Illinois	708
California	909	Illinois	815
California	916	Illinois	847
Caribbean	809	Indiana	219
Colorado	303	Indiana	317
Colorado	719	Indiana	812
Colorado	970	Iowa	319
Connecticut	203	Iowa	515

Iowa	712	New Jersey	609
Kansas	316	New Jersey	908
Kansas	913	New Mexico	505
Kentucky	502	New York	212
Kentucky	606	New York	315
Louisiana	318	New York	516
Louisiana	504	New York	518
Maine	207	New York	607
Manitoba	204	New York	716
Maryland	301	New York	718
Maryland	410	New York	914
Massachusetts	413	New York	917
Massachusetts	508	Newfoundland	709
Massachusetts	617	North Carolina	704
Michigan	313	North Carolina	910
Michigan	517	North Carolina	919
Michigan	616	North Dakota	701
Michigan	810	Nova Scotia & Prince	
Michigan	906	Edward Is.	902
Minnesota	218	Ohio	216
Minnesota	370	Ohio	330
Minnesota	507	Ohio	419
Minnesota	612	Ohio	513
Mississippi	601	Ohio	614
Missouri	314	Oklahoma	405
Missouri	417	Oklahoma	918
Missouri	573	Ontario	416
Missouri	816	Ontario	519
Montana	406	Ontario	613
Nebraska	308	Ontario	705
Nebraska	402	Ontario	807
Nevada	702	Ontario	905
New Brunswick	506	Oregon	503
New Hampshire	603	Oregon	541
New Jersey	201	Pennsylvania	215

Pennsylvania	412	Texas	713
Pennsylvania	610	Texas	806
Pennsylvania	717	Texas	817
Pennsylvania	814	Texas	903
Quebec	418	Texas	915
Quebec	514	Texas	972
Quebec	819	Utah	801
Rhode Island	401	Vermont	802
Saskatchewan	306	Virginia	540
South Carolina	803	Virginia	703
South Carolina	864	Virginia	804
South Dakota	605	Washington	206
Tennessee	423	Washington	360
Tennessee	615	Washington	509
Tennessee	901	West Virginia	304
Texas	210	Wisconsin	414
Texas	214	Wisconsin	608
Texas	281	Wisconsin	715
Texas	409	Wyoming	307
Texas	512		

NORTH AMERICAN AREA CODES IN NUMERIC ORDER

201	New Jersey	214	Texas
202	District of Columbia	215	Pennsylvania
203	Connecticut	216	Ohio
204	Manitoba	217	Illinois
205	Alabama	218	Minnesota
206	Washington	219	Indiana
207	Maine	250	British Columbia
208	Idaho	281	Texas
209	California	301	Maryland
210	Texas	302	Delaware
212	New York	303	Colorado
213	California	304	West Virginia

305	Florida	419	Ohio
306	Saskatchewan	423	Tennessee
307	Wyoming	441	Bermuda
308	Nebraska	501	Arkansas
309	Illinois	502	Kentucky
310	California	503	Oregon
312	Illinois	504	Louisiana
313	Michigan	505	New Mexico
314	Missouri	506	New Brunswick
315	New York	507	Minnesota
316	Kansas	508	Massachusetts
317	Indiana	509	Washington
318	Louisiana	510	California
319	Iowa	512	Texas
330	Ohio	513	Ohio
334	Alabama	514	Quebec
352	Florida	515	Iowa
360	Washington	516	New York
370	Minnesota	517	Michigan
401	Rhode Island	518	New York
402	Nebraska	519	Ontario
403	Alberta	520	Arizona
404	Georgia	540	Virginia
405	Oklahoma	541	Oregon
406	Montana	562	California
407	Florida	573	Missouri
408	California	601	Mississippi
409	Texas	602	Arizona
410	Maryland	603	New Hampshire
412	Pennsylvania	604	British Columbia
413	Massachusetts	605	South Dakota
414	Wisconsin	606	Kentucky
415	California	607	New York
416	Ontario	608	Wisconsin
417	Missouri	609	New Jersey
418	Quebec	610	Pennsylvania

612	Minnesota		810	Michigan
613	Ontario		812	Indiana
614	Ohio		813	Florida
615	Tennessee		814	Pennsylvania
616	Michigan		815	Illinois
617	Massachusetts		816	Missouri
618	Illinois		817	Texas
619	California		818	California
630	Illinois		819	Quebec
701	North Dakota		847	Illinois
702	Nevada		860	Connecticut
703	Virginia		864	South Carolina
704	North Carolina		901	Tennessee
705	Ontario		902	Nova Scotia & Prince
706	Georgia			Edward Is.
707	California		903	Texas
708	Illinois		904	Florida
709	Newfoundland		905	Ontario
712	Iowa		906	Michigan
713	Texas		907	Alaska
714	California		908	New Jersey
715	Wisconsin		909	California
716	New York		910	North Carolina
717	Pennsylvania		912	Georgia
718	New York		913	Kansas
719	Colorado		914	New York
770	Georgia		915	Texas
801	Utah		916	California
802	Vermont		917	New York
803	South Carolina		918	Oklahoma
804	Virginia		919	North Carolina
805	California		941	Florida
806	Texas		954	Florida
807	Ontario		970	Colorado
808	Hawaii		972	Texas
809	Caribbean			

COUNTRY CODES IN ALPHABETIC ORDER

Albania	355	Cayman Islands*	809
Algeria	213	Central African Republic	236
American Samoa	684	Chad	235
Andorra	33	Chile	56
Angola	244	China	86
Anguilla (Barbuda)*	809	Colombia	57
Antigua*	809	Congo	242
Argentina	54	Cook Island	682
Aruba	297	Costa Rica	506
Ascension Island	247	Croatia	385
Australia (incl. Tasmania)	61	Cyprus	357
Austria	43	Czech Republic	42
Bahamas*	809	Denmark	45
Bahrain	973	Djibouti	253
Bangladesh	880	Dominica*	809
Barbados*	809	Dominican Republic*	809
Belgium	32	Ecuador	593
Belize	501	Egypt	20
Benin	229	El Salvador	503
Bermuda	809	Equatorial Guinea	240
Bhutan	975	Ethiopia	251
Bolivia	591		
Botswana	267	Faeroe Islands	298
Bosnia-Herzegovina	387	Falkland Islands	500
Brazil	55	Fiji Islands	679
British Virgin Islands*	809	Finland	358
Brunei	673	France	33
Bulgaria	359	French Antilles	596
Burkina Faso	226	French Guiana	594
Burundi	257	French Polynesia	689
Cameroon	237	Gabon	241
Canada	1	Gambia	220
Cape Verde Islands	238	Germany, East	37
		Germany, West	49

Ghana	233	Libya	218
Gibraltar	350	Liechtenstein	41
Greece	30	Luxembourg	352
Greenland	299	Macao	853
Grenada (incl. Carriacou)*	809	Macedonia	389
Guadeloupe	590	Madagascar	261
Guam	671	Malawi	265
Guantanamo Bay	53	Malaysia	60
Guatemala	502	Maldives	960
Guinea	224	Mali Republic	223
Guinea-Bissau	245	Malta	356
Guyana	592	Marshall Islands	692
Haiti	509	Mauritania	222
Honduras	504	Mauritius	230
Hong Kong	852	Mayotte Island	269
Hungary	36	Mexico	52
Iceland	354	Micronesia	691
India	91	Monaco	33
Indonesia	62	Montserrat*	809
Iran	98	Morocco	212
Iraq	964	Mozambique	258
Ireland	353	Namibia	264
Israel	972	Nauru	674
Italy	39	Nepal	977
Ivory Coast	225	Netherlands	31
Jamaica*	809	Netherlands Antilles	599
Japan	81	Nevis*	809
Jordan	962	New Caledonia	687
Kenya	254	New Zealand	64
Kiribati	686	Nicaragua	505
Korea	82	Niger	227
Kuwait	965	Nigeria	234
Lebanon	961	Norway	47
Lesotho	266	Oman	968
Liberia	231		

Pakistan	92	Suriname	597
Palau	680	Swaziland	268
Panama	507	Sweden	46
Papua New Guinea	675	Switzerland	41
Paraguay	595	Syria	963
Peru	51	Taiwan	886
Philippines	63	Tanzania	255
Poland	48	Thailand	66
Portugal (incl. Azores)	351	Togo	228
Qatar	974	Tonga	676
Reunion Island	262	Trinidad/Tobago*	809
Romania	40	Tunisia	216
Rwanda	250	Turkey	90
Russia	7	Turks and Caicos Islands*	809
Saipan (incl. Rota)	670	Uganda	256
San Marino	39	United Arab Emirates	971
Sao Tome	239	United Kingdom	44
Saudi Arabia	966	United States	1
Senegal Republic	221	Uruguay	598
Seychelles	248	Vatican City	39
Sierra Leone	232	Venezuela	58
Singapore	65	Western Samoa	685
Slovenia	386	Yemen Arab Republic	967
Solomon Islands	677	Yugoslavia	381
South Africa	27		
Spain (incl. Balearic Isl)	34	Zaire	243
Sri Lanka	94	Zambia	260
St. Helena	290	Zimbabwe	263
St. Kitts*	809	SAT East Atlantic	871
St. Lucia*	809	SAT West Atlantic	874
St. Pierre/Miquelon	508	SAT Pacific	872
St. Vincent/Grenadines*	809	SAT Indian	873

*809 is an area code, not a country code. You can reach these locations by dialing '1'+ 809 + the number.

COUNTRY CODES IN NUMERIC ORDER

1	United States and Canada	57	Colombia
7	Russia	58	Venezuela
20	Egypt	60	Malaysia
27	South Africa	61	Australia (incl. Tasmania)
30	Greece	62	Indonesia
31	Netherlands	63	Philippines
32	Belgium	64	New Zealand
33	Andorra	65	Singapore
33	France	66	Thailand
33	Monaco	81	Japan
34	Spain (incl. Balearic lsl)	82	Korea
36	Hungary	86	China
37	Germany, East	90	Turkey
39	Italy	91	India
39	San Marino	92	Pakistan
39	Vatican City	94	Sri Lanka
40	Romania	98	Iran
41	Liechtenstein	212	Morocco
41	Switzerland	213	Algeria
42	Czech Republic	216	Tunisia
43	Austria	218	Libya
44	United Kingdom	220	Gambia
45	Denmark	221	Senegal Republic
46	Sweden	222	Mauritania
47	Norway	223	Mali Republic
48	Poland	224	Guinea
49	Germany, West	225	Ivory Coast
51	Peru	226	Burkina Faso
52	Mexico	227	Niger
53	Guantanamo Bay	228	Togo
54	Argentina	229	Benin
55	Brazil	230	Mauritius
56	Chile	231	Liberia

232	Sierra Leone		297	Aruba
233	Ghana		298	Faeroe Islands
234	Nigeria		299	Greenland
235	Chad		350	Gibraltar
236	Central African Republic		351	Portugal (incl. Azores)
237	Cameroon		352	Luxembourg
238	Cape Verde Islands		353	Ireland
239	Sao Tome		354	Iceland
240	Equatorial Guinea		355	Albania
241	Gabon		356	Malta
242	Congo		357	Cyprus
243	Zaire		358	Finland
244	Angola		359	Bulgaria
245	Guinea-Bissau		381	Yugoslavia
247	Ascension Island		385	Croatia
248	Seychelles		386	Slovenia
250	Rwanda		387	Bosnia-Herzegovina
251	Ethiopia		389	Macedonia
253	Djibouti		500	Falkland Islands
254	Kenya		501	Belize
255	Tanzania		502	Guatemala
256	Uganda		503	El Salvador
257	Burundi		504	Honduras
258	Mozambique		505	Nicaragua
260	Zambia		506	Costa Rica
261	Madagascar		507	Panama
262	Reunion Island		508	St. Pierre/Miquelon
263	Zimbabwe		509	Haiti
264	Namibia		590	Guadeloupe
265	Malawi		591	Bolivia
266	Lesotho		592	Guyana
267	Botswana		593	Ecuador
268	Swaziland		594	French Guiana
269	Mayotte Island		595	Paraguay
290	St. Helena		596	French Antilles

597	Suriname	809	Montserrat*
598	Uruguay	809	Nevis*
599	Netherlands Antilles	809	St. Kitts*
670	Saipan (incl. Rota)	809	St. Lucia*
671	Guam	809	St. Vincent/Grenadines*
673	Brunei	809	Trinidad/Tobago*
674	Nauru	809	Turks and Caicos Islands*
675	Papua New Guinea	852	Hong Kong
676	Tonga	853	Macao
677	Solomon Islands	871	SAT East Atlantic
679	Fiji Islands	872	SAT Pacific
680	Palau	873	SAT Indian
682	Cook Island	874	SAT West Atlantic
684	American Samoa	880	Bangladesh
685	Western Samoa	886	Taiwan
686	Kiribati	960	Maldives
687	New Caledonia	961	Lebanon
689	French Polynesia	962	Jordan
691	Micronesia	963	Syria
692	Marshall Islands	964	Iraq
809	Anguilla (Barbuda)*	965	Kuwait
809	Antigua*	966	Saudi Arabia
809	Bahamas*	967	Yemen Arab Republic
809	Barbados*	968	Oman
809	Bermuda	971	United Arab Emirates
809	British Virgin Islands*	972	Israel
809	Cayman Islands*	973	Bahrain
809	Dominica*	974	Qatar
809	Dominican Republic*	975	Bhutan
809	Grenada (incl. Carriacou)*	977	Nepal
809	Jamaica*		

A P P E N D I X   G

Telecommunications Acronym Dictionary

The telecommunications industry is as expansive in its use of acronyms as the computer industry. The following is a list of acronyms used in this book, without definitions. Definitions for most acronyms are indexed by their full name in the glossary.

AAC	Alternate access carrier
AAL	ATM adaptation layer
AC	Alternating current
ACD	Automatic call distributor
ACP	Action control point
ACTS	Automatic coin telephone system
ADPCM	Adaptive differential pulse code modulation
ADSI	Analog display service interface
ADSL	Asymmetric digital subscriber line
AF	Audio frequency
AIN	Advanced intelligent network
AIS	Automatic intercept system
ALI	Automatic location information
AM	Amplitude modulation, Active monitor
AMA	Automatic message accounting
AMI	Alternate mark inversion
AMIS	Audio messaging interchange specification
ANI	Automatic number identification
AOS	Alternate operator service
APD	Avalanche photo diode
API	Application program interface
APPC	Advanced program-to-program communications
ARP	Address resolution protocol
ARQ	Automatic repeat request
ASCII	American standard code for information interexchange
ASIC	Application specific integrated circuit

ASN	Abstract system notation
ATM	Asynchronous transfer mode
AUI	Attachment unit interface
AWG	American wire gauge
B8ZS	Bipolar with 8-zero substitution
BACP	Bandwidth allocation control protocol
BBS	Bulletin board system
BCD	Blocked calls delayed
BCH	Blocked calls held
BCR	Blocked calls released
BECN	Backward explicit congestion notification
BER	Bit error rate
BERT	Bit error rate test
BHCA	Busy hour call attempts
BIOS	Basic input/output system
BLER	Block error rate
BOC	Bell operating company
BRI	Basic rate interface
BSA	Basic service arrangement
BSC	Binary synchronous communications (bisync)
BSE	Basic service element
BTA	Basic trading area
CAC	Carrier access code
CAD	Computer aided dispatch, Computer aided design
CAMA	Centralized automatic message accounting
CAS	Centralized attendant service
CATV	Community antenna television
CBX	Computer branch exchange
CCIS	Common channel interoffice signaling
CCITT	Consultative Committee on International Telephone and Telegraph
CCS	Centum call seconds
CCS	Common channel signaling
CCTV	Closed-circuit television
CDDI	Copper-distributed data interface

CDO	Community dial office
CDPD	Cellular digital packet data
CDR	Call detail recorder
CELP	Code excited linear prediction
CEPT	Conference European on Post and Telecommunications
CGSA	Cellular geographic serving area
CIF	Common intermediate format
CIR	Committed information rate
CLASS	Custom local area signaling services
CLID	Calling line identification
CMIP	Common management information protocol
CNM	Customer network management
CNS	Complementary network services
CO	Central office
CO-ACD	Central office automatic call distributor
COCOT	Customer owned coin telephone
CODEC	Coder/decoder
CPE	Customer premises equipment
CPU	Central processing unit
CRC	Cyclical redundancy checking
CSMA/CD	Carrier sense multiple access with collision detection
CSTA	Computer-supported telecommunications application
CSU	Channel service unit
CTI	Computer telephony integration
CTS	Clear to send
DAL	Direct access line
DAMA	Demand-assigned multiple access
DAP	Directory access protocol
DAS	Dual attachment station
dB	Decibel
DBS	Direct broadcast satellite
DC	Direct current
DCA	Document content architecture
DCE	Data circuit-terminating equipment
DCO	Digital central office

DCS	Digital crossconnect system
DCT	Discreet cosine transform
DDD	Direct distance dialing
DES	Data encryption standard
DHCP	Dynamic host configuration protocol
DIA	Document interchange architecture
DID	Direct inward dialing
DISA	Direct inward system access
DLCI	Data link connection identifier
DMI	Digital multiplexed interface, Desktop management interface
DNIC	Data network identification code
DNIS	Dialed number identification system
DNS	Domain name service, Directory naming service
DOC	Dynamic overload control
DOV	Data over voice
DQDB	Distributed queue dual bus
DSA	Directory systems agent
DSI	Digital speech interpolation
DSMA/CD	Digital sense multiple access with collision detection
DSP	Directory service protocol
DSX	Digital service crossconnect
DTE	Data terminal equipment
DTMF	Dual-tone multifrequency
DUA	Directory user agent
EAS	Extended-area service
EBCDIC	Expanded binary-coded decimal interexchange code
EDI	Electronic data interchange
EDIFACT	EDI for administration, commerce, and transport
EF	Entrance facility
EFS	Error-free seconds
EGP	Exterior gateway protocol
EIA	Electronic Industry Association
EIRP	Effective isotropic radiated power
EMF	Electromagnetic force

EMI	Electromagnetic interference
EAOSS	Exchange access operator service signaling
ER	Equipment room
ERL	Echo return loss
ESF	Extended super frame
ESP	Enhanced service provider
ESS	Electronic switching system
ETC	Enhanced throughput cellular
ETN	Electronic tandem network
FCC	Federal Communications Commission
FDDI	Fiber-distributed data interface
FDMA	Frequency division multiple access
FEC	Forward error correction
FECN	Forward explicit congestion notification
FOD	Fax on demand
FEX	Foreign exchange
FM	Frequency modulation
FRAD	Frame relay access device
FTP	File transfer protocol
GB/S	Gigabits per second
GCD	Graphic codepoint definition
GFC	Generic flow control
GHz	Gigahertz
GOS	Grade of service
GUI	Graphical user interface
HDTV	High-definition television
HEC	Header error control
Hz	Hertz
IC	Independent company
ICMP	Internet control message protocol
IDF	Intermediate distributing frame
IEC	Interexchange carrier
IETF	Internet Engineering Task Force
if	Intermediate frequency
IML	Incoming matching loss

IMTS	Improved mobile telephone service
INMARSAT	International Maritime Satellite Service
INWATS	Inward wide area telephone service
IP	Internet protocol
ISDN	Integrated services digital network
ISM	Industrial, scientific, medical
IVR	Interactive voice response
IVS	Interactive video system
KB/S	Kilobits per second
KHz	Kilohertz
KWH	Kilowatt hour
KTS	Key telephone system
LAN	Local area network
LAPD	Distributed link access procedure
LAMA	Localized automatic message accounting
LATA	Local access transport area
LCR	Least-cost routing
LEC	Local exchange carrier, LAN emulation client
LED	Light-emitting diode
LEOS	Low earth orbiting satellite
LES	LAN emulation server
LIT	Line insulation test
LLC	Logical link control
LTD	Local test desk
LU	Logical unit
MAC	Media access control
MAP/TOP	Manufacturing automation protocol/technical and office protocol
MAPI	Mail application programming interface
MAU	Multistation access unit
Mb/s	Megabits per second
MCU	Multipoint control unit
MCVD	Modified chemical vapor deposit
MDBS	Mobile database station
MDF	Main distributing frame

MDIS	Mobile data intermediate station
MDT	Mobile data terminal
MHz	Megahertz
MHS	Message-handling system
MIB	Management information base
MIF	Management information format
MIME	Multipurpose Internet mail extensions
MLN	Main listed number
MPEG	Motion Picture Experts Group
MTA	Message transfer agent, major trading area
MTU	Maximum transfer unit
MTBF	Mean time between failures
MTS	Message telephone service
MTSO	Mobile telephone switching office
MTTR	Mean time to repair
MVIP	Multivendor integration protocol
NAR	Network access restriction
NAU	Network access unit, Network addressable unit
NCP	Network control program, Network control point
NCTE	Network channel terminating equipment
NEXT	Near-end crosstalk
NFAS	Nonfacility associated signaling
NIC	Network interface card
NID	Network interface device
NLM	NetWare loadable module
NMCC	Network management control center
NNI	Network-to-network interface
NPA	Numbering plan area
NRZ	Nonreturn to zero
NRZI	Nonreturn to zero inverted
NSC	Network services complex
NSN	National significant number
NT1	Network termination 1
NT12	Network termination 12
NT2	Network termination 2

NTN	Network terminal number
NTSC	National Television Systems Committee
OCR	Optical character recognition
ONA	Open network architecture
OPX	Off-premise extension
OSI	Open systems interconnect
OSP	Outside plant, Operator service provider
OSPF	Open shortest path first
OSS	Operations support system
PA	Prearbitrated
P/AR	Peak-to-average ratio
PABX	Private automatic branch exchange
PAD	Packet assembler/disassembler
PAL	Phase alternate line
PAM	Pulse amplitude modulation
PASP	Public service answering point
PBX	Private branch exchange
PCM	Pulse code modulation
PCS	Personal communication service
PDU	Protocol data unit
PIC	Primary interexchange carrier
PIN	Personal identification number
POP	Point of presence
PPP	Point-to-point protocol
PRI	Primary rate interface
PSK	Phase shift keying
PSTN	Public switched-telephone network
PT	Payload type
PU	Physical unit
PVC	Permanent virtual circuit
QA	Queued arbitrated
QAM	Quadrature amplitude modulation
RCF	Remote call forwarding
rf	Radio frequency
RIP	Routing information protocol

RISC	Reduced instruction set computer
RMATS	Remote maintenance and testing system
RMON	Remote monitoring
rms	Root mean square
rn	Reference noise
ROM	Read-only memory
ROTL	Remote office test line
RSL	Received signal level
SAR	Segmentation and reassembly
SAS	Single attachment station
SCC	Satellite communications control
SCP	Service control point
SCSA	Signal computing system architecture
SDLC	Synchronous data link control
SDN	Software Defined Network
SDNCC	Software Defined Network control center
SECAM	Sequential coleur avec memoire
SF	Single frequency
SIP	SMDS interface protocol
SIR	Sustained information rate
SIT	Special identification tones
SLIP	Synchronous line interface protocol
SMDR	Station message detail recording
SMDS	Switched multimegabit data service
SMI	Structure of management information
SMR	Specialized mobile radio
SMS	Service management system
SMSA	Standard Metropolitan Statistical Area
SMTP	Simple mail transfer protocol
SNA	Systems Network Architecture
SNMP	Simple network management protocol
SOHO	Small office–home office
SONET	Synchronous optical network
SP	Signal point
SPC	Stored program control

SRL	Singing return loss
SSB	Single sideband
SSCP	System service control point
SSTDMA	Spacecraft switched time division multiple access
STP	Signal transfer point
SVC	Switched virtual circuit
SVD	Simultaneous voice data
TAO	Telephony application object
TAPI	Telephony applications programming interface
TC	Telecommunications closet
TCAM	Telecommunications communication access method
TCM	Trellis-coded modulation
TCP/IP	Transmission control protocol/internet protocol
TDM	Time division multiplexing
TDMA	Time division multiple access
TDR	Time domain reflectometer
TE1	Terminal equipment type 1
TE2	Terminal equipment type 2
TEMPEST	Transient electromagnetic pulse emanation standard
THT	Token holding timer
TIA	Telecommunications Industry Association
TLP	Transmission level point
TMGB	Telecommunications main grounding busbar
TRT	Token rotation time
TTRT	Target token rotation time
TSAPI	Telephony systems applications programming interface
TUR	Traffic usage recorder
UA	User agent
UCD	Uniform call distribution
UDP	User datagram protocol
UNI	User network interface
UPS	Uninterruptable power supply
USB	Universal serial bus
VAN	Value-added network
VCI	Virtual channel identifier

VF	Voice frequency
VLAN	Virtual LAN
VNL	Via net loss
VOD	Video on demand
VPI	Virtual path identifier
VPN	Virtual Private Network
VRU	Voice response unit
VSAT	Very small aperture terminal
VTAM	Virtual terminal access method
VU	Volume unit
WA	Work area
WATS	Wide area telephone service
WDM	Wavelength division multiplexing
XPD	Cross-polarization discrimination

GLOSSARY

A Bit: In T-1 carrier, the signaling bit that is formed from the eighth bit of the sixth channel.

A Law: The coding law used in the European 30-channel PCM system.

Absorption: The attenuation of a lightwave signal by impurities or fiber core imperfections, or of a microwave signal by oxygen or water vapor in the atmosphere.

Access Tandem: An LEC switching system that provides access for the IECs to the local network. The access tandem provides the IEC with access to more than one end office within a LATA.

Access Time: The time required for a hard disk to retrieve information requested by a file server. Access time consists of seek time plus rotate time.

Access: The capability of terminals to be interconnected with one another for the purpose of exchanging traffic.

Acoustic Coupler: A method of connecting a modem to a voice circuit with a handset adapter that picks up modem tones through the mouthpiece and sends them to the modem through the earpiece of a handset.

Adaptive Differential Pulse Code Modulation (ADPCM):   A method approved by CCITT for coding voice channels at 32 kb/s to increase the capacity of T-1 to either 44 or 48 channels.

Adaptive Equalizer: (1) Circuitry in a modem that allows the modem to compensate automatically for circuit conditions that impair high-speed data transmission. (2) A circuit installed in a microwave receiver to compensate for distortion caused by multipath fading.

Adaptive Integration: A voice mail feature that enables the mail system to give personalized service to callers depending on the called party's personal preference. Includes such features as transfer to a personal assistant and variable treatment according to the time of day.

Address Resolution Protocol (ARP):   A protocol that translates between IP addresses and Ethernet addresses.

Addressing: The process of sending digits over a telecommunications circuit to direct the switching equipment to the station address of the called number.

Advanced Intelligent Network (AIN):   An interface between the LEC switching system and an external computer that can provide special and custom services to subscribers independently of features offered by the switch manufacturer.

Aerial Cable: Any cable that is partially or completely run aerially between buildings or poles.

Agent: In ACD an agent is a customer contact person, also known as a telephone service representative. In network management an agent is software that resides on the managed device and communicates with the network management workstation.

Alerting: The use of signals on a telecommunications circuit to alert the called party or equipment to an incoming call.

Algorithm: A set of processes in a computer program used to solve a problem with a given set of steps.

Alternate Access Carrier (AAC):   A common carrier that builds a local access network, usually of fiber optics, to provide access service to the IECs in competition to the LECs.

Alternate Mark Inversion (AMI):   See Bipolar Coding.

Alternate Operator Service (AOS):   An operator service provider, not connected with a major IEC, that handles operator functions such as coin, third number, collect, and credit-card billing.

Alternate Routing: The ability of a switching machine to establish a path to another machine over more than one circuit group.

Alternating Current (AC):   Current flow that changes over time from a peak positive value to a peak negative value.

American Standard Code for Information Interexchange (ASCII):   A seven-bit (plus one parity bit) coding system used for encoding characters for transmission over a data network.

American Wire Gauge (AWG):   The American standard method of designating wire size. The higher the number, the finer the wire.

Ampere: A unit of measure of current flow.

Amplitude Distortion: Any variance in the level of frequencies within the passband of a communication channel.

Analog: A transmission mode in which information is transmitted by converting it to a continuously variable electrical signal.

Analog Display Service Interface (ADSI):   An interface between a display telephone set and the central office that supports interactive features.

Angle of Acceptance: The angle of light rays striking an optical-fiber aperture, within which light is guided through the fiber. Light outside the angle of acceptance escapes through the cladding.

Answer Supervision: A signal sent from a switching system through the trunking network to the originating end of a call to signal that a call has been answered.

Antenna Gain: The increase in radiated power from an antenna compared to an isotropic antenna.

Application Program: A computer program that performs a specific function such as word processing or spreadsheet.

Applications Processor: An ancillary processor to a PBX that performs a specific function such as message handling.

Area Code: See Numbering Plan Area.

Armored Cable: Multipair cable intended for direct burial that is armored with a metallic covering that serves to prevent damage from rodents and digging apparatus.

Aspect Ratio: The ratio between the width and the height of a video screen.

Asymmetric Digital Subscriber Line (ADSL):   A technology for multiplexing a compressed video signal over the voice channel in a subscriber loop.

Asynchronous Transfer Mode (ATM):   A broadband connection-oriented switching service that carries data, voice, and video information in fixed-length 48-byte cells with a 5-byte header.

Asynchronous Transmission: A means of transmitting data over a network wherein each character contains a start and stop bit to keep the transmitting and receiving terminals in synchronism with each other.

Atmospheric Loss: The attenuation of a radio signal because of absorption by oxygen molecules and water vapor in the atmosphere.

Audible Ring: A tone returned from the called party's switching machine to inform the calling party that the called line is being rung.

Audio Frequency (AF):   A range of frequencies, nominally 20 Hz to 20 kHz, that the human ear can hear.

Audio Messaging Interchange Specification (AMIS):   A standard that permits networking of voice mail systems from different manufacturers.

Audiotex: A voice mail service that prompts callers for the desired service, and delivers information in audio form.

Autodial: Automatic dialing of a number that is programmed into a telephone or PBX.

Automated Attendant: A feature of voice mail and stand-alone systems that answers calls, prompts callers to enter DTMF digits in response to menu options, and routes the call to an extension or call distributor.

Automatic Call Distributor (ACD):   A switching system that automatically distributes incoming calls to a group of answering positions without going through an attendant. If all answering positions are busy, the calls are held until one becomes available.

Automatic Coin Telephone System (ACTS):   A coin telephone service that rates calls, collects coins, and completes other types of calls without intervention by an operator.

Automatic Intercept System (AIS):   An LEC service system that intercepts calls to disconnected numbers and routes them to a call transfer announcement.

Automatic Location Information (ALI):   Emergency equipment that enables a 911 center to determine the location of a caller using a table lookup function.

Automatic Message Accounting (AMA):   Equipment that registers the details of chargeable calls and enters them on a storage medium for processing by an off-line center.

Automatic Number Identification (ANI):   Identification of the calling line that is delivered from the calling station to the IEC for the purpose of billing the call. ANI is similar to calling line identification (CLID) and comes from the same source, except that CLID may be blocked by the caller, where ANI, which is used on long-distance and 800 calls, cannot be blocked.

Automatic Repeat Request (ARQ):   A data communications protocol that automatically initiates a request to repeat the last transmission if an error is received.

Automatic Route Selection (ARS):   A software feature of PBXs and hybrids that selects the appropriate trunk route for a call to take based on digits dialed and the caller's class of service.

Availability: (1) The ratio of circuit uptime to total elapsed time. (2) In a switching system, the ability of every input port to reach every output port.

Avalanche Photo Diode (APD):   A light detector that generates an output current many times greater than the light energy striking its face.

Average Bouncing Busy Hour (ABBH): A method of determining the traffic load on a switching system by determining the load during the busiest hour of the day for a one-week period, and averaging them.

B Bit: In T-1 carrier, the signaling bit that is formed from the 8th bit of the 12th channel.

B Channel: The 64 kb/s "bearer" channel that is the basic building block of ISDN. The B channel is used for voice and circuit-switched or packet-switched data.

Back-to-Back Channel Bank: The interconnection of voice frequency and signaling leads between channel banks to allow dropping and inserting channels.

Backboard: A board made of wood or plastic on which terminating blocks are mounted in a wiring system.

Backbone Cable: Cabling connecting a main distributing frame to intermediate distributing frames located in telecommunications closets.

Backoff Algorithm: The process, built into a contention network, used after collision by the media access controller to determine when to reattempt to acquire the network.

Backplane: A network of wiring with sockets into which printed circuit cards can be placed.

Balance: The degree of electrical match between the two sides of a cable pair or between a two-wire circuit and the matching network in a four-wire terminating set.

Balanced Modulator: An amplitude modulating circuit that suppresses the carrier signal, resulting in an output consisting of only upper and lower sidebands.

Balancing Network: A network used in a four-wire terminating set to match the impedance of the two-wire circuit.

Balun: A device that converts the unbalanced wiring of a coaxial terminal system to a balanced twisted-pair system.

Band: A range of frequencies.

Bandpass: The range of frequencies that a channel will pass without excessive attenuation.

Bandwidth: The range of frequencies a communications channel is capable of carrying without excessive attenuation.

Banyan Switch: A high-speed switching system that takes its name from the many branches of a banyan tree. A banyan switch is bidirectional and chooses its path from the address contained in the header of an incoming packet. If an address bit is a 1, the upper path of the switch is taken. Otherwise the switch takes the lower, or 0, path.

Baseband: A form of modulation in which data signals are pulsed directly on the transmission medium without frequency division.

Basic Input/Output System (BIOS): A collection of software routines that a computer uses to communicate with its peripherals.

Basic Rate Interface (BRI): The basic ISDN service consisting of two 64 kb/s information or bearer channels, and one 16 kb/s data or signaling channel.

Basic Service Arrangement (BSA): An ONA term referring to the fundamental switching and transport service obtained by an information service provider to serve its customers over the PSTN.

Basic Service Element (BSE): Functions of the telephone network broken down into essentials that are defined in the FCC's Open Network Architecture plan.

Battery: A direct-current voltage supply that powers telephones and telecommunications apparatus.

Baud: The number of data signal elements per second a data channel is capable of carrying.

Beacon: In a token ring network, beacons are signals sent by stations to isolate and bypass failures.

Bearer Channel: A 64 kb/s information-carrying channel that furnishes integrated services digital network (ISDN) services to end users.

Bell Operating Company (BOC): One of the 22 local exchange companies (LECs) that were previously part of the Bell System.

Binary Synchronous Communications (BSC or Bisync): An IBM byte-controlled half-duplex protocol using a defined set of control characters and sequences for data transmission.

Binary: A numbering system consisting of two digits, zero and one.

Bipolar Coding: The T-carrier line coding system that inverts the polarity of alternate 1s bits. Also called alternate mark inversion (AMI).

Bipolar Violation: The presence of two consecutive 1s bits of the same polarity on a T-carrier line.

Bipolar with 8-Zero Substitution (B8ZS): A line coding scheme used with T-1 clear channel to send a string of eight zeros with a deliberate bipolar violation. The 1s bits in the bipolar violation maintain line synchronization.

Bit Error Rate (BER): The ratio of bits transmitted in error to the total bits transmitted on the line.

Bit Rate: The speed at which bits are transmitted on a circuit; usually expressed in bits per second.

Bit Robbing: The use of the least significant bit per channel in every sixth frame of a T-1 carrier system for signaling.

Bit Stream: A continuous string of bits transmitted serially in time.

Bit Stuffing: Adding bits to a digital frame for synchronizing and control. Used in T carrier to prevent loss of synchronization from 15 or more consecutive 0 bits.

Bit: The smallest unit of binary information; a contraction formed from the words BInary digIT.

Block Error Rate (BLER): In a given unit of time, BLER measures the number of blocks that must be retransmitted because of error.

Blocked Call: A call that cannot be connected immediately because no path is available at the time the call arrives.

Blocked Calls Delayed (BCD): A variable used in queuing theory to describe the behavior of the input process when the user is held in queue upon encountering blockage.

Blocked Calls Held (BCH): A variable used in queuing theory to describe the behavior of the input process when the user immediately redials upon encountering blockage.

Blocked Calls Released (BCR): A variable used in queuing theory to describe the behavior of the input process when the user waits for a time before redialing when encountering blockage.

Blocking: A switching system condition in which no circuits are available to complete a call, and a busy signal is returned to the caller.

Bonding: The permanent connecting of metallic conductors to equalize potential between the conductors and carry any current that is likely to be imposed.

Boot: A program that starts another program.

Branch Feeder: A cable between distribution cable and the main feeder cable that connects users to the central office.

Branching Filter: A device inserted in a waveguide to separate or combine different microwave frequency bands.

Break: An interruption in transmission on a circuit.

Breakdown Voltage: The voltage at which electricity will flow across an insulating substance between two conductors.

Bridge: Circuitry used to interconnect networks with a common set of higher-level protocols.

Bridged Tap: Any section of a cable pair that is not on the direct electrical path between the central office and the user's premises, but which is bridged onto the path.

Bridger Amplifier: An amplifier installed on a CATV trunk cable to feed branching cables.

Broadband ISDN (B-ISDN):   A broadband service based on the use of ATM and SONET.

Broadband: A form of LAN modulation in which multiple channels are formed by dividing the transmission medium into discrete frequency segments. Also a term used to describe high-bandwidth transmission of data signals.

Broadcast Address: A network address that includes all stations on the network that are intended to receive a transmission.

Brouter: A local area network bridge that is capable of routing.

Buried Cable: A cable that is buried in the ground without being enclosed in conduit.

Bus: A group of conductors that connects two or more circuit elements, usually at a high speed for a short distance.

Busy Hour Call Attempts (BHCA):   The number of call originations that occur during the hour or hours in which a telecommunications system carries the maximum number of calls.

Busy Hour: The composite of various peak load periods selected for the purpose of designing network capacity.

Busy Season: An annually recurring interval in which call volumes reach a peak for a specified period of time such as 10 days.

Bypass: Routing circuits around the facilities of a local exchange carrier by some form of technology such as lightwave or microwave.

Byte: A set of eight bits of information equivalent to a character. Also called an octet.

C Message Weighting: A factor used in noise measurements to describe the lesser annoying effect on the human ear of high- and low-frequency noise compared to mid-range noise.

C Notched Noise: A measurement of C message-weighted noise in a circuit with a tone applied at the far end and filtered out at the near end.

Cable Racking: Framework fastened to bays to support interbay cabling.

Caching: The use of memory in a file server to read more information than is requested, storing it so the next information request can be served from memory instead of from the disk.

Call Detail Recorder (CDR):   An auxiliary device attached to a PBX to capture and record call details such as called number, time of day, duration, etc.

Call Progress Tones: Tones returned from switching systems to inform the calling party of the progress of the call. Examples are audible ring, reorder, and busy.

Call Sequencer: An electronic device similar to an automatic call distributor that can answer calls, inform agent positions of which call arrived first, hold callers in queue, and provide limited statistical information.

Call Store: The temporary memory used in an SPC switching system to hold records of calls in progress and pending changes to permanent memory.

Call Warning Tone: A tone placed on a circuit to indicate that the call is about to route to a high-cost facility.

Call-back Queuing: A trunk queuing system in which the switching system signals the users that all trunks are busy and calls them back when a trunk is available.

Call-by-Call Service Selection: An ISDN feature that lets more than one service be assigned to a single channel. ISDN-compatible switching systems communicate across the D channel to select the appropriate service.

Called Party Control: The provision in a 911 system for the called party to supervise a call and to hold it up for tracing.

Calling Line Identification (CLID):   A service offered by LECs in which the calling line number is delivered with the call. Note that this CLASS feature is often confused with automatic number identification (ANI).

Capacitance: The property of an electronic circuit element that stores an electrical charge.

Capacity: The number of call attempts and busy hour load that a switching system is capable of supporting.

Carbon Block Protector: A form of electrical protector that uses a pair of carbon blocks separated from ground by a narrow gap. When the voltage from the block to ground exceeds a specified value, the blocks arc across to ground the circuit.

Carried Load: The amount of traffic that a switching system or trunk group carries during a set period of time; usually one hour.

Carrier Access Code (CAC):   A five-digit code consisting of the digits 10 plus a three-digit carrier identification code. For example, the CAC for MCI is 10222.

Carrier Sense Multiple Access with Collision Detection (CSMA/CD):   A system used in contention networks where the network interface unit listens for the presence of a carrier before attempting to send and detects the presence of a collision by monitoring for a distorted pulse.

Carrier-to-Noise Ratio: The ratio of the received carrier to the noise level in a satellite link.

Carrier: (1) A type of multiplexing equipment used to derive several channels from one communications link by combining signals on the basis of time or frequency division. (2) A card cage used in an apparatus cabinet to contain multiple circuit packs. (3) A company that carries telecommunications messages and private channels for a fee.

Cell Relay: A data communications technology based on fixed-length cells.

Cell-Site Controller: The cellular radio unit that manages radio channels within a cell.

Cell: A hexagonal subdivision of a mobile telephone service area containing a cell-site controller and radio frequency transceivers. Also, a group of bytes conditioned for transmission across a network.

Cellular geographic serving area (CGSA):   A metropolitan area in which the FCC grants cellular radio licenses.

Centralized Automatic Message Accounting (CAMA):   A LEC message accounting option in which call details are sent from the serving central office to a central location for recording.

Mobile Telephone Switching Office (MTSO):   The electronic switching system that switches calls between mobile and wireline telephones, controls handoff between cells, and monitors usage. This equipment is known by various trade names.

Central Office (CO):   A switching center that terminates and interconnects lines and trunks from users.

Central Processing Unit (CPU):   The control logic element used to execute instructions in a computer.

Centralized Attendant Service (CAS):   A PBX feature that allows the using organization to route all calls from a multi-PBX system to a central answering location where attendants have access to features as if they were collocated with the PBX.

Centrex: A class of central office service that provides the equivalent of PBX service from an LEC switching machine. Incoming calls can be dialed directly to extensions without operator intervention.

Centum Call Seconds (CCS):   See Hundred Call Seconds.

Channel Bank: Apparatus that converts multiple voice frequency signals to frequency or time division multiplexed signals for transmitting over a transmission medium.

Channel Service Unit (CSU):   Apparatus that interfaces DTE to a line connecting to a dataport channel unit to enable digital communications without a modem. Used with DSU when DTE lacks complete digital line interface capability.

Channel: A path in a communications system between two or more points, furnished by a wire, radio, lightwave, satellite, or a combination of media.

Chrominance: The portion of a television signal that carries color encoding information to the receiver.

Circuit Pack: A plug-in electronic device that contains the circuitry to perform a specific function. A circuit pack is not capable of stand-alone operation but functions only as an element of the parent device.

Circuit Switching: A method of network access in which terminals are connected by switching together the circuits to which they are attached. In a circuit-switched network, the terminals have full real-time access to each other up to the bandwidth of the circuit.

Circuit: A transmission path between two points in a telecommunications system.

Cladding: The outer coating of glass surrounding the core in a lightguide.

Class 5 Office: The former designation for an end office in the AT&T/BOC switching hierarchy that directly serves end users. See End Office.

Class of Service: The service classification within a telecommunications system that controls the features, calling privileges, and restrictions the user is assigned.

Clear Channel: A 64 kb/s digital channel that uses external signaling and therefore permits all 64 kb/s to be used for data transmission.

Client: A workstation in a local area network that is set up to use the resources of a server.

Clock: A device that generates a signal for controlling network synchronization.

Closed Circuit Television (CCTV):   A privately operated television system not connected to a public distribution network.

Cluster Controller: A device that controls access of a group of terminals to a higher-level computer.

Coaxial Cable: A single-wire conductor, surrounded by an insulating medium and a metallic shield, that is used for carrying a telecommunications signal.

Code Blocking: The capability of a switching system to block calls to a specified area code, central office code, or telephone number.

Code Conversion: The process of registering incoming digits from a line or trunk and converting them to a different code required for call routing.

Code Excited Linear Prediction (CELP):   A speech-encoding algorithm that enables speech to be digitized at 8.0 kb/s with quality approximately equal to that of analog FM systems.

Coder/Decoder (Codec):   The analog-to-digital conversion circuitry in the line equipment of a digital CO. Also, a device in television transmission that compresses a video signal into a narrow digital channel.

Coherence Bandwidth: The bandwidth of a range of frequencies that are subjected to the same degree of frequency-selective fading.

Coin-free Dialing: The ability of a caller from a coin telephone to reach an emergency or assistance operator without using a coin to place the call.

Collimate: The condition of parallel light rays.

Collision Window: The time it takes for a data pulse to travel the length of the network. During this interval, the network is vulnerable to collision.

Collision: A condition that occurs when two or more terminals on a contention network attempt to acquire access to the network simultaneously.

Committed Information Rate (CIR):   In a frame relay network the CIR is the speed the carrier guarantees to provide. Frames above the CIR are carried on a permissive basis up to the port speed, but are marked discard eligible.

Common Carrier: A company that carries communications services for the general public within an assigned territory.

Common Channel Interoffice Signaling (CCIS):   The AT&T common channel signaling system used in North America.

Common Channel Signaling (CCS):   A separate data network used to route signals between switching systems.

Common Control Switching: A switching system that uses shared equipment to establish, monitor, and disconnect paths through the network. The equipment is called into the connection to perform a function and then released to serve other users.

Communicating Word Processor: A word processor that includes protocols for enabling memory-to-memory transfer over a telecommunication circuit.

Communications Controller: See Front-end Processor.

Community Antenna Television (CATV): A network for distributing television signals over coaxial cable throughout a community. Also called "cable television."

Community Dial Office (CDO): A small CO designed for unattended operation in a community, usually limited to about 10,000 lines.

Compandor: A device that compresses high-level voice signals in the transmitting direction and expands them in the receiving direction with respect to lower-level signals. Its purpose is to improve noise performance in a circuit.

Complement: A group of 50 cable pairs (25 pairs in small cable sizes) that are bound together and identified as a unit.

Complementary Network Services (CNS): An ONA term referring to a service residing on the user's side of the telephone line. The user purchases CNSs to connect to an information service provider.

Composite (CX) Signaling: A direct-current signaling system that separates the signal from the voice band by filters.

Computer-Aided Dispatch (CAD): A feature used by many public agencies that employs a computer to track the location and availability of emergency personnel.

Computer Branch Exchange (CBX): A computer-controlled PBX.

Computer-Telephony Integration (CTI): Marriage of the PBX with a host computer or file server. The PBX provides call information to the computer, and accepts call-handling instructions from the computer.

Concentration Ratio: As applied to CO line equipment, it is the ratio between the number of lines in an equipment group and the number of links or trunks that can be accessed from the lines.

Concentration: The process of connecting a group of inputs to a smaller number of outputs in a network. If there are more inputs than outputs, the network has concentration.

Concentrator: A data communications device that subdivides a channel into a larger number of data channels. Asynchronous channels are fed into a high-speed synchronous channel via a concentrator to derive several lower-speed channels.

Conditional Routing: An ACD feature that routes calls based on variables such as number of agents logged on, length of oldest waiting call, etc.

Conditioning: Special treatment given to a transmission facility to make it acceptable for high-speed data communication.

Conference European on Post and Telecommunications (CEPT): The European telecommunications standards-setting body.

Connection-Oriented: A circuit that is set up over a network so that the originating and terminating stations share a defined path, either real or virtual. For example, a telephone call uses a connection-oriented circuit.

Connectionless: A data transmission method in which packets are launched into the network with the sending and receiving address, but without a defined path. For example, LANs use connectionless transmissions.

Connectivity: The ability to connect a device to a network.

Consultative Committee on International Telephone and Telegraph (CCITT):
An international committee that sets telephone, telegraph, and data communications standards. Now known as the International Telecommunications Union (ITU-T).

Contention: A form of multiple access to a network in which the network capacity is allocated on a "first come first served" basis.

Control Equipment: Equipment used to transmit orders from an alarm center to a remote site to perform operations by remote control.

Converter: A device for changing central office voltage to another DC voltage for powering equipment.

Core: The inner glass element that guides the light rays in an optical fiber.

Coverage Path: In a PBX the coverage path determines where the call will be routed if the called telephone is busy or does not answer.

Critical Rain Rate: The amount of rainfall where the drops are of sufficient size and intensity to cause fading in a microwave signal.

Cross-polarization: The relationship between two radio waves when one is polarized vertically and the other horizontally.

Cross-polarization Discrimination (XPD):   The amount of decoupling between radio waves that exists when they are cross-polarized.

Cross: A circuit impairment where two separate circuits are unintentionally interconnected.

Crossbar: A type of switching system that uses a centrally controlled matrix switching network consisting of electromechanical switches connecting horizontal and vertical paths to establish a path through the network.

Crossconnect: A wired connection between two or more elements of a telecommunications circuit.

Crosstalk: The unwanted coupling of a signal from one transmission path into another.

Current: The flow of electrons through an electrical circuit.

Custom Local Area Signaling Service (CLASS):   A suite of services offered by LECs. Examples are Calling Line Identification (CLID), distinctive ringing, automatic callback, etc.

Customer Premise Equipment (CPE):   Telephone apparatus mounted on the user's premises and connected to the telephone network.

Cutover: Any change from an existing to a new telecommunications system.

Cyclical redundancy checking (CRC):   A data error-detecting system wherein an information block is subjected to a mathematical process designed to ensure that errors cannot occur undetected.

D Channel: The ISDN data 16 kb/s channel that is used for out-of-band signaling functions such as call setup.

Daisy Chain: A local area network configuration in which nodes are directly connected in series.

Data Circuit-Terminating Equipment (DCE): Equipment designed to establish a connection to a network, condition the input and output of DTE for transmission over the network, and terminate the connection when completed.

Data Compression: A data transmission system that replaces a bit stream with another bit stream having fewer bits.

Data Line Monitor: A data line impairment-measuring device that bridges the data line and observes the condition of data, addressing, and protocols.

Data Link: A circuit capable of carrying digitized information.

Data network identification code (DNIC): A 14-digit number used for worldwide numbering of data networks.

Data Over Voice (DOV): A device that multiplexes a full-duplex data channel over a voice channel using analog modulation.

Data Service Unit (DSU): Apparatus that interfaces DTE to a line connecting to a dataport channel unit to enable digital communications without a modem. Used with CSU when DTE lacks complete digital line interface capability or alone when DTE includes digital line interface capability.

Data Terminal Equipment (DTE): Any form of computer, peripheral, or terminal that can be used for originating or receiving data over a communication channel.

Data: Digitized information in a form suitable for storage or communication over electronic means.

Datagram: A single unacknowledged packet of information that is sent over a network as an individual unit without regard to previous or subsequent packets.

Dataport: A PCM channel unit that provides direct access to a digital bit stream for data transmission.

dBm: A measure of signal power as compared to one milliwatt (1/1,000 watt) of power. It is used to express power levels. For example, a signal power of –10 dBm is 10 dB lower than one milliwatt.

dBrn: A measure of noise power relative to a reference noise of –90 dBm.

dBrnc: A measure of noise power through a C message weighting filter.

dBrnc0: A measure of C message noise referred to a zero test level point.

Decibel (dB): A measure of relative power level between two points in a circuit.

Dedicated Access Line (DAL): A line, usually provided over T-1, that connects the customer's premises to the IEC.

Dedicated Access: The interconnection of a station to an IEC through a dedicated line.

Dedicated Circuit: A communications channel assigned for the exclusive use of an organization.

Delay: (1) The time a call spends in queue. (2) The time required for a signal to transit the communications facility.

Delta Modulation: A system of converting analog to digital signals by transmitting a single bit indicating the direction of change in amplitude from the previous sample.

Demand Assigned Multiple Access (DAMA): A method of sharing the capacity of a communications satellite by assigning capacity on demand to an idle channel or time slot from a pool.

Demarcation Point: The point at which customer-owned wiring and equipment interfaces with the telephone company.

Demodulation: The process of extracting intelligence from a carrier signal.

Dependency: A sequential relationship between tasks. For example, if one task must finish before another can start, a finish-to-start dependency exists.

Diagnostic: Test programs used for error and fault detection in apparatus or a circuit.

Dial-one WATS: A long-distance service that carries a fixed monthly fee that entitles the user to purchase service at a discount.

Dial-up: A data communications session that is initiated by dialing a switched telephone circuit.

Dialed Number Identification Service (DNIS):   A service offered by most 800 carriers that reports to the PBX which 800 number was dialed. The PBX can then use the 800 number to route the call. DNIS on 800 circuits is equivalent to DID on central office trunks.

Digital Access Crossconnect System (DACS):   A specialized digital switch that enables crossconnection of channels at the digital line rate.

Digital Service Crossconnect (DSX):   A physically wired crossconnect frame to enable connecting digital transmission equipment at a standard bit rate.

Digital Speech Interpolation (DSI):   A method of increasing the carrying capacity of a circuit group by dynamically assigning voice channels only when the users are speaking.

Digital Switching: A process for connecting ports on a switching system by routing digital signals without converting them to analog.

Digital: A mode of transmission in which information is coded in binary form for transmission on a network.

Digroup: Two groups of 12 digital channels integrated to form a single 24-channel system.

Diplexer: A device that couples a radio transmitter and receiver to the same antenna.

Dipole: An antenna that has two radiating elements fed from a central point.

Direct Broadcast Satellite (DBS):   A television broadcast service that provides television programming services throughout a country from a single source through a satellite.

Direct Control Switching: A system in which the switching path is established directly through the network by dial pulses without central control.

Direct Current (DC):   Current that flows through a circuit in only one direction.

Direct Distance Dialing (DDD):   A long-distance calling system that enables a user to place a call without operator assistance.

Direct Inward Dialing (DID):   A method of enabling callers from outside a PBX to reach an extension by dialing the access code plus the extension number.

Direct Trunks: Trunks dedicated exclusively to traffic between the terminating offices.

Direct-to-Line Multiplex: A system that modulates individual channel frequencies directly to their final carrier line frequencies.

Directional Coupler: A device inserted in a waveguide to couple a transmitter and receiver to the same antenna. Also a passive device installed on a CATV cable to isolate the feeder cable from another branch.

Discard Eligible: In a frame relay network, frames above the committed information rate are marked discard eligible. In case of congestion the carrier can discard such frames to preserve network integrity.

Disk Duplexing: In a file server a duplexed disk provides redundancy of both the hard disk and the controller. Transactions are written to both disks to provide backup.

Disk Mirroring: Similar to disk duplexing except that the controller is not duplicated.

Dispersion: The rounding and overlapping of a light pulse that occurs to different wavelengths because of reflected rays or the different refractive index of the core material.

Dispersive Fade Margin: A property of a digital microwave signal that expresses the amount of fade margin under conditions of distortion caused by multipath fading.

Distortion: An unwanted change in a waveform.

Distributed Control: A switching system architecture in which more than one processor controls certain groups of line ports.

Distributed Processing: The distribution of call-processing functions among numerous small processors rather than concentrating all functions in a single central processor.

Distributed Queue Dual Bus (DQDB):   The protocol used in the 802.6 metropolitan area network.

Distributed Switching: The capability to install CO line circuits close to the served subscribers and connect them over a smaller group of links or trunks to a CO that directly controls the operation of the remote unit.

Distributing Frame: A framework holding terminal blocks that interconnect cable and equipment and provide test access.

Distribution Cable: Cable that connects the user's serving terminal to an interface with a branch feeder cable.

Diversity: A method of protecting a radio signal from failure of equipment or the radio path by providing standby equipment.

Domain Name Service (DNS):   Translates host names to IP addresses.

Downlink: The radio path from a satellite to an earth station.

Download: To send information from a host computer to a remote terminal.

Downstream Channel: The frequency band in a CATV system that distributes signals from the headend to the users.

Drop Wire: Wire leading from the user's serving terminal to the station protector.

Dual Tone Multifrequency (DTMF):   A signaling system that uses pairs of audio frequencies to represent a digit. Usually synonymous with the AT&T trademark Touch-Tone.

Dumb Terminal: A terminal that has no processing capability. It is functional only when connected to a host.

Duplex (DX) Signaling: A direct current signaling system that transmits signals directly over the cable pair.

Dynamic Overload Control (DOC):   The ability of the translation and routing elements in a CO to adapt to changes in traffic load by rerouting traffic and blocking call attempts.

Dwell Time: In frequency hopping spread-spectrum radio, dwell time is the time the system stays on one frequency before changing to another.

E&M Signaling: A method of signaling between offices by voltage states on the transmit and receive leads of signaling equipment at the point of interface.

Earth Station: The assembly of radio equipment, antenna, and satellite communication control circuitry that is used to provide access from terrestrial circuits to satellite capacity.

Echo Cancellation: A protocol used to obtain full-duplex data communication over a two-wire line.

Echo Canceler: An electronic device that processes the echo signal and cancels it out to prevent annoyance to the talker.

Echo Checking: A method of error checking in which the receiving end echoes received characters to the transmitting end.

Echo Return Loss (ERL):   The weighted return loss of a circuit across a band of frequencies from 500 to 2,500 Hz.

Echo Suppressor: A device that opens the receive path of a circuit when talking power is present in the transmit path.

Echo: The reflection of a portion of a signal back to its source.

Effective Isotropic Radiated Power (EIRP):   Power radiated by a transmitter compared to the power of an isotropic antenna, which is one that radiates equally in all directions.

Electromagnetic Interference (EMI):   An interfering signal that is radiated from a source and picked up by a telecommunications circuit.

Electronic Data Interchange (EDI):   The intercompany exchange of legally binding trade documents over a telecommunications network.

Electronic Mail: A service that enables text-form messages to be stored in a central file and retrieved over a data terminal by dialing access and identification codes.

Electronic Switching System (ESS):   A stored program controlled switching system used in Class 5 offices.

Electronic Tandem Network (ETN):   A private telecommunications network that consists of switching nodes and interconnecting trunks.

Emergency Ringback: A feature that enables a 911 center to connect a caller to the appropriate Public Service Answering Point (PASP) and to enable the PASP to rering the circuit if the caller disconnects. This enables the PASP to connect to the caller to get additional emergency information.

End Office: The central office in the LEC's network that directly serves subscriber lines.

End-to-End Signaling: A method of connecting signaling equipment so it transmits signals between the two ends of a circuit with no intermediate appearances of the signaling leads.

Enhanced 911:   An emergency service in which information relative to the specific caller, such as identity and location, is forwarded to the 911 agency by the serving central office.

Enhanced Service Provider (ESP):   Companies that use the PSTN to provide services to the public.

Enterprise Network: A private network of both switched and dedicated facilities that enables users to connect to services wherever they are located without concern about how to establish the session.

Entrance Facility (EF):   The physical structure and cable connecting the main equipment room to the common carrier's facilities.

Entrance Link: A coaxial or fiber-optic facility used to connect the last terminal in a microwave signal to multiplex or video terminating equipment.

Envelope Delay: The difference in propagation speed of different frequencies within the passband of a telecommunications channel.

Equal Access: A central office feature that allows all interexchange carriers to have access to the trunk side of the switching network in an end office.

Equipment Rooms (ER):   Building areas intended to house telecommunications equipment. Equipment rooms also may fill the functions of a telecommunications closet.

Erlang: A unit of network load. One Erlang equals 36 CCS and represents 100 percent occupancy of a circuit or piece of equipment. Also used to define the input process under the BCC (Erlang B) and BCD (Erlang C) blockage conditions.

Error-Free Seconds: The number of seconds per unit of time that a circuit vendor guarantees the circuit will be free of errors.

Error: Any discrepancy between a received data signal from the signal as it was transmitted.

Ethernet: A proprietary contention bus network developed by Xerox, Digital Equipment Corporation, and Intel. Ethernet formed the basis for the IEEE 802.3 standard.

Extended Super Frame (ESF):   T-1 carrier framing format that provides 64 kb/s clear channel capability, error checking, 16 state signaling, and other data transmission features.

Facility: Any set of transmission paths that can be used to transport voice or data. Facilities can range from a cable to a carrier system or a microwave radio system.

Facsimile: A system for scanning a document, encoding it, transmitting it over a telecommunication circuit, and reproducing it in its original form at the receiving end.

Far-end Crosstalk (FEXT):   The amount of crosstalk measured at the distant end of a receive circuit when a signal is applied at the near end.

Fax on Demand (FOD):   Equipment that prompts a caller to enter digits from the dial pad identifying information needed and a fax number. FOD equipment retrieves the information from a database and automatically faxes it to the caller.

File Transfer Protocol (FTP):   A protocol used by TCP/IP networks to transfer files from one system to another.

Flow Control: The process of protecting network service by denying access to additional traffic that would add further to congestion.

Foreign Exchange (FEX):   A special service that connects station equipment located in one telephone exchange with switching equipment located in another.

Four-wire Circuit: A circuit that uses separate paths for each direction of transmission.

Frame Relay: A data communications service that transports frames of information across a network to one or more points. Cost is based on three elements: committed information rate (CIR), access circuit, and port speed.

Front-end Processor: An auxiliary computer attached to a network to perform control operations and relieve the host computer for data processing.

Full-duplex: A data communication circuit over which data can be sent in both directions simultaneously.

Gas Tube Protector: A protector containing an ionizing gas that conducts external voltages to ground when they exceed a designed threshold level.

Gateway: Circuitry used to interconnect networks by converting the protocols of each network to that used by the other.

Gauge: The physical size of an electrical conductor, specified by American Wire Gauge (AWG) standards.

Generic Program: The operating system in a SPC central office that contains logic for call processing functions and controls the overall machine operation.

Glare: A condition that exists when both ends of a circuit are simultaneously seized.

Grade of Service: (1)The percentage of time or probability that a call will be blocked in a network. (2) A quality indicator used in transmission measurements to specify the quality of a circuit based on both noise and loss.

Ground Start: A method of circuit seizure between a central office and a PBX that transmits an immediate signal by grounding the tip of the line.

Half-duplex: A data communications circuit over which data can be sent in only one direction at a time.

Handshaking: Signaling between two DCE devices on a link to set up communications between them.

Hang-on Queuing: A trunk queuing system in which the switching system signals users that all trunks are busy and allows them to remain off-hook while they are held in queue until the call can be completed.

Heat Coil: A protection device that opens a circuit and grounds a cable pair when operated by stray currents.

High Usage Groups: Trunk groups established between two switching machines to serve as the first-choice path between the machines and handle the bulk of the traffic.

Hit: A momentary loss of signal in a transmission system.

Holding Time: The average length of time per call that calls in a group of circuits are off hook.

Horizontal Wiring: The wiring from the equipment rooms or telecommunications closets to the work area.

Hundred Call Seconds (CCS):   A measure of network load. Thirty-six CCS represents 100 percent occupancy of a circuit or piece of equipment.

Hybrid: (1) A multiwinding coil or electronic circuit used in a four-wire terminating set or switching system line circuits to separate the four-wire and two-wire paths. (2) A key telephone system that has many of the features of a PBX. Such features as pooled-trunk access characterize a hybrid.

Impedance: The opposition to flow of alternating current in an electrical circuit.

Impulse Noise: Short bursts of high-amplitude interference.

Independent Telephone Company (IC): A non-Bell LEC.

Inside Wiring: The wiring on the customer's premises between the telephone set and the telephone company's demarcation point.

Integrated Services Digital Network (ISDN): A set of standards promulgated by CCITT to prescribe standard interfaces to a switched digital network.

Integrated Voice/data: The combination of voice and data signals from a workstation over a communication path to the PBX.

Interactive Voice Response (IVR) also known as Voice Response Unit (VRU): Equipment that acts as an automatic frontend for a computer system, enabling callers to conduct their own transactions. The IVR prompts the caller to dial identification digits plus digits to complete transactions such as checking account balance, transferring funds, etc.

Interexchange Carrier (IEC): A common carrier that provides long-distance service between LATAs.

Interface: The connection between two systems. Usually hardware and software connecting a computer terminal with peripherals such as DCE, printers, etc.

Intermediate Distributing Frame (IDF): A crossconnection point between the main distributing frame and station wiring.

Intermodulation Distortion: Distortion or noise generated in electronic circuits when the power carried is great enough to cause nonlinear operation.

International Telecommunications Union (ITU): An agency of the United Nations that is responsible for setting telecommunications standards.

Internet Protocol (IP): A connectionless protocol responsible for delivering data from host to host across an internetwork.

Inverse Multiplexer: A device that combines multiple 64 kb/s or 56 kb/s channels into a higher-speed bit stream. It is often used to combine multiple switched 56 or ISDN channels for videoconferencing.

Jabber: A single or steady stream of Ethernet frames longer than the maximum.

Jitter: The phase shift of digital pulses over a transmission medium.

Jumper: Wire used to interconnect equipment and cable on a distributing frame.

Key Telephone System (KTS): A method of allowing several central office lines to be accessed from multiple telephone sets.

Latency: The time it takes for a bit to pass from origin to destination through network.

Leased Line: An unswitched telecommunications channel leased to an organization for its exclusive use.

Least-Cost Routing (LCR): A PBX service feature that chooses the most economical route to a destination based on cost of the terminated services and time of delay.

Level: The signal power at a given point in a circuit.

Line Conditioning: A service offered by common carriers to reduce envelope delay, noise, and amplitude distortion to enable transmission of higher-speed data.

Link: A circuit or path joining two communications channels in a network.

Loading: The process of inserting fixed inductors in series with both wires of a cable pair to reduce voice frequency loss.

Local Access Transport Area (LATA):   The geographical boundaries within which Bell Operating Companies are permitted to offer long-distance traffic.

Local Area Network (LAN):   A narrow-range data network using one of the non-switched multiple access technologies.

Local Automatic Message Accounting (LAMA):   A LEC message accounting option in which call details are recorded in the serving central office.

Local Exchange Company (LEC):   The operating telephone company that serves a particular franchised area.

Look-ahead Overflow: An ACD feature in which the system looks at the target queue of an overflow command to ensure that queue conditions are such that overflow is permitted.

Look-back Overflow: An ACD feature in which the system looks back at the queue from which a call overflowed. If queue conditions improve in the original queue the call can be completed there.

Loop Start: A method of circuit seizure between a central office and station equipment that operates by bridging the tip and ring of the line through a resistance.

Loopback Test: A test applied to a full-duplex circuit by connecting the receive leads to the transmit leads, applying a signal, and reading the returned test signal at the near end of the circuit.

Loss: The drop in signal level between points on a circuit.

Low Earth Orbiting Satellite (LEOS):   A global personal communications service technology using a constellation of satellites orbiting the earth at a few hundred miles for communications with handheld units.

Main Distributing Frame (MDF):   The cable rack used to terminate all distribution and trunk cables in a central office or PBX.

Management Information Base (MIB):   A database contained in an SNMP-compatible device that defines the object that is managed.

Maximum Transfer Unit (MTU):   The maximum amount of data that can be transferred across a data network as defined by the network protocol.

Mean Time Between Failures (MTBF):   The average time a device or system operates without failing.

Mean Time to Repair (MTTR):   The average time required for a qualified technician to repair a failed device or system.

Message Switching: A form of network access in which a message is forwarded from a terminal to a central switch where it is stored and forwarded to the addressee after some delay.

Message Telephone Service (MTS): A generic name for the switched long-distance telephone service offered by all interexchange carriers.

Message Transfer Agent (MTA): In a messaging system the MTA transfers messages between the user agents and other MTAs.

Messaging: The use of computer systems to exchange messages among people, applications, systems, and organizations.

Messenger: A metallic strand attached to a pole line to support aerial cable.

Microwave: A high-frequency, high-capacity radio system, usually used to carry multiple voice channels.

Milestone: An event that is defined by the project team as significant.

Milliwatt: One one-thousandths of a watt. Used as a reference power for signal levels in telecommunications circuits.

Mobile Data Terminal (MDT): A wireless terminal that permits one-way or two-way data communications. The MDT may be vehicular or handheld.

Modeling: The process of designing a network from a series of mathematical formulas that describe the behavior of network elements.

Modem Pool: A centralized pool of modems accessed through a PBX or LAN to provide off-net data transmission from modemless terminals.

Modem: A contraction of the terms MOdulator/DEModulator. A modem is used to convert analog signals to digital form and vice versa.

Modulation: The process by which some characteristic of a carrier signal, such as frequency, amplitude, or phase is varied by a low-frequency information signal.

Multi-drop: A circuit dedicated to communication between multiple terminals that are connected to the same circuit.

Multiline Hunt: The ability of a switching machine to connect calls to another number in a group when other numbers in the group are busy.

Multiple Access: The capability of multiple terminals connected to the same network to access one another by means of a common addressing scheme and protocol.

Multiplexer: A device used for combining several lower-speed channels into a higher-speed channel.

National Significant Number (NSN): In the ITU-recommended international dialing plan the NSN is the maximum number of digits permitted within a country.

Near-End Crosstalk (NEXT): The amount of signal received at the near end of a circuit when a transmit signal is applied at the same end of the link.

Network: A set of communications points connected by channels.

Network Access Restriction (NAR): A software restriction built into Centrex systems to limit the number of simultaneous trunk calls the subscriber can place.

Network Administration: The process of monitoring network loads and service results and making adjustments needed to maintain service and costs at the design objective level.

Network Channel Terminating Equipment (NCTE): Apparatus mounted on the user's premises that is used to amplify, match impedance, or match network signaling to the interconnected equipment.

Network Design: The process of determining quantities and architecture of circuit and equipment to achieve a cost/service balance.

Node: A major point in a network where lines from many sources meet and may be switched. Also, circle or box on a PERT chart. A node may represent a task or an event.

Noise: Any unwanted signal in a transmission path.

Nonfacility Associated Signaling (NFAS):   The capability in a primary rate ISDN network of using one 64 kb/s D channel to control the signaling of multiple PRIs.

Octet: A group of eight bits. Also known as a byte, although a byte can have other than eight bits.

Off-Premise Extension (OPX):   An extension telephone that uses LEC facilities to connect to the main telephone service.

Off-hook: A signaling state in a line or trunk when it is working or busy.

On-hook: A signaling state in a line or trunk when it is nonworking or idle.

On-net: In a virtual network, an on-net call is one that uses a dedicated access line (DAL).

Open Network Architecture (ONA):   A telephone architecture that provides the interfaces to enable service providers to connect to the public switched-telephone network.

Open Systems Interconnect (OSI):   A seven-layer data communications protocol model that specifies standard interfaces that all vendors can adapt to their own designs.

Overflow: The ACD process in which a call is routed to a queue other than the original one.

Overhead: Any noninformation bits such as headers, error checking bits, start and stop bits, etc. used for controlling a network.

Packet Assembler/Disassembler (PAD):   A device used on a packet-switched network to assemble information into packets and to convert received packets into a continuous data stream.

Packet Switching: A method of allocating network time by forming data into packets and relaying it to the destination under control of processors at each major node. The network determines packet routing during transport of the packet.

Packet: A unit of data information consisting of header, information, error detection, and trailer records.

Parity: A bit or series of bits appended to a character or block of characters to ensure that either an odd or even number of bits are transmitted. Parity is used for error detection.

Patch: The temporary interconnection of transmission and signaling paths. Used for temporary rerouting and restoral of failed facilities or equipment.

Peak-to-Average Ratio (P/AR):   An analog test that provides an index of data circuit quality by sending a pulse into one end of a circuit and measuring its envelope at the distant end of the circuit.

Peg Count: The number of times a specified event occurs. Derived from an early method of counting the number of busy lines in a manual switchboard.

Permanent Virtual Circuit (PVC):   In a data network a PVC is defined in software. The circuit functions as if a hardware path was in place, but the path is shared with other users.

Personal Communications Service (PCS):   A radio-based service that allows subscribers to roam anywhere, using a telephone number that is not associated with a fixed location.

Personal Identification Number (PIN):   A billing identification number dialed by the user to enable the switching machine to identify the calling party.

Point-of-Presence (POP):   The point at which a carrier meets the customer-provided portion of a circuit. For LECs the POP is usually on the customer's premises. For IECs the POP is usually on the carrier's premises.

Point-to-Point Circuit: A telecommunications circuit that is exclusively assigned to the use of two devices.

Poisson: A curve that describes the distribution of arrival times at the input to a service queue.

Poll Cycle Time: The amount of time required for a multidrop data communications controller to make one complete polling cycle through all devices on the network.

Polling: A network sharing method in which remote terminals send traffic upon receipt of a polling message from the host. The host accesses the terminal, determines if it has traffic to send, and causes traffic to be uploaded to the host.

Postalized Rates: A method many IECs use for billing long-distance calls. With postalized rates the cost is sensitive to talking time, but not to distance.

Power Fail Transfer: A unit in KTS that transfers one or more telephone instruments to central office lines during a power failure.

Primary Rate Interface (PRI):   A 1.544 mb/s information-carrying channel that furnishes integrated services digital network (ISDN) services to end users. Consists of 23 bearer channels and one signaling channel.

Private Automatic Branch Exchange (PABX):   A term often used synonymously for PBX. A PABX is always automatic, whereas switching is manual in some PBXs.

Private Branch Exchange (PBX):   A switching system dedicated to telephone and data use in a private communication network.

Propagation Delay: The absolute time delay of a signal from the sending to the receiving terminal.

Propagation Speed: The speed at which a signal travels over a transmission medium.

Property Management System (PMS):   A computer application used in the hospitality industry to handle functions such as check-in/check-out, room status, etc. The PMS is often linked to the telephone system to provide such functions from the PMS terminal.

Protector: A device that prevents hazardous voltages or currents from injuring a user or damaging equipment connected to a cable pair.

Protocol Analyzer: A data communications test set that enables an operator to observe bit patterns in a data transmission, trap specific patterns, and simulate network elements.

Protocol Converter: A device that converts one communications protocol to another.

Protocol: The conventions used in a network for establishing communications compatibility between terminals, and for maintaining the line discipline while they are connected to the network.

Protocol Data Unit (PDU): A formatted data message, the size and structure of which depends on its position in the protocol stack. For example, a frame is a data-link layer PDU, a packet a network layer PDU, and an X.400 message is an application layer PDU.

Public Data Network (PDN): A data transmission network operated by a private telecommunications company for public subscription and use.

Public Switched Telephone Network (PSTN): A generic term for the interconnected networks of operating telephone companies.

Pulse Code Modulation (PCM): A digital modulation method that encodes a voice signal into an eight-bit digital word representing the amplitude of each pulse.

Queuing: The holding of calls in queue when a trunk group is busy and completing them in turn when an idle circuit is available.

Redundancy: The provision of more than one circuit element to assume call processing when the primary element fails.

Reference Noise (rn): The threshold of audibility to which noise measurements are referred, –90 dBm.

Registration: The process the FCC follows in certifying that customer premise equipment will not cause harms to the network or personnel.

Remote Access: (1) A family of products that allow users who are away from the office to dial into the LAN and access its resources. (2) The ability to dial into a switching system over a local telephone number in order to complete calls over a private network from a distant location.

Remote Call Forwarding (RCF): A service offered by most LECs that allows a user to obtain a telephone number in a local calling area and have calls automatically forwarded at the user's expense to another telephone number.

Remote Maintenance and Testing System (RMATS): A service offered by PBX manufacturers and vendors that enables the vendor to access a PBX over the PTSN and perform testing and administrative functions.

Remote MONitoring (RMON): A network management function that enables the manager to monitor network functions from a remote management workstation.

Reorder: A fast busy tone used to indicate equipment or circuit blockage.

Repeater: A bidirectional signal regenerator (digital) or amplifier (analog). Repeaters are available to work on analog or digital signals from audio to radio frequency.

Response time: The interval between the terminal operator's sending the last character of a message and the time the first character of the response from the host arrives at the terminal.

Restriction: Limitations to a station on the use of PBX features or trunks on the basis of service classification.

Return Loss: The degree of isolation, expressed in dB, between the transmit and the receive ports of a four-wire terminating set.

Ring: The designation of the side of a telephone line that carries talking battery to the user's premises.

Riser Cable: See Backbone Cable.

RJ-11: A standard four-conductor jack and plug arrangement typically used for connecting a standard telephone to inside wiring.

RJ-45: A standard eight-conductor jack and plug arrangement typically used for connecting a telephone or data terminal to inside wiring.

Routing Script: See Vector.

Routing: The path selection made for a telecommunications signal through the network to its destination.

Rules-based Messaging: An E-mail feature that enables a user to screen messages based on criteria that the user specifies.

Runt: An Ethernet frame shorter than the 64-byte minimum.

Segment: See Subnet.

Serial Interface: Circuitry used in DTE to convert parallel data to serial data for transmission on a network.

Server: In a telecommunications network servers are the trunks or the service process, such as call center agents, that fulfill the users' service requests. In a LAN servers are devices that provide specialized services such as file, print, and modem or fax pool services.

Service level: In a call center, service level is defined as the percentage of calls answered within an objective time interval.

Short: A circuit impairment that exists when two conductors of the same pair are connected at an unintended point.

Sidetone: The sound of a talker's voice audible in the handset of the telephone instrument.

Signal-to-Noise Ratio: The ratio between signal power and noise power in a circuit.

Signaling System No. 7 (SS7): An out-of-band signaling protocol between public switching systems.

Simple Mail Transfer Protocol (SMTP): A protocol for delivering messages across a TCP/IP network.

Simple Network Management Protocol (SNMP): A management protocol for monitoring and controlling network devices.

Simulation: The process of designing a network by simulating the events and facilities that represent network load and capacity.

Singing: The tendency of a circuit to oscillate when the return loss is too low.

Skill-based Routing: An ACD function that routes calls based on a table showing the skills of each agent.

Split: A designated group of answering stations in an automatic call distributor (ACD).

Spread Spectrum: A radio modulation method that transmits its signal over a broad range of frequencies (direct sequence method) or rapidly jumps from one frequency to another (frequency hopping). Spread spectrum provides excellent security and resists interference.

Station Message Detail Recording (SMDR): The port in a PBX that provides information such as called and calling station, time of day, and duration on long-distance calls. The SMDR port is usually connected to a call-accounting system to produce the necessary reports.

Station Range: The number of feet or ohms over which a telephone instrument can signal and transmit voice and data.

Statistical Multiplexing: A form of data multiplexing in which the time on a communications channel is assigned to terminals only when they have data to transport.

Store-and-Forward: A method of switching messages in which a message or packet is sent from the originating terminal to a central unit where it is held for retransmission to the receiving terminal.

Structure of Management Information (SMI): The framework that defines network management variables in a network management system.

Subnet: A group of workstations in a LAN that are separated from other subnets by a bridge or, more frequently, a router.

Subscriber Carrier: A multichannel device that enables several subscribers to share a single facility in the local loop.

Subscriber Loop: The circuit that connects a user's premises to the telephone central office.

Supervision: The process of monitoring the busy/idle status of a circuit to detect changes of state.

Switched Multimegabit Data Service (SMDS): A high-speed connectionless data transport service offered by LECs and some IECs.

Sustained Information Rate (SIR): The maximum guaranteed rate at which data can transit an SMDS network. SIR is similar to committed information rate (CIR) in a frame relay network.

Switched Virtual Circuit (SVC): A logical link between points on a carrier network that is set up and disconnected with each session.

Synchronous: A method of transmitting data over a network wherein the sending and receiving terminals are kept in synchronism with each other by a clock signal embedded in the data.

System Integration: The process of bringing software and equipment from different manufacturers together to form an operational unit.

Systems Network Architecture (SNA): An IBM data communications architecture that includes structure, formats, protocols, and operating sequences.

T-1 Multiplexer: An intelligent device that divides a 1.544 mb/s facility into multiple voice and data channels.

Telecommunications Bonding Backbone: A backbone cable run between equipment rooms and telecommunications closets and the building's telecommunications main grounding busbar.

Telecommunications Closet (TC): In a telecommunications wiring plan, a satellite closet containing a junction between backbone and horizontal cable.

Telecommunications Grounding Busbar: A grounding point for telecommunications services and equipment in each telecommunications equipment room and closet.

Telecommunications Main Grounding Busbar (TMGB):   The central grounding point for telecommunications equipment rooms and closets. The TMGB is bonded to the electrical ground and to the building's metal framework.

Telecommunications: The electronic movement of information.

Telephony Applications Programming Interface (TAPI):   A programming interface developed by Microsoft that connects PCs to telephone instruments to enable computer-telephony applications.

Telephony Services Applications Programming Interface (TSAPI):   A programming interface for Novell servers that enables developers to write computer-telephony software for applications that work on Novell servers.

Terminal: (1) A fixture attached to distribution cable to provide access for making connections to cable pairs. (2) Any device meant for direct operation over a telecommunications circuit by an end user.

Text Messaging: The use of a computer-based network of terminals to store and transmit messages among users.

Thermal Noise: Noise created in an electronic circuit by the movement and collisions of electrons.

Throughput: The effective rate of transmission of information between two points excluding noninformation (overhead) bits.

Tie Trunk: A privately owned or leased trunk used to interconnect PBXs in a private switching network.

Time Division Multiplexing: A method of combining several communication channels by dividing a channel into time increments and assigning each channel to a time slot. Multiple channels are interleaved when each channel is assigned the entire bandwidth of the backbone channel for a short period of time.

Timed Overflow: In an ACD this feature allows a call to overflow to an alternate queue after it has waited in the original queue for a specified period of time.

Tip: The designation of the side of a telephone line that serves as the return path to the central office.

Token Passing: A method of allocating network access wherein a terminal can send traffic only after it has acquired the network's token.

Token: A software mark or packet that circulates among network nodes.

Topology: The architecture of a network, or the way circuits are connected to link the network nodes.

Traffic Usage Recorder (TUR):   Hardware or software that monitors traffic-sensitive circuits or apparatus and records usage, usually in terms of CCS and peg count.

Transceiver: A device that has the capability of both transmitting and receiving information.

Transducer: Any device that changes energy from one state to another. Examples are microphones, speakers, and telephone handsets.

Translations: Software in a switching system that establishes the characteristics and features of lines and trunks.

Transmission Level Point (TLP):   A designated measurement point in a circuit where the transmission level has been specified by the designer.

Transmission: The process of transporting voice or data over a network or facility from one point to another.

Transmission Control Protocol (TCP):   A protocol for providing reliable end-to-end delivery of data across an internetwork.

Trap: A message sent by an SNMP-managed device to indicate that a threshold or alarm has been reached.

Traveling Class Mark: A feature of switches used in electronic tandem networks to carry the class of service of the user with the call so downstream tandems know what features and restrictions to apply.

Trunk: A communications channel between two switching systems equipped with terminating and signaling equipment.

Uplink: The radio path from an earth station to a satellite.

User Agent (UA):   In a messaging system the UA is the user's interface to the system. The UA provides for message composition, receipt, sending, and handling.

Utilization: The ratio of the time a resource is used to the total time it is available. For example, if a circuit carries 25 CCS of traffic during the busy hour, its utilization is 25/36=69.4 percent.

Value Added Network: A data communication network that adds processing services such as error correction and storage to the basic function of transporting data.

Vector: A series of routing and call-handling instructions in an ACD.

Video on Demand (VOD):   The delivery of video services to customers in response to their specific request. VOD is contrasted to conventional cable television where all channels are delivered over the medium.

Videotex: An interactive information retrieval service that usually employs the telephone network as the transmission medium to provide information with text and color graphics.

Virtual Circuit: A circuit that is established between two terminals by assigning a logical path over which data can flow. A virtual circuit can either be permanent, in which terminals are assigned a permanent path, or switched, in which the circuit is reestablished each time a terminal has data to send.

Virtual LAN (VLAN):   A LAN composed of users that are attached to different hubs. Users can be assigned to a LAN segment regardless of their physical location.

Virtual Network: A switched voice network offered by interexchange carriers that provides service similar to a private voice network. Virtual networks offer reduced rates for on-net calling, which is available from stations with a direct T-1 connection from the user to the IEC.

Voice Mail: A service that allows voice messages to be stored digitally in secondary storage and retrieved remotely by dialing access and identification codes.

Voice Response Unit (VRU):   See Interactive Voice Response.
Voice Store-and Forward: See Voice Mail.

Wide Area Telephone Service (WATS):   A bulk-rated long-distance telephone service that carries calls at a cost based on usage and the state in which the calls terminate.
Wiring Closet: See Telecommunications Closet.
Wireless: A radio or infrared-based service that enables telephone or LAN users to connect to the telecommunications network without wires.
Work Area: In the EIA/TIA 568 specifications the work area is the area in which the station jack is located to feed the terminating devices.

BIBLIOGRAPHY

Bellcore. *BOC Notes on the LEC Networks,* 1994.

Black, Uyless. *Emerging Communications Technologies.* Englewood Cliffs, NJ: Prentice Hall, 1994.

Comer, Douglas E. *Networking with TCP/IP* Volume I: *Principles, Protocols and Architecture* 2nd ed. Englewood Cliffs, NJ: Prentice Hall, 1991.

Comer, Douglas E. and David L. Stevens. *Networking with TCP/IP* Volume II: *Design, Implementation and Internals.* Englewood Cliffs, NJ: Prentice Hall, 1991.

Comer, Douglas E. and David L. Stevens. *Networking with TCP/IP* Volume II: *Client-Server Programming and Applications.* Englewood Cliffs, NJ: Prentice Hall, 1993.

Feit, Dr. Sidnie M. *SNMP: A Guide to Network Management.* New York: McGraw-Hill, 1995.

Flanagan, William A. *Asynchronous Transfer Mode User's Guide.* New York: Flatiron Publishing, Inc., 1994.

Gladstone, Steve. *Testing Computer Telephony Systems and Networks.* New York: Flatiron Publishing, Inc., 1994.

Green, James H. *The Irwin Handbook of Telecommunications Management,* 2nd ed. Burr Ridge, IL: Richard D. Irwin, 1996.

Minoli, Daniel. *Video Dialtone Technology.* New York: McGraw-Hill, Inc., 1995.

Motorola, *The Basics Book of ISDN,* 2nd ed. Mansfield, MA: The Motorola University Press, 1993.

National Fire Protection Association. *National Electric Code 1996.*

Newton, Harry. *Newton's Telecom Dictionary,* 8th ed. New York: Flatiron Publishing, Inc., 1994.

Radicati, Sara. *Electronic Mail.* New York. McGraw-Hill, 1992.

Radicati, Sara. *X.500 Directory Services.* New York: Van Nostrand Reinhold, 1994.

Schatt, Stan. *Understanding Network Management: Strategies and Solutions.* New York: Windcrest/McGraw-Hill, Inc., 1993.

Smythe, Colin. *Internetworking: Designing the Right Architectures.* Wokingham, England: Addision-Wesley Publishing Co.

Sokol, Phyllis K. *EDI: The Competitive Edge.* New York, McGraw-Hill, 1989.

Stallings, William. *Local and Metropolitan Area Networks,* 4th ed. New York: Macmillan Publishing Company, 1993.

Taylor, D. Edgar. *The McGraw-Hill Internetworking Handbook.* New York: McGraw-Hill, 1995.

Trowt-Bayard, Toby. *Videoconferencing: The Whole Picture.* New York: Flatiron Publishing, Inc. 1994.

INDEX